FROM R⊕ARING HATE

—— TO ——

RAMR⊕D STRAIGHT

*A Journey from Hitler's Germany
to the US Marine Corps*

PETER S. BECK

PUBLISHED BY FIDELI PUBLISHING INC.

ISBN: 978-1-60414-635-6

Published by Fideli Publishing, Inc.

DEDICATION

__All__ profits from the sale of this book will be donated to the Injured Marine Semper Fi Fund located at the Wounded Warrior Center, Building H49, Camp Pendleton, CA 92055

The wars in Iraq and Afghanistan have seriously wounded thousands of America's young men and women, some with lifetime disabilities, and our government, while paying for an initial two weeks of family visits, has made no provisions for the families of these brave warriors to stay near them for longer periods of time during their months and sometimes years of recuperation. The Injured Marine Semper Fi Fund underwrites the expenses of these families and also funds special equipment for the wounded warriors, often not covered by any other source, once they are released from their recuperation and/or hospitalization.

As of this writing, the Injured Marine Semper Fi Fund has issued more than 50,000 grants to more than 8,500 of our wounded and critically ill service members providing over $67 million in assistance to those who need it most.

As medevacs continue to arrive stateside from Afghanistan carrying wounded warriors with multiple amputations and shrapnel injuries and as more service members are diagnosed with the "invisible injuries of war"- Post Traumatic Stress Disorder (PTSD) and Traumatic Brain Injury (TBI), the caseload of this phenomenal fund continues to grow.

Readers desiring to make a donation to the Injured Marine Semper Fi Fund can do so by sending a donation to:

The Injured Marine Semper Fi Fund
825 College Boulevard, Suite 102
PMB 609
Oceanside, CA 92057

All donations to the fund are fully tax deductible and the Fund has the highest rating as a charity.

To do anything less would not uphold the sacred motto of our Corps:

Semper Fidelis — Always Faithful.

Peter S. Beck

* * *

LIVING THE DREAM

A true story of an escape from Nazi Germany,
immigration to the United States by way of South America
and
service in the United States Marine Corps,
including combat in Vietnam with the First Marine Division.

CONTENTS

THE JOURNEY TO FREEDOM
February 27, 1939, to August 30, 1940

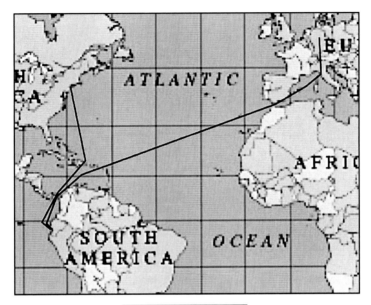

Iron Cross, First Class, awarded to Louis Beck in World War I.
It was the key to obtaining timely exit visas from Nazi Germany in 1939.

From Berlin, Germany, to Genoa, Italy, by Lufthansa airplane.
February 27, 1939

From Genoa, Italy, to Guayaquil, Ecuador, South America,
on the Italian Motor Ship *Orazio*.
March 1, 1939, to March 18, 1939

From Guayaquil, Ecuador, to New York City,
on the Chilean ship *Aconcagua*.
August 20, 1940, to August 30, 1940

LIVING THE DREAM AS A U. S. MARINE
1956 - 1978

1956	Syracuse, N.Y. to Quantico, Va. and The Basic School
1957	Quantico, Va. to Camp Fuji, Japan, and 3rd Marine Division
	Camp Fuji, Japan, to Luzon, Philippines
	Philippine Area to Okinawa, Japan
	Okinawa to the South China Sea for the Indonesian Alert
	Indonesian Area to Subic Bay, Philippines
1958	Subic Bay to Parris Island, S. C. and MCRD
1959	Parris Island to Washington, D. C. and
	"The Oldest Post in the Corps," Marine Barracks, 8th & I
1962	Camp Lejune, N. C. and 2nd Marine Division
	Camp Lejune to Europe as Landing Force, Mediterranean
	Gibraltar
	Golfe Juan, French Riviera
	Corsica and training with the French Foreign Legion
	Valletta, Malta
	Bomba, Libya, and desert training with the Libyan Army
	Messina, Sicily
	Pilos, Greece
	Patras, Greece
	Pireaus, Greece (Athens)
	Sardinia and training with the Italian Carabineri
	Barcelona, Spain
	Porto Scudo, Sardinia
	Genoa, Italy, (Sister City of Guayaquil, Ecuador)
1963	Camp Lejune to Landing Force, Caribbean
	Vieques, Puerto Rico
	San Juan, Puerto Rico
1964	Camp Lejune to Spain for Operation *Steel Pike*
	Gibraltar
	Huelva, Spain
	Santander, Spain
	Bilbao, Spain
	San Sebastian, Spain
1965	Camp Lejune to Guantanamo Bay, Cuba, and
	Marine Barracks, Naval Station
1966	Guantanamo to Quantico, Va. and Amphibious Warfare School
1966	Quantico to Washington, D. C., to Supply Dept., HQMC
1968	To Vietnam via Okinawa, and combat with 1st Marine Division
1969	Vietnam to Sydney, Australia, for R&R and return
1969	Vietnam to San Diego, Calif. and duty with MCRD
1972	San Diego to Honolulu, Hawaii, and duty with CINCPAC
1975	Honolulu to Okinawa, Japan, and 3rd Marine Division
1976	Okinawa to Washington, D. C, and HQMC; The Last Hurrah!
1978	Washington, D. C. to Retirement in the San Francisco Area

* * *

PERSONS WHO ARE PART OF THE MILITARY STORY

U. S. MARINE CORPS

Alexander, Bob, Maj, 1/7
Austin, Randall, LtCol, Koh Tang
Bateman, John, Lt., PLC/TBS/PISC
Bethel, Bill, LtCol, 1/7
Bouker, John G., Col/MajGen, 3rd Mar
Bowlin, Jerry (Buzz), Lt/Col, PLC/TBS
Brennan, Joseph P., Lt, TBS
Burke, Douglas, SSgt, 7th Mar
Campbell, Tom, Maj/Col, J3-CINCPAC
Carter, Nick, Maj, 1/7
Challener, Robert, LCpl, 1/7, KIA
Chen/Schenn, Byron (Barney)Capt/Col
Codispoti, Gildo, Col, 7th Mar
Coffman, R, P., LtCol/Col, 7th Mar
Davis, Charles E., Lt/LtCol, Gitmo
De Peau, Bob, Cpl, 7th Mar
Derning, Edmund, Col, MCRD, SD
Doehler, William F., Maj/BGen
Dowd, Jack, Lt. Col, 1/7, KIA, NC
Gestson, Johann S., LtCol, CINCPAC
Givens, Jim, Maj, 7th Mar
Harris, H., Capt, MarBks, Wash, KIA
Higgins, Bill, 1st Lt, 1st Tank Bn
Hittinger, Russ, LtCol, KIA
Hoar, Joseph, Maj/Gen
Holcomb, Thomas, Gen, CMC
Hood, Webb, Col, G-4, 2nd MarDiv
Josslyn, William R., Col/MajGen
Krulak, Bill, Maj, 7th Mar
Lang, Frank, MajGen, CINCPAC
Lee, Howie, Maj, HQMC, MOH
Marousek, Andrew V., LtCol, 1/2
McLaughlin, John N., MajGen/LtGen
McMonagle, James, Col/MajGen
Memmer, George, Capt, BLT 1-2
Moore, B., Cpl, (Bennie X), 7th Mar
Moore, Brian S. Gy Sgt, 3/3
Mundy, Carl. LtCol/Gen, CMC
Nichols, Robert, Col/LtGen, 7th Mar
O'Donnell, Andrew, LtGen, HQMC
O'Keefe, Keith, Maj/Col, MarBks, DC

Pate, R. McCall, Gen, CMC
Pirhalla, Paul, Col/ HQMC
Platt, Jonas M., Col/MajGen, MB, DC
Rauchle, A. J., LtCol, 3/3
Richards, Robert M., Col, 1st Mar, NC
Rouse, J.M., LtCol, 3/3
Schoepper, Al, LtCol, Marine Band
Simpson, Ormond, MajGen,1st MarDiv
Smith, George W., Capt/MajGen
Spanjer, Ralph (Smoke), MajGen
Stanton, J. H. (Culebra Joe), Lt/Col
Steele, Ort, Maj/MajGen, 3rd MarDiv
Tye, Charles, Capt/LtCol, AWS
Tyler, Paul R..MajGen, QMC
Uren, Bill, Maj, 1/7, WIA
Von Harten, W. (Skeeter) R., Lt/Col
Walker, Tony (Cold Steel), Col, Gitmo
Wilson, Louis H,.LtGen, CMC, MOH

* * *

U. S. NAVY

Bulkeley, John D., Vice Adm, MOH
Gayler, Noel, Adm, CINCPAC
Germano, Vince, Lt/Capt, CHC
Kaufman, Draper L., Capt/VAdm, NC
La Boone, Jake, Capt, CHC, CINCPAC
Scranton, Bill, Doctor, MC, 1/7
Wyse, Edward C., Capt

* * *

U. S. AIR FORCE

Abbodongo, Joe, LtCol, Red Horse Sqd
Rodriquez, Rod, Chief MSgt, CINCPAC
Treyz, Fritz, BGen, CINCPAC Staff
Young, J. A. BGen, CINCPAC Staff

* * *

FOREWORD

This book is being written because I have a story to tell, and the time to tell it is getting shorter since I celebrated my 77th birthday in June 2012. I have led a full life, and I have seen much of the world. The highlights of my life are still the escape from Nazi Germany, and the twenty-two years I spent on active duty in the United States Marine Corps. My Marine Corps was a totally different organization from the Marine Corps of today. When I joined the Corps in 1955, America had finished a World War just 10 years before and the Korean War had ended in a stalemate in 1953. Political pressures centered on home grown issues, and the military strength of the country was considered one of our largest assets. Americans were expected to serve their country, and a national draft was in place requiring men 18 years and older to register for the draft and to be prepared to be called up to serve their country when the need arose.

Born in Berlin, Germany, my journey to the United States and my assimilation into the American culture is the basis for this book. Influences from many different places somehow pointed me in the direction of the United States Marine Corps. This book deals with those influences, and then, once inside the Corps, this book relates my personal experiences. It could be called a trip through time because some of the things I write about hardly exist anymore. The Corps and our Country have undergone significant changes; however, the essential Corps values imbued in my heart and my mind remain unchanged and could probably be traced back to Tun Tavern in Philadelphia in the year 1775, which is when the Continental Marines, the forerunner of the United States Marine Corps, were established before we became an independent nation.

The incidents related in this book are all true, and the facts discussed in this memoir are as accurate as I can make them, relying on my memories, records, letters uncovered in recent years, which date back to 1914, and the surviving photographs which have traveled with me and my family from Berlin, Germany, to the present day. If there are errors, they are caused by the long years between happening and writing and a 77 year old brain (and perhaps too many Birdbath Martinis).

Our escape from Germany was very traumatic for my family, and my father never discussed the details of it. Growing up, I knew very little about our personal exodus. My father told very few stories, and it is only because he spent an evening with my wife, Cathie, on the front porch of his house in Yorktown Heights in Westchester County, New York, that I know the exact details of our eventual successful escape from Nazi Germany in 1939.

This dearth of information about my past remained until April 2007 when I received a package from Tom Selldorff of Weston, Massachusetts. Tom is my stepbrother, the son of my father's third wife, Dorothy Hertenried. While replacing the air conditioning system in his attic, a packet of papers from Germany dating back to 1914 was found. The papers dealt with my father and they were a treasure trove of information not previously known to me. Through these papers, other photographs, which I already had in my possession, and a few other documents, I was able to piece together the early history of my family.

Living The Dream is a current Marine Corps saying, usually uttered in a tongue and cheek manner, when a group of Marines begin telling each other how tough they have it in the Corps. During recruit training, a Drill Instructor once informed his recruits that they were "living the dream" of becoming Marines. The irony stuck, and whenever a Marine may be feeling sorry for himself, some other Marine simply reminds him that he is Living the Dream. For those Marines, past or present, we are all living the dream because we have served our country in the *Green Machine*. In my case, my dreams encompassed more than simply being a Marine.

My dreams were of freedom, opportunity, choices, and most important of all, the right to live my life free of oppression in a country composed of citizens who originally came from every corner of the earth. I was accepted in America based solely on my accomplishments, and there were no restrictions on how high I could climb.

The important point throughout this book is that my service in the Marine Corps was the high point of my life. During that career, I met and kept three lifelong friends and comrades in arms. The contributions to my life made by Skeet Von Harten, Chuck Davis and Barney Chen/Schenn enhanced my experiences and improved the quality of my life immeasurably.

I hope the chapters that follow will share my love of Corps and Country with the reader. You will discover that, in America, I was living my dreams and the Corps gave shape and substance to those dreams.

Peter S. Beck
10 November 2012

ACKNOWLEDGEMENT

Writing a book about your life over a seventy-seven year span requires a lot of thought, research and, most importantly, time. Once embarked on the project, the writer seems to feel that every small aspect of his life is of the utmost importance and must be described in minute detail. Nothing can be omitted if the work is to be a true reflection of the life being chronicled.

This usually results in an inordinately long manuscript filled with minutia that in the end is only interesting to the writer. Due to the writer's involvement with the story, (after all, it is his life) he cannot bring himself to delete a single stroke of his work. This is what happened with this book. It began as a 1350 page manuscript meant solely for the immediate family and friends of the writer.

When several readers prodded the author to produce a book with commercial appeal, based on his lengthy manuscript, the writer turned to his old and dear friend of over 53 years for assistance. Colonel Byron Thomas Schenn, USMC (Retired) graciously agreed to help and devoted many months of his time, thought and intellectual prowess to the production of this book.

He developed and arranged the photographs in this book from a large group of unsorted pictures and documents. Where no pictures were available, and he felt there should be, he was able to find them. This included old ships pictures and passenger manifests that were over 70 years old and resident in South American archives. He wrote witty and appropriate captions for these pictures and then arranged them in the sequences which are contained in the book.

Following this huge task, he undertook the job of editing my manuscript to a workable and interesting story that would appeal to all readers. In the process, he devoted months of arduous detailed work making each sentence and paragraph meaningful while at the same time reducing the volume of the book to a size that would not intimidate either the reader or the publisher.

Without my friend Barney, who appears often in this book, this work would not have been possible. There is no truer test of a long established friendship founded on love, honor, and mutual respect than to come through when asked for assistance. Barney met every challenge and helped me produce this book. While I may have put the words down on paper, Barney made them readable and interesting and, along the way, I incurred a debt to my friend that I can never repay.

I am glad he is my friend but, what is more important, I am honored to be his. We have known each other for 53 years, and God willing, there will be many more Chicago hot dogs (or any other kind) and good quality red wine.

Semper Fidelis, **my dear friend…**

and you can take that to the bank!

CHAPTER 1

THE JOURNEY TO FREEDOM

I was born in Berlin, Germany, on the third day of June 1935, at the Landhaus Klinik, a hospital in the Wilmersdorf section of Berlin. The hospital survived World War II and is now a Red Cross facility serving the needs of Berliners. This was my beginning, and this book tells of my exodus from Germany where my family escaped the clutches of the Nazi regime. I am a survivor of the country of my birth, and I honorably served my adopted country in time of war as a United States Marine. What follows is my story.

In 1935, the Jews of Berlin predominantly inhabited the Wilmersdorf and the Charlottenburg sections. In June 1935, I joined that group. My father, who was born in Berlin to a seventh generation Berlin family, was named Ludwig Adolf Helmuth Beck. He was born on December 3, 1899, which made him 35 years old at the time of my birth. My mother, Margarete Herzberg Beck, was also born in Berlin on January 27, 1906, which made her 29 years old when I was born. My parents were married in Berlin on March 22, 1934, after a courtship of several years.

My father worked for his father, Adolf Beck, who owned a textile mill and a costume jewelry manufacturing business. My father's brother, Kurt Beck, also worked in this business. The two brothers were salesmen and traveled throughout Europe selling the products my grandfather manufactured. My grandmother was named Emma Rudolph. She was not Jewish and, therefore, in the strictest interpretation of Talmudic Law, my father was considered a non-Jew, because it is the mother that passes the religion to her children and not the father. Whatever the case, my father considered himself Jewish, and documents relating to him since 1914 classified him as a Jew. Later, the fact that he married a Jewish woman made him a Jew in the eyes of the Nazi regime anyway.

My mother was a fashion model in Berlin and was closely associated with manufacturers of expensive women's clothing. This provided an opportunity for my parents to meet, since my father was selling textiles to several clothing manufacturers in Berlin. They met, and a two-year courtship evolved which culminated in their marriage.

While serving in the German Army in World War I, my father was severely wounded fighting the French. He sustained four machine gun bullet holes in his left arm, shrapnel in both knees (some of which remained for the rest of his life), and damaged vision in his left eye from an explosion near his face. At one time, he served as the company commander of his unit because all officers had been killed or wounded and evacuated.

After being wounded, he was evacuated to a field hospital where the surgeons decided they had to amputate his arm. He pleaded with them to save his arm, and he finally found a surgeon who was willing to try. The operation was a success, and for the rest of his life, his left arm was shorter than his right arm, and his left hand had reduced mobility. This infirmity required that he always wear custom made suits and shirts, a condition I think he rather liked, since he always enjoyed wearing good clothing. His rank while in the German Army was Muskatier in the 30th Infantry Regiment.

For his actions in combat, he was awarded the *Iron Cross,* First Class; the Iron Cross, Second Class; the Honor Cross of the World War with Swords (commonly called the Hindenburg Cross); and the Wound Badge. The Iron Cross, First Class, was always worn on the left breast of the uniform and was the highest award for valor that Germany could bestow. Recipients were issued a card which stipulated that the bearer could always get immediate service from any government agency in Germany. This card would be invaluable to him many years later.

After spending almost two years in a hospital recovering from his wounds, my father was declared 65 percent disabled and granted a lifelong pension. Throughout his life, this pension was paid to him by the German Government, and it is only through the documents relating to his pension payments that I have been able to piece together the fabric of his early life. This was because, to receive his disability pension payments, he was required to inform the authorities in writing every time he changed addresses, got married, and when he had children. Throughout his life, this pension was paid to him by the German Government. During Hitler's regime the pension was suspended, however, after the war the new German Government paid him all his back pension payments with interest, and continued to send him monthly payments until he died.

One of the few war stories he told me was that when he was finally released from the hospital in 1920, he was wearing his uniform with all his medals when he went to a train station to catch a train to Berlin. On the station platform, a group of hooligans assaulted him for losing the war! Luckily, a policeman broke up the altercation and escorted my father onto the train. He never wore his uniform again, and rarely spoke of his military service unless it was with other veterans.

My father continued to live in Berlin and work for his father, and from the pictures I have of his younger days, I see a very good looking and healthy appearing successful businessman who drove a Mercedes convertible and wore custom made clothing. One photograph I have shows him wearing a derby with a very stylish suit and carrying a walking stick while standing in, what appears to be, a very well-manicured park. It is my favorite picture of him.

If you could pick the place where you were to be born, a Jewish baby would never have selected Berlin, Germany, in 1935! What was happening at the time, and how did those events affect our family? To understand fully, we need to review German history. How could Adolf Hitler, an Austrian, be elected Chancellor and Reichs President of Germany in 1933, just two short years before my birth?

Germany entered the First World War from a position of strength, empowered by tremendous growth, both economically and socially. In many historical works, the period leading up to the First World War was called the Imperial Period. This period began in 1871, which is when Kaiser Wilhelm ascended to the throne in Germany, and ended in 1918 when Germany was defeated by the Allied powers of that time. The lengthy period of Kaiser Wilhelm's reign was considered one of Germany's most prosperous and successful periods. It was a period much longed for after the debacle of defeat, inflation, and depression that followed Germany's loss of the First World War.

During the years of prosperity, many changes took place inside the country which provided a better life for the average German. A limited form of religious freedom developed in a country that was predominantly Protestant, as Catholicism, long on the periphery of German society, became an accepted religion. Catholics began to join political parties and formed a voting bloc courted by politicians who previously had ignored them. Besides the Catholics, Germany's Jews enjoyed a far greater degree of freedom and were accepted within German society. With these changes came increased commerce with the rest of the world, and through this flourishing economy, a standard of living developed which made Germany the most prosperous society in Europe.

By the year 1910, statistics of the time show that 24 percent of all German Jews lived in Berlin. When the Kaiser declared war on August 4, 1914, he granted a general amnesty to all Germans, regardless of religious affiliation, social standing, or ethnic background, urging his people to rise as "one folk" to attain the common goal of victory for Germany.

For the first time in the long military history of Germany, Jews were recruited for military service and were even allowed to become officers. German Jews viewed this as an opportunity to prove their love for Germany and to eventually become accepted as full-fledged Germans. The census of Berlin in 1914, revealed that approximately 50,000 Jews were eligible for military service, and during the four year course of the war, over 18 percent of all German Jews served in the German Army. Of these, 4,000 Jews were promoted to officer rank, and a total of 1,500 Jews of all ranks were awarded the Iron Cross, First Class, for valorous combat actions. My father was one of those so decorated. Over 12,000 Jews died in combat during World War I, of which 1,917 were Berlin Jews.

In tracing the genealogy of the Beck family, I visited the huge Jewish cemetery in the Weissensee section of Berlin, and while I found the graves of all eight generations of Becks, I also discovered a large memorial park in the center of the cemetery dedicated to those 1,900 plus Berlin Jews who had lost their lives in World War I. The irony was not lost on me!

When Germany was defeated in 1918, odious fines and punishments were levied on the German people by the victors. These fines severely affected German society, and soon horrendous economic consequences ensued as the mark became almost worthless on the international exchanges. A nationwide depression followed which led to political unrest and general distrust of the German monarchy.

The German people demanded an end to the monarchy, and called for a general election to select a Reichs President (President of Germany) and Chancellor. Heated political activities began in earnest during 1932, a full year before the general election of 1933. Three viable candidates emerged: Paul Von Hindenburg, the revered old man with the flowing mustache; Ernst Thaelmann, the urbane statesman; and Adolf Hitler, the relative political newcomer and head of the Nationalist-Socialist German Workers (Nazi) Party. Each of the candidates promised to renew Germany's former strengths.

Adolf Hitler and his Nazi Party won the election, and in 1933, just two years before my birth, he became the Chancellor and Reichs President of Germany. Shortly after taking office, Hitler began a plan to develop and improve the German/Aryan race. He quickly found a scapegoat upon which he could blame almost all the faults of the current German society, and he decided that the Jews of Germany were the ideal targets. While he blamed Jews in general, he was very careful to exclude Jews who had been decorated for valor in combat or who had fought on the front lines during World War I. My father qualified on both counts and experienced no problems.

Almost immediately after his election, Hitler and his representatives began issuing decrees against Jews which would begin his "cleansing" of the Aryan race. In 1933, the following decrees became law:

- All non-Aryan civil servants in any branch of the government were to be retired, and only front line combatants from World War I were exempted.
- No Jew could participate in or be a member of governmental councils.
- Jews could not have any positions of authority in the National Labor Front.
- Jews could no longer take examinations to become doctors, dentists, pharmacists or lawyers.
- All university professors had to prove their Aryan backgrounds which immediately eliminated all Jews from any university position.

After my birth, my grandfather urged his two sons to leave Germany as quickly as possible. He did not see a bright future for Berlin Jews, even though most of them felt that Hitler would not be taken seriously and would soon be defeated in an election. My father, because of his war hero status, felt that he was not threatened at all and, with a new baby at home, did not feel he needed to leave.

While my father elected to remain in Germany, my Uncle Kurt immigrated to Australia in 1935, changed his first name to Ken, and served in the Australian Army during World War II. Although he was married, he never had any children, and he died in 1989 of Alzheimer's disease. My cousin, Steffi Beck, immigrated to London in 1936 and married a Jewish business man named Michael Borchard. She had one son who had two sons of his own, Jonathan and Terrence. Jonathan Borchard lives in London and runs a machinery parts business, and Terrence Borchard now lives in New Jersey, where he is a sales representative for a European machinery manufacturing company. My mother's brother, Hans Herzberg, had already immigrated to Argentina in 1922. He never left Argentina, and I know nothing about him. Thus, the Beck clan departed Germany on the advice of my grandfather, except for my father, who continued his life in Berlin with no interference from the new Nazi regime.

I am amazed that the legislation coming from the Nazi's did not wave a red flag in front of my father. Many of these directives were published in 1933 or 1934 before I was born. My father, because he was a war hero, was exempt from these directives, however, the rest of his family was not, nor were any of his Jewish friends. Because my father's friends and family members had money, they quickly left the country, and those that could, immigrated to the United States, England or Australia. Entrance requirements became more difficult after thousands applied for immigration between 1933 and 1937 and the countries tried to stem the already large influx of potential immigrants.

One of the most famous Berlin Jews to leave in 1935 was the Director of the Berlin Institute of Applied Physics. He had been the Director of the Institute for over 20 years when he departed for the United States and Princeton University. His name was Dr. Albert Einstein. What irony, because it was his *Theory of Relativity* that led to the development of the atomic bomb which eventually ended World War II in 1945.

In 1935, more directives concerning Jews were issued by the Nazi regime. For example:

- No Jew could become a citizen of Germany.
- No Jew could obtain a doctoral degree from any German university.
- Jewish doctors, lawyers and pharmacists lost their licenses to practice in Germany.
- No Jew could own either property or a business.
- No Jew could marry a Christian, or even have any kind of sexual relations with a Christian, under any circumstances.

Finally, on August 17, 1938, a decree was issued that required every Jewish male in Germany to take the middle name of *Israel*, and every Jewish female was required to take the middle name of *Sara*. This allowed the Nazi authorities to identify immediately that the person with this middle name was Jewish. I have documents that verify this decree and show me as Peter Israel Beck, my father as Ludwig Israel Beck, and my mother as Margarete Sara Beck. On October 5, 1938, all German Jews were required to have the letter "J" stamped in red ink on their passports.

While hindsight is always 20/20, I can't understand how any Jew living in Germany would even consider remaining in that country. That may be easier to say now, looking back on what eventually happened there. As far as my father was concerned, I honestly believe he always considered himself to be a German first and then a Jew. Also, since we were all redheaded with a fair complexion and blue eyes, we were exactly what Hitler's description of the perfect "Aryan" was, therefore, I am sure we were able to pass as Germans. Besides that, our surname was Beck, one of the most common and popular surnames in Germany.

Despite the decrees written since Hitler had taken power, and the constant harassment of the Jews in Germany, by 1937 only 48,000 of the 160,000 Jews living in Berlin had decided to leave Germany. Sadly, my father was a part of this startling statistic. This meant that 70 percent of the Jewish population in Berlin thought that things could not get any worse and decided to see it through to the end. The end, however, was too horrendous for any of them to imagine.

The pictures I have of that period show my family living a very good and prosperous life in Berlin. We took vacations to the seashore in Holland and to the Black Forest in Bavaria, and we enjoyed living in one of the most vibrant cities of the time. Obviously, my father had been lulled into a false sense of security because of his heroism in World War I, and the fact that he did not have a Jewish name. The Chief of Staff of the German Army under Adolf Hitler was named Ludwig Beck, the same name as my father. He was listed, along with my father, in the Berlin telephone book of 1937 and 1938. My father told me that he would occasionally get telephone calls for General Beck by mistake.

The night of November 9, 1938, Kristallnacht, or "The Night of Broken Glass," changed the lives of Jews all over Germany forever. Any German Jew who clung to the notion "things will get better" and that Hitler would not be taken seriously was proven to be disastrously wrong! It is beyond my abilities to understand what sobering thoughts went through the minds of the Jews of Berlin when they saw all of their businesses destroyed, every storefront window broken, and their shops looted. Every synagogue in Berlin suffered damage. Through all these events, the police ignored the perpetrators and watched as destruction rained down on every Jewish property.

The Jews remaining in Berlin were astounded that, by 1938, Hitler had already been in power for over five years. The events of Kristallnacht ended any illusions they might have had about continuing a normal life in Germany. With the realization that they were no longer safe in Germany came panic and chaos, as Jews began to look for any escape. Foreign embassies in Berlin and consulates throughout Germany began to see a daily influx of German Jews desperately attempting to leave Germany.

The three countries which seemed to be choices for most Berlin Jews were Palestine, England and the United States, all of whom had been fairly liberal in their entrance policies before Kristallnacht. With greater demand for entry came more restrictions, and fewer applicants were accepted. Compounding the problem was that the Nazi's required the presentation of a valid *entry* visa from a country before issuing an *exit* visa to that country. This made obtaining an entry visa from another country critical for any Jew. Each foreign government immediately established quotas for Jewish immigration, and Palestine even went so far as to restrict further entry by allowing only people who had specific skills to obtain the valued entry visa. Even with these barriers in place, records show that over 50,000 German Jews immigrated to Palestine during these times.

For the Jews remaining in Berlin, life became progressively harder as Jews were arrested for the slightest "offenses" and sent to concentration camps where they would serve their sentences and then be released. Later on, release from a concentration camp would only be by death! The handwriting was on the wall, and the walls were closing in on the Jews who remained in Germany. My father finally recognized the peril he and his family were in, and he tried desperately to obtain entry visas from any country. Unfortunately, he was unable to get any country to provide such visas. He was on the verge of accepting his fate when he received a telephone call from a friend who worked in the Argentinean Embassy.

The call came on Friday, February 24, 1939. My father's friend told him that the Argentinean ambassador was leaving Berlin for the weekend and that he (the friend) could provide him with three legitimate entry visas for Argentina, but they would only be valid for the weekend while he (the friend) had authority to verify the entry visas in the absence of the ambassador. Since the ambassador was scheduled to return to Berlin on Monday, February 27, my father had a very small window in which to act, so he rushed to the embassy on Friday evening and picked them up. The escape from Germany had just begun!

The next morning my father went to the district headquarters of the Nazi government to obtain his three exit visas since he now had "valid" entry visas to Argentina. When he arrived, there was a long line of Jews waiting to be processed. A Schutzstaffel (SS) Major was sitting at a desk in front of the line with several other SS personnel. They were taking their time and were in no hurry to issue exit visas to the desperate people waiting. As the hours passed, it became very clear to my father that unless he took some kind of instant action, there was no way he would get his exit visas that day, and there was no other opportunity for him to do so, since the office would be closed on Sunday and on Monday the Argentinean ambassador would return to Berlin.

Since drastic times required drastic action, my father stepped out of the line and walked to the front where the SS Major was sitting. He took out the card he had received when he was awarded the Iron Cross, First Class, and placed it in front of the Major. As he laid the card on the desk he said to the Major, "Based on my war record, I am entitled to immediate service, and I demand three exit visas according to the terms of this card." The Major was startled; however, he picked up the card, read it, saluted my father, and instructed his personnel to issue three exit visas to my father immediately. Again, my father's heroism in the face of overwhelming odds saved his life and the life of his family.

The year 1939 was very late in the game to be able to get out of Germany. Only 50,000 Jews were able to escape in that year and luckily we were three of them. The fate of the remaining 90,000 Jews is well known to anyone who is familiar with history. The saddest statistic of all is that in 1933, there were 160,564 Jews living in Berlin, and on November 1, 1946, only 7,274 Jews had survived.

It was imperative that we leave Germany immediately. My father had heard there was an organization in Genoa, Italy, which was assisting Jews in obtaining passage to South

America, so he decided to go there. On Monday morning, February 27, 1939, we flew out of Berlin to Genoa, Italy. I don't remember very much about the trip except that my ears began to hurt terribly, and I started to cry. The same thing happened when we landed in Genoa. Looking back on that day, instead of crying, I should have been laughing, because through my father's bravery, we had been spared the wrath of Hitler and we were now on our way to a new life.

We arrived in Genoa late in the afternoon on Monday, February 27, 1939. At that time, the Italian-Jewish Humanitarian Agency was helping Jews obtain legal entry visas and boat passage to Chile, Argentina, and Ecuador. These countries had agreed to lessen their entry requirements, and had instructed their consuls in Genoa to issue entry visas to whomever could present proof of sufficient funds.

Apparently, my father left Berlin with a considerable amount of money, because, in just a few days, he had obtained three valid entry visas to Ecuador and three passenger tickets on the Italian ship, M.S. *Orazio*. On March 1, 1939, we boarded *Orazio* for the Ecuadorian port city of Guayaquil. *Orazio* was one of two ships regularly taking Jewish refugees to South America. The other ship was the *Virgillio*, and each ship had accommodations for 423 passengers. The ships belonged to the Associates Italia di Navigazione Company in Genoa, and they always departed with a full passenger load.

There is an interesting follow-on story about what became *Orazio*'s last trip. *Orazio* and her sister ship, *Virgillio*, continued taking Jews to South America despite warnings from the Nazi government that this activity had to stop. On the afternoon of January 20, 1940, a powerful explosion rocked the engine room of *Orazio*. The ship had departed Genoa the previous day and was still in the Mediterranean Sea near Toulon, France, headed for Valparaiso, Chile. Fire spread throughout the ship very rapidly, and the captain transmitted an SOS. Four French Navy ships responded, but by the time they arrived, *Orazio* was well on its way to destruction. The Navy ships were able to save most of the passengers and crew, but the final report showed that 48 passengers and 60 crew members had lost their lives.

The official maritime report concluded that the cause of the explosion and fire was probably sabotage. Italian authorities have always maintained that the cause of the explosion was an act of sabotage by the Nazi's in retribution for not ending the ferry service of Jews to South America. *Orazio* was towed back to Genoa where she was demolished for scrap metal and never replaced. This act of sabotage had reduced the Jewish ferry program to South America by 50 percent in one day. The survivors erected a monument to Marconi, the Italian inventor of the radio, because it was a radio transmission that summoned the French rescue ships to the site of the tragedy. The monument still stands in Genoa today in the Piazza Marconi.

We arrived in Guayaquil on March 18, 1939. Guayaquil is located at the mouth of the River Guayas, which flows into the Golfo de Guayaquil and the Pacific Ocean. The Spanish built a shipyard there to build the large ships that transported the gold and silver they had plundered from the New World back to Europe. The ships returned, loaded with material the Spanish needed to colonize the cities they had captured. Guayaquil was always the most progressive city in Ecuador. The most revered man in Ecuadorian history is Simon Bolivar, El Liberador (The Liberator), who overthrew the Spanish and returned Ecuador to local rule. Every year, the biggest holiday is Simon Bolivar Day which commemorates this historic event.

My father rented an apartment, and we began our new life. He started a small neckwear manufacturing company, and my mother worked for him as the sewing machine operator and operations manager. In very little time, we spoke only Spanish, and while I was only four years old at the time, I remember speaking Spanish while we lived there.

I attended kindergarten and made friends with the children in the school. On Simon Bolivar Day, the school presented a military pageant. One lucky boy was selected to play Simon Bolivar, and I was selected to be the drum major of the troops as they marched in to the auditorium. I have a photograph of that day, and it shows the entire pageant on the stage of the school. Simon Bolivar is dying on the top of a large platform behind the Ecuadorian flag, and I am standing on the left side of the picture at the head of a line of troops. We are all in uniform, and it looks like it was a grand pageant.

Life was good for us in Guayaquil. The neckwear factory grew, and more workers were employed. The weather was always hot and humid, and we were always wet or damp, but after a while you became accustomed to your environment. Around March or April of 1940, I developed a cough that would not go away. At first, it was ascribed to the weather and the humidity, but when the cough became persistent, my parents took me to a doctor who immediately ordered X-rays of my chest. What the X-rays revealed was a shock to my parents, because it confirmed that I had tuberculosis. At that time, there was little that could be done for my condition, and the doctor recommended that we leave the tropical climate and go where there was a more moderate climate with better medical facilities. Thus, just before I was to turn five years old, my parents were faced with a major new problem -- my health.

My mother had an uncle, Julius Hesslein, who had left Germany before 1930, and was now a naturalized citizen living in New York City. Besides Uncle Julius, our family doctor from Berlin, Dr. Fritz Riesenfeld, had left Germany immediately after Adolf Hitler was elected in 1933, and immigrated to the United States. He changed his name from Fritz to Fred, took the medical licensing exams, and was licensed to practice medicine in the United States. My mother wrote to her Uncle Julius, and my father wrote to Dr. Riesenfeld and told them about my illness and requested assistance.

Because there were thousands of refugees trying to get into the United States in 1940, the only way anyone could immigrate without being part of an assigned quota was to have a sponsor who was an American citizen, and who would guarantee complete support for one full year after arrival. This meant providing not only the money necessary for living expenses, but they were also required to provide a place for the family to live. Finding a sponsor to commit to these conditions was very difficult. At first, my mother's uncle refused, but when she informed him that if he did not agree to sponsor us, it was a certainty that I would perish from my disease, Uncle Julius relented. He signed the necessary papers which provided our family with the much sought after entry visas into the United States.

On the morning of August 20, 1940, our family departed Guayaquil in a ship from Valparaiso, Chile, named *Aconcagua*. The ship made regular voyages from Valparaiso to New York City through the Panama Canal, stopping at Guayaquil, Cristobal in the Canal Zone, and Havana, before arriving in New York. After making the two stops in the Caribbean, we arrived in the United States of America on Friday, August 30, 1940.

As our ship sailed past the Statue of Liberty on our way to the commercial piers of Manhattan, the true significance of this arrival did not register in my five year old brain. It was not until many years later that I realized the good fortune my family had just experienced. By the time of our arrival in America, Hitler had invaded and captured Poland, Denmark, Norway, France, Belgium, the Netherlands and Luxembourg. Both the Battle of the Atlantic and the Battle of Britain were in progress. The city of my birth was being bombed, and Hitler had begun the extermination of the German Jewish population. Over 95 percent of the Jews of Berlin did not survive World War II. While war was raging in Europe, my family stood at the rail of the ship as we sailed up the Hudson River, viewing the skyline of New York City and looking forward to our new and unknown life in America.

CHAPTER 2

EARLY YEARS IN AMERICA

Our sponsor, Uncle Julius, came from a family of accountants in Berlin. He arrived in New York in the winter of 1930, shortly after the Great Depression of 1929, and landed an entry level accounting job at J.P. Morgan. While his fellow countrymen were struggling in Europe, Uncle Julius climbed the corporate ladder fairly quickly, and in 1936, he left J.P. Morgan and opened his own accounting office in the Empire State Building. When my mother contacted him, he was living on the upper west side of Manhattan on West 79th Street in a very upscale apartment house.

Uncle Julius had no children, and was married to a German Jew he had met in New York. They enjoyed a very good life. While he was certainly not thrilled over our extended stay, he did agree to sponsor us and guarantee our livelihood, as well as our accommodations for one year. This probably saved my life and allowed my parents to gain a foothold in our newly adopted country.

The second person my parents contacted shortly after our arrival was Doctor Riesenfeld, our family physician from Berlin. In 1940, he had a thriving practice in internal medicine in Manhattan and was on the staff of Mt. Sinai Hospital. Mt. Sinai Hospital is one of the oldest and largest teaching hospitals in the country. It is internationally acclaimed for excellence in clinical care, education and scientific research in almost every aspect of medicine. Dr. Riesenfeld had arranged to get me admitted to Mt. Sinai Hospital as a charity case for treatment of my tuberculosis. How lucky for me to be able to be treated at this outstanding hospital upon my arrival in the United States.

My father found employment at the R. H. Macy flagship store at 34th Street and Herald Square as a shipping clerk. My mother worked as a sewing machine operator in a neckwear manufacturing plant. This was the classic "sweatshop," but it provided the money our family needed, and there was no hesitation for two educated and highly skilled people to take the most menial jobs to survive in their new country.

My parents shared a bedroom in Uncle Julius' apartment, and when I was released from the hospital, I also slept in the same bedroom. Since my parents were working, they enrolled me in a rather unique day care center, called Children's Colony, which was located almost around the corner from Uncle Julius' apartment. Children were required to wear a uniform, and I remember the uniform being dark trousers, a white shirt and a dark blue cardigan sweater with the school logo on it. There was strict discipline, daily classes, closely supervised physical activity, and mandatory naps on folding cots. I have no bad memories from Children's Colony.

After work, my parents would pick me up at school, take me home to Uncle Julius' apartment, and then go to the local public school where they took English lessons. This is a noteworthy fact: Immigrants arriving in the United States then wanted to assimilate into the American culture and knowledge of English was required to become a naturalized citizen. While they retained their ethnicity, their primary desire was to become an American. This was aided by the United States, which insisted that all documents, examinations, ballots and any other official documents required for any purpose, were to be published only in English. If you could not read English, you were out of luck because you needed the English language skill to move forward in your newly adopted country. Quite a difference from the way things are today. In San Francisco alone, official city documents are now printed in 17 different languages, and that includes voting ballots.

One day, while my mother was at work, the production manager of the neckwear manufacturing plant died of a sudden heart attack. My mother went to the owner of the company and told him her husband was a university trained, textile engineer (my father had a degree from the University of Berlin in textile engineering). The owner of the plant told my mother to bring my father in the next day, and after a brief interview, he was hired. This new job paid much better than the job at Macy's, and it also made it possible for my mother and my father to work together in the same place.

Uncle Julius was getting very impatient for us to find a place of our own. By the first of January 1941, we moved into our own apartment located in Washington Heights in upper Manhattan. The neighborhood was a cultural mix of German Jews, Irish, Italians, Puerto Ricans, Greeks, Poles and Czechoslovakians. Our new home was right on the corner of Broadway and 170th Street.

In less than four months, we had our own apartment. I continued attending Children's Colony where my parents would leave me on the way to work. I was still going to Mt. Sinai Hospital for outpatient treatment. On days I needed treatment, my parents took me to the bus stop to wait for a double-decker bus, because those busses had a single seat over the right front wheel, and this seat was directly across from the driver. My parents would put me in this seat, ask the driver to tell me when he got to Mt. Sinai Hospital, and then I would get out and go to the area where I received treatment. After treatment was completed, I would wait for another double-decker bus and go home the same way, getting off at the end of the line. Imagine having a five-year old child doing something like that today!

I remember these times as being very good, and while I did not see much of my parents, my days at Children's Colony kept me busy and safe. On the day after Labor Day in 1941, I began elementary school at Public School (PS) 173, which was located on Fort Washington Drive and 173rd Street, about four blocks from my apartment and within easy walking distance. PS 173, like all other public elementary schools of the time, used one teacher to teach the initial grades which encompassed arithmetic, spelling, penmanship and geography. My teacher was a strict Irish woman who ran a taut ship and brooked no wayward behavior of any kind. A strict disciplinarian, she was also a very good teacher who cared deeply for her students. After all this time, I still remember her name; it was Mrs. Sophie Claire Conroy who signed her correspondence using her initials. I remember that you never wanted to take home a note to your parents that bore the signature of S. C. Conroy! I enjoyed my first year of school.

One Sunday in December, I was on the street playing with my friends when someone came running down the street yelling, "The Japs bombed Pearl Harbor, the Japs bombed Pearl Harbor." It was Sunday morning in Honolulu, Hawaii, on December 7, 1941. I think everyone who was alive then remembers exactly where they were when they heard the news for the first time. The streets seemed to fill up with people pouring out of their apartments. I ran home to our apartment. My parents were sitting in the living room listening to the radio and trying to figure out what to do next.

The next morning, Monday, December 8, men from all over the United States rushed to recruiting offices as President Franklin Delano Roosevelt declared war, stating that December 7, 1941, would be, "A date that would live in infamy," at least for the next few years! Among the hundreds of thousands of volunteers was my father who rushed to the recruiting office to volunteer for service. He was told that, while they appreciated his patriotism, a 41 year old, severely wounded, World War 1 veteran who was not a citizen of the United States, was not eligible to serve. My father was devastated, but immediately volunteered to be our area air raid warden when the program was instituted several months after the war started.

With the declaration of war, things began to change immediately, and all of us became participants in the war effort. Critical materials were rationed and hard to obtain. Gasoline, the most critical of all materials, was rationed first. Vehicles were classified as either being Category A, B or C. Every vehicle was required to have a sticker on its' windshield that displayed the A, B or C classification, and this sticker dictated how much and how often you could buy gasoline. This rationing began almost at once, and lasted for quite some time after victory was attained in 1945.

Shortly thereafter, all materials began to be rationed. Food was the first item after gasoline that was needed for the war effort, and a point system was instituted for all civilians. You could only buy a certain quantity of meat, and you always had to use points, besides money. Points were issued monthly as a ration book containing pages of tear off square coupons, each coupon being one point, so that you could save your points for special occasions; otherwise you ate canned meats such as SPAM, which was an acronym for spiced ham. Coffee was scarce, so a form of "fake" coffee was manufactured from vegetables that tasted somewhat like coffee. For women, all forms of silk and nylon were no longer used in the manufacture of clothing, as this material was essential in the manufacture of parachutes and other war equipment. Tires and all other things made of rubber became almost impossible to obtain.

Everyone on the home front, as it was called, made sacrifices for our men in uniform and small flags, which had a white background and a red border with a blue star in the center, began appearing in the windows across America. Each family that had a member serving displayed this flag in the window of their homes, and if more than one person was serving, there would be another blue star for every member of the family serving. One family in America had a flag with five blue stars for the O'Sullivan boys, all serving together on the same ship. If you saw this flag with a gold star, it meant that someone in that family had lost their life fighting for our country. It was a sad thing to see, and there were many of these flags as time passed. Unfortunately, the O'Sullivan family flag became a flag with five gold stars, as all five brothers lost their lives when their ship, USS *Juneau*, was sunk in the Pacific.

In New York City, a very aggressive air raid preparedness policy was put into place. Since New York City was one of the most important cities of the world, there was always the thought that it would be attacked by bombers or rockets in much the same way that London was being bombed. All neighborhoods in New York City had air raid wardens. My father proudly served as an air raid warden, and he felt that in this small way he was doing his share to fight the war. I remember that he was very conscientious about his duties, and, eventually, he was promoted to the chief warden for our neighborhood. This meant that besides his armband, he also wore a badge identifying him as the chief warden. He was extremely proud of that badge.

The years 1941 and 1942 were memorable times. The country was on a war footing, and everyone was doing their share to help the war effort. In the age before television, live pictures of combat footage were shown in the movie theaters by means of the newsreels that preceded every main feature. These newsreels were updated constantly and served as the only moving picture link between the home front and the war front. Newspapers published daily war maps to keep troop movements current, and reporters filed stories from the front lines that were published in all newspapers and read religiously every day.

On the home front, we were encouraged to conserve all kinds of materials for the war effort, and schools regularly had drives to collect essential materials like scrap metal, rubber, silk, and even cooking oils and fats. People started growing vegetables in their window boxes and these small gardening efforts were called "victory gardens."

I started second grade at PS 173 in September 1942, and shortly after school started our class held a scrap drive to collect as much metal as possible. I went home and told my father about the scrap drive and asked him to help me collect tin cans and other metals for the drive. One morning, as I left for school, my father gave me an envelope and told me to take it to the scrap drive. When I got to school, I gave the envelope to the teacher who opened the envelope and out fell my father's medals from World War I. This included his coveted Iron Cross, First Class, and his Wound Badge. The teacher was dumbfounded, but there was a note in the envelope that said my father could not think of a better thing to do than to have his old German medals help fight the Nazis. The significance of this gesture was lost on me at the time, but what a tremendous sacrifice it must have been for my father, and what a singular act of patriotism his contribution represented.

I never forgot that day, and many years later after I became an officer in the Marine Corps, I asked him to request a new set of medals from the German Government. They complied, and sent him an entirely new set of medals which he gave to me. I still have those medals framed and displayed on my wall at home. They are a part of our family legacy, and I have placed them next to my own medals from Vietnam. I hope someday in the future, the sacrifices we made for our country prove to be worthwhile.

As the war progressed, more patriotic activities occurred on a daily basis. In grammar school, boys were learning to tell the difference between American and enemy aircraft by studying the silhouettes. Posters appeared to tell us to buy war bonds and to keep our mouths shut because, *Loose lips sink ships,* or *The slip of a lip could sink a ship*! Almost no pleasure vehicles were seen anywhere, and food, clothing and almost all items manufactured for civilians were scarce. This included medicines, which were being sent to the front lines for our combat troops. If you traveled downtown in New York City, you saw only men in uniform. Times Square, known as *The Great White Way* because it was always lit up with so many neon signs, was blacked out as the signs had been shut off for the war effort.

In September of 1943, I began the third grade. The country was still engaged in the war, both in Europe and the Pacific Theater. Newsreels depicted our efforts in both areas, and the patriotic wave that swept across America continued to build and grow as more money and materials were needed to fight our two front war.

In February 1944, my mother suddenly became seriously ill. She went to see Dr. Riesenfeld, and nothing seemed to be able to ease her discomfort and her unusually high fever. It was necessary to take her to Mt. Sinai hospital in March, and because I had no one to look after me, my father's friends from Berlin, Emil and Trudy Kamp, agreed to have me live with them while my mother was in the hospital. My mother was diagnosed with spinal meningitis, a highly infectious disease. My father spent his every waking minute with her when he wasn't working. Because my mother had such an infectious disease, I was not allowed to visit her, but I spoke with her on the telephone from time to time. I remember I made her a plastic necklace in one of my craft classes at school which Emil Kamp took to my father to give to my mother.

One Friday in early May, the Kamp's were getting their apartment ready for a party that was going to be on the following day. I remember that everything was set up early on Saturday morning, and then the Kamp's left and I remained with a local girl who was staying in the apartment with me until the Kamp's returned. Early in the afternoon the Kamp's returned, and my father, along with many other people, was with them. I remember that almost all the people were Germans, and they seemed to know each other.

My father took me into the Kamp's bedroom and told me my mother had died on Thursday, May 4, from her disease. She had made the ultimate sacrifice because, if the antibiotics that could have saved her life had been available to civilians, she might have survived her illness. He told me that the people present had just come back from mother's funeral and that, for the time being, I would stay with the Kamp's until he could figure out what to do with me. I remember I was very hungry, but my father was extremely upset and he was crying. I don't think I fully understood that I had lost my mother forever. If I had, I'm sure that I would have joined my father in his vale of tears.

After we left the bedroom, many of the people at what was obviously a wake for my mother, came over to me to tell me how sorry they were that my mother had died. The only feelings I can remember from that time were of being numb and very hungry. In a way, because of the unavailability of the antibiotics required to treat my mother's spinal meningitis, my mother also became a victim of World War II, and I lost my mother at the age of eight.

My mother's illness, medical bills and hospital stay had totally exhausted my father's savings. There was no money available to take care of me, so my father began contacting charitable organizations to see if he could find one that would be willing to take care of me for a year. He felt that if he could do this at their expense, he could get back on his feet financially and take care of me properly.

All Jewish agencies refused his request since Jews were suffering in Europe, and all monies being raised were going to help the poor Jews caught in Hitler's holocaust. Finally, he received a letter from Father Flanagan of Boy's Town, informing him that Boy's Town would take care of me for one year. It looked like I was going to be going to Omaha, Nebraska, for a year when, at the last minute just a few days before my departure for Boy's Town, my father received a letter from the Quakers.

The Quakers stated they would care for me for one year, and that they would do so by sending me to a private school called Mohonk School for Boys, located in the Mohonk Mountain House in New Paltz, New York. Since this was only ninety miles from New York City, my father decided to accept the offer from the Quakers. He sent Father Flanagan a letter telling him that an offer closer to home had come at the last minute, and he had accepted it.

MOHONK SCHOOL FOR BOYS

In June 1944, I completed third grade at PS 174. After the July 4 holiday, I departed the Kamp's apartment with my father and took a train to New Paltz in Westchester County. We were met there by a Mr. Milbut, who identified himself as one of the Master's of the Mohonk School for Boys. He drove us up a long winding road into the mountains. Near the crest of one mountain, we came upon a magnificent lake called Lake Mohonk, and there, on the side of the lake, was a massive stone building that looked like a castle to me. This was the Mohonk Mountain House where I would be spending the next year of my life.

The Mountain House was opened as a resort hotel in 1877 by brothers Alfred and Albert Smiley, who were Quaker schoolmasters from Massachusetts. It stands today as a world class hotel and resort, and the building you see today is quite similar to the one my father and I saw for the first time in July 1944. At that time, Mountain House was open only in the summer and the resort was closed after Labor Day. The Mohonk School for Boys was located in a wooden building attached to the east side of the stone hotel. Mr. Milbut showed my father the room I would be living in alone until around September 1 when my roommate would report to school. He was an "old boy," having already completed two years at the school, and the staff thought it would help me to room with someone who already knew the ropes.

Mr. Milbut also said he lived at the school and would begin teaching me several subjects from July to September to prepare me for the arrival of the regular students. While I did not know it at the time, he turned out to be one of the finest teachers I have ever had, for he was well versed in the classics, mathematics, geography, Latin, Spanish, German, and world history. He was a Princeton graduate and a strong believer in the Quaker faith, with a sincere mission to teach and educate his charges, academically, socially and morally.

Tomorrow we would travel to New Paltz where Mr. Milbut would buy me appropriate clothing for my one year at Mohonk. From what he saw of my belongings, apparently I did not have clothing suitable for Mohonk School year round. Since I had no money and I was a Quaker charity case, everything bought for me would be gifts from the Quakers. The next morning, we bought complete outfits for the one years stay at the school. I had never owned so many clothes in my life, and all the clothes were top of the line brands.

On the drive to New Paltz and back, Mr. Milbut explained some things about the school and what would be expected of me. To begin with, Mohonk was not an ordinary school. It had been founded by Mabel Smiley in 1920 with the express intention of having a special kind of school that concentrated on educating young boys intellectually, socially, and with high integrity and moral standards. The entire course of instruction and the day-to-day activities would reflect the Quaker traditions of hard work and strong moral fiber.

According to the school brochure, Mohonk emphasized three things: personal health, a sound curriculum, and individual attention for each boy. A 1921 school bulletin pointed out that the school differs from the average school in that there are no fixed classes. Boys were advanced as rapidly as their abilities warranted. They were required to ride horses daily, look after and clean their own room's, and perform daily physical chores for the good of the entire school community. These chores were as much a part of the school educational process as their individual classes.

All meals were eaten in a formal dining room with the boys required to dress in coat and tie. A Master sat at the head of each table for discipline, table conversation and to enforce proper table manners. After dinner, which was the noon meal, a half hour rest period was required. After the afternoon nap, outdoor physical activities began in earnest. Vigorous physical activity was always required and took many forms. Boys would build log cabins in which they would spend nights sleeping, once the cabins were completed. In the winter, they would saw large ice blocks from the frozen lake which were then transported to a large icehouse where the ice was stored until it was used in the main house for refrigeration and food preservation.

Ice hockey was played by all boys, and there were competitions in both downhill and cross-country skiing. In the warm months, there was baseball, football, tennis as well as boat racing, swimming and diving. Horseback riding was mandatory, and it was done in both winter and summer. A large part of the riding curriculum was the care and feeding of the horses and maintenance of the stables. The boys performing all of these activities ranged from 10 to 14 years of age.

Discipline was strict. The Masters assigned "demerits" for any infractions of the rules, and when a boy attained an unacceptable number of demerits, he was required to walk them off for the number of hours assigned to the total number of demerits attained. The walking was always done outdoors, either around the small golf course or the entire lake. During July, I became familiar with all of these things.

Since the hotel was open in the summer, I ate at a staff table with Mr. Milbut, the house nurse, and the Headmaster of the school and his wife. We dressed for each meal, and while I remained fairly quiet during meals, I listened to the conversations and always answered when spoken to by any of the adults. I learned that Quakers respected their food and that you were required to eat everything you put on your plate. If you wanted it, you ate it; there were no leftovers. I guess this was a precursor to the adage, "Take all you want but eat all you take."

In the mornings, Mr. Milbut began testing me to see where I would fit. Since there were no formal grade levels in the school, he was interested in my existing knowledge and how capable and willing I was to expand my horizons. The school was trying to assess my abilities, since the school was listed as a private school for boys in grades 5 through 9. This was particularly interesting when you consider that I was nine years old at the time, and had just completed the third grade in the New York City public schools system. Mohonk was about to launch me into the fifth grade, since that was their starting point in the school.

Mr. Milbut spent the summer months indoctrinating me in the way the school operated, and he kept to the same sort of schedule the school would demand once it began in September. Every morning I was awakened at 6 a.m., cleaned my room, bathed and dressed for breakfast in coat and tie. At 7 a.m., I was seated at the staff table in the dining room and ate breakfast. From 8 a.m. to noon I had classes with Mr. Milbut. The classes were varied, but I do recall that they covered a vast array of subjects. I learned mathematics, penmanship and spelling. I read assigned books and wrote book reports, and, not to leave any stone unturned, I also learned about the Society of American Friends, which is the formal title of the Quakers.

I discovered that the Quakers were a simple congregational sect that conducted local meetings for communal worship and church business. I also learned that Quakers did not attend established churches, took no oaths of office and refused to bear arms. During and after World War I, the Quakers were instrumental in providing relief services in Germany, and they were highly regarded by the German population. Perhaps this is one of the reasons my father, in desperation after the death of my mother, turned to the Quakers for help. After Kristallnacht in Germany, the Quakers became active in relief efforts and championed a child refugee act in the United States to assist the children of Jews who were being persecuted in Germany. With this background, I began to understand how a Christian sect could take in a Jewish refugee child.

My summer classes always ended at noon. Since it was summer, I was allowed to swim in the lake with the hotel guests. I could take out the hotel rowboats or, on some designated days, I would go on two or three hour hikes with Mr. Milbut along the many wooded trails around the lake, or hike to the top of Skytop, the tallest mountain on the property. Swimming was my favorite activity. I found I was good at it and never got tired, and I could swim in the lake for hours at a time. This mandatory physical activity was my introduction to rigorous exercise, and I found that I enjoyed it and looked forward to my daily requirements. The need for exercise is something that has remained with me all of my life, and I am sure that it was instilled in me during my stay at Mohonk. It certainly came in handy during my twenty-two years in the United States Marine Corps. In the late afternoon, I reported to the hotel kitchen for my chores, which consisted of doing whatever was needed at the time.

On the day after Labor Day, the students of Mohonk School arrived, and I was introduced to my roommate for the year. His name was Robert, and I found him to be a friendly sort who was a good roommate, albeit somewhat shy. There was a total of forty students in the school and, as I recall, there were five or six teachers. There were four hours of classes daily from eight in the morning until noon. The basic reading, writing, arithmetic and social studies composed the core curriculum, while Latin was mandatory. We received individualized instruction, and we used the repetition method, meaning that we kept repeating something until we got it right. Sometimes, written errors had to be corrected by writing the correction one hundred times on a piece of paper.

As I mentioned earlier, discipline was dispensed using demerits and there were unusual ways to work off demerits. Besides the standard walking off of demerits, one could also work off demerits. For example, students could roll the tennis courts of the hotel, using heavy iron rollers that took three students to pull, or one could work on the maple sugar detail which meant taking buckets of sap from maple trees and pouring the sap buckets into steaming vats that were making maple syrup. I do not have a single unpleasant memory of any time I spent at Mohonk School.

In the winter, when the lake froze over, the most difficult demerit detail was the cutting of ice blocks from the lake. This was an important task since it provided refrigeration year round for the hotel and the school. Each student's demerits were posted on a school bulletin board, and the demerits had to be paid for before participation in any after school activities was allowed. Winter meant ice hockey, and we were avid players. I wasn't a particularly good skater, so I played goalie quite often, which did not exactly thrill me as I was not fond of being hit with hockey pucks. I turned out to be a fairly decent skier, especially in the downhill, where I won quite a few medals and ribbons.

The school was truly fabulous. I can't imagine learning any more than I learned in Mohonk in one school year. The teachers were highly intelligent, totally dedicated, and highly competent as teachers. They took a sincere interest in all of us, and our success was their success. I honestly don't know what "grade" I was in at Mohonk. I only remember that we were constantly studying and learning and working and playing outdoors. It was a good life.

While the level of instruction at Mohonk was outstanding, I remember one particular class that still stands out in my mind over 65 years later and, as luck would have it, it was a class taught by Mr. Milbut. One of his most avid interests was American railroads, and he believed you could learn the geography of the United States by learning the names of the railroads that traversed the country from the East coast to the West coast, and from Canada to Mexico. Towards that end, Mr. Milbut had a large map of the United States on the wall which showed the outline of the country, and then there were rail lines all over the map. He also had pictures of railroad logos, and he would distribute ten or twelve logos to each student. Our job was to tell him where those railroad lines traveled.

Believe it or not, it was a terrific way to teach geography. After all these years, I still remember some of those railroad lines, many of which no longer exist. For example, there was the Delaware and Lackawanna called The Anthracite Line because it hauled coal; the Memphis, El Paso and Pacific Line, famous because it never went to any of the three destinations in its' name; there was the Mobile and Gulf Line that was only 11 miles long and did not go to either Mobile, Alabama or the Gulf of Mexico; the Bellefontaine and Indiana, which became the Bee Line because it was easier to spell; the Alaska Railroad which was nicknamed "The Moose Gooser," and finally the Acme, Quanah and Pacific. Mr. Milbut would tell us that railroads routinely put Western, Pacific or Atlantic in their names to make them sound bigger than they were, even though most of them did not go there.

During the school year my father would call, and on rare occasions he would come to visit me. I always looked forward to his visit, and he always wanted to speak with Mr. Milbut to see how I was doing. Mr. Milbut gave him glowing reports about my school work, but felt that my deportment (personal conduct) could always stand some improvement as I fancied myself some sort of wit (which continues to this day). I liked Mr. Milbut very much, and he seemed to like me just as much, but, unfortunately, after I left Mohonk, I never heard from him again.

All good things must end, and my days at Mohonk were ending at the end of the school year. There was no way my father could ever afford to keep me at Mohonk. The Quakers gave me a precious gift. At the age of ten, I was fairly certain that doing 5th grade work was probably going to be very easy for me, no matter where I went to school. They allowed me to keep all my clothes and, as a farewell present, I got to keep the ice hockey skates.

I had received a wonderful education, both scholastically and physically. I was self-confident. I was prepared to take on any challenge and, most importantly, I realized that anything in life worth attaining required hard work. I owe this to the American Society of Friends, who truly were friends to a depressed and sad little boy who had just lost his mother. I have never forgotten their kindness.

I was at Mohonk when the war in Europe ended. The Germans surrendered unconditionally on May 7, 1945, and it was announced in the United States on May 8. Unfortunately, Adolf Hitler chose to commit suicide in Berlin rather than be captured by the Russians. I remember that there was much celebrating at the school, and our teachers told us that for the rest of our lives, we would always remember May 8, 1945. Sadly, they were wrong. A war in Europe that took the lives of millions of people is hardly remembered today.

The country was, however, still, at war with Japan, and the Allied powers began their final preparations for the invasion of the Japanese homeland. At Mohonk, Mr. Milbut showed us the island hopping campaigns going on in the Pacific. We saw islands called Guadalcanal, Tinian, Pelilu, Guam, New Guinea, Bougainville, Tarawa, Iwo Jima, and Okinawa. Mr. Milbut showed us how each island came closer and closer to the main islands of Japan. The United States Marines were receiving rave reviews for their bravery in these island campaigns, and many movies featuring the Marines were being made in Hollywood.

The school year ended on June 24, 1945, and I said farewell to my teachers and classmates, none of whom I would ever see again. I had just turned ten years of age, and my whole life was about to change drastically.

OLGA AND NORTH CAROLINA

On the train from New Paltz to New York City my father dropped a bombshell on me. He told me that while I had been at Mohonk, he had joined a social club composed mainly of German immigrants, and he had met a woman he liked very much and who wanted to have children. When he told her he had a ten year old boy, she was very enthusiastic about meeting me, and they spoke often of providing me a home with a father and a mother.

My father was a man of immediate action and acted on what he thought was right, and did not confer with anyone else. He obviously did this in combat, where he was so successful, and he continued to act in this manner throughout his life. For example, he did not believe I should attend my mother's funeral, so I did not. It was his decision and, as far as he was concerned, that was the correct decision. He went on to tell me he was so interested in providing me a home with a mother that he had married the woman, and she was waiting to meet me. He also informed me that we were moving to North Carolina.

I was doubly surprised. First, I was very apprehensive about my new "mother," and furthermore, why in the world were we going to North Carolina? We arrived at our apartment, and I met Mrs. Olga Jablon Beck. She spoke fluent German, although she was Polish, and fluent English. She was about 5 feet 6 inches tall and had red hair and blue eyes. This was quite a surprise to me since my mother also had red hair and blue eyes. She had been living in the United States for over ten years when I met her, and she was already a naturalized citizen. She seemed nice at the time and told me how happy she was to meet me.

My father had accepted a job with the Wellco Shoe Corporation of Waynesville, North Carolina, where he would be the production manager. The company had contracts with the US government to manufacture boots and hospital slippers. My father had sublet our apartment, and we had to vacate it within three days. He had bought a car, a 1940 Studebaker President, and it would take us to Waynesville. I remained quiet during the trip. I was depressed and uncomfortable since, again, something significant had happened in my life and I had no input into it. At ten years of age, I was simply confused.

We arrived in Waynesville in July 1945. While the South is hot in July, Waynesville was cool and breezy. In the height of the summer, the average temperature was 70 degrees because Waynesville is located at an altitude of 2,713 feet in the Great Smoky Mountains. We immediately moved into a house the shoe company had rented for my father which belonged to a man serving in the Army. When the owner returned from Europe, we would be relocated. It was a luxurious house, directly across from the Siler farm which manufactured pork sausages.

My father began inquiring about schooling for me and was informed that the public school system was not particularly good, but there was a small private school in Waynesville called St. John's School, which was run by the Catholic Church. After a visit to the school and discussions with the Nuns, it was agreed that, in September, I would start the fifth grade.

On August 6, 1945, an atomic bomb was dropped on Hiroshima, Japan, causing 90,000 casualties and destroying the city almost instantaneously. The Americans called on Japan to surrender immediately and warned the Japanese that more atomic bombs would be dropped on other cities if the Japanese did not surrender. To the shock and amazement of the entire world, the Japanese did not surrender. On the morning of August 9, 1945, another B-29 bomber dropped the second atomic bomb over Nagasaki. On August 15, 1945, under orders from the Emperor of Japan, the Japanese surrendered and World War II was over. Waynesville had a big celebration; automobile horns sounded, flags waved everywhere and total strangers embraced each other in happiness and joy.

Throughout the summer, I noticed a disturbing pattern developing at home. Whenever my father was present things were calm, and my life was good, but after he departed, Olga would begin to find fault with everything I did. There was no pleasing her, and we quickly developed an adversarial relationship that ended the moment my father came home, and then began again when he departed for work the next day. My reaction to this was to spend as much time away from home as I possibly could. This habit lasted for the entire six years we were together, and would lead to some severe self-esteem problems for me down the road.

Mr. Siler, the hog farmer and sausage maker neighbor, took a liking to me and I spent hours with him watching the meat smoking process and the hog raising going on at his property. Mr. Siler had only daughters, so I think having a young boy around the farm gave him some pleasure, and it certainly made my days far more enjoyable. I also performed some light chores around the farm for which Mr. Siler always paid me. This really made me feel good about myself, but I never told my parents about the money I was earning.

Waynesville was a small town. It had one Main Street, where all the shops were located, as well as the court house and the post office. One of the shops on Main Street was an auction house that sold expensive antiques and art objects to summer tourists. It was owned and operated by a Miami Beach businessman named Mr. Fink, who was not only the owner, but also the auctioneer. The town's local newspaper, the *Waynesville Mountaineer*, had its' offices on Main Street and was published once a week on Wednesdays.

The closest large city was Asheville, located 30 miles southeast of Waynesville, where the courts and government agencies were located, as were the big stores. It was in Asheville that I first saw separate colored and white facilities. Drinking fountains, waiting rooms and all public entities were clearly labeled "white" or "colored." I didn't understand what this meant until my father explained it to me. He simply told me that these were the rules for living in the South and that if something was labeled "colored," I could not go into it. He told me that this was very similar to what we had experienced in Germany, only this time it was another group of people that were being discriminated against. I often snuck a drink at a "colored only" drinking fountain, just because I thought it was a great trick to pull on the southerners.

Jews were also discriminated against in the South, but in a much more subtle manner. Hotels and lodging houses, as well as golf courses and private clubs, all had signs posted outside their properties proclaiming that the property was "Restricted." Restricted was the southern way of saying that Jews were not allowed inside. Even America in 1945 discriminated against Jews.

After Labor Day, I began school at St. John's. My teacher was Sister Cordea, who I remember as one of the most beautiful women I had ever met, up to that time. She was also a wonderful teacher, however, when she was dispensing discipline her beauty faded very quickly as one of the three white knots of her white rope belt that she wore around her habit, descended on the top of your head. It was rumored, but never substantiated, that Sister Cordea had some lead weights tied into that infamous third knot. I didn't doubt it, because I was a favorite target of hers, as my habit for unsolicited remarks continued at St. John's.

I met many new friends at St. John's, but the one that stands out even today was what I would have to call my first girlfriend, Miss Sally Stovall. Sally was the daughter of one of the wealthiest men in town and lived in a large mansion on top of a hill. Her mother, whose name was Margaret, was kind to me from the moment I met her, and I never forgot the kindness and love she gave me. Often, she would pick me up downtown in the Chrysler Imperial and drive me to the house for Cokes and cookies. Once accepted by the Stovall family, Sally and her mother became my second family.

Besides spending time with the Stovall's, I got my first real job in Waynesville when I was hired as a paper carrier by the *Waynesville Mountaineer*. I was issued a cloth bag from which I would sell newspapers. The papers sold for a nickel and I got two cents for every paper I sold. I spent every Wednesday walking up and down Main Street selling the *Mountaineer*.

After I completed my newspaper rounds, Mrs. Stovall and Sally would pick me up, and we would drive to the local gas station where Mrs. Stovall bought us a bottle of Coca Cola. In those days, Coke came in a 5½ ounce bottle and on the bottom of each bottle, printed right into the glass, was the bottling company location where the bottle had originated. Since the bottles were returnable and used repeatedly, it was quite possible to get a bottle from as far away as California or Florida. We would finish our Cokes and then look at the bottom of the bottle, and whoever had a bottle that came from the furthest distance from Waynesville, won the game for the day. It was great fun and I remember the joy of winning to this day. Mrs. Stovall was a wonderful person and, in many ways, she was the mother I wished for but never found after the loss of my own mother.

One Wednesday, as I was walking down Main Street, Mr. Fink was standing outside his auction house. He asked me if I walked by every Wednesday, and I told him I did. He then asked me to come back to the auction house in a few hours with any papers I did not sell. When I returned to the auction house, I saw that it was full of people who were seated in rows of seats, bidding on large works of art. When Mr. Fink saw me, he stopped the auction and told the group about me, saying that I was working for money to go to college. He called me to the front of the gallery, took all my papers out of my shoulder bag and began to auction each paper to the seated audience. Most people paid a dime for the paper and a few even paid a quarter. Mr. Fink gave me all the money he collected, and he always sold all my papers.

We did this every Wednesday for the whole time I lived in Waynesville. Mr. Fink enjoyed doing it, and the audience apparently got a big kick out of the paper auction. I sold all my papers, and I made quite a bit of money. I soon became the most successful paper carrier and no one, except Sally and her mother and Mr. Fink, ever knew my secret. Mr. Fink told me that the newspaper auction put the crowd in a better mood to bid on art items after we completed the sale of my papers. I was glad that I was contributing to Mr. Fink's business, and he always treated me extremely well.

One Sunday, I went to church with Sally and her mother. They were Methodists and I was baptized as a Methodist because they were doing baptisms, and I thought it would be a nice thing to do for the Stovalls. I never told anyone about this, but I guess I decided to cover all my bases, even at ten years of age. After my baptism, I became even closer to the Stovalls.

In April 1946, I went to Asheville with my father and watched him become a citizen of the United States. He was sworn in at a ceremony in the Asheville Court House and was given an American flag and an American flag lapel pin, as well as his citizenship papers, which he proudly showed to all of his business associates. I was proud of my father because he was so happy to become an American. He was proud of that fact until the day he died, always professing his love for his adopted country.

We were notified that the owner of the house in which we were living was returning from Europe. The company procured another one for us, and we moved to it on the thirteenth hole of the golf course of the Waynesville Country Club, which was really out in the country. The house itself was nicer than the one we left and had a commanding view of a truly magnificent golf course.

Shortly after my father became a citizen he was able to locate my grandmother in Berlin through the Red Cross. She had survived the heavy allied bombing and was living in a bombed out building with some of her old friends. The fact that she was not Jewish had obviously saved her life. The Nazi's, however, had killed her husband, my Jewish grandfather, early in 1942. He was seriously ill in a hospital bed in Berlin when the Nazi's systematically killed the old, sick Jewish people in the hospital by ordering the hospital staff to inject them with drugs that would kill them instantly. That is what happened to my grandfather. He was indeed a victim of the Nazi Holocaust but was saved from the horrors of the gas chambers of the concentration camps.

Once my father found out where my grandmother lived, he began to send her weekly CARE packages of food and essential items for health and comfort. CARE was an organization that was founded in the United States in 1945, and the letters meant, "Cooperative for American Remittances to Europe." The purpose of the organization was to send lifesaving packages to the survivors of the war in Europe. The first 20,000 CARE packages arrived in Europe in May 1946, and I am sure my Grandmother was one of the first people in war-torn Berlin to receive such a package. The first CARE packages were US Army surplus food packages that were left over from the war.

The summer of 1946 became quite profitable for me as my newspaper sales continued at the art gallery. Mr. Fink had discovered that the "newspaper auction" as he liked to call it, was good for business so he decided to embellish his patter to his clients when I arrived every Wednesday afternoon with a full bag of *Waynesville Mountaineers*. I was now going to go to medical school, Mr. Fink told his assembled clients. I had decided I wanted to become a doctor and was working to save every penny I made for college and then medical school. While the previous year had netted me dimes and occasional quarters for my five-cent papers, now it seemed as though the least I ever got was a quarter, quite a few fifty-cent pieces and even an occasional dollar bill! I was becoming a very good businessman, thanks to Mr. Fink.

There was one significant disappointment for me at St. John's which revolved around my inability to serve as an altar boy. Father Tait, the young pastor of St. John's Church, was my teacher in the catechism classes we were all required to take, and I was one of his best students. I asked him why I couldn't serve as an altar boy, and he told me that I was not

Catholic and, therefore, I could not be an altar boy. I never could understand how I could be one of his best students, but still remain unqualified for altar boy duty.

My father continued sending weekly CARE packages to my grandmother in Germany and soon, letters began arriving from Berlin, in which my grandmother detailed the horrors of World War II for her. She had been chased through Berlin by allied bombs, buildings were destroyed around her and food and water supplies were almost nonexistent. Berliners lived in fear of the Russian invaders who raped, pillaged and burned wherever and whenever they could.

In May 1945, after the unconditional surrender, Berlin was divided into four zones, with each of the victorious forces administering a part of the city. Luckily, my grandmother was in the British Sector of Berlin, because, while the American, French and British Sectors, enjoyed relative normalcy, the Russian Sector of east Berlin lived under draconian, communist regulations. As the Russians began to make life ever more problematic for the survivors, my father decided he would bring my grandmother to the United States.

One morning in April 1947, my father told me we were going to Asheville for a court proceeding. I dressed in a suit, shirt and tie, had my picture taken on Main Street, and we drove to the courthouse. We were ushered into a courtroom and there, behind a large bench, sat a judge in his robes. Soon my name was called, and I was escorted before his bench. The judge asked me if I knew why I was there, and I replied that I did not. I remember the judge to be a very kindly man who explained to me that I was becoming a citizen of the United States. He asked me if I wanted to become a citizen, and my enthusiastic "yes" resulted in applause in the courtroom.

The judge asked me my name, and I told him it was Peter Beck. He then asked if I had a middle name and I replied I did not. The judge then informed me he was filling out my new citizenship papers, which required the newly taken photograph of myself in my suit and tie. He further stated that, in the United States, almost everyone had a middle name, and if I wanted one, this was the time to tell him. He asked me if there was a name I liked and I told him I liked the name Steven. I don't to this day know where that name came from, but it popped into my mind at that exact moment, and that was the name I told the judge. The next question the judge asked was, "Is that with a 'v' or a 'ph.'" I didn't have the slightest idea what the judge was talking about, but I said that it was with a "v." That is how I became known as Peter Steven Beck and not Peter Stephen Beck! I might be one of the few people in America who gave themselves their own middle name.

In early May 1947, we were informed we would have to vacate the golf course house because the owners would be coming from Florida for the summer months. This time, my father rented an apartment in a small complex within the town borders of Waynesville. The apartment was much closer to St. John's, and this also meant I could walk to the Siler Farm to visit Mr. Siler.

I returned to St. John's in September 1947, entering the seventh grade. My association with Sally Stovall and her family continued and Sally and I became inseparable at school. We were both the same age and in the same grade, and we spent all our time together.

My father, with the help of the American Red Cross, had arranged to bring my grandmother to the United States. One day in early December 1947, my father took a train to New York City where he met the plane bringing my grandmother from Berlin. Two days later, I met my grandmother for the first time since I had been a small child in Berlin. I remembered nothing about her from those days, and the person I met in Waynesville was a 75 year-old woman who was so crippled by arthritis, she required two canes to walk. She was alert and clear of mind and spoke only German. She moved into my bedroom, and I slept on the sofa in the living room. I spoke often with my grandmother, but after the initial conversations, there was little else to talk to her about since I was twelve years old and, sadly, had little interest in what had happened to her during the war.

The situation in Berlin was not good. Food shortages continued, and the restrictions the Russians placed on travel throughout Berlin made life more difficult than it already was because of bombed out buildings, reconstruction, food rationing and shortages of all types of goods and services. My father continued sending CARE packages to my grandmother's friends, and letters indicated that they were getting along better than most people in Berlin.

In June of 1948, I completed the seventh grade and became an official teenager. Life at home was cramped but, since the arrival of my grandmother, Olga's constant denigration ceased because my grandmother was always in the house. I remember wondering how my grandmother could even enjoy being with us. She couldn't go anywhere, she didn't speak the language, and besides my father, Olga and me, she knew no one in the entire United States. She spent hours writing letters to her friends in Berlin.

In September 1948, I began the eighth grade at St. John's, little knowing that 1948 would become another pivotal year in my life. In November, my father came home one day and informed us that he had been offered a job in New York City with a men's fashion company. The salary was far more than what he was receiving in Waynesville, and since he had only sublet our apartment in Washington Heights, we could return to New York City. He waited until the Christmas break at St. John's, and we then left Waynesville.

It was a very bittersweet time for me. I was leaving the Stovall's, who had been my family in North Carolina. I was saying goodbye to Sally, who I was convinced was the only girl for me, and whose loss would ruin my life. Nevertheless, I was left with no options, and on a dreary evening in December 1948, I bid farewell to the two women I truly loved, and whose memory would remain with me for the rest of my life. Three years in North Carolina was not enough, but it was all that I was allowed.

CHAPTER 3

GROWING UP IN NEW YORK CITY

Returning to New York City in the winter of 1948, I was not the same person I was when I left the city after my mother's death in 1944. In four years,

- I had attended an exclusive boy's boarding school for one year,
- became an American citizen,
- spent three years in the American south,
- attended a private Catholic parochial school, and
- I was a Jewish boy who had been baptized a Methodist.
- My attitudes were very different, perhaps enhanced by the fact that I was also a teenager who knew everything and feared nothing.

On the first day of school in January 1949, my father took me to Junior High School (JHS) 115. We were ushered into the principal's office, and I was surprised to see that Mrs. Conroy, my old teacher from PS 173, was now the principal of Humboldt Junior High School (the official name of JHS 115). Mrs. Conroy told my father that, in view of my unusual education, she would test me and see where I would be assigned for the second half of the school year. When the tests came back, I was placed into the 9th grade.

After returning to our apartment, I went out on the street. Looking back on that moment, I now realize that my immediate future was going to be determined by which direction I turned when I got to the corner of 170th Street and Broadway. I turned towards 169th Street and Broadway, and started walking to that corner. Without my knowledge, I had just opted to grow up Irish-Catholic. Had I turned in the other direction towards 171st Street and Broadway, I would have grown up German-Jewish.

As I walked towards 169th Street, I noticed a group of boys about my own age standing on the corner. Since I was redheaded with blue eyes, they were friendly towards me and asked what I was doing in their area. I replied that I had just moved into the neighborhood. They asked the usual questions like which school I went to, and I told them JHS 115. At that point, one of the boys said, "Well, I guess you're in Incarnation Parish," to which I answered yes. He went on to say, "We're all in St. Rose of Lima Parish, because the dividing line is right here at 169th Street." This was a stroke of luck for me later on, because I could always claim Incarnation Parish activities when I didn't go to Mass with them at St. Rose of Lima.

The boys I met were the Lynch twins, Kevin and Sean, and Gerry Quinn, George Duncan, Patrick O'Halloran, and Tom Day. All these boys were Irish immigrants, and not a single member of their families had yet been born in the United States. They were all members of a gang called the Celtics, and they advised me that if I wanted to get along on 169th Street, I'd better join or never show my face on 169th Street again. I decided to join the gang and keep my Jewish heritage a very private affair. From then on, I was a Catholic German, which, while not Irish, was marginally acceptable to the group.

The first week in January 1949, I started the 9th grade at JHS 115 and met many great kids there. George Zografi, whose father owned a pharmacy on St. Nicholas Avenue, Steve Katz, who lived on 173rd Street right by the schoolyard, and Vernon Jacobs, who lived on 172nd Street and, like me, had escaped from Nazi Germany with his parents in 1936.

All these kids had working papers, and because of them, they had after school jobs. I immediately applied to get my own working papers which had been instituted in New York City to eliminate the exploitation of children in the workplace. For many years, in the early 1900s, children were used in many factories and stores and were paid almost nothing. They worked in poor conditions for little pay and with utterly no regard for their safety or well-being. The Working Paper Law in New York City stated that no merchant or employer in the City of New York could hire anyone below the age of 13. In addition, all 13 to 17 year-old children were required to have papers attesting to their age, address, and authority to work within the city limits.

Through a stroke of luck, the day after I got my working papers I went into the Broadway Pharmacy, located at 168th Street and Broadway, and asked if there was any opportunity for a part-time job. The owner, a Mr. Harkavy, said he needed a boy to deliver prescriptions, and that he would pay me 50 cents an hour plus I could keep all the tips I would receive. Mr. Harkavy had graduated from Columbia University, and since the pharmacy was around the corner from the world famous Columbia-Presbyterian Medical Center, he got a large amount of business from the doctors at the hospital. When I reported for work after school, I was busy until I had to go home at 6 p.m. every evening. I made quite a bit of money from tips, and I enjoyed working for Mr. Harkavy. I would rush home after work, eat dinner, and then go out on the street until 9 p.m., which was my bedtime.

One day, George Zografi, from JHS 115, invited me to his Boy Scout Troop meeting. The scout troop met at the Broadway Temple Methodist Church which was entirely underground. You walked into a small building at the street level and then went down for five floors. On the bottom floor was a complete basketball court and four bowling alleys. The scout troop met every Friday evening in the basketball court.

The scout troop was very impressive. It had six patrols of about ten boys each, and each patrol had a totem pole as a patrol flag which was held by a patrol member. Every boy was in uniform, as were all the leaders. The meeting was conducted in a very military manner, with each patrol reporting to the scoutmaster who took the report. Then the patrols broke up for classes in various scouting skills. I was very impressed, and I told my friend, George Zografi, that I thought I'd like to join. George took me to the Scoutmaster, Mr. Chaves, who had been the Scoutmaster of Troop 718 for over 20 years. He arranged to meet my parents the following week and explain what was expected of me as a Boy Scout.

Mr. Chaves visited my parents the next week. He informed my father about the Boy Scout movement and told him that Troop 718 was the oldest Boy Scout troop in New York City, having been formed in 1912. My father had only one question for Mr. Chaves, and that was, "What is the highest rank in Scouting?" Mr. Chaves told him that it was an Eagle Scout. My father then turned to me and said that if I joined, I would become an Eagle Scout or there was no reason to join. I agreed, and the next Friday evening I was inducted as a Tenderfoot Scout into Troop 718.

The following weekend, I went downtown to the official Greater New York Council Boy Scout store and bought a complete uniform. I was in, and it felt great. When I told the Celtics about the troop, Tom Day and George Duncan also joined, thus, unknown to Mr. Chaves, he had three new scouts who also happened to be members of a tough Irish street gang, a fact about which he was totally unaware and remained unaware.

Just before the New Year 1949, I met Rose Mary Fitzgerald, who lived on 169th Street and was an immigrant from County Waterford in Ireland, and whose brother, Kevin, was one of the parish priests at St. Rose of Lima Church. Rose Mary was in 8th grade at St. Rose of Lima School, which is the school that all my Irish friends attended before going to a Catholic high school. Rose Mary and I became boyfriend and girlfriend, and it lasted until 1953 when I was in college. She was truly the love of my life, at the time, and there are so many wonderful memories of our times together that I think about her even to this day.

My Grandmother and I shared a bedroom in our apartment, but my grandmother was truly unhappy. She wanted to return to Berlin, because, as she told my father, she wanted to die with her friends around her in a country that she knew. Things were not so good in Berlin. The Russians had blockaded Berlin in June 1948, and the allied forces were forced to establish the Berlin Airlift to fly supplies into Berlin, since that was the only way that the people living in the allied sectors of Berlin could receive supplies.

The blockade was finally lifted on May 12, 1949, and the Federal Republic of Germany was formed on May 24, 1949. My 79 year-old grandmother then returned to Germany. She lived for another five years and died on March 14, 1954. She was much happier in Germany, and my father continued to send her food parcels and other items until she died. After her death, he continued sending packages to her friends who had taken such good care of her.

School was progressing very well for me. In February 1949, we were informed that in May we would be taking our first State Regents exams. Passing these exams was necessary to be promoted to the next grade. New York had an exceptional educational system. Exams for all subjects taught in high school were prepared in the state capital by a committee of educators. The test was prepared in secret, and then on one day throughout the state, the exam was administered to every student in the state at the same time. This was an outstanding system, and it takes the testing process out of the hands of local teachers whose only job under this system is to teach their students. If you failed the Regents exam, you failed the class, and you had to repeat it the following year. There were no appeals, no excuses, and no exceptions.

Besides the Regents exams, there was also the issue of which high school you were going to attend. Living in Washington Heights, my district high school was George Washington High. Except for the Catholic kids, who would be going to parochial high schools, everyone in my neighborhood was going to George Washington in September 1949. I included myself in this group.

One day, after a Boy Scout meeting, my friend, George Zografi, told me he was going to be taking the test to get into Stuyvesant High School. I had never heard of Stuyvesant, or for that matter, of a special test to get into Stuyvesant. George told me that Stuyvesant was one of three high schools in the city that required entrance exams. The other two were Bronx High School of Science and Brooklyn Technical High School. These schools were extremely difficult to get into, but they were open to students in all five boroughs, and they were public schools, so they were also free. He told me that the test would be given in two weeks at JHS 115 and that I should apply to take it. He said that the test was given only once a year and he, Vernon Jacobs, and Steve Katz, were going to take it. If they passed, that would mean they would be going downtown to Stuyvesant in September, instead of going to George Washington with everyone else. I decided to take the test.

I went to see my counselor at JHS 115, and she helped me fill out the necessary paperwork. She informed me that the test was the same test for all three specialized high schools and that when you took the test, you had to check which school you wanted to attend. I didn't pay that much attention to the issue, because if my friends were all going to Stuyvesant, then that was where I wanted to go. I never told my father I was taking the test because I had no idea how important acceptance to Stuyvesant was in New York City. I was just taking the test to stay with my friends. I didn't study for the test, and I didn't even know where Stuyvesant was, except that it was downtown.

On the day of the test, there must have been at least 250 students at JHS 115 who were going to take it. Of course, some were competing for Bronx Science and others were competing for Brooklyn Tech. I got my test papers, checked the box for Stuyvesant, and took the test. Looking back, the test was pure English, math and science and, as we were told, our score on the test would be placed on a list and the top 250 grades in the entire city, meaning all five boroughs of New York, who had selected Stuyvesant, would be admitted to the school. The rest of the students would have to go to their district high schools.

Three weeks later the city wide results were published, and each high school published a list of the students it had accepted. George Zografi, Steve Katz, Vernon Jacobs, and I were accepted to Stuyvesant and would be starting the sophomore year in September 1949. I casually mentioned to my father that I had taken a test for Stuyvesant and got accepted. He had no idea what that meant until he went to work and told some of his colleagues that his son had gotten accepted at Stuyvesant, and they all told him what a fantastic accomplishment it was. Suddenly, my father was extremely happy for me, and I could thank George Zografi for it. Since I had gotten accepted at this school, I now made it my business to find out something about it.

STUYVESANT HIGH SCHOOL LOGO

I had, again, been very lucky concerning schools. I had been accepted to one of the most prestigious public high schools in the entire United States just because I wanted to go to school with my friends! In 1949, Stuyvesant High School accepted only 250 boys each year. There was apparently terrific competition and much studying, preparation and tutoring involved to prepare to take the test and earn one of the coveted 250 spaces available. Entire families were devastated if their son failed to be accepted, and given the number of boys taking the test each year, over 97 percent of applicants were denied admission.

Stuyvesant was founded in New York City in 1904. Together, with the Bronx High School of Science and Brooklyn Technical High School, it was one of the three original Specialized High Schools in the city. Gaining admission to one of these three schools was purely by academic testing. They were pure meritocracies, which means that the only thing that was considered was your score on the entrance exam. Nothing else has ever been considered for admission. There are no quotas, and no "special considerations." Stuyvesant is noted for its strong academic programs, having produced four Nobel laureates. Stuyvesant High School is left out of the annual national list of the top 100 High Schools in the country because its' standards are so high and its students score too high on all national testing. It is not considered to be on a par with regular high schools. The Bronx High School of Science and Brooklyn Tech are also excluded from the national ranking.

In 2007, the test for admission to Stuyvesant was taken by 28,000 New York City 8th graders, and only 850 were offered admission to the school. This 3 percent admission rate is similar to the admission rate that was being used in 1949 when I took the test. Stuyvesant was located between 14th and 15th Street on First Avenue in the lower east side of Manhattan, a one-hour subway ride from my home in Washington Heights. The new Stuyvesant High School is a ten story modern building on Battery Point at the tip of Manhattan.

While acceptance at Stuyvesant proved to be a highlight of my year during 1949, I also was accepted into the Scout troop drum and bugle corps where I played the snare drum. During a scout meeting, Mr. Chaves stated that the troop was low on equipment and that it needed more to go on the annual two week summer camping trip to Camp Manhattan at the Ten Mile River Scout Camp Reservation. George and I told Mr. Chaves that we knew a man at the New York Central Railroad who we were sure would donate excess equipment to our troop. Mr. Chaves was very excited about this news, as was his assistant scoutmaster, Jim Morris, who had been a Marine during World War II.

What neither of these two men knew was that the Celtics regularly broke into railroad cars on the New York Central siding near the Hudson River. During some of our forays into the railroad cars, George and I noticed that every passenger car had an emergency compartment built into the car. The compartment was covered with a glass panel which stated that the glass was to be broken only in the case of a railroad emergency. In those days, railroad accidents were not uncommon. This usually left the passengers stranded, and that is why the emergency compartments existed in the passenger cars.

Inside each emergency compartment the following items were stored: one collapsible canvas water bucket, two long handled axes, two short handled axes, one canvas water bag for storing water, three flashlights, one crowbar, one sledgehammer, and several boxes of field rations. George and I made a quick assessment, and we felt that ten cars were all that we needed to outfit Troop 718 for the summer. George, Tom Day and I broke into ten cars and stole the equipment in the middle of the night.

The following Friday evening, we presented the equipment to Troop 718 amid much fanfare. Each piece of equipment was marked "NYC" in a black diamond, the symbol of the New York Central Railroad. We thought we were pretty sharp until Mr. Chaves asked us for the address of the man who had donated the equipment, because he wanted to send him an official letter of thanks from the Boy Scouts. We told Mr. Chaves we would get him an address. We left the meeting greatly worried, as we didn't have the slightest idea how we were going to get out of this situation. We decided we needed help, so we went to Jim Morris, our assistant scoutmaster, and told him the truth. He was flabbergasted that we would do such a thing, but, since he liked us and didn't want to see us get in trouble, he told us he would handle the situation. He warned us never to do that again, and to not speak about the incident again under any circumstances. Mr. Chaves did not ask us again for the address after we had spoken to Jim Morris, and the equipment went to summer camp with the original markings taken off and replaced with Troop 718 markings.

Rose Mary and George could not understand why I wasn't going to a parochial school, so I told them that my father could not afford it. While they accepted my explanation, it must have been hard to imagine my father not being able to afford sending me to a parochial school when their fathers, who were both truck delivery route drivers, could somehow afford to send their children to a private, parochial school. The fact that I got accepted at Stuyvesant helped my explanation, since everyone in New York City knew how hard it was to get accepted into that school.

School work was also progressing well. I looked forward to graduation from JHS 115, entering my sophomore year at Stuyvesant High School in September, and my first summer trip to Boy Scout Camp with Troop 718. My schedule was certainly full, and it adhered to my father's desire to "always remain busy and occupied."

THE STUYVESANT PERIOD:
BOY SCOUTS AND HIGH SCHOOL

Our Boy Scout troop had been assigned the first two weeks of the summer of 1949 to go to Ten Mile River Scout Camps. That was good news, but it also meant that we got to spend the hottest time of the summer on the streets. The Ten Mile River Scout Camps were a truly special place. In 1924, Franklin Delano Roosevelt was the Governor of New York, who in his youth, had been an avid Boy Scout, and who remained active in the scouting movement as the President of the Boy Scout Foundation of New York City. Roosevelt formed a committee to search for a very large tract of land which contained lakes, streams, swamps, timberland, sufficient area for the construction of extensive hiking trails, and had to be almost a complete wilderness environment.

Eventually, in 1927, 1,100 acres were bought near Narrowsburg, New York and the Ten Mile River Boy Scout Reservation was born. On my first trip there in the summer of 1949, I found that the reservation consisted of five major camps, one for each borough of the city. Our camp was Camp Manhattan. Each week, 3,500 Boy Scouts from the five boroughs, spent at least one week in these camps. Each borough camp was totally self-sufficient.

I fell in love with Ten Mile River and wanted to stay the whole summer, but my father could not afford it, so I went about gaining the most out of my two weeks as possible. I quickly earned Second Class Scout rating and earned credits in swimming, rowing, canoe-ing and sailing. During each period a troop was in summer camp there would be secret elections for the Order of the Arrow, which was an honor society based on Indian lore, and you could only get into the Order if your fellow scouts elected you. Only the best and most worthy scouts in each troop were elected.

The day before we were to return to New York City, I heard that a scout, who was a dishwasher in the mess hall, had fallen and broken his arm. I ran to Mr. Morris and asked him if he could help me get that job for the remainder of the summer. My quick action in this case resulted in my receiving a scholarship for the rest of the summer. I became a dishwasher on the mess hall staff, and moved into the staff cabins on the day the troop left to go home.

The next six weeks were hard work and entailed at least three hours of work per meal in the mess hall, but I also finished all my First Class Scout requirements, except for the six months service as a Second Class Scout. This meant, that having finished the First Class Scout requirements, I could start earning some of the 21 merit badges I needed to become an Eagle Scout. When I returned to the city in late August, I was well on my way towards my Eagle Scout goal, plus, I had secured a promise of a job as a dishwasher at the camp the following summer for the entire eight-week program.

In September 1949, I started school as a sophomore at Stuyvesant High School. My classes started at noon and ended at 5 p.m. In those days, Stuyvesant had split sessions, with the freshmen and sophomores going from noon to 5 p.m. and the juniors and seniors going from 7 a.m. to noon. While this was only five hours of class, it was always an intense five hours of classroom instruction, and there were no breaks, no recess, and no lunch time. In fact, Stuyvesant didn't even have a cafeteria.

Getting to Stuyvesant was another adventure. Since we had to be at school by noon, we left Washington Heights at 10:30 a.m. every weekday morning. We were given free subway passes by the Board of Education, and we would meet at the 168th Street subway station and catch the world famous "A train," downtown. Probably one of the most famous jazz songs ever written is *Take the A Train*, written by Bobby Strayhorn and first performed by Duke Ellington. He wrote that song because it was the train you took from downtown up to Harlem, and all the after-hours clubs that were there. We just happened to take it from uptown, through Harlem, on our way downtown to school. Our route took us about one hour each way, and was taken twice a day for the entire three years that I attended Stuyvesant. On hot days, we would ride between the cars until the conductor would chase us back inside. On cold days, the temperature inside was warmer, but smelly, because there were always more people than seats. We were very lucky, because getting on at 168th Street, we always got seats for the ride downtown.

The beginning of Stuyvesant was a real eye opener. The competition was so strong, that from the first day, you could cut the academic tension with a knife. Everyone took college preparatory classes. The only unanswered question was, which college. I had to take chemistry, algebra, English, history, German (this was a break for me since it was one of the required languages being taught) and Latin. I had so much Latin at Mohonk and St. John's that luckily, Latin was not much of a problem for me, but the rest of the work was demanding.

The teachers were there to teach, and they were not disciplinarians. It was up to you to pass the Regents exams in each subject, and the teachers gave you all the information you needed. In every class and every subject, grades for all tests taken were publicly posted for all to see, and all grades were displayed in percentages. A perfect grade was 100 percent, and a failing grade was anything under 65 percent, but woe be to anyone at Stuyvesant who got below a 75 percent in any test, for they became the constant butt of jokes, ridicule and scorn.

When we arrived at Stuyvesant, usually around 11:30 a.m., we had just enough time to get a sandwich at *Ptomaine Joe's*, before going to class. Since there was no lunchroom or cafeteria at Stuyvesant, the pushcarts and catering wagons all vied for our trade. Invariably, we were drawn to a small sandwich shop that was located directly across the street from the main entrance to the school. Many years ago, some Stuyvesantian had dubbed it "Ptomaine Joe's," and that's what it was throughout my three years at the school. Besides Ptomaine Joe's, there were pushcarts selling knishes, hot dogs, flavored ice cones (for some reason, they were called Italian ices) and ice cream. The city closed 14th Street to traffic from 11 a.m. to 1 p.m., Monday through Friday, so that the students could eat their lunches on the street. It was great fun, and it was the social hour before total immersion in serious studying and classroom work.

At noon, the bell rang, and the freshman and the sophomores went into school as the juniors and seniors ran out to repeat the whole lunch process on the street. I can just imagine all the "concerned parent's groups" today who would be up in arms over this system, but it was a great system for the times, and it was a total "New York experience." I treasure the memories of lunches on the street at Ptomaine Joe's.

I kept my job at the pharmacy and went to work at 7 a.m. to begin delivering prescriptions to the hospital. I worked until 10 a.m. and then went to the subway station to meet my friends and take the train to school. I always made enough money to buy lunch and even to buy something for dinner before going home.

I continued my scouting activities and became very active in Troop 718, becoming the Patrol Leader of the Eagle Patrol, advancing to First Class rank by January 1950, and taking all the merit badges that I could take in the city.

School was very difficult, but I soon learned that if you studied exactly what the teachers taught you in class, you would always pass the exams. I rarely put in any extra time and spent more time working and hanging out with my friends. It is important to point out that in 1949, two of the top three public high schools in New York City were for boys only. Only Bronx Science admitted girls, so they were never a distraction at Stuyvesant. The three schools were also different in another way. Although all three schools were predominantly Jewish, they were open to any student who could pass the entrance examinations. Conversely, today in 2012, all three schools are coed and predominantly Asian.

Stuyvesant boys were quite eclectic. There were also many tough boys going to the school, including a basketball player named Jack Molinas, who would end up shaving points while playing for the professional Detroit Pistons. Later, Jack Molinas was gunned down in Hollywood by the mob for interfering in some activities where the mob felt he did not belong. The truth was, that while some of the student body certainly was to be avoided, all of them were smart, and all of them deserved to be in Stuyvesant. Most of them graduated, because once you got in, you were a fool not to avail yourself of one of the best free educations available in the entire United States.

Being located directly on the A train line meant that we were literally only 25 minutes from Broadway. By Broadway, I mean the *Great White Way* that stretched from 34th Street to 59th Street, and included all theaters, movie houses and nightclubs that were known all over the world. Times Square was at 42nd Street, and it seemed to be the hub of all activity. Just walking around Times Square was an adventure. Usually a draft card, which showed that you had registered for military service, was your entry into the New York City adult world. You had to register on your 18th birthday.

Stuyvesant really put pressure on us. We took only three Regents exams in JHS 115, but every final exam in Stuyvesant was a Regents exam, and that meant that during Regents exam time, the school was like a pressure cooker. We formed a study group to prepare for our Regents Exams, using study guides, which contained sample questions, from previous exams. This reinforced my theory, that by studying for the exams using previous questions, you could pass any of them. You simply wouldn't be able to earn a college scholarship for high grades, which George Zografi. Vernon Jacobs and Steve Katz all accomplished, and I did not.

At any rate, we took our sophomore year Regents exams, and while I scored in the 80th percentile, the other three in my study group all scored in the 95th percentile. In my defense, the only thing I can say about that is that I probably had more fun than they did, and this was a pattern that would follow me for the rest of my life. Having passed the exams, we were finishing our first year in Stuyvesant, and in September 1950, we would all become "Sunrisers," a term used to identify juniors and seniors who began classes at 7 a.m. every morning.

Summer arrived, and I was off to Camp Manhattan to start my second year on the staff of the Boy Scout camp I loved so much. Two other notable events happened in June of 1950. First, I became 15 years old. I thought I was the "cat's meow," after all, there just wasn't anything you could tell someone who had just turned 15 in New York City! The real historic event, however, was that the North Koreans invaded South Korea on June 25, 1950, and the United States supported the efforts of the South Koreans to throw off the invaders from the North. The draft again began calling up young men to serve in the "police action," as President Truman called it, and reserve units all over America were being called to active duty. Thus, in just five years after the Second World War, American men found themselves engaged in combat again.

I did not grasp what impact this news might have on my summer, since once school ended I was off to the Ten Mile River Scout Camps. I had secured a position as a dishwasher the previous summer, so I reported one week before camp opened to help prepare the camp for thousands of campers who would soon be arriving from the city. We cleaned cabins, mowed lawns, painted fences, repainted signs, unclogged plumbing, and did whatever projects the camp director felt had to be accomplished. Then, again, one of my lucky charms must have come into play.

The Camp Quartermaster, who was the camp supply clerk, post office manager and canteen manager, had an appendicitis attack and had to be rushed to the hospital. It was not a simple case, and he had to stay in the hospital for several weeks. I volunteered to take the job until he returned, and the camp director gave me the opportunity. I was designated as the Assistant Quartermaster in the absence of the Quartermaster, and I performed all his duties for the rest of the summer. The real Quartermaster came back after four weeks, but by that time I had done such a terrific job that the camp director let me stay on in this newly minted position.

I looked forward to the arrival of Troop 718 on the fourth week of camp. I learned that the Troop would come to camp with only one leader, and that was Mr. Chaves, our Scoutmaster. All other adult leaders had been in the Marine Corps Reserve, and their unit was called up to go to Korea. By the time Troop 718 arrived at camp, all assistant scoutmasters were already on their way to Korea. Luckily, every one of them came home when the war ended. They had all seen combat in World War II, and we were afraid that their luck might run out, but it did not.

I was elected into the Order of the Arrow in 1950, and immediately became involved in the Indian ceremonies that the Order performed in camp. I had already earned Indian Lore Merit Badge, so my interest in American Indians came in handy when I became the Ceremonial Chief for the Order of the Arrow ceremonies. It was great fun, and I enjoyed the Indian ceremonies very much. The following year I would perform a hoop dance at a scout jamboree held in Madison Square Garden.

My summer at Ten Mile River was a very successful on two fronts. First, I had secured the job of Camp Quartermaster for the 1951 camping season, and second, the George Zografi method of taking all of our field merit badges at summer camp, was really working for me. There were seven merit badges we could earn at camp, and all of them were required for Eagle Scout. One of them was pioneering, which was an extremely interesting merit badge and required knowledge of how to make emergency bridges, rope ladders, slings and other field expedient items for emergency situations. Later, I would actually use some of these skills in Vietnam.

Returning to the city, I realized that my job at the pharmacy was running out. As a Sun Riser at Stuyvesant, I had to leave the 168th Street Station by 5:30 a.m. This meant that any job I took after school would have to start at 1 p.m., since I got out of school at noon. Mr. Harkavy at the Pharmacy agreed that it would be very difficult for him to accommodate my schedule. I still needed an after-school job, and with some help from the

City of New York employment office, I found a job as a page in the New York City Library System. The job itself entailed replacing books in their proper locations in the library shelves, repairing torn books, filing new arrivals and all other tasks that the full-time librarians required. The pay was better than the Pharmacy, but since there were no tips, I wound up making less money at the library.

Life as a Sun Riser was exciting. The classes got progressively more difficult, as I was now taking zoology, physics, mechanical drawing, architectural drafting, geometry, and calculus. Along with these, I continued my German studies because it was an easy grade, and I felt I needed all the help I could get in the purely academic environment I found myself in at Stuyvesant.

I became a "forever morning person" at Stuyvesant. Getting up at 5 a.m. and starting classes at 7 a.m. makes you appreciate the morning, and forces you to engage your brain early and keep it going for the rest of the day. I still find that mornings are my favorite time of each day, and I seem to be wide awake as soon as I am conscious. Remember, by the time the bell rang for the first class at 7 a.m., we had already completed a one-hour train ride to school. We never ate breakfast and waited for lunch at Ptomaine Joe's.

When I began my sophomore year I had arrived at a crossroads in my life. I didn't know it at the time, but my decision in this single issue would influence the rest of my life. As a junior and a senior, the boys of Stuyvesant were rapidly approaching the time when they had to make life decisions. This meant that many of the students had to decide what they wanted to become in life, and then aim their studies and efforts towards getting into the right college or earning a state scholarship to help with college. These boys were the ones who took their studies seriously and spent almost all of their time studying to earn high grades.

There was another element at Stuyvesant, and probably the best way to describe these boys would be to call them "wise guys." They were all smart (or they wouldn't be at Stuyvesant), but they had attitudes that said that they were prepared to deal with whatever came along, and the time to have fun was now. Their studies would take care of themselves, and since they were all juniors and seniors, they had already proven that they could pass the Regents examinations and would all get into college somewhere.

While the bookworms studied and concentrated, the wise guys lived on the edge constantly. They had fake draft cards so they could drink in the bars of New York, they cut classes to shoot pool at Julian's Billiard Academy on 14th Street and Union Square, and they initiated and regularly attended an event that became a New York City wide, high school tradition. It was called *Saint Paramount's Day*. While George Zografi, Steve Katz and Vernon Jacob opted to become and remain bookworms, I opted and actively participated in all the wise guy activities.

Stuyvesant High School was run like a university. You went to classes with different teachers who taught only that subject. When that class was finished, you had five minutes to get to your next class, and this went on throughout the school day. Attendance was taken in each classroom, but the teachers were not particularly interested in who was there or who was not. The goal of the school was to prepare a student for the Regents examinations and acceptance to college, and whether a student attended every class was rarely even an issue. If a student was inclined to miss a class from time to time, it was never noticed in most cases. The wise guys loved this feature of life at Stuyvesant.

As I had mentioned previously, the Stuyvesant wise guys had begun a practice called St. Paramount's Day. Word would circulate throughout the school that the following Wednesday, for instance, would be St. Paramount's Day. This meant that any Stuyvesant student that wanted to participate would meet at the entrance to the Paramount Theater at Times Square and Broadway in time for the first performance, which began at 8:30 a.m. This was a movie followed by a live performance of either a famous band or a famous singer or entertainer. I can remember Louis Armstrong playing our high school song with his band, Frank Sinatra welcoming all the Stuyvesant students, and Dean Martin and Jerry Lewis making jokes about the Stuyvesant students who cut class to see their show. I can remember Benny Goodman and his band playing the Stuyvesant Marching Song, all from the stage of the Paramount Theater at 9:45 in the morning, immediately after seeing the newest Paramount Pictures movie release. The price to see the movie and the stage show was about $1.25.

My father always insisted that when I was not going to school, I should be working, so I always had an after-school job. Through his connections in the garment district, my father got me a job at a company called Raxon Fabrics, which had offices and workrooms in the heart of the garment district. If you saw pictures of it today, you would see people pushing carts loaded with dresses and fabric through the streets of the district from one company to another, or to the post offices for mailing of packages containing samples of dresses and fabrics. This job was much more exciting than the library job, so I quit the library and went to work in the garment district. My job was to take the customer's order, wrap it, and then wheel it to the post office for shipment. This was in the days before UPS and FedEx would come to your door and pick up the shipments.

Life on the streets of the garment district was exciting and always active. I generally worked from 1 p.m. to 6 p.m. and then took the subway home. If I wanted to eat dinner downtown, there were many restaurants in the garment district and around Times Square to eat. There was a diner near the 34th Street Post Office that was my favorite spot. I remember that they always had very good soup, and for fifteen cents, I could get a big bowl of hot soup and a large roll. If I wanted anything else, there was a hot dog pushcart between 34th and 35th Street that was always available. I never went hungry.

While I was at Stuyvesant, my extracurricular activities were running on the varsity track team. I was on the mile relay team, and our team ran in the Milrose Games High School Mile Relay event at Madison Square Garden. We came in last in a field of six. I was also on the varsity swimming team, 50 and 100 yard freestyle events, and played the kettledrums in the high school symphony orchestra. My scouting activities continued on schedule, and I became a Star Scout.

The Regents exams came and went. I passed them all, again with grades in the low 80th percentile, while my three friends from Washington Heights passed all of their regents exams with grades in the 95th through 99th percentile. I had begun to think that George Zografi must be a genius, or maybe he just spent a lot more time studying than I did. The guys at Stuyvesant were talking about going to college, but I still had my senior year to worry about that, so I wasn't very interested in their discussions.

Summer came, and I returned to Ten Mile River Scout Camps as the Camp Quartermaster. I knew this would be my last summer at the camp, because the next summer I would be graduating from high school, and I was either going to go to college or go to work full time. In either case, scout camp would be out of the question. I was determined to make the most of my last summer and enjoy it to the fullest.

I earned all my required outdoor merit badges, and I worked like a beaver. I got sailing, canoeing, woodworking and rowing merit badges and then, after four more attempts, I finally got the Bird Study Merit Badge. I had conquered the final obstacle for Eagle Scout as far as I was concerned, because I would have no problems with the rest of the requirements. First, though, I had become a Life Scout, which I did.

When I left Ten Mile River at the end of August 1951, I said goodbye to a wonderful time in my life. The Boy Scout program, as it existed then, was a wonderful means to teach self-reliance, creativity, integrity and good citizenship. It is unfortunate that, over the years, the program was watered down, reduced in intensity, tailored to be performed by boys who could not meet the exacting standards of the old methods, and had age requirements reduced to make scouting "available" to more boys. Like so many things, reducing the standards and the requirements did not make the program better, it just made it different, and, therefore, future scouts never had the opportunity to experience the things we did, in the manner that we experienced them. In my own case, almost all the things I learned in scouting helped me at some point later in my life.

Returning to Stuyvesant in September 1951, meant I was entering my senior year and that there had to be some consideration given to what I was going to do with the rest of my life. My association with the Celtics steered me in the direction of the New York City Police Department, which was heavily constituted with Irish and Italian employees. There was a school called the Delehanty Institute that guaranteed that its' students, who enrolled for the full course, would pass the citywide exam for incoming police officers. Rose Mary, who was entering her junior year at Mother Cabrini High School, thought it would be a good idea for me to go to Delehanty and take the police test. If we were going to get married, she thought that having a cop in the family would be a good thing. I surfaced the issue with my father who did not favor this course of action.

I had gotten into some trouble with the Celtics and had to appear in Juvenile Court. A friendly judge suggested that my father take me to Columbia University and have me tested to determine if I was college material. The City of New York paid for the test, and the results were that I was suited for college and that I would make an excellent chemical engineer. I continued my studies in Stuyvesant, and worked on my Eagle Scout requirements, as well as hanging out with the Celtics and getting into occasional fights with other competing gangs who would intrude into our territory. These fights were fought with fists and sticks and guns were never used. You could get injured in these fights by brass knuckles, metal garbage can lids and an occasional bicycle chain, but you could never get shot.

Meanwhile, school continued and the seniors were talking about going to college. Applications were being sent out and, because each application cost money, my father limited me to three applications. I applied to Hobart College in Geneva, New York, St. Lawrence College in Canton, New York, and Union College in Schenectady, New York. I got accepted at Hobart and St. Lawrence but did not get accepted at Union College.

When my father saw how expensive it was to send me to these colleges, all of which were private schools, he told me that based on my attitude and behavior, he wanted me to prove to him that I would be serious about college work and attend a cheaper state college for one year after graduation from high school. This way, I would show him that I could do the work and graduate with a degree.

My counselor in high school located a small state school on the New York-Canadian border called Champlain College that had been set up to help returning Korean War veterans adapt to college life. The average age of the students was much higher than the normal 18 to 20 years of age of college students then, and the counselor felt that this environment would help me get serious about going to college. It was also a fairly small school with only 1600 students, located in Plattsburgh, New York, right on the shores of Lake Champlain. I filled out an application, and was accepted to enter the Freshman Class in September 1952. I would be 17 years old then and probably one of the youngest students in the school.

In the winter of 1951, I began taking the New York City Life Guard classes that were being taught at the 23rd Street YMCA. Each year, the New York City Department of Parks and Recreation, conducted training for life guards for the pools and beaches that they operated all over the city, and they needed over 1,200 life guards to man these pools and beaches each summer. The top 250 candidates were allowed to select where they wanted to work, and the remainder of the list was assigned to a pool or beach, depending on the needs of the Department. It was to your benefit to finish as high on the list as possible. I passed the course, earned my second Senior Life Saving Certificate, and finished in the top 250. I selected Rockaway Beach as my place of employment for the summer of 1952.

With my summer job assured, I concentrated on completing my Eagle Scout requirements, which I did. George Zografi, George Duncan, Tom Day and I became Eagle Scouts in April of 1952. There was a ceremony, called a Court of Honor, conducted by the church in which all four of us received our Eagle Scout badges. Since I did not want Olga there under any circumstances, I never told my father about the Court of Honor, and I was the only one of the four Eagle Scouts who did not have a family member present. After the ceremony, I took the Eagle Scout medal home and showed it to my father who was very pleased that I had earned the highest award in Scouting.

In May 1952, we were hit with Regents exams all month long. These were important tests because those seniors who attained high grades were automatically awarded State of New York Scholarships that were worth a lot of money at any state operated college or university. I took the Naval Reserve Officers Training Corps examination, and if I passed I would get a four-year scholarship to any one of the top four-year universities in the country. I failed the test and did not get any scholarship offers. George Zografi, Steve Katz and Vernon Jacob all earned state scholarships and made the school honor roll.

I finished my high school education with an overall grade of 82 percent for four years of purely academic work. My 82 percent placed me fourth from the bottom of the Stuyvesant High School graduating class. Our valedictorian had a grade of 100 percent over four years, the Salutatorian had a grade of 99.99 percent over four years, and then it went down from there. This is what happens when you go to a top academic high school. If I were to take my 82 percent average today, it would equate to a 2.9 grade point average over 4 years. Not exactly fabulous, but certainly not too bad considering that I did very little more work than what was required.

Regardless of my final average, I departed Stuyvesant with credits in algebra, geometry, trigonometry and calculus. In the Sciences, I had credits in biology, chemistry, zoology and physics, I had taken world history, and American history, American and English literature, German, Latin, mechanical drawing and automotive mechanics. I had been on the varsity track and swimming teams, and played in the school orchestra. Not exactly an average high school experience! I often wondered what I could have done had I applied myself in that wonderful academic environment. I will continue to ask myself that question for the rest of my life.

I was notified by the City of New York that all life guards had to report to their stations by the 15th of June, because that was the day the outdoor pools and beaches opened for the summer season. This was going to be a problem for me because our graduation from Stuyvesant would be on June 26. The ceremony would take place at the Academy of Music, a large, former vaudeville theater that was then a movie theater. Stuyvesant always had their graduation ceremonies in this theater because the school auditorium was too small. We had no senior prom or any other rites of passage, except taking our exams, earning our diplomas and applying to college. I never knew about the proms until long after I left Stuyvesant and I was glad we didn't have such a thing. It would have been a waste of time, as far as I was concerned.

Since I had to report to Rockaway Beach on the 15th of June, I went to the Principal's office to inform him that I could not make graduation because my summer job would already have begun. He told me that I was not alone, that at least 25 percent of the graduating class would already be working, and the school would mail our diplomas to us. This made me feel better, and besides, I was not looking forward to graduation, as I was winning no awards except I was receiving a coveted Stuyvesant High School diploma. To this day, when I tell someone from New York City that I went to Stuyvesant High School, their immediate reaction is always, "Oh, you were one of the smart ones!" That has to be worth something.

The letter I received from the Department of Parks and Recreation stated that I had been assigned to the Beach 96th Street Lifeguard Station. This station supervised the beaches from 96th Street up to 115th Street in Rockaway Beach. I was to report to a Lifeguard Captain, Bill O'Rourke, who was the Chief Life Guard of the 96th Street Station. The area that I would work in included Rockaway's Playland at the Beach, a large amusement park right off the Boardwalk, and all the Irish bars from Beach 100th Street to Beach 110th Street.

THE SUMMER OF 1952: ROCKAWAY BEACH

On the 15th of June, I reported to the Beach 96th Street Life Guard Station. Rockaway Beach is a neighborhood on the Rockaway Peninsula in the New York City borough of Queens. It is the largest urban beach in the United States, stretching for miles along the Rockaway Peninsula facing the Atlantic Ocean. Rockaway Beach was known as the *Irish Riviera* because of the large percentage of Irish Americans who lived there and spent their summer vacations there. My experiences with the Celtics and my redheaded, blue-eyed appearance made me a natural for assignment to the Beach 96th Street Station, where every lifeguard assigned to the station was an Irish-American, except, unknown to them, the one German Jew in their midst.

We were issued official uniforms which were all orange color, including one bright orange pith helmet, and then briefed by the Captain of the Station, Bill O'Rourke. He had over ten years experience as a New York City lifeguard, and he had been the Captain of the Station for the past four years. He was also the owner of one of the wildest bars in Irish Town, called Bill O'Rourke's Snake Pit.

At this initial gathering of the 96th Street Shack (Lifeguard stations were called shacks) for the summer of 1952, Chief O'Rourke outlined the procedures to be followed by all lifeguards. To begin with, every Sunday morning all lifeguards would attend the Sunday Morning Mass at St. Rose of Lima Church. The Mass began at 7 a.m., and we were expected to meet in the church parking lot at 6:30 a.m. and then Chief O'Rourke would lead us into the church. He had been doing this for the past ten years. Never did he ask if there was anyone in the group that was not Catholic or not Irish.

My three years of parochial school and my five years dating Rose Mary Fitzgerald came in handy. The unusual thing about this situation is that the Catholic Church in Rockaway Beach had the same name as the parish church from my neighborhood in Washington Heights, which was also the church where Rose Mary's brother, Joe, was one of the parish priests. The other aspect of my requesting duty in Rockaway was the fact that Rose Mary's family always came to Rockaway Beach for two weeks every summer, renting one of the hundreds of small "beach bungalows" that were spread all over Irish Town from Beach 94th Street to Beach 115th Street. To call them bungalows was a joke, as the "bungalows" were the size of a two-car garage and were built in long rows. There were easily 40 to 50 of them in one row, and they were furnished with enough beds to sleep four people.

The Irish were hard working and hard drinking people in those days, and most of them held blue-collar jobs that did not make it possible for them to take fancy vacations. Since most of them were union members, they usually took their union mandated two weeks vacation in Rockaway Beach. The beach was much cooler than the city, and the ocean breezes provided a cooler and more comfortable sleeping environment in July and August.

During the day, they would spend their time at the beach or go to Playland-at-the-Beach. You could go on a date at Playland with about ten dollars, and that would be enough for two adults to go on all the rides, dance in the dance arcade, and get enough to eat. In the evening, the families would eat at one of the many small restaurants in Irish Town, and then the adults would go to the bars where they would drink, socialize, listen to Irish music, generally played by Irish bands which would come over from Ireland for the summer.

It was a magical time for me. Among the more famous Irish bars of the time were; McQuire's (owned by the basketball playing brothers, Al and Dick, from St. John's University), Sligo House, the White House, Harbor Rest, Maher's, Smyth's, the Park Inn, the Mermaid Inn, Boggiano's (the only Italian bar in Irish Town), McWalter's, The Last Stop Inn (it closed at 5 a.m. daily), and Riordan's. Chief O'Rourke's Snake Pit was one of the hundreds of small bars that were interspersed between the giants listed above. The drinks were cheaper in these small bars, but there was no music and fewer women. It was just a place for the boys to hang out, drink, get drunk and fight.

Listening to Chief O'Rourke's instructions, we were further informed that he viewed the lifeguards of the 96th Street Shack as one family, and we worked together, and we played together. We were entitled to one day off a week, but no one could take off on a Friday, Saturday or Sunday, because on the weekends there were hundreds of people on the beaches and he needed every lifeguard on duty. There were only three rookies in the Shack; me, a guy named Kenny Vincent, who was a biker from Brooklyn and a tough looking guy from the Bronx named Bobby Ahearn. Everyone else were returnees who had worked there in previous summers. I remember one lifeguard, who was about 50 years old, named Frank Finnerty. He was a legend in Rockaway Beach because he had been a summer lifeguard since 1930, all in the 96th Street Shack. He preferred to work alone, but regulations had changed, and the Department of Parks and Recreation required two lifeguards per beach whenever the beach was open.

The beaches were always accessible to the public, but lifeguards were on duty from 9 a.m. to 6 p.m., seven days a week from the 15th of June to Labor Day. After that, the beaches were not manned by anyone until the following summer. Rockaway Beach was renowned for its' unusually large waves, and the few people who were surfing in the New York City area, used Rockaway Beach almost exclusively. In addition, body surfing was much more popular because the waves were very big and you didn't need a surfboard.

My original plan was to commute to the beach from Washington Heights, but it was a two-hour train ride each way. Considering Chief O'Rourke's idea of what he thought our group of lifeguards should be, I realized I needed to live in Rockaway Beach for the whole summer. Apparently, all three of us rookies had the same idea, and Chief O'Rourke directed us to a house on Beach 104th Street that was located on the end of the street facing Jamaica Bay. We went to see a Mrs. Mary Flanagan, the owner of the Sea Breeze Boarding House. It was essentially a barracks that had a large number of rooms on each of its' four floors, with a bathroom at each end of the hallway on each floor. Kenny, Bobby and I rented a room together for the summer. We were simply renting a bed to sleep in, and hoping that we could sleep elsewhere occasionally. We were all earning $50 a week, and the room cost $25 a week for all three of us. This cost us $ 8.35 a week, and that was a bargain. It left us money to eat and drink and still save some for college. Bobby and I were going to college in the fall, but Kenny only wanted to drink and party, so that was pretty much the direction we all followed.

The lifeguards had been summoned to duty on 15 June to prepare for the official opening of the beach season on Friday morning, June 27. This gave our Shack less than two weeks to get ready for the season. The 96th Street Shack was responsible for beaches from Beach 96th Street to Beach 115th Street. This was a total of twenty separate beaches and each beach had a large lifeguard station situated in the middle of the beach. The lifeguard station was a very large 8 to 10 foot high wooden chair that had ladders on both sides. The chair at the top was big enough for two lifeguards to sit in, side by side. Each beach in our district was separated by stone jetties that went out into the ocean for about thirty feet. The purpose of these stone jetties was to break up the riptides and reduce the strength of the constant waves. One lifeguard station was responsible for one beach, jetty to jetty.

Besides the lifeguard chair, every beach had two flotation devices, one surfboard, two body boards and two torpedo floats. A torpedo float was a flotation device that was shaped like a torpedo and "shot" to the victim. Every two beaches had a catamaran rowboat that was launched into very heavy surf so that the lifeguard could row through the surf to the victim. The time before the opening was used to prepare equipment, paint and place lifeguard chairs, and conduct drills.

During the beach season, it was normal to have at least one hundred people on my beach during the week, and well over two hundred per day on the weekends. We were always busy, and we were always pulling people out of the surf. While we rarely had a really dangerous case, we were in the water constantly while the beach was open, pulling people out who had become either panic stricken or tired when they met with a situation they could not handle.

After a week of work on the beach, the Chief Lifeguard assigned teams for the summer. I was assigned to Beach 103rd Street, and my partner was Kenny Vincent, the tough biker from the Bronx, an unusual decision in that we were both rookies. Kenny was also my roommate in the boarding house, along with Bobby Ahearn. I liked Kenny, and I never wanted to make him angry. He had a mean temper, which I saw firsthand that summer in numerous bar fights that he always won. Kenny was 21 years old, stood 6 feet 1 inches tall and had the body of a weight lifter. Since I was tall and skinny, it gave me a sense of security to work with Kenny.

Through a stroke of luck, the crew on the beach next to us was Frank Finnerty, the legendary, twenty year veteran lifeguard and none other than Bobby Ahearn, who had been assigned to work with Frank, even though Frank would prefer to work alone. It was made very clear, that the only lifeguard to row the catamaran from our beach would be Frank Finnerty. Frank was a big man, over six feet tall and his body was solid and burned brown from years in the sun. He was an outstanding long distance open water swimmer, and it was great having him as a back-up.

Bobby Ahearn, like me, was tall and skinny. He was also six feet tall, a great swimmer, but also a guy you did not want to cross. His nickname was "Ratshit," and he had a group of friends from his neighborhood that would come to the beach often and party with him all night long. His associates appeared to be the local tough guys from their neighborhood, and Bobby appeared to be their leader. Bobby was smart and had graduated from Power Memorial High School (the school that later produced Lou Alcindor, who became Kareem Abdul Jabar in the NBA) and had received a scholarship to Iona College that he was beginning in the fall. We probably had more in common than most of the other guys, since we were both headed to college. Bill O'Rourke, the Chief Lifeguard, had graduated from Regis High School, a very good academic parochial high school for boys, where over 85 percent of the graduates went on to seminaries to become priests. Bill O'Rourke did not wind up going to a seminary, but perhaps that explained why he felt the need to march us to Mass every Sunday morning.

Living with Kenny and Bobby was exciting, and since both were older than me, it struck me that it was a good thing I had my fake draft card. I was the only one in the 96th Street shack that was under eighteen years old and, therefore, I was also the only one who was drinking illegally. This was never a problem in Irish Town, where proof of age was only checked if the bar owner thought there might be an Alcoholic Beverage Control Inspector lurking around the premises. I got to know several of the lifeguards very well, and strangely enough, Bill O'Rourke took a liking to me, primarily because I had a big mouth and wasn't afraid to use it, especially with Kenny Vincent by my side, which was most of the time when we hit the Irish bars.

On Friday, June 27, the Rockaway Beach summer season officially opened. The beach was always open since you could simply walk down from the boardwalk and go swimming at your own risk. The city overcame liability by posting signs at each boardwalk stairway, and on each lifeguard station chair simply stating, "No Lifeguard on duty. Swim at your own risk." We went to work at 9 a.m. daily, took down the signs, and got on our chairs. Once on the chairs, we were on duty until 6 p.m. If we wanted lunch, we had to bring something with us, but because we were in the water so often, we rarely ate between 9 a.m. and 6 p.m., choosing only to drink water or an occasional soda.

The first people began arriving at the beach by around 9:15 a.m. and they immediately staked out a location, spread their blankets, set up their chairs and planted their umbrellas in the sand. They were there for the day. When the swimming began, we had to watch every swimmer. Staying in close to the shore was no problem, but children playing in the waves would get knocked down often and we would run into the surf and grab them before the rip tide started to carry them out. In other cases, people who thought they could swim would swim out too far, get tired, and we could see the early signs of fatigue by the way they were thrashing around in the water. With these people, one of us would grab a torpedo buoy and swim towards the person while the other one remained in the chair watching the rest of the beach.

Both Kenny and I were constantly blowing our whistles and signaling swimmers to swim in certain directions, either to the right or to the left. We could see the rip tide patterns from the chair and thus, by alerting swimmers before they swam into the rip tides, we could avoid unnecessary rescues. Later in the season, if things got slow we would direct swimmers into the rip tides so that we could jump in and rescue them. This was particularly true for young, good-looking girls. Rescuing a damsel in distress was a great way to meet new girls at the beach.

At the end of the first day I was exhausted. I was waterlogged and physically tired, but then I found out that the parties would begin at the Snake Pit at 7:30 that evening. We had time to shower, put on our street clothes (nothing orange…ever), grab something to eat at the Pot O' Gold Diner or the Shamrock Inn, and then wander over to the Snake Pit where the evening's activities were being planned. It was Friday night, and the start of the first weekend party at the beach. Thankfully, I was 17 years old and could take the pace, but then so could Frank Finnerty, and he was over 50!

The summer continued at this pace. The only thing to break this daily routine was my day off, which turned out to be each Wednesday, and the Sunday morning Mass March at St. Rose of Lima's Church. The Mass March was a thing of beauty and, looking back on it today with a clear head and aged eyes, it was a public relations coup that J. Walter Thompson, of that famous Madison Avenue advertising agency, would have appreciated and envied. While Bill O'Rourke was a failure as far as Regis was concerned, (he decided that he did not want to be a priest), his love of the Catholic Church never wavered. Thus, the Sunday Morning Mass March was his way of giving back to a church that, in his heart of hearts, he felt he had disappointed.

Each Sunday, we met in the church parking lot at 6:30 a.m. We were required to wear our orange sweat suits and at exactly 6:50 a.m., we marched down the aisle, sitting in the first four or five pews on the left side of the church. It was a wonderful sight and one that must have brought tears to the eyes of Father F. X. Quinn, the Pastor of St. Rose of Lima Church. There was Bill O'Rourke, Chief Lifeguard and Keeper of the Faith, leading 50 orange-clad lifeguards down the center of the church, and quietly standing in the aisle as we filed into our seats. The front row seat was always reserved for Bill, and he took his seat after all of us were seated, having knelt properly, made the sign of the cross and reverently bowed our heads in silent prayer as we waited for Mass to begin. Maybe Bill *should* have been a priest. We participated in the Mass, and we all received communion (yes, even Peter S. Beck, German Jew). I was certainly being a much better Catholic than a Jew in those days.

Rose Mary and her family rented one of the bungalows in Irish Town, and this year they would arrive at Rockaway Beach on Sunday, July 20, for the last two weeks of July. I was looking forward to her arrival, as I loved her very much and she was truly the only girl in my life, at that time. I would not yet have experienced the unbelievable Annie Bianco caper, that would begin to unfold for me at Rockaway Beach, beginning on August 7, and that almost caused me to get myself whacked by the mob! That was one of the most exciting events of my entire life and, looking back on it today, I am extremely grateful to two "gumbahs," who may no longer be alive as I write these words. More about this incident later.

Rose Mary arrived at Rockaway Beach, and an outstanding two weeks began that allowed me to break the mold of the nightly drinking and fighting, and spend some time with my girlfriend and her family. It is important to point out that even at this late point in my relationship with Rose Mary, she never knew that I was not a Catholic. I had never brought it up, and I knew that if I did, our relationship would be over. I had given the matter quite a bit of thought and was convinced that if Rose Mary and I ever got married, I would convert to Catholicism, and that would be that! I was a long way from that point. I was 17, I was a lifeguard, and I was going away to college, hardly the time to make a life changing decision. Rose Mary and I went for long evening walks, sometimes under the boardwalk for some groping, pseudo-sexual experiences, and then to Playland to ride the roller coaster, go through the Fun House and just enjoy each other's company. The prospect of taking Rose Mary into one of the Irishtown bars never arose and would never have been tolerated. We spent every spare moment I had together during her two weeks at Rockaway. When she left to return to the city, we swore to each other that we were soul mates forever, and would soon be making plans to spend the rest of our lives together.

Monday was my return to the wild days of summer in Rockaway, and on Tuesday morning I met Annie Bianco who plopped herself down on her blanket right by my lifeguard station chair. Annie was about 5 foot 5 inches tall, had dirty blond hair and was unusual for the beach in that she wore a one piece bathing suit, not something the young women were wearing then. She was pretty, had a great figure and seemed content to sit by my chair and enjoy the sun. Kenny Vincent, my partner, tried to get her into a conversation, but she didn't appear to be interested. When Kenny went to walk the beach in front of our station, Annie began talking to me. She asked me what I was doing that evening and if I had anyone special with which to spend time. I told her that I was probably going to Bill O'Rourke's Snake Pit bar, and then would wind up at Gildea's later that evening. I truthfully told her that I did not have anyone special here at the beach.

At 17, the prospect of meeting an older woman, and Annie was definitely older than 17, proved to be a rather heady aphrodisiac. I finished my shift, showered in the locker room, and then continued to the Snake Pit to begin another rowdy evening at Rockaway. I was surprised to see Annie at the bar. She was dressed rather well for the beach, and she asked me if I wanted to get something to eat. Since I had "scored" early, my buddies from the shack gave me an envious look as we departed. Annie wanted to go to Far Rockaway for dinner, and she had her own car. This was getting better and better. As we drove out of Irish Town and continued towards Far Rockaway, I found out quite a bit about Annie Bianco (I have changed her name to protect her identity).

Annie was 21 years old, and when she was 13 she was accidentally run over by a New York City police car. The injury made it impossible for her to ever have children and left an ugly scar on her body from below her bust line to her pelvis. She spent close to a year in the hospital recovering from her injuries. Her family sued the City of New York on her behalf, and the settlement payment was made just after her 21st birthday. While she never told me how much money she had received, she appeared to be financially self-sufficient and was spending the summer at Rockaway Beach to figure out what she would do with the rest of her life.

She was driving a brand new 1952 Chevrolet Bel-Air Coupe, which she had bought for cash, and she was staying at a house on Beach 116th Street which she had rented for the summer. She was living alone. She also told me that one of her brothers was the first man electrocuted at Sing Sing Prison. I thought I was a pretty cool guy, going out with an older woman who lived alone, had her own car, had money and a notorious brother.

After dinner, we drove back to Irish Town, hit a few bars, and then continued to Annie's house where I spent the night. After that night, I spent a lot of time with Annie. She was fun, uninhibited and didn't appear to have a care in the world. Since Wednesday's were my day off, Annie suggested we go into New York City and see her brother, George, who was visiting from Florida. She said he was a bookmaker around the Miami area and was only in New York for a few days.

I met her brother George, and after some pleasantries and a cold beer, he asked me if I would like to make a quick 50 bucks. This certainly sounded like a good deal to me, so I asked him what I had to do to earn the 50 dollars. He told me I should go down to the street with his sister and go to a place where there were two phone booths, side by side. Then, I was to call a phone number he gave me, and at the appropriate time, bet on the horse that Annie would give me from the other phone booth. I was to place the bet in George Bianco's name, and that was all I had to do. This sounded pretty easy to me, so off I went with Annie to the twin phone booths on Lexington Avenue and 23rd Street.

Annie seemed to know what she was doing, and she told me that she would place the call first. She instructed me to place my call and dial all the numbers except the last one. When she signaled me, I was to dial the last number and bet on the horses name she gave me. I did what she told me and waited for her signal. I got the signal, dialed the last number and repeated, "100 dollars on Angel's Flight in the 7th race for George Bianco," got a verification number and hung up. Annie and I then went upstairs, I gave the verification number to George, and he gave me a 50 dollar bill. I said goodbye to Annie, and rode up to Washington Heights to see Rose Mary and visit my father. I returned to Rockaway Beach around 11 p.m. The 50 dollar bill was burning a hole in my pocket, but I would put it away in my college fund. All in all, it was one hell of a day off.

On Thursday morning, I didn't see Annie and I didn't see her on the weekend either. Life at Rockaway was as hectic as ever, and the weekends were always extremely busy. We always looked forward to Mondays, because the traffic at the beach and on the boardwalk reduced itself by at least fifty percent. Monday morning arrived, and Kenny and I were sitting in our lifeguard chair, watching the relative few swimmers in the water. The surf was fairly calm, and we were both looking forward to an uneventful day.

Around 10 a.m., two unusual men walked up to our lifeguard chair. They shook the chair and yelled up to us, "Which one of you is a friend of Annie Bianco?" I told them I was, and they told me to get down off the chair. These two men were wearing suits on the beach and they looked like they were pretty tough guys. I turned downright scared very quickly. I hemmed and hawed and told them that I could not leave my station and that I couldn't get off the chair until my shift was over or unless I had to rescue someone in the water. They cut to the chase very quickly and made it abundantly clear that either I came down, or they were going to come up and drag me off the chair.

I got off the chair, and they forcibly escorted me under the boardwalk behind the beach. When we got there, the two men hit me in the face, in the body and in the stomach. I was totally scared and started crying and yelling and asking them what the hell they were doing and why were they beating me up. They finally stopped hitting me, and they wanted to know how well I knew Annie and George Bianco. I told them the truth. I told them that I had never met George Bianco until last Wednesday when Annie introduced me to him in the city. I told them that I had met Annie about two weeks ago, right here at the beach. These guys were definitely mob guys, and they were laughing as I told them the story. While I was telling them all of this my nose was bleeding, my stomach hurt, and I felt that at any moment they were going to start on me again.

Finally, one of the guys turns to the other and says, "You know what, I believe this dumb bastard." They then asked me if I had any idea of what I had become involved in with Annie and George Bianco. I told them that all I knew was that he gave me 50 dollars to place a bet for him on the telephone, and that was all I knew. Apparently, I sold my case very well because they then asked me if I knew what "past posting" was. I told them I had never before even heard the term. They then told me that George and Annie used me to place a bet on a horse race that had already been run and that I was placing a bet on the winner of the race, seconds before the book closed on the race. That was why two telephones were used. Annie was talking to someone at the track, and when the winner crossed the finish line he told Annie the name of the horse. Annie told me, I made the bet, and within seconds the book in New York was closed, but not before George Bianco's bet was registered by his bookie as a legitimate bet.

It just so happened that the bookie was a mob bookie and George Bianco had made off with a large amount of the mob's money. The guys punched me around a little more, and then gave me a warning to never do that again. I did not feel like such a wise guy after that beating. They then told me that if Annie ever came to see me again, to stay away from her because they were going to settle some scores with her and her brother George. They left the area quickly and I returned to my lifeguard station, bloody and scared, and not in the best shape to help anyone who might need assistance in the surf.

Kenny asked me what that was all about, but I just told him that I had gotten myself into some trouble but that I thought that I was now in the clear. Kenny didn't ask any further questions, but he seemed impressed that some mob guys were doing a number on me. I suppose I had gained a certain level of street credibility with Kenny. I hoped that I would never experience something like that again, and I promised myself to watch what I was getting myself into in the future. I saw Annie at the beach the next day. I still had plenty of visible scars on my face and arms from the midday visit of the two mob guys. She asked me what happened, and I told her that she probably ought to think very seriously about leaving Rockaway Beach as soon as she could. I made it very clear that I didn't want to see her anymore, and just like that she was out of my life, because she walked up towards the boardwalk and I never saw her again. She may have been telling the truth about her presumed innocence, but I didn't believe her and besides, the two mob guys had convinced me otherwise.

The 1952 calendar was very accommodating to the beach season in Rockaway. Labor Day fell on Monday, September 1, so the official beach season for the City of New York, concluded on Tuesday, September 2. We had a big end of season bash at the Snake Pit, and Bill O'Rourke outdid himself at St. Rose of Lima church as we gathered for our last Sunday processional at 6:30 a.m. The parish knew it was one day away from closing day at the beach, and there was a larger than usual crowd in the pews when we did our usual march in. During the sermon, the priest mentioned the lifeguards and closed by hoping to see all of us back at the beach again next summer. I had never thought about returning, but the seed was planted, and I must admit that even I, the German Jew, had a feeling of solidarity with the Irish lifeguards and the people of St. Rose of Lima parish.

It had been an exciting summer. Our record of no drownings was, unfortunately, broken on the beach directly in front of Playland. There wasn't even an investigation, based on the strength of the eye witnesses and their statements asserting that the victim had been drunk, and the lifeguards did all they could, which the police concluded in their report. It was still a great place to work, and I had met a tremendous group of guys, had saved over $400, and had the time of my life. The going away party was quite a blast and Bill O'Rourke asked me to come back for another season. Everyone departed with promises of returning next year, but even I, a naive 17 year old, knew it probably would never happen. As I left Rockaway Beach to return home, I realized that, in a few days, I would be departing for Champlain College in Plattsburg, New York and beginning yet another new life.

CHAPTER 4

COLLEGE DAYS

CHAMPLAIN COLLEGE

Champlain College required incoming freshmen to be at the college on Monday, September 8, 1952, for orientation week. My father had decided to drive me there, and since I had to report at 8 a.m., we would travel the 300 plus miles upstate by departing New York City early on Sunday morning. We would stay at the Union Hotel in Plattsburgh on Sunday night, and then he would drop me off at Champlain College on Monday morning and return to New York City. As we drove up Route 9, I suddenly realized I was going to spend more continuous time with my father than I had spent in a very long time. My father had always been so busy working, and when he came home there was rarely any family interaction that I could recall. It seemed strange to me to be in the same car with my father and not have very much to say. There were hardly any topics of common interest, so the trip went extremely smoothly for both of us.

We spent time together discussing the sights we were seeing and trying to determine how long it would take us to reach Plattsburgh. Since this was before interstate highways and major expressways, routes always wound through small towns. Our stops along the way were particularly interesting to both of us, since neither of us had been above New Paltz, and each new small town was a revelation of some sort. The leaves begin to turn in September, so as we progressed north, we were engulfed in a cascade of changing autumn colors that seemed to underscore the importance of my trip to a new life in college. The other aspect of Route 9 was that it parallels the Hudson River all the way to Lake George, and the scenery is absolutely beautiful in late August and early September. As we traveled further north, the temperature became cooler, and the air became clearer and crisp. I was enjoying the trip, and, while we didn't speak of any weighty subjects, I was enjoying having my father all to myself. By early evening, we arrived at Plattsburgh and checked into the Union Hotel.

The Union Hotel was an old hotel in 1952, and, while the rooms were adequate, the cocktail lounge, named "The Drum Room," was almost a revolutionary war museum. There were old pictures of uniformed soldiers, some old battle paintings and several regimental drums mounted on the molding. My father suggested we enjoy a cocktail. I was

53

very impressed with myself that I was going to a real cocktail lounge and have a drink with my father. We sat down at a table and the waiter asked what I wanted to drink. Up to this time, I had never had a cocktail. I had drunk plenty of beer in Rockaway Beach in the Irish bars, but never a cocktail. Now I was faced with a decision I was not qualified to make, however, being quick witted, I said I would have a "7 and 7," without having any idea what I had just ordered. My father seemed impressed, and I told him that I had heard people ordering that drink and always wondered how it tasted. My father smiled and said he had no idea that I was so worldly. Neither did I.

The information I had received from the school told me I was assigned to Clinton Hall in a four man room, and that I was to report to the front of the dormitory at 8 a.m. on Monday, the 8th of September. Champlain College was located on the site of the old Plattsburgh Barracks, a United States Army base dating back to the Civil War, and was on the west shore of Lake Champlain.

Champlain College was established in 1946 as a two-year college to assist returning World War II veterans under the GI Bill to become eligible to attend a four-year college where they could receive degrees. The plan worked initially; however, there was not as large a continuing student body as was anticipated, so by 1950, Sampson College and Mohawk College were merged with Champlain College, which then became a four-year liberal arts college. It also became the first college of the newly formed State University of New York system (SUNY).

In September 1952, Champlain College had an enrollment of 1,600 students, both male and female, of which over 50 percent were veterans of either World War II or the Korean Conflict. It was into this environment that a 17 year old New York City Jew, with a distinctly eclectic background, was introduced on that Monday morning. I remember saying goodbye to my father on the steps of Clinton Hall where I shook his hand and thanked him for making it possible for me to attend college. I promised him I would do well, and that I would not get into trouble.

I found out several months later that my father returned home to our apartment from our trip, packed his belongings, and moved out of the apartment, leaving Olga and taking up residence at the Latham Hotel. Strangely, he never mentioned any of this to me when we were driving to Champlain. I also found out that he had established a relationship with an artist he had hired to design neckwear fabrics. Her name was Dorothy Hertenried, and he would spend the rest of his life with her. Luckily for him, the rest of his life then meant he would enjoy 27 years with Dora, who, besides his beloved wife, Margarete, would prove to be the second love of his life.

I returned to my room and waited for my campus guide. The remainder of my roommates arrived, and I was surprised to learn that all of them were Korean War veterans; two had been in the Army and one had been in the Marines. All three had seen combat, and as I recall, they were all in their mid to late twenties. They were attending Champlain College to get an education, and they were certainly not interested in the college life, other than to get enough credits to transfer to a better known university. All three of them were bachelors, and as I looked at them, I realized why Champlain College had been recommended to my father. This was not a group that was going to go out drinking, smoking a pipe, and singing the Whiffenpoof Song in some local tavern. They were serious about a college education. They were interested in me only to the degree that they could not understand how, at 17 years old, I could already be in college, and they thought I could help them get reacquainted with school work and studying. I was about to change my entire life-style, just to get along with my roommates.

In short order, our campus guide arrived and took us on a tour of the campus. He informed us that Champlain College was going to close at the end of 1953 and that we were the last class. He went on to tell us that it was extremely important to get good grades in our first and only year at Champlain, because the State of New York was going to pay for each Champlain student to apply to three colleges of his or her choice to transfer to for the 1953 college year. How was that for motivation?

I could see that I would enjoy my one year at Champlain. It was a beautiful campus with old buildings, all situated around a large quadrangle. No matter where you walked on campus, you could see the lake. Later on, in the middle of the winter, I would not enjoy the lake that much, as the icy blasts coming from there chilled you right down to your bones. It got so cold at Champlain, that in the middle of the winter when the entire lake froze solid, you could drive a car on the ice from Champlain College in Plattsburgh, New York to the University of Vermont in Burlington, Vermont, located on the opposite shore of the lake. I know this to be true because I saw it done. It was a real stupid trick because the ice was never uniformly frozen, but some nut at the college did it. He did not return over the lake but drove around it back to college. As it turned out, he was very lucky, because the local police informed him that he was not the first person to try it, he was only the first person to succeed.

Classes began on September 15, and we were then immersed in college life in earnest. The courses were all required subjects that included freshman math, freshman English, a science lab, a language, one elective, physical education, plus one class from your proposed major. I selected an English class because I could write fairly well and thus, without knowing it, I would begin my major field of study and become an English major. In those days, colleges demanded that all freshmen take the required courses before selecting a major field of study, the argument being that if you could not meet the basic education requirements, there was no sense in continuing at the college level.

Classes at Champlain were challenging, and they were also very small. With an enrollment of 1,600 students, I do not ever remember having more than 25 people in any class, and this was for the required freshman courses. Instruction was fast paced but thorough, and the professors were interested in the students. I have fond memories of the Champlain professors, and I found that my strong academic background from Stuyvesant, even though I finished fourth from the bottom with an 82 percent average, made all my classes at Champlain almost a repetition of my senior year in high school. Consequently, I did not have to study real hard, but I did spend a lot of time with my roommates, and found that I was able to help them get the feel of doing hard academic work, something none of them had tried for a long time.

Although Champlain was a small school, it did have varsity sports, and I was a member of the school soccer team. We played other colleges in the area, primarily in Vermont, and we also had a heated rivalry with McGill University in Montreal. Since Champlain College was only 30 miles from the Canadian border, weekend trips to Montreal occurred regularly, and any student with a car found it very easy to have passengers pay for their entire trip. The drinking age in Canada was also 18 at the time, so Americans were certainly attracted to the pleasures of Montreal.

In November, I hitched a ride back to New York City and met Dora for the first time. My father had arranged a small room at the Latham Hotel where he was living, and Dora, my father, and me enjoyed our first Thanksgiving dinner together. Dora was actually named Dorathea Hertenried.

DORATHEA NEUMANN/HERZ-HERTENRIED/BECK

"Dora" became my stepmother. She was born in Vienna, Austria, in 1907, the daughter of Dr. (PhD) Richard Neumann, a General Director of textile enterprises in Vienna, and the owner of an extensive and well known art collection. When the Germans annexed Austria in 1938, Dr. Neumann fled Vienna to Paris with some of his art works, but was forced to leave much of it behind in Vienna which was then confiscated by the Nazis. When the Germans occupied France, he fled to Spain and then to Cuba.

Daughter Dorathea remained in Vienna with her husband, Dominique Herz-Hertenried. Both were subsequently arrested by the Gestapo and detained in prison in Vienna. They were eventually released, for unknown reasons, and traveled to Spain and then on to Cuba where Dora's father was now living after leaving France. Dr. Neumann was working in the textile industry and was later named honorary professor at the University of Havana, He laid the foundation for the establishment of Havana's Palacia de Bellas Artes. Information about Dr. Neumann is from *Sotheby's, Important Old Masters and Sculptures*, Catalogue note, Sophie Lille, New York, 2012.

Dora lived outside of Havana for over ten years where she and her family enjoyed a lifestyle that was rarely experienced by many others. Her family became friends with Ernest Hemingway and Fidel Castro's family, Fidel being only a young man at the time. She learned and spoke fluent Spanish, along with the French, Italian, German and English she already knew.

Dora's husband died in Cuba and she immigrated to the United States in 1952 and lived in New York City. She became a naturalized citizen in June 1955. Dr. Neumann later moved to New York City where he died in 1961.

Dora was an inventor, an artist, a writer and a poet and possessed an extremely active and inquisitive mind. She had a delightful personality, was an outstanding cook and, to my knowledge, had very little fear of anything.

It was abundantly clear to me that my father and Dora had been friends for a long time and, what is more important, I could see that my father was very happy with her. The fact that her apartment was only a few blocks away from the Latham Hotel made me wonder if Dad ever spent much time at the hotel. Shortly after I met Dora, Dad moved in with her and gave up the room at the Latham Hotel. It was almost as though he was waiting for my approval, which he received from me in glowing terms. I liked Dora very much, almost from the first minute I met her. I would like her more and more over the next 27 years that she and my father were destined to spend together.

When I got back to Champlain, I began studying for final exams for the first semester. I did very well in my exams, and I wound up with a 3.7 grade point average. While this appears high, it must be remembered that the competition at Champlain certainly was not comparable to eastern colleges, and the majority of the students at Champlain were just beginning to get back into the habit of studying and taking exams.

Christmas arrived quickly, and I returned to New York City. I had two weeks to spend in New York, and I spent most of it with my girlfriend Rose Mary. New York at Christmas time is magical. Rockefeller Center is decorated with herald angels and the ice rink is framed by a towering Christmas tree which is placed in front of 30 Rockefeller Plaza every Christmas. Radio City Music Hall has its' Christmas special show, St. Patrick's Cathedral is decorated for the holidays, and the store windows up and down 5th Avenue glisten with decorations and sparkling gifts of the season. When you coat all of this very lightly with the snow that always seemed to fall in New York at this time, you have a picture that only Norman Rockwell could duplicate in all its' glory.

The two weeks passed far too quickly, and soon I was back in Champlain, beginning my second semester of my freshman year. Dean Amy Gilbert, the highly competent Dean of the College, announced that Champlain was indeed closing. The State of New York had decided to keep only one four year liberal arts college open, and while they would have preferred to keep Champlain, the property that the college occupied belonged to the federal government and they wanted the land back to build a Strategic Air Command radar base.

We were informed that we could transfer to Harpur College in Binghamton, New York, or the college would pay for us to apply to three colleges or universities of our choice. In the end, I applied to Princeton University, St. Lawrence College, and Syracuse University. I thought I would probably get into St. Lawrence, a small private college in Canton, New York, situated on the banks of the St. Lawrence River. It was famous because it was the alma mater of movie star Kirk Douglas, who was born Isadore Demsky in Amsterdam, New York. It also had one of the best college hockey teams in the country. I did not think I would get into Princeton, but since the State of New York was paying for the application fees, I figured I would try anyway.

I was shocked to find out several weeks later, that I had been accepted to all three schools. Naturally, I wanted to go to Princeton, but the cost was over twice the amount of either Syracuse or St. Lawrence. As I remember it, Syracuse would cost $750 a year, St. Lawrence would cost $700 a year and Princeton would cost $1,800 a year, and that was just for tuition. Since I had no scholarship, my father would have to pay the entire bill, and there was no way we could afford Princeton.

While I wanted to go to St. Lawrence College, some friends of my father convinced him that I should go to Syracuse. The argument in favor of Syracuse was that it was an internationally known university that would be more helpful to me in the future than St. Lawrence, which was an excellent school, but hardly known outside of New York State. His friends won, and when the time came to make a decision, I opted to attend Syracuse University in 1953. It was sad to see the Champlain College family split up. The school year came to a close in June, and I had completed my first year of college with an overall grade point average of 3.5. I looked forward to beginning my sophomore year at Syracuse in September.

I had decided to return to Rockaway Beach for my second year as a lifeguard, needing only a one and half hour endurance swim to re-qualify for my old job at Beach 96th Street. I took the test during one weekend in April and was again assigned to Bill O'Rourke and his crew of Irish hellions. Returning to Beach 96th Street was a grand experience, especially since I was now one of the "old lads," and was able to look down at the three rookies who had been lucky enough to have entered the fold. Kenny Vincent had decided not to return to the beach, so I was partnered with Bobby Ahearn, the tough Bronx gang lord, who had just completed his freshman year of college at Iona College in New Rochelle, New York.

We returned to the Sea Breeze Boarding House and rented a room for the summer from Mrs. Flanagan. The surprising thing about our return there was that Mrs. Flanagan seemed pleased to see us. Since we were making more money as second year lifeguards, we decided to keep our humble abode as a two man room and pay the extra rent. This proved to be a much better situation for both of us.

Bill O'Rourke assigned me to my old beach at Beach 103rd Street, and I was pleased to see that my old friend, Frank Finnerty, was going to be back at Beach 102nd Street for the 10th year in a row. Although Frank preferred to work alone, Bill O'Rourke always assigned the best rookie as Frank's partner. This year, it was a Sean O'Donnell, who was supposedly heading to Notre Dame in the fall. Sean concentrated on being a good lifeguard, which he was. He was also a great party animal, in which endeavor he excelled. Being six foot two inches tall and looking like a Greek god probably didn't hurt him any either.

The summer was almost a rerun of the previous year. Many parties in Irish Town, the regular Sunday morning marches to Mass at 6:30 a.m., led by our wannabe priest, Wild Bill O'Rourke, and hundreds of surf rescues throughout the summer, all of which were successful. Rose Mary graduated from Mother Cabrini High School with honors and received a full scholarship to Manhattan College. She came to Rockaway for her usual two weeks in August, and there was no sign of Annie Bianco, who, the grapevine had informed me, had moved to Florida.

I spent a fair amount of time trying to prepare myself mentally for going to Syracuse in September. Champlain had been a small, relatively easy college, but Syracuse was an internationally known university, and I worried that I might have a hard time fitting in to my new environment. I think I was primarily concerned with a major field of study, because, as a sophomore, I had to declare a major when I registered.

Before long, it was time for the final march to Mass of the summer at St. Rose of Lima Church. It happened to be on September 6, 1953, with the beaches closing on Tuesday, September 8, the first day after Labor Day. As usual, we marched into the church, and the parishioners were there to say farewell. As I prayed with my friends, I knew that this was going to be my final Sunday in Rockaway, and that next summer I had to make more money to offset my increased expenses at Syracuse. I said my farewells to all of my lifeguard buddies, and especially to Bill O'Rourke, whom I never saw again, but who has remained in my memory.

SYRACUSE UNIVERSITY

Syracuse began on the 14th of September. I had never been to Syracuse, and I was surprised to find out that the university sat on a hill, called Piety Hill, that overlooked the entire city. In 1953, Syracuse had an enrollment of 10,000 students, just a tad larger than the 1,600 souls that comprised the student body at Champlain. I found an enormous university with 16 different colleges, including a medical school, a nursing school and a forestry school, not to mention the famous Crouse College of Music, the Maxwell School of Government, the College of Performing Arts, the Business School, the Law School, the Engineering School, the College of Architecture, and the College of Liberal Arts.

Besides the varied colleges and schools of specialization, Syracuse also had a tremendous athletic department. In the middle of the campus stood Archbold Stadium, a 25,000 seat, open arena, where the Saltine Warriors (Later known as the Syracuse Orange) played their intercollegiate football games in the fall. There were lacrosse fields, track fields, a baseball diamond, plus an entire separate athletic department for women, all within the confines of the athletic department area on campus. In 1953, Syracuse was still competing in intercollegiate boxing and staged regular fights with other universities on Friday nights in the gymnasium. Several collegiate boxers went on to limited professional boxing careers. One of them, Nicholas Georgiade, became a movie star after he was cast as Robert Stack's assistant in the long running television show, *The Untouchables*. I was tremendously impressed with what I saw at Syracuse.

All incoming freshmen and transfer students were required to live in college dormitories. There were plenty of dormitories, although the majority of them were old World War II metal buildings that were erected in 1946 when Syracuse University welcomed close to 10,000 returning veterans under the GI Bill, which paid for their education. This generous gesture by Syracuse tripled their enrollment overnight, and the university continued to grow from that point forward.

Another little known aspect in the continued growth of Syracuse was their acceptance of Jewish students. Most universities then had quotas for Jews. While it was not a published statistic, there was rarely more than a 4 to 5 percent population of Jewish students at any major university during the late '40s and early '50s. Medical schools were so hard for Jews to be accepted into, that New York City and Philadelphia, built Jewish Medical Schools to accommodate the large number of Jewish students desiring to enter medical school.

Syracuse had no quota system for Jews, and when I arrived, close to 50 percent of the student body was from the five boroughs of New York City and the surrounding areas. That meant that close to 50 percent of the entire student body was Jewish. When you look at all the endowed chairs and buildings at Syracuse University today, you can see what a wise course of action Syracuse followed. The Jewish alumni of Syracuse had been extremely generous and supportive of a university that drew no ethnic, racial or cultural barriers at a time when everyone else was doing something that would never be acceptable today.

Syracuse was spread out in all directions from the central campus, and the university ran a bus service from Sky Top and the Collendale dormitories, the upper class dormitories, which were located closer to the campus, and housed the scholarship athletes from all the varsity teams. The bus dropped off students directly at the main entrance to the central campus where Sims Hall was located, a women's freshman dormitory and the site of the college cafeteria. Every Syracuse student who had bought the semester meal plan was required to eat in the Sims Cafeteria Dining Room which served three hot meals per day, seven days per week.

Since my father's assets were limited, I had applied for student aid from Syracuse as a job to help me earn my meals. I was hired as a dishwasher at the Sims Hall cafeteria, and in exchange for these duties, I received free meals throughout the school year as long as I kept my job as a dishwasher. The cafeteria had a large staff of student employees, all of whom were working only for meals and receiving no salaries. The dining room was so large it had music during meal hours, played at a piano located in the center of the dining hall. The piano player was also a student, and the student playing piano while I was at Syracuse was named Lanny Okun. After graduation he went to Hollywood where he wrote many songs and melodies for movies and television shows. Among his Hollywood compositions were the theme music for *Love Boat* and *Fantasy Island*.

When I moved to Collendale, I was placed in a five-man room, the very cheapest living arrangement possible at the university. We were placed in the rooms alphabetically, and I met one of the new dorm residents immediately, since he was moving in when I arrived. He was a freshman scholarship lacrosse player from Manhasset, Long Island, and his name was Jim Brown. He wasn't there very long, because he walked on to the football field during the opening practice and asked for a tryout. Apparently, Coach Ben Schwartzwalder liked what he saw and before the practice session was over, he was changed to a full football scholarship and was moved in with the rest of the football team that had been living elsewhere.

Living at Collendale meant I had to adjust my life to the campus bus schedule. As the weather got colder, which usually begins in Syracuse in early October, waiting for a bus was not much fun. Registration for classes was held in the huge gymnasium. The trick was to register for the right classes that would give you the required number of credits for graduation, and that would also qualify you for your declared major field of study.

My counselor extracted my file which contained my grade transcript from Champlain College. She seemed impressed with my grades, particularly with the grade point average I had attained at Champlain. After looking over my transcript, she informed me I was accepted as a full fledged sophomore, having met all of my required freshman courses while at Champlain, and could, therefore, concentrate on my major field of study for the complete three years I had remaining at Syracuse. This is where the problem began. I told her I did not have any idea what I wanted to study, and had no desire to go to medical school, law school, become an engineer or architect, and I wasn't even sure that I wanted to go into business. She then asked me what I enjoyed doing. I told her that I liked to read, and that writing came extremely easy for me. Those must have been magic words for her, because she then informed me that I would become an English Major. I thought that this was a reasonable solution, so in just ten minutes, I decided to become an English major in the College of Liberal Arts.

I registered for literature courses, Shakespeare, creative writing, poetry, and since a language was required for the English major degree, I tried to enroll in Beginning German, but was quickly found out, and began my German studies with Goethe and Schiller. If I kept that up, after three years, I would become extremely well educated in the arts and classics, but not exactly on a fast track to getting a great job. These things were not of any great concern to me. I was 18, I had come upon a program that didn't look as if would require a great deal of effort on my part, and I looked forward to beginning classes the following Monday.

I looked at my class schedule and noticed that all my classes began at 8 a.m. While this meant that I had to be ready early each morning, this was nothing new to me, and it fit right into my early morning habits that I had developed so well at Stuyvesant High School. The other side of the coin was that all my classes were over every day by 2 p.m., which left plenty of time to study in the huge Carnegie Library, located right in the center of the university grounds.

When I went to classes there in 1953, the Hall of Languages building had not received any major renovations since it had originally been built in 1870. All the classrooms were built like small amphitheaters with a stage for the professor, whose offices were located to the left of the stage as you sat in the classroom. When the bell rang to start class, the professor would come out of his office, walk directly to the podium in the center of the raised stage, and begin his lecture. It was a wonderful system, and because an English major was considered to be a difficult field of study, during my entire time at Syracuse my classes were never larger than 25 students. This made learning easier and gave us an opportunity to interact with the professor in a manner which must be almost impossible today.

As classes progressed, incoming students received letters telling them that the following week would be "Rush Week" for all incoming students. This meant that the 54 fraternities and 38 sororities on campus would be holding open houses during the week.

The purpose of these open houses was for incoming students to decide if they wanted to pledge one of the fraternities or sororities. All fraternities had kitchens and dining rooms and meals were prepared in the house by a professional chef. Obviously, this cost money and some fraternities were so expensive that the cost alone would determine who would or would not be able to join. In those days, there were Christian and Jewish fraternities and sororities, and they were exceptionally good about deciding who would get in and who would not without ever asking anyone their religion. In my case, with my German name and my red hair and blue eyes, I received several offers from some decidedly Christian houses, all of which appealed to me, and all of which I was seriously considering as possible organizations I would like to join.

Then I discovered Phi Epsilon Pi, located on Euclid Avenue, about five blocks from the main entrance of the university. When I knocked on the door of the fraternity, I was met by a guy in his underwear wearing a miner's helmet with the light on, and all the other lights in the house were off. He informed me that I was an hour early, but asked me to come in and wait in the living room. He explained that he was washing dishes in the kitchen and didn't want to get his clothes wet, and since he had this neat miner's helmet to work with, there was no need to turn on any lights. I immediately fell in love with the place. It turned out that the fraternity was an all Jewish fraternity, but they had a ground rule for membership: If you were not from the five boroughs of New York City, you were not welcome. One of the first questions they asked every prospective brother was where they were from. If someone answered anything other than New York City, interest in you as a potential member was rapidly lost.

An hour passed as I watched a strange group of guys prepare for the open house. First, no one in that fraternity had the standard collegiate crew cut. They all wore what was called in those days, "DAs," which meant *duck's ass*. This meant that your hair was greased on the side and combed to the rear of your head, so that both sides converged in the center rear of your head and formed a duck's ass appearance. The top of your hair was grown long and was combed in a form of a pompadour. If you've seen the movie *Grease* recently, you will see exactly how they all looked. Instead of the white tee shirt and V-neck sweater commonly worn at all colleges in those days, all the brothers wore white-on-white dress shirts, open at the collar with khaki pants and brown shoes and not the customary white buckskin shoes. They all had strong New York City accents, and at least in my case, I felt as though I was home again.

I got along well with all the brothers, and before I left that night, the President of the fraternity told me I was in and handed me a pledge pin, if I wanted it. This was against all rules and was called "pocket pinning," because prospective brothers received pledge pins only after they had formally accepted the written invitations and registered with the Pan Hellenic Council. Rules were rarely followed at the Phi Ep house. I kept the pin and looked forward to becoming a Phi Ep.

During the second evening of rush week, I met a fellow whose name was Bob Zirt. He was a saxophone player in the university football marching band that billed itself as "A

Hundred Men and a Girl." The girl at this time was the famous Alta Burg from Pennsylvania, the national baton twirling champion, who had received a four year scholarship to come to Syracuse and be "the Girl." Syracuse awarded a full scholarship every four years to the national champion so that its' marching band could continue to be nationally recognized and continue to call itself "A Hundred Men and a Girl." I don't think they ever counted the band members, because I sure never saw one hundred on the field at any one time, but I bet the university could have produced one hundred names. Everyone was too busy watching "the girl" anyway.

Bob Zirt confided in me that he would really like to join Phi Ep, but he didn't have a chance because he came from Ellenville, New York, which is a small town in the heart of the Borscht Belt in the Catskill Mountains. I liked him very much, especially when I heard him imitate the musical styling's of Stan Getz, one of my favorite jazz saxophonists. I approached Gene Cutler, the President of Phi Ep, and pleaded his case. I told him that I thought he would be a great addition to the fraternity. I asked Gene to tell the brothers that they ought to give him a chance.

The next day, Gene informed me that the brothers had said No! In one of those moments where you do things that you really don't know why you did them, I told Gene that if Bob Zirt was blackballed, they could have the pin he gave me back because I was no longer interested in joining Phi Ep. I did, however, tell him that if they accepted Bob Zirt, they would have two definite new members, because I was in to stay. The next evening, Bob Zirt was the most excited guy I had ever seen because Phi Ep had pocket pinned him that night. I was glad for him, but to this day, I don't know what made me do what I did.

When the pledge class for Phi Ep was announced, we learned that 27 students had selected Phi Ep as their fraternity. This meant that this was going to be the largest pledge class that Phi Ep had ever had. We would be pledges for the remainder of the school year and would be initiated into the fraternity just before Spring Weekend in April of 1954. Looking back on it today, aided by the maturity of almost fifty plus years, there is no way I would have tolerated the idiotic and juvenile behavior of the fraternity system of the 1950s. Hindsight is always 20/20.

Bob Zirt and I became good friends during the pledge period, as did Hugh Fordin, who was a drama major from Brooklyn, and he became one of us. The fraternity called us the three musketeers. We liked the name. Bob, Hugh, and I did everything together and, while they were freshmen and I was a sophomore, I was the youngest of the three. I remained close friends with Bob and Hugh for many years after college.

Thanksgiving arrived and I did not plan to leave Syracuse. Dad was living with Dora, and I didn't want to go to New York City and live in a hotel, so I had decided to stay in my dorm room and spend the holidays alone. Bob Zirt found out I was not going anywhere and he invited me to his house in Ellenville for the holiday. Bob said his family always had a very nice Thanksgiving dinner, kosher of course, and that he had already asked his mother, who definitely wanted me to share dinner with them. It was a trip of several hours from Syracuse to Ellenville. We pulled into the driveway of a huge house that stood on a large hill overlooking a river and a long valley, and had a five car garage attached to the house. There was no room for Bob's car, because every space was taken with four Cadillacs and one Lincoln. I guess the suspicion I had that Bob might have more money than my family was fairly accurate.

Bob introduced me to his mother and father who treated me like a member of the family. I also realized that the Zirt family was strictly kosher and obeyed all the rules of Judaism. This came as a surprise to me since I had never seen Bob observe any kosher rules at college. I discovered that Ellenville was in the heart of the Borscht Belt, an area of hotels and summer resorts where the Jews of New York City came to vacation in the summer. I had a wonderful Thanksgiving time with the Zirts. After the weekend, Bob and I headed back to Syracuse for final exams that would end our first semester at Syracuse. Bob was a business major, and it was his family's intention that, upon graduation, Bob would go into the family business.

We had many extracurricular activities at Syracuse. Bob was in the band. I had walked-on to the varsity swimming team and was trying to make the team and, of course, the constant demands and hazing of the brothers of Phi Epsilon Pi took up most of our available free time. This did not leave much time for studying, and neither one of us devoted much effort to the principal reason for which we were at Syracuse. I had discovered that if you took really good notes, and never cut a class, the professor was giving you the exam questions during his lectures. Every professor in the English Department spent the bulk of each class lecturing, and at the end of the semester the tests contained at least 85 percent of the subject matter that had been discussed in class. Therefore, simply attending class, listening and taking good notes without reading any of the assignments, could always produce a C grade. Not exactly a great ambition, however, it did result in a degree.

The other thing that was very helpful is that Phi Epsilon Pi had what was purported to be the very best "test files" on campus. Every brother and every pledge of Phi Ep, was required to submit all the test questions, in writing, that they could remember immediately after taking their respective tests. The method was simple. You put the name, date and number of the class at the top of the paper and then, if the questions were multiple choice, you wrote down as many questions as you could remember. If the questions were essay questions, you wrote down the subject matter of the essays. If you could get a copy of the test and bring it home, you were a real hero. We had many heroes in Phi Ep. With the arrival of computers, I can only imagine the data available on examinations and examination questions that exist in colleges and fraternities today.

I finished my first semester at Syracuse with a 2.8 average. This was a direct reflection of the amount of time I spent studying, and the increased degree of difficulty of many of my classes. While I used the degree of difficulty argument to explain my lower grades to my father, the truth of the matter was that I was having a lot of fun at Syracuse, and studying was not my highest priority.

I spent much time with my friend from Brooklyn, Hugh Fordin. Hugh was a drama major, and his goal was to go into the theater, but, not as an actor. Hugh wanted to be a director and producer, and all of his efforts were made in that direction. Since we both lived in New York City, we decided to spend some time together in the city. Hugh's parents owned a large luggage store which took up half a block on 44th Street, and I met both of his parents for the first time at their store. Like the Zirt's, they treated me as though I was one of their long lost sons. They were wonderful people, and I remember them with great affection and fondness.

Christmas vacation arrived, and going home to New York City for the holidays meant that I would be able to warm up at home. The Christmas break was a momentous one for me. To begin with, it was three weeks in duration, and this meant that under my father's rules, I had to have a job for the time I was at home. Luckily, through his contacts in the fashion industry, he got me a job as a neckwear salesman at A. Sulka, a very high end men's furnishings store on Madison Avenue and 50th Street. Peter Sulka, the owner of the company, was a close friend of my father's from Europe, and he always needed extra help over the holidays. I went to work daily in my Brooks Brothers suit, wearing one of my father's super expensive ties, and sold neckwear to people for holiday gifts that started at $100 per tie, and went up from there.

Many radio and television stars came to shop at the store, since Rockefeller Center and NBC headquarters were almost around the corner from the store. I remember selling a necktie to Steve Allen, who was one of my idols, and five ties to Ed Sullivan, who came in to buy some last minute gifts for his staff and didn't much care what the ties looked like, as long as they had that all important A. Sulka label in them. As I remember it, he had me pick five ties and wrap them up. I guess if you got a $100 Sulka tie from Ed Sullivan for Christmas, you were going to wear the tie whether you liked it or not. Sulka ties were all very classy, so the chances of a disappointed gift receiver were almost nonexistent.

Christmas of 1953 stands out in my mind for another reason. I had decided I did not want to continue my relationship with Rose Mary. The main reason was that there were plenty of girls at college, and I did not want to be committed to one girl at the age of 18. Rose Mary was a wonderful girl who was loyal, pretty, and very smart. Looking back on that particular situation, it was a perfect example of the grass being greener somewhere else, and not realizing how good you had it. This was a very difficult concept to grasp at the age of 18. Rose Mary had been a wonderful friend, and there was really no reason to break up with her, however, I hit on the perfect way to do it, and it was probably inevitable anyway.

I took Rose Mary out to dinner, and after dinner I told her that I was not a Catholic and that I was Jewish and had been lying to keep going with her. I also told her that none of my Irish friends knew this fact and that the Celtics certainly didn't know it either. Rose Mary told me that she was through with me, but she would not tell anyone else my secret. She was true to her word, and we parted as friends. I later found out that she married an attorney from Manhattan College. I never saw her again, but I have thought about her my entire life. She was a wonderful girl.

The holiday season in New York City is very special, and for returning college students, it was a particularly exciting time. Parties, Broadway shows, night clubs, dinners in the Village, and almost daily evening visits to the garden court of the Biltmore Hotel, where people met each other "under the clock." The entrance to the garden court of the Biltmore had a huge wrought iron gate with a large arch over the entrance to the court itself, and perched high above the arch was a large, antique Tiffany clock. Everyone would say, "I'll meet you under the clock" and you knew that meant, I'll meet you in the garden court of the Biltmore Hotel. When you were "under the clock," the pickings were good, and you could generally always meet someone, provided you had enough money to pay for drinks and/or dinner later. This was not generally the case with me, or my friends, but the chase was more fun anyway.

When I was in New York, I always stayed at the Latham Hotel on 28th Street, a fact that I did not share with any of my classmates or friends. I always gave Dora's apartment address as my home address, and this worked fine for me. I always looked forward to Christmas holidays in New York while I was in college, because of the great holiday atmosphere in the city. New Year's Eve of 1954 was spent at a great party that my friend Hugh Fordin's family had in a private hotel suite in the Astor Hotel. The Astor was practically right on Times Square, so we got to see the ball come down on the New York Times Building exactly at midnight. Bob Zirt came into town for the party, and then Hugh and I put him back on the train for Ellenville early on the morning of January 1, 1954.

School began again on January 11, so we departed New York City for the frozen tundra of the upstate New York ice belt. In the second semester of my sophomore year, I needed an elective class and asked my counselor to recommend a class that would not require either papers or essay test questions. She recommended a class called, A Survey of Fine Arts. The class met three times per week in Crouse College, the music and fine arts school located next door to the College of Liberal Arts. The class was held in a huge auditorium, and at each class, slides were shown of paintings, sculptures, architectural details or any other type of art work. Professor Fleming would lecture on each slide, telling us the name of the work, the artist who made it or painted it, what period it was from, and then he would give us the history of the art work. The exams were also taken in the auditorium, and the professor would show a slide and then ask about the slide. If you were paying just a little bit of attention, you could easily get a C in the class, and all you had to do was show up and listen. The class was full of scholarship athletes, and the football and basketball teams were very well represented. A funny thing happened to me in that class. I absolutely fell in love with the topic, and I wound up taking the class, in ever increasing detail, for the rest of my time at Syracuse. I amassed so many fine arts and art history credits, that I accomplished a minor in art history, along with my major in classical literature.

Of my entire college education, the classes that have remained with me for life are the art classes I took with Doctor Fleming. I got to know him personally, and he became one of my three favorite professors of all time. The other two were Doctor William Terhune, who taught Shakespeare and who dressed in the costume of a character in the play we were studying, and thereby made learning Shakespeare a joy and a memorable experience, and Doctor Dorothy Little, who taught me Non-Aristotelian Semantics, and opened new areas of my brain that would never have been opened had our paths not crossed.

In the spring, we were inducted into Phi Epsilon Pi, and we were told we would be living in the fraternity house during the coming school year. I had also experienced my first football season at Syracuse. There were a total of five home games played at Archbold Stadium. The games were always on Saturday afternoon and they were preceded by Friday night parties at all fraternity houses, followed by the standard walk to the stadium on Saturday mornings.

During my stay at Syracuse, the university was still affiliated with the Methodist Church and drinking was not allowed on campus. Thankfully, I cannot recall a time when the drinking ban was enforced, as long as students behaved themselves and were not in open violation of the rules. I don't recall any open drunkenness on campus, but I do recall students being escorted away from danger by their classmates. The university made it very clear that they might look the other way, but, if you brought attention on yourself, you were gone, and by gone, they meant expulsion.

The football season saw teams like Boston University, Penn State, Cornell, Maryland, and to end the season, the annual game with our arch rival at the time, Colgate University. Colgate weekend was always homecoming at Syracuse, and the entire week before the Colgate game, all sorts of hijinks occurred at both campuses. I am very glad I was able to experience the fun of Colgate weekends. The memories remain vividly clear in my mind, and they always elicit a smile.

With all the extracurricular activity, my studies were relegated to a very low priority. My system of never cutting a class, always taking good notes and remembering everything the professor said, was assuring me a minimum of C's with the usual B in German, and an A in my Survey of Fine Arts course. Unfortunately, my freshman pledge brothers were falling on hard times academically. Hugh, the drama major, got more involved with the drama department, and he wound up with a 3.0 at the end of his freshman year. Bob, who was a business major, had a tougher road to travel, but he also finished the year with a 2.9 grade point average. Considering that they both were transitioning from high school, they and their parents seemed happy with the results.

My classes were more difficult, in that every class I was taking required a term paper that would reflect a full semester's work and research per class. I put off all my papers to the last week before they were due, but was able, nevertheless, to complete all my papers in the required amount of time and receive a C on each paper. Considering that each paper only involved one week's work, it seemed like a good trade-off.

The reality of things then was, that until I began attending Syracuse University and subsequently pledging Phi Epsilon Pi, I had never experienced very much of Jewish life. I understood about 80 percent of the Yiddish language, but only because 80 percent of the language is based on German root words. I knew nothing about the High Holy Days, eating Kosher, and for that matter, I knew nothing about being Jewish. I have often thought that my pledging an all Jewish fraternity, particularly an all Jewish fraternity made up mostly of New York City Jews, must have been some sort of subliminal desire to reestablish my ethnic heritage. Until that time, I was basically an Irish Catholic, if only by inclination and upbringing. I have thought about that particular fact for most of my life, and I can't remember a single incident or thought on which I can focus, which determined that while at Syracuse University, I would suddenly become a Jew again, if not in religion, certainly in orientation and ethnic emotion. While I had only completed my first year at Syracuse and my sophomore year of college, the next two years would bring more illuminating experiences that would also remain with me for the rest of my life.

As the first year ended it became necessary for me to find summer employment. By keeping my job at the cafeteria, I had managed to get free board for my first year, but I now needed to make some more money to assist my father in meeting my college expenses. Bob Zirt suggested I go to work in the Borscht Belt for the summer. He felt certain he could find me a job as a busboy in one of the resort hotels. Ten weeks of hard work could easily assure me at least a thousand dollars (mostly from tips), and that would go a long way to defraying some of the costs that my father was meeting for me. My father never complained about the cost, but I just felt an obligation to help him help me.

THE BORSCHT BELT:
WORKING MY WAY THROUGH COLLEGE

Bob Zirt had called his father, and in short order I had been promised a job as a busboy at the Jefferson Hotel in Warwarsing, New York. I later discovered that any summer job at a Borscht Belt hotel was highly coveted due to the inordinate amount of money, primarily from tips, that could be earned. Going to work in the Borscht Belt for the summer was going to be another totally Jewish experience, and one that would, as so many other things then, influence my thinking and remain with me for the rest of my life.

The Borscht Belt was an informal term for the summer resorts of the Catskill Mountains located in Sullivan and Ulster Counties in Upstate New York. While the resorts were frequented primarily by Jews who originally immigrated from Eastern Europe, primarily, Hungary, Poland and Russia, and who shared a common language known as Yiddish, German Jews were rarely encountered in any Borscht Belt location. Borscht is a beet soup, eaten hot or cold, with a dollop of sour cream in the middle of the bowl, and very popular with people who originally lived in Eastern Europe. New Yorkers called the Borscht Belt the *Jewish Alps* or *Solomon County* (a play on Sullivan County).

Borscht Belt hotels came in all sizes and shapes. The fanciest resorts were first class hotels with pools, tennis courts, social halls, a theater, basketball courts, a basketball team staffed with professional players (NBA), and a large staff to ensure all guests were treated like royalty. Some of these famous hotels were Brickman's, Brown's, the Concord, Grossinger's, the Granit and Kutscher's Hotel and Country Club, the home of the best basketball team in the entire Borscht Belt region. The team at Kutscher's was staffed by NBA players such as Lew Alcindor, Bob Cousy, Bones McKinney, Bill Russell, and coached by such luminaries as Red Auerbach, Joe Lapchick, Nat Holman and Claire Bee, to name just a few of the Hall of Fame coaches who came to the Borscht Belt in the summer.

To my recollection, Brown's Hotel, which introduced Jerry Lewis, Grossinger's, which launched Eddie Fisher's career, and the Concord, which had Mel Brooks, Woody Allen and Milton Berle, were the top three hotels for talent, but the list of entertainers who got their start in the Borscht Belt reads like a Who's Who of American show business. Many of the comedians who broke in at the Borscht Belt hotels would continue to refer to their days there in the routines they used for the rest of their lives. Comedians who got their start, or regularly performed in Borscht Belt resorts, in addition to the one's mentioned above, included Joey Adams, Morey Amsterdam, Shelly Berman, Al Bernie, Lenny Bruce, George Burns, Red Buttons, Sid Caesar, Jack Carter, Myron Cohen, Billy Crystal, Bill Dana, Rodney Dangerfield, Phyllis Diller, Betty Garrett, Shecky Greene, Buddy Hackett, Mickey Katz (the father of Joel Grey), Danny Kaye, Alan King, Robert Klein, Jack E. Leonard, Jerry Lewis, Jackie Mason, Jan Murray, Carl Reiner, Don Rickles, Joan Rivers, Jackie Vernon and Henny Youngman. Certainly an astounding list of entertainers, made all the more astounding by the fact that every one of them was Jewish!

After the first class hotels came second and third class hotels, all of which had to have a swimming pool, a social hall, a main dining room and a small theater. In some of the hotels, the social hall doubled as the theater, since entertainers would travel a circuit, and consequently, smaller hotels only needed a theater when the circuit riders came to their hotel, generally on a preset schedule throughout the summer. When entertainers were not present, every hotel had to have an in-house band for dance instruction and nightly dances. The smaller the hotel was the smaller the band. Interestingly enough, smaller hotels could also not afford the expense of having a dance instructor on their permanent staff, so similar to the entertainers, dance instructors would also "ride a circuit" where they would give dance lessons, primarily in the Mambo, the Tango, the Cha-Cha-Cha and the Rumba, on scheduled days. Dance lessons were always a popular feature in the daily activities schedule of all the hotels.

The summer staffs of the hotels were also very interesting. The waiters and busboys were usually Jewish college students who held on to their jobs as long as they possibly could. Like the pecking order of the hotels, it was the goal of every waiter to work at one of the first class hotels, and it was the goal of every busboy to become a waiter and join the quest to get to a first class hotel. This was not an easy accomplishment, and it was almost impossible, unless you knew someone who could assist you on the way up.

The reason for all of this was that the Borscht Belt was based on a "tip economy." Guests paid their tips weekly, usually after the Sunday luncheon, because that was the time people usually left for home. Sundays were always tense times for waiters and busboys. If you were a waiter at a first class hotel, you could count on a ten-dollar tip per week from each person sitting on your station. A station usually comprised four tables of ten people per table, so the waiter could count on a minimum of $400 per week in tips alone. This would occur if everyone tipped only the minimum, which rarely happened. Busboys in first class hotels could usually count on a seven-dollar tip per person, per week. Thus, first class hotels were referred to as "10 and 7 houses," which described the expected tips for the waiters and busboys.

In 1954, if you could earn $3,200 for the summer as a waiter or $2,240 as a busboy, you earned all of your college expenses for the coming year. Tuition at Syracuse in 1954 was $700 per year, which did not include books or room and board, not to mention any spending money. This explains why these jobs were so very desirable. Second Class hotels were described as "8 and 5 houses" and third class hotels were described as "7 and 3 houses." In any case, working at any of these hotels during the summer months, meant you had most of your college expenses fairly well covered for the coming year. You just had a lot more disposable income if you were lucky enough to work at a "10 and 7 house."

The minimum hourly wage in New York in 1954 was 75 cents per hour. Waiters and busboys at all hotels received this minimum wage salary only, and their hours were tightly controlled with daily requirements to clock in and out for every shift. Even at 75 cents per hour, management was not going to pay one penny more than required. The fact that you were working for tips made the hourly salary almost meaningless, and no one complained.

As for the rest of the staff, the lifeguards were mostly Jewish, as were members of the house band. Bands generally came from colleges where they had been formed to play at the local campuses on weekends. The maids were never Jewish, nor was the kitchen staff, who seemed to be either Hispanic or non-Jewish, eastern European, usually Russians or Poles. Like the waiters and busboys, a good kitchen staff was difficult to find. If a good chef was found, every effort was made to keep him happy, working and, most importantly, sober. They ruled the kitchens like tyrants and made life miserable for everyone else, but as long as the food was good and the customers were happy, no one cared if the staff was happy.

The Jefferson Hotel in Warwarsing was a high third class or a low second class hotel, depending on your point of view. The clientele returned to the hotel every summer, and the staff was rarely replaced unless employment could be found at a higher class hotel that promised higher wages or greater tips. Bob Zirt's father had gotten me the job at the hotel because he was a friend of one of the owners, Jack Levine. Jack was a formidable boss who ran a tough operation, took no guff from anyone, and always made a profit. I was determined to do a good job and make sure that nothing derogatory concerning me ever got back to Mr. Zirt.

Bob Zirt dropped me off at the Jefferson Hotel which would be my home for the next two months. My impression of my living quarters were less than favorable. I never thought there would be any place that could make my former summer residence at Mrs. Flanagan's Sea Breeze Inn at Rockaway Beach look luxurious, but the "bungalow" at the Jefferson Hotel accomplished this feat in a heartbeat. The bungalow was a bunkhouse with a shared bathroom and hooks on which to hang your clothes. There was no air conditioning and no fans of any type, and the place was hot and smelly by 8 a.m. every day. By noon, the place was ripe, and it rarely got much better until late in the evening when the air cooled, and the temperature became somewhat bearable.

Unknown to me, this would be the hardest work I had ever done at this point in my life. The daily routine for waiters and busboys was extremely demanding. While the Jefferson was a "7 and 3 house," many of the guests tipped in the "8 and 5 house" manner, so we really worked hard to impress the guests at our tables. On the first day, waiters were paired off with busboys and there was a waiter/busboy team for every station of forty guests (four tables with ten persons per table). There were ten stations in the dining room, so a full hotel meant there were four hundred guests staying at the Jefferson when the hotel was 100 percent occupied.

I was paired with a second year waiter from Columbia University whose name was Isaac Shapiro. Ike had gone to Bronx Science High School, had won a scholarship to Columbia, and was studying to become a Doctor. Ike and I began our day at 6 a.m. in the dining room. We polished the silverware on our station, folded clean linen napkins, wiped and shined both juice glasses and water glasses, placed fresh flowers in vases, cut fresh bread from the loaves that had been baked during the night, placed butter in dishes and cleaned and wiped all the plates on our station. These chores were to be completed by 6:30 a.m. so we could eat the breakfast that was prepared for the dining room staff. We ate whatever the chef prepared.

At exactly 7 a.m., the dining room opened for breakfast, and the hordes of guests descended as though they had just completed a three week hunger strike. We soon got to know our guests' idiosyncrasies, and prepared for them as best as possible. When one guest requested and received a special item, thirty nine other guests thought they would like to "try that also!" Never a dull moment in the dining room, and immediately following breakfast, which ended at 10 a.m. for the late sleepers, we broke down the settings from breakfast and prepared for lunch.

The Jefferson, like most hotels in the Borscht Belt, was Kosher. This meant that there were two sets of dishes that could never be mixed, because one set was used to serve only dairy meals and the other was used to serve only meat meals. Besides the dishes, which were rotated between dairy and meat meals, there were also two sets of silverware. The silverware was stored in wooden, wheeled credenzas, and were rolled out to our stations, depending on which type of meal was being served. Both sets of silverware had to be maintained in a clean state, subject to the inspection of the headwaiter at any time. These requirements kept us extremely busy all the time.

Breakfast was always dairy, as was lunch, and the meat meal was always served in the evening. Dairy meant that under no circumstances could you serve meat with any dairy dish. You could serve fish, such as Lox (smoked salmon) or white fish, but no meat of any kind. Thus, Lox and eggs was a popular favorite for breakfast, as were pancakes, cheese and vegetable omelets, blintzes, waffles and poached or boiled eggs. Potatoes were fine, as long as they were not cooked in lard or rendered meat fat.

For the meat meals, no dairy products could be served. If you got a steak and a baked potato, there was no butter or sour cream to put on the baked potato because you were eating meat. It was a healthy way to eat, which was the whole idea behind the Kosher tradition. Kosher also required that the premises be maintained in an extremely clean manner. The waiters and busboys were expected to help with kitchen cleaning after all the station cleaning was completed in the dining room.

We earned our money through hard work over long hours. While the money was extremely good, I was already wondering what I would do next summer to continue to earn money for college. I wasn't sure I would be particularly eager to return to the Borscht Belt, no matter how much money I made. My doubts were wiped away after the first week when I received $150 in tips. This was a good omen and made the hard work well worth the effort. The time passed very quickly because we were working close to sixteen hours per day.

The season ended, and during the end of season party, I was assured a position as a busboy for the summer of 1955, as long as I let the headwaiter know one month in advance. This was a good omen, and I left for Syracuse feeling very good about myself with $3,000 in my pocket. This was a lot of money in 1954, and my father was very pleased with my summer efforts. I had earned a year's tuition, plus book money and nominal spending money in ten arduous weeks of work in the Borscht Belt. All I needed was a job at Syracuse to earn my board, and I was home free for the year.

The Borscht Belt has changed to the point where today it is nothing like what I experienced in 1954. To have worked there is an experience I will always treasure. The New York Jews, the comedians, the dance bands, the mambo and rumba lessons, the social director, and all the things we read about today, and that serve as material for the surviving Borscht Belt comedians like Billy Crystal, Mel Brooks, Woody Allen and Jackie Mason, were all there and were simply routine. These are things I lived through and enjoyed. I did not know I was living a piece of history that would soon disappear from the landscape forever.

For $90, I bought a 1933 Dodge Coupe. I named my car *Rozinante* after Don Quixote's horse, and painted the name on the hood and a large orange "S" on both doors of the car. I headed back to Syracuse, needing only a raccoon coat and megaphone to look like a typical college kid of the Roaring '20s! Bob Zirt followed me to make sure Rozinate made the trip.

RETURNING TO COLLEGE

I returned to Syracuse, encountering no problems with my "new" car Rozinate, and moved into the fraternity house at 423 Euclid Avenue. The fraternity house was a three-story house that had been bought by the fraternity in the late 1940s. The attic was converted into a 75-man dormitory by putting up 40 double decker bunk beds. Every space below the attic was made into study rooms and places to store personal gear. Each study room had three to four desks and two closets, so space was at a premium. On the first floor, there was a living room/lounge and a large dining room which also served as a chapter room for our weekly meetings. There was a large, institutional style kitchen with a scullery and pantry, plus a professional chef who was the only paid employee of the fraternity. The basement contained a television room and a bar. On occasions, the television room could be converted into a poker room or a porno movie theater, depending on which entrepreneurial fraternity brother was hosting the particular event.

Also, located in the basement were the fraternity test files, reputed to be the very best on campus. The files were very serious business, and were kept locked at all times. Every year, a brother was appointed to maintain and manage the files, and in return for this work, he received free board for the year. It was always some pre-med or business major, who got the job, since "flakes" would only wreak havoc with the files, and this was unacceptable.

My study room consisted of Bob Zirt and my friend from Brooklyn, Hugh Fordin. Besides the three of us, the only non-Jew in the fraternity, a fellow named Bill Gaffney from the Bronx, became our fourth member.

I rushed down to Sims Dining Hall to see if I could get my old job back, but it had been given to a football player as a part of his scholarship. This really threw a wrench into my financial plan, and I went to the campus employment office to see if there was anything available to earn board for the year. As luck would have it, there was a job opening for a waiter at the Pi Beta Phi Sorority house. I went to the sorority house for an interview with the housemother, a Mrs. Melby, who was an older woman who had been at the sorority for the past fifteen years. She was a no nonsense type who made it clear that waiters, of whom there were three, would have nothing to do with the girls in the sorority, would arrive on time, do their work, and depart the premises quickly, and always by the rear door. In exchange for this work, the sorority would provide free meals to their waiters. I told her I was an experienced waiter, and based on my experience and my assurances that I would conform to her rules, she hired me, and my board for the 1954-55 school year was secured.

The next step was registration, and while I had just turned 19, I was entering my third year of college and the requirements of my major were getting to be very demanding. I was getting into classical literature, scientific German and, just to maintain my sanity, History of Fine Art, television scriptwriting and public speaking. While all students were subject to the military draft, there was no requirement to participate in ROTC (Reserve Officer's Training Corps), which both the Army and the Air Force sponsored at Syracuse. This meant that any student who had two years of ROTC could, upon graduation, become an officer in either the Army or the Air Force and serve three years on active duty.

Life in the fraternity house was an eye-opening experience. Most of the brothers came from backgrounds that involved a lot of money. They had experienced many of the costly aspects of living in New York City by the time they got to college. They read *The New Yorker*, drank J&B Scotch or Beefeaters Gin, knew all the in places to go in the city, and had attended many theater productions. They wore Brooks Brothers clothing, cashmere sweaters and blue blazers. They bet on football and basketball games, played poker and, if they wanted a sexual experience, drove to a mob brothel in Utica, New York, where, for five dollars, they could alleviate their sexual tensions. They seldom dated coeds, because it "was simply a waste of time, since you were not going to get laid anyway." Their parents were either professionals (doctors, dentists or lawyers) or owned their own businesses.

Money rarely was a problem for the brothers of Phi Ep. They did not participate in very many campus activities, meeting only the most basic requirements of the Pan-Hellenic Council, which allowed them to keep functioning as a fraternity. They openly flaunted the unofficial dress codes of the 1950s college student that dictated white buckskin shoes, khaki pants, white tee shirts and cashmere sweaters, together with a crew cut and a blue blazer with a white button down shirt for formal events. While they all had the appropriate clothing, and even wore them when the occasion dictated, Phi Eps wore "ducktail" haircuts, pegged pants, white-on-white shirts and plain brown shoes. Pegged pants were taken in to thirteen inch cuffs that hugged your shoes, and you could never put them on without first taking off your shoes. A jacket and pegged pants comprised the "zoot suit" appearance. The Phi Eps were nicknamed "the greaseballs" on campus, because to keep their ducktail haircuts in place required lots of hair pomade. These were my newly acquired standards which came fairly easy for me, since I was already wearing these clothes before I got to Syracuse. This is probably the reason I felt so comfortable in the fraternity.

Although the campus was "dry," the bar at our house was always open, and a beer keg was constantly ready to draw a drink for any thirsty brother. The television was constantly on, and a small core of regulars stayed up every night from 11:30 p.m. to 1 a.m. to watch the Steve Allen Show (which became the original Tonight Show).

Living at the fraternity house was much different from living in a university dormitory. First, there was always something going on, and it very rarely had anything to do with studying. The first thing I encountered was football weekends. I had attempted to walk on to the football team, but wound up becoming a human tackling dummy, so my football career at Syracuse was extremely short. I did make the swimming team, but my times for the 50 and 100 meter freestyle events were far too slow to compete on an NCAA level. Being a lifeguard at Rockaway Beach had been fun, but it certainly did not qualify me to swim competitively at the college level.

Football weekends always started on Friday night and went through to Sundays. There were dates for anyone who wanted one, and there was always a party at the fraternity house. There was a pre-game party, a post game party, and a Sunday morning party. Football weekends were particularly attractive to our alums, who seemed to come in droves, and partied as hard as any of the current crop of brothers. Every fraternity was required to have a sign against the team Syracuse was playing, and the signs were judged weekly with a trophy awarded for the best sign. They never gave a trophy for the worst sign, because if they had, Phi Ep would have had a closet full of trophies. As it was, I don't remember Phi Ep winning anything during my three years, but we sure did have a lot of fun. We also were the only fraternity that recycled the signs. If we played a team that we had played the previous year, we simply reassembled the sign we had used before, and displayed it in front of our house. The alums never knew, and most of the judges didn't get it either, and we had more time to party since we didn't have to make new signs. Since we played Colgate every year, our Colgate sign was so old by the time I got there that we made a new one, which, I was later informed, lasted until Colgate cancelled Syracuse because our teams were going in different directions.

The academic year passed quickly. My grades were mediocre, meaning I was getting C's in everything, but I was not studying at all and simply attending classes regularly. I had discovered that if I never cut a class, I would always get enough material to pass any class. Of course, I would probably get a C, but since they did not put your grade point average on your diploma, it didn't much matter to me. In that regard, in my entire three-year career at Syracuse, I never missed a single class, and I handed in every paper that was due on the last day that was allowable. For some of my classes, I never even bought any of the books, using the library for important works, and borrowing other people's books just so I would have something to carry into class. This is not a way to get on Dean's list, or to become competitive for entering graduate school, but in my case, neither of those two options interested me.

I went home to New York for both Thanksgiving and Christmas. My father and Dora had an apartment in the Murray Hill section of Manhattan between Park Avenue South and Lexington Avenue. Dora was great fun to be with, and she was a fabulous cook. She prepared my favorite meals, and my all-time favorite meal is Weinerschnitzel with red cabbage and hot German potato salad. I thought I had died and gone to heaven. The schnitzel, which were nothing more than very flat and thin, breaded veal cutlets, were always perfectly prepared, and it was a joy to visit with her. She also made my father extremely happy, which made her truly special in my book.

When I left to return to Syracuse after the holidays, I could not remember when I had a better time with my father or just "being at home." I also had made some money working for Peter Sulka, again as a holiday sales clerk in his Fifth Avenue salon, and as usual, the normal run of celebrities came in to do their annual Christmas shopping, buying extremely overpriced silk ties, shirts, scarves and jackets.

In the spring semester, I walked onto the lacrosse team and made the team as a defensive player. I made the traveling team and played against West Point, Annapolis, Johns Hopkins and Maryland. Dad and Dora came to see me play at West Point, and as luck would have it, I got knocked out in the first quarter, and did not play again because my head hurt.

The spring semester of 1955 was a turning point in my life. As I mentioned previously, all young men in 1955, over the age of 18, were required to serve their country. We had to register with our local draft boards, and this meant that unless you had a student exemption, when your number came up, off you went for two years of service in the Army. If you wanted to serve in another branch of the military, you could enlist in the Navy, the Air Force or the Marines, but you then had to serve for three years instead of two. The only way to avoid the draft in 1955 was to get yourself declared 4-F, which meant that you were physically unable to serve. In order for that to happen, you needed a letter from a doctor who would have to certify that you were physically unable to tolerate military duties.

Since all college students had exemptions, the military requirements became automatic upon graduation. If you got accepted to a medical, dental or law school, you could extend your exemption, but at some point, especially when you graduated from one of those schools, you were immediately subject to the draft and military service. Only a 4-F classification could keep you out of the service. Almost all the brothers in Phi Ep knew a doctor. Most of them either had fathers, uncles or cousins that were doctors, and, if that wasn't the case, their fathers had means to obtain a letter from a doctor, certifying that their sons were physically unfit for military duty.

One evening, a group of brothers were sitting around drinking beers and talking about avoiding military service. Each of them was almost assured of a 4-F classification through their personal connections with a willing doctor, and they were happy that they didn't have to go into the military. Since I was drinking right along with them, I suddenly lost my temper and called them all a bunch of cowards and informed them that I was going to enlist in the Marine Corps the next day. They thought I was crazy.

The next afternoon, I went to the Syracuse recruiting office of the U. S. Marine Corps and spoke to a sergeant about enlisting after I graduated from college. The sergeant informed me that since I was a college student, I could enroll in the officer program, and he recommended that I take some prescreening tests for Officer's Candidate School. He told me that he could administer the tests in Syracuse but that if I passed the tests, I would have to go to Buffalo to be accepted into the officer program. The office that procured officers for the Marine Corps was located in the Old Post Office Building on Swan and Ellicott Streets in downtown Buffalo, and if I passed the tests, the Sergeant was certain that I would be accepted. I agreed to take the tests, and the following morning I went back to the recruiting office and took about six or seven different tests. The Sergeant told me he would call me with the results in several days, as the tests were being forwarded to Buffalo for grading and evaluation.

The following week the sergeant informed me that I had passed the tests and that I was to report to the Officer Selection Office in Buffalo on Friday morning for processing which would take about a day, and it included a physical exam. The Marine Corps would provide transportation from Syracuse to Buffalo and back. Little did I know then that this would be the first of many travels with the Marine Corps. I arrived in Buffalo at exactly 8:30 a.m. on Monday, February 7, 1955. I took a cab to the Old Post Office Building and went to the Marine Corps Officer Selection Office, ready to present myself promptly at 9 a.m.

I was met by a sergeant who informed me that a Major Reynolds would be processing me, except for the physical examination, which would be performed by a Navy Doctor who would be arriving at the office by 10 a.m. Major Reynolds told me that most Platoon Leaders Class (PLC) candidates were Freshman who went to boot camp for six weeks twice before graduating, but since I was a Junior, I had to do it all in one twelve week session before graduation and commissioning. He immediately informed me that if I wanted to continue, I would have to sign a paper that said I had been told these facts, and that I agreed to take both Junior and Senior PLC sessions at Quantico in the coming summer, and that I understood that the time would be 12 weeks with no break in between sessions.

I readily agreed and signed, not realizing that I had just agreed to a mind and body altering experience from which I would be forever changed. The physical followed some routine paper work and a large number of signatures to various documents. After the doctor cleared me for enrollment in the program, I was sworn in and became a Corporal in the United States Marine Corps Reserve. My first duty assignment would be at Marine Corps Schools at Quantico, Virginia, where I would report for duty for twelve weeks of training. I was now officially a United States Marine, but only on paper. Earning the title, *Marine*, would start in June and I would be severely tested.

I returned to the fraternity house, and my fellow fraternity brothers were totally amazed that I had gone through with my promise to join the Marines. They seemed perplexed that a Jew would enter the service voluntarily, and especially the Marine Corps, which had a reputation of having officers primarily from the South, with all the biases that came with that distinction. They were positive that I would not survive basic training.

I got a grade point average of 2.8 for the first half of my junior year and finished the year in May with a grade point average of 2.7. Not exactly burning up the academic portion of my college career, but I had survived another year of college, had passed all of my classes, had all the credits I required, and had managed to make the money I had earned in the summer last throughout the school year.

After I returned from Buffalo, I went to the 4th Tank Battalion, the Marine Reserve unit in Syracuse, and obtained a full issue of military utility uniforms, which included a fully lined, foul weather winter parka, the kind they were issuing to troops in Korea. I wore the parka to class throughout the winter, also wearing my *Mongolian piss cutter* (a Marine expression from the Korean War), which was a fur lined cap with earflaps that Marines wore in Korea along with their parkas. I was never cold again on my long walks to morning classes, plus I received the added benefit of having other students mistake me for a veteran student, which gave me quite a bit of credibility on campus.

CHAPTER 5

QUANTICO, 1955

PLATOON LEADERS COURSE, USMC

When school ended for the summer, I returned to New York and waited for my orders to Marine Corps Schools (MCS), Quantico, Virginia. I received a three-page telegram directing me to report to Quantico on Sunday, June 5, 1955, for training in the Junior PLC Program. The telegram went on to say that the telegram itself was my voucher to obtain a train ticket from New York City to Quantico on Saturday, June 4. There was no mention of a return ticket, and I was not that concerned about one at the time. I went to Grand Central Station and obtained my US Government train ticket. My train was scheduled to arrive at Quantico at 4 a.m. on Sunday, not exactly a good arrival time, as my prospective Drill Instructors would soon inform me.

Dad and Dora celebrated my 20th birthday on June 3, by taking me to dinner at my favorite New York City restaurant called Asti. It was an Italian restaurant, and all staff working there were opera singers, many of them with contracts at the Metropolitan Opera House. At a certain time each evening, the house lights dimmed, all service stopped, and the entire staff sang an opera. It was one of Caruso's favorite restaurants, and Pavarotti and many other famous opera stars stopped by when they were in New York. On rare occasions, they would even join in the singing. One night, I was lucky enough to hear the world famous Beverly Sills as she sang a complete aria. Unfortunately, the Asti restaurant is now closed.

On Saturday, I began packing the few things I was instructed to take to Quantico. I was really nervous about my upcoming adventure, especially since I would not be making very much money during the summer. The Marine Corps paid officer candidates at the rate entitled by their rank, and we went through training as both a Corporal for the first six weeks, and a Sergeant for the second six weeks. This meant that at first I would receive Corporal's pay, which was $85.80 per month, and for the second six weeks, I would receive Sergeant's pay, which was $99.37 per month. I estimated that for the entire 12 weeks of training, I would earn $277.75. I asked my father how he felt about this situation, since it meant that he would have to pay the bulk of my senior year college expenses. I told him that I would continue to work for my meals, but tuition, books and my room fees at the fraternity, would have to be paid by him. He was totally supportive and told me that if I made it through the training and became an officer, it would be worth it to him.

I left New York on Saturday afternoon, June 4 and arrived at Union Station in Washington late in the evening. I found out my connection to Quantico came to Union Station only twice a day and the next train would not depart until 3 a.m. Sunday. There wasn't much to do but wait in the station, and at 2:30 a.m., I boarded my train for Quantico. At 4 a.m., Sunday, June 5, 1955, I stepped off the train at the Quantico station and my Marine Corps career was about to begin.

I was surprised to see that I was the only person getting off the train, as I expected to be joined by other young men eager to begin their Marine training. As I looked up and down the station platform, I saw two Marines dressed in summer khaki uniforms approaching me; one was a Sergeant, and the other one was a Staff Sergeant. They asked me if I was arriving for training in the PLC program, and when I responded affirmatively, they directed me to follow them. At this point, no one spoke, and I was doing what I was told to do. I got into a van and was driven to the Training and Test Regiment area, a group of brick buildings and Quonset huts located at the extreme southern end of the base. A Quonset hut is a lightweight prefabricated structure of corrugated galvanized steel having a semicircular cross section. The name comes from their site of first manufacture, Quonset Point, Rhode Island.

There was no conversation, and I did not attempt any. When we arrived at the Regiment, I was instructed to enter a Quonset hut near where the van had stopped. As soon as I entered the Quonset hut, the screaming and yelling began. I had made the mistake of arriving hours before anyone else, causing the drill instructors (DI's) to get up earlier than normal. I arrived sporting my very best ducktail haircut, and wearing a pair of 13 inch pegged pants. Needless to say, I was grist for the mill of these already irritated DI's. My manhood was immediately assaulted, then my hair, then my New York accent, then my posture, and then my arrogance of arriving at 4 a.m. on a Sunday. I had been through some tough times on the streets of New York, but these guys were really working me over, all the time predicting that I would not make it and that they would personally see to it.

Since it was still very early, they placed me in a metal wall locker which accommodated me standing up. The DI's locked the wall locker and left me there for about two hours. This was my introduction to the Marine Corps, and it was not exactly a very happy way to start my basic training. To say that I began questioning my logic in joining the Marine Corps was an understatement. Around 6:30 a.m., a DI unlocked the wall locker and told me to get outside and join the rest of the candidates who had arrived during my incarceration in the wall locker.

We stood at attention, waiting for the next injustice to be performed on us, and we were not disappointed. We were immediately run down to the Post barber shop where we formed a single line. I was called to the front of the line because the DI's did not like my hair and wanted me to be the first candidate to receive his boot camp haircut, meaning that every bit of hair would be shaved off of my head. I honestly didn't care about the haircut, but I was concerned that due to my early arrival, every DI already knew my name. This was not good! After we got our haircuts, we were marched and run to the supply warehouse where we were issued all the clothing we would need in training. We were also issued a rifle, a cartridge belt, two Marine Corps packs, a blanket, sheets and a pillowcase, boots, sneakers, socks, underwear, a bucket (in which to do our laundry), clothespins, a washboard and sundry other materials that would be required.

All this activity was carried out at an extremely fast pace, and there was constant yelling by our drill instructors. Quantico is very hot in the summer, and this day was extremely so. We all were dripping with sweat, and on we moved until our drill instructors told us to stop. We were in a loose formation in front of some red brick barracks, and this is where we were broken down into platoons. Since the Marine Corps likes to do things efficiently, we were broken down into forty man platoons arranged in alphabetical order.

Naturally, I wound up in the first platoon, which was composed entirely of men whose names ended in A through D. After we were assigned to platoons, we met the drill instructors who would be training us for the next six weeks. We met our Platoon Commander, a First Lieutenant Batchelder, our Senior Drill Instructor, a Staff Sergeant Roth, and the Assistant Drill Instructor, Sergeant Evans. These three Marines were going to control our lives totally, and we'd better be ready to do anything they asked and do it quickly without any holdups. They were going to set a torrid pace, and it was up to all of us to keep up.

We were hurried into the 1st Platoon squad bay where twenty double bunk beds awaited us. Each bed, which was called a "rack," had a wall locker, with which I was already intimately familiar, and a foot locker, which was a wooden trunk painted Marine Corps green. We were instructed on how to store our gear, where and how to hang our uniforms, where to store our rifles and all of our rifle cleaning gear, how to place our shoes and boots, and finally, how to make our racks. Everything we did or owned was going to be under constant inspection and we had to pass.

We were then instructed on how to wear the utility uniform properly since we would be spending most of our time wearing it, and how to store the rest of our gear. Everything had to be in a specific place, and every man in the platoon had to store his gear in exactly the same manner. Because the weather was so hot, we were issued silver helmet liners, which were nicknamed "chrome domes," which we were required to wear outdoors at all times. The silver color of the helmet liners reflected the sun and was considered to be a cool alternative to overheating your whole body through your head. We always wore two canteens on our cartridge belts so we would never run out of water. It was our responsibility to keep the canteens filled. As we assembled in the squad bay, I realized that I was very hungry since I had not eaten anything since I arrived at Quantico. I wondered if this was another form of harassment.

I looked at my watch, and realized it was only 11:30 a.m. I felt as if I had been at Quantico for a long time already! This was going to be a very long six weeks, and in my case, it would be an impossible twelve weeks. We were assembled again outside our squad bay and marched and run to the mess hall. This was my first experience with a Marine Corps mess hall, however, it resembled the dining hall at Boy Scout camp. We took metal trays that were separated into sections so that the messmen could slam whatever was being served into each section. It was normal to get mashed potatoes, gravy and vegetables, all mixed together, and if we were going to get ice cream, that always wound up, in or near the gravy. We got our food, sat down at long tables, and began to eat. There was no conversation and the DI's hovered over us to insure that we ate quickly, ate everything on our trays, and did not talk. The food was good, there was plenty of it, and it quickly disappeared.

After lunch, we assembled outside the mess hall and were marched and run to a class that was being held in a metal building called a Butler building. These metal buildings must have been the idea of a sadist, as they were very quickly heated by the sun and were always hot inside. There was no relief from the heat inside these buildings, even though they always had two large pedestal fans working at each side of the front of the building. This was supposed to keep the air circulating, however, the only thing the fans circulated was heat and humidity.

The purpose of this first class was to inform us about what the next six weeks would be like. Except for a few twelve week PLC's, almost all the PLC's were college freshmen. They were almost all either 18 or 19 years old, and I, having attained the ripe old age of 20 just two days ago, was one of the older men in the program. The freshman had to complete just six weeks and then they did not have to return until their junior year of college when they would return for another six weeks of training.

The Regimental Commander, a Colonel Houser, who looked like Superman in a Marine uniform, informed us that the next six weeks would be very difficult for us. He told us that it was the purpose of the junior PLC program to identify those individuals who could not complete the program, either because of physical problems, mental capacity or the inability to adapt to military life. He further informed us that the attrition rate in junior PLC's was 40 percent and that only six out of every ten men who start the PLC program are able to complete it. He explained that there were three ways to fail in the program. The first way was for our DI's to recommend that we be dropped from the program. The second was for our peers to vote us out of the program, and finally, any one of us could drop on request (called DOR, in the program), which meant that we only had to go to our drill instructor or platoon commander, and request to be dropped from the PLC program. I could see why attrition was so high.

The Colonel then went on to explain why the regiment was named the Training and Test Regiment. We were going to be trained, and then we were going to be tested on everything we learned. This training and testing would set the pace throughout the six weeks, and would cover all phases of military life, from physical fitness, to marching, to field exercises, to drilling on the parade ground, to leadership and our ability to endure stress and respond to immediate situations.

It was emphasized that we were being tested on our abilities to lead troops into combat, and if this is not what we thought we were doing, then the time to drop out was right now. The Colonel closed by saying that from the moment we walked out of the Butler building, we have accepted the challenge, and our stressful training would begin. If there was anyone who wanted to drop out, now was the time to raise your hand and let him know that you are not suitable for the Marine Corps. No one raised their hands, and so the lecture was over, we were marched out of the building, and the training began in earnest. My bunkmate was a fellow from LSU who also happened to be a junior in college, and who was also there for the twelve week period. His name was John Henry Bateman, and he was a true son of the South. He had a great attitude, and nothing seemed to faze him. We hit it off instantly.

The training was heavily skewed towards physical fitness and leadership. In almost everything we did, our physical fitness and endurance was constantly tested. Whether on the obstacle course or the pugilstick fighting classes, or even just taking the Marine Corps Physical Fitness Test, we were being evaluated on our abilities to endure and continue, no matter how difficult the stress might become. Besides this aspect of the training, each week a different candidate was assigned a leadership position within the platoon. The position could be platoon leader, squad leader, fire team leader, squad clerk or guidon bearer. Our performance was always evaluated by the DI's and our peers, and the reports were posted openly for all members of the platoon to see. There was no whining or excuses, and we learned to take complete responsibility for our actions.

On top of these requirements, we were taught close order drill, and we competed against other platoons to show our proficiency in drill and the manual of arms. We spent hours on the drill field, sweating in the hot Virginia sun, and then we would follow drill periods by running the obstacle course every day. We noticed that everyone in the Training and Test Regiment ran the obstacle course, and one of the fastest on the course was Colonel Houser who would run it with his swagger stick in his mouth! The swagger stick was carried by all officers in the Marine Corps, supposedly to keep their hands out of their pockets. It was discontinued in 1960 by the Commandant of the Marine Corps, who called the swagger stick "an optional item of interference."

The individual ratings came out weekly, and I found myself rated 20 out of 40. Not exactly a great mark, but sufficient to keep out of the range of being dropped from the program. In my own mind, I was continuing my "gentleman C" position. During the first two weeks, SSgt Roth had identified me as someone who was going to be harassed by him. He spent an inordinate amount of time trying to get me to screw up in any way possible. If I took a wrong step in drill, he was all over me, if I hesitated on the obstacle course, he was right behind me, yelling obscenities and screaming at me. He seemed to have a personal grudge against me, and try as I might, I could not get him off my back. One night after a particularly backbreaking day and many rebukes from SSgt Roth, I called my father and told him that I was seriously thinking of dropping out. I told him that a drill instructor obviously had it in for me and that I did not think I could take it much longer. My father told me that if I dropped out I would have to live with that for the rest of my life, and he thought I should stick it out no matter what. He was sure I could do it, so he simply said,

"Stay there and complete the job." As usual, my father was right, and I decided to stick it out and not let SSgt Roth drive me out just because he didn't like me. I also swore to myself not to give him any reason that would allow him to recommend me for discharge.

I vowed that I would complete the course. This proved to be a more difficult task than I had imagined, as the next few weeks would soon prove. Along with field work and physical fitness, we also had classroom work that dealt with Marine Corps history, weapons nomenclature, field sanitation, first aid and orienteering, which was primarily a class in how to use the lensatic compass, and how to orient your position on a map. All classroom work ended with written tests, and your grades from these tests were added into your overall class standing. Leadership points were the most important, and every leadership position that you held was evaluated and graded. Failing in a leadership position was usually a sure way to a discharge, since an officer was expected to be a leader and if you could not lead, you probably would not be a very good officer. In the first three weeks of training we lost eight candidates, six were discharged by the staff and two dropped out voluntarily. I think SSgt Roth was disappointed that I was still around, but, as long as I performed, there was little he could do to drive me out.

In the second peer grading period, I was graded 16 out of 32. I seemed to be destined to finish in the middle of the pack, but that was OK with me, because those kinds of grades made me untouchable to SSgt Roth. At the end of the fourth week of training, we departed on a field exercise in which we would have a mock war against another company. We were going to stay in the field for several nights and then return to our base just before the weekend.

On the first night in the field, SSgt Roth was going around telling us where to pitch our two-man tents. The area that he had picked out for me was covered with poison ivy, and I told him that I was extremely allergic to it and asked him to please move me to another place. SSgt Roth simply laughed in my face and told me to pitch my tent and shut up. I did what I was told, and the next morning I was covered in festering blisters of poison ivy. SSgt Roth looked concerned, and I was immediately evacuated to the Quantico Naval Hospital, where I joined about twenty other candidates all covered with severe cases of poison ivy.

The Marine Corps, in typical barracks humor, dubbed the ward, *The Ivy League*, and the room was kept air conditioned to a fairly low temperature to help dry out the blisters on our skin, all of which were covered with bandages and calamine lotion. We stayed in bed, trying to move as little as possible in order for the blisters to break and then heal. Once a day, an officer from the Regiment came by to see how we were doing. I was totally shocked when SSgt Roth came by to see me. I told him that I hoped that I had proved to him that I truly was allergic to poison ivy. He laughed, and said that he couldn't wait to get me back in training. After five days in the hospital, a captain came to see me. He told me that since I was a 12-week PLC, the rules stated that a 12-week PLC could not miss more than five days of training or he would be disqualified from the course. This meant that if

I wanted to complete the course, I had to return to training by the next day. This was a tough decision, as I was still draining from my blisters.

The captain also informed me that the medical staff thought I should remain in the hospital, but that if I did that I would be dropped from the PLC program. The only way I could return to training was to sign a release and a waiver, indicating that I knew I had to stay in the hospital, but wanted to leave to continue training. The captain just happened to have the necessary paperwork with him, so I signed the documents, packed up my gear, was given a large supply of calamine lotion and bandages, and returned to my platoon.

We had five days to go to finish the first six weeks, and I was on track to finish with my platoon. SSgt Roth continued giving me a hard time every chance he got. I did notice that he occasionally smiled when he was harassing me, and it did not seem that he was as angry with me as he had been previously. He knew he had caused my poison ivy, but since that was between him and me, the issue was never discussed. I finished my first six weeks with my blisters healed about 50 percent. The problem was that during the day, the extreme heat and activity always seemed to irritate the blisters and make them burst open, and then at night, they had a chance to heal slightly. It was a vicious cycle, and it would continue into the next six weeks.

The Junior course finished on a Friday morning, and since I did not have to report to the Senior PLC course until the following Monday, I went to Quantico town where I rented a hotel room with air conditioning. I stayed in bed, covered in calamine lotion, all weekend. The lack of activity plus the air conditioning did wonders for my festering blisters. I left my hotel room only to get a hamburger and a coke at Diamond Lou's, a Marine hangout on the main street of Quantico. By the time Monday morning rolled around I had been 75 percent healed.

On Monday morning, I joined the first platoon of my new company, and was very pleasantly surprised to see that there were twenty candidates in the platoon who had completed the first six weeks with me. We were joined by twenty new candidates who had arrived the previous day and who were now ready to begin their second six weeks of training. It had been two years since these candidates had completed their first six weeks of training, and I felt that those of us who had just completed the first six weeks had a distinct advantage over these new candidates.

We waited in our new squad bay for our two new drill instructors, and our new platoon commander. Unfortunately, there was nothing new for me. In walked 1st Lt Batchelder, SSgt Roth and Sgt Evans. Having finished six weeks with a junior PLC group, they were now assigned a senior PLC group. I think I noticed an evil grin cross the face of SSgt Roth when he saw me in the formation. While portions of my arms and legs remained bandaged and draining, I was prepared to take whatever he was going to dish out. There was no doubt in my mind that I would complete the 12-week course.

Senior PLC was different from junior PLC. The staff assumed that we had basic knowledge about the training, and for the next six weeks we would be getting advanced training in all the aspects that were covered in the junior PLC program. The leadership assignments became more demanding, and the grading was much tougher. More was expected from us at every turn. We were required to be faster, better and more capable than the standards that had been satisfactory in the junior course.

The staff kept reminding us that we were just ten months away from becoming Marine Officers, and this was certainly going to be our final testing period. The staff said that they had to be diligent in grading and evaluating our potential, because once we completed the course there was no turning back. Peer evaluations became more important, and each week a candidate was discharged. It was very obvious to me that this was serious business, and if you wanted to complete the course, hard work and dedication was required.

The training began with a bang as we went over the obstacle course for time, and then were evaluated for drill competence. I thought that it was extremely unfair for the new six week candidates, but apparently most of them had kept in shape in preparation for the second six weeks. I was secretly glad that I had signed up for the 12 week course, because it would be very difficult to go through all of this again two years from now. Our group of forty candidates was reduced during the second six weeks much more rapidly than it had been during the junior program. The staff was dead serious when they said that they would be far more demanding of the seniors, and they proved it.

There were far more discharges, and I was surprised when we had two "drop on requests," because these guys were so close to the end. They dropped out with only three weeks to go. My poison ivy continued to irritate me constantly and so did SSgt Roth. He took every opportunity to get on me about something, and he kept at it with a vengeance. Whatever kindness had coursed through his body when I was in the hospital and he came to visit me had most certainly been replaced with abject cruelty. Nevertheless, I would not let him get to me, and I made it a point to try to stay one step ahead of him always. I wondered why he had such a bias against me, but perhaps his toughness made me want to finish the course that much more. After another three day war in the field, this time I was placed far away from poison ivy, we marched back to the base for our final exams, the only thing standing in our way to completing the course.

The last day finally arrived, and I looked around and saw 28 smiling faces getting ready to graduate. We had lost 12 candidates, and as I look at the picture of our graduating platoon, I see 28 very self-assured and competent young men. All we had to do now was graduate, and we would be commissioned second lieutenants upon graduation from college. We would leave Quantico as Sergeants in the United States Marine Corps Reserve.

On the night before graduation, SSgt Roth asked me if I was going home on Saturday after we graduated. I told him I was planning to take a bus to Washington and then take a train to New York City. SSgt Roth told me that he wanted me to wait for him outside the auditorium where we would be graduating. After the ceremony, SSgt Roth asked me to accompany him to his car, and he took me to his quarters where his wife had made a lunch for the three of us. As I sat down to lunch at his house, SSgt Roth finally explained why he had been so hard on me.

He told me he was Jewish, and he saw from my record book that I was also Jewish. There were not many Jewish officers in the Marine Corps, and he wanted to be sure I would be a good one. He told me that he felt that I would be a very good officer, and that is why he wanted to have lunch with me. He wished me well and hoped to see me sometime in the future. The next time I saw SSgt Roth was in Vietnam in 1969 when he was the Sergeant Major of the 3rd Marine Regiment, and I was the Executive Officer of the 1st Battalion of the 7th Marine Regiment.

I had arrived at Quantico on Sunday, June 5, and I was leaving on Saturday, August 27, just 12 weeks after getting off the train and spending my first two hours in the Marine Corps locked in a wall locker. I had certainly had a life changing experience, and as I thought about returning to college for my senior year, I began focusing on my future for the first time in my life. If nothing else, the Marine Corps had already taught me about self-reliance and the importance of taking responsibility for your own actions.

I knew, as I boarded the bus to Washington, that in exactly ten months, I would be commissioned as a Second Lieutenant in the United States Marine Corps. After my commissioning, and for the next three years after that date, I would go and do everything that the Marine Corps asked of me without question and without hesitation. I did not have to worry about graduate school or employment, because Uncle Sam had already taken care of those issues for me. I had just completed the most arduous 12 weeks of my life, and there were many times throughout those 12 weeks that I did not think I would finish.

I found out that if I wanted something badly enough, I could push myself to the utmost limits of my capabilities, and I also discovered that my capabilities were far greater than I had ever imagined. I had overcome adversity, humiliation, prejudice, weakness, apathy, and fear. Not too bad for just 12 weeks of your life. I was also leaving as a Sergeant which would enable me to participate in drills at the Reserve Center in Syracuse during the school year. Since I had earned a whopping $237.12 for the entire summer, I felt that drill attendance would help me ease some of the financial burden on my father. I looked much different from when I had arrived at Quantico. I was leaner, and some might say, meaner. I also felt a lot different about myself, and I was full of self-confidence. After all, I was a U. S. Marine, wasn't I?

I arrived in New York's Grand Central Station at 6 a.m. on Sunday. I didn't want to wake Dad and Dora, so I took a cab to the Biltmore Restaurant which was a New York City landmark, in that it never closed and always served great food. You could tell where the restaurant was by looking for the long line of yellow taxis and green and white police cars that were always parked around it. You could get breakfast, lunch or dinner anytime you wanted at the Biltmore, so shift workers, doctors, nurses, taxi drivers, students, truck drivers, deliverymen and any worker who was up early or late, gravitated there.

I stayed in our apartment for the next six days, and my poison ivy finally dried up. On Saturday evening we went to dinner at Asti Restaurant, and on Sunday morning, Hugh Fordin, my Brooklyn fraternity brother, picked me up in his brand new 1955 Chevrolet

Bel-Air convertible, a black and white dream machine, for the return trip to Syracuse and the beginning of my senior year of college.

Hugh was shocked at my appearance. I don't think he expected to see the person he picked up in front of my apartment building. He was full of questions, and I was only too eager to share my experiences with him as we drove up the New York State Thruway. Mentally, I felt totally different. I was more relaxed and far more assured than I had ever been. The Marine training had imparted that inner peace that comes with the knowledge that you are capable of doing anything you want to do and that perseverance and hard work will always make things happen. I was ready to live the rest of my life in a different manner, because I now had goals and the ambition to become the best Marine officer possible.

CHAPTER 6

SENIOR YEAR AT SYRACUSE UNIVERSITY

BA DEGREE AND SECOND LIEUTENANT, USMC

The trip to Syracuse with Hugh Fordin was uneventful. Hugh had worked in his parents' luggage store all summer, and had gone to almost all the plays that were currently playing on Broadway as he was a drama major, and was particularly interested in going into the theater as a producer. He had no interest in acting, but he seemed genuinely skilled when it came to the administrative side of the theater. Hugh had been elected President of the *Boar's Head Society* at Syracuse, and this was a high honor.

The Boar's Head Society was the drama school honors society, and all the truly good drama students were members. I remember that Suzanne Pleshette, who later became a famous movie and television star, was a member, as was Bob Dishy, who later became a very well-known movie and television character actor. Lanny Okun, who later became a top Hollywood musical director, having written the theme to *The Love Boat* television series, as previously mentioned, was a member. Gil Katz was also, and he later became a top film and television director and producer. Under the name of Gil Cates, he produced the annual Academy Awards television show. Through Hugh, I went to all the campus theater productions. I even dated Suzanne Pleshette once; however, she was not interested in someone who was going into the Marines when he graduated. One year after graduation, Suzanne got her first big break in a Jerry Lewis movie called *Geisha Boy* in which she played Jerry's love interest as an airline stewardess.

So, my senior year at Syracuse started. I was lucky enough to get my old waiters job back at the Pi Beta Phi house, where I had made a firm friend of Mrs. Melby, the housemother, and the sorority president, a wonderful girl from Buffalo named Marie Cappriano. Halfway through my senior year I found out that Marie's father was the head of the Mafia in Buffalo, New York. I do remember that one morning, while I was setting up breakfast at the sorority house, a black Cadillac pulled up to the front of the sorority house and a man in a suit rang the doorbell and asked for Marie. Marie came down and drove away in the Cadillac. She came back for lunch, and I heard her say her father had come down to visit her because he had some business in Syracuse. Memories of my Rockaway Beach boardwalk experience flooded my mind, and I was mighty glad that the business was not with me.

Before returning to Syracuse for my senior year, my father had asked me for a favor. He had heard that if you made Dean's List (a 3.5 grade point average or higher), the Dean sent a letter to your parents, and he asked me to make Dean's List, just once, so he could get a letter to show his business cronies. I promised him that I would, even though this meant that I would certainly have to study for one semester. I went to registration with this goal in mind, and signed up for courses in which I knew I could do well, and that were still required for my major completion. I took Greek Mythology (a memory course), Non-Aristotelian Semantics (a discussion and non-subjective English course), German Opera (another memory course), Spanish Literature (a course that sounded very interesting to me), a Survey of Fine Arts (the third year in this wonderful course) and Physical Education. I figured this combination of courses would not only get me 18 units of credit, but would also make it possible to make Dean's List as I had promised my father.

It turned out exactly as I had planned. I got A's in everything, except Spanish Literature, in which I was very lucky to get a B. I made Dean's List and my father did get a letter from the Dean of the College of Liberal Arts, attesting to my wonderful academic skills. I thought my father would be extremely proud of me, however, he told me that this just proved that if I had worked harder at Syracuse, I could have been an honor student. I guess I should have seen that coming.

The prospect of graduating was made even sweeter when I was notified that the Dean of the Liberal Arts College wanted to see me in his office. The Dean congratulated me on my summer in the Marine Corps, and informed me that the University was giving me two full years of academic credit for Military Science for my 12 weeks of PLC training. Apparently, successful completion of the ROTC program at Syracuse, got you 2 years (12 units) of credit for military science, and since I had successfully completed the PLC program, the University felt that I should get credit as well. I was thrilled, especially when the Dean informed me that only one other student at Syracuse University had also completed the PLC program, and that he and I would be commissioned at graduation. I was also informed that we could, if we wanted, graduate in uniform. I was unable to do so since I had not bought any officer's uniforms yet, and would not get them until I arrived at Quantico. The extra credit meant I needed only a single unit (1 credit) in the second semester of my senior year to graduate. I later found out that Dean Faigle had been an officer in the Marine Corps during World War II, and had pushed to get Marine officer candidates full credit for ROTC if they finished their program.

The winter of my senior year was a very good one. I was elected the Parliamentarian of the fraternity and officiated at all meetings, having to be totally conversant with Robert's Rules of Order which governed all official meetings. The football season was very successful as the great Jim Brown was running all over opponents. Syracuse was on its' way to a winning season, and Colgate was soundly defeated. The Phi Ep ice sculpture for Winter Weekend, won a third place trophy, the first one in the fraternity's history at Syracuse, and our academic average was no longer the lowest of all the fraternity's on campus. I think we were still near the bottom, but our brother's always graduated, and those that needed to get to graduate school (medical, dental and law) always seemed to get accepted somewhere. At Thanksgiving, I went home to Dad and Dora's and had a wonderful weekend with them.

Finals for the first semester of my senior year followed the Christmas vacation. I spent another great Christmas in New York City, and while I personally have never liked the crass commercialism of the Christmas season, the combination of Christmas decorations, cold weather and the general feeling of good will that prevails in cynical New York for a short time, with a little snow added in for good measure, is unbeatable.

As I finished my first semester of my senior year and achieving Dean's List status, I began to seriously realize that the best part of my life to date was rapidly ending. As I went to register for my last semester at Syracuse, I was told by a registration clerk that I only needed one credit to graduate. This meant that I only had to take a one-hour course once a week to get my Bachelor's Degree in June. I was also told by the same clerk that University regulations required full time students to take a minimum of 12 credit hours a semester. So much for my one credit course holiday. I registered for the second part of Non-Aristotelian semantics, a course in television script writing in the School of Drama, a public speaking course, also in the Drama school, and the Survey of Fine Arts course that I truly enjoyed. That added up to 12 credits.

My classes went very well, and I remember enjoying everything I was doing because I realized there would not be another year for me at Syracuse. Graduation day was scheduled for Saturday morning, June 2, 1956. The graduation ceremony would be conducted in Archbold Stadium, our old, venerable football arena, and all students receiving degrees would graduate at once. This meant that roughly 3,000 students would be receiving their degrees from all the varied schools. It also meant that I could forever tell everyone I graduated from college at 20 years of age, because I would turn 21 on the day *after* graduation. I would also require a waiver from the Marine Corps because I would be only 20 years old on the day I was commissioned, and the Marine Corps required second lieutenants to be college graduates and 21 years of age. Since I would be 20 years old on the 2nd of June, the day of my commissioning, and 21 years old on the 3rd of June, I had to have a one-day age waiver from the Marine Corps. I received the waiver which remained in my official records throughout my career in the Marine Corps.

The last six months at Syracuse went very quickly. My classes were a breeze, and I established very warm relationships with two professors at the University. The first was Dr. Dorothy Little, who had a PhD from Yale University in English. She was a brilliant woman who had never married and enjoyed the academic life to the hilt. She wrote poetry and short stories, and was a free lance writer for magazines. She lived in a small house near the campus which had been built in the very early 1900s. The downstairs was dominated by an old Victorian sitting room lined with bookshelves from floor to ceiling. There was an old fireplace in the room, and several large, overstuffed chairs, as well as several small sofas. Dr. Little called it her salon, and she invited selected students to have afternoon tea with her where she would discuss literary subjects in considerable detail. I was privileged to be one of the students who were invited frequently, and I never missed an opportunity to attend one of her teas. When my parents came for graduation, she insisted on having them to tea. They never forgot her graciousness and her keen mind. I have never forgotten her, and my university experiences were highlighted by the wonderful literary teas I enjoyed in Dr. Little's salon. The other professor that stands out in my mind is Dr. William Terhune, a PhD in Classical Literature from Harvard University, and the Chairman of the English Department at Syracuse. I was extremely lucky to have him as a professor for all of my Shakespeare classes, and several Spanish and German classical literature classes as well.

As graduation came closer, I began to wind up my activities on campus and prepare myself for real life. I had a wonderful four years, in two decidedly different colleges, and those four years formed my lifestyle for the rest of my life. Looking back on those years, at the age of 77, I am amazed at how much of my life was influenced by those four years of college. My college career was orchestrated in such a manner that derived the largest possible benefits from it.

Going to Champlain College for my freshman year turned out to be a godsend, as the first year of college can be highly traumatic. Champlain was a small college with a very supportive and dedicated community of professors and students. The primary purpose of Champlain College was to educate, and while we had student activities, there were no football stadiums, fraternity houses, large, influential alumni, and spoiled, rich students. I got a solid education, surrounded by serious students whose aim was to secure an education and a college degree. My three war veteran room mates grounded me in such a way, that being from the streets of New York City didn't make much of a difference in Plattsburg, New York. Their maturity and motivation to succeed rubbed off on me and influenced me in a positive manner.

When I arrived at Syracuse to start my sophomore year, I was ready to take on more responsibility and was not intimidated by the large campus and the huge student body. Joining Phi Epsilon Pi was also a turning point in my life. Until that time, I had not had very much interest in my Jewish heritage. I had grown up in an Irish Catholic neighborhood and being Jewish just didn't seem to make much difference. Once I got into Phi Ep, being Jewish suddenly became important. Being in the company of 75 men who had all grown up Jewish, was a new experience for me, and I learned almost everything about my religion and my heritage from the brothers of Phi Epsilon Pi.

Life with my fraternity brothers was never dull. We went to every movie opening in Syracuse and always stayed after the movie to read the credits. The next day there would be questions concerning the movie, and woe be unto the brother who could not come up with the name of the head gaffer, the best boy, or the make up artist of the movie we had seen the previous day. To this day, I continue to read the credits of movies with keen interest, and there is always some piece of information in those credits that I find most interesting.

I learned about Scotch whiskey at Phi Ep, and, for many years, I drank J&B Scotch because *The New Yorker* Magazine advertised the brand. I also drank Beefeaters Gin, because that was what you ordered if you wanted to impress someone at the Algonquin Bar or Toots Shor's. Besides, Beefeater also advertised in *The New Yorker*. Unlike most college kids who swore by *Playboy* Magazine, which began publishing in December of 1953 (Marilyn Monroe was the first centerfold), Phi Eps all read *The New Yorker* and *Vanity Fair* from cover to cover. Our daily conversations were always based on things written in these two magazines, and to remain current in our fraternity house, the two magazines were required reading. We read *Variety*, the show business newspaper and were all conversant with show business knowledge. The more frequently you went to Europe, the greater status you enjoyed in our house. Being familiar with London, Paris and Rome was fairly standard, but, since we were all Jews, no one was going to Germany in the 1950s.

The fraternity brothers were bright, irreverent, funny, lazy, rich, uncaring and had the world by the tail. It was a terrific way to spend my college days and, besides all the fun I had at the fraternity, I managed to leave Syracuse with a degree in Classical Literature. The degree was written entirely in Latin and still adorns the wall of my den, where I am writing this memoir. In that regard, I want to make a strong case for getting a degree in the Humanities and not in some specific science. While I left Syracuse with no specific skills,

- I had read the great books,
- studied the great artists, and the great writers,
- became proficient in a romance language,
- was familiar with most of the finest written poems, short stories and essays of our time,
- I could write a coherent sentence and put a well-crafted letter or essay together, and
- I could write a succinct report and use vocabulary that could impress, if I so desired.

In short, I was ready for whatever life was going to throw at me and, based on my education, I would be able to handle it. The skills I acquired in college helped me succeed throughout the remainder of my life.

On Thursday, May 31, 1956, Roy Place, a PLC, and I went to Dean Eric Faigle's office. In the Dean's office was Mr. Roy Simmons, the Syracuse lacrosse coach, the boxing coach and the defensive line football coach. Along with his coaching duties, Mr. Simmons also was a physical fitness instructor. He had been an All-American football player at Syracuse in the 1920s and a Captain in the Marine Corps. With the Dean and Mr. Simmons, was the local Marine Recruiter. Roy and I were administered the oath of office as Marine Officer's by Roy Simmons, and we left the Dean's office as Second Lieutenants in the United States Marine Corps Reserve. The Marine recruiter gave us our first salutes as Marine officers, and as custom dictated, we each gave the recruiter a dollar bill for giving us our first salute. Besides our first salute, the recruiter also gave us our orders to report to The Basic School in Quantico, Virginia, on 4 June 1956, for nine months of training on how to become an Officer of Marines.

On Saturday morning, June 2, 1956, I graduated from Syracuse University, and Dad and Dora came for the ceremony. That graduation was the first graduation I had ever attended, and I remember Dad and Dora, sitting with thousands of parents in the stadium, were immensely proud. In honor of my graduation, my father gave me a beautiful LeCoultre chronograph watch, which I still have to this day, and a Marine Corps swagger stick which was required to be carried by all Marine Corps officers in 1956. I treasured it because he had "With all my love, Dad" engraved on the silver tip of the stick.

We drove back to New York City immediately after graduation where an even bigger surprise awaited me. My father had bought a used, but beautiful 1954 Chevrolet Bel-Air Coupe for me as my first real car. It was light blue and white and had less than 10,000 miles on it. It had belonged to a business associate of my father's, and he had bought it from him for a very good price. It would serve me very well, and I was genuinely happy as I departed for Quantico in my new car on Sunday, June 3, 1956. I was ready to conquer the world!

I was an Officer in the Marine Corps, had a college degree, was on my way to beginning a new life, and I was doing it all on my 21st birthday.

CHAPTER 7

OFFICER'S BASIC SCHOOL – QUANTICO, 1956

The drive from New York City to Quantico, Virginia, was uneventful. I was celebrating my 21st birthday and beginning an intensive nine-month course on how to become a Marine officer. Before leaving home, I had a conversation with my father in which I thanked him for everything he had done for me, and the sacrifices that I knew he had made for me. I told him that as of this date, June 3, 1956, I was totally responsible for my own well-being, and I did not expect any financial support from him. I told him that college had prepared me for life, and by beginning as a Marine officer, I would certainly be able to take care of myself. I also told him that the best thing he could do for me was to spend his money on himself and Dora and enjoy life. God knows, he most certainly deserved it. We parted with a hug and a kiss. It was an old German custom to kiss your father, and I continued this custom with great pride until my father's death. As I got into the car, my father gave me a hundred dollar bill and told me it was for good luck and to use it wisely. I do not recall whether I did or not.

My new monthly salary would be $237.12 per month, plus $42.88 per month for subsistence (food), and $68.40 per month allowance for living quarters, if none were furnished for me. As a Reserve officer, I would also receive a $300 clothing allowance to buy a green winter service uniform and a khaki gabardine summer service uniform and caps, which are called *covers* in the Marine Corps. Covers consist of a frame type barracks cap and a green and a khaki garrison cap, called overseas caps or *piss cutters* by Marines. Khaki uniforms and caps are no longer authorized for wear. We also had to buy uniform dress shoes, khaki ties, shirts, rank insignia, and metal emblems. The rest of our uniforms had been issued to us during our summer training, so I arrived at Quantico with a full seabag of utility (work) uniforms, boots, and underwear.

At the main gate of Marine Corps Schools (MCS), I was directed to the Provost Marshal's office where I had to register my car by showing proof of ownership and proof of insurance. After producing the required documentation, I was issued a metal plate for my car license that identified me as an officer and a resident of the base.

MCS, Quantico's main function was to provide military education at almost all levels of command. It housed the:

- *Training and Test Regiment,* which provided screening and training for all officer candidates.
- *The Basic School,* a 9 month long school for newly commissioned second lieutenants (it is currently only 6 months long).
- *Amphibious Warfare School* (AWS), an advanced six month school for senior captains and majors.
- *Command and Staff College,* a senior command school for lieutenant colonels and colonels.

Besides these schools, MCS also housed the Presidential Helicopter Squadron (HMX-1), the FBI Academy, Marine Corps Air Station, Quantico, and the support troops required to run both the schools, the aviation units and the widely spread out base.

I drove to Camp Upshur, about 20 miles into the forest away from the main part of MCS, where The Basic School was then located. It was an old World War II Quonset hut camp. On my way, I passed the FBI Academy which was almost entirely hidden in the trees. The area was off limits to everyone except agents and students of the Academy. The location was not general knowledge in 1956, and the FBI intended to keep it that way. My first impression of Camp Upshur was one of complete surprise. It was literally a village composed of Quonset Huts and Butler Buildings. Butler buildings were all metal buildings that, unlike the semicircular Quonset huts, were square, and had high ceilings and a metal roof. As the sun got hotter, these buildings turned into ovens.

I went to the administration building where I was assigned to Company E, which was called E or Echo Company because the letter E was pronounced "echo" in the phonetic alphabet then in use in the Marine Corps. I reported in and joined the 1st Platoon. We were assigned to units alphabetically, so the 1st Platoon was all A's, B's and C's, with a few basketball players added. In 1956, the Marine Corps competed in intercollegiate sports in football, basketball and baseball. All major Marine bases had teams, and the teams at Quantico were the best. The reason was very simple; Basic School was full of second lieutenants who had just completed varsity sports competition on the college level. In 1956, there was a Heisman Trophy winner and 16 All-American football and basketball players attending The Basic School. The football players were assigned to G Company, the basketball players were assigned to E Company, and several of them wound up in my platoon.

In Echo Company there were 187 second lieutenants. They came from all over the United States, and all were graduates of some of the finest colleges in the country. In my 75 man platoon, there were graduates of Notre Dame, Yale, LSU, Stanford, Syracuse, and Duke, just to name a few of the more well known schools. I think every major college in the country was represented in our class, which was designated as Basic Class 3-56. This meant that we were the third class of 1956, and there were usually five classes each year. Classes 1-56 and 2-56 were already in session at Camps Barrett and Goettge, two other camps located in a different part of the Quantico forest. The fifth class was always held for the 17 percent of the graduates of the US Naval Academy (Annapolis) who had elected to be commissioned in the Marine Corps instead of the Navy. One member of my platoon was different, not because of the school he attended, but because his mother was a famous movie star of that time. He did his three years as an officer, and then became a well known and exceptionally successful developer in Southern California.

There were two categories of second lieutenants: Regular officers and Reserve officers. Regular officers were designated as being in the USMC, and they came from the US Naval Academy and the Naval Reserve Officer Training Corps (NROTC), which paid for four years of college for every midshipman in the program. NROTC officers enjoyed the same status as graduates of the Naval Academy. This category was considered to be regular officers who would remain in the military as a career. They had an initial four-year obligation of service, after which they could decide if they wanted to remain or be separated. The second category was Marine Corps Reserve officers, and they were designated as being in the USMCR (the R meaning Reserve) They came from the Platoon Leaders Course (PLC) and other officer candidate programs, and they had only a three year military obligation after which it was assumed they would return to civilian life or apply for retention as a regular officer. I was one of the USMCR officers.

Officers from both categories were integrated in the companies, and we had more reserve officers than regular officers in our class. In 1956, the majority of the second lieutenants were not married. In our platoon, 30 were married, which left 45 bachelors living in our Quonset hut. The married officers went home after classes, but had to return the following morning by 6 a.m., ready to begin that day's training. I was glad I was single, as it was harder for the married officers to meet all the time requirements.

After the platoon was formed, there was a week to take care of administrative matters which included buying winter and summer service uniforms. While regular officers paid for their uniforms, reserve officers' $300 clothing allowance generally paid for both uniforms and dress shoes. During this week, we got to know the members of our platoon. We also got to know Captain George W. Smith, USMC, who would be our staff platoon leader for the nine months of school. The group was diverse, and we were about the same age, which meant 21 or 22 years old. All were college graduates and, since they had selected the Marine Corps, they were full of life, had a great thirst for adventure and were generally up for anything. It was going to be a big fraternity of hard working men who, when they had free time, would probably play just as hard as they worked.

During that first week, Captain Smith gave us some idea of what we could expect at Basic School. First, he made it very clear that we were Marine officers, and we were expected to act accordingly. We were to be careful how we conducted ourselves away from the base, and he stressed that the Marine Corps expected us to set the example for enlisted

Marines. In other words, he expected us to act like officers, and the longer we were in Basic School, the more we would learn about being an officer. We worked a five and a half day work week, and around 1 p.m. on Saturdays we were free to go where we wanted. At 6 a.m. on Monday we had to be in uniform and ready to go.

Platoon members were assigned to double decker metal bunk beds, and each had a wall locker and a wooden foot locker. The remainder of our belongings were stored in the trunks of our cars. My bunk mate was Stephen W. Blodgett, a three year reservist from Yale University. He was a quiet, pleasant man, who was somewhat shy, but who met every challenge very well. Looking back on it today, I think his biggest challenge was having me for a bunk mate, since I must have been the opposite of everyone he had grown up with. Next to me were two soul mates with whom I would begin a lifelong friendship that continues to this date. One was John Henry Bateman, (my bunkmate from PLC), from LSU, born and raised in Baton Rouge, Louisiana, and a member of DKE fraternity, known across the campuses of the United States as "the drunken Dekes." John was a sterling member of the fraternity and a genuine example of their hallowed nickname. The other mate was Joseph P. Brennan, a graduate of Villanova University and a resident of Atlantic City, New Jersey, where his parents owned and operated a seaside resort hotel. Nick Brennan was the consummate Irishman, funny, easy-going and always ready to share a story and a drink at the drop of a hat. The four of us were all reserve officers, and none of us intended to make the Marine Corps a career.

During that first week, as we got to know each other, the laws of natural selection seemed to have occurred, and everyone was talking about the first weekend liberty in Washington. Before the week had ended, platoon members began to plan for the weekend trip to our nation's capital. Since money was always an issue, we would form into groups of five or six and one would be designated the driver. We would pile into the designated driver's car for the 30 mile trip to Washington, and then we would get one or two hotel rooms and share accommodations. The only requirement was that there be sufficient beds and towels in the room. Hotel managers seemed to recognize that we were all second lieutenants without much money, and they always were quite generous with us. I think they also knew there would be no trouble with us because our careers at the Basic School depended on good behavior.

On my first liberty, I went to Washington with Jerry (*Buzz*) Bowlin, a Montana State graduate who had been in the PLC program with me; Tom Regan, a basketball player from Seton Hall; Ed Peterson, a basketball player from Wagner College; and my buddies John Bateman, and Nick Brennan. After getting one large room at the venerable Willard Hotel, one of the most historic hotels in the country which still exists today around the corner from the White House, we went to the Old Ebbitt Grill for a few beers and lunch before going to the Ambassador Hotel to see if we could meet women.

Bachelors would usually wind up at the Hi-Hat Lounge of the Ambassador Hotel because it was a very large cocktail lounge. It was a given that everyone in the place was either single, or acting single, and if there was an attraction between a man and a woman, things could develop into some kind of arrangement for the weekend. While six of us checked into the hotel room, six of us rarely went back to the hotel room to spend the night. It was a glorious time, much more innocent than things are today, and a lot more fun. The women were mostly coeds from local universities or secretaries from the thousands of government offices. Both men and women were looking for partners, and many couples who met at the Hi-Hat Lounge later wound up getting married.

Each weekend went pretty much along those same lines. Sometimes we went to shows at the Casino Royal, a supper club located around the corner from the Ambassador Hotel, or there were occasional visits to the strip clubs on 14th Street. Places like the Blue Mirror featured famous strippers of the day such as Candy Cane, Rusty Gates, and later, Anne Howe, a former Marine Corporal. Comedians like Red Foxx and Rusty Warren also played in these clubs. The price of admission was usually a three drink minimum which did not represent a problem to any of us, either in volume or price.

We drank a lot, partied hard, and then piled into our car at about 4 a.m. Monday morning to return to our platoon hut and get ready for training which would begin promptly at 6 a.m. when we were required to muster in formation and march to breakfast. Only a 21 year old could do something like that, and I am in total wonder at my former recuperative abilities. We would get a cup of coffee, eat breakfast and be ready for whatever the gods of war were going to throw at us that day.

During our initial week, Captain Smith told us that we would be trained in leadership, tactics, weaponry, intelligence, administration, general subjects, and the most important course in the Marine Corps, physical fitness. We were constantly told we would get older every year, but the troops we would be leading would always be 18 or 19, so we better be up to the test and be physically qualified to lead them by example. It was a lesson I would never forget for the rest of my life. Besides the core course subjects, we were also assigned leadership positions within our platoon on a weekly basis. One of us would be the platoon leader, and other platoon positions such as platoon sergeant, squad leaders and platoon clerk were assigned and graded by Captain Smith.

Since we would be assigned military occupational specialties (MOS) based on the needs of the Marine Corps, our performance in leadership roles throughout instruction would aid our commanders in determining which officers were assigned duties as infantry officers, artillery officers, tank officers, supply officers or aviation control officers. Almost everyone wanted to become an infantry officer, but troop leading skills featured heavily in the selection process.

The officer corps of the Marine Corps in 1956 was predominantly southern, and almost 60 percent of them had graduated from southern universities. This culture brought with it the customs and courtesies of the Old South, the social traditions of southern living, and the cooking of "down home southern fare," which was prevalent in our messhalls and our clubs. Grits, hot sauce, southern fried chicken, chicken fried steak, biscuits and gravy, collard greens and sweet potato pie, were messhall staples that Marines of all ranks learned to like. My first encounter with my all-time favorite, *Tabasco sauce*, was in a Marine messhall. Southern customs and traditions required interpretation, and Captain Smith was able to inform us and train us in the art of being "southern gentlemen."

Captain Smith enhanced the regular course of instruction through his unique leadership skills. He believed officers should learn to ride horses, so he would take our platoon to the Base stables to learn to ride. Nothing was funnier than to watch a heavy football lineman try to get on a horse in the proper manner and ride around a corral using all the correct terminology and posture. We enjoyed the experience, and the process brought us closer together as a group. None of us became equestrians, but we laughed a lot and we got to know our platoon commander very well.

Another of Captain Smith's projects was to encourage each of us to open a savings account at the Navy Federal Credit Union, which took only five dollars to do. He told us we would thank him later in our lives. As I write this memoir, I am pleased to report that I have been saving my money at the Navy Federal Credit Union ever since that summer day in July 1956.

Everyone should have a pair of shoes to be proud of, claimed Captain Smith, and the best pair of shoes made at the time was the Florsheim Imperial. He arranged with an officer's uniform store in the town of Quantico, Al Bolognese and Sons, to obtain these shoes for his lieutenants. These shoes cost $150.00 a pair in 1956 and through Captain Smith's intervention, we were able to pay for the shoes over a nine month period with no interest. I bought a pair of Florsheim Imperial wingtip cordovan leather civilian dress shoes, and to this day, fifty-five plus years later, they are still the best pair of shoes I have ever owned. I still wear them on special occasions. Captain Smith was a wonderful leader, and through my years in the Marine Corps I was privileged to serve with him on two other occasions; once when he was a Major, and again when he was a Major General.

The weeks in Basic School went flying by. We would go on two to three day field exercises, we would go to firing ranges where we qualified with the rifle, the pistol and the Browning Automatic Rifle (BAR). We were awarded shooting badges for our accomplishments, and were required to wear them as a part of our uniforms. We drilled under the direction of the assigned weekly leaders, and we became proficient in calling cadence and marching units from one point to another. All of our actions were observed and graded, and each fourth week we received leadership grades that placed us in the position of one to seventy-five within our platoon.

The hard physical work, the field exercises, the classroom work and the living together in a hot, cramped Quonset hut, made us into a close group of friends. Most of those friendships have endured the test of time, and when we had our 50th reunion in San Diego, the joy of seeing each other and reliving the tales of our Basic School experiences underscored how much serving together in the Marine Corps meant to all of us. That particular reunion was made even more special to us as 83 year old Major General George W. Smith, USMC, Retired, was our Guest of Honor.

As Basic School progressed, it became fairly obvious that we were being trained to become infantry troop leaders, and everything we did revolved around leading troops in combat. We learned to: read maps, to call in artillery fire, to plan tactical assaults and to operate at night. We fired every weapon in the Marine Corps arsenal. Those of us who had seen the John Wayne movies were thrilled when it became our turn to storm an "enemy pillbox" with a fully loaded flame thrower on our backs and let loose a heavy burst of flame. I think each of us felt as though we had just stormed ashore on Iwo Jima!

We also learned, in addition to administrative functions, how to:

- maintain service record books and unit diaries,
- apply the Uniform Code of Military Justice and how to participate in court-martials,
- maintain good order and discipline through the administration of non-judicial punishment,
- monitor our supplies and inventories of munitions and weapons,
- employ military intelligence,
- use medical and dental personnel,
- use civil engineering personnel,
- load amphibious ships,
- deal with foreign diplomats, and
- act in foreign countries.

We heard lectures from:

- Colonel Joe Foss who talked about Marine aviation during the Battle of Midway,
- the famous Colonel Gregory (Pappy) Boyington and listened to tales of his Black Sheep Squadron,
- Colonel John Smith, a Native American, and a World War II ace, who received the Medal of Honor for his air battles in the South Pacific,
- a colonel who, as a second lieutenant during the Makin Island Raid, led a platoon ashore under the cover of darkness to make a reconnaissance of the Japanese positions before the full scale landing,
- unit commanders who stormed ashore on D-Day at Iwo Jima,
- survivors of the Bataan death march and others who survived Japanese prisons after being captured on Wake Island,
- members of Carlson's Raiders who told tales of the Raider Battalion,
- the battalion commander who led the breakout to the sea from the Chosin Reservoir battle,
- Marines who were in the major World War II and Korean battles, and other Medal of Honor recipients.

We learned field engineering, radio communications, field sanitation, field cooking, and logistics. We became experts in making after action reports, and we participated in numerous patrols against enemy forces. The "enemy" forces were always played by enlisted Marines from Schools Demonstration Troops Battalion, which was formed specifically to provide enemy troops for all Basic School field exercises.

The enlisted troops were highly motivated to beat us at every turn, and received extra days of liberty for every victory over the "3rd Lieutenants," as they liked to call us. I remember one particular battle in which the enemy troops were led by a first lieutenant who ran across a field faster than I had ever seen anyone run with full gear. Later, I found out the speedy lieutenant was none other than the famous Jim Ryan, the American Olympic gold medal winner in the marathon.

We usually worked a five day week with inspections on Saturday morning. After the inspections, we were released for liberty, and we dispersed to points on the eastern seaboard. My group of liberty buddies stayed together for the entire nine months. One of our best weekends came when a Saturday morning inspection was cancelled, allowing us to depart on Friday evening. We piled into Buzz Bowlin's station wagon and off we went to Atlantic City, New Jersey, to stay at the hotel owned by Nick Brennan's mother.

We drove to Somers Point, a town near Atlantic City, where the Rock and Roll Clubs were located. It was summer at the Jersey Shore, and the place was hopping with women, small 7 ounce bottles of Rolling Rock Beer, and great bands playing live music at clubs all along the seashore strip. The most famous of these rock and roll clubs was Tony Mart's, and it became our headquarters. Playing there that weekend was a group called Eddie and the Cruisers who became famous, and even had a movie made about their lives.

Tony Mart's was always the liveliest place to go, and women from all over the eastern shore would move between the major bars of Somers Point. It was a wild time, and going to the Jersey shore became one of our favorite activities, especially during the summer months before schools started. If we could not get a room at the hotel owned by Nick's mother, we'd camp out on the beach and shower in the public locker room. After all the field work during the week at Quantico, sleeping on the beach for the weekend was nothing. We also discovered we were not alone, as far as sleeping on the beach, but we could well have been the only Marine Corps officers sleeping there.

On other weekends, when we didn't go to Somers Point, we'd go to Washington and chase secretaries, airline flight attendants and college coeds. We drank a lot, and we partied a lot, but we always returned to Quantico and sobered up by 6 a.m. Monday morning when the work week began. I remember one particular Monday morning when we learned that we would be departing for a 50 mile march in full pack with weapons at 6:30 a.m. I am convinced we did not sober up until we had marched about 20 miles. I was sweating so profusely that I think every drop of alcohol departed my body on the Hill Trail of Quantico, a 50 mile length of sheer agony after drinking all weekend.

Whenever we went to the field, we always returned to the base over a cable suspended over a stream that ran alongside Camp Upshur. There was a footbridge over the stream, but the Marine Corps felt that we would develop our upper body strength by going hand over hand on a suspended cable to the other side of the stream with our full pack, helmet and weapon. If you couldn't hold on, you fell into the stream and had to march back to the hut, soaking wet and embarrassed. For the first several months, I fell into the stream every time I tried to cross. It got to the point that Captain Smith would hold me back for last so that when I fell into the stream, the entire platoon could enjoy my fall. Finally, after about two months, my upper body strength developed and I never fell in again. I found out later that my good humor over my initial inability to cross over the cable, and my subsequent soaking, was a positive leadership trait since I didn't whine about falling in all the time, and I finally conquered my ineptness by making it over the cable. While laughing at my many dumps into the stream, my classmates always shouted encouragement as I began to cross the cable. When I finally made it across, I did so to an ovation from the entire platoon.

On Saturday, November 10, 1956, we attended our first Marine Corps Birthday Ball. This is almost a religious event in the Marine Corps, as it celebrates the founding of the Marines at Tun Tavern in Philadelphia on November 10, 1775. The birthday is celebrated with a cake cutting ceremony and formal ball (where and when possible), and it follows a prescribed format. A message is read from the current Commandant of the Marine Corps, followed by a reading of Marine Corps Order No. 47, Series 1921, which summarizes the history, mission, and tradition of the Corps. It was implemented by Major General Commandant John A. Lejeune, who further directed that the order be read to all Marines on 10 November of each year. Thereafter, 10 November became a unique day for U. S. Marines throughout the world. A birthday cake is brought before the Commander and Guest of Honor, and the cake is cut with a ceremonial sword. The first piece goes to the Guest of Honor, the second piece of cake always goes to the oldest Marine present who then passes it to the youngest Marine present (with a clean fork, of course). The Marines' Hymn is played to end the ceremony followed by dinner, drinking and dancing, and everyone has a great time. I have celebrated the birthday on 10 November every year since 1956, and I will continue to do so as long as I live. Long live the Marine Corps!

At Quantico, the Birthday is a big event and every lieutenant is encouraged to bring an escort, which in southern terms means bringing a date. We always found dates for these kinds of affairs at Mary Washington College, an exclusive girl's college in Fredericksburg, Virginia. All you had to do was to go to the college, tell them you needed a certain number of young ladies in ball gowns, and they would come, some eager to snare a Marine lieutenant for a husband. Some were successful, and many Marine officers wives are alumnae of Mary Washington College.

I went home for Christmas, and my father insisted I accompany him to visit his customers wearing my green uniform. I went to lunch with him and his cronies and everyone was very interested to hear about Marine officer training. The subject always came back to being Jewish in the Marine Corps, and they were always surprised to hear that I was not experiencing any anti-Semitism. They were also surprised that I was a Marine, because they did not know anyone who had ever been in the Marine Corps.

When I went to see my Boy Scout troop in uniform, I was received as the conquering hero. I was glad I made the trip, and I think Jim Morris, who was now the Scoutmaster having succeeded Mr. Chaves, was particularly proud. He had been a Marine in World War II and Korea, so he was most certainly biased. I have often reflected on the fact that it might very well have been Jim Morris who first placed the idea of the Marine Corps in my head while listening to his Marine war stories around countless campfires during my Boy Scout days.

My Christmas and New Year's holiday in New York was most enjoyable. I had no "girlfriend," but I did go to the Biltmore Hotel Garden Court in my Marine winter green uniform. I became very successful in picking up young coeds who were interested in the military, particularly the Marine Corps. The Ivy League schools sent many graduates to the Marine Corps, certainly not in the numbers of the southern schools, but if an Ivy Leaguer wanted to become an officer in the military, he usually chose the Marine Corps over the other branches. I guess elitism never dies. I met a few interesting women with whom I went to Broadway plays and had dinner in small Greenwich Village restaurants. For music, I would take dates to the Blue Note, still located on West 3rd Street in the Village. We'd hear the Dave Brubeck Quartet, the Modern Jazz Quartet, Lionel Hampton, Cal Tjader, John Coltrane and almost all the great names in jazz.

Before departing on Christmas leave, we had been given questionnaires which asked us to list the three MOS's we desired. Over 90 percent of the platoon requested infantry officer as the first choice, and we knew most of the Basic School lieutenants did also. Since Captain Smith was a tank officer, almost all of us chose tanks as our second MOS choice out of respect for him. Tanks were a limited field and the officer requirement was small, but since Captain Smith reviewed all the requests, we were certain he would be pleased. The third choice for most of the officers in our company was artillery, although I wrote down motor transport, thinking that leading a truck company would be more exciting than firing cannons. We were also asked to list the three geographic areas where we desired to be assigned; the East Coast, the West Coast or Overseas. Overseas meant you would be shipped out of the country for a 15 month period, with the Marine Corps determining where in the world you would be sent.

The geographic selections ran true to predictions. The married officers elected the geographic areas from which they had come originally, and the bachelors requested overseas without exception. The assignments were now in the hands of the Basic School staff who would determine who would go where as soon as they received the staffing requirements from Headquarters Marine Corps (HQMC) in Washington. HQMC would notify the staff how many second lieutenants were required in all three geographic locations, and how many were required in each MOS. The staff would then match the best officers with the immediate requirements of the Marine Corps. Our request forms were simply a guide. If they could satisfy our requests, they would, but in all cases, the needs of the Marine Corps came first. We would receive our assignments the first week following Christmas leave.

While driving back to Quantico after Christmas leave I realized that, in the next two months, there would be a significant change in my life. To begin with, I would be an Officer of Marines, and somewhere in the world was a group of young Marines who would have me as their leader. I prayed that I was up to the task. Furthermore, wherever I went I was going to be entirely on my own, responsible for my actions, and solely reliant on my skills to make a way for myself in the Corps. All of my education and Marine Corps training was going to be tested in the arena of real military life. No more training exercises or studying for tests. In fact, the only tests I would face in the future would be tests that my decisions influenced, and which would ultimately achieve results. No excuses and no whining. Reality sets in and you either sink or swim. I intended to swim.

New Year's Day, 1957, was on a Tuesday and we were not required to be back at Basic School until Thursday morning, January 3. Assignments would be announced on Friday afternoon just before weekend liberty. On Friday morning, we stood our usual Saturday morning inspection, and then we filed into the classroom to hear where we would be going. We still had one major tactical problem before graduation, and that would begin on Monday, January 7. It was the famous *three-day war* in which the lieutenants were formed into tactical units and went into the field to fight a war with the Schools Troops, who were the aggressors. The only difference in this exercise was that due to "combat deaths," command assignments were changed rapidly throughout the three days.

After being seated, the Basic School Commanding Officer, Colonel William K. Jones, spoke to us about our choices. He told us that all of us would not get what we wanted. We would be disappointed in both our MOS assignments and our geographic assignments. He went on to say that our assignments reflected the needs of the Marine Corps and he expected us to perform to our full capabilities, no matter what or where we were assigned. He told us that the assignments were final, and that no changes would be made or entertained. He then concluded his talk by emphasizing that there were no bad assignments in the Marine Corps. We would all be leading troops at some level, just under different circumstances. Our company commander, Major Robert L. Autry, then began reading off the assignments. He did it by MOS and then gave us our official orders that specified where and when we were to report to our first duty station.

As luck would have it, I was given an infantry MOS, (0301) and my orders directed me to report to the 3rd Marine Division, headquartered at Camp McGill, Japan. My orders further directed me to report to the Department of the Pacific in San Francisco, California, by Monday, February 11, 1957, for further transportation to the 3rd Marine Division. Since we were graduating from Basic School on February 2, I was not given much time to say good-bye to the USA.

As the assignments were handed out, there were many disappointments. Many married officers were going overseas and some bachelors were staying in the US. Officers who wanted to go to the West Coast got East Coast assignments, and those who wanted to remain on the East Coast had orders to Camp Pendleton, California. There was much grumbling, some of it well-founded. Two officers, one married and one single, received the same MOS, Air Traffic Control Officer, and while both would have to go to Air Traffic Control School, the married officer was going overseas and the single officer was staying on the East coast. Both officers agreed to switch duty stations, but the Marine Corps turned a deaf ear to their requests. They went where they were directed and there was no appeal. These two officers were not alone. Many bachelors were extremely disappointed that they did not get overseas assignments, especially when so many married officers did get them, but, again, a simple "needs of the Marine Corps" statement ended all discussion. All my weekend liberty crew got what they wanted, and most of the members of the first platoon received what they had requested. We felt our platoon leader, Captain Smith, had influenced the selection process in our favor, and we now appreciated him even more.

All my weekend liberty crew received infantry assignments, except John Bateman, who became an artillery officer and was assigned to the Army Artillery School at Fort Sill, Oklahoma. A large group of lieutenants were assigned to Naval Air Station (NAS), Pensacola for flight training, and a few lawyers went directly to the Navy JAG Corps (then the Marine Corps did not have a separate Judge Advocates General Corps). We had one tank officer, about seven air traffic control officers, one motor transport officer, five supply officers, two communications officers, one intelligence officer and one public affairs officer. The rest of us went to the infantry -- the *ground pounders.*

Captain Smith addressed our platoon in the hut after the assignment debacle. He told us we should consider ourselves lucky to be Marine officers, and if we did not perform satisfactorily during the three day war, we could have our MOS's changed. He really motivated us to do an outstanding job, and he also told us that we had two weeks to prepare for the big war.

The three-day war started on a Monday morning. We hiked to the war zone and received briefings on the situation. Lieutenants were assigned every command position from regimental commander down, and we never knew what position we would be assigned. While we may have started out as a member of a platoon, in short order we could wind up as a platoon leader, company commander, regimental commander, supply officer, communications officer and all the assignments in between. We coordinated air and ground units using helicopters for ground troop deployment and fixed wing aircraft for bombing runs, which were simulated using real napalm. We used tanks in a frontal assault, flame throwers for pillbox neutralization and we called in artillery strikes. After each engagement, casualties were assessed as were the efficacy of our tactical schemes, all of which we were forced to devise. If we were declared dead, we left one unit and reported in to another as a replacement. At night we were responsible for night patrols, security, harassing and interdiction fires, which were all called into a coordinated fire control center, and we still had to prepare for night attacks.

Every instructor participated in this exercise and they were judges, facilitators, critics and agents of harassment. We got very little sleep, we were constantly challenged and evaluated, and at a moment's notice, we could be declared dead and given a new assignment. The intensity of the three-day war was legendary in Basic School lore, and each basic class swore that their three-day war had been the toughest ever. It was rough and it served as our final examination, the results of which would fortify our instructor's decisions that we were prepared to join the Fleet Marine Forces in the field. My assignments during the three-day war were platoon leader, company first sergeant and assistant battalion operations officer. Many years later I would remember the three-day war in great detail when I served as the operations officer of an infantry battalion in Vietnam in actual combat.

After the three-day war, we celebrated with a Mess Night, which is a formal dinner modeled after British officers traditions with all the pomp and circumstance. Mess Nights were enormously popular, especially since we would wind up toasting just about every person with any title on the face of the earth. This led to good times and a few inebriated Marines. To the best of my knowledge, Mess Nights continue to be held in today's Marine Corps, although the emphasis on drinking has been practically eliminated. When we finally settled down, we realized that nine of us were going to be traveling to San Francisco on the same set of orders.

Graduation Day arrived and we said our farewells. Some of us would never see each other again, while others had forged lifelong friendships that would withstand the ravages of time. I drove to New York and went to LaGuardia Airport, presented my travel voucher to American Airlines, and was issued a ticket for a flight to San Francisco. I would be arriving there on Sunday, February 10, 1957.

CHAPTER 8

FLEET MARINE FORCE, PACIFIC

FIRST DUTY AT SEA AND IN THE FIELD
WITH 3RD MARINE DIVISION

I arrived in San Francisco on Sunday, February 10, 1957. I had never been there, in fact I had never been on the American West Coast. California was predominantly featured in the movies, and everyone seems to think that the entire state is covered with palm trees, beautiful women and lots of sunshine. I went to the Marines Memorial Club, a club and hotel in San Francisco that is both a living memorial association for Marines, and a hotel located in the heart of downtown San Francisco.

All the names on my set of orders were second lieutenants, and we were directed to report to the Department of the Pacific on Monday morning, February 11, 1957. Since we were new to San Francisco, we were drawn to the Marines Memorial. We didn't know how long we would be staying, since our further transportation to the Orient was in the hands of the Department of the Pacific. The club was very accommodating. After checking in, I went to the bar on the 12th floor and ran into Tom Agnew and Buzz Bowlin, both from my platoon in Basic School, and both headed to the Orient on the same set of orders.

San Francisco, in 1957, was a wonderful place to be if you were in the military. The city had served as a point of embarkation during both the Korean War and World War II and was very pro-military. Everywhere you went in uniform people smiled and waved. We were still the conquering heroes. The first night in San Francisco, I talked Buzz and Tom into going to Fisherman's Wharf as I had heard about the place, and had seen it in several movies. We went to Number 9 Fisherman's Grotto Restaurant for dinner right on the wharf. In those days, the wharf had a thriving and active fishing industry, and boats were unloading their catches right on the piers. We were in uniform and seated at a window table overlooking the activity on the wharf. We ordered lobster and shrimp dinners, had a few cocktails, and were having a very good time. When it came time to pay the bill, the waiter informed us that our meals and drinks had already been paid for by a gentleman who was no longer in the restaurant. He had simply asked the waiter to tell us *Semper Fidelis*, and to wish us good luck. This was one of the first examples I can remember of the adage that is still valid to this day, *Once a Marine, Always a Marine*. We never knew who our benefactor was, but it was certainly a gesture I still recall vividly.

The following morning we reported in to 100 Harrison Street, (Normally, Marines referred to the address rather than to constantly say Department of the Pacific), where we were informed that there was no transportation available. In those days, the military used the Military Air Transportation Service (MATS, which became the Military Airlift Command, and currently is the Air Mobility Command), flying out of Travis Air Force Base, located in Fairfield, California. Since there was no flight available, we would have another 24 hours before we had to report in again, and we were informed we could do it by telephone. If there was no transportation yet available, we would have at least another 24 hours in San Francisco.

We wound up staying in San Francisco for nine days awaiting transportation, and we drew our regular pay plus a per diem to pay for our hotel and meal costs. We went to the Blackhawk Jazz Club and listened to the Modern Jazz Quartet, we went to the Purple Onion, where we were entertained by a New York City comedian named Woody Allen, and a black comedian from Philadelphia named Bill Cosby. We rented a car for a day and traveled to Muir Woods, followed by a great dinner in Sausalito, and we found the famous Yankee Doodle Bar, located across the street from the Sir Francis Drake Hotel. We found another bar not far from the Marines Memorial Club called the Half Note, and its' claim to fame was that the bar was lined with shelves containing 8 mm film canisters of people drinking and partying in previous times at the bar.

The entertainment was a continuous showing of wild times in the bar, all captured on 8 mm film. If you did something outrageous or simply got commode hugging drunk, the bartender, at the proper moment, would take an 8 mm movie camera mounted on a light bar and shoot pictures of the event. There were hundreds of films of drunks, half naked women, and many great times being enjoyed by the patrons. If you were lucky enough to have a film made of your antics, the bartender gave you a card with a number on it. If you came back after two weeks and asked for that number, the bartender would get out the canister of film with that number, load it on the bar projector, and show the movie. Before we left for the Orient, we had six cards documenting our wild times at the Half Note.

After nine days, we finally got word to report to Travis Air Force Base the following morning for our trip to Japan, and we boarded a US Navy Constellation to Honolulu, Hawaii. Upon arrival, we were informed of a problem with the next leg of our flight, and we would have to spend two nights at the Royal Hawaiian Hotel right on Waikiki Beach while we waited. Uncle Sam was paying all our expenses. I was really enjoying my new life as a Marine Second Lieutenant, and I couldn't believe I was getting paid for the job.

I had never seen San Francisco before this trip, and now I was visiting Hawaii in February. It couldn't get much better than this. We went to the beach in front of the hotel and rented surfboards. Since we knew nothing about surfboarding, we paddled out to where the Hawaiian beach boys were all congregating on their boards. They caught waves while we cut our feet on the coral under the water. We spent several hours trying to surf, but finally gave up in frustration as we were getting sunburned. We received a call at the hotel informing us that a flight was scheduled to leave for Japan from Hickam Air Force Base on the following morning. Our Hawaiian holiday had just been cancelled!

In 1957, MATS depended primarily on two aircraft to carry cargo and troops to the Orient. One was the Lockheed Constellation, an aircraft that was in use commercially by many American airlines, and the C-124 Globemaster, a purely military aircraft designed to haul a maximum number of troops and/or a mix of troops and cargo. The Globemaster, because of its' higher payload, was more popular with the military, and by 1957, several of them had crashed over the ocean and disappeared. The macabre nickname among the military for the Globemaster was the "Crowd Killer." We had no control over which aircraft would fly our trip, and we were greatly relieved when it turned out to be a Constellation. We boarded the plane with great enthusiasm.

The loadmaster informed us that we would stop at Midway Island to refuel. Midway Island, 1,130 miles from Honolulu, was a major refueling point in the middle of the Pacific Ocean for military and commercial airlines. We arrived at Midway in the middle of the night, and were met by a military bus that took us to a small messhall where we were served a hot breakfast and coffee. Midway was the home of the famous Gooney birds, which were large, almost ostrich sized pelicans that lived all over the island, and posed a real threat to aircraft. They were obviously sleeping, because we did not see a single one, but the permanent personnel assured us that they were there, and they dodged them on a regular basis. We departed Midway on the last leg of our trip to Tokyo and Haneda International Airport, which was 2,720 miles away.

As I sat belted into my canvas seat, I thought about the past ten days, and came to the conclusion that I had made an excellent choice in joining the Marine Corps and requesting an overseas assignment. I had always been fascinated with travel, and the thought of traveling halfway around the world where I would be spending 15 months appealed greatly to me. I had never been to San Francisco or Honolulu, and here I was flying towards Japan, having spent nine days in San Francisco and having gotten sunburned, while trying to surf, at Waikiki Beach in Honolulu.

I had no idea what awaited me in Japan, but I felt I was prepared for anything. I was landing in a country that had been our enemy just a short twelve years before. They had been a very formidable enemy, and it had taken two atomic bomb attacks to persuade the Japanese to surrender. The surrender was unconditional, and an occupying military government, under General of the Army (5 Stars) Douglas MacArthur, was established to govern Japan. The bombing of those two Japanese cities saved thousands of American lives, because the ultimate goal of World War II was to invade Japan. While pictures of the devastation of Hiroshima and Nagasaki are horrible, the benefit of the attack was that no additional American lives were lost. The military government, primarily General MacArthur, ruled Japan as a benevolent dictator until 1952, when the peace treaty Japan signed took effect, and the ruling government became a constitutional monarchy.

The Marine Corps had a major presence in Japan and occupied bases all over the islands. The 3rd Marine Regiment, the tank battalion and several artillery battalions, plus the Division headquarters was stationed on mainland Japan, while the 9th Marine Regiment, a forward element of the 3rd Marine Division Headquarters, and almost all other support troops were stationed on Okinawa. Once we landed in Japan, we would travel to Camp McGill, a former Japanese Army Base, where the Division Headquarters was located, and we would then receive our assignments.

We arrived at Haneda Airport early on Sunday morning, February 24, 1957, and boarded busses to Camp McGill, which would take about three hours. It was very cold in Tokyo, and we were uncomfortable in our summer weight uniforms that had seemed so perfect in Hawaii. The first thing we noticed about Japan was the smell. In 1957, Japan still had open sewer trenches, and they were on every street. If you had to urinate, you simply stood over an open sewer trench and did your business in public. It was totally acceptable, and everyone, male or female, did it. The people were generally much smaller and more petite. Bicycles were everywhere, and while motorcycles and scooters were the motorized choice of transportation, bicycles were by far more prevalent. We motored through Tokyo and Yokohama to the city of Yokosuka, where the US Navy had a huge base, and where ships of the US Pacific Fleet regularly made ports of call. The surrounding areas of Yokosuka, especially those areas immediately around the bases, catered to US servicemen.

After arriving at Camp McGill in the early afternoon, we were directed to a building containing a large dormitory with about forty single metal beds, each bed having a pillow and two blankets placed on each of the mattresses. We were told we would be spending the night here, and those of us who would be remaining in mainland Japan would be driven to the Camp Fuji area. Officers assigned to Okinawa would go to Atsugi Naval Air Station and take the approximately one hour and fifteen minute flight to the island.

We placed our gear on a bunk and reported to the Administration Building for processing. First, the Paymaster collected our American currency, and in its place we were issued Military Payment Certificates (MPCs). The MPCs were bills in the same denomination as American currency and were used only by American troops overseas. The purpose of these MPCs was to eliminate a black market in American currency by taking it entirely out of circulation. MPCs were legal tender all over Japan, and we used them exactly as we would have used American currency. When we left the base to go into the local economy, we were supposed to exchange our MPC's for Japanese Yen. This was never necessary, as MPCs were accepted all over Japan, even though they were not supposed to be used outside any military base. To show you how things were in 1957, compared to 2012, one dollar was worth *380* yen in 1957. In 2012 one dollar is worth *80* yen. Quite a change in the last 55 years!

After receiving our MPCs, we were briefed on American/Japanese relations. We were admonished that we were representatives of the American government and that we were expected to act appropriately. We were not to show any victorious attitude to the Japanese. After the briefing, we were informed where we would be going. I was listed among the officers that would be reporting to the 3rd Marine Regiment headquartered at Camp Fuji. This meant I would be remaining in mainland Japan. Tom Agnew, a liberty buddy of mine from Basic School, would also be staying here, as well as Loren Brandt, who would be joining the tank battalion at Camp McGill. There were nine officers headed to the 3rd Regiment at Camp Fuji, and the rest were going to the 9th Regiment on Okinawa. We went to the Officer's Club and toasted our good fortune. The officers going to Okinawa were not very happy, but I looked forward to enjoying my tour of duty in mainland Japan.

By the time we got back to the barracks it had gotten very cold. There was no heat in the barracks, so we turned in, and noticing that there were approximately twenty empty bunks, we took blankets from the empty bunks so we could sleep warmly. In the middle of the night, a draft of ten officers arrived, and there was much complaining that there were not enough blankets for the new arrivals. One officer, a very tall first lieutenant with a strong southern accent, was trying to get comfortable in the bunk next to mine. Since I had taken an extra blanket, I threw him one of my blankets. The following morning he introduced himself to me. His name was Skeet Von Harten. He thanked me profusely for giving him an extra blanket, never realizing that he was only getting a blanket back which he should have had in the first place. At any rate, I accepted his thanks and wished him well with his forthcoming assignment.

The bus trip to Camp Fuji took several hours, and the areas we traveled through were mostly rural, small villages, where people were working in rice paddies, and where the industrial reawakening of Japan had not yet happened. The scenery was beautiful, and as we drove higher up into the mountains we could see snow on the peaks of many of them. After about an hour, we could clearly see the outline of Japan's most famous mountain, Mount Fuji, which is a dormant volcano.

We arrived at Middle Camp Fuji (there were three camps, South, Middle and North), which was the headquarters of the 3rd Marine Regiment. The Regimental Commander, Colonel John G. Bouker, greeted us and welcomed us to the Regiment. We then reported to the Regimental Adjutant who told us the units where we would be assigned. Three second lieutenants were assigned to the 3rd Battalion of the 3rd Marines, which happened to be located at Middle Camp Fuji. I was one of the three officers, as was Alton A. Scott and Harry Kelly. The three of us reported to the 3rd Battalion Headquarters and met Lieutenant Colonel A. J. Rauchle, the Battalion Commander.

LtCol Rauchle informed us that 3/3 (the Marine Corps way: denotes the 3rd Battalion of the 3rd Regiment), had just returned from a long deployment to the Indian Ocean and had only returned to Japan in the past month. He further told us that the Battalion was losing many of its' officers because they had completed their 15 months overseas tour of duty. One company in the battalion had only one officer, and he was the company commander who was departing for the US in three days. Because this company would be without any officers, LtCol Rauchle told us that he had decided to send all three of us to the same company. He then did an unusual thing. He asked us to tell him our service numbers.

My service number was the lowest (more senior) of the three officers, so I was designated the new Company Commander of H Company (Hotel) of 3/3. Harry Kelly, who had the next lowest number, was designated as the executive officer and Al Scott became a platoon leader. In that instant, I was assigned to a job normally held by an experienced captain, Harry Kelly was assigned a job normally held by a senior first lieutenant, and only Al Scott was assigned to the job we all should have normally been assigned, namely infantry platoon leaders.

We checked into the BOQ, which is somewhat of a misnomer, since every officer serving in the Fleet Marine Forces overseas was a "bachelor," because families were not allowed overseas with units that could be deployed on 24 hours notice. We each got a single room and an assigned maid. Every officer in Japan and Okinawa had a maid. These local women would work for three officers at a time, and they would clean our rooms, wash our clothing, shine our shoes and take care of everything we owned, for the price of $10 each per month. We would return from the field covered with mud and dirt, strip off our clothes, leave them on the floor and go to the showers. When we returned, our dirty clothes were gone, our field gear was stripped and being washed, and our boots were being cleaned and shined. It did not take long to get accustomed to this lifestyle.

We were issued Camp Fuji winter uniforms of dark green wool trousers and shirts which were much warmer than what we arrived with. Once in the warmer uniform, we went to Hotel Company to check in and were met by Captain Robert T. Roberts, a mustang officer (a slang term for an officer who was commissioned from enlisted ranks, normally without a college degree), who was returning to the US. I informed him that I was the designated company commander and he was extremely interested in turning over the company to me just as soon as possible. In 1957, the Marine Corps required a company commander to sign for every item of equipment belonging to the company. Signing for weapons meant that every weapon had to be inspected and have their serial numbers checked against the numbers listed on the Consolidated Memorandum Receipt (CMR), which was the document that one company commander signed to relive the other company commander. I worked long and hard to accommodate Captain Roberts, but in the end, I could not locate three rifles that were listed on the CMR.

Captain Roberts told me the weapons were at Camp McGill at the armorer's shop being repaired, and he assured me that I could sign the CMR and everything would be fine. He could not rotate to the US without my accepting the CMR. I decided not to approve the CMR unless I had seen everything so I refused to sign. This made Capt Roberts very angry until I told him that I would help him out and sign the CMR. I did sign it, but I wrote at the bottom of the document, "With the exception of three rifles (listing their serial numbers), which I did not visually sight."

After completing the CMR, I called a meeting with my two officers and the staff noncommissioned officers who had been running the company. In 1957, every noncommissioned officer in H company was a combat veteran. They had either been in World War II or the Korean War, which had ended in 1953. The Company First Sergeant, Master Sergeant Victor Martinez, and the Company Gunnery Sergeant, Gunnery Sergeant Brian S. Moore, were veterans of both wars. The remainder of the NCO's were all Korean veterans, and they were definitely older than their 21 year old company commander. There is a tradition in the Marine Corps that company commanders are called either "Skipper" or the "Old Man." I think Gunnery Sergeant Moore took great delight in announcing to the assembled NCO's that he was introducing "the old man" to the unit. I did not miss the irony, nor did Gunnery Sergeant Moore.

After meeting with the officers and NCO's, I addressed the company. I told them that I had not expected to be a company commander when I arrived at Camp Fuji, that I was a brand new second lieutenant just out of Basic School, that I had never had any real command experience and was inexperienced. I also told them that I was from New York City, I wasn't born yesterday, I was smart, and that I learned fast. Then I told them that they could work with me and we would have a good unit, or they could work against me and I'd find out eventually, and that would be their problem. I ended the meeting thanking them for their attention and promising them that I would give them 100 percent effort always.

After the meeting, Gunnery Sergeant Moore said, "Skipper, please let me buy you a drink in the Staff NCO Club. In my thirty years in the Marine Corps, you are the first officer that ever admitted he didn't know shit." I went with Gunny Moore for that drink, and for the rest of his life, both in and out of the Marine Corps, Gunnery Sergeant Moore remained a close friend of mine. He was a wonderful character, and I would not have been successful as a company commander without his support and guidance.

On our first night in Middle Camp, we went to the Battalion Officer's Club, which was located on the second floor of the Battalion Headquarters building. There was a long bar and a piano in the center of the room. In those days, officers would gather around the piano and sing songs. The songs were old Marine songs from World War I, World War II and Korea. There always seemed to be someone who could play the piano in the group, and in the case of the 3rd Battalion, we were blessed to have twin brothers, Winfred and Wesley Wedge, Win and Wes, who were both first lieutenants, had played in the Stanford University Marching Band, and who entertained nightly. Win played the piano and Wes was an expert on the trombone. On that first night about halfway through the evening, the officers started singing, "Out the window he must go, he must go, he must go, out the window he must go, Ah so deska!" This was a signal that every new officer present was to be initiated into the Battalion Officer's Club.

The initiation took the form of being grabbed by your fellow officers and thrown out of the second floor window into the bushes below. Before I knew it, I went sailing through the window, hit the bushes, rolled over on my side, and went back upstairs to the club where everyone cheered and bought me a drink. It was a lot of fun and no one ever got hurt that I can recall. I can't imagine anyone approving that behavior these days. It is really too bad, in my opinion, because it was just another special bond between Marine officers that has passed from our history and our customs and traditions. I'm certainly not saying it was a smart thing to do, just something wild and crazy that we always remembered many years later when we thought about our first days overseas in Japan.

After taking over the company, I learned the distressing news that on March 1, 1957, the 3rd Marine Regiment would be loading aboard ships of an amphibious task force for a one month Division size field exercise on the island of Luzon in the Philippines. We would meet up with the rest of the Division, which was located in Okinawa, and when the exercise was completed, the 3rd Marines (my unit), would switch with the 9th Marines (the unit on Okinawa). This meant that I had about two weeks in Japan before boarding a ship for the Division exercise and then relocating to Okinawa.

On March 2, the Regiment loaded aboard ships for the Philippine Sea. We would rendezvous with ships carrying the remainder of the Division and then implement a division sized landing, fully supported by fixed wing and helicopter squadrons, on Dingalan Bay. This operation had the interest of headquarters all the way to Washington, and the Commandant of the Marine Corps, General Randolph Pate, was coming to observe the landing. We were also informed that Ramon Magsaysay, the newly elected President of the Philippine Republic, and a strong supporter of the United States, would also view the landing.

Running a Marine rifle company of about 300 men and being responsible for all of their equipment and support facilities is a formidable task. This is a reason the job is usually assigned to a seasoned officer with the rank of captain. A captain has a minimum of five years experience and, as an infantry officer, has served at various levels within the company framework. To give this job to a second lieutenant on his very first assignment was so unusual, that, even to this day, when I tell other Marines that my first job out of Basic School was that of a rifle company commander, they are incredulous. I was able to do the job because some inner sense told me that if I did not have the support of the staff noncommissioned officers in the company, I would surely fail. The opposite occurred because in my very first meeting with the Staff NCO's, I had apparently won over the company first sergeant and the company gunnery sergeant with my candor and determination to succeed. Without their continuous support, I would not have been able to survive. It was a lesson I would take with me for the rest of my life.

Life in the company continued at a very hectic pace. Unfortunately, all our efforts were centered on preparing the company for embarkation aboard ship and for permanently departing Middle Camp Fuji. I could just visualize the grins on the faces of the Marines, who only a few short weeks ago were devastated that they were going to Okinawa and not staying in Japan, when the reality of the situation was that I was going to have about a month in Japan, and they were going to have 14 months in Japan. There wasn't much time to feel sorry about that turn of events, as my practical education in leadership was continuing at breakneck speed.

On 10 March, 3/3 departed Middle Camp Fuji for Yokosuka to load aboard ships to take us to the Philippines. I remember the drive through the streets of Gotemba where young women were standing in front of their houses or the baths and bars crying and waving heartfelt good-byes to the troops. The troops, in turn, were waving their good-byes, convinced that they would never find another "true love," as Gunnery Sergeant Moore liked to say. The truth of the matter was, of course, that in a month's time, these women would be welcoming the troops of the 9th Marine Regiment to Middle Camp Fuji and to all the pleasures that Gotemba had to offer.

Preparing a unit to embark aboard ship is a tedious and detailed operation that requires a tremendous amount of planning. Every item going aboard ship must be measured, weighed and inventoried. It must then be loaded aboard the ship in the reverse order from which it would be required, since the last item loaded aboard the ship becomes the first item unloaded. This makes strategic planning extremely important, since making a landing over a hostile beach with a case of toilet paper instead of a case of rifle ammunition would not allow your unit to survive very long. This strategy simplifies, but in my opinion, defines combat loading succinctly. First In, Last Out was, and continues to be, the mantra of all embarkation officers.

With a great deal of work, long hours and instant learning, Hotel Company loaded aboard USS *Renville* (APA 227), on March 10. I was not prepared for life aboard an amphibious assault ship. To say that accommodations were sparse for everyone would be an understatement. USS *Renville* was my first encounter with the US Navy's amphibious fleets, and, unknown to me at the time, it would be far from my last encounter. The amphibious Navy in 1957 was still composed of ships used to win World War II. *Renville* had been built in 1944 and saw service in World War II as one of the assault ships that landed troops over Red Beach on D-Day during the Normandy Invasion. She also participated in the Battle of Okinawa, returned troops from the Pacific Theater to the United States after the end of the war, and participated in the Inchon Landing during the Korean War. Probably her most famous claim to fame was that the ship had been used in the movie, *In Harm's Way*, starring Kirk Douglas and John Wayne.

There was always tension between the Sailors and Marines, primarily because neither side could ever understand why anyone would want to be in the other service. Marine officers always put the troops first, and Navy officers seemed to be constantly separated from their troops. There were parts of the ship marked with signs that said, "Officer's Country," which was off limits to ordinary Sailors or Marines. It was a system I could never understand, and one that Marines felt disrespected their position as enlisted men.

Along with naval customs aboard ship, living accommodations were highly uncomfortable. My rifle company lived in a hold that had 250 bunks strung on metal chains suspended from the overhead to the deck. Each chain had five bunks on it, and if you were on the top (fifth) bunk, to get to your bunk you had to climb the other four bunks like a ladder. Many Marines preferred to sleep on deck, but this was against the rules and was quite dangerous while the ship was at sea. The officers did not fare much better. There was a transient officer's bunk room that had bunks suspended on chains, however, our bunks were only three deep, and we had mattresses laying in a metal box while our troops had canvas tied on a metal frame suspended from their chains.

USS *Renville* had a crew of 56 officers and 480 enlisted men, and when Marines came aboard, they were able to accommodate 86 Marine officers and 1,475 enlisted men. The 17 landing craft on the ship were on the main deck level, ready to be lowered over the side by cranes to load Marines and their equipment into them. All equipment was loaded into holds of the ship so that, when we left Yokosuka, we were fully loaded in all aspects, with absolutely no wasted space anywhere aboard the ship. These tight quarters could easily lead to additional tensions, and it was the job of Marine leaders to assure that this did not happen.

Once underway we had a daily routine to ensure the troops would be occupied and maintain their physical conditioning. In such close quarters, sanitation is of the utmost importance, and the bunk areas and all the heads (toilets) were meticulously cleaned every day. It was a two edged sword. We needed to keep the troops busy, so we conducted constant inspections. The constant inspections insured clean quarters, and when we weren't inspecting, we were conducting classes and physical exercises. When the time came to make our landing in the Philippines, the troops were definitely very happy to leave the ship.

As we steamed through the South China Sea on the way to Dingalan Bay in Central Luzon, I reflected on how quickly my life had changed. In two short months, I had gone from a carefree shavetail (second lieutenant) to a company commander, responsible for the lives and the livelihood of 300 men. I had become a thinking, alert, and responsible individual in these two months. The amazing thing for me was the fact that I was still only 21 years old, but life had thrown some hard fast balls at me, and so far, I was able to hold my own. I was, however, very worried about the field exercise itself.

Once we landed, it would be my responsibility to get my unit from point A to Point B and to participate properly in the field exercise. While I had the help of my officers and staff noncommissioned officers, ultimately, the manner in which we performed during the landing and the subsequent field exercise would be entirely on my shoulders. I had to move my troops, feed my troops, and get them through the exercise without injury, all the time adhering to a specific battle plan that would require our company to perform certain tasks at various destinations and at specific times.

This exercise was the first full Division sized operation, about 15,000 troops supported by both fixed wing and helicopter aircraft, that the Marine Corps had conducted since the end of World War II. This was also my introduction to being an infantry officer. We arrived at Dingalan Bay and remained in the operating area preparing for landing on D-Day on the morning of March 17. I thought it most appropriate that my first landing would be on St. Patrick's Day. I could only imagine my Irish friends in New York City celebrating, what to them was the most important holiday of the year, while I was riding in a landing craft, waiting to land with my troops over one of the landing beaches.

On D-Day, the 17 landing craft aboard *Renville* would be put into the water before first light, and they would join the rest of the landing craft from the other amphibious ships. Each landing craft was equipped with a wooden, triangular sign in the bow of the boat that had a number designation painted on all three sides of the sign. For example, the number designation may read, "1-14," and this would mean that the landing craft was assigned to the first wave as the 14th boat in the wave. Upon signal, all boats assigned to the first wave would form a straight line, from right to left, and head to the beach, with the goal being that all boats in the wave hit the beach at the same time. This rarely happened but, it was always fairly close. As the landing craft grounded on the beach, the ramps in front of each boat would drop, and the troops would charge onto the beach and move inland. The goal was to get off the beach and into the first growth of trees or bushes as quickly as possible.

Getting into the landing craft from the ship was an art that was practiced over and over. No amount of practice can prepare you for the first time you go over the side with all your equipment, rifle, ammo, helmet and assorted other gear, and climb down a cargo net into a landing craft that is bouncing up and down in the waves as it waits alongside the ship to embark the troops. Approximately 36 fully loaded Marines can fit into an LCVP (Landing Craft, Vehicle or Personnel) or a Jeep and a fully loaded trailer or a combination of vehicles and troops. Once you get aboard the landing craft, it goes to a designated area and circles with other loaded boats assigned to the wave. All boats await the signal from the wavemaster, a Navy officer who controls the forming of the waves and then dispatches them to the beach. The problem is that once you are loaded aboard the landing craft, it could be several hours before your boat receives the signal to move ashore. During that time you are in a confined space, circling in an open boat, smelling diesel fumes and being rocked back and forth by the waves. Many get seasick, and the Navy does not provide seasick pills!

The morning of D-Day was fairly cool, and the seas were not rough. We ate breakfast very early because we were going over the side at 6 a.m. In the Navy, D-Day breakfasts for troops going ashore are always steak and eggs. This was a holdover from World War II, and I often wondered how many Marines who hit the beaches in assault landings had this steak and eggs breakfast as their very last meal. Once in the landing craft, we headed to the rendezvous area where we immediately began circling while we waited for the wave-master's signal.

After about one hour, we received the signal to form up and head for the beach. We were in the second wave, and as we headed in we were passed by landing craft that had already deposited troops on the beach in the first wave and were returning to pick up more troops and equipment. Our boats grounded on the shoreline, and the ramps went down. We stormed ashore, and then my job began. I moved the troops over the beach rapidly to the first area on my battle map, where we would wait for orders from our Battalion head-quarters, which was already ashore and operating inland. By the time I got the company to our designated area, I was soaking wet with sweat, and worried that my entire unit was not with me. A quick check by the Company Gunny reassured me that all units had reported in, and we were in good shape for the move inland.

Suddenly, we were ordered to remain in our assembly areas and have company commanders report to the battalion headquarters. We were informed that the President of the Philippines, Mr. Ramon Magsaysay, had been killed in a helicopter crash on the island of Cebu on his way to view the landing. The helicopter had flown into Mount Manunaggal, and there were no survivors. We were instructed to erect camp in our assembly areas and await further orders. Our maneuvers inland were curtailed, and there was an official mourning period in the Philippines. What had promised to be a huge Division landing with opposition from the Philippine Marines and Army, turned into a series of field exercises, which finally culminated in a Division sized maneuver into a designated enemy area approximately 25 miles inland from the landing beaches. Towards the end of the field exercise, some Philippine troops returned to the field exercise areas, and we were able to conduct operations against an "enemy" aggressor force.

At the end of the two weeks, we marched back to the landing beaches and set up camp in the tree lines surrounding the beaches. It took several days to reload our equipment, and engineers and pioneer battalions were busy day and night steam cleaning all equipment. After two weeks in the hot Philippine sun, and living in the field under fairly Spartan conditions, we simply walked into landing craft and returned to our ships by climbing cargo nets. We cleaned our spaces, took hot, salt water showers, and cleaned our web gear and weapons. We then went to the troop spaces to begin our routine inspections while on our way to our new bases on the island of Okinawa. Hotel Company troops responded very well, and the noncommissioned officers made our company look extremely good. The Colonel was impressed with our company, and made it a point to tell me so during our final briefing.

The trip to Okinawa took several days, and during that time I read whatever information I could find on Okinawa. I knew it was a prefecture of Japan, but it was under US Military control, and the island had an American High Commissioner. Since the American victory on Okinawa in 1945, in one of the bloodiest and costliest battles of World War II, the island was still being held by American forces. Although the Okinawans had never been very fond of the Japanese, they seemed well adjusted to the American presence and occupation, at that time.

The troops felt good about their performance on Operation *Strong Back*, the name Division had given to the operation, and we were wondering what our new base would be like. We arrived at White Beach, which had been used as a landing beach by US Forces during World War II, and tied up alongside the pier to unload. The troops left first and following their debarkation I had to go back aboard ship so the Navy could inspect all the spaces that the troops had used. We passed our inspections and were cleared to load aboard busses that would take us to our new home, Camp Sukiran.

Sukiran had been a former US Army barracks built in the early 1950s. Unlike buildings in Japan, almost all buildings in Okinawa were built of solid concrete with very strong tile roofs and bars covering most windows. The reason for this type of construction was that Okinawa was hit by typhoons, and the very forceful and dangerous winds could do much damage. Buildings withstood typhoon winds because of the solid concrete construction. It was a lesson that had been learned the hard way when a typhoon swept the island in 1948, and destroyed almost 80 percent of all houses.

Sukiran was located north of Naha, the major city of Okinawa and the capital of the Ryukyu Islands. The small town of Ginowan was located outside of the base perimeter, so we passed through it on the way to Camp Sukiran. The scenes we had seen at Camp Fuji, where all the girls were tearfully waving goodbye, were repeated on the streets of Ginowan. Ginowan and Gotemba could have been interchangeable. Both towns had hundreds of girls working in bars, restaurants and souvenir shops, and there must have been at least 50 bars that we could see from the windows of the busses. The girls were laughing and waving happily as the troops passed by, and I could easily imagine the same scene being repeated for the 9th Marines as they rode through Gotemba to Camp Fuji.

Our battalion debarked in front of an area that had twelve buildings arranged in a row. Each building was two stories tall and had a red and yellow sign painted on the street side of the building. There was a Marine Corps emblem at the top of each building sign, and then in gold letters were the designation of the unit that had previously occupied the building. I could see that the twelve buildings had been the location of the 3rd Battalion, 9th Marines. We only had to change one number to make the buildings our own. This was the new home of 3/3, and each building housed one complete rifle company. My company marched to a building that proclaimed that Company H of 3/9, had previously been there.

When the Regiment left Japan on its way to the Philippines, an advance party from each battalion was dispatched to Okinawa. The job of these advance parties was to prepare the sites that we would be occupying upon our arrival in Okinawa. So, while we were sweating it out in the Philippines, the advance parties were fixing, arranging and marking all areas in preparation for our arrival.

A Marine infantry battalion is an extremely lightweight and mobile unit. Like all units in the Marine Corps, they are designed for rapid deployment, generally by amphibious shipping, therefore, almost all support functions are either task organized (assigned as needed) or centralized at the highest command level possible. A battalion has a messhall, a field medical unit, a chaplain and sufficient supplies, weapons, ammunition, radios and equipment to function for 14 days without resupply. Marine Infantry companies carry enough equipment with them to fulfill their missions, however, all support and logistics originates at the battalion level or higher. Because of these limits, what greeted us at Camp Sukiran was like a dream come true.

Camp Sukiran had been constructed to meet US Army specifications. The Army tends to carry far more equipment than a first strike Marine unit, and Army companies are totally self-sufficient. The barracks at Camp Sukiran emphasized this huge difference between our organizations. The barracks assigned to Hotel Company was a two-story building. The top floor housed all platoons in separate troop bays, with each troop bay having separate showers and toilets. This alone was a luxury that our troops had never experienced in the Marine Corps.

The first floor contained a complete kitchen and messhall, a supply storage area, an armory, company offices and staff noncommissioned officer's quarters. We were told that our battalion would disperse their cooks and bakers from the battalion messhall and staff each company messhall in the camp. Hotel Company drew Sgt Theron Lang, from New Iberia, Louisiana, as our company Mess Sergeant, and Cpl. John Beaver, from Portland, Oregon, as assistant Mess Sergeant and baker. Hotel Company troops would continue to provide all other mess related duties, such as dishwashers, line servers and general kitchen help. In those days, all Marines drew two weeks of mess duty per year, and this practice continued, only now, they were providing these services to their own company messhall instead of to the battalion messhall.

The troops of the company were just as dumbfounded as I was. Here, we were moving into a concrete building, completely self-contained and self-sufficient. We had left old Quonset huts and spartan field conditions, even while in camp at Fuji. All things considered, we clearly felt that we had gotten a good deal. We moved in quickly, and within 24 hours we were enjoying our first meal in the Hotel Company messhall. Our Mess Sergeant, Sgt Lang, was a 15-year veteran of the Marine Corps. He was a superb cook, and his SOS, creamed beef on toast, lovingly referred to as *shit on a shingle* by all Marines, was the best I have ever eaten. I have a copy of his secret recipe which he gave me in 1957.

Two days after we moved in, I was approached by an Okinawan gentleman who identified himself as Mr. Ishigaki, our company laundry man. Local entrepreneurs had set up laundry companies where they employed many women who washed and ironed clothes in a centralized location. The laundry operation worked in the following manner: Each platoon had two maids assigned to the platoon for immediate washing. All other clothes were collected daily and taken away to be washed. The clothes were returned the next day, washed and ironed. For this service, each man in the company, paid $5 per payday. The arithmetic was easy enough: 300 men equaled $3,000 a month (There were two paydays a month). Mr. Ishigaki informed me that he wanted to retain our company business since he had already obtained the business of two other companies in the battalion. He indicated that if he got our business, he would gladly pay me $300 per month, or 10 percent. I told him that I did not want the money, but I wanted him to throw a monthly "laundry party" for the officers and staff noncommissioned officers of the company. He was delighted, since a party would cost him very little, and he would retain a lucrative contract. He readily agreed, and left the building smiling and probably wondering why the dumb American officer refused his offer of "cumshaw" (a bribe).

Two days after my meeting with Mr. Ishigaki, a new company commander reported to Hotel Company. I had mixed feelings about his arrival. I was enjoying my role as a company commander, but, on the other hand, I realized that I was in a captain's job as a second lieutenant, and eventually, a captain would arrive. Captain Kenneth T. Hughes was our new company commander. He came from Camp Pendleton where he had been a company commander with the 5th Marine Regiment, and was now beginning his 15 month overseas assignment.

Captain Hughes was 6 feet 3 inches tall and was a graduate of the University of Nebraska. He had been in the Marine Corps for seven years and was a gung ho type with a great personality. He had played football at Nebraska, and was a man who enjoyed life and enjoyed being around the troops. I liked him instantly. He asked me to remain as the Company Executive Officer, and together we ran a great company. I told him about my arrangement with Mr. Ishigaki concerning the laundry parties in lieu of the customary bribes, and he liked that arrangement. He was a regular guy who was not impressed with his rank.

Daily life in Sukiran settled into the routine of a regular Marine infantry company. Monday mornings began with inspections and classroom work, along with physical training and other garrison type issues. On Tuesday morning, the company took off for field exercises that lasted until Thursday evening. We returned to camp late Thursday night and took Friday to clean our gear and take care of whatever administrative issues required attention.

The troops were paid on the 15th and the 30th of each month, and they were always paid in cash (Military Payment Certificates in lieu of dollars). All second lieutenants took turns being pay officers, and we hated the duty. We would go to the Paymaster with a company roster, officers and enlisted, and draw the exact amount of cash to pay every man in the company. As the Marine was paid, he signed his payroll signature next to his name, along with the amount of money he was paid. When you collected all the signatures, you should be out of money. If you were short, it came out of your pocket. You signed for the entire amount of cash, and you either returned a completed pay roster, fully signed, or you returned the pay roster and the money for all unsigned spaces if you could not find all the Marines listed on the roster. In the interim, you walked around with about 10 to 20 thousand dollars in cash, usually carried in an empty ammunition box, and armed and prepared to protect the governments' money. In all the times I was a pay officer I never broke even, and it usually wound up costing me about twenty dollars per payday of my own money. I was not alone in this, because the sheer volume of cash, coupled with counting exact amounts to every trooper, usually led to some small errors. Years later, the Marine Corps implemented paychecks.

Except for Sailors returning from a long cruise and departing on liberty, there is nothing quite like Marines descending on a village with a fistful of cash on payday night. These nights always required an augmented military police presence, and there was a constant shuttle of intoxicated Marines being thrown into military vehicles and returned to their barracks.

Each camp had a thriving community of bars, restaurants, souvenir and embroidery shops, and clothing and tailor shops located right outside the camp boundaries. Our community in Sukiran was Ginowan, and a little further down the road, Koza BC (the BC meant business center). These communities were filled with bars, each one with a contingent of women working there as bar hostesses. The job of the hostess was to sell as many drinks to the troops as possible and also have the troops buy them drinks which were usually tea and water but looked like whiskey. The hostesses all worked for the bar owner, usually an older woman called mama-san. If the girl liked you, you could buy her services for a short time or all night, and the price was always negotiated with the mama-san. You never left the premises of the bar since all bars also had several bedrooms in the rear. The bars were all generally the same and had American names. The few I remember were named Bar Viewing the Moon, Bar American Eagle, Bar Jazz Club, Bar Judy, Bar Warm Arms, Bar Everly, Bar Rock and Roll, and Bar Nothing. Being Jewish, I always felt that there should have been a Bar Mitzvah, but the humor would have been lost on both the Marines and the Okinawans.

Many young Marines had their first sexual experiences in these bars, and oddly enough, quite a few wanted to marry these women. In those days, Marines were required to get permission from their commanding officers to marry overseas, and permission was never granted. Liberty meant leaving the base and going to one of the many bars to enjoy the company of your true love, as Gunnery Sergeant Moore liked to say.

Days evolved into weeks, and I could not believe I was getting paid for having so much fun at work, in the field, and on liberty. Officers did not cruise the bars very often. We had an active Officer's Club where we enjoyed each other's company. We ate meals at the Officer's Club, and the bar was well stocked and had regular Happy Hours, where martini's cost ten cents each and beers were a nickel. Often, after consuming so many cheap drinks, some officers decided that cruising the bars might be fun. We rarely went to the bars our troops frequented, and more often than not, we picked a few bars in several towns that seemed to cater to officers, which meant that the prices were higher, and this fact alone kept out the troops.

There was an officer in our group from a small town in New Mexico named Billy Brown. Billy was a Reserve officer who intended to return to his home town to teach school. He was a straight arrow and rarely drank, and it was our objective to get him drunk, get him a woman, and get him tattooed. We promised him that he would return home with a Marine Corps emblem tattooed on his arm and that he would experience the pleasures of at least one bar girl before he returned to the States. Our opportunity came one happy hour when Billy had too many 10 cent martinis. We had already located a Japanese tattoo parlor near Naha, and several of us were toying with the idea of getting a Marine Corps emblem tattooed on our arms. It would have to be on our shoulders where no one could see it, because officers were not allowed to get tattooed. Only officers who had tattoos before commissioning were excluded from this rule. Most of our mustang officers had tattoos, and getting one meant that we might be mistaken for a mustang, which would be a great honor and make us much more acceptable to the troops.

On the night in question, Billy was fairly drunk, as were the rest of us, and we went to the tattoo parlor. I had our company corpsman (medic), a sailor named Blazek, with us, and he had his field kit with him. We got to the tattoo parlor, and there were four of us, me, Billy, Joel Martin, and Blazek. We swore we would all get tattooed, and that no one would back out once the process began. Doc Blazek cleaned all needles and equipment with alcohol. I volunteered to go first. It was only then that I discovered that this was a real Japanese tattoo artist and that he used bamboo needles. He used the emblem on our ID card as an example, and began to tattoo me.

It was incredibly painful, but I realized that if I showed any fear or pain, I would probably be the only one with a tattoo. I bit my tongue and sat there for about 45 minutes while the tattoo artist finished. I almost fainted, but I did not let on how painful it actually was. Joel was next, and he must have caught on right away, because he also made no sound. Finally, it was Billy's turn. I think he started yelling with the first needle prick, but he stayed the course and the tattoo was completed. The surprise of the evening was that Doc Blazek, a gung-ho Navy Medic, also got one, and the four of us found an open bar to celebrate our accomplishment. The second part of our promise to Billy was completed at a bar in Naha. I still have that tattoo, fifty-five years later, and Billy, who wound up becoming the principal of a high school, still has his, as far as is known.

Joel Martin had to have his tattoo removed because he was assigned embassy duty in Turkey, and the State Department ordered him to Bethesda Naval Hospital to have the tattoo removed. I never thought that they did a good job, since his scars looked far worse than the tattoo, but he didn't have a tattoo, just an ugly scar that he carried around for the rest of his life. I preferred the tattoo, and I'm glad I never got assigned to embassy duty. That is the story of how I got my tattoo. Many years later in San Francisco, I tried to get the tattoo recolored and selected a Japanese tattoo artist. He took one look at my tattoo and told me that it was a classic tattoo done in the old Japanese manner, and he would not desecrate the work of a true artist who practiced the ancient art of bamboo needle tattooing. That is why my tattoo looks like it does today, in deference to the ancient art of bamboo needle tattooing.

One day, Mr. Ishigaki came to inform Captain Hughes that he had planned a great laundry party. He told us that we would enjoy a traditional Japanese dinner followed by genuine Geisha entertainment. The evening arrived, and the company officers and staff noncommissioned officers departed camp in several taxis which took us to a very large complex of Japanese style houses. We entered the establishment, leaving our shoes outside, and were escorted to a large room where a woman dressed in a formal kimono was playing a samisan, a Japanese type of three stringed guitar. Lighting was dim, and we were escorted to our places in a large dining room where we would be sitting on the tatami mats covering the floor. The entire setting was very elegant, and I felt Mr. Ishigaki was going overboard on this party. In a short time, several women, also attired in very formal kimonos, entered the room and sat next to each Marine present. They served the meal and sang in chorus to certain songs played on the samisan. They also danced formal Japanese dances, and for once, I actually felt we were absorbing some real Oriental culture. Not all the staff noncommissioned officers were enjoying themselves, but the more sake they drank, the better they liked the show.

Suddenly, the lights went out, and a mama-san came through the building telling us to lie on the floor and not make a sound. We suddenly saw blinking red lights reflected on the dark paper and wood walls and doors of the house. The next thing we heard was English being spoken, and flashlight beams were working their way through the halls of the building. Suddenly the doors slid open, and beams of flashlights revealed about 15 Marines lying on the floor with about 15 kimono clad geisha girls. We, in turn, looked up at about five US Army Military Policemen who instructed us to get up and file out of the building. When we were outside, the MP's inquired what we were doing there.

Captain Hughes identified himself as the senior officer present and told the MP's that we were there for a dinner party, and if they looked inside, they could see that the tables were set with food and that we were being entertained by the geisha girls. The MP's then inquired if we knew that we were in a brothel that had been placed in an off limits category because there had been several incidents in the place, and it had been closed down to all American military personnel. Of course, we did not know this, but the MP's said that all of us were under arrest, and we were taken to the Army stockade. A few telephone calls were made by Captain Hughes from the stockade, and we were subsequently released. Unfortunately, the incident did not end there. Captain Hughes was relieved of his command and assigned duties as the Assistant Battalion Operations Officer, and I was relieved as the company executive officer and made a platoon leader.

The new company commander was a senior first lieutenant, named William Rivers Von Harten, a Citadel graduate from Beaufort, South Carolina, and another southern gentleman. His nickname was "Skeeter" and he was 6 foot 5 inches tall and had played basketball for the Citadel. By a strange coincidence, Skeeter was the officer I had given a blanket to that cold night at Camp McGill when we had both first arrived in Japan. Skeeter remembered me from that night, and implored the battalion commander to let me remain as the executive officer. Apparently, he made a strong case, and I was reinstated as the company executive officer. After a thorough investigation of the off limits bordello caper, it was determined that we were just at the wrong place at the wrong time, and the matter was totally dropped. The incident never made it into our official records, and Captain Hughes' career was saved. He would retire many years later as a colonel.

While still on Okinawa, I was called into the office of LtCol Rauchle, our battalion commander, who was an Old Corps Marine who had begun his service in 1932. He insisted on formal dining in the field using a little known piece of equipment that I have never seen since those days in Okinawa, which was an item of equipment in every battalion called an Officer's Field Mess Chest. This chest contained metal plates, cups, silverware and complete dining service for twenty-four persons. It was a holdover from pre-World War II days, but I must admit it was a very special treat to sit in a tent in the field and eat off of these plates. It was an experience I will never forget, and in some ways, ties me back to Marine Corps lore many years before I ever thought about becoming a Marine. At any rate, LtCol Rauchle wanted me to apply for a regular commission. This meant I would become a career Marine, and I told him that I wasn't sure I wanted to go in that direction. He told me that even if I wasn't sure, I should apply because I may never have the opportunity again. There were over 150 officers applying, and he did not know how many would be selected. He told me I could always say no if I were selected. With that much pressure, and being about 90 percent in favor of becoming a regular officer, I applied for a regular commission, and LtCol Rauchle gave me a very favorable endorsement.

Life in Okinawa was a blast. We worked hard, we partied even harder, and all of us were having the times of our young lives. On weekends, we would drive all over the island and visit some of the most famous World War II battlefields. We looked at Suicide Cliff where thousands of Japanese, both military and civilian, committed suicide rather than allow themselves to be captured by Americans. We toured Sugarloaf Ridge, where so many Americans lost their lives, and we visited the sprawling city of Naha. We visited the two main industries of Okinawa, and watched as skilled glass blowers made works of art that found their way into American homes. We saw skilled weavers, making the world famous Bingata cloth, which was used to make elegant and very expensive kimonos.

We did not ignore our more earthy sides. We were well known in bars throughout most of the areas in Southern Okinawa, especially Koza, BC, which seemed to have the best bars and the best women in all of Okinawa. We harassed the Air Force officers and their wives who were stationed at the mammoth Kadena Air Force Base. Marine officers were admitted to the Kadena Officer's Club, but they certainly weren't welcome. The Air Force, in 1957, was allowed to bring their families to Okinawa. This made going to the Kadena Officer's Club a bitter sweet experience for Marines, since it was the one place on the island where you could see beautiful American women. Of course, they were all married to Air Force officers, but in some rare cases, that did not seem to matter. The Kadena club was like a big city nightclub. I remember one "big band" group that sounded exactly like the famous Stan Kenton Orchestra.

The club also had slot machines and great food, and for Marines, it was like a quick trip to the States. I remember one night I was quietly being escorted out of the building by Air Force Security. On the way out I passed a bank of slot machines, and I recall telling the security guards that I had one nickel chip in my pocket, and if they would let me put it in a slot machine on my way out, I would leave quietly. They agreed. I put the chip in the slot machine and hit a $250 jackpot. Bells rang, lights flashed and the club manager gave me twenty-five $10. MPC certificates. I know this to be true, because I woke up the following morning and could not remember where I had gotten those twenty-five $10 MPC certificates. It became quite a story at the Kadena Officers Club.

June, July and August of 1957 went very quickly. The standard routine of four days in the field and one and a half days at the base was fairly constant. The troops were in excellent spirits, which was good, when our battalion was informed we were going to be moving to a Quonset hut camp which had formerly been a Japanese ammunition dump. We said goodbye to Camp Sukiran and moved to a remote camp in a hilly part of Koza village overlooking the Kadena Air Base. Camp Bishigawa became the new home of the 3rd Battalion, 3rd Marine Regiment. The camp was truly austere. We had all the necessary components required to maintain an infantry battalion, but in comparison with the luxury of Camp Sukiran, we had just moved back in time by simply taking a short truck ride. The company facilities disappeared and we returned to the Marine Corps way of doing things. Our 12 Quonset huts were painted white to reflect the sun, and it felt as though we were again a front line expeditionary force. Our training continued, and we had to find new bars with new women for our off duty entertainment. This was not a problem, as Koza BC was the hotbed of bars and restaurants in the central part of the island.

In September, our battalion received a warning order to be prepared to board ships and sail towards Indonesia at a moment's notice. Southeast Asia was relatively stable in 1957. President Sukarno, in answer to a perceived threat from a US backed coalition of nations called the South East Asia Treaty Organization (SEATO), was threatening military action against the coalition. He formed the Bandung Conference, which espoused neutralism for the remaining non-SEATO nations in the region. To add to the concern of American leaders, Sukarno had made trips to both the Soviet Union and China, and bought weapons from Eastern European countries, although only after being turned down by the United States. The US decided it had to guarantee the safety of US Nationals living in Indonesia. To accomplish this, Washington decided that a Marine Expeditionary Force should be launched to the South China Sea, fully prepared to land in Jakarta to evacuate US nationals. If other issues developed while the troops were ashore, they obviously had to be dealt with, and the Marines would be the force to do it.

In late September, 3/3 was designated as the landing force of the task force that was being formed on Okinawa. The amphibious squadron, with the Marine expeditionary force, would depart from Okinawa to an undetermined spot in the South China Sea. We were informed that the situation in Indonesia would dictate the duration of the operation. Once aboard ship, all tours of duty were extended until the squadron made a port where personnel could be transferred and replaced. This was the atmosphere that energized our training, and made our preparations for going aboard ship far more serious than departing for another field exercise.

In September, LtCol Rauchle received orders to report to Headquarters Marine Corps. Along with these orders, he was also selected for promotion to the rank of colonel, a promotion that he richly deserved. We had a wonderful farewell party for LtCol Rauchle, who was that rare senior officer who could blend firmness with compassion, strictness with a sense of humor, and intelligence with the ability to relate to every Marine under his command. He was a terrific role model for leadership, and there are many traits that I learned from him that remained with me throughout both my Marine Corps and civilian careers. We had a change of command ceremony at Camp Bishigawa and LtCol Rauchle was relieved of command by Lieutenant Colonel J. M. Rouse. It would fall to LtCol Rouse to lead us into our next adventure in the South China Sea.

On the 30 September, 3/3 received its' marching orders. We were to proceed to White Beach where we would become a part of an amphibious squadron which would take this task organized unit to the South China Sea. Events in Indonesia had continued to become alarming to the United States. In July, the Indonesian Communist Party had again gained seats in the Indonesian Parliament, and concern increased that President Sukarno would ally himself with both the local communists and the Mainland Chinese.

Under the guise of "protecting American nationals," the Marine expeditionary force was formed and dispatched with a mission to invade the island capital of Jakarta, remove all Americans, and as many foreign nationals as desired evacuation, and then rapidly depart. The assumption was that this operation would be orderly, and without bloodshed, however, no Marine unit has ever gone into a foreign country without the expectation of some form of combat. To do otherwise would be foolhardy and would greatly imperil our troops. While we did not expect any combat in Indonesia, there certainly was no guarantee that we would not be tested under fire. We trained as though we would be, and continued to expect trouble once we landed.

Our orders specified that 3/3 would board ships of Amphibious Task Force 26, for extended operations in the South China Sea. Hotel and India Companies would embark, along with the Headquarters and Service Company of the Battalion, aboard USS *Bexar* (APA 237). Bexar was a better ship than *Renville*, which had taken us from Japan to the Philippines, and then to Okinawa, but, it was not very much different in its accommodations and available space. The truly unusual thing about *Bexar* was that its commanding officer was a legendary Naval officer who was famous for forming the Navy's Underwater Demolition Teams (UDT) in World War II, and who had commanded UDT 5. He was twice awarded the Navy Cross for heroism. He was a tall, handsome and extremely competent officer whose name was Draper L. Kaufman. Later, he would become a vice admiral and the 44th Superintendent of the United States Naval Academy.

The Captain loved Marines, and the crew reflected this in their dealings with embarked personnel. It was an extremely lucky circumstance for both parties because, unknown to anyone at the time, we were destined to spend the next two and half months at sea. We departed Okinawa on October 12 for Indonesia. Once aboard ship, we were told that the situation in Jakarta was extremely fluid, and the Marines would not be ordered in unless the US State Department felt that American lives were in danger. It was a constant drill for all embarked troops. One day we were going in, and the next day we were not. During all the time at sea, we could only plan on a course of action and prepare for the worst, not knowing what we might meet once we were ashore.

I realized that this was the life of a Marine, and I remembered what LtCol Rauchle had told me when we were discussing my application for a regular commission. He had said that in the entire history of the Marine Corps, there had never been a twenty year period that Marines were not engaged in some kind of war, declared or undeclared, and that if I accepted a regular commission, he could guarantee me that sometime in my twenty year career, I would be going to war. If that was something I couldn't accept, then I should not accept a regular commission. Well, here I was, still a reserve officer and the specter of war was hanging over my head in a very real manner. Only incidents and decisions being made in Jakarta and Washington would determine whether I was going to experience combat at the age of 22. It certainly got my attention.

We arrived at our station in the South China Sea approximately two weeks after departing Okinawa. Every day, Captain Kaufman would brief all hands on the situation in Indonesia by getting on the ship's intercom system and reading all current news reports and dispatches he had received in the past 24 hours. Along with his daily updates, Captain Kaufman made it a point to walk through all troop spaces on a daily basis. He always stopped and spoke with the troops, putting them at ease with his easy manner and sincere interest, which, in my opinion, is impossible to fake. He was a true leader, and he made life aboard a crowded troop ship far more bearable.

On the 1st of November, the ship received a message from Headquarters Marine Corps which stated that effective that date, all second lieutenants from Basic Class 3-56 had been promoted to first lieutenant. There were 14 officers from my class aboard ship, and we went running to the Ship's Store to buy silver bars so that we could get rid of the hated gold bars that identified us as "new recruits." The Ship's Store did not have any silver bars in stock, and obviously would not have any until we put into port somewhere and were resupplied. This created a dilemma for us new first lieutenants until one of our group came up with an ingenious idea. He suggested that we cover our gold bars with the silver foil in cigarette packs and then attach our bars to our uniforms. This worked beautifully, and for the rest of our time aboard ship, we were known as *cigarette foil lieutenants*. At least we were not wearing gold bars any longer.

Keeping troops from being bored was not a problem on this deployment. We all knew we could be going into combat, and we spent our time studying maps and aerial photographs of the areas where we might be landed. It is amazing how much the threat of war does to keep everyone fully focused on their mission. It was hot and humid, and there was no air conditioning aboard ship. Portholes and hatches were kept open, and the ocean breezes provided the only cooling available.

We remained on station in the South China Sea, sailing in "square circles" as the troops liked to say, until December 15th. The situation in Jakarta had stabilized in that President Sukarno had a firm hold on the island country, and whatever opposition there was to his regime, the US included, could not gain any foothold. His assurances to the US State Department that all American interests in Indonesia were safe, convinced the American government that, at least for now, a ready strike force of Marines in the South China Sea was not necessary. Electing to be cautious, the US decided it might be prudent to place the strike force in the Philippines, rather than returning them to Okinawa. On December 23, the strike force made port at the US Naval Base in Subic Bay on the island of Luzon. It would be the first time in 2½ months that any of us had set foot on solid ground.

When an amphibious squadron makes port in any place around the world, the standard operating procedures are that only 50 percent of the crew and embarked troops are allowed liberty at any one time. The other half must remain aboard ship in case of an emergency departure that would insure that at least half of the force was available to go. Based on this, 750 Marines were set loose on the Naval Base on the morning of December 24. These men had not had a drink in 2½ months and had 2½ month's pay in their pockets.

The base and the adjoining town of Olongopo was in for an amazing experience. On the evening of the 23rd, the officers and noncommissioned officers of the Battalion met and agreed to split into two groups to patrol our own troops and try to keep them out of the hands of the Navy Shore Patrol. One group would patrol the base, and the other group would be responsible for the town of Olongopo. There was no doubt in anybody's mind that we were headed for a disaster, but we could not deny our troops liberty. I drew the base patrol group, and we were primarily tasked to watch all the enlisted clubs and to be especially watchful for the possibility of fights between the Marines and Sailors.

We off-loaded several of our 3/4 ton trucks to serve as patrol vehicles and "paddy wagons" to return troops to our ships, if needed. We patrolled in groups of two, one officer and one noncommissioned officer per team. Liberty for the troops started at 8 a.m., and we didn't have to wait too long for the first altercation. Almost all the troops wanted to go off the base. This would have inundated Olongopo with such a large group of Marines that the local constabulary determined that only 300 Marines at a time could go into Olongopo. This would enable both the women and the local bars to adequately serve and satisfy the troops.

The remainder of the troops would have to go to enlisted clubs on the base and drink beer and eat hamburgers. By noon, the Marines had drunk all the beer available in the base clubs. The beer that was rushed to the clubs from the warehouses was warm and did not gain the approval of the drinking Marines. Bottles and cans began flying. Sailors and Marines began mixing it up, whistles and sirens went off all over the base, and our local patrols went to work. Our Marines would not listen to anyone in a sailor's uniform. It became necessary to form flying squads, diving into large groups of fighting Marines and Sailors and bodily pulling them apart. Once we got Marines in our grasp, we placed them in a truck where they were ordered to stay. As we filled up each truck, we drove them back to the ships and turned them over to their respective duty officers. This went on all night until all Marines and Navy Corpsmen returned to their ships. Through our quick reaction, none of the embarked troops wound up in the brig.

Our reaction force, however, did not impress the admiral in charge of the base. His immediate reaction was to restrict all Marines to their ships, and to prohibit them from going ashore. He called for an immediate meeting with all embarked Marine commanders and ship's captains. It was Christmas morning, 1957.

Fortunately for all Marines, Captain Draper L. Kaufman, USN, the captain of our ship, *Bexar*, attended the meeting. He was a hero to all Navy men, and he made a logical and cool-headed recommendation: Let the Marines go ashore, on the base for Christmas services, open the enlisted clubs and have the Officer's Wives Club put on a buffet for the troops. All base wives were encouraged to attend, with their children, and Captain

Kaufman would personally vouch for the Marine's conduct ashore. This scheme worked like a charm, and many Marines will always remember Christmas in Subic Bay. Captain Kaufman had turned a red-hot crisis into a memorable day for 1,500 embarked Marines.

The day after Christmas, the "cigarette foil lieutenants" rushed to the Base Exchange and bought official first lieutenant bars. We celebrated New Year's Day aboard ship, and were informed that we would be building a camp on the outskirts of the Subic Bay Naval Base. It would be a temporary tent camp, and the Seabees would help build it. They laid water pipes for showers, built water treatment tanks, and installed electricity to the large tents we were erecting while they were working.

In just two weeks Camp Driftwood was completed, and all embarked Marines disembarked from their ships and moved into the tent camp. It was extremely hot in the Philippines, and the canvas of our tent camps absorbed the heat relentlessly, making it almost impossible to remain inside a tent in the middle of the day. We worked tropical hours, meaning that training began at 6 a.m. and was over by 1 p.m., at which time the troops were free to do whatever they wanted, either on base or ashore in the town of Olongopo. Trouble continued in Indonesia, but it never escalated to a point where the US government felt that it was necessary to send in the Marines. We remained in our camp at Subic Bay.

In January 1958, LtCol Rouse informed me that of the 153 applicants for a regular commission from the 3rd Marine Division, only four officers were selected, and I was one of them. This meant that if I accepted the regular commission, I would automatically add one year to my service obligation. As it stood, I could leave the Marine Corps in June of 1959, having served three years on active duty. As a regular officer, I would have to serve four years on active duty before I was eligible to request separation. Since there were so many heartbroken officers who had placed their hopes for the future on a regular commission, I felt that I could not refuse mine. I signed on the dotted line and accepted a regular commission. I was now assured of a war within the 20-year period that I would be serving in the Marine Corps, or at least that's what LtCol Rauchle had "guaranteed" me.

Training continued in the Philippines. Our troops were honed to a very fine edge, and the training was a means to keep them busy. The main activity of the Battalion was liberty in Olongopo, and it was an activity that all hands, officers and enlisted, embraced with reckless abandon. Olongopo was a village that became a city, thanks to the huge, sprawling Naval Base and Air Station located at Subic Bay.

The base provided civilian employment to Filipinos, and it also provided a very good livelihood to every entrepreneur who had established a business near the base. There were bars, restaurants, souvenir shops, tailor shops, art galleries, luggage stores, clothing stores, electronics stores and any other type of establishment that might appeal to American Sailors and Marines. The bars catered to specific clientele, and either the troops went there for a specific reason (strip club, bordello, rock and roll club, etc.) or a group of troops adopted a bar, and then insured that the bar would cater to their tastes. As an example, many bars provided guitars, pianos and drums for troops to play music, especially country and western music, so it didn't take long for almost all bars in Olongopo to develop their own niche market. There were enlisted bars, staff noncommissioned officer bars and officer bars. They were not designated as such, but through natural selection, they became such.

All transportation in Olongopo was by Jeepneys, a vehicle that in 1957 was unique to the Philippines. It was a Jeep that had only a front seat, and the remainder of the vehicle, had been taken down to the frame and a body was welded onto the rear of the vehicle that contained two rows of benches with a canopy over them. The vehicles drove up and down Grand Avenue endlessly, and you could hop on and off anywhere along the route. Each Jeepney was unique, in that the drivers would decorate them with lights, horns, statues, flags or anything else to get your attention.

Most of the officers from the 3rd Battalion found their way to The Grandillia, a bar and restaurant run by a woman named Lisa Macapagal. Lisa was an attractive woman, in her late twenties or early thirties, but there was no doubt that she was in charge of everything in the place. She had a staff of about twenty girls, all of them younger than her. They were all quite beautiful and, as might be expected, they were all "available." The Grandillia was the very last bar on Grand Avenue, and, therefore, it was the most expensive "Jeepney" ride to get there from the main gate.

To keep the peace in the town of Olongopo, the admiral at Subic Bay had established a midnight curfew. This meant that all military personnel had to be off the streets by midnight, every night. Military personnel caught on the street after midnight were taken to the base brig. The curfew was lifted the following morning at 6 a.m. This presented a unique set of problems. If you remained in Olongopo after midnight, you had to find a place to hide or sleep until 6 a.m. and then get to the base after 6 a.m. in time for morning roll call. There was an art to doing this, and it was amazing to see the number of Jeepney's appearing at the main gate of Subic every morning at 6:01 a.m., and dropping off troops.

On my first night in town, I had found my way to the Grandillia, where I had more than my share of alcohol. By the time Lisa, the owner of the bar, was able to get some food into me, it was past midnight, and I was stuck in town for the night. I had to get back to my unit because there was no way that I would be able to justify my late arrival to LtCol Rouse. I began to panic as I visualized another situation that would probably not be too good for my career in the Marine Corps. Lisa, who I had just met that evening, decided that she would help me get back on base in order for me to stay out of trouble. She told me that delivery trucks were routinely let onto the base during the night, especially vehicles that were supplying food to base messhalls. She was a friend of a local dairy owner who regularly delivered milk to the base in a refrigerated truck, which usually entered the base through the main gate at about 4 a.m. She persuaded the dairy owner to let me ride into the base in the refrigerated portion of the truck, which was never inspected, and that is how I got back onto the base at 4:30 a.m. The walk to Camp Driftwood took about an hour, but I made it back in time and no one was the wiser. As usual, I had dodged a bullet on my very first night of liberty. I wondered if I would ever learn.

The following night I returned to the Grandillia to thank Lisa for her help. She seemed very pleased to see me, and told me that she had helped me because I had red hair, and red hair was a lucky omen to her. She also told me that I was a funny drunk and that she liked me very much. She also told me that I could stay with her anytime, and it would not cost me a penny. It seemed that I had found myself a Filipino girlfriend in just one day, and I soon became the envy of all my contemporaries. No one could figure out how I had been able to captivate the owner of the best bar in Olongopo, and apparently she made no secret of the fact that she considered me to be her boyfriend. Since I was drinking her whiskey, eating her food, and sleeping in her bed, I had absolutely no objection to the arrangement.

As far as I was concerned, life was good. Lisa was an intelligent and capable woman. She was attractive, and she was also an extremely successful business owner. She had an outgoing personality, and seemed to know everyone in town. She was most certainly a prize catch, and she did not want or demand anything from me in return, except to be loyal to her. It was not difficult to fulfill her expectations.

Life in this Asian paradise continued relatively unabated. The troops, many meeting and sleeping with women for the first time, came in endless processions, requesting permission to marry the Philippine women they were semi-living with in Olongopo. In every instance, they were refused, and they sulked off, convinced that all officers were complete fools and did not understand what it meant for a Marine to be "in love." The training and conditioning continued during normal training hours, although tropical hours made working in the hot sun debilitating and extremely unpopular. Olongopo and its pleasure haunts were much more appealing.

Skeet Von Harten, our company commander and my good friend, ran a great company, and all the troops respected him and would follow him anywhere. January February and March came and went quickly, and then I realized that both Skeet and I would be receiving orders very soon. This fact was also not lost on Lisa, who realized that soon I would have to depart, and we would never see each other again. She was still convinced that my red hair was a lucky omen, and she desperately wanted to have a child with me because she was sure that the child would have red hair, and, therefore, enjoy a lucky life. I told her that I did not want to marry her, and she told me that she did not want to marry me. She only wanted a red headed child.

In late April 1958, Skeet and I received orders to the Marine Corps Recruit Depot in Parris Island, South Carolina, for duty as Series Officers. On April 8, 1956, at the Recruit Depot in Parris Island, a Drill Instructor by the name of Staff Sergeant Matthew McKeon, had marched his platoon through a deep swamp in the middle of the night as punishment for not performing well at the rifle range the previous day. This form of punishment was fairly common at the time.

The recruits got filthy dirty, were wet to the bone, and returned to their barracks convinced that they must do better, because they did not want to go on another "midnight conditioning march" in Ribbon Creek, which was the name of the swamp located behind the target lines at the rifle range. The only problem with the night march that Sergeant McKeon took is that somehow during the march, his troops became disoriented, and six young Marine recruits drowned. The incident made headlines. SSgt McKeon was court-martialed and subsequently defended by a flamboyant, but brilliant civilian lawyer, named Emile Zola Berman, who was able to place the blame on the Marine Corps for allowing the incident to occur.

This made the Marine Corps revise their training procedures to the point that every four platoons going through recruit training (called a series) had an officer permanently assigned as the supervisory authority and his title was Series Officer. Our orders indicated specifically that Skeet and I were being assigned to Parris Island to become Series Officers. We were to report to Parris Island by May 15, 1958. I didn't even know where Parris Island was, but, lo and behold, it was next to Beaufort, South Carolina, the hometown of one Skeeter Von Harten. He assured me that I would love it in Beaufort, especially since he had been born and raised there and knew everyone in the whole town. I would not be a stranger.

I said goodbye to Lisa and she was very loving and tearful, but she assured me that life would go on for her and that business was booming at the Grandillia. She was a good businesswoman, and she would not miss any opportunity to make money. She had single-handedly made an unofficial Officer's Club out of her establishment, and it was well known that her club and restaurant was the most successful business venture in Olongopo.

On the morning of April 30, Skeet and I boarded a Navy Constellation at Cubi Point Naval Air Station for a flight to Okinawa to retrieve our gear, and then board a flight to Travis Air Force Base in California. From there, we would connect with a commercial flight to spend 30 days leave at home before reporting for duty at Parris Island.

I booked a flight to New York City on Wednesday, which left me time to go to the Half Note Bar on Sutter Street and look at the 8 mm films taken of our nine man group of second lieutenants when we were on our way to the Orient, just a scant 15 months ago. It was funny, looking at our shenanigans, and it brought back many fond memories of the way we were. While 15 months doesn't sound like a long time, in that period I had served as a rifle company commander in Japan, Okinawa and the Philippines, I had been on a two month alert to go into combat, I had been promoted to first lieutenant, and I had made a decision to make the Marine Corps my career. I'd say that was an active period, especially since I was only 22 years of age.

I arrived in New York City, and Dad and Dora met me at the airport. It was great to see them both again, and they both looked healthy and happy. When my father saw my tattoo, he was surprised but not shocked. He told me that I could not be buried in a Jewish cemetery because I had a tattoo, but it did not upset him, and it did not upset me. Frankly, I had never planned on being buried in a Jewish cemetery, and besides, at 22 years of age you are immortal anyway.

My thirty days leave was spent visiting old friends, seeing a few Broadway plays, listening to great jazz on 52nd Street and at the Blue Note. I also bought my first new car, a brand new British Triumph 3A sports car. It was a two-seater, pure sports rally car and was one of the hottest cars at the time. I remember I paid $2,700 for it. It would be the car I would drive to South Carolina, where I was to report to Parris Island for duty no later than Monday, June 9, 1958.

On Friday, June 6, I left New York. I had celebrated my 23rd birthday on June 3rd with Dad and Dora at my favorite restaurant in New York City, Astii. It was a memorable birthday celebration, and it was made even more memorable for me because I could see that Dad and Dora were thoroughly enjoying themselves. Since they both spoke Italian, the owner of Asti always treated us with great respect. One of the things I truly enjoyed about going out to dinner with Dad and Dora in New York was the fact that they spoke so many languages. This always assured us of personalized service. We always had a marvelous time, and I have fond memories of dinners together.

CHAPTER 9

PARRIS ISLAND, SOUTH CAROLINA

MARINE CORPS RECRUIT DEPOT

Parris Island is one of the 660 sea islands located in Beaufort County in the South Carolina Low Country. It is located near the Broad River and connects to the mainland of Beaufort, the county seat, by a long causeway rising out of the surrounding marshes and wetlands. To a recruit entering Parris Island on his first day of recruit training, there is a feeling of complete isolation from the rest of the world. Parris Island couldn't be a better geographic location available to underscore the contention that, for the next 12 weeks, your body belongs to the USMC. The drill instructors are also greatly aided by the fact that the waters surrounding Parris Island are inhabited by alligators that are quite visible at different hours of the day. Recruits are warned not to attempt to swim off the island, as the alligator risk is very real and dangerous. With the fact that the island is isolated and surrounded by alligators, the drill instructors tell their recruits that the only way off the island is as a U. S. Marine who has completed his 12 weeks of boot camp. Further motivation, at least initially, is rarely needed.

The Marine Corps has two recruit depots: One in Parris Island that trains all recruits who enlist east of the Mississippi River, and one in San Diego that trains recruits that enlist west of the Mississippi River. Marines at Parris Island like to call Marines who trained at San Diego *Hollywood Marines*. Parris Island is much colder in the winter, much hotter in the summer, and about 1000 percent more isolated. The recruit depot in San Diego is located downtown next to the San Diego International Airport. By comparison to that location, Parris Island is as close to Devil's Island as is possible in the United States. There is nothing near it, and the only views of real civilization are the views across the Broad River where the houses of Port Royal and Beaufort can barely be discerned. They are so far away, that swimming to them would be close to impossible for most of the recruits, even if there weren't any alligators in the water.

I was assigned to the 3rd Recruit Training Battalion. My job was to oversee the training of about 300 recruits every 12 weeks. The recruit platoons were composed of 75 recruits per platoon, and there were four platoons to a series. Each series had a Senior Drill Instructor and each platoon had three drill instructors. There was at least one drill instructor with each platoon seven days a week, 24 hours per day. There was never a time in the 12 week training cycle that recruits were not supervised by a drill instructor. My job was to insure that training was being conducted properly and that the drill instructors were not abusing their recruits. My team of 13 DI's was outstanding, and their enthusiasm for training recruits never waned. Even though there was little time between series, I thoroughly enjoyed recruit training. There is a certain satisfaction of seeing 300 young men change so completely in just 12 weeks. Many times, their own parents would not recognize them when they came to the Island for their graduation.

Skeet Von Harten, my friend from Japan and Okinawa, was assigned as a company commander. He was a senior first lieutenant who would soon be promoted to captain, so he was assigned a job of greater responsibility. He also took me under his wing in the town of Beaufort. While the 40 bachelors who lived in the BOQ were constantly complaining about how far in the sticks Parris Island was, I was busy meeting Skeet's friends in town, going on fishing trips, going out on shrimp boats with the local shrimpers, and meeting quite a few southern belles. My earlier time in North Carolina was definitely an advantage, as Southerners don't take kindly to "Yankees."

We had good times in Parris Island. We would go to Savannah, and Charleston on weekends, chase girls in Beaufort, usually school teachers, and do a whole lot of drinking, which continues to this day to be a great southern tradition as long as it is bourbon. The bachelors of the Parris Island BOQ were an eclectic group. We had great parties, water fights, and food fights, more like a fraternity house than a bachelor officer's residence. I remember nine of us carrying a Renault 4CV, a very small French car, into the room of an officer, just to be crazy. We had a party once where we put a Dixieland band on the roof of the building, and they played music all night for one of our parties. That was the talk of the base for several months, especially since the band got drunk and we had a very hard time getting them off the roof. We finally had to call the Base Fire Department for assistance.

Life at Parris Island was one of constant activity. Since recruits were being trained in 12-week cycles, once you picked up a new group of recruits, your time was totally allocated to training. While the drill instructors had to be with their platoons always. Scheduling did allow some free weekends during the training cycle, and, at least for the officers, every night off. The BOQ was totally away from all other facilities on the base. It was essentially an officer's complex that housed the BOQ, the Officers Club, the officer's swimming pool and the Officer's Guest House. Located around the complex were the quarters of senior officers, each house having a wonderful waterfront vista. Except for the isolation, it was an idyllic duty station with very rewarding accomplishments for those directly involved in recruit training.

In that regard, the sole reason for the existence of Parris Island was to train recruits. There were no other missions, and that meant that every one stationed on Parris Island was vested in the awesome task of training the next generation of United States Marines. We were a small but proud group who worked at least 12 hours per day without any complaints. Since we did not have time to leave the base very often, when we did have time, we invariably went to either Savannah, Georgia, which was only 30 miles south of the base, or Charleston, South Carolina, which was 70 miles north of the base. There were great bars, clubs, restaurants and women in both places, and I can never recall that anyone ever had a bad time in either of these classic southern cities. We were always glad that General Sherman had decided to spare Savannah on his march to the sea from Atlanta during the Civil War.

I was also fortunate to share a suite of rooms in the BOQ with my old friend, John Henry Bateman of Baton Rouge, Louisiana. We had gone through officer's training together and had served on Okinawa at the same time. John had become an artillery officer and was originally assigned to Parris Island as a series officer. His good looks and southern charm were quickly noticed, and in a very short time, John became the Commanding General's aide-de-camp. John and I shared many wonderful times together, and almost all of my memories of Parris Island days include John Henry Bateman. Although John was a regular officer like me, he left the Marine Corps after five year's and returned to Baton Rouge, where he became a highly respected executive of one of the largest banks in the United States. He honored me by attending my surprise 70th birthday party my wife, Cathie, arranged for me on June 3, 2005, in San Diego, California.

While I had thoroughly enjoyed my first tour of duty in the Fleet Marine Force, I was finding that life at a "Post and Station," the Marine Corps way of describing non-combat tours of duty world-wide, was even more enjoyable. For me, the introduction to the city of Beaufort by Skeet Von Harten, made all the difference in the world, and I was very much a part of the local scene. I was accepted in the homes in Beaufort, and through Skeet, I became extremely popular in the City of Beaufort. I was a rarity, to say the least, a "Yankee" that people liked and spent time with at social events. I was introduced to Jack Daniels and coke, never mixed, but always drunk in succession, first the Jack Daniels straight and then followed by a Coke chaser. We spent many weekends at the fishing camp of Skeets father, a rustic cabin, set on a spit of land, in the middle of some Carolina wetlands. Not a single fishing line ever got wet, but a lot of Jack Daniels and coke was consumed as we spent the weekend playing poker.

We had shrimp and oyster cookouts and all the seafood was fresh caught. It was a wonderful life, and I enjoyed it very much. I often wondered what would have happened if I hadn't offered my blanket to Skeet on that cold February night in Japan. That single gesture cemented a lifelong friendship between us that endures to this day. With the enjoyment of my time off in Beaufort, and the satisfaction I was deriving from my job in recruit training, I felt as though I had truly hit the jackpot in the Marine Corps and I celebrated my 24th birthday on June 3rd with a big party at the Officer's Club.

I was happy and content living in the BOQ with the other 40 bachelor officers. That was another interesting fact. There were 40 bachelor officers living at the BOQ, not because there was a requirement that officers assigned to Parris Island be bachelors, although given the hours we were required to work, it was certainly an asset, it was just that young men did not get married as early as they did in later years. The Marine Corps way of life required a dedicated woman, who was willing to endure long periods of separation and having to do things on her own. That type of woman is not easy to find, and most Marine officers I knew were not in a hurry to get married anyway.

I was getting tired of driving my tiny Triumph sports car, so I traded it in for a new 1958 Ford Fairlane 500 coupe. It was white with gold trim, had dual exhausts and a very powerful 5.8 liter, V8 engine. When the windows were lowered, it looked like a hardtop convertible because there were no center posts in the car. It was a very sharp looking car, and I "souped" it up a little more by adding glass packed mufflers that roared when you accelerated, and fender skirts over both rear wheels. My drill instructors all insisted on test driving it, and it turned out to be the talk of the base for a few weeks.

This wonderful life was interrupted one morning in April 1959, when I received a call from my roommate, John Bateman, informing me that the Commanding General wanted to see me in his office within the next half hour. I could not imagine why the Commanding General wanted to see me. I rushed back to the BOQ, put on a fresh uniform and reported to the General's office as directed. The Commanding General of Parris Island was Major General Robert B. Luckey, a veteran of World War II, having been a Major during the Guadalcanal campaign. He had been an artillery officer, and I firmly believe that is why he selected my friend, John Bateman, an artillery officer, as his aide-de-camp. I rushed into the office, and John had a big smile on his face. I asked what was going on, but he told me that the General would tell me. He also told me not to worry, I was going to receive some very good news.

I was quite apprehensive as I entered the General's office. I did not need good news. I was happy at Parris Island. I had only completed less than one year on a programmed three-year tour of duty, so it was difficult to imagine what news could be better than the situation I was currently enjoying. The General informed me I had been selected for duty at the Marine Barracks in Washington, and I was scheduled to report there by April 15, 1959, for duty as a parade platoon commander. This meant that I had just ten days to get to Washington and report for duty. While I should have been honored with the assignment, I was devastated and did not want to leave Parris Island.

The General seemed surprised by my reaction. Marine Barracks, Washington, was a prime assignment for a young officer, and selection for assignment there was very difficult to obtain and was considered to be a high honor. A candidate for the Barracks usually had to be six feet tall or over, he had to be single, and he had to have had extensive troop leading experience. Usually, officers were assigned to the Barracks for a full three year term, however, two first lieutenants had resigned their commissions and replacements were required for the commencement of the annual parade season that would begin on May 1. There was no time to train replacements, so the Marine Corps decided to pick one officer from the Recruit Depot at Parris Island, and one from the Recruit Depot at San Diego. There was a stipulation that both officers had to be currently working on the drill field and have already completed a 15-month tour overseas. I was the officer from Parris Island and Jerry Bowlin, a classmate of mine from Basic School, was the officer from San Diego.

I had no choice in the matter, and everyone at the Recruit Depot was full of congratulations for me and kept telling me what an honor it was to be selected for duty at *8th and I*, which is what the Barracks was commonly referred to in the Marine Corps because it was located at 8th and I Streets, Southeast, in Washington. I continued to have mixed feelings about the "honor." Regardless, I packed my new car and departed Parris Island within two days in order to report to the Barracks in time to rehearse for the upcoming parade season.

CHAPTER 10

WASHINGTON, D.C. — THE FIRST TIME

THE OLDEST POST OF THE CORPS

My mixed emotions about being assigned to the most prestigious post in the entire Marine Corps centered on the fact that I felt that I did not deserve such an honor. There were far more deserving first lieutenants in the Marine Corps who should have been selected ahead of me, and once at the Barracks I was not sure that I could meet the high standards expected of officers assigned there. Not only did officers participate in all types of ceremonial events, they also served as official escorts for dignitaries, senators, and congressmen. They also served as White House aides when needed. All officers had to have the highest security clearances to serve in the security force at Camp David, the President's mountain retreat in Maryland. I felt that my background, and my already established reputation as a fairly "wild and crazy" kind of junior officer might not play very well in the hallowed halls of Marine Barracks.

Marine Barracks, Washington, D.C. was established in 1801 and is traditionally known as the *Oldest Post in the Corps*. The Barracks complex is one of the oldest government buildings in continuous use in Washington, D.C. and is a National Historic Landmark, the official residence of the Commandant of the Marine Corps since 1806, and the main ceremonial grounds of the Corps. The Barracks is also the home of the famous Marine Band which has played for every President since John Adams in 1801. John Philip Sousa, the American March King, was the Director of the Marine Band from 1880 to 1892. Other buildings besides the barracks are a band hall and a row of five officer's quarters. The five quarters buildings house three senior general officers and the commanding officer of the Barracks. The fifth building, called the Center House, was the Bachelor Officers Quarters (BOQ) at the end of the row, and definitely not in the center where it had once been located. Center House housed seven bachelor officers with each officer living in almost Victorian style rooms.

On April 18, 1959, I reported for duty to Colonel Jonas M. Platt, the Commanding Officer of Marine Barracks. He welcomed me, informed me I would be living in the Center House and on Friday, May 1, I would be the platoon leader of the second ceremonial platoon of Marine Corps Institute (MCI) Company for the opening of the 1959 parade season. He went on to say he was certain I would be ready in that short two week rehearsal period to take my place with the rest of the Barracks ceremonial officers. He then sent me to meet my company commander, Captain John H. Gary III, a VMI graduate, who informed me that the company would begin rehearsals at 8 a.m. the following morning. In the meantime, he suggested I get moved in to the Center House and check to see if I had the required uniforms.

When I returned to my car, I found that it had been completely emptied, and all my personal belongings had already been moved into my newly assigned room on the third floor. My clothes had been hung in my closet, my uniforms had been taken to the tailor shop to be cleaned and pressed and would be returned by 4 p.m. that day. My leather shoes were being polished by one of the seven Marine stewards who worked at the Center House under the direction of the Chief Steward, Gunnery Sergeant Theodore F. Cherry.

There were six individual rooms on the second and third floors and one suite for the senior officer. Each room had a fireplace, no longer in use, but a holdover from the early days of 1904. There was a small shower, and toilet on each floor that was shared by all residents on that floor and each room had a sink. It was living as though you had suddenly been shuttled back to another time, but it was also very elegant and quite exclusive. There was no other group of officers in the entire Marine Corps who lived the way I was going to live for the next three years.

The first floor of the Center House housed an elegant drawing room, a small library, a bar built like a small British pub and a dining room. The meals were served in a formal fashion and were prepared by the house stewards who also served the meals. The senior house officer, Major Lester Stone, who was also the senior Marine White House Social Aide, sat at the head of the table and officiated at each meal. All other officers sat at the table in order of their rank seniority.

Each new officer was welcomed to the Barracks with a small cocktail party attended by all officers of the Barracks. I was greeted in this manner and was also welcomed into the smaller group of bachelor officers who lived in the Center House. Besides Major Stone, there was Captain Byron (Barney) T. Chen, not a Chinese officer, but an American of Polish descent whose grandparents immigrated from Russia and changed their name from something like Chenofski to Chen, thinking it was more American. Instead, Barney Chen was always thought to be Chinese until you met him and saw that he was a 6 foot 2 inch tall Caucasian Marine. Living there also was Captain McClendon G. Morris, from the University of North Carolina; Captain John Hamilton Gary, III, from VMI, my company commander; First Lieutenant Bobby G. Overcash, White House Social Aide; First Lieutenant. Wayne M. Wills, a former Brigade Commander at the US Naval Academy; First Lieutenant Tom Ryan, from Ohio State University; and First Lieutenant Willem Van

Hemert, an immigrant from The Netherlands who had been commissioned from the US Army. These were my new roommates at the most elite BOQ in the Marine Corps.

Colonel Platt, who lived two doors from the Center House in the Commanding Officer's Quarters, came to the party. He was a very gracious and charming Marine. I could see why he was the commanding officer and there was no doubt in my mind that he would become a general officer in due time. It was certain that a Barracks commanding officer, primarily because of the selective nomination process to become the commanding officer, would be selected for general officer rank when their name came before the selection board.

During the welcoming cocktail party, Colonel Platt asked me what qualification scores I had shot with the rifle and pistol. I told him that I was not a very good shot and that I was a marksman (the lowest rating) in both the rifle and pistol. Colonel Platt then told me that before the parade season began he expected me to shoot expert (the highest rating) with both the rifle and pistol. He told me that all parade officers were expected to be "double experts." He further instructed Captain Herkimer Harris, one of the premier shooters in the Marine Corps, to take me to Quantico and make me an expert shooter. Captain Harris was assigned to the Barracks as a weapons instructor in the Marine Corps Institute, the Marine Corps correspondence course school located at the Barracks.

I went to Quantico and in three days I learned how to fire the rifle and the pistol, and I shot officially for record as an expert in both weapons. This was the first time in my short Marine Corps career that I had ever shot expert, and for the rest of my career I always shot expert with both weapons. When I retired from the Marine Corps I had shot expert with the rifle and the pistol for 18 consecutive years. That was just one of the many things I owed to Colonel Platt, not to mention Captain Herk Harris, a USMC Distinguished Marksman, and a member of the U.S. Marine Corps Rifle and Pistol Team. Unfortunately, Captain Harris was later killed in action in the Vietnam War.

When I returned to the Barracks as a double expert, I made quite an impression on Colonel Platt. Apparently he received a very good report about my enthusiasm on the weapons ranges from Captain Harris, and he was pleased that I had accomplished the expert rating so quickly. I now had exactly one week to get ready for parade season.

May 1 through September 4 was the official parade season, and this meant that Marine Barracks would conduct two parades a week; every Tuesday afternoon at the Marine Corps War Memorial (commonly called the Iwo Jima Memorial) in Arlington, Virginia, and every Friday evening at the Marine Barracks. Both of these ceremonies are open to the public and draw large crowds. The Barracks parade regularly was drawing over 700 spectators to the evening parades which were held on the Barracks Quadrangle. Every Friday morning, temporary bleachers were set up to accommodate the crowds. Since that time, permanent bleachers have been installed, and the spectator capacity has greatly increased.

A mistake in this arena would not be good. I counted every step I took and made sure I hit my marks exactly when the other officers hit theirs. Every movement had to be exactly correct and in total unison so that the entire two ceremonial marching units on the parade ground did everything perfectly and together. Even a slight hesitation would be noticed because of the coordinated movement of all troops. It was, and continues to be, a great military spectacle to watch. I returned to the Barracks about 20 years after I had left and I was still able to count every step and knew exactly when a facing movement would be made and when a sword was to be drawn or returned to scabbard. Nothing had changed, and the movements were still the same. Why change a successful formula? The parades continue to amaze and impress all who see them, and troops from the Barracks also put on military shows throughout the country and around the world.

I was under a great deal of stress concerning my first parade. Most officers go through this stress before their first parade, and the only relief is a successful one with no mistakes. Friday evening, May 1, arrived, and I was about as tight as a high wire in a circus. I kept repeating the movements in my head and counting out the required steps. I also reminded myself not to stand at rigid attention because to do so could cause you to faint. There is a trick to standing ramrod straight while not actually being ramrod straight, and the secret is to make sure that your knees are not locked. The parade began, and there was no turning back. My troops knew it was my first parade, and they were all wishing me luck. As it turned out I had a perfect parade, no mistakes, no hesitations and all facing movements and marching steps were in perfect unison with the other five officers on the parade ground.

When we passed in review for the final phase of the parade, I felt as though someone had just taken a huge weight off my shoulders. The post parade celebration in the Center House was a gratifying and exuberant feeling. Colonel Platt congratulated me on an outstanding job and informed me that I would remain as the second platoon leader for the entire parade season of 1959. Although I was very happy about this turn of events, I still experienced a level of stress that I was unfamiliar with and found somewhat distressing.

As the parade season progressed, I was introduced to the other duties assigned to officers at the Barracks. I stood parade duty at the Marine Corps War Memorial, I participated as an honor guard for Marine officer funeral's at Arlington National Cemetery, I participated in numerous honors ceremonies for visiting heads of state and I stood at attention for fairly long times until our presence was no longer required at a varied number of social functions presented by President Eisenhower. I became familiar with his cabinet, especially Secretary of State Christian Herter and Secretary of Defense Hugh McElroy, who made numerous calls on the President in the White House. The Attorney General of the United States, Herbert Brownell, also was a frequent visitor and was always included in all social events. While most of Eisenhower's cabinet attended the numerous social events, on occasion, the three cabinet members mentioned above, State, Defense and the Attorney General, were always in attendance.

I became a very close friend of Captain Barney Chen. We seemed to strike a similar chord in almost everything we did at the Barracks and our closely allied sense of humor, plus our enjoyment of good times, was a ready prescription to lighten the severe pressures of serving at The Oldest Post in the Corps.

Officers serving at 8th and I were required to have all approved uniform items in their possession, except for the boat cloak, a uniform item dating back to Revolutionary War days. Although still available for purchase, it was no longer a required uniform item. In retrospect, I am sorry I never bought one just to have it today. Assignment to 8th and I meant spending a great deal of money on additional uniforms not normally required at other duty station in the Marine Corps.

In spite of all these regulations, traditions and customs, life at the Barracks was bearable for me as long as Barney and I could visit the numerous establishments in the Capitol. We particularly enjoyed going to the Potomac River waterfront and visiting the old oyster bars that were located near the foot of the 14th Street Bridge. While all these places are now long gone, when we were in Washington they were thriving. Our favorite was a place called Cy Ellis's Oyster Bar which was on the quay. They served fresh oysters shucked in front of you which were delicious, cold and salty, and an oyster boat was tied up on the river. The waterfront establishments eventually disappeared, but Cy Ellis did reopen somewhere near 14th Street in downtown Washington. Without the river, the sawdust, and the ancient wooden oyster barge, it simply wasn't the same.

Barney and I had achieved a reputation for being party animals, and this was no doubt enhanced with the discovery of a new bar and restaurant that opened in Southwest Washington two blocks from FBI National Headquarters called the *Market Inn*. After enjoying a 50 year run as one of the truly "in places" to go or be seen in Washington, the Market Inn no longer survives, having closed on December 31, 2009. Barney and I were at their opening night. We kept going there throughout our tours of duty in Washington and became such regulars at the establishment that John Mandis, the owner, affixed brass plaques in our honor on the back of two chairs. When the chairs wore out those plaques were removed and placed on a wall and remained there to the very last day of business.

With all the partying, there were many mornings when I was hung over, and while I was able to perform all of my ceremonial duties, I was identified as someone who seemed not to take the mission of the Barracks "too seriously." This placed me in the position of not always being too sure of my place in the Barracks and created a level of stress that I was not quite able to deal with properly.

One of the brighter spots of that time was that at every Friday evening parade, there were plenty of single women. If there was an attractive one, it was not difficult to invite her to the Center House for a drink. The atmosphere at the Barracks was always so "charged," and the "old world" charm of the Center House so overwhelming that no young lady could help but be impressed. It was in just such a circumstance that I met Evelyn McCormick, a secretary at the Department of Agriculture. She was a beautiful young, single woman who just happened to be two years older than I was. While I was 24 and Evelyn 26, I told her that I was also 26 just to make sure that I was playing on an even field. We hit it off very well and became an "item" at the Barracks. She was well-educated, having graduated from Georgetown University, and was the daughter of a college professor who could trace her family tree back to one of the First Families of Virginia (FFV).

Her mother, Gloria McCormick, whose maiden name was Mosby, claimed to have been a distant relative of that famous Confederate Rebel, John Singleton Mosby, who served on the staff of Confederate General J.E.B. Stuart. Gloria McCormick was extremely proud of her southern background which she never failed to discuss with anyone who would listen. She welcomed me into the family, no doubt visualizing a splendid southern wedding, complete with uniformed Marines and Southern belles in flowing gowns. She was always very courteous and genuine with me, and I enjoyed her company.

Parade season ended on Friday evening, September 4, 1959. I had successfully completed the season without a single mistake on the parade ground, and my platoon had been selected "best in the parade" three times by the weekly judges who graded every parade. Election Day was rapidly approaching in November, as was the annual Marine Corps Birthday Ball, which in Washington was a highlight of the Capitol's social season. The ball was held every year at the swank Shoreham Hotel and invitations were hard to come by. The guest list for the ball was controlled by the Commandant of the Marine Corps, who in 1959, was Randolph McCall Pate. All Marine activities in the Washington area were allocated an attendance quota, and everyone else was invited at the discretion of the Commandant. It was a hot ticket.

I had been notified that I was the youngest Marine officer in the Washington area and that I would be receiving the second piece of birthday cake at the Marine Corps Ball ceremony which, according to tradition, would be held on 10 November 1959, a Tuesday. I previously covered details of the Birthday Ball celebration when I was in Basic School. When a birthday cake is cut, the first piece of cake goes to the Guest of Honor and the second piece goes to the oldest Marine present, who then passes it to the youngest Marine present. I had planned to ask Evie to the Ball, but since the issue of my age was playing a major part in the ceremony, I told Evie that I had to work that evening and that I would take her out the following evening, which was November 11, Veteran's Day.

I attended the ball without a partner and waited for the cake cutting ceremony. I was honored when I found out that the oldest Marine present would be General Thomas Holcomb, the 17th Commandant of the Marine Corps, who was 80 years old. General Holcomb was one of the giants of the Marine Corps, and we stood side by side at the cake cutting ceremony. The Guest of Honor that evening was Secretary of Defense Hugh McElroy, and cutting and presenting the cake was the Commandant of the Marine Corps, General Randolph McCall Pate. I have a picture on the wall of my den that shows me receiving the piece of cake given to the youngest Marine. General Holcomb is at my right, and Secretary McElroy is applauding as I accept the cake from General Pate.

Parade season is a magical time at Marine Barracks. The afternoon parades on Tuesdays at the Marine Corps War Memorial are a popular tourist attraction, but the Friday night parades at Marine Barracks are a "reservations only" event that is performed to a packed house throughout the parade season. Admission is free, and the parade begins promptly at 8 p.m. and lasts for approximately an hour and a half. The pomp and circumstance of precision military marching and stirring marches played by the Marine Band and the Marine

Drum and Bugle Corps, performed under night skies and illuminated by perfectly placed spotlights, are crowd-pleasers that always leave the spectators amazed. Marching in these events is an honor, and it is an assignment that remains fresh in their minds of participants throughout their Marine Corps careers.

Since the parades are such a tourist magnet, there was always an opportunity to meet young women. Since they were at the parade, it followed that they must be attracted to the military and, therefore, it was quite easy to "cut one out of the herd" and invite her into the Center House for a cocktail. We cut a dashing figure in our "white-blue-white" uniforms (white dress cap, blue coat and white trousers), with leather Sam Browne belts and swords. We would casually look at the young women passing by on their way out of the Barracks grounds to see if there were any good looking woman we could pick out that we might select for an after parade drink. Since things had not worked out with Evie McCormack, I was, again, on the lookout!

One Friday evening I spied a young blonde woman who was wearing dark sunglasses in the middle of the evening. I was intrigued by that affectation, and I determined that I would try to meet her after the parade just because she was wearing sunglasses in the dark. She walked by me with another young blonde woman who was not wearing sunglasses. They were both attractive women, and they were dressed very well. I introduced myself and invited them to the Center House, which they happened to be standing in front of, for an after parade cocktail.

Once we got in the bar, I found out both young women were airline stewardesses. The one with the dark glasses, Sharron Shire, worked for Capital Airlines, and the other woman, Mary Anne Jorgensen, worked for American Airlines. Sharron was 5 feet 10 inches tall, was thin, with curly blond hair and had a deep tan that seemed to go well with the sunglasses. It turned out that she wore the sunglasses because she needed glasses and didn't like wearing them so she opted for prescription sunglasses. She flew the Miami to Washington run for Capital Airlines and roomed with Mary Anne who flew from Washington to Los Angeles for American Airlines.

Barney Chen immediately picked up Mary Anne, and we had a ready-made foursome. We decided to go to dinner at the Market Inn so we walked to the Naval Gun Factory, just down the street, to get Sharron's car which had to be moved one hour after the parade. We drove to the Market Inn in Sharron's brand new white 1960 Dodge convertible with red leather interior, a really flashy car which had been given to her by her father. As the evening wore on, I found out that Sharron, at the age of 18, went to work for a local Florida airline called Mackey Airlines, which regularly flew from Miami and Fort Lauderdale to the Bahamas and Cuba.

She had been flying since she was 18 and I met her in 1960 when she was 21 years old. I was impressed with the whole package; the new flashy convertible, the long legged, willowy blonde with the sunglasses, and the perfect tan. The fact that she was an airline stewardess was a definite plus in those days. These attributes impressed me enough to ask her out again. She agreed. We dated from May through September, and sometime in

September 1960 I asked Sharron to marry me. She accepted. We decided we would get married in New York City around Thanksgiving.

After parade season ended I took Sharron to New York City to meet Dad and Dora. They took us to dinner and a Broadway play. Both Dad and Dora assured me they thought Sharron was "very nice." We returned to Washington, and Sharron was happy to be back at Hunting Towers and a lifestyle with which she was totally comfortable.

In October, I returned to New York City to find a Catholic Church that would marry us. Sharron was essentially a non-practicing Catholic, and I was a Jew who was not going to convert. It seemed like an almost impossible task to accomplish. I drove around the neighborhood and then up 5th Avenue looking for a Catholic church. The first one I came upon was the world famous St. Patrick's Cathedral at 50th Street and 5th Avenue, the Cathedral of New York City.

I went in and met the rector of St. Patrick's. I informed him I was interested in getting married there and that I was Jewish and the woman I was marrying was a Roman Catholic, and I would agree to raise my children as Catholics. The Monsignor said there was no way I could get married in St. Patrick's under any circumstances. I then played my trump card and informed him I was going to see Cardinal Spellman, the Military Vicar of the Armed Forces. I told the Monsignor that I would inform Cardinal Spellman that I had promised to raise my children as Catholic, and I was marrying a Catholic woman who had never been married before, and who had promised her mother, on her death bed, to be married in a Catholic church. The Monsignor hastily reconsidered and informed me that I could get married in the Lady Chapel, a small chapel behind the main altar of the Cathedral.

He informed me that it was a favorite location for small weddings, and, since he was unable to conduct the wedding himself, he would assign a Maryknoll Missionary who was on a sabbatical leave from his posting in China, to officiate at my wedding. He asked me to wait in the office and meet with the Maryknoll priest, a Father John Kelly Walsh. In a few minutes, I met a very old priest with white hair and the smile of a leprechaun. He had blue eyes, which seemed to twinkle, was somewhat stooped and greeted me with a warm and enthusiastic handshake. He told me he had been in China for almost 45 years and spent every seventh year here at St. Patrick's because he was New Yorker, and he missed the comforts of America. He seemed genuinely amused that I had pressured the Monsignor. He also said he was only too happy to work with me on my forthcoming marriage.

We left the office, and he took me to see the Lady Chapel. It was, and still is, a very beautiful chapel, located behind the main altar of St. Patrick's. Since there would be only seven people at the wedding, us, my best man, Barney Chen, Sharron's Maid of Honor which would be her sister Audrey, her father, "GJ," plus Dad and Dora, the chapel seemed just perfect. After some discussion, Father Walsh said, "Let's see, Sharron is a non-practicing Catholic, Peter you are a Jew, and your Best Man has a Chinese surname. Yes, there is no way you can get married at the main alter, but Lady Chapel will be fine." Father Walsh looked at his calendar and told me that the best date for him in November would be Thursday, the 24th. This happened to be Thanksgiving Day, but it seemed perfect to me, so I agreed on the date and told him we would all assemble at the Lady Chapel at 5 p.m. on that date, which was the time he suggested.

I returned to the Barracks quite proud of my accomplishment and very thrilled that I would be getting married in one of the most famous places in New York City. When I told Sharron about my New York adventure she seemed quite pleased. The next issue was where to go on our honeymoon. I suggested Montego Bay on the island of Jamaica and Sharron agreed. We made reservations at a rather unique hotel called the Hacton House, and we would depart from Idlewild Airport on the morning of November 25.

Since we were such a small group, there certainly wasn't any need to reserve a restaurant for the wedding dinner, especially since it was Thanksgiving Day and most people would be home enjoying a holiday meal. As I thought about a restaurant, I remembered that the world famous Waldorf-Astoria Hotel was located only two blocks from St. Patrick's Cathedral. We could walk there and have dinner in the famous Peacock Alley Restaurant. I was certain I could pull it off.

I departed the Barracks for the wedding on Monday, November 21, 1960. I had taken two weeks leave, and this would accommodate the wedding, my honeymoon and a move to our new home in Burke, Virginia. I had made friends with a Marine aviator who was assigned to the Barracks by the name of Keith O'Keefe. Keith's wife, Natalie, was the daughter of Judge Paul Brown, who owned a three-bedroom house near his plantation on Burke Road located next to Major O'Keefe's home. Since we could carpool to the Barracks, I rented the house, and it was to this house that the newly married Beck's would move into upon their return from Montego Bay.

Looking back, I remember that Colonel Platt was being transferred to take over the 6th Marine Regiment at Camp Lejeune, North Carolina. The Barracks was losing a great C.O., and I was losing a friend and mentor who had personally guided and nurtured my young career in the Marine Corps. I was sorry to see Colonel Platt go and that he could not share in my happiness at getting married. I will always be grateful to Major General Jonas Mansfield Platt, USMC (deceased). He is my personal hero.

We arrived in New York on the evening of 21 November. On Thanksgiving morning, we got everything ready to go to the airport the following morning. We would be flying to Jamaica through Nassau in the Bahamas, and the weather reports showed only tropical weather and sunny skies. I hoped that my marriage would match the weather we were going to encounter.

We were married in the Lady Chapel. After the ceremony a light rain began to fall, so we hailed a cab for the two block trip to the Waldorf-Astoria Hotel and the Peacock Alley Restaurant. The Maître'd asked if I had a reservation. I was surprised to see the room was full. I told him we had just gotten married, and I needed a table for seven. Several of the diners noticed my uniform and Sharron's white wedding dress and began applauding. Barney came in wearing his uniform adorned with the medals he had been awarded in China and several World War II medals and more of the diners applauded. The headwaiter immediately made room for us, and we had a wonderful evening in the Peacock Alley of the Waldorf-Astoria without any reservations. Many of the diners sent over drinks and kept coming by our table to congratulate Sharron and me. I couldn't have planned it any better. To this day I tell people I got married in St. Patrick's Cathedral and had my reception at the Peacock Alley Restaurant of the Waldorf-Astoria. Yes, we did, and it is all true.

The following morning, Dad drove us to Idlewild (now JFK) Airport in Jamaica, New York, for our flight to Montego Bay in the island of Jamaica. We found the hotel to be an old time British era hotel, full of eccentrics, including the owner of the hotel, a Major Nyland, who walked around the property with a large parrot on his shoulder. Sharron was not impressed by the hotel, but I loved it, and felt it was a real tropical hotel that Somerset Maugham would have loved.

We returned to Washington and moved into our house in Burke, Virginia. I began to commute to the Barracks daily with Major O'Keefe, now my next door neighbor, and Barracks life resumed as normal. I remained the platoon leader of the second platoon of the MCI Company, and even during the winter months we continued weekly rehearsals.

President John Fitzgerald Kennedy was inaugurated as the President of the United States on January 20, 1961, and my platoon was designated to be the security troops around the inaugural stand in front of the Capitol. It would be from this stand that President Kennedy would be sworn into office as the 35th, and the first Catholic, President of the United States by the Chief Justice of the United States, Earl Warren. My troops were wearing dress blue uniforms and heavy green wool overcoats as the weather had turned extremely cold. The inauguration was scheduled for 10 a.m., and in typical Marine Corps fashion, we had been standing out in the cold since 8 a.m.

The inauguration began promptly at 10 a.m., and when Cardinal Cushing began to give the invocation, an electrical fire broke out in the podium and smoke came pouring out while he was speaking. There was a great deal of activity all around the Cardinal, and the fire was extinguished in short order. The Cardinal kept speaking throughout the emergency efforts, and my troops remained at attention throughout the event. To this day no one knows what caused the fire. I insist it was God's way of showing that He wasn't very happy with Cardinal Cushing's extremely long invocation. The rest of the ceremony went off without a hitch. I was proud to be a part of President Kennedy's inauguration. I was also able to verify, at very close quarters, that Jackie Kennedy was as beautiful as everyone said she was.

We kept rehearsing endlessly for the upcoming parade season, and during one such extended rehearsal period, to break the monotony for my troops, I assumed the age-old sword dueling stance and pretended to challenge the adjacent platoon commander to a duel. He finally understood what I was trying to do, but just before he began to draw his sword the Barracks Executive Officer appeared in the walkway.

He was livid, called an end to the rehearsal and commanded me to follow him into his office. I received a long lecture as to my total lack of dedication to the Marine Corps and the mission of the Barracks, my warped sense of humor and, finally, I was informed that I was relieved of duties as a parade officer. I thought the punishment way out of line. I attempted to explain what I was doing, however, LtCol William F. Doehler, an Annapolis graduate and former enlisted Marine, had long ago lost both his empathy for his fellow Marines and his sense of humor. He had been the Barracks Operations Officer (S-3) and, after promotion to Lieutenant Colonel, was moved up to Barracks Executive Officer.

The following day I was assigned duties as the Barracks Special Services Officer and given my own office in the Band Hall of the U.S. Marine Band. The job description for this position is roughly to conduct all athletic events at the Barracks, to include all intramural competitions, to care for and maintain the Barracks mascot, a purebred English bulldog named Chesty, to write and publish a Barracks newspaper and to maintain the Barracks gym and all athletic equipment. In addition, I would serve as a Parade guide for visitors, be a fill-in in the event one of the regular marching officers became ill, and march in whatever parades, ceremonies or funerals that I may be assigned. Thus, my days of regular parade duty at the Marine Barracks came to a rather abrupt ending. When the 1961 parade season began on May 5, 1961, I was the main gate parade guide and one of my clerks, Lance Corporal Frank Coniglio, was assigned the duty of marching the mascot across the Center Walk to begin every evening parade to the accompanying "oohs and ahhs" of the spectators.

I was not particularly disappointed in my new job. I liked my new office in the Band Hall, and I became friends with the Leader of the Marine Band, Lieutenant Colonel Albert Schoepper. I listened to rehearsals, participated in concerts performed in the White House as a guide and security detail and thoroughly enjoyed getting to meet a group of Marines that I would never otherwise have met. All the members of the U.S. Marine Band are professional musicians. They are recruited for duty with the Band only and only in Washington, D.C. They do not go to boot camp, but spend hours learning to march, under the tutelage of a regular Marine noncommissioned officer who has served as a drill instructor at a Recruit Depot. This Marine is designated as the Drum Major of the Marine Corps, and he is charged with making the band a top notch marching unit. They have never failed to accomplish the task, and the Marine Band is the finest musical and marching organization in the land. I also was allowed to sit in on auditions for the band. They were extremely difficult as each potential band member is required to play three instruments and was provided with music for each one just seconds before they were required to play the instrument. Only the truly best musicians became permanent members of the U.S. Marine Band.

On July 31, 1961, General Pate, the former Commandant of the Marine Corps who had given me the piece of cake at the 1959 Marine Birthday Ball, died. His funeral would be held at Arlington National Cemetery. Since he was a four star general, four platoons of Marines were required, and I was detailed to one of the platoons. I thought it very ironic that I was burying the officer who only two short years ago had given me a piece of cake at the Birthday Ball. I was very touched during the funeral, and proud to be a part of the ceremony. I felt that I had a special bond with General Pate.

Life in Burke was also very pleasant. We participated in many local events and were welcomed into the home and family of Judge Brown. Keith O'Keefe and his wife, Natalie, also included Sharron and me in their social circles and we got to meet many "old southern" Northern Virginia society. Christmas 1961 turned out to be a very special period for me in Northern Virginia as the entire region was blanketed in snow, making the holiday season memorable and enchanting. We lost power, warmed ourselves by fireplace heat and sledded through the hills surrounding our house. We cut down a local pine tree for a Christmas tree, and we anticipated the arrival of our first child, which was scheduled for some time in March 1962. It was a magical winter and holiday period, and we shared it with the O'Keefe's and the Brown's, in much the same manner that the Confederates must have celebrated the holidays during the Civil War. The charming manners and customs of old southerners can make even the hearts of "dyed in the wool" northerners melt, and believe that adage, The South will Rise Again!

In January 1962, I was promoted to the rank of captain. Shortly thereafter, I received notification that I would be transferred to the 2nd Marine Division at Camp Lejeune, North Carolina. While I had certainly enjoyed my tour of duty, and it enhanced my career, I don't attend Barracks reunions and, except for Barney Chen/Schenn, do not keep in touch with any other officer with whom I served at the Barracks.

The Barracks had no medical facility, and we were authorized to obtain civilian medical care. The Naval Gun Factory, the site of our closest Navy medical facility, did not have an obstetrician, and we were fortunate to receive prenatal care from a highly respected Northern Virginia physician who had hospital privileges at George Washington University Hospital. Sharron had an easy pregnancy and on March 22 she went into labor, and we rushed her to the hospital. Early in the morning of Friday, March 23, 1962, Eric Louis Beck was born. I chose the middle name of Louis, in honor of my father, and that is how Eric Louis Beck became a reality. Sharron did not stay in the hospital long, and in a few short days we moved Eric to our house in Burke, Virginia.

On April 18, 1962, I received the orders directing me to report for duty to the 2nd Marine Division by May 18. The official departure from the Barracks is always a ceremony. The departing officer is given the opportunity to request three songs which are then played by the Marine Drum and Bugle Corps. The three songs I requested were John Philip Sousa's stirring march, The Stars and Stripes Forever, The March of the Women Marines (a rarely played March that has always been one of my favorites because it has a wonderful drum portion in the march) and the theme from the movie Exodus.

After the "play off," the departing officer goes to the Center House where he is presented with a sterling silver, glass bottomed tankard, suitably engraved with his name, rank and dates of his tour of duty at the Barracks. The tankard is then filled with beer, and if he can drink the tankard of beer in 2.5 seconds or less, his name is engraved on a wall plaque as a member of the "2.5 Second Club." I had practiced for the event and was able to down the beer in 2.3 seconds, which resulted in my name being added to the plaque. I was also cited as one of the few officers who had received all three pieces of silver that the Barracks presented to officers for significant events. It has been a tradition that officers who get married while at the Barracks receive a sterling silver wine bucket suitably engraved with the name of the bride and groom along with the date of the marriage. If an officer has a child while at the Barracks, he receives a sterling silver baby cup with the child's name and birth date engraved on the cup and upon the departure he is presented with the sterling silver tankard. I received all three during my tour of duty which, it turned out, was very rare. At the time of my departure, no one could recall another officer who had accomplished the "trifecta."

My son Eric kept the silver baby cup until it was, unfortunately, melted during a forest fire in 2004 in San Diego when he lost his house to the raging fire. I bought another silver cup for him and presented it to him as a Christmas gift in 2008. While it does not look like the old fashioned heavy silver Victorian cup which was presented to me in 1962, it does represent the silver cup and is suitably engraved to remind Eric of the special gesture to him by the Officers of the Marine Barracks in Washington.

CHAPTER 11

FLEET MARINE FORCE, ATLANTIC

THE 2ND MARINE DIVISION

Sharron, baby Eric and I departed Burke, Virginia, for Jacksonville, North Carolina. I had rented a three-bedroom house in a civilian housing area because military quarters were not available. Before reporting for duty, I located Colonel Platt, who was the Commanding Officer of the 6th Marine Regiment. As an infantry officer and a newly promoted captain, it was very important to obtain a command. This was considered a requirement for further promotion and, at the rank of captain, a rifle company was what every infantry captain desired. This was, unfortunately, not always attainable since there are only 36 rifle companies in a standard Marine infantry division.

I asked Colonel Platt if there were any rifle companies available in the 6th Marine Regiment. He did not have any companies needing a commander, but he did tell me that his good friend, Colonel Robert M. Richards, the Commanding Officer of the 2nd Marine Regiment, had a few openings, and he would speak to him on my behalf. I thanked Colonel Platt and told him how glad I was to see him and how much I appreciated his efforts.

I reported for duty on Friday, May 18, 1962, and was introduced to the Division Commanding General, Major General Frederick M. Wieseman, who informed me that I was being assigned to the 2nd Regiment. He directed me to report to the Regimental Commander, Colonel Richards. Somehow, I felt that Colonel Platt had again gone to bat for me. I reported to the 2nd Marine Regiment for duty and was introduced to Colonel Richards, a Navy Cross recipient from World War II, who told me that he heard good things about me from Colonel Platt and that, on the strength of Colonel Platt's recommendation, he was sending me to the 1st Battalion for duty as the commanding officer of Delta Company. For an infantry captain, it was the answer to my prayers. Little did I know that I was about to meet the worst officer I ever encountered during my twenty-two year career in the Marine Corps.

Lieutenant Colonel Patrick William Williams was the Commanding Officer of the 1st Battalion (the name of this commander has been changed to a fictitious name). I reported to him, and I was truly happy to begin my duty in the 2nd Marine Division. LtCol Williams immediately took the wind out of my sails by informing me he did not like officers who used connections, and furthermore, he particularly did not like officers from "8th and I." Apparently, unknown to me, LtCol Williams was going to give Delta Company to another officer when he received word that Delta Company was to be assigned to me. He did not like someone above him making assignments within his battalion. He also knew I had just reported from Marine Barracks, Washington, and it didn't take a genius to figure out that Colonel Platt, my former C.O. in Washington, must have pulled some strings for me. He further said he would keep a close eye on me, and at the first sign that I couldn't perform, he intended to relieve me as a commanding officer. Welcome to the 1st Battalion I thought.

I reported to Delta Company where I met the company First Sergeant, Vernon Loveall. First Sgt Loveall called the company staff together and introduced me as the new commander. I said a few words to the staff and retired to my office hoping I had made a favorable first impression. Being a company commander was not a new experience for me since I had already had that duty with the 3rd Marines in Japan and Okinawa.

First Sgt Loveall informed me that our battalion was scheduled to depart on a six-month deployment to the Mediterranean as the 6th Fleet rapid deployment force, and our embarkation and departure date was already set for September 20. Again, embarkation was nothing new to me either since I had successfully embarked Hotel Company out of Japan to the Philippines and then Okinawa.

I looked forward to the challenge, but I was having a difficult time dealing with the fact that I would be leaving Sharron with a six-month old baby as I departed for a six months deployment in the Mediterranean Sea. While I rationalized that this was what a Marine wife was faced with, and they knew about long deployments, I had doubts about whether Sharron would be emotionally and physically up to the task. My view of her then was not that of a reliable and supportive partner, but rather of an attractive woman who needed to be kept active and interested in what was happening around her. She was not a person, in my mind, who could handle all the stresses associated with being a mother of a small baby with her husband at sea. Like it or not, that was the way it was going to be, and I hoped for the best.

Preparing a rifle company for such a long deployment meant many hours of preparation, inspection and training. There were many nights in the field, surf landing practices, night marches, field food preparation exercises, tent inspection, field equipment testing, repair and replacement of faulty or worn out equipment, and physical conditioning. At 90 days before embarkation, we set a personnel cutoff date, which meant that no new people would either come into or get out of the unit. This enabled us to train the team that would depart for the Mediterranean, and build a solid group that knew they were staying together for the next nine to ten months.

Throughout all of these preparations LtCol Williams was all over us. He inspected everything and everyone. He was unforgiving and dogmatic, never demonstrating the slightest trace of a sense of humor or compassion. He was all business in a chilling and very intimidating manner. A successful deployment was usually a sure way for him to make colonel, and conversely, a poor deployment would almost guarantee him that he was at his terminal rank with no hope of further promotion.

The Executive Officer, Major Kenneth High, was the exact opposite of LtCol Williams. He was kind, understanding, and seemed to follow LtCol Williams trying to repair the damage he had caused to the morale of the troops. One of the most interesting things about LtCol Williams is that the senior officers above him thought he was an outstanding officer. The reason for this is that whenever a senior officer was in our area, LtCol Williams suddenly became the best officer you could wish for, kind, clever, witty and friendly. This demeanor lasted only until the senior officer departed the area after which LtCol Williams reverted to the horrible leader he truly was.

He watched me like a hawk, but I never gave him any reason to relieve me. One time, in the privacy of his office with the door closed, he threatened me by telling me that he was going to break me on the Mediterranean cruise. I looked him in the eye and told him it would take a better man than him to do that. He got livid, his face turned red, and he picked up a pistol magazine laying on his desk and threw it at me. I was standing at attention in front of his desk, and the pistol magazine hit me in the face. I didn't move. I stood there and looked him square in the face, and at that moment he knew that he had gone too far. He regained his composure and then ordered me out of the office. I decided not to do anything about the incident, but to wait and see what happened next. I think LtCol Williams probably spent an anxious 48 hours waiting for the other shoe to drop, but I did nothing. The next time I saw him he was all business, but I noticed that the edginess he had previously displayed towards me was somewhat subdued. I hoped that it would remain that way. As it turned out, it did.

I told Sharron about the deployment date, and she said that the Battalion Officers Wives Club was already preparing for the deployment and that a group of wives were planning to go over to one of the major ports during our deployment and she was planning on going. By the end of August, we had not yet received our itinerary, so the Battalion Officers Wives Club could make no plans where to meet us for a reunion in Europe.

We did know that we would be departing for the Mediterranean from the port of Morehead City, North Carolina, a port located about 20 miles north of Camp Lejeune. On September 1, the battalion officers met with Captain Alan B. Pridmore, USN, who was the Commodore of Amphibious Squadron 4. He told us that the seven ships of the squadron were:

- USS *Mount McKinley* (AGC 7, an amphibious command and control ship.
- USS *Telfair* (APA 210), USS *Fremont*-(APA-44)) and USS *Chilton* (APA-33) which were amphibious assault ships.

- USS *Fort Mandan*-(LSD-21) and USS *Ashland* (LSD-1). An LSD was a Landing Ship, Dock, which could flood an interior well deck for water launching amphibious vehicles.
- USS *Waldo County* LST 1163, which was a type of landing ship that could land tanks and heavy equipment directly on the beach.

Unit ship assignments were also announced at this meeting, and my company was assigned to USS *Telfair*, which would be our home for the next six months. We would be spending Christmas and New Year's in Athens, Greece, and this would be the destination to which some of the officer's wives would travel to join their husbands. Their trip would not be subsidized, and all expenses would be borne by the individuals who would be traveling.

The mission of the amphibious squadron was to make a landing in a hostile environment anywhere in the Mediterranean on extremely short notice. Once committed, the landing force must be prepared to engage an enemy force immediately upon landing and hold a beach head until reinforcements arrived. The landing force must also be prepared to evacuate American nationals from any location in the Mediterranean, either by air, land or sea. This makes it necessary to task organize each landing force unit with the necessary troops and equipment to accomplish all of these missions without the need for immediate reinforcement.

Our organization, to be known as Landing Force Mediterranean 3-62, was composed of one each of the following elements:

- Infantry battalion
- Helicopter squadron
- Artillery battery with six 105 mm howitzers
- 8 inch howitzer platoon, self-propelled with two guns
- Tank platoon with five heavy tanks
- Antitank assault platoon, consisting of the *Ontos* antitank vehicles, each carrying six mounted 106 mm recoilless rifles.
- Amphibious tractor platoon with six amphibious tractors capable of operating in water or on land, and carrying twenty troops inside the hull of each vehicle.
- Reconnaissance platoon
- Force supply detachment
- Landing support platoon (engineers)
- Motor transport platoon, with all of their trucks
- Division support platoon (personnel and payroll services)
- Pioneer battalion platoon (beach landing support)

- Equipment maintenance platoon
- A medical detachment of doctors, dentists and medical support personnel sufficient to establish a front line medical facility.

All of these personnel and their equipment were a part of the landing force, and all of them fit aboard our seven-ship task force. Space aboard ship was always at a premium, and embarked Marines spent their time being overly crowded and eager to get off the ship. Being alone aboard ship was never an option.

We were informed that, for security reasons, the task force would only go into three ports of call with all seven ships. These ports would be Genoa, Italy; Barcelona, Spain; and Athens, Greece. At all other times, the task force would be split into two units so that if there was an enemy strike, at least 50 percent of the force would remain ready to carry out the mission. My task force component would always be separated from the command unit, meaning that we would rarely be in a liberty port with LtCol Williams and the staff. We also found out that while the main task force would be celebrating the 187th Birthday of the Marine Corps on November 10 in Taranto, Italy, our component would be celebrating it in Valletta, the capital of the island of Malta. The prospect of seeing less and less of LtCol Williams made me personally very happy.

On September 18, after months of briefings, exercises, inspections and physical training, Battalion Landing Team (BLT) 1-2, embarked aboard ships at Morehead City and departed for the Mediterranean. The crossing of the Atlantic was extremely slow as we had to sail as slow as the slowest ship in our convoy. This meant that all the ships had to keep the LST *Waldo County* in sight. With a full load of troops, tanks, amphibious tractors and the heavy landing ramps always attached to her sides, she did not cut a dashing figure through the waves.

We arrived in Gibraltar on October 1, but we could not leave the ship because we had not received permission to land there. We crossed the Straits and continued to our rendezvous with the 2nd Battalion of the 6th Marine Regiment which we would be relieving as the landing force. On the designated date, we had a formal relief ceremony aboard *Mount McKinley*. Our troops were not required to attend, and immediately following the change of command our troop element, composed of USS *Telfair*, USS *Fort Mandan* and USS *Waldo County* (the slow LST) departed for Golfe Juan, a small coastal resort town on the French Riviera and our first liberty port in the Mediterranean.

It was early October, no longer the tourist season. The weather was much warmer than North Carolina had been and all of us looked forward to getting off the ship and walking on land. Liberty instructions were rigid and uncompromising. Our mission was to be a force in readiness so at no time could an embarked unit have more than 50 percent of its personnel ashore. This was for the same reason that our amphibious squadron was always split. Readiness was paramount, and that was the watchword throughout our force. I drew up rosters for my company to insure that we always had 50 percent of our troops aboard ship. I found out that many troops did not want to go ashore but would rather remain aboard ship with half the troops gone. These personnel became a part of the crew for the duration of the voyage, however, I made sure that they knew they would have immediate priority whenever they desired to go ashore.

During the second month of our tour, I cancelled this policy. I found out that most of the troops who elected to stay aboard ship, did so out of shyness or a reluctance to observe or live in a foreign culture. I sponsored tours for my "reluctant nellies," and forced them to go ashore. I got tremendous assistance from the local American Express offices in the various ports we visited, and as a group we toured many local places of interest.

My officers and I escorted the troops on these enforced tours, and I thoroughly enjoyed them. I made sure that, at some point, we stopped at a local restaurant where the troops could sample the local foods and wines. I think the wines won out over the food, but we enjoyed the tours and this made me feel very good about my new policy of forced indoctrination. The feedback I received from the troops seemed to indicate that they also enjoyed the tours. I like to think that there are men throughout America who look back on their tour of duty in the Mediterranean and tell their grandchildren about the overly enthusiastic Marine Captain who took them on forced tours in Europe. I hope they tell the tales with humor and fond remembrance.

We arrived at Golfe Juan on October 7, anchored in the protected harbor and then went ashore in small boats that dropped us off at a pier which the Navy always called the "fleet landing." It was from this landing that you returned to your ship, and if you missed the last boat, which departed at midnight, you were considered to be "AWOL" (absent without leave). The fleet landing was in a small harbor filled with yachts and sailboats belonging to the rich who inhabited the Cote De Azur during the season. You could take a bus to Cannes, Nice or Monte Carlo. Cannes was located to the south of Golfe Juan, and Nice and Monte Carlo were north. Interestingly, both areas were serviced by the same coastal road, and were well within our allowable liberty distance range which required that we could be no more than two hours away from the ship.

While officers were required to wear civilian clothes on liberty, the troops were required to wear their uniforms. While the officers enjoyed the anonymity, the troops always felt discriminated against. Ultimately, there was a certain benefit to wearing a uniform as most of the troops found out after their first forays into the mysteries of "foreign shores."

My first adventure on the French Riviera was to travel to Cannes. I had read about Cannes and had seen it in numerous movies, plus almost all the beautiful people on the Riviera seemed to congregate in Cannes. It was the site of the famed Cannes International Film Festival, and the place where topless beaches reigned supreme. I arrived in Cannes on the coastal bus from Golfe Juan and found my way to the world famous Majestic Hotel. This was an international landmark often seen in movies or written about in novels. I went to the bar, ordered a drink, and sat back to contemplate my good fortune at being on the French Riviera, being a rifle company commander, and being a Captain of Marines. In my mind it simply didn't get much better than that.

As I was sitting at the bar minding my own business, I was approached by an attractive young woman with dark hair and an excellent command of English. She introduced herself and told me that her name was Jacqueline Boniface and that she lived in Nice. She asked me if I was an American Marine, a fact that was rather easy to ascertain since I had my hair cut "high and tight," and looked as if my clothing had been stuffed in some closet for quite some time.

We spoke for a long time and then she took me to a small restaurant for dinner and drinks. I enjoyed her company, but I was very wary about her motives. While I could not see any reason for her kindness to me, I did not fully trust her. At around 10:30 p.m. I informed her that I had to get back to my ship, which was anchored in Golfe Juan. She informed me that this was on the way to Nice and that she would be happy to drive me back to Golfe Juan. I agreed, and we got in to her black Mercedes coupe. She took me directly back to the fleet landing dock while I was constantly looking in the rear view mirror to see if she was being followed. She dropped me off at the dock and asked me if I was planning to go on liberty again tomorrow. I told her that I was, and she said she would meet me at the dock at noon if I wanted her to. I jumped at the offer and told her I would meet her tomorrow. I then boarded the liberty boat and returned to the ship.

I did not discuss my good fortune with anyone. The following morning I was curious to see if there would be anyone waiting at the dock in a black Mercedes. I arrived earlier than noon and shortly she arrived in her car, and I drove off with her. She drove me to the perfume factory town of Grasse where we had another wonderful day. In the late afternoon, we headed towards Monte Carlo, and she seemed intimately familiar with all the places we visited. I must admit that, for the next five days, I enjoyed one of the most exciting times of my life. I felt as though I was in some movie being made in Hollywood with the benefits of a wonderful looking woman, coupled with absolutely delightful weather, all of which was enjoyed from a sleek, high powered car.

At the end of my six day liberty, I said farewell to my benefactor without ever finding out her motivation or, for that matter, what it was she did for a living that allowed her to live in an obviously privileged lifestyle that most people can only dream about. She never asked me for any money and was quite free with her own. I would say that this was a once in a lifetime experience except, thanks to the U.S. Marine Corps, this would prove to be wrong as later events in life unfolded.

As our ship departed Golfe Juan, most Marines seemed to look longingly towards the shore. Perhaps I joined them. We were now the 6th Fleet Landing Force and our amphibious squadron headed towards the island of Corsica where we would conduct two weeks of field exercises. The only thing I knew about Corsica was that it was the birthplace of Napoleon Bonaparte.

We conducted an amphibious landing near St. Florent on October 16. Once ashore our units began to move inland against an "aggressor" force that was already on the island and would act as the "enemy power" during the field exercise. In our briefings before the landing we were given a scenario which was to be the premise under which we, as the Sixth

Fleet Landing Force, was to land on the beaches of St. Florent. What we were not immediately told was that the aggressor force that we would face was the world famous French Foreign Legion.

The island itself is split into a northern and southern section, with the capital city of Ajaccio located in the southern portion of the island. Our landing and subsequent field operations were conducted in the more mountainous regions of the north and proved to be a strong motivator for the troops. The Foreign Legion took their role of aggressor very seriously and moved mostly at night in attempts to infiltrate our positions. Both sides used blank ammunition and the judges, who determined either victory or defeat, were both American and French. We received resupply by helicopter and remained ashore for two weeks.

At the conclusion of the exercise, which proved very beneficial to both forces, we enjoyed two days of military contests, field meets, and a large cookout, featuring the best of what our combined field cooks could offer. Our troops were amazed that the Foreign Legion received a daily ration of red wine and fresh baked baguettes of bread with canned cheese. While American troops cannot legally drink on duty and no alcohol is ever served aboard ship, rules were disregarded during the two day "stand-down" in honor of the time honored Legion traditions. While our troops marveled at the rations of the French, the Legionnaires were very taken with our "C" rations. There were many trades made during those two days with our troops enjoying French bread and red wine and the Legionnaires downing ham and limas and beans and franks.

The troops were further impressed by the multinational nature of the Legion. While all the officers were French, the troops were from all over the world and spoke many languages. All orders, however, were given in French, and all Legionnaires spoke French fluently. I found a few Germans in the group and was able to converse with them quite well. I had some doubts that some of the older German noncommissioned officers had as they stated, "Never served in the German army during World War II." After all, it was only 18 years since the end of that war. What was probably far more important during our exercise with the Foreign Legion was the possibly world shattering crisis that was occurring between Russia and the United States over the island of Cuba.

Just before our relieving the 2nd Battalion, 6th Marines as the landing force, an American U-2 spy plane flying over Cuba detected what appeared to be long tubes being transported on large flatbed trucks. Additionally, there appeared to be bare sites throughout the island that were newly excavated and which were all on the US side of the island facing Florida. Overflights of other aircraft detected the silhouettes of Russian MIG fighters on the ground. Subsequently, Cuba shot down an American U-2 plane, and the pilot was killed, the only casualty of the Cuban Missile Crises.

President Kennedy confronted Premier Kruschev and finally got an admission from the Russian Premier that Russia was positioning missiles with nuclear warheads on the island of Cuba in direct answer to the stationing of US missiles with nuclear warheads in Turkey. What followed was a series of crises which resulted in a naval blockade of Cuba, twenty-four hour per day aircraft surveillance, and a positioning of American troops entirely around the island who were prepared to invade at a moments notice.

All of this military saber rattling was accompanied by international calls for immediate arbitration with the Secretary General of the United Nations, U Thant of Burma, pleading for calm from both the United States and Russia. During all of these issues, the Marine Corps dispatched the 2nd Battalion of the 8th Marine Regiment to Morehead City, North Carolina, where they loaded aboard ship and headed towards Cuba. This unit would be the first wave landing force if the invasion of Cuba was directed, and it was also the unit that was scheduled to relieve our battalion in the Mediterranean in February 1963.

When 2/8 left for Cuba, our landing force in the Mediterranean was ordered to remain there "indefinitely," as our time in the Mediterranean would be dictated by conditions in Cuba. During the next two weeks, Russia and the United States came closer to a nuclear war than ever before or since. In the end, Premier Kruschev agreed to take his missiles, planes and troops out of Cuba, and the United States agreed to remove their missiles from Turkey. In the interim, an American armada of ships and troops totally blockaded Cuba allowing nothing to leave or enter the island. The entire confrontation ended on October 28, 1962, at about the time we were enjoying our two day beach "stand down" with the Foreign Legion on the island of Corsica.

The exercises on Corsica were very successful with the Legionnaires keeping the action fast and furious throughout the two weeks ashore. Their experiences in Indochina made them highly mobile and flexible to any situation that developed on the ground. They were particularly capable in night operations and moved throughout the exercise area in total darkness with considerable ease and accuracy. We learned a lot about night movement and night land navigation from the Legion. It was a lesson that would serve me very well a few years down the road when I became familiar with the country the Legion called French Indochina and we called Vietnam.

On October 31, we began to back load our ships. This is a lengthy process using the principle of "last out, first in," meaning that we had to reload all of our equipment and supplies in the exact order that we unloaded it to have it ready to unload during the next landing, in the appropriate order of necessity, which, might be another training exercise or the real thing.

Along with back loading in the proper order, all equipment had to be steam cleaned before re-embarkation. This was because our ships had to be protected from insect or rodent infestation. One particular animal that presented a real problem was called the Mediterranean snail, which, if uncontrolled, could cause irreparable damage to crops in the United States if it were ever to arrive on American soil alive. All of this was accomplished by individual units and the landing support platoon that steam cleaned everything on the beach head. On November 4, we were totally loaded and ready to depart Corsica. Before departure, we were informed that the Cuban Missile crisis response had only caused our landing force to be extended in the Mediterranean by one month, and our relief by 2/8 was now scheduled for March 7, 1963.

This was one of the times that our squadron would split up, and half of the ships departed for Taranto, Italy while our component departed for the island of Malta. Since both components would be in port over the Marine Corps Birthday on 10 November, we were instructed to schedule an official Birthday Ball in Malta. Each component had a Commanding Officer of Troops, which in our case was Captain George W. Memmer, the commanding officer of the embarked artillery battery, and who was a mustang (former enlisted man who had received a commission) with about twenty years of service. This made him the senior embarked Marine officer in our component of ships and, therefore, conducting the Ball fell in his hands.

I had never heard of Malta before receiving our sailing orders. It is an island country today that in 1962, when I visited the country, was a member of the British Commonwealth. The capital of the island empire was the port and harbor city of Valletta, the largest city on the island, which is protected by an ancient fort dominating the harbor entrance. Valletta has a deep-water port and ships from all over the world regularly anchor there.

Our convoy arrived early in the morning, and we displayed the flags of Malta and the United Kingdom from our masts. As we neared the harbor, our convoy received a 17-gun salute from the fort which was flying the American flag during the gun salute. We, in turn, returned the gun salute with a 17-gun salute of our own. This was a first for me, and it made me think about what it must have been like so many hundred years ago when sailing ships entered the port of Valletta either as a friend or a foe. The fort looked very imposing, and it remains so to this day.

George Memmer and I went to the best hotel in Valletta, the five-star Phoenicia Hotel, located just outside the walls of the original city of Valletta and built by the British in 1930. It was an elegant hotel in 1962 with a British staff and everything about the hotel was formal and very "British." The hotel manager was delighted to undertake a formal Marine Corps Ball in their main ballroom, and was even able to recommend several girls schools and British nurses who might be invited to attend the ball as guests of the U.S. Marine Corps. George established ball committees and on Saturday, November 10, 1962, we had a grand Birthday in the famed Hotel Phoenicia.

Almost every British nurse working on Malta arrived at the Ball, and two complete girls schools of 17 and 18 year old young women arrived with their chaperones. We had briefed the troops that these women were not working girls or bar girls and that they were to treat them with courtesy and respect. We tried to impress on the troops that they were representing their country and standard, gross Marine liberty conduct, would not be tolerated.

The hotel manager had assisted us in booking a local band that knew the latest American music, and we also invited local dignitaries as well as members of the diplomatic corps. Our troops wore their green uniforms, as did the officers. Captain Memmer, however, had packed his "dress blues" so he wore them at the ball. All officers were detailed to additional chaperone duty and the evening went off without a hitch.

We had strategically positioned a few jeeps outside the hotel, and these were used to transport those Marines who had consumed too much alcohol back to their ships. It was a memorable Marine Corps birthday, and of all the birthday balls I have attended over the years, it is right up there among the best. The people were great, the ladies enthusiastic and friendly, and quite a few of our Marines fell in love that night. It was one of those things that only happen once, and you could never plan for something like that to happen again. I am sure that the Marines who participated in the Ball, even today, remember their stay in Malta with fondness and nostalgia.

We departed Malta on 13 November for Bomba, Libya, where we were scheduled to conduct desert operations with the Libyan Army in the Sahara Desert. This was another first for me. The beach at Bomba is wide, and the sand is almost white. It presented no problem for our landing and facilitated a smooth movement inland where we were immediately assaulted by hot desert winds and a glaring, white hot sun.

We encountered Bedouin tribesmen, camel caravans, and old World War II German tank hulls, preserved for eternity in the hot African desert. We also experienced the extreme desert heat of the Sahara which, on occasion, has been measured to be 136 degrees Fahrenheit. This presented a serious problem for our troops, and we had to be extremely careful to cover ourselves as much as possible during daylight hours.

At the end of our two weeks of desert warfare exercises, we were ready to jump into the ocean off the Bomba beaches, which we did with considerable enthusiasm. The water in late November felt like the waters of the Caribbean and served as a transition from the grueling days spent in the Sahara. Libya is an interesting country. I was glad to have seen it, intrigued by the famous Sahara desert and impressed by the Bedouins, but I was glad to leave Libya for our next port of call which, for our group, was the Sicilian city of Messina.

We arrived in Messina on 28 November and spent five days touring the island. We saw the snow covered peak of Mt. Etna, and I took my "nervous nellies" to the world famous Greek theater in Taromina. The troops were very excited to be able to stand anywhere within that giant outdoor amphitheater and to hear perfectly what someone standing at the opposite side of the open theater was saying. The bus ride up to Taromina and the base of Mt. Etna was very exciting as we traversed many steep and winding mountainous roads in a large Italian tourist bus.

We departed Messina on 3 December for Pilos, Greece, where we would conduct field exercises near the famous Greek fort that housed the guns of Navaronne during World War II. It was our first contact with Greece and the Greek people, both of which we found to be outstanding. After a week in Pilos we departed the area on our way to Patras, Greece, for another liberty call.

When we arrived at Patras on 12 December, I was detailed to shore patrol duty for the entire length of our stay in Patras, which would be until 17 December. Again, we had split up our group, and the other component went to the island of Corfu for their liberty call. In this case, they certainly got the better deal. My experience as a Shore Patrol Officer remains in my mind to this day, and it was one I would never want to have missed.

Whenever American forces landed in a foreign port in those days, one officer, usually a captain or above in rank, was assigned to the local police as a liaison officer to assist the local police in dealing with American forces ashore. This officer is called the Shore Patrol Officer, and he travels with the local police forces. Whenever an issue arises which involves American forces, the Shore Patrol Officer is expected to clear up the matter with the local police. This usually works exceptionally well except for three countries who simply treat the Shore Patrol Officer as a witness to their police methods. The three countries were Spain and Franco's Guardia Civil, Italy and their Carabinieri and Greece and the Greek police.

When we landed in Patras, I was dispatched to the local police chief who assigned me to the waterfront police station. I was initially treated with reserve, but when I made it clear that I was here to learn from them. I was accepted and treated in a friendly and supportive manner. This improved when I went to dinner with the local constabulary the night before the troops would be arriving for liberty. It was at this point, in a small Greek taverna (a restaurant that serves food, wine and has a house band, that traditionally opens at 9 p.m. and remains open until 1 or 2 in the morning), that I was introduced to the wonders of Ouzo, that anise-flavored alcohol that turns milky white if you add water to it, and the locally produced wine, distilled for hundreds of years by the Achaia-Clauss Winery of Patras, called Retsina. Retsina is made from the grapes of the white saviatiano grape and then combined with white pine resin. Retsina, a Greek favorite, takes some getting comfortable with since it tastes like kerosene.

Not wishing to insult my hosts, I drank both profusely, wound up dancing with the men in a circle and throwing plates on the floor of the Taverna, an established Greek custom to signify our approval of both the music and food. I had a great time and departed the Taverna with the policemen who took me back to the police station and showed me the small room where I would be staying during our liberty stop at Patras.

The following morning, somewhat hungover, I met with the Chief of Police who informed me what the ground rules would be for our visiting Marines and Sailors. The primary point that the Chief made was that in Greece you are presumed guilty until you can prove your innocence, or until the local police feel that you are innocent. He went on to say that the police are the law and American laws do not work in Greece. He wanted me to be sure to inform the troops that if a policeman stops you, don't run and don't object because the police will hit you and lock you up immediately. If you choose to continue to run, they will shoot you.

These seemed like plain and simple instructions to the Chief, but they hit our troops like a ton of bricks. I made it very clear to all commanders aboard ship that the police in Greece are the law and that our troops better understand this before they go ashore. I went on to say that I would be with the Chief but that my ability to help our troops was limited directly to what the Chief chose to do and what he allowed me to do. I told the commanders that if their troops obeyed the law they would have a great time in Patras. Since Patras was an international port city there were many bars, tavernas, restaurants and women ashore and the police took a liberal attitude to drinking and women, as long as no one caused any trouble. I returned to shore and began to prepare for the first onslaught of troops that would begin at noon. The troops from our ships began arriving at the liberty boat docks and spread out throughout the city.

I had discussed with the Chief of Police the possibility that quite a few of the troops would get drunk on the very strong Ouzo and Retsina. He laughed and agreed with me and said that he had already instructed his force that drunks would simply be driven back to the liberty boat dock and returned to US custody with no problem. This was a giant step forward for us, and I began to see the benefits of having a "permanent" Shore Patrol Officer ashore. Liberty ashore was always over at midnight, which meant that the last boats departed the liberty boat dock at 12:15 a.m. With the cooperation of the Patras Police, we rounded up strays until about 12:30 a.m. and released the last boat from the dock closer to 1 a.m.

Greek society, in those days, began late at night and Patras was still active and vibrant at 1 a.m. The Chief decided that I was a pretty good guy and took me under his wing. We went to dinner together, which was like going out with a "rock star," since the Chief was known throughout Patras and was apparently very well liked. Women flocked to the Chief who was, like so many Greek men, a reincarnation of Zorba the Greek. He was garrulous, uninhibited, full of life and very friendly. All of these traits masked his unusually cold and almost brutal efficiency when dispensing his brand of justice.

It was quite an experience having an entire city at my disposal as long as I was accompanied by the Chief. One day I spent the entire morning in the main police station observing what went on with the population of Patras, especially when they ran afoul of the law. I saw two teenage boys brought into the station for shop lifting. The desk sergeant hit both boys across the face and threw them into a holding cell. A telephone call was made to the fathers of the two boys, and they were directed to report to the police station. Upon their arrival, the desk sergeant, a large, strong and imposing figure of a man, hit the fathers and yelled at them in Greek. He then released the boys to the custody of their fathers. I always wondered what happened to them after they left the station, but I must admit it seemed like a good method to me. Our liberty call at Patras was uneventful. We had no incidents and the troops had a wonderful time. Both the women and wine were apparently to the liking of everyone.

On my last night ashore the Chief took me to dinner at his favorite taverna where he presented me with a patch of the Patras Police Force. Our landing force had plaques made before our departure from Camp Lejeune which had a Marine Corps emblem on the plaque with a metal plate on the bottom of the plaque that said, "With Thanks and Appreciation from Landing Force 1-2, United States Marine Corps-1962." The plaques were made to give to diplomats and consulate officials who helped us along the way, but I had decided that if the Chief was good to our Marines, I would give him one of those plaques. Since he truly had been very good to our troops, I took the plaque to our last dinner not knowing he was going to give me a patch, and, as it wound up, we exchanged gifts.

I departed Patras with some bottles of Ouzo and Retsina which the Chief insisted I take with me, and surrendered the alcohol to the Officer of the Deck when I got aboard ship. The alcohol would be held for me until our return to the United States. My experience in Patras was unique, and I believe it was simply the result of the fact that the Chief and I enjoyed each other's company.

On 17 December, we departed Patras for a rendezvous with our other component somewhere in the Mediterranean. This was an exercise for the ships, and it was designed so that the entire amphibious squadron could make port at Pireaus, the deep water port city of Athens, the capital of Greece, which lay about seven miles inland from the port. The Officer's Wive's Club had selected Athens as the location to which they would fly to reunite with their husbands. A travel agent in North Carolina had negotiated attractive rates at the Athenee Palace Hotel (now the Hilton Athens Palace Hotel) which was a 5 star hotel located near the palace and the thriving and always busy downtown section of Athens.

The squadron arrived in Piraeus on Friday 21 December, and we were not scheduled to depart until January 6, 1963. The group of wives that had arrived a day earlier met the squadron on the pier where our ship tied up. I spotted Sharron right away because she was still wearing her sunglasses in lieu of regular glasses. Piraeus is an ancient city. It is the deepest harbor in all of Europe and the third largest port in the world. To sail into Piraeus is an experience in itself. There are huge passenger terminals, cargo terminals, ship building facilities, cranes, railroads, breakwaters, piers, and industrial buildings, scattered throughout the port area. At any given time, there are ships from many nations of the world anchored in the harbor, and there is round the clock activity.

When we arrived in Greece in December 1962, the country was ruled by a monarchy and King George II was the reigning monarch. As the troops learned in Patras, Greece was essentially a "police state," where many basic human rights enjoyed in the United States were nonexistent. Probably the most important one of these, as far as the troops were concerned, was that you were presumed guilty until you could prove your innocence. This was a strong motivator to stay out of trouble. The officers and noncommissioned officers whose wives had made the trip to Athens were granted shore leave for five days and this was probably the best thing that LtCol Williams had ever done. I believe he did it because his wife, who was not present, had urged him to do it since she was the President of the Wives Club and was looking out for her constituents.

In 1960, an award winning black and white movie came out entitled *Never on Sunday.* It starred Melina Mercouri, a well-known Greek actress, playing the role of a prostitute in Piraeus who meets an American student of the Greek classics. The film is rich in Greek culture, music and dance. The theme from the movie, a Bouzouki band number entitled, "Never on Sunday," won the Oscar for 1960 as the best music from a motion picture. The film was very popular in the United States, and it was particularly topical for all the people who had seen the film and who were now visiting Greece for the first time.

I met Sharron at our hotel in downtown Athens. She updated me on Eric, showing me pictures of his rapid growth and assuring me that he was fine while being cared for by our next door neighbor, also a Marine wife. We then proceeded to do all the things tourists do in foreign cities. We celebrated New Year's Day in downtown Athens and watched the fireworks from the Acropolis as we welcomed in 1963. On January 5, the wives returned to the States and on the morning of January 7, our amphibious squadron departed the port of Piraeus on our way to another training exercise, this time on the island of Sardinia.

Exercise areas in the Mediterranean are issues that are determined at the highest levels of the American Defense Department. Negotiations are undertaken, and agreements reached that reserve specific areas in specific countries for a specified number of days. These agreements are usually consummated more than three to four years before the date of the actual exercise. If aggressor forces are to be used in the exercise, the host country usually designates who that aggressor will be. In the case of the French on Corsica, they designated the French Foreign Legion for our first landing and the French Marines for our second landing, which was actually a landing scheduled for the 2nd Battalion, 8th Marines. Since they were delayed in arriving in the Mediterranean due to the Cuban Missile Crisis, we made the landing in their place.

For the Sardinia exercise, we would go up against field elements of the Italian National Police, the Carabineri. The island of Sardinia belongs to Italy and is the second largest island in the Mediterranean. We were going to conduct our landing exercise in Porto Scudo, and we were scheduled to remain in Sardinia for ten days. We arrived in the exercise area on January 12, and our landing was scheduled for dawn on January 14. Again, the inland area around Porto Scudo was mountainous and craggy, and the weather had turned colder which made use of field stoves and warmers necessary.

The Carabineri were nothing like the Foreign Legion and seemed to treat the exercise as a chance to get away from patrolling the different parts of Italy from which they came. They were friendly, easy to spot, and turned out to be nothing more than gracious hosts. We maneuvered through various assigned areas of operation and then had another two day "stand down" on the beach of Porto Scudo. This time we conducted a static display of all of our equipment and school children were bussed in to the beach area for tank rides, athletic contests and American hamburgers and hot dogs. They loved the food and couldn't get enough of it, especially the Coca-Cola.

We backloaded on 25 January and headed to our next liberty port, Barcelona, Spain, which became another highlight of our deployment. Our trip to Barcelona would again comprise the entire amphibious squadron, and we were informed that all personnel who had been granted leave in Athens would be expected to take the bulk of the duties aboard ship in Barcelona. I volunteered to be the Shore Patrol Officer, but that job went to one of the captain's on LtCol William's staff aboard *Mount McKinley*. Since he had to deal with LtCol Williams on a daily basis, I felt that he more than earned the honor. I volunteered to be the Officer of the Deck as often as I could, but the captain of our ship, Captain Edward C. Wyse, USN, a submarine hero of World War II, did not agree with LtCol Williams' policy of "punishing" people who had taken legitimate leave in Athens.

Captain Wyse established a standard duty roster which afforded all personnel equal time in Barcelona. While this irritated LtCol Williams, there was nothing he could do about it since Captain Wyse outranked him and besides, no one aboard can usurp the power of a ship's captain. Our liberty in Barcelona began on January 31 and would last until Friday 8 February. I took the "nervous nellies" on several tours in Barcelona because there was so much to see. They visited replicas of Columbus's ships, they shopped in stores on the famed Ramblas, and they ate dinner in a restaurant that had a wonderful demonstration of flamenco dancing as the main event of the evening.

Before releasing them to their own devices, I clearly warned them that of all the countries we had visited so far, Spain could be the most dangerous. I told them that Spain was a dictatorship under General Francisco Franco and that the State Police, the Guardia Civil, was the most feared police in the Mediterranean. Spain was a tightly controlled, well run country, with just about every aspect of Spanish life regulated and controlled by the regime. Restaurants were told what they could charge for meals, depending on their location and the quality of their food and service, hotel rates were price fixed and all other business ventures were regulated by the state. To a visitor, Spain was clean, efficient and organized. This perspective was probably not shared by the Spaniards.

Our landing force had one unfortunate incident in Barcelona which made a lasting impression on the troops. One of the Marines from another unit in our squadron got into an argument with a taxi driver over the fare. The Marine had been drinking and decided to leave the cab without paying his fare. The cab driver called a policeman who was patrolling the street and the policeman yelled at the Marine to halt. The Marine ignored the order and the policeman shot him dead in the street. All we could do was to collect the body and take him home in his ship's freezer. It was a sad event and a brutal illustration of life in Franco's Spain. I was very glad that I had been emphatic with my troops concerning their behavior in Barcelona, and it was not necessary to say I told you so. We all mourned the needless loss of life and were secretly glad we did not live in Spain.

We departed Barcelona on 9 February on our way, again to Porto Scudo in Sardinia for another landing. This field exercise lasted only a week and was an opportunity for us to repair and maintain our equipment, which was unloaded, inspected and serviced before being reloaded. At the conclusion of the exercise, we headed to another liberty port and arrived in Genoa, Italy, on the 19 February. This would be our last port of call in the Mediterranean, as we were scheduled to make one last landing in Aranci Bay, in the northern part of Sardinia, and then head to Majorca, where we would be relieved as the landing force in the Mediterranean by the 2nd Battalion of the 8th Marine Regiment on March 7, 1963. From there, we would be heading home to Camp Lejeune.

Genoa, Italy, was another great port of call. The city has an ancient breakwater built out of huge stones which fully protects the harbor. Our squadron of seven ships was forced to anchor outside the breakwater and trips by small boat from our ships to the fleet landing inside the breakwater took almost 45 minutes each way. We were only scheduled to be in Genoa for five days, and we were sailing to our last landing in Sardinia on February 24.

Genoa is a thriving and active metropolis, and our American consulate in Genoa is an active agency. The fact that I had left from Genoa for Ecuador in 1939, after escaping from Nazi Germany, was not lost on me, and I wondered from where the M/S *Orazio* departed on her way to Ecuador. It is interesting, that as of this writing, the city of Guayaquil, Ecuador, is listed as a sister city of Genoa.

We visited the restaurant, shops and historic sites of this old and venerable city, enjoying the sights and aromas of what was our final port of call for this deployment. We departed Genoa on 24 February and made another landing at Porto Scudo where we renewed our acquaintance with the French Foreign Legion for one more week. We then departed for our change of command ceremony on 7 March in Majorca. After six months in the Mediterranean Sea, we were headed home.

We had an extremely rough crossing of the Atlantic with high winds and highly turbulent seas. Our ship, USS *Telfair*, was tossing so strongly that it was necessary to close the galley (kitchen) for three days. There were a few times during those three days that I thought we weren't going to make it. The seas were so rough, and we were beaten around so constantly that I felt that, at any minute, our ship was going to break in half. We managed to eat only sandwiches which the Navy cooks were able to prepare and distribute throughout the ship. A large contingent of Sailors and Marines became seasick, and there was little call for the sandwiches. Finally, after three days, the storm subsided and we continued on our way without further incident.

After we returned to Camp Lejeune on March 18, I got reacquainted with my soon to be one year old son, Eric. He was a happy baby, and nothing seemed to bother him. He laughed a lot, and he was truly a little bundle of joy. We also received word shortly after my return that we had been assigned government quarters aboard the base. We moved into a three-bedroom fully furnished house in Paradise Point. It was the only time in my life that I lived in a community that was composed of families that were identical. We were all college graduates, we were all about the same age, all of our wives were about the same age, and we had about the same number of children, all at about the same age. We all received the same amount of pay and we were all well aware of that fact, plus, we all had the same political inclinations. No wonder that the Marine Corps chose to name the housing area "Paradise Point."

It was a magic time socially as there were many potluck dinners and Saturday evening house parties. Everyone would baby-sit for the other and, most importantly, everyone trusted everyone else. A feeling of unity ran through the community since we were all in the Marine Corps together. I have never lived in a community like that since, nor do I believe that I will ever again.

Shortly after our return we had a change of command ceremony. LtCol Williams was being sent to command another battalion, and I did not envy the Marines of his new unit. Lieutenant Colonel Andrew V. Marousek became our new commanding officer, and the effect of the change was mind boggling. Where LtCol Williams was taciturn, cold and totally humorless, LtCol Marousek was open, friendly and sincerely interested in the troops. Shortly after his arrival he told me that he was appointing me the Battalion Logistics Officer (S-4) due to the departure of the current logistics officer. It was time, he said, for the current crop of company commanders to be assigned staff jobs so other captains could get a shot at a command.

At first I was disappointed. Then I found out that the other company commanders were going to either regimental or division level staff assignments, and I, at least, was staying with the battalion. The battalion logistics officer is an extremely important job. All equipment, supplies and embarkation procedures are the responsibility of this office and excellent job performance in this assignment is particularly helpful for promotion and future assignments. As I took over as the Battalion S-4, LtCol Marousek informed me that our battalion was scheduled for a Caribbean deployment on September 30, 1963.

This meant that we would have six months of training in Camp Lejeune before deploying aboard ship again. This time, however, it would only be for three months. Pre-deployment training began almost immediately. Officers, staff noncommissioned officers and enlisted men began rotating out of the battalion as replacements arrived to fill all the vacancies caused by normal tour terminations. Tours of duty in the battalion were generally two years. Officers could expect to remain in the 2nd Division for three years, but if you got one year of command you were considered lucky.

I was one of the lucky ones, having commanded a rifle company in a deployed battalion. This was considered an excellent asset to have in your record when you became eligible for promotion. There was no question that during your tour of duty in an infantry division you could count on staff duty to round out your assignment. In all cases, your job performance in all duties and your attitude was constantly being observed and documented in the semiannual officer's fitness reports which were required to be completed on each officer by all commanding officers.

In October, our battalion would be deploying to Camp Francisco Garcia, a minimal, field base camp, on the island of Vieques, located south of the main island of Puerto Rico. The camp was named in honor of Marine Private First Class Francisco Garcia, a native of Puerto Rico, who lost his life during the Korean War and was decorated with the Medal of Honor. The purpose of a battalion of Marines in the Caribbean was thinly veiled as a training deployment but was, in actuality, a force in readiness to deal with unstable governments and dictatorships in the region. While Haiti had a dictator, the only threatening dictator in the Caribbean at the time was Fidel Castro in Cuba.

Preparing for our next deployment under LtCol Marousek was a great pleasure. He listened, he asked questions, and he included his staff in his decision making process. He had become aware of the unrest within the battalion under LtCol Williams. No one "bad-mouthed" the former CO (that would be considered whining and not a smart thing for a Marine officer to do), but there were plenty of suggestions made about our upcoming deployment, usually couched in terms such as "we learned from our last deployment that there are better ways to do certain things."

Based on the Marine Corps assignment system, fully one-third of the Marine's who had made the Mediterranean deployment remained with the battalion for the Caribbean deployment. This gave the battalion a core of experienced Marines who would serve as trainers and facilitators for the new group of Marines who had joined our battalion since our return from Europe.

The nature of the Caribbean deployment was different from our Mediterranean deployment in that we did not remain with our ships. Once in the landing area of Vieques Island we would land everything onto the island, and the ships would depart. If we needed to reload for a contingency matter, there was a very strong chance that a different amphibious squadron would arrive to take us to the trouble zone. In this manner, the Navy could have more flexibility with the limited resources of their amphibious fleet in the Atlantic. I made several trips to Norfolk, Virginia, to view the ships that I would have to load for our Caribbean deployment. Unlike our Mediterranean deployment, we would go in fewer ships since we did not need a command and control vessel.

The helicopter air detachment would fly to the island from their base at the Roosevelt Roads Naval Air Station in Puerto Rico and remain at the Vieques Island airstrip at Camp Garcia. The jets would participate in our exercises, do their bombing and napalm runs and then return to their air-conditioned barracks at Roosevelt Roads. The battalion took on a more friendly and cooperative attitude while remaining sharp and professionally motivated. Mrs. Marousek was extremely energetic in the formation of a far more active Officers Wives Club, and plans were made for the wives to meet their husbands in San Juan, Puerto Rico, over Christmas. The ladies had regularly scheduled weekly luncheons at the Officers Club, and the wives of the battalion felt more connected to the unit than they had ever been under our previous commander.

The battalion trained hard, and when we stood our Commanding General's Inspection before our deployment, we received outstanding marks all around. As the logistics officer of the battalion, I was literally working day and night. I had to procure new equipment, repair old equipment, prepare embarkation plans, work with individual rifle company commanders to get their units ready for deployment and prepare the battalion command group for deployment. I found that I had a natural talent for logistics work because I could easily conceptualize, and the more hectic the pace became the smoother things seemed to work out. I learned how to choose good people and how to delegate work so that there was an equal distribution of labor. We always seemed to meet our deadlines. This did not go unnoticed, and our logistics section received high praise from the Regiment, the Division and the Navy in Norfolk.

Our embarkation at Morehead City could not have gone more smoothly. Monday morning, September 30, as the 2nd Marine Division Band played the *Marine's Hymn* and *Over the Seas, Let's Go Men,* an old World War I barracks song, 1/2 departed again for a training deployment, this time to the Caribbean to relieve 1/8, as the landing force in the Caribbean.

Vieques Island today is no longer the site of a training base since the Department of Defense, bowing to protests from Puerto Rican politicians and land activists, left the island in 1978. It had been a forward training base in the Caribbean since 1939. The honeymoon lasted 39 years and was still in force when our battalion arrived on the scene, late at night on October 7. The plan was always the same. Early at dawn the battalion would execute a full scale landing across the beaches of Vieques Island and then move inland to Camp Garcia. There they would relieve 1/8 and take over the camp as 1/8 back loaded for their return to Camp Lejeune.

We followed all the procedures for amphibious operations dictated by the Marine Corps for amphibious landings on a foreign shore. One of those protocols would forever make an impression on, and generate a nickname for one young Marine first lieutenant. Because of one single incident he received a nickname that would stick with him throughout his lengthy and successful career as a Marine. To this day, Colonel Joseph H. Stanton, USMC (Retired), is still known as *Culebra Joe,* a title that, over the years, he has come to accept and embrace. To understand what occurred it is necessary to note that the island of Vieques sits next to the island of Culebra. While Culebra is smaller than Vieques, both islands look similar, and both belong to Puerto Rico.

The distance between the two islands is only eight miles, which is the length of Vieques Sound. Our convoy, anchored in the middle of the sound, provided a four-mile assembly area to launch the landing craft on their way into the beaches for the landing. The plan called for the 1st Platoon of the 2nd Reconnaissance Battalion, under First Lieutenant Joe Stanton, to depart the ship at dark, paddle ashore in rubber boats and set up markers for the landing craft to home in on the following morning when the actual amphibious landing would take place. The platoon departed the ship, and we "hit the rack" in order to be ready for our dawn landing. At first light, the troops from all the ships went into their landing craft, and the first wave was launched past the line of departure on its way to Vieques Island.

What the first wave saw, as well as what all subsequent waves saw, was a perfect job of beach marking except it was on the beach of Culebra Island! In the dark, the Recon Platoon had paddled to the wrong island and had spent the entire night marking it for the landing. Thus, was "Culebra Joe" Stanton born. A lesser officer would probably have been unable to take the heat, but Joe Stanton was able to laugh about it after he was promoted to captain. He always thought that his mistake in Culebra would cost him his career. It did not, and he retired as a colonel.

Our landing went smoothly, and we moved into our new home at Camp Garcia for the next three months. Once settled, we started a training schedule that included much field work and weapons firing. The island had excellent ranges, and every infantry weapon carried by, or attached to, the battalion was fired and registered for accuracy. Tanks were able to fire at field targets and artillery units fired their 105 mm howitzers at targets deployed at multiple known distances.

The island of Vieques was a rural island, and those inhabitants who did not work for the US Government, either at Camp Garcia or the various weapons firing ranges, were either farmers or shop owners in the two small towns on the island. Directly outside of the main gate of Camp Garcia was the islands' largest town, Isabella Segunda. The other town located almost at the direct opposite location on the island was the town of Esperanza.

On the afternoon of November 22, 1963, the officers of the battalion were in a meeting to discuss the upcoming one weeks' field exercise when a sergeant came running into the Quonset hut yelling that the President of the United States had been shot. It was 1:30 in the afternoon, and it was a moment that I shall never forget. I think that you can ask anyone who was alive on that day where they were when they heard about President Kennedy's assassination in Dallas, Texas, and they will give you the details almost verbatim. We stopped all activity, waiting for word from higher headquarters, as some of us thought that the shooting might be the prelude to some international plot and we had to be ready to move quickly. As it turned out, we received the word to continue with our current activities, but that we were to increase our readiness status if immediate relocation was required.

For several weeks, as the country and the world mourned the loss of our President, US military units worldwide were placed on full alert. Finally, after the funeral and the subsequent shooting of the assassin, Lee Harvey Oswald (a former Marine) by Jack Ruby, a Dallas night club and strip joint owner, we were ordered to return to normal routine and to continue our training on Vieques Island. Christmas was rapidly approaching, and the battalion was scheduled to load aboard ship and sail to San Juan, the capital of Puerto Rico, for Christmas leave and a reunion with our wives who would meet us there.

We back loaded aboard amphibious ships and proceeded to San Juan. The wives who had made the trip to Puerto Rico were all staying at the Caribe Hilton Hotel, which was the finest hotel available and which graciously gave us military discounts. The hotel was right on the ocean on a peninsula of land and had a beautiful white sand beach and a magnificent pool. In addition, there was a very active casino in the hotel, and it was very convenient to Old San Juan and the Condado area for shopping and night life.

I took a few days leave and spent Christmas and New Year's Eve with Sharron in the Caribe Hilton. We visited the sights in Puerto Rico such as Morro Castle, the Bacardi Rum Factory (which had relocated to San Juan from Cuba after Castro took over), the rain forests and all the trendy shops in the Condado area. In addition, we partied with the other couples and had a great time together. The wives flew home on January 2, and we departed for Camp Lejeune the next day. We arrived back at our battalion area by 9 January, and training and life within the battalion returned to our normal status while in the United States.

I continued as the logistics officer of the Battalion for another six months and then received orders to the 2nd Marine Division Headquarters for duty as an assistant G-4 (Division Logistics Officer), effective on July 9. I was assigned to the Division Headquarters to prepare for a full division sized landing to take place in Huelva, Spain, during October and November of 1964. The name of the operation was Operation *Steel Pike*, and it was to be the largest amphibious landing operation conducted by the United States since the end of the Second World War. Over 25,000 Marines and supporting elements would be landed across the beaches of Huelva, Spain, either by landing craft or by helicopter.

It was a monumental logistics and operations nightmare. To make the operation a success, more hours had to be worked than could be accounted for in any given 24 hour period. The Navy was prepared to muster almost every available amphibious ship in the Atlantic Fleet, and was also going to include aircraft carriers, oilers, replenishment ships, destroyer escorts and amphibious landing ships that launched Navy Seals and Marine Recon personnel under cover of darkness. During the operation, the 2nd Marine Division would essentially be "at sea," with only a small cadre of support troops left behind to continue to operate Camp Lejeune. The operations office (G-3) and the logistics office (G-4) of the Division were open for business 24 hours a day, 7 days a week, during the hectic pre-deployment planning phases which started on July 1, 1964.

The Division was scheduled to embark aboard ships during a one-week period in late September, with units loading aboard ships at Morehead City on an incremental schedule, which required rapid loading and deployment to accomplish the entire division embarkation in one weeks-time. In the case of this operation, one weeks-time meant a duration of 168 hours since embarkation continued at Morehead City and Norfolk around the clock. Once the ships were loaded they would depart from the port and proceed to a specific location in the Atlantic where the entire convoy of ships would consolidate and move towards Europe in a combat convoy formation with exterior destroyer security.

From the point of view of gaining experience, when the operation was concluded I would be one of the very few officers on active duty that had ever participated in the loading out of an entire division for a combat operation. I had been ordered to the Division for this assignment because of the smooth embarkation and debarkation that my battalion had accomplished during our Caribbean deployment. Since everything went well, I got the credit, although over 7 officers and 22 enlisted men were involved in the effort. That is the Marine Corps way. If things go well, the officer in charge gets the credit, if things go bad then the officer in charge gets the blame. This is why I have always stressed to all of my subordinates that if you are willing to take all the credit you must be prepared to take all the blame. I have found that sharing all the credit and assuming all the blame is what truly makes an outstanding leader.

Embarkation week was set for September 14 through September 20 with the entire armada scheduled to rendezvous in the Atlantic by September 24. Remember, the convoy, to maintain unit integrity, had to travel as slow as its' slowest ship. The details of logistics planning for an exercise of this scope would require a separate book, however, suffice it to say, everyone worked hard, and I worked harder than I have ever worked before or since. It was the kind of challenge where everything you planned and prepared for execution was going to be tested immediately. If you were wrong, your mistakes could cause delays, injuries or, in a few rare cases, fatalities. There were no second chances. The division had to get underway, fully loaded, prepared to land and fight on a foreign shore, and the logistics planners had to make it happen.

The Division logistics officer was a Colonel Webb Hood. Colonel Hood was an intelligent strategic planner who did not make mistakes. After retirement, he served for many years as the treasurer of the worldwide Navy Federal Credit Union. It was an honor and a privilege to work for him, and I always remember my year with him with great fondness. A few words about our endless hours spent in the planning of this operation. Life aboard ship is very insular and crowded. Everything that is required to sustain life is aboard the ship; food, water, light, heat, sleeping arrangements, barbershops, laundries, dry cleaners, a prison, a morgue, a hospital, dental offices, etc. The ships furnish these services for their Sailors and sometimes grudgingly provides them for embarked Marines. Each Marine, when they go aboard ship, is issued two sheets and one pillowcase. Each week they are laundered, and clean sheets and pillowcases are issued from the laundry. For years, Marines returned from deployments missing hundreds of sheets and pillowcases per ship. It was not a big mystery to figure out what was happening. The Navy was using Marine supplies to make up their own shortages.

We attacked this problem, trying to figure out how we could save our own linen from the Navy, and in the process, save thousands of dollars from our own operating budget. Through some stroke of luck, I came up with the idea of using green sheets and pillowcases for embarked troops. Since the Navy used white, there was no way they could steal green sheets and pillowcases and claim them for themselves. This idea was implemented and remains to this day aboard ships to distinguish between Marine and Navy linen. I got a certificate of commendation from the Commandant of the Marine Corps for this idea, especially after they figured out how much money they were saving.

The Division staff was going to embark aboard USS *Pocono* (AGC 16) and *Pocono* would serve as the Headquarters for the landing force and the communications central for all units. Liaison officers from every embarked unit, ground or air, would be required for duty aboard the command and control ship. This made accommodations for junior officers (captains and lieutenants), sparse and extremely crowded. Again, I would be living in a 36 bunk space, with 12 columns of 3 bunk chains supporting the beds. Use of the head (toilet and the shower) was closely controlled and scheduled, with everyone forced to take "Navy showers." This means that you get wet, turn off the water, soap down and wash yourself and then turn on the shower to rinse off. There is a chain attached to the shower head to facilitate the on and off process, and it is designed to conserve water aboard ship.

I was assigned the duty of working with all Division embarkation officers and coordinating the loading plans, all of which had to be presented to the Commanding General for his ultimate approval. Supplies and equipment for an entire division had to be inventoried, staged and accommodated in the holds of the more than 75 ships that would be participating in the exercise. Aviation supplies and equipment, as well as spare parts and emergency fuel, also had to be accommodated.

Months of intricate planning were culminated when we managed to complete the load out in the required seven days. I think that when I collapsed on my bunk aboard *Pocono*, as we steamed to our rendezvous point, was the first time I was able to relax. The Division had selected Huelva because of its' strategic location in the south of Spain, very near to the border of Portugal. It was an area of Spain that boasted almost 150 miles of unobstructed beaches bordering the Atlantic Ocean. The entire fleet could easily anchor near the landing beaches, and the beaches were so long and so wide that several waves of landing craft could land simultaneously from a series of different locations within the landing zone. On D-Day, besides having five landing beaches, there were enough air corridors to allow helicopters to bring in two additional infantry battalions. The heavy helicopters could also begin ferrying in artillery on D-Day plus 1, which made the entire area ideal for a full scale division sized landing.

Being on the major command and control ship (translated, this meant that the General and the Admiral in charge of the entire operation were embarked on our ship) allowed *Pocono* the opportunity to call on ports that none of the other ships could enter. For example, when we arrived in the Mediterranean we had to make a formal call on the Governor General of Gibraltar. We were granted liberty in Gibraltar, and while I could have taken the ferry across the strait to Tangiers, I did not want to take a chance of missing the departure of the ship and I didn't go. Those that did go had a great time and all made it back in time, but I was too "gung-ho" then to risk not making muster. We were also informed that after the operation, the command ship would make formal calls at Santander, Bilbao and San Sebastian, all located in northern Spain on the Bay of Biscay. The remainder of the task force would return to the Mediterranean and visit Barcelona, Valencia, Cartagena, Almeria and Malaga. The Spanish government made every effort to obtain as many US dollars as possible before our return to the United States. Besides, the embarked troops had certainly earned a liberty call.

Operation *Steel Pike* began in earnest on October 12, 1964. On D-Day, we had the misfortune to lose nine Marines who were involved in a helicopter midair collision over the beach at Huelva. Later in the exercise, we lost another Marine who was run over by a tank while asleep in his sleeping bag. The loss of ten Marines on a training exercise, no matter what size the landing force, is unacceptable. Our commanding general subsequently retired in 1965 at the rank of Major General. Besides the fatalities, the exercise was very successful. We proved that we could move a landing force of 25,000 Marines halfway around the world with all of their supplies and equipment and have them ready to fight an enemy force immediately upon landing. Observers from foreign military organizations were impressed, and I am sure informed their respective governments that the U.S. Marines were a force to be reckoned with in the future. We remained ashore through 20 October when the operation was declared a success, and we began to back load aboard our ships immediately.

The reward for the outstanding exercise, disregarding the fatalities, was that immediately upon back loading the armada would split up and proceed to various liberty ports.

Following two weeks of liberty we would proceed back across the Atlantic in smaller convoys that would allow a more rapid return. When the back load was completed, we departed the Huelva area on 24 October on our way north, sailing past Portugal, around the northern tip of Spain and making our first stop at Santander for a few days. We then departed for Bilbao and San Sebastian where one of the most unusual events of my trips to the Mediterranean was about to occur.

When our ship landed in Bilbao on 28 October, the American Consul came on board with a request from the American ambassador to Spain, the Honorable Robert F. Woodward. The consul stated that a bus would arrive at the pier the following morning to go somewhere for an entire day. He was tasked to fill the bus with 60 servicemen from the "armada," and that the detail was to include at least one officer. No one was interested in going, however, at the evening staff meeting the General asked for a volunteer to take the troops and act as the officer in charge. I volunteered. The General assigned quotas and in short order we had the 60 troops requested. The interesting point of all of this is that, at the time, no one had the slightest idea of where we were going or what we were doing.

The next morning I found my detachment of 60 "volunteers" standing in formation on the pier. They were in their green uniforms and looked quite good, however, their moods were not. A very modern, spotlessly clean, European touring bus equipped with reclining seats and an onboard toilet arrived to pick us up. The driver, who spoke limited English, informed me that we were going to the city of Guernica, high up in the Pyrenees Mountains. I was amazed that, while our group was heading up into the Basque Country mountains, not a single representative from the US Government saw fit to accompany us on the journey. Just before 10 a.m. we arrived in Guernica. The bus stopped in the middle of a large city park, which was the city center, and fronted both the city hall and the very modern convention center.

As we got off the bus, we were met by at least 200 people who cheered us as we disembarked. We were escorted to a temporary platform where we were officially welcomed by the Alcalde (Mayor) of Guernica, Senor Pedro Unceta. He went on to say that the city was hosting a formal luncheon in the convention center for our group, but first, we would be given a tour of the Astra Weapons Factory, which the mayor and his family happened to own ever since it had been established in 1908. At the mention of all of this, there was an increased level of interest throughout the group.

The mayor was a very personable and good looking gentleman who was genuinely proud to be hosting the Marines and, in short order, the Marines seemed to return the favor. Our first stop was the weapons factory where, since 1908, the famous Astra pistols had been manufactured. The pistols were small handguns called the Victoria mini, which held nine 6.35mm cartridges in its magazine. The factory had produced pistols for the Spanish Army, the French Army and the German Army. All models were on display, and each Marine was given an opportunity to fire one of the mini pistols in the factory's indoor firing range.

During the weapons factory tour, which was conducted by at least ten of his employees, all in white coats with Astra emblems embroidered on the coats and ear protectors for firing on the indoor range, the Mayor asked me to join him in his personal office. He poured me a glass of Spanish wine and then asked me directly why only a captain was assigned as the officer in charge. I felt that this question was coming, and I had a prepared answer. I told the Mayor that there were several colonels who wanted to lead the tour but that the General felt that the young troops would relate more easily to a junior officer, one who was an experienced troop leader, and, therefore, I had been selected both for my experience and my youth. This seemed to fully satisfy the Mayor, and his demeanor towards me became even friendlier. The Mayor then informed me that, after the factory tour, our group would return to the town square for a formal luncheon in the Convention Center.

The men at the luncheon were either government officials, merchants, farmers or entrepreneurs, and they considered it an honor to be our hosts. I would be sitting at the head table with the Mayor and the City Council. We arrived at the Convention Center, and I was amazed at the detailed arrangements that had been made for us. There was a very large square of tables at which 30 places were set on each side of the square. This would accommodate 120 people (60 Marines and 60 citizens) plus the Mayor and me who were fit into what was designated as the head table or the top of the square.

The hall was decorated with many Basque flags representing the various Basque provinces in Spain and France plus the flags of Spain and the United States. The meal began with a toast to the United States, and the troops drank what would become the first of many glasses of good Spanish wine. The meal was served by young women from the city and this immediately brought the attention level of the troops to new heights. As the wine flowed and the meal progressed, it was obvious that both the Marines and the local citizens were thoroughly enjoying themselves.

At the conclusion of the meal, which lasted over three hours, the Mayor spoke of the historical significance of Guernica. He explained that Guernica, as the spiritual capital of the Basque region, had been viciously attacked the morning of April 26, 1937, by German fighter bombers that began an indiscriminate bombing of the marketplace, located in the middle of the city. The bombing attack then spread out throughout the remainder of the city. When the three hour attack ended the city was destroyed, and over 1,700 people had been killed. This figure represented two-thirds of the population of the city of Guernica at that time.

Following the Mayor's speech he informed us that another of Guernica's claims to fame is the birth of the sport of Jai Alai. He went on to say that all the Jai Alai players who were playing in the Florida frontons in 1964, were Basque and they were all currently in Guernica for a tournament before departing for Florida for the start of the 1964 winter Jai Alai season. He then told us that in honor of the visit of the U.S. Marines to Guernica we were going to the fronton to view a match that was being played in our honor.

We were introduced to the players, and when we noticed that the entire fronton was packed with spectators, all of whom cheered our arrival, we saluted the townspeople and took our places in the stands. Before the commencement of the tournament, the Jai Alai players selected three of the biggest and strongest looking Marines and asked them to step out onto the court. The players strapped a cesta-punta on the hand of each Marine. This is a woven basket that is strapped to your hand (right or left depending on your choice), and which is used to catch the pelota (ball) before returning it to the front wall. Pelotas have been clocked at 188 miles per hour coming off of the front wall when thrown by an experienced player. The players explained how to throw the pelota from the cesta-punta and then asked the Marines to try it. The crowd cheered the Marines, but not a single Marine could get the ball to the front wall. All three Marines had the pelota fall out of the basket before they could even wind up to attempt a throw.

The Marines were excellent sports. The players and the crowd applauded them, and the matches began in earnest. The matches were over by 8 p.m., and the Mayor addressed us again. When he finished I addressed the Mayor and the crowd telling them how much we had enjoyed our visit to Guernica, and that the day would be a day that we would never forget. I presented the Mayor with a 2nd Marine Division plaque that had our standard engraving on it that said, "Presented on behalf of the 2nd Marine Division with great respect and admiration 1964." If we had known what kind of event we were attending, the ship in Bilbao had the capability to personalize any plaque, but, once again, without any prior information it was impossible to do so in this case. I regretted having to give the Mayor such a "boilerplate" plaque, but he seemed to be truly impressed, and he walked us to the bus. We loaded the troops aboard and the Mayor, and I did our Spanish farewell with hugs and warm handshakes. It had been a wonderful and memorable day and one that I recall with genuine fondness, even 50 plus years later.

After a few more days of liberty in Bilbao, we prepared for our return trip to the United States. Because *Pocono*, as the command and control ship for the entire Division, was not required to be a part of the convoy for the return trip, the ship proceeded independently, and we arrived in Morehead City on 9 November. This allowed the General and staff to attend the Marine Corps Birthday Ball which was held in the Officer's Club at Camp Lejeune on Tuesday evening, 10 November, 1964.

After returning to Camp Lejeune, I learned two very important things. The first was that my wife Sharron had become pregnant with our second child, and the second was that based on my excellent performance of duty in the Division logistics office I was assigned a secondary MOS of 0402, which meant that I was now a logistics officer, besides being an infantry officer. What the 0402 MOS meant was that if a logistics MOS rated officer reported into a unit and a logistics officer was required, anyone with a secondary MOS of 0402, was most probably going to be assigned to logistics type duties. While this did not make me very happy, a secondary MOS was an indicator to a promotion board that the officer being considered for promotion had mastered another skill besides infantry troop leading. If nothing else, in the case of limited promotion opportunities, it seemed logical that a board would pick an officer with several skills instead of just a single skill.

In March 1965, I was selected for duty at Marine Barracks, Naval Base, Guantanamo Bay, Cuba. Since there were huge political problems with Fidel Castro and the base was under constant threat from the Cuban Army, Marines assigned there were considered to be in a potential combat zone and could not take their families to Guantanamo Bay. Considering this hardship, the tour of duty for Marines in Guantanamo Bay (called *Gitmo*) was considered a hardship tour and, therefore, lasted only 13 months.

The orders I had received directed me to report to Marine Barracks by March 15, 1965. At the time I received those orders, Cuba was as close to a fighting war as we could get. Patrols worked the Cuban fence line, and occasionally one side would shoot at the other. It was considered an honor to be selected for duty in Cuba.

I departed Camp Lejeune in February and rented a two-bedroom house in Deerfield Beach, Florida, near Sharron's parents, for Sharron and Eric. I spent one month of leave in Deerfield Beach then departed for Cuba in a US Coast Guard KC-130 aircraft from the Opa-Locka Airport. As I flew to my new duty station, I had a chance to reflect on my life in the Marine Corps to date. I had served in two infantry battalions, one in the 3rd Marine Division and one in the 2nd Marine Division. I had been stationed at one of the Marine Corps Recruit Depots as a Series Officer training recruits, and I had completed a three year tour of duty at the Marine Barracks in Washington. I was now headed to a semi-combat environment in Cuba, a position for which I had supposedly been personally selected, and I had only been on active duty for nine years. I was a Captain of Marines, I was married with one child and another one on the way, and I was all of 30 years old. It had been a pretty full life so far, and I wondered what awaited me in Cuba.

We carefully avoided flying over Cuba, so our plane took a course towards the island of Hispaniola, the island where both Haiti and the Dominican Republic coexist, where we would veer northwest through the Greater Antilles and approach Guantanamo Bay from the ocean side of the island. We landed at the Naval Air Station on 15 April 1965. My tour of duty in Cuba had begun.

Peter S. Beck: From Birth in Hitler's Nazi Germany to Retirement as a U. S. Marine Corps Officer

Berlin, Germany, in 1935, the year of my birth.

My Mother, 1931 Margarete Herzberg.

My Birthplace. Landhaus Klinik, Berlin, June 3,1935.

My Father, 1931 Ludwig (Louis) Beck

My Mother "The Model"

Last photo of me in Berlin, 1939.

My Father "The Dandy"

With Cousin Steffi Beck
in London. She left
Berlin in 1936.

Uncle Kurt Beck left
Berlin for Australia in 1936.
He served in World War II.

My Father's
German Army Wound Badge.

These weathered 1919 records revealed that
My father received 65% disability for wounds
suffered in World War I. He received a
disability pension for the rest of his life.

Iron Cross,
First Class

Iron Cross,
Second Class

The Honor Cross of
the World War, 1914-1918

Awarded to my Father in World War I.
The Iron Cross was our Ticket to Freedom in 1939.

Mother and me on deck
enroute to Ecuador, 1939.

Me in Quayaquil,
Ecuador, 1939.

In my first uniform as
a drum major in 1939.

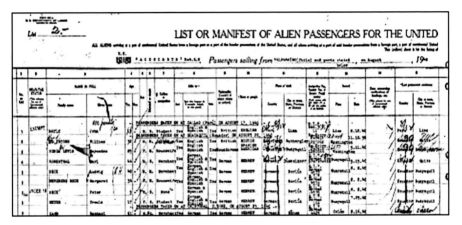

LIST OR MANIFEST OF ALIEN PASSENGERS FOR THE UNITED

Three "Alien" Becks going to America, at last! (Lines 5, 6 and 7).

Welcome to the Promised Land.
New York, August 30, 1940.

War Rages in Europe.
Summer of 1940.

Mohonk Mountain House in New Palz, New York. Home of the Mohonk School For Boy's where I was sent after my Mother died in 1944.

Dad and me by the Studebaker in front of our new home near Waynesville, North Carolina. 1945 to 1948.

Certificate of Naturalization for my Father and my Certificate of Citizenship. We are now citizens of America! 1946.

As a First Class Scout, looking to the future. I became an Eagle Scout in April 1952.

I passed the city wide examination to attend Stuyvesant High School in Manhattan and graduated from there in June 1952.

Syracuse University where I received a Bachelor of Arts Degree on June 2, 1956. I was also commissioned a Second Lieutenant in the Marine Corps Reserve.

Where I started my Marine Corps career after joining the Platoon Leaders Program while a Junior at Syracuse University. I was sworn in as a Corporal in the Marine Corps Reserve on February 7, 1955, here in the Old Post Office building in Buffalo, New York.

THIRD MARINE DIVISION
Fleet Marine Force, Pacific

3rd Battalion, 3rd Marines
Camp Fuji, Mainland Japan, 1957
Okinawa, Japan, 1958
Philippine Islands, 1958
Division Staff, Okinawa, 1975-76

At Graduation,
Officers Basic School,
February 2, 1957.

My first duty station, Camp Fuji, Japan, and my first command as Company Commander of "H" Company, 3/3.

Company Headquarters tent in Camp Driftwood at Naval Base Subic Bay, Philippines, 1958.

As a Series Officer with my DI Team at
MCRD, Parris Island, SC, 1958.

Col J. Platt introduces CMC, Gen.
D. M. Shoup, during a Mess Night
at MarBks, Washington.

First Lieutenant at MarBks,
Washington, D.C.
1959

On Parade at Marine Barracks, Washington, D.C.
(8th & I), "The Oldest Post of the Corps."
I am the leader of the second platoon.

The 184th Marine Corps Birthday Celebration at the
Shoreham Hotel, Washington, D.C., on November 10, 1959.

Traditionally, the youngest Marine present receives the second piece of cake
and in 1959, I was that Marine. I received the cake from General R. Mc. Pate, the
Commandant of the Marine Corps. Observing the proceedings in the background were the Secretary of Defense, the Secretary of the Navy and the Chief
of Naval Operations.

Col Jonas M. Platt and the Officers of Marine Barracks, Washington, D.C, 1960.
I am in the next to the last row (smiling). Three of the officers shown were later
killed in action in Vietnam.

SECOND MARINE DIVISION
Fleet Marine Force, Atlantic
1st Battalion, 2nd Marines
Assistant G-4, Headquarters, 2nd Marine Division
Camp Lejune, NC, Caribbean and Mediterranean.
Operation "Steel Pike"
1962-1965

Leading Delta Company, 1/2,
on a conditioning march in
the rain, Pilos, Greece, 1963.

Taking a break enroute to
Barcelona, Spain.

Landing in Sardinia.

At Vieques, Puerto Rico,1964.

Operation *STEEL PIKE* in Spain

MINNEAPOLIS TRIBUNE 5
Mon., Oct. 26, 1964

U.S., Spanish Forces Stage Mock Invasion

HUELVA, Spain —(AP)— A massive mock invasion by U.S. and Spanish forces was to begin at dawn today on sandy beaches near where Christopher Columbus embarked on his voyage in 1492.

Billed as the largest amphibious exercises since World War II, "Operation Steel Pike" involves a landing force of 28,000 U.S. Marines and several thousand Spanish troops.

Under Vice Adm. John S. McCain Jr. and Spanish navy Capt. Martel Vinicgra, the attackers were to disembark from a fleet of 80 U.S. and 14 Spanish warships and transports under conditions simulating amphibious warfare.

Among the observers were the U.S. secretary of the Navy, Paul H. Nitze; the Spanish naval minister, Adm. Pedro Nieto Antunez; Sen. Richard B. Russell, D-Ga., ranking member of the Senate Armed Services Committee, and Rep. L. Mendel Rivers, D-S.C.

The Division G-4 area during Operation *Steel Pike* at Huelva, Spain, October 1964. I am on the right standing next to Colonel King, the AC/S-G4.

The Bag Man has our liberty money!

Father Lou visits me in Miami, Florida, in July 1965 before my return to Gitmo after the birth of my son, Paul.

Colonel "Cold Steel" Walker and the Officer Staff of Marine Barracks, Naval Base, Guantanamo Bay, Cuba. 1965

The Guard Company at Marine Barracks,
Guantanamo Bay, Cuba, 1965.

At the sentry pillbox at the
main gate from Cuba to Gitmo.

I am the "Sheriff of Gitmo."
1965

The Naval Brig Staff at Guantanamo. I am
the Brig Officer and I just received a plaque
upon my transfer to Junior School (AWS) in
Quantico, Virginia, 1965.

Admiral Bulkeley's answer to Castro.
He cut the water line into Gitmo from
Cuba at the main gate and put this
sign up so that the Cuban sentries
could photograph it.

Promotion to Major at HQMC
by my first wife, Sharron, and Maj Gen.
Paul Tyler, Quartermaster General
of the Marine Corps. 1966.

The White House, Washington, D.C.

Shaking hands with President Lyndon Johnson after my friend, Major Howie Lee, received the Medal of Honor for heroism in Vietnam.
October 1967.

FIRST MARINE DIVISION
Fleet Marine Force, Pacific

1st Battalion, 7th Marines
Headquarters, 7th Marines
Vietnam, 1968-69

Me with Lt Col Bill Bethel (left), CO, 1/7, at Dai Loc District HQ,

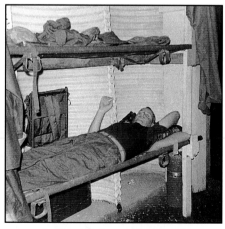

In the 1/7 Command Bunker.
My first night with the Battalion
Vietnam, September, 1968.

"Rambo Beck" without a flak jacket and helmet, which makes me an idiot. With SSgt Lorenzo and 1st Lt. Thompson. Vietnam, 1968.

Alpha Company, 1/7, with captured NVA rockets ammo and one of our fake NVA flags.

Maj Nick Carter, 1/7 Executive Officer (right) and me at Hieu Duc District HQ, Vietnam, 1968.

Maj Nick Carter (right) with Mr Cu, our laundryman and me with Ho, our captured NVA barber. 1968.

Welcome to Headquarters of 1/7 outside the old French Fort in Dai Loc. I was the Executive Officer of the the Battalion at this time, January 1969.

My driver and all-around great Marine, the "famous" Benny X, reinforcing our "hooch" after a mortar attack.

Colonel Gildo Codispoti,
CO, 7th Marines.
One hell of a Marine and a great
and fearless combat leader.

Me and SSgt Douglas Burke
experiencing the Vietnam
monsoon season, 1969.

The operations tower at Fort Courage,
Hill 55, Vietnam, 1969.

Sgt Bob DePeau, my tower
operator at Fort Courage, Vietnam
1969.

That's me hooking up an external
load of water trailers to a CH-53
hovering over the strip at
Fort Courage, Vietnam, 1969.

Me and my good friend, Bill Krulak,
Assistant Operations Officer of the
7th Marines, outside the Regimental
Operations bunker. 1969.

I have just informed Lt Gen H. Nickerson, CG, III MAF, Maj Gen O. Simpson, CG, 1st Mar Div and BGen D. Robertson, ADC, 1st Mar Div, that the reviewing stand I had built for a parade was made from an old outhouse. Vietnam, 1969.

Receiving the Legion of Merit Medal for service in Vietnam at a parade at MCRD, San Diego, in Jan. 1970.

Cathie, my second wife, whom I met at MCRD, San Diego, 1971.

Cathie and me in New York City where I introduced her to my parents in 1971.

193

Drinking a cold Primo beer after completing a 3 mile PFT run with the Boss, Maj Gen Ralph "Smoke" Spanjer. Hawaii, 1974.

Dad and Dora visit us in Hawaii in 1975 and get married after being together for 27 years. Dad is still "The Dandy."

A Japanese reenactment of our wedding done on Okinawa in 1975.

Our last Marine Corps Birthday Ball before retirement, Washington, D.C. 1977.

Receiving the Joint Services Commendation Medal from Maj Gen Lang upon departing Hawaii for Okinawa, 1975.

Lt Gen Andy O'Donnell presents me with the Meritorious Service Medal upon my retirement from the Marine Corps on March 31, 1978.

SEMPER FIDELIS

LIEUTENANT COLONEL PETER S. BECK
U. S. MARINE CORPS, 1956-1978
0302/0402/3002

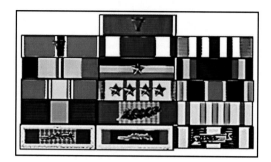

PERSONAL AWARDS

Legion of Merit with Combat "V" for exceptionally meritorious conduct in performing outstanding service in combat in Vietnam with the 7th Marines, First Marine Division in 1968-1969.

Bronze Star Medal with Combat "V" for heroic actions in combat on Hill 55, Vietnam, on 27 May 1969.

Meritorious Service Medal for outstanding service with the Plans & Policies Division at Headquarters Marine Corps. Presented upon retirement.

Joint Services Commendation Medal for meritorious service while serving as Executive Assistant to the Director of Operations for Commander in Chief, Pacific Command at Headquarters in Hawaii.

Combat Action Ribbon for participating in ground combat operations.

Vietnam Gallantry Cross, Bronze Palm Class (Foreign decoration).

Vietnam Armed Forces Honor Medal, 1st Class (Foreign decoration).

UNIT AWARDS

Presidential Unit Citation, 2 awards to the 1st Mar Div.

Navy Unit Commendation to 1st Battalion, 7th Marines, 1st Mar Div

Vietnam Meritorious Unit Citation of Gallantry Cross Color with Palm and Frame (Foreign award).

Vietnam Meritorious Unit Citation of Civil Actions 1st Class Color with Palm and Frame (Foreign award)

SERVICE AWARDS

National Defense Service Medal for military service during the Vietnam War.

Vietnam Service Medal with 4 combat engagement stars.

Navy-Marine Corps Overseas Service Ribbon for duty with 3rd Mar Div, Okinawa, Japan.

Marine Corps Drill Instructor Ribbon for service in Recruit Training Regiment and as Director, Drill Instructor School, MCRD, San Diego.

Republic of Vietnam Campaign Medal to recognize military service in Vietnam (Foreign award).

BRONZE STAR MEDAL
WITH
CHIVAS REGAL DISTINGUISHING DEVICE

AWARDED TO
MAJOR PETER S. BECK, USMC
**FOR HEROIC ACTIONS ON 27 MAY 1969
HILL 55, QUANG NAM PROVINCE, VIETNAM**

A SPECIAL AWARD

with an *unauthorized* distinguishing device
which is a replica of a bottle of Chivas Regal scotch.

While I did receive the Bronze Star Medal with the Combat "V" device, this special one of a kind award was made and presented to me by my good friend of over 53 years duration, Colonel Barney Chen/Schenn, USMC, Retired. The presentation was made on 10 November 2011, at an appropriate place, the Bar at the Marines Memorial Club in San Francisco, California.

Barney said the exploit should not go unnoticed any longer, and Chivas Regal should be recognized for their contribution to the war effort.

We toasted with . . . Chivas Regal, of course!

**My Stepmother, Dorathea Neumann Hertenried.
Photograph taken in Paris, France, circa 1975.**

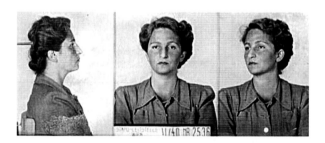

*Dorothea Herz-Hertenried, Wien
Geboren am 8. August 1906*

Official photographs taken when Dora was arrested by the Gestapo in June 1940 and detained in a prison in Vienna for 90 days. She was then mysteriously released and warned to leave the country, which she did.

IN MEMORIAM

Lou and Dora Beck

*Two of the finest people I was
fortunate enough to meet in my lifetime.
Great friends, great role models,
and loving and adoring parents.*

It doesn't get much better than that !

Lou 1899-1979
Dora 1906-1980

CHAPTER 12

GUANTANAMO BAY, CUBA

"GITMO"

To say I was reporting for duty in Cuba would be a misnomer. Since Castro had taken over the island in 1959, the only place on the island that Americans were allowed was the sprawling Naval Base in Guantanamo Bay. Located at the southeastern end of the island of Cuba, the base had been in continuous operation as a US base in the Caribbean since the end of the Spanish-American War in 1898. It is the oldest overseas US Naval Base in the world, and the only base in a country with which the United States does not have diplomatic relations.

The US is in Guantanamo based on a lease signed in 1903 and modified again in 1934, with the total agreement of both the Cuban and the US governments. The lease states that Guantanamo Bay is leased to the United States and the only way the lease can be broken is if both sides agree, simultaneously, to void the lease. This is an interesting clause, since, over the years, each country has wanted to break the lease, but never at the same time, therefore, the lease held as it does to this day.

During the Spanish-American War, the US Fleet in the Caribbean rode out the summer hurricane season in Guantanamo Bay. The Marines aboard the ships pushed the Spanish off the island, with the support of Cuban Scouts. The land then became the US Naval Station, Guantanamo Bay, which covers about 45 square miles and is abbreviated as *GITMO*.

The lease between the US and Cuba was signed in 1903, and the lease price was $2,000 in US gold coins per year. In 1934, this amount was increased to $4,085 in US dollars, and the lease was made permanent. Since the Cuban Revolution, the government under Fidel Castro has cashed only one rent check from the US government. The Cuban government maintains this was done only because of the confusion in the heady days following the successful revolution, while the US government maintains that the act of cashing the check constitutes an official validation of the treaty as written. All the remaining rent checks remain uncashed.

Until the revolution, thousands of Cubans commuted daily to jobs on the base. In mid-1959, vehicular traffic was stopped, and workers were required to walk through the base's several gates. Because the Cuban government prohibited new recruitment of Cuban workers, only workers already employed were allowed to continue until their retirement. When I landed at Gitmo, there were only 650 workers crossing into the base through a single, heavily fortified gate. This was from an original figure of over 4,000 workers before Castro.

During the Cuban Missile crisis of 1962, all military families on Gitmo were evacuated to the United States. After the crisis was over, Navy families were allowed to return to the base, but the Marine Corps remained in a combat status on the base and Marine dependents never returned to Gitmo.

Since 1939, the base's water had been supplied by pipelines that drew water from the Yateras River, and the US government paid for this service. In 1964, the monthly fee paid to the Cuban government for water was about $14,000 per month for about 2.5 million gallons per day. In 1964, the Cuban government stopped the flow. The base had about 14 million gallons of water stored in tanks on the base, and strict water conservation was put in place immediately. The US first imported water from Jamaica by barges, and then built two desalination plants on the base.

When the Cuban government accused the US of stealing water from Cuba, Rear Admiral John D. Bulkeley, USN, the Base Commander, and a World War II Medal of Honor recipient (he commanded the PT boat that evacuated General MacArthur from the Philippines), ordered the pipeline to be cut and a section removed. The point where the water pipeline was cut was in full view of the Cuban guards at the main gate of the base, and the sections that were removed were put on permanent display at the main gate in full view of the Cuban gatehouse and the Cuban Army guards.

After the 1959 revolution, some Cubans sought refuge on the base. In the fall of 1961, Cuba had its troops plant an 8 mile barrier of cactus along the northeastern section of the fence. US troops placed 75,000 land mines across the no-man's land between the US and the Cuban border, while the Cubans did the same, creating the second largest minefield in the world and the largest in the Western Hemisphere. The press referred to this no-man's land around the base as *The Cactus Curtain*.

In 1996, the US removed all of their mines and replaced them with motion and sound sensors, but the Cuban mines remain in place. It was this atmosphere that greeted me upon my arrival at Gitmo in 1965. While I thought I was going into a combat zone in Cuba, U.S. Marines had landed in Da Nang, Vietnam, on March 8, 1965. My fellow Marines were now engaged in a real shooting war while I was playing around with the Cuban Army in Gitmo. The irony of the whole issue was that Marines in Vietnam and Marines in Gitmo were both considered to be engaged in combat related duties. In reality, the Gitmo Marines were on a picnic compared to the Marines in Vietnam.

I landed in Gitmo at the Naval Air Station that was separated from the main base by the lower portion of Guantanamo Bay. The only way to get across to the main base was by ferry, which was a bulky landing craft of World War II vintage. I was met by a Warrant Officer who identified himself as the Adjutant of the Marine Barracks. I got into his jeep, and we drove through the huge main base to Marine Point, the name Naval personnel gave to the enclave housing the Marine Barracks and the official quarters for Marine families who were no longer allowed to be at Gitmo. The actual name of the place was Deer Point, and it was an idyllic location on a spit of land jutting into lower Guantanamo Bay.

We arrived at the Barracks, and I reported for duty to the Commanding Officer, Colonel Anthony Walker, one of the legendary characters of World War II, who, in 1965, was in his 27th year of service in the Marine Corps. Colonel Walker had been a football player at Yale and had received a commission as a second lieutenant in the Marines. When the war broke out in 1941, he was a first lieutenant and became one of the first Marine officers to be engaged in combat when he landed with his platoon on Guadalcanal. Because of heavy casualties he became a company commander, and when his company ran out of ammunition during a firefight, he ordered his troops to fix bayonets and led them in a successful bayonet charge that apparently terrorized the Japanese and saved his company. For his actions that day he was awarded the first of two Silver Stars he would receive in World War II, and he was forever tagged with the nickname of *Cold Steel Walker*, a name I felt he rather enjoyed.

He was a big man, standing about 6 feet 3 inches tall, and looked like he could still play the lineman's position at which he had distinguished himself at Yale. He had a brusque way about him, spoke in a very loud voice and had the habit of always looking over his glasses at you as though he was admonishing a young schoolboy. He was a tough old bird with a thick Boston accent and a heart of gold well hidden beneath his rather gruff and intimidating persona. In short, he was an outstanding field commander, and I could tell instantly that my days in Gitmo would be challenging and eventful.

Colonel Walker welcomed me to the Barracks and informed me that I was assigned duties as the Commanding Officer of the Guard Company, with additional duties as the 10th Naval District Brig Officer. This meant I was taking over a unit of 300 Marines composed of three officers, ten staff noncommissioned officers and approximately 295 infantry troops, whose sole duty was to guard the perimeter fence line surrounding the base facing the Cuban military posts. My Marines also manned the only open gate to Cuba which allowed workers access to the base to continue their employment until they qualified for retirement. When they became eligible for retirement, they were forced to quit their jobs and return to Cuba permanently.

During my initial meeting with Colonel Walker, he brought me up to date on the pressing issues at the base. The first matter was the importance of the Brig. Since Gitmo was considered a combat zone, it was necessary to fill sand bags continuously for use as reinforcements at all the perimeter fence guard stations. The hot sun and humid weather eroded the bags quickly so new bags were constantly needed. These bags were supplied by the brig which used prison labor to fill them. This made the brig a real hard labor facility, as prisoners would fill sand bags eight hours per day. This was accomplished in the sand dunes surrounding the base and was always done under armed Marine guards.

Naval commanders had the authority to sentence Sailors to the brig for thirty days for minor infractions aboard ship. Ship's captains waited until they pulled into port at Gitmo to sentence their troublemakers to a thirty day brig sentence. The brig was always operating at capacity, and our sandbag supply never ran out. It was essential that the brig be kept difficult but extremely fair, and void of any problems, either from the prisoners or the guards. Towards that end, Colonel Walker informed me that the brig personnel were the cream of the crop at the Barracks, and my initial inspection of the brig a few days later confirmed that point. Furthermore, the Colonel informed me that the morale of the fence guards was of the utmost importance. The job was boring, but had to be performed at the highest state of readiness, twenty-four hours a day, seven days a week. Troop morale had to be maintained at a high level at all times, and it was my responsibility to see that it was. He charged me and my officers to ensure that this mandate was constantly carried out.

If Cuba ever decided to attack the base, it would occur at the fence line, and we were the first line of defense for the base. Supporting units from the 2nd Marine Division, such as tanks and artillery, were available to us at the base, but had to be alerted to prepare for action. We were the eyes and ears of the base, the first responders, as Colonel Walker liked to say.

The final issue was the plush quarters the Marine Corps had for Marine families at Deer Point. Since the Marines secured the base from the Spanish during the Spanish-American War in 1898, they selected the prime piece of real estate on the base for their headquarters. They had managed to hold on to the property by erecting the Marine Barracks on the site and then building ten beautiful Caribbean island style homes. Each house had three bedrooms with a large kitchen and dining room, an open, airy living room protected from the sea breezes by screened windows and louvered window frames. Large electric fans cooled each room and blew the island breezes throughout the house. Wicker furniture accented the Caribbean nature of the surroundings. There was also a staff of gardeners who maintained the palm trees, bushes, lawns and vines that decorated each house and protected it from the glaring Cuban sun.

When Marine Headquarters decided that Marine families could not go to Cuba, based on the possible combat threat to the base and the need to keep Marines always "at the ready," the Navy made a concerted effort to reclaim the houses for Navy families. The Commandant of the Marine Corps countered the move and designated all housing at Deer Point as bachelor quarters. When I arrived, all the houses were occupied by Marines, with either an officer or a senior staff noncommissioned officer assigned to one bedroom per house. Thus, there were three Marines living in each house on Deer Point in the lap of luxury. I was assigned to a large house overlooking the bay that already housed two first lieutenants, both of whom worked for me as guard officers. Since I was a captain, I was the senior officer and received the master bedroom in the house.

I went about the business of meeting my command, both at the Guard Company and at the Brig, which was fully separated from all other activities on the base. I drove around the entire base with my executive officer, First Lieutenant Charles E. Davis, a Naval Academy graduate who had opted to go into the Marine Corps. Chuck was a 6 foot 4 inch tall, Force Reconnaissance Marine, who was a paratrooper, scuba diver and underwater swimmer, having gone to the Navy UDT (Underwater Demolition Team, forerunner of today's SEALS) schools. Chuck had been a three-year All-American at the Naval Academy, but not, as most people thought when they saw him, in football, but rather in baseball, where he was one of the best collegiate pitchers in the country. He was the captain of the US baseball team when they competed in the Pan American Games, and was heavily recruited by professional baseball teams while at Annapolis, most notably the Baltimore Orioles and the New York Yankees. His initial five-year military obligation upon graduation made it impossible for him to accept any offers.

Over time, we became very close friends. Chuck and I drove all over the base, and Chuck, having both a genius IQ and a sincere interest in history, gave me a detailed history of the Gitmo base. Originally, Gitmo was strategically vital to the Navy as a coaling station. Navy ships ran on coal, and the location of Gitmo made it ideal to service all Atlantic Fleet ships on training exercises in the Caribbean. A large logistics base was developed which made it capable of conducting heavy ship repairs. Along with that capability, machine parts were manufactured, and it boasted a complete metal foundry.

With all these activities, it became necessary to hire and train skilled labor, and the local Cubans proved themselves both capable and highly intelligent. A large naval hospital was built, and almost the entire nursing and orderly staffs were composed of Cuban trained professionals. Quarters were built, and community support activities were conducted which kept life on the base pleasant and entertaining. Officers employed the services of local maids and butlers. Officers clubs were as plush as any stateside country club, and weekends could be spent in the large city of Santiago de Cuba, home of the giant Bacardi Rum Distillery, where there were wonderful, restaurants and night clubs. A train ride of several hours would take you to the bustling capital of Havana. Sailors and Marines who had experienced Cuban duties in the old days all spoke glowingly of the great times they had while on the "Cuba Station."

My duties as Brig Officer of the 10th Naval District put me under the direct command of the Base Commander, Rear Admiral John D. Bulkeley, USN, the most decorated naval officer of World War II, and one of the most unusual and inspirational leaders of men I have ever met. Admiral Bulkeley's biography is worth reading, and his exploits during the war were written about in a book entitled, *They Were Expendable*. Later, the book was made into a movie with the same name, starring Robert Montgomery and John Wayne. During my tour of duty, I became personally friendly with the Admiral, who always referred to me as "the Captain of my Marines". There are many stories about the Admiral at Guantanamo, and there will be a few in this chapter. As I got to know him, he would joke with me that he always resented the fact that the actor Robert Montgomery played him in the movie when he personally felt that it should have been John Wayne!

My company of Marines, who manned the fence line and the main gate post, were composed of Marines from all over the United States. They were trained infantrymen, and it was my responsibility to maintain their training and keep them poised to react to any acts of aggression by the Cubans.

The nature of duty at Guantanamo required that at least 50 percent of Marines speak Spanish. The Marine Corps, in an attempt to be 100 percent fair to all concerned, sent 25 percent of our Spanish speaking Marines from Puerto Rico and 25 percent from Mexican extraction, usually from Texas, California, and the states of the Southwest. Thus, I had 50 percent of my Marines that spoke Spanish, but only 25 percent who could be put on duty at the main gate. It seemed that the Cubans felt that Puerto Ricans spoke a "bastardized" Spanish and refused to speak with them, while, according to the Cubans, the Mexican-American Marines spoke a more distinct "Castilian" dialect of Spanish, and, therefore, were acceptable to the Cubans crossing over from Cuba into the base. My Puerto Rican Marines were great on the fence line, where they traded curses on a continuing basis with the Cuban soldiers on the other side of the Cactus Curtain. They could also easily intercept radio traffic between Cuban units using our more sophisticated radio surveillance equipment.

Life on the base was isolated. While Navy personnel did have their families with them, they could not go anywhere and were restricted to the base. "Island fever" was a common malady, and the base command provided every form of entertainment possible. There was an excellent system of clubs for all ranks, there were several well run base restaurants, the base theaters played the most current movies, there were bowling alleys, swimming pools, roller rinks, pool halls, handball and tennis courts and beaches that were right on the Caribbean. Intramural sports at every level were played throughout the year, with complete uniforms and regulation playing fields. League play in every sport was closely controlled, and there were championship tournaments in every sport. Because of the unique environment of the base, civilians were allowed to play on command sponsored, teams. Since the Cubans loved baseball, the Naval Hospital, which employed the largest number of Cubans on the base, had the best baseball team. The Naval Hospital team were the "Yankees" of the base.

Because there was a considerable need for civilian labor, the 650 line-crossers were extremely valuable to the base, however, every month that figure was reduced as another Cuban worker reached his retirement date. For those Cubans who decided to defect from Cuba and remain on the base permanently, an entire village was built to house them and to provide them with some form of indigenous recreation, most specifically, Cuban music.

Since we did not have enough Cubans remaining on the base to service the many areas requiring local labor, the base began to contract with Jamaicans through a Kingston, Jamaica, hiring office. These workers were granted one-year employment contracts and were also housed in a civilian housing area. This turned out to be a mistake, because the

Cubans and the Jamaicans did not like each other. One of the major areas of disagreement was over music, which could be heard coming from the civilian village at all hours of the night. While the Cuban music was mellow and jazz-like, the Jamaican music tended to be far louder and more robust, with many ska and calypso beats, not to mention homemade steel band drums. Friday and Saturday nights, when work was not required, and the liquor flowed, my brig received a large number of drunks from both sides of the village.

While the base police maintained order, those personnel, both Cuban and Jamaican, who did not observe the rules, were sentenced to jail. The jail was my brig, and so I wound up with a military brig and a civilian jail, where I had to segregate the Cubans and the Jamaicans. It made for a constant challenge for me and my brig guards, and it became an enormous problem as the Cuban population dwindled, and the Jamaican population increased. I was running a three culture detention center which required extremely close attention to detail, and the highest levels of security, both inside the facility and outside on work details.

Since the military situation was a never changing threat condition, my officers and I were essentially on duty 24 hours a day, 7 days a week. Without the civilian population, there were over 9,500 Sailors and Marines on the base, plus the Navy families. It was essentially a small city with all the problems and challenges such an environment presents. It was a common sight to see armed Marines walking around the base which gave Marines somewhat of a "cowboy" image, an image that we did very little to dispel. We drove around the base in jeeps, with large "whip" radio antennas that also had flack jackets, helmets, a rifle, extra ammunition, flares, radio batteries, first aid supplies and other combat essential items in a locked box welded onto the chassis of the jeep, a classic "Southern Sheriff" persona. Inside the jeep was a permanently attached radio that could contact any post on the fence line, as well as the Barracks and the Guard Company communications center.

While the fence line extended entirely around the base, the Guard Company was only responsible for the fence line surrounding the main base. The remainder of the base, which was on the other side of the bay, was guarded by units of the 2nd Marine Division, who were sent to Guantanamo for three month periods of duty. Besides the 2nd Division Marines, Marines assigned to the squadrons based at the airfield on the other side of the bay, also augmented the guard forces of the 2nd Marine Division troops. This, then, comprised our armed camp, and it was the responsibility of the Marines at Gitmo to ensure the safety of the base at all times. If we received an alarm, we only had to jump into our jeeps, and rush out of the base onto the dirt roads leading to the main gate and the perimeter fence line.

Due to this constant state of alert, we were always treated with respect by the Navy and especially their families, who seemed to look upon us as their local police force. While we lived "at the ready," we certainly availed ourselves of all the good things about being stationed at Gitmo. We ate at the Officer's Club, where we were allowed to carry weapons at all times, we enjoyed tennis and swimming, keeping our weapons locked in our lockers, but always having our radios at the ready, no matter where we were.

We played intramural football, where I was the center on the Marine Barracks team and my friend, Chuck Davis, was the quarterback, and we played intramural baseball, where Chuck Davis was our right fielder and best hitter on our team. We played the games at a first class ballpark, and I was the public address system announcer for all of our baseball games. Since baseball was the favorite sport of Cuba, many Cubans participated on the intramural teams of the facilities where they worked. This made the baseball season especially active and the ballpark was filled for every game.

In 1965, the commanding officer of the Naval Hospital decided he wanted to win the baseball championship of the base, and he fielded a team made up entirely of Cuban hospital employees, who also happened to be exceptionally talented baseball players. There were two leagues in the intramural competition, with the champion of each league playing the other for the base championship. At the end of the regular season, the Naval Hospital won their league, having literally destroyed every team they had played by very wide margins.

In the other league, Marine Barracks won and thus, the stage was set for the championship game two weeks after the regular season ended. Colonel Walker decided he wanted to win the championship, and told Chuck Davis he would pitch the championship game. Chuck had purposely not pitched during the regular season because he felt that, based on his experience and skill, it would be unfair and he had not pitched in a meaningful game since leaving the Naval Academy four years earlier.

Colonel Walker, true to his "Cold Steel" nickname, found out that the Barracks Executive Officer, Lieutenant Colonel Charlie Stephenson, had been an All-American catcher at Holy Cross University. LtCol Stephenson had not caught a ballgame in over ten years, but Col Walker ordered Chuck and LtCol Stephenson to practice in utmost secrecy, so that on the day of the big game they would comprise the battery for the Marine Barracks against the Naval Hospital's Cubans. They had two weeks to get ready, and Colonel Walker relieved them of all other duties so that they could prepare for the game.

Each day, LtCol Stephenson and Chuck would train in almost total secrecy behind the main Barracks building. The maintenance department had built a pitcher's mound and set up a plywood shield behind home plate. They practiced religiously, and Marines would stop by and watch them. It took a few days for LtCol Stephenson to learn how to handle the extremely fastballs that Chuck could throw, and it took a little longer to master the curves and the sinkers that came at him. By the end of the first week, anticipation was high for the championship game that would be played on a Saturday afternoon.

The Base newspaper, the *Guantanamo Bay Gazette*, which came out daily, kept writing about the excellence of the Naval Hospital team. Since it was a Navy publication, the newspaper, anticipated a strong showing and a definite victory from the Naval Hospital team. About four days before the game, word leaked out that the Marine Barracks had a surprise for everyone. Naval officers soon discovered that First Lieutenant Davis of the Marine Barracks was also the former Midshipman Chuck Davis, the Naval Academy All-American pitcher. Not only was he the same, he was going to pitch for the Marine Barracks in the championship game, and this gave the game a much greater level of importance. The

Admiral indicated he would attend the game and throw out the first pitch. A Naval Academy alum and a great friend of the Marines, the Admiral could show no partiality, but we all felt that he secretly would like to see the Marines defeat the Naval Hospital "Cubans."

The day of the game came, and the stands were packed. I had never seen such a crowd at the ballpark, and fans brought folding chairs to sit alongside the outfield because the stands were packed very early. The Navy Band played the *National Anthem* and the Admiral threw out the first ball, and the game got underway. As each Cuban batter came to the mound, convinced that they could get a hit off the Marine Barracks pitcher, they returned to the bench utterly confounded by the range and speed of the pitches being thrown to them. In the end, the Marine Barracks won the game 4 to 0, and Chuck Davis threw a no-hitter against the semiprofessional Cuban baseball players of the Naval Hospital team. It was a magnificent accomplishment. Admiral Bulkeley later presented him with a beautiful silver trophy from Tiffany's in New York City. Chuck cherishes that trophy to this day, because after that game he never threw another pitch, having completely thrown out his arm in the winning effort.

In another sport, the Marine Barracks football team, where I was the center, was playing for the base championship against the Base Seabees. The game came down to the final minute, with the Marine Barracks team on the Seabee three-yard line. All I had to do was center the ball to Chuck Davis, and he could easily run the ball in for the winning score. My moment came, the crowd was silent and, for some inexplicable reason, I centered the ball over Chuck's head and we lost the game. It was not funny then, but we laugh over that play to this day. As Chuck was quick to point out, a captain playing center was not going to guarantee anything! I still laugh over that play, just thinking about it right now as I am writing these words. I guess the look on my face, as I realized what a bonehead play I had just made, is what makes Chuck laugh to this day. I know how Bill Buckner of the Red Sox felt on his ignominious day, having been there myself.

Social life at the base revolved around athletics, tennis and swimming at the officer's club, and dancing at the various venues. I was never a particularly good dancer, but Chuck was a superb one, and the ladies at the clubs all wanted to dance with him. He taught me the art of dancing in the privacy of our wonderful home at Deer Point.

Our military duties were discharged with the same degree of enthusiasm. It was no small challenge to keep the fence line troops on their toes. We knew that especially in the hours of darkness, when there was no sound and little activity, attention spans tended to wander and, in some cases, sentries could fall asleep. Sleeping on watch is a dangerous thing to do and, in the Marine Corps, is subject to immediate and rather harsh punishment. A reduction in rank is generally guaranteed, with a court-martial usually included in the punishment.

In addition, notations are made in your official record. If you were considering remaining in the Corps, your chances for reenlistment were considerably less. I felt it was my responsibility to ensure that my troops did not suffer the serious indignities associated with sleeping on watch, so I devised a system that turned out to be downright fun for the officers and staff noncommissioned officers of the Guard Company, and served to keep all the fence line troops on their toes. Technically, "the game" started at midnight each evening, but I never published a timetable, and this also served to keep everyone alert. The game was an easy one. There were 27 posts on the fence line, stretching from the "Water-gate" at the mouth of the bay that entered the Base, all the way to the ocean, where the base land ended by culminating at the shores of our recreational beach on the Caribbean shore.

The Cactus Curtain extended for about 300 yards between our fence line and the Cuban guard stations. The area was bare and cut back and full of antipersonnel mines, interspersed with occasional vehicular and antitank mines. In a like manner, the areas in front of our guard stations were similarly mined, but the areas behind our guard stations, which were on the base side of the guard towers, were full of trenches and heavy vegetation. It was purposely kept that way, because if there was an all-out crisis, the trenches and brush would serve to camouflage the reinforcing troops who would move into position in those trenches immediately upon receiving an alarm. The trenches also had built in gun positions and wire connections to implement immediate readiness and instant communications between the reinforcing troops and the guard towers. The sand bags that were constantly being filled by the prisoners at the Brig were used to reinforce the fighting positions, and to replace sandbags that had deteriorated due to the hot sun.

I decided we would use the trench line as a way to sneak up on our guard towers at night and check on the alertness of the troops. This was not exactly a safe practice, since we were sneaking up on armed troops, but the troops knew better than to fire into the base, instead of across the fence line, so the risk was never that great. Besides sneaking up on the troops, we all carried wire cutters and wire connectors that allowed us to eavesdrop on the troops. We kept off the radios, because the Cubans could easily monitor our radio transmissions, but they could not monitor our wire communications and all of our posts were wired into one another. The posts would identify themselves by number, each number indicating the location of the post. While the wire network was supposed to be used for official business only, at night it became a "Bravo Sierra" network (Bravo Sierra denoting the letters B and S or "Bullshit" network). The troops would gossip and just amuse each other over this network, and when we tapped into it, we would whisper a post number and try to get a conversation started. If we trapped an unsuspecting trooper into conversation, another member of our team snuck up very quietly to the post, and the purpose of that was to tap him on the helmet while he was talking and saying something rather colorful to the trooper. The sentence always included the words, "You are dead, Marine!"

It did not take the troops very long to figure out our scheme, but we still managed to trap our share of unsuspecting fence line guards. The Admiral heard about what we were doing and insisted on going out with us from time to time. I was privileged to go out with him on many nights, and I really got to know him. He was a phenomenal human being and an outstanding officer. We would sit under the stars on many nights and the Admiral would take out a planisphere (an adjustable map of the constellations in the skies) and point out all the stars that sailors use to navigate. He told me many World War II stories, especially stories relating to General MacArthur and the role of PT boats in the Pacific Theater of Operations. He also enjoyed surprising the troops, although no one was more surprised than a PFC fence line guard being tapped on the helmet by a two star Admiral, who also happened to be a recipient of the Medal of Honor.

The Brig was also an activity that required constant supervision. With the influx of the Jamaican contract workers on the base, the brig was rapidly becoming a civilian prison, and we had to severely reduce the number of Sailors we could accept from Atlantic Fleet ships which were in port for their annual readiness inspections. The problem was what to do with the civilians. While we could hold Cubans, since they had no other place to go, it was easier to deport the Jamaicans back to Kingston, without trial, just to get them off the base.

Every week, our Brig Guards accompanied Jamaicans, in chains, to the airport where they put them on airplanes to Jamaica. Once on the plane, the prisoners were as docile as puppies, since they were going home, usually with two weeks severance pay. This cleared up enough cells to handle the next consignment of weekend drunks that seemed to turn up at the brig every week.

Ship Captain's implored the Admiral to make more room at the brig because of the positive effect 30 days of hard labor had on their sailors. We built a tent camp, complete with a field mess and canvas cots, a typical Marine Corps field encampment and put the sailors into this tent camp for their 30 days of hard labor. Apparently, the hard labor of filling sand bags 8 hours per day and, what the sailors considered even harsher living conditions, served to significantly reduce discipline problems in the Atlantic Fleet. In contrast, the Marine guards thought the brig camp much too easy, and hardly up to the standards of typical Marine field deployments.

Meanwhile at Gitmo, the CIA had begun a secret operation in an attempt to undermine the communist regime of Fidel Castro. It was an operation that required assistance from the Marines of the Guard Company, and we were briefed on what was going to be happening in Gitmo soon. Dubbed, Operation *Brain Drain*, the CIA sent operatives into Cuba. Their purpose was to approach professionally qualified Cubans and persuade them to defect to the United States. They were especially targeting doctors, dentists, lawyers, engineers, architects, journalists and accountants. The only requirement was a valid university degree and a minimum of three years of experience in the field for which they held a degree. If they had a family, their entire family was also included in any effort to defect. The United States' position was simply that the defector and his family had to manage to get to the Naval Base through the "Watergate," the point where Guantanamo Bay entered the base.

Small watercraft were secreted on the shores of the upper bay near Boqueron and Caimanera, the two towns located on the upper portion of the bay, belonging to Cuba. At night, our Watergate was always well lit. Besides floodlights, we also had a rotating beacon that shined across the lower part of the bay, in timed increments. Once on the upper portion of the bay, there was no way anyone in a small boat could miss the entrance to the Watergate on the lower part of the bay. Through careful navigation, it was possible to traverse the upper portion of the bay in complete darkness, avoiding any Cuban Navy patrol boats until just before the Watergate.

Once in sight of the Watergate, the Marines would protect the entrance to the lower bay with 50 caliber machine guns, mounted on each side of the Watergate, to protect any boats attempting to enter the base. Conversely, these machine guns could impede the progress of any Cuban Navy vessel attempting to enter the base. Once on the Naval Base, the defector and his family would be flown to the Opa Locka Naval Air Station in Miami, Florida, for relocation in the United States. Often, the defector spent less than one hour on the base, because the CIA kept planes at the ready on the Gitmo airfield. This was done as a means to underscore the validity of the program, since the defector always had means to communicate with people left behind in Cuba.

To implement this plan, a cadre of Spanish language trained Marines began arriving at Gitmo. Under the command of Colonel John J. Donahue, USMC, a Defense Language Institute trained linguist, he and his team met all incoming defectors, interrogated them and accompanied them to Opa Locka for processing. In the next few days, they returned to Gitmo to begin the process again.

The operation proved to be an enormous success, however, there were two serious drawbacks. The first one and the most obvious was that it did not take long for the Cuban Navy to become aware of increased activity on upper and lower Guantanamo Bay. Patrols increased, and several defectors were killed, along with their families, in the small boats that were trying to get them to freedom. The Cubans would tow the bodies to the Watergate and then let them float into the base, a grim reminder that peace and freedom is never cheap. Even with the deaths, the flow of defectors never ceased, and flights were departing Cuba almost nightly, carrying Cuban professionals to their new homes in the United States.

The Cubans were to be relocated all across the United States, providing much needed professional services. Once in Opa Locka, however, the defectors wanted to remain in Florida and more specifically, in the Greater Miami area. Since the CIA could not direct them to go anywhere in the United States, Operation Brain Drain became the Cubanization of Miami. The thriving and robust Cuban population of Miami today began with the brave defectors of Operation Brain Drain, who embraced America by forming a vibrant and politically active society less than 150 miles north of Havana.

I have always enjoyed visiting Miami because I was involved in the relocation of the Cuban Nationals who went on to become US Senators and Congressmen, and several others have served and are now serving as Mayor of Miami. A stroll down the famed "Calle Ocho," (8th street) the center of the Cuban community in Miami, is all one needs to see that democracy works in wondrous ways. Perhaps someday, these Cuban-Americans will reinvigorate a Cuba without Fidel Castro.

Our lives at Guantanamo were full and extremely busy. On July 2, 1965, I received word that Sharron had given birth to a boy, which we named Paul, at Holy Cross Hospital in Fort Lauderdale, and mother and new son were both doing fine. On July 4, I received word that Paul had an extremely high fever and that he was not responding to any medication. The doctors in Fort Lauderdale felt that my presence was necessary, and I was immediately flown to Miami in one of the CIA planes. By the time I got to the hospital, Paul's fever had broken, and his temperature returned to normal. The doctors could not explain the fever and made a diagnosis of "fever of unknown origin."

I returned to Gitmo aboard another CIA plane and continued with my myriad duties, again settling into my role of being "the Captain of Admiral Bulkeley's Marines." In August, Colonel "Cold Steel" Walker went home and was replaced by Colonel Richard S. Johnson, a southern gentleman and an excellent officer. The problems in Gitmo began to increase as more Jamaican contract workers arrived at the base. It was a given that Jamaicans and Cubans simply did not like each other. Since Jamaicans could go home to Jamaica anytime, it seemed to underscore the helplessness of the "political prisoner" Cubans, who had to make a life for themselves aboard the base, and did not qualify for immediate resettlement in the United States.

The Navy retired Admiral Bulkeley in 1988. He was promoted to the rank of Vice Admiral after his Gitmo tour of duty and made the Admiral in charge of all ship inspections with an office at the Old Navy Yard in Washington. He lived there in a beautiful old set of government quarters for another 21 years of active duty. On the day he retired in 1988 he had completed 55 years of continuous service to the Navy and the United States.

After he retired, the Navy kept him busy lecturing at the Naval Academy, where he had graduated in 1933, and just being a perfect role model for all young sailors, as the bravest and most decorated naval officer in the history of the Navy. He died at the age of 85 in 1996, at his Maryland home. He was a phenomenal human being, and I was honored to have served under him. One of my most prized possessions is an official photograph of him inscribed by him which reads, "To Pete Beck from your shipmate and friend, with esteem." I was privileged to have served under the Navy's version of our own Marine General, "Chesty" Puller. Admiral Bulkeley's' decorations included the Medal of Honor, the Navy Cross, two Army Distinguished Service Crosses, two Distinguished Service Medals, two Silver Stars, two Legions of Merit and a Purple Heart. They just don't make them like that anymore.

In November 1965, we began getting reports of Marine battles in Vietnam. Officers I had been commissioned with in 1956 were now leading units in combat, half a world away. I felt that I was not carrying much of a burden in Cuba where Chuck and I played tennis in the afternoon, had a steak dinner in the club and drank Mateus rose' wine out of crockery bottles that, when empty, we threw against the coral walls of the club, simulating our own version of hand grenades. Stalking the troops at night to ensure constant attention on the fence line seemed like a cake walk, when compared to our comrades in arms, who were stalking the Viet Cong and the North Vietnamese regulars in the rice paddies, valleys, and mountains of Vietnam.

Among the many Navy dependents living on the base, I met a young woman, Roxanne, who was the daughter of a Commander in the Medical Service Corps and the administrator of the Naval Hospital. She was 25 years old, had been voted Miss Coast Guard of 1964, and was working as a civilian nurse at the hospital, We became extremely close friends spending almost all of our free time together. Her father knew I was married and simply told me, "I respect you as an officer of Marines, and I know you will do the right thing." He never interfered in my relationship with his daughter and because of Roxanne, my remaining time at Gitmo was idyllic and extremely happy. Her father was correct. I did the right thing, not because I wanted to, but because his daughter did. For the first time, I admitted to myself that I wished I was not married, because Roxanne and I shared something truly special that we never had a chance to develop further than a very deep friendship, which, under different circumstances, certainly would have blossomed into something much more meaningful and lasting.

Our friendship lasted through March 1966, when I received orders to attend the Marine Corps Amphibious Warfare School (AWS) in Quantico, Virginia. This school, which was of five-month duration, was formerly called the "Junior School." It was a period of formal training for company grade officers that prepared them for promotion to the rank of Major. Non-selection to this school probably meant that your future in the Marine Corps was limited.

My last week at Gitmo was extremely traumatic. I was saying goodbye to my troops, for whom I had a genuine fondness and respect, and I was leaving my brig guards, who were all outstanding and dedicated young Marines. I was leaving the Gitmo community at large, a community composed of US Navy personnel, Cuban line-crossers and Cuban exiles and Jamaican contract workers, many of whom were jovial and intelligent workers and good people. I was also leaving Roxanne, who had already broken my heart anyway, so it was probably a good thing to be leaving at that time. Given just a little more time, I do not think that she or I could have resisted much longer.

The last week was full of going away parties. The brig guards presented me with a handsome plaque that they had the machine foundry shop cast for me. It was the seal of the Marine Barracks at Guantanamo Bay, and it was cast out of solid bronze and hand painted then mounted on a beautiful piece of wood. I still have the plaque and treasure it because of all the fond memories it evokes. On the night before I was to leave, the Cubans asked me to attend a picnic in my and Chuck Davis' honor. Chuck had received orders to the Force Reconnaissance Company at Camp Pendleton, California, and we would be departing Gitmo within one week of each other. The Cubans at the picnic were both line-crossers and exiles.

The line-crossers had obtained an overnight pass from the Cubans, and that meant that they did not have to return to Cuba at the end of their shift. They would remain on the base with some exile friends after the party. Line crossers rarely had any problems from the Cuban soldiers on the other side of the fence. Line crossers were allowed to bring in three Cuban cigars every day, which they could then sell on the base for extra money.

They could leave the base each evening with a pack of American cigarettes, but the pack had to be opened, and there could only be 19 cigarettes in the pack. This was supposed to stop black market activities in Cuba, but it really didn't matter to a prospective Cuban buyer, and each base worker left with their 19 cigarette pack every evening. Sometimes, the Cuban soldiers would confiscate a pack for themselves, but only occasionally, so as not to discourage the daily movement of American cigarettes into Cuba.

The picnic began on a point of land near the officers club, and the Cubans brought all of their instruments. Cubans do not party without music, and our picnic was not going to be an exception. Several Jamaican contract workers from the officers club also were in attendance, and they brought some steel drums and cooked all the food except for the Cuban delicacies. The music started, and the rum flowed, and Chuck and I heard the longest single rendition of "La Bamba" ever heard on this earth. La Bamba is almost a round, where the number of verses is limited only by the imagination and wit of each singer, as he raises his hand and sings yet another lyric, always funny and usually dirty. Each verse is followed by much applause, laughter and an immediate challenge to the next singer to top the verse just rendered. I think that the song itself must have lasted for over four hours, with appropriate breaks for food and libation. The party extended long into the evening, and it seemed to underscore the fact that the curtain was coming down on my Cuban experience.

I was leaving a great duty station, and many good friends I would never see again. At the end of the party, both Chuck and I were presented with a small flag set to remind us of the friends we were leaving behind. The flag sets were small silk flags of the countries of Cuba and Jamaica, set into a two flag pedestal. I still have that flag set in my den today, and they were right. Every time I look at it, I think of my Cuban and Jamaican friends and the year we shared together at Guantanamo.

The next morning, March 29, 1966, I boarded a Navy Constellation aircraft for the flight to Miami airport. At Gitmo, I had made a friend that would remain one of my truly best friends to this day. There is not a single month that goes by that I do not speak with Chuck Davis, who retired as a Lieutenant Colonel and now lives outside Phoenix, Arizona. My year with him was very special. We had some marvelous times together and to this day, when we get together and recount those days in Gitmo, we always laugh out loud. It was an assignment that turned out to be a once in a lifetime opportunity, and we both grabbed it and ran with it, enjoying every minute.

I was privileged to meet and work for one of the true heroes of World War II, and number myself among those people that he liked and with whom he enjoyed spending time. I had served under the legendary "Cold Steel" Walker, and managed to satisfy his high standards of job performance. I had been a commander of two units at the same time, the Guard Company and the Naval Brig, and had managed to leave both places in excellent shape, with no unfavorable incidents occurring during my tenure as commander. I had made good friends with both Cubans and Jamaicans, who I would never see again, but who enriched my life as much as I hoped my actions and attitudes towards them had enriched theirs.

Finally, in the not so happy department, I had met a wonderful woman whom I would have married in a heartbeat, except for the fact that I was already married. I would never forget Roxanne. After Gitmo, I only saw her once, several years later, for a few hours in Washington, D.C. where she was living with her Naval officer husband.

So that was my Guantanamo experience. While the Marine Corps direct involvement in Vietnam broke out during my tour of duty and my peers were either on their way over or coming back from their first real combat experience, the Marine Corps considered my year in Gitmo to be combat-related duty, and I would not be eligible for assignment to Vietnam until 1969. Since I was going to AWS in Quantico beginning in April, I would receive an assignment upon graduation in August, and then I would have to serve in that duty station before getting a chance to see any combat duty in Vietnam. As a professional infantry officer, this would not help my promotion prospects.

CHAPTER 13

QUANTICO AND WASHINGTON, D.C. — AGAIN

AMPHIBIOUS WARFARE SCHOOL (AWS)

I looked forward to attending Amphibious Warfare School (AWS), secure in the knowledge that to have received the assignment meant I was definitely considered to be a candidate for promotion to the rank of Major sometime during my tenth year of service. This was the third time I would be stationed at Quantico, first during my Platoon Leaders Class in the summer of 1955, then during my Basic School period in 1956 and 1957 and now for AWS in 1966. I was determined to do well in AWS so I could ensure favorable consideration for promotion when the promotion board met in 1966.

We arrived at Quantico on April 6, 1966 and moved in to a townhouse in Thomason Park, an area set aside for officer students. My neighbors were Captain Bill Krulak, whose father was a Major General and Captain Pieter Hogaboom, whose father was a Lieutenant General, both in the Marine Corps. We were all going to AWS when it began on Monday, April 11, 1966.

On Monday morning, I reported to the Amphibious Warfare School, an impressive red brick building that certainly could have passed as any Ivy League college classroom building. The building had white columns in the front, administrative offices and conference rooms on the first floor, and a large auditorium that could seat the entire enrollment of each class, which usually numbered about 150 captains, most of whom were soon coming into the promotion zone for major. The second floor was entirely allocated to classrooms and instructor's offices, which gave the entire place a feeling of returning, again, to our college roots.

The interesting aspect of this class was that over three quarters of them had just returned from a tour of duty in Vietnam. As we assembled in the auditorium for our initial orientation lecture by Colonel Lowell D. Grow, a Marine aviator and the Director of the School, I could see many officers wearing at least two rows of ribbons, signifying their combat tour in Vietnam. As a ten-year veteran of the Marine Corps, I was wearing a single ribbon, the National Defense Service Medal ribbon, an award given to every military person serving on active duty. It was considered so inconsequential by Marines that it was dubbed the "*Shirley Highway Medal*," named for the old main highway that connected Quantico, Virginia, to Washington. The sarcasm was that this medal was for those officers fighting the horrible commute between Quantico and Headquarters Marine Corps. Since Marine Corps regulations required the wearing of all award ribbons as a part of your uniform, I felt somewhat embarrassed to have to wear my "Shirley Highway ribbon" in the company of officers who were wearing Silver Stars, Bronze Stars and Purple Hearts, not to mention Vietnam campaign medals with battle stars.

As Colonel Grow addressed the new students of AWS, he informed us that we would be required to study diligently, that our classes were difficult and that our progress would be monitored throughout the course of instruction. Graduation depended on the successful completion of a case study paper to be written on a subject to be approved by our faculty advisor. We were also informed that we had to select a classic, military themed book and that, along with the term paper, a 15 page book report was also required. To assist us in this task, the school had a list of 35 books which were considered acceptable for the required book report.

As far as testing was concerned, there would be a midterm examination and a final examination. Any grade below 75 percent was considered to be failing. As usual, the Marine Corps did not fool around and the standards were set high. There was no doubt in anyone's mind that our grades at this school would have an impact on our future in the Corps. All students took the same classes, had the same report requirements, and took the same exams at the same time.

The assembled class was an amalgam of every type of company grade officer in the Corps. Half the class came from aviation units and were composed of officers with aviation related skills and occupational specialties. The other half came from officers with ground related skills. This made for interesting classroom discussions with divergent opinions and field experiences, not to mention the occasional bias, but it also permitted us to see "how the other half lives."

Whenever we were broken down into work groups or discussion groups, these divergent MOS groups were always placed in the same group. Thus, we had an aviator, either helicopter or fixed wing, an air traffic control officer, a supply officer, an artillery officer, an intelligence officer, a tank officer, an engineer, a communications officer, an administrator and an infantry officer, all trying to come up with the "school solution" to case studies presented to us by the staff.

Staff instructors were mostly Marine officers. Navy Seabee officers instructed us in the aspects of field construction projects, such as forward operating base air fields, mobile pontoon bridges and fuel depots. Navy Medical Service Officers instructed us in field sanitation, medical evacuation procedures, triage requirements and immediate field first aid methods.

In our class, we had in our midst an accomplished artist who was a graduate of the Philadelphia Art Institute and had worked as a graphic artist before joining the Corps. He was an experienced infantry officer, with a tremendous sense of humor, and I had been stationed with him at Parris Island. One day, during an extremely boring two-hour lecture, he drew a caricature of the instructor, in some compromising situation, specifically related to something about which he was lecturing. While the entire caricature was rendered in a cartoon style, the instructor's face was almost a perfect portrait. The entire rendition was in several colors, and it was always finished within the period of the lecture being presented.

Captain Charlie Tye, the artist and mysterious cartoonist, chose his pen name from the name of a piece of engineering equipment used in surf landings called the Anthony Crane. Each caricature was signed Anthony Crane, and it was always placed on the bulletin board located outside the lecture hall, when no one could see who placed the drawing on the board. Each drawing was funnier and more clever than the previous drawing and the staff soon began to go to the bulletin board after lectures to see who the mysterious Anthony Crane had just lampooned. The students thought the drawings hilarious, but except for me and Captain Josh Bridges, a helicopter pilot who sat on the other side of Charlie during lectures, no one knew the identity of the infamous Anthony Crane. It turned out to be a secret that was never revealed because of the potential problems that Charlie might encounter with individual staff members who may not feel as entertained by his drawings as students and the rest of the staff. I found out several months after we graduated, that Colonel Grow, the school's Director, had saved every caricature and put them into a bound scrapbook, because they were not only extremely well rendered, they were also highly topical and humorous.

Charlie Tye and I also formed a group of officers that became an almost nightly study group, at least that is what we told our wives, and we met regularly in the back booth of Diamond Lou's Bar and Grill on Main Street in downtown Quantico. Over short beers, bought individually, we would study the topics covered in the classroom. This group was composed primarily of infantry officers, none of whom would later prove to be general officer material. It seemed that I was always attracted to the rebel type of officer, meaning one who was competent and professional when he had to be, but one who also had a bit of a wild hare streak inside that made him far more fun and much more interesting to be around.

Our group of approximately ten officers scored well on the midterm exam, and we all took time off from our nightly gatherings at Diamond Lou's, to work on our term papers and book reports. Our goal was to finish the requirements quickly to allow us more time to "study" in the back booth of Diamond Lou's. I began saving the individual beer receipts just to see how many beers we would consume during study sessions.

The curriculum at AWS was designed to train captains and majors in the nuances of command and control areas that we were going to experience as potential majors and lieutenant colonels. While the Basic School trained second lieutenants, this school dealt with areas of responsibility not expected of junior officers. We learned how to write five paragraph orders, (essentially war plans) at the battalion and regimental level. We learned how to coordinate field intelligence with actions occurring on the ground, we learned how to coordinate close air support, and how to plan and use helicopter operations in the field. We learned logistics, ship-to-shore movement, embarkation and debarkation, beach operations, field reconnaissance, artillery and fire coordination, and what we could expect in a combat situation.

As far as the combat experiences were concerned, we had at least 20 to 30 front line experienced infantry officers and Marine aviators who had just returned from Vietnam. Their personal experiences were great classroom examples and led to many hours of classroom discussions. There was never a doubt among any of the students, that all of us would get Vietnam experience, and, unfortunately, seven students among us would lose their lives there.

I wrote my book report on one written by T. E. Lawrence (Lawrence of Arabia), entitled *The Seven Pillars of Wisdom*. This book, written during Lawrence's time with the Arab Legions, gives excellent insight into the Arab mentality, their willingness to fight and die, and their total inability to work in unison with other sects, tribes or military units. The issues described in his book are every bit as true today, as they were when Lawrence was maneuvering around the desert in a robe and burnoose, leading his Arab troops.

The book, when read today, forces the reader to question why no one took the time to understand the Arab mentality before jumping off against an enemy that has been harboring hatred of western ideals for close to a thousand years. I was interested in the fact that, in the entire class of 150 students, I was the only one to select this book from the 35 books contained in the list of books acceptable for a term book report.

My term paper was written on the use of a flexible, folding metal wing that could be attached to the side of an amphibious cargo ship, producing a single helicopter landing platform, from which troops and supplies could be loaded aboard during amphibious operations. The concept had been developed by the Army Corps of Engineers, however, the subsequent development and construction of the LPH class of ships (Landing Platform Helicopter) by the Navy, which was an amphibious assault ship, negated the future utility of the flexible, folding helicopter landing wing. Nevertheless, it turned out to be an excellent topic, and I received one of the highest marks in the school for my term paper.

Social life at Quantico were fairly restricted. Since all of us were captains with ten years of service, our monthly base pay was the staggering sum of $715.08. In my case, this amount of money had to support a family of four, and there was not much money left for anything other than the essentials. Our housing, which was furnished by the government, did not cost us anything, so things like housing and utilities were already taken care of by the government as long as we lived in the government furnished quarters. Still, all the students were in the same economic status.

We socialized at each other's homes with potluck dinners and weekend parties, and the camaraderie between all of us was genuine and supportive. I remember one incident very clearly that is worth recounting as an example of how well we all got along. One day, the sound on my television went out, and I did not have the money to get it repaired. By some quirky coincidence, my next door neighbor, Bill Krulak's television set also broke down, but he could only get sound but no picture. We solved our joint problem by putting one television on top of the other so we could watch television with our families. Naturally, both families were together during all the television shows we watched. To this day, we laugh about this story, but it is an example of what a close community we were in those days at Quantico.

During the last week of July 1966, we began to study in earnest for our final exam, which was to be administered on August 5. One week later we would receive orders telling us where we would be going upon graduation. Our study group began serious efforts at Diamond Lou's Bar. We continued our tradition of beer and study, and most of the other students in the class, knowing about our little group felt that we were not taking the course very seriously. I found that hard to believe, since we had passed all the exams with decent grades, had handed in all required papers, either early or exactly on time, and actively participated in classroom discussions. I think that the idea of studying in a bar downtown, instead of in the school library, rubbed many of the other students the wrong way. They were probably the ones, who later on in their careers became general officers, but I bet they did not have as much fun as we did.

With the final exam scheduled for the next day, our last study group met at Diamond Lou's Bar at 5 p.m. on August 4. We had been warned that the final exam consisted of 100 questions and that the exam was broken down into the 20 different subjects we had covered in school. This meant that the exam would consist of five questions from each of the 20 categories covered during the school term. I told my study group that I bet that I could predict at least 65 percent of the questions that would be asked. They asked me how I could do this, and I told them that I had been keeping good notes during all lectures, and had written down everything that each instructor repeated more than twice during his course of instruction. I figured if an instructor repeated something often, it would probably be a test question. It was a foolproof system in college, and I did not think it would be any different at AWS.

To prove my point, I pulled out all the bar receipts I had been collecting from Diamond Lou's and wrote a question and an answer on each receipt. When I finished my writing a few hours later, Charlie Tye took the receipts home with him and stapled them together into one continuous garland of paper receipts. Apparently, sometime during the night, Charlie managed to get into the AWS building and draped our garland of questions and answers all over the bulletin board where he usually put his Anthony Crane cartoons. When the students arrived for the final exam on Friday morning, they gravitated to the bulletin board and started reading the questions and answers. After the exam, students went back to check the garland, still adorning the bulletin board, and found that of the 100 questions on the exam, the garland contained 80 of those questions with the correct answers. Charlie and I had the last laugh, but no one, except our study group, and those friends of ours who knew that a certain group of "rebels" studied at Diamond Lou's, ever figured out who put the questions and answers on the bulletin board.

Graduation was scheduled for August 12, and we were instructed to report to the school at 8 a.m., on August 8 to receive final grades and our new orders. Since we had all graduated, the Marine Corps assumed we were going to be promoted to the rank of Major within the next few months. All captains graduating from AWS would be receiving orders to fill majors billets wherever they were being assigned.

I carried the primary MOS code of 0302, which signified I was an infantry officer. All infantry officers in the Marine Corps are also "unrestricted line officers," which means that an infantry officer can be assigned to almost any job in the Marine Corps, because being an infantry troop leader is not considered a highly "technical or specialized" skill. Most other ground combat MOSs were also unrestricted, but most of the highly skilled or technical officers remained in positions in their primary MOS. Since infantry and other ground combat officers were logically considered the most flexible, they were candidates for esoteric, and sometimes strange and unusual assignments. Thus, I spent the weekend wondering where the fates or "assignment gods," were going to send me. Monday morning finally arrived, and we hurried to our home rooms to receive our orders.

We had been informed that final grades would be posted on the school bulletin board on Tuesday morning, and the grades would remain on the board until Friday. I hurried to my home room, picked up my envelope and saw that I was ordered to report to Headquarters, U.S. Marine Corps, for duty with the Supply Department. My orders further instructed me to report directly to the Quartermaster General of the Marine Corps, Major General Paul R. Tyler, for further assignment within the Supply Department. As an infantry officer, I was devastated by these orders.

SUPPLY DEPARTMENT, HQMC

In the Marine Corps, we infantry officers had a name for supply officers, whom we saw only as paper-shufflers who remained "in the rear with the gear." We derisively called them "bean counters." I just could not understand how I could have been assigned to the Supply Department. After graduation, I went to Washington to see if a mistake had been made in my case. I arrived at Marine Headquarters in the Navy Annex building, located in Arlington, Virginia, next to Arlington National Cemetery.

The Supply Department was located on the third floor of the Headquarters building, and the assignment section was a few doors from the office of the Quartermaster General of the Marine Corps. I went into the assignment section and spoke to a colonel who was in charge of all Supply Department assignments. I asked him what job I was going to be assigned upon my arrival at Headquarters, and he told me I would be assigned duties as the Industrial Engineer of the Marine Corps, working directly for the Quartermaster General of the Marine Corps. While the title sounded impressive, I asked the colonel if there were any prerequisites for the job since I was not a supply officer and carried an infantry MOS. The colonel informed me that the job required an industrial engineering degree. I told him that I had a degree in classical literature, which, at least in my mind, did not exactly qualify me as an industrial engineer. The colonel seemed to agree with me, and asked me to wait while he consulted with Major General Tyler, the QMG (Quartermaster General) about my case.

He returned in about ten minutes, and asked me to accompany him to General Tyler's office where I met a very professional looking general officer. He was seated behind a large polished oak, almost antique desk, which, I thought, probably belonged to the very first Quartermaster General back in Philadelphia in 1775. The general informed me that he had been briefed on my apprehension of becoming the Industrial Engineer of the Marine Corps. The general also explained that there were no industrial engineers available, and since I was an "unrestricted officer," I would have to show my flexibility and take the job and run with it.

As to my not being a supply officer, the general indicated that the job might benefit from having an infantry officer deal with the problems I would face. He seemed to have an excellent sense of humor, and he smiled as he sentenced me to three years of duty within the *Black Brotherhood*, as the supply department at Headquarters Marine Corps was nick-named. He also informed me that my department was totally staffed by civilian personnel and that the top four civilians were all industrial engineers.

I was there solely to provide leadership and to brief the Commandant of the Marine Corps on a monthly basis. The general shook my hand, and congratulated me on being selected to the rank of Major. The promotion list had just come out, and the general had checked to see if I had been selected. Since I was, I would be taking over the job when I relocated to Washington. I departed the Headquarters building, elated that I had been selected for promotion to Major, but not too happy that I was going to spend the next three years in the Supply Department.

We located a house in Alexandria, Virginia, on Sheldon Drive, which was only 12 miles from my new office, and I bought it for $23,500. Several of the houses near me were occupied by Marines. One of them belonged to Lieutenant Colonel Russ Hittenger, a Marine with whom I had served on Okinawa, and who was a very good friend. He was heading to Vietnam in a few weeks, and his wife and children would remain in the house in Alexandria. There were quite a few "Vietnam widows" in the area, meaning they remained in their Alexandria homes, awaiting the return of their Marine from the war. I was happy to learn that my good friend, Barney Chen, was also stationed at HQMC in the G-1 Division. Still single, we would see a lot of him during our time in Alexandria.

After I reported to my new job in the Supply Department, the first thing that I did was to write a letter to the Commandant of the Marine Corps, volunteering for immediate assignment to Vietnam in a combat infantry unit. I went on to say that I had been assigned to one year in Cuba, while the first elements of Marine units were fighting in Vietnam and since my tour of duty in Cuba counted as a "combat related" assignment, the war in Vietnam might be over before I got a chance to serve there.

I received a letter from General Leonard F. Chapman, the Commandant, in which he congratulated me on my patriotism, and informed me that, in view of my request, he was personally shortening my tour of duty at HQMC, from three years to two years and that on September 1, 1968, I would receive orders to Vietnam. He then went on to say that copies of my letter and his reply would be filed in my permanent records. I think he was doing this just in case the war ended before I got a chance to go there, and the letters would show any promotion board in the future that I wanted to go, and even took extraordinary means to try to get a combat assignment.

My civilian staff consisted of five industrial engineers and one engineering deputy who was my first assistant and deputy head of the section. Civilians in the government services all have ranks and the ranks go from GS-1 (GS stands for Government Service) all the way up to GS-15. My deputy, a fellow named Jerry Collins, was a GS-13. The main mission of the industrial engineering office was to oversee the repair and rebuild schedule of all major items of equipment in the Marine Corps. This was accomplished at two rebuild facilities, one located at Barstow, California, and the other located in Albany, Georgia.

At each of these locations, there was a major assembly line that rebuilt all equipment needing repair or equipment that, through long periods of use, required rebuilding. With the war in Vietnam, equipment battle casualties were being flown to Barstow and Albany for repair and rebuild, which made both facilities busy enough to be working three shifts around the clock, seven days a week. All of this work was coordinated through a document called the Master Work Schedule, which accounted for all programmed repair work throughout the year. Extra repairs and rebuilds, caused by battle damage, were add-ons that had to be fit into the existing work schedule.

The industrial engineering department developed the Master Work Schedule based on the needs of the Marine Corps, and was responsible for insuring that the rebuilt equipment went back to the operating forces to maintain operational effectiveness and efficiency. The work going on at Barstow and Albany was so critical that the QMC had to be briefed weekly on the progress of the Master Work Schedule, the amount of additional equipment being introduced to the repair facilities due to combat damages, and when all the equipment would find its way back to the forces in the field. We were rebuilding tanks, trucks, jeeps, artillery pieces, radios, and anything else being used in the field for which rebuilding an item was faster than trying to procure new equipment.

My industrial engineers monitored performance constantly by telephone or message traffic. Once a month, Jerry Collins and I traveled to Barstow and Albany, to get a first-hand look at progress and at the problems being encountered due to the high rate of unscheduled battle damaged equipment that was being introduced into the Master Work Schedule, and which had to be repaired immediately and returned to the field.

In mid-September, my promotion to Major came through, and I was promoted to that rank in General Tyler's office. I was now a field grade officer, and was guaranteed twenty years service in the Marine Corps and would qualify for retirement.

Every month, General Tyler and I briefed the Commandant of the Marine Corps on the status of the supply chain going back to Vietnam. General Chapman was a no nonsense officer and wanted straight answers to his questions. Any officer that was not prepared to brief the Commandant in his area of expertise only got one chance. Each time we were scheduled to brief the Commandant, I spent the previous 48 hours going over everything I thought might come up. I prepared charts and graphs, and presented photographs of actual work in progress, as I always took a camera with me whenever I visited Barstow or Albany. I think the pictures were a real asset for me during these presentations, because it seemed to assure the Commandant that when I said I'd seen this last week, my pictures underscored my statements.

While the Commandant never specifically said anything to me, he must have told General Tyler that he liked my briefings. The more often I briefed the Commandant, the more comfortable I became in his office. I got the distinct impression, after several briefings, that the Commandant simply allowed me to make my report, give him a status of where we were, and when we were going to complete specific equipment, without any further questions or comments. At the end of my briefings, the Commandant always thanked me and was very pleasant with me. General Tyler was happy with this arrangement, and while the Commandant never made a comment about the quality of my briefings, General Tyler always was highly complimentary. Of course, the briefings were just talking, and the result, which was the completion of the work and the shipment of the repaired equipment back to the field, is really what it was all about. If that was meeting the deadlines, then everything else was fine.

I did do one thing that seemed to annoy General Tyler, and even though I knew it did, I never stopped doing it. Before every briefing I gave to General Tyler, I would preface my remarks with the comment, "As the General knows, I am not a Supply Officer, but…" this was just my way of reminding the General that I was an infantry officer, and being in the supply department was not my idea. Since my briefings were always very good, thanks in no small part to the tremendous support I was receiving from Jerry Collins, I do not think General Tyler minded my constant whining about not being a supply officer, especially since the Commandant of the Marine Corps was always very complimentary to General Tyler.

A few words about Jerry Collins. He was originally from New York where he had graduated from Brooklyn College with an engineering degree. He had received a commission in the Marine Corps, served his three years, and then obtained a civilian job at Headquarters Marine Corps at the age of 26. When I met him, he had been in the Supply Department Industrial Engineering Division for over 30 years and knew everyone in the business. He was also Jewish, and while I do not think that was ever an issue with anyone I knew, Jerry always thought it was. He was a fine man, and he helped me immensely to get through an extremely tough job in which I had no previous experience.

1967 passed very quickly for me. One of my friends, Howie Lee from Brooklyn, New York, was scheduled to receive the Medal of Honor for valor in Vietnam as a rifle company commander. He had been blinded in both eyes by flying metal fragments, wrapped an empty bandolier around his eyes, and with his radio operator, reported on enemy positions. He stayed on top of a hill in the midst of a vicious Viet Cong attack, fighting off the enemy all night, while bleeding from a head wound and unable to see. At dawn, they had repulsed the enemy and killed all the attackers, losing only a few men in the all-night firefight. At dawn, Howie was immediately evacuated to a field hospital and was flown to Japan and then directly to the National Naval Medical Center in Bethesda, Maryland, where he was treated, three days after being wounded. With very strong electromagnets, the doctors were able to pull the steel fragments out of his eyes, and they saved his vision.

Now, he was going to the White House where President Lyndon Johnson, would place the Medal of Honor around his neck. Howie was allowed to invite 150 guests to the ceremony, and I was one of his official guests. After receiving the medal, a formal receiving line was formed in the parlor outside the oval office. Standing at the head of the receiving line was the President, followed by Howie, his wife and two children, and then followed by the Secretary of Defense, the Commandant of the Marine Corps and the Secretary of the Navy. As we went through the line, we shook hands with the President and then we congratulated Howie and left the room. The entire process was exceptionally well orchestrated, and the ceremony came to a close as scheduled.

A few weeks later, Howie presented me with a photograph of me shaking hands with President Johnson. Unknown to Howie, there was a secret camera in the room that took a picture of every one of Howie's Marine comrades shaking hands with the President. The pictures were then sent to Howie, who autographed each one and presented them to his friends. I still have my framed picture of that day hanging in my den.

I remember going to the Marine Corps Ball in 1967 and sitting at a table with Howie Lee, another officer named Patrick Collins, who was very highly decorated in Vietnam, plus an aviator who had received the Navy Cross in Vietnam. Then there was me with my one medal, the "Shirley Highway" medal. I must say I felt embarrassed, inadequate and certainly out of place. Every now and then Howie would say to me, "Boy, that must have been one tough battle on the Shirley Highway," as only one New Yorker could say to another! Little did I know that my time would come sooner than I realized.

I had nothing but pleasant experiences in the Supply Department. I attended the Department of Defense Maintenance Conference at the Rock Island Arsenal in Rock Island, Illinois, where each service sent their head of maintenance. The Air Force and Army each sent a general, the Navy sent an admiral and the Marine Corps, in its infinite wisdom, sent me, a lowly major, and a junior one at that. Each of us was scheduled to speak about what our service was doing in the maintenance area and, since I was a major, I was the last to speak. Recognizing the absurdity of a major, mingling with flag grade officers, and having observed their obvious discomfort, I decided to wow them all with a great presentation. I started out my presentation with a good New York joke that got everyone laughing, and then related real time episodes in maintenance from my numerous trips to Barstow and Albany. I talked about battle damage, turnaround times, difficulties experienced in parts procurement, outsourcing, single source providers and labor issues.

Since the flag officers only worked from notes prepared for them by their staffs, I gave the attendees real hands-on information. My question and answer session with the attendees lasted twice as long as any of the other presenters, and, upon my return to Headquarters Marine Corps, the QMC called me into his office to present me with a Commandant of the Marine Corps Certificate of Commendation for my work at the worldwide conference. Apparently, the general in charge of the conference had written a personal letter to the Commandant about my presentation. This underscores the importance of having one really good joke in your head that you can use at any time and that is always guaranteed to get a laugh.

On the advice of Jerry Collins, I took several night classes at George Washington University on industrial engineering issues. This enabled me to be up to date on the latest technical jargon, especially when I was briefing the Commandant in our monthly meetings. One class I took was on Program Evaluation Review Techniques, (PERT) a fairly new idea at the time, which, when I used the terminology in my briefings, made me appear to be on the cutting edge of industrial engineering.

I enjoyed the classes at George Washington, and I was able to grasp the ideas discussed in the classroom. It got to a point that I would learn something in class and then use it in a briefing within a few days after learning the subject. It made me look extremely good, and I am sure that General Tyler thought I was some kind of genius, based on how quickly I was catching on to the disciplines of industrial engineering. Little did they know that I owed it all to a great civilian employee who had decided to become my mentor.

Life in 1967 was not much fun for the Marine Corps. There were funerals conducted every day at Arlington Cemetery, and the Marine Corps insisted that Marines from Headquarters attend the funerals of Marines killed in combat. I remember going to the funerals of several close friends, many of whom I had served with in my 11 years of service. I particularly remember the funerals of Captain Dick Hatch and Captain Bill Leftwich, two outstanding Marine officers who, had they lived, would definitely, in time, have become generals. There was the funeral of J. J. Carroll, an officer with whom I had served with in the Mediterranean, and, unfortunately, too many others to remember their names at this late date in my life.

On the brighter side of things, Barney Chen practically lived at our house. I saw him every weekend, and we would go to Washington Redskins games as often as we could get tickets from John Mandis, who owned the Market Inn. We would go to the Market Inn early on a Sunday morning for breakfast. In those days, Washington was a "blue law" state, which meant that they could not serve alcohol on Sundays. The Market Inn got around that law by having everyone join an "eating club" on Sundays. Since it was a private club, alcohol flowed freely, both in the Market Inn and on the bus on our way to the stadium. Members, who paid $5.00 to become a member for the day, would be served breakfast and drinks, then driven to JFK Stadium in a chartered bus that also served drinks enroute, watch the game, return to the Market Inn after the game, have more cocktails and then leave whenever they were ready. This entire process took twelve hours or more, and made for some less than loving receptions upon my arrival home.

Tickets to Redskins games, then and now, were almost impossible to obtain. Season ticket holders willed their tickets to relatives and, unless you knew someone, there just were not any tickets to be had anywhere. If you are familiar with NFL history, you might remember that the Washington Redskins, then, had a unique helmet design. It was a single feather that began at the rear of the helmet and ended on the top of the helmet, making it look like each player was wearing a single feather as an Indian head dress.

The NFL, always looking for ready identification, decided that all teams should have logos on each side of their helmets so television viewers could easily identify the teams that were playing. The Redskins decided that they would have a contest to design a new, NFL approved helmet. I submitted a drawing of a flaming arrow, from my Boy Scout days, and enclosed a letter with my design that said I was a big fan of the Redskins, and that if my design was accepted by the team, the only reward I wanted was the opportunity to buy two season tickets. After a few weeks, I received a letter from the Redskins, informing me that my design had been accepted by the team, with a few modifications, and if I took the letter I received to the Redskins office, I would be able to buy two season tickets, and keep them for as long as I wanted them. I rushed to the office, bought the two season tickets and still have those tickets to this day.

The year 1968 started off with a bang. The Tet offensive in Vietnam caused many casualties and equipment failures. Our plants were working full shifts, 24 hours per day, and my job kept me extremely busy. I also realized that the promise that the Commandant of the Marine Corps had made to me would soon come to fruition. In July 1968, I received orders to report to the 1st Marine Division, Fleet Marine Force, in the Republic of Vietnam by September 20, 1968, I would be detached from my duties at HQMC on August 1, 1968, and granted 30 days leave, after which I was to report to Camp Pendleton, California for pre-deployment training.

Sharron was very unhappy with my orders, and I never told her that I had volunteered for early assignment to Vietnam. This would be a case of her not understanding and being angry with me when I needed her to be supportive. General Tyler seemed surprised that I was leaving HQMC after only two years, and even offered to have me stay a third year, however, I could not miss the opportunity to again remind the good General that I was an infantry officer, and apparently, there was a need for infantry officers in Vietnam.

On my last day in the Supply Department, General Tyler gave me a small reception in his conference room. All of my staff was there, as well as other high ranking supply officers with whom I had interacted, during my two years in the department. The General began by awarding me another Certificate of Commendation for my work in the Supply Department, and then with a great big smile, he said the following: "Major Beck, since you have been in the Supply Department, you have never missed an opportunity to remind everyone, that you are not a Supply Officer and that you are an Infantry Officer, serving in the Supply Department. Up until this moment, that was always true, but, from now on, it will never be true again. I hold here in my hands, an official document that from this date forward, assigns you the secondary MOS of 3002, which just in case you might not know, is the MOS of a Supply Officer. Congratulations!" Apparently, everyone in the room except me, knew this was coming and everyone erupted in applause, punctuated with good-hearted laughter. The General gave me the orders and I could see that they were signed by him and countersigned by the Commandant of the Marine Corps.

I had become an official Supply Officer, without ever going to Supply School, just because the Quartermaster General of the Marine Corps said so, and the Commandant of the Marine Corps endorsed the action. I laughed just as hard as everyone else and, I must admit, I was deeply touched. For the rest of my Marine Corps career, I was an infantry officer, a supply officer and a logistics officer. I wore all three titles with considerable pride. Looking back on those three titles, it was the supply and logistics training that helped me achieve success in civilian life, just a little more than my infantry officer background. Being an infantry officer, however, made civilian leadership come somewhat easier, once I realized that I could not shout at civilians or threaten to send them to the brig if they didn't do what I wanted them to do.

I had wanted Sharron and the family to remain in Alexandria while I was in Vietnam, but Sharron said there was no way she would do that. She wanted to stay in Florida, and so we sold the house, for a $2,000 profit. I moved the family to Deerfield Beach, Florida, where I found a house almost around the corner from her parent's house, and rented it for one year. Since I had almost two weeks before I was due at Camp Pendleton, Sharron and I took a one-week vacation to Nassau, in the Bahamas.

Like Jamaica, I never felt that Sharron was particularly enjoying herself, but we ate at excellent restaurants, swam in the beautiful, blue Caribbean Sea, and relaxed on the beach of the Nassau Beach Hotel. One evening, when we were out to dinner in a highly exclusive restaurant, I saw the English race car driver, Sterling Moss, in one of the booths and went over to introduce myself. I told him I was going to Vietnam in a week and that my wife and I were spending a few days away from our children before my departure. He could not have been nicer. We wound up drinking with him into the early morning hours, and it was a pleasant memory in a somewhat unpleasant period of my own personal life.

I departed for Camp Pendleton on Sunday morning, September 1, 1968. As my first commanding officer had warned me, "Sometime in your twenty year career, you are going to go to war. If you can't handle that, then do not make the Marine Corps your career." In my case, it happened in my 13th year of service. Like it or not, I was getting what I had asked for. I was on my way to combat!

I kissed Sharron goodbye, and made that hollow promise that just about all military men make to their wives, "Don't worry, Honey, I'll be OK, and I'll see you in 13 months." I hoped I was going to be right.

CHAPTER 14

VIETNAM

WITH THE 1ST MARINE DIVISION

As the airplane taxied into position for take off from Miami International Airport, there were a thousand things going through my mind. I was leaving two children, aged six and three, whom I might never see again, and I wondered how my wife Sharron would handle the separation and the huge tide of antiwar sentiment that was raging through the country. Fueled by a liberal press, whose reporters lived in fear of being called up for service in Vietnam, Americans were receiving doses of daily predictions of doom, accented by photographs of the dying and the dead a half a world away in a jungle. Young men of draft age (there was still an obligation to serve your country in those days), were evading draft notices by running away to Canada, and college campuses throughout the country erupted in a chorus of doom and gloom, calling for the overthrow of the duly elected government. American flags and draft cards were burned, and service members from all branches of the armed forced were vilified as "baby killers" and monsters. The *Summer of Love* blossomed in San Francisco, composed primarily of dope smoking, unwashed and over indulged hippies, who had neither respect for themselves, their country or the preservation of our nation.

Many felt that to live in America was a god given right, but there was no need to protect that right. Americans were force fed nightly television reports of the war, bringing small unit encounters and napalm attacks into the living rooms of the nation on a continuous basis. Photographs of caskets returning from the war zone, each covered with an American flag, made the front pages of America's newspapers more often than any other news story. In short, the country hated the war, felt it was wrong, and did not support it, however, Americans took their anger at the war out on the troops who were called upon to fight it.

I counted myself among the troops fighting the war, but because I was a career military officer, I looked on my role in this war as that of a mercenary whose motivation to fight and die had been sealed with a contract executed between me and the United States Marine Corps. My loyalties were to the Marine Corps and to those troops under my command. In my mind, that was what I was fighting for, namely doing my very best to get them and me home in one piece. I was going to fight because I had made a contract, and, as I was warned 13 years ago, signing that contract guaranteed me a shot of combat in some yet undeclared or declared war. As they say in Las Vegas, my number had come up, and it was time to put the chips on the table and play the hand I was dealt.

Even today, so far removed from those times, as I write these sentences, my anger at the American people has never subsided. The press fueled the traitorous actions of so many cowardly citizens, none of whom ever considered the irreparable damage they were doing to the unfortunate young men who, because of their socioeconomic groupings, were unable to avoid the draft. The privileged, through the numerous ploys and venues available to their families who had enough money to send them to college, Canada, or some plush National Guard or Reserve assignment which kept them from going to Vietnam, were almost certainly guaranteed immunity from the horrors of war. The bitterness continues, and probably will continue, for the rest of my life, because I cannot bring back the 58,000 persons whose names are engraved on that marble wall in Washington, D.C.

PRE-DEPLOYMENT

My uneventful flight ended in San Diego where I rented a car and drove to Camp Pendleton. I was directed to Camp Las Pulgas, located in the middle of the huge base, where a special field grade officer's pre-deployment orientation class was going to be conducted. After the two-week training period, we would be transported to Norton Air Force Base in San Bernardino, where we would be flown directly to Okinawa for processing before reporting for duty in Vietnam.

On September 2, 1968, our group of 35 majors and lieutenant colonels, assembled for our first class. The purpose of the course was to familiarize us with the enemy's order of battle (military organizations), their weapons, their fighting spirit, their tactics and their guerilla warfare techniques. Days were spent learning about booby traps and then going into the field and seeing how these booby traps were deployed. I remember that we learned the history of the Republic of Vietnam and its governmental organization. We studied the command and control organization of all allied forces in Vietnam, the organizations of the North Vietnamese Army and the Viet Cong guerilla force. We became familiar with the concept of tactical operations against these enemy forces, and combat support available in Vietnam to all allied forces. There was also a section on combat service support, including medical evacuations and hospitals, plus all other types of logistical support required by allied troops in the field. The final section was devoted to civil operations, often called the battle for the hearts and minds of the Vietnamese people.

Our classroom work was often boring but certainly necessary, however, once we got in the field, everyone's eyes and ears were glued to the instructors. We learned about the varied tactics employed by both the North Vietnamese regulars and the guerilla Viet Cong. Their operational concepts were decidedly different, and you did not find out who you were fighting until you engaged the enemy. This required split second decisions and tactical changes that needed to be implemented almost as a second sense to respond to the enemy's threats. We learned about the Viet Cong's use of tunnel networks to move into and out of areas of operations.

Often, tunnel entrances were disguised with vegetation or even cooking pots situated in the center of a house in a local village. We learned that a haystack in the middle of a field could house five fully armed fighters, who would strike at the appropriate time when you were least expecting such actions. We learned about caves dug into the sides of riverbanks that were only accessible from the water, and would exit on dry land beyond the river's edge. We were instructed about entire guerilla bases set up in underground bunkers, housing anywhere from three to twenty soldiers, all of whom entered the bunkers from a river entrance and exited into an open rice paddy for night operations.

One of our instructors had been a "tunnel rat," meaning he was a small, thin Marine who would always be the first man to go down into a tunnel complex to flush out enemy soldiers. He told us of entire hospitals set up in tunnel complexes, and from firsthand experience, gave us a feel of how dangerous these tunnel complexes were. He told us about a tunnel complex discovered in the Ben Cat Area in 1965 that was composed of five large bunkers, each capable of housing up to 20 soldiers, with tunnels leading away from each of the bunkers to distances of over 300 yards from the main bunker complex.

While these lectures were extremely important to us, the lectures on booby traps were even more astounding. The enemy, long on courage and cunning, but very low on supplies, used anything, including our own weapons, against us as homemade, ingenious booby traps. An Explosive Ordnance Disposal (EOD) Major, with two tours of duty in Vietnam already completed, briefed us on these devices. For example, there were cartridge traps, which were nothing more than an unexpended round of ammunition set into the ground over a nail pounded into a board. When you stepped on a piece of grass attached to some bamboo slats, your weight on the bamboo slats pushed the cartridge down onto the nail, and the cartridge was then fired up into you, or the next person behind you, depending on your speed.

Booby traps were the favorite devices of the Viet Cong. Grenades, spike traps, poison arrows, and a variety of other means were employed to harass, slow down, confuse and kill friendly troops. The forms of these weapons were limited only to the imagination of the designer. Grenades were commonly used in booby traps because they are light in weight, easy to carry and conceal, and readily adaptable. They were frequently put in trees, or on fences and trails commonly used by US forces. The most common method of exploding these grenades was simply to straighten the pin that served as a security device for the grenade, and then attach the pin to a taut trip wire. When you pulled on the trip wire with your foot, or any part of your body, the pin came out of the grenade and it armed and you became a casualty.

Munitions, especially unexploded mortar and artillery rounds, were also employed as booby traps. Later, during my tour of duty, I would come under attack one night from an American 2,000 pound unexploded bomb, originally dropped by a B-52 bomber on the Ho Chi Minh trail, that was hurled through the air by a dynamite charge placed under the bomb at an angle, with a trip wire attached to the fuse of the bomb. When the small explosion went off, it hurled the bomb in the air, arming the fuse, which was tied to another trip wire, causing the bomb to explode upon impact. I had the extremely bad luck of having a bomb impact on one of our artillery ammunition dumps, but that is a story told later in this chapter. Booby traps were emplaced most frequently on the most convenient routes, such as main dirt roads suitable for motorized traffic, rice paddy dikes, trails, river fords, foot bridges, approaches and gates entering specific areas, usually with an open field in the front or back.

Spiked foot and mantraps were also common booby trap types found throughout Vietnam. The spikes were usually sharpened bamboo stakes, or they could be barbed wood or metal spikes emplaced in wooden, concrete or metal blocks. These spiked devices were placed in holes, along routes of movement, and carefully concealed to prevent detection. They could also be placed above ground as bamboo "whips" that would hurl a spiked board of Punji sticks at you as you crossed a specific point and triggered a device that activated the whip. The bamboo whip consisted of a bamboo pole about ten feet long, two fragmentation hand grenades, and materials for securing them all together. One grenade is tied to each end of the pole. One end of the pole is buried, and the pin of its grenade is secured to the ground so that removal of the pole detonates the grenade. The pole is then bent into a bow with the free end fastened to the ground. The safety pin of this grenade is also secured to the ground. The prime target of the whip is jungle clearing equipment or jungle clearing personnel on foot patrols. When the device is activated, the bamboo pole whips up, and the grenade is detonated about ten feet off the ground. Any attempt to remove the pole, in case it is spotted, will detonate the grenade placed at ground level. A deadly and very effective device, it was manufactured in the field by a clever enemy.

Other, even more clever devices, were employed to hurl activated grenades directly at you as you walked along a trail. By the time the grenade got to you, it exploded practically on your head, and you were either dead or very seriously wounded. Most of the Punji stick devices used against American troops were always covered with poison or animal dung, which made the wound received become infected almost immediately.

I can't remember all the devices, but the one's that come readily to mind are

- rice paddy Punji stick booby traps, always placed on the dikes, which was the only place you could walk without getting wet;

- Punji bear traps, which were two boards full of rusty nails, placed on two bricks in a hole. When you stepped in the hole, the boards separated, and each side of your foot was impaled on a board full of rusty nails;

- treadle pivoted spike boards,which were rusty nails placed on a board that shot up in your face when you stepped on a concealed foot treadle;

- spiked foot bridges, that collapsed in the middle of the bridge, and deposited you into a Punji stake pit, and finally,

- a swinging mace, that was heavily concealed along a foot path, and was activated by a trip wire that released a mace (a round ball covered with exposed rusty nails) directly at you so fast that it was impossible to get out of the way. If you encountered a flying mace, you were definitely going to get wounded at the very least, if not killed.

These classes got our attention, and certainly underscored the belief that we were headed for very dangerous times in the very near future.

We lived in a BOQ and in the evenings would go to the bars or restaurants of Oceanside or Fallbrook, and tell each other how anxious we were to get into combat. We'd go to Marty's Valley Inn in Oceanside, which seemed to be the watering hole of choice then, and demonstrate how macho we all were by drinking large quantities of alcohol, and champing at the bit to mix it up with the Viet Cong. In the privacy of my room, later at night, I wondered what the hell I had gotten myself into, and I wondered, secretly, if I was going to be up to the challenge of functioning as an Officer of Marines in combat. I was aware that I had volunteered for early deployment, but now, in the reality of the pre-deployment training, I felt very unsure about my decision, even though I knew there was nothing I was going to do to change the inevitable trip to Vietnam.

Perhaps I would get an assignment in the rear or with some supply unit, after all, I was a certified supply and logistics officer. These were thoughts I shared with no one, and I continued to be the macho Marine during training that everyone else was. Secretly, I wondered how many of my macho friends felt the same way I did. I called home every evening and spoke to Sharron. Everything was fine at home, and Sharron appeared to be in good spirits, and was very supportive in her comments to me. Eric and Paul were fine, and she was spending much time with her parents. The family was in excellent shape, and I never spoke about the self-doubts that I entertained. I simply promised to take care of myself and return in one piece, as though I could guarantee such a thing.

We completed our pre-deployment training, boarded a World Airlines 707 at Norton Air Force Base, and headed to our initial stop in Okinawa. I hoped a peace initiative might be successful during my tour of duty in Vietnam. It was Sunday, September 15, 1968. With a great deal of luck and good fortune, I would be returning to the United States on October 15, 1969. On the day I departed for Vietnam, it was also exactly one year since the American Secretary of State Dean Rusk, expressed doubt that reports from French and Canadian sources, indicating North Vietnamese interest in opening discussions to end the war, displayed any shift in Hanoi's announced position. Things did not look that good after all.

Our plane arrived in Okinawa on September 17, and we were immediately transported to Camp Hansen, near Kin Village, where we were processed to continue on to Vietnam. We packed our belongings in one cardboard box, wrote our home address on the box and sealed it. We were given a receipt for the box, and it was placed in storage. We were told we would either reclaim the box on our way home, or the box would be mailed to our next of kin. Leave it to the Marine Corps to cut right to the chase!

We had our immunization (shot) record reviewed by medical personnel, received a few more especially for Vietnam, received our 782 gear (field packs and cartridge belts, poncho liners, ponchos, entrenching tools (shovels) holsters, magazine pouches, helmets and helmet liners, flack jackets, shelter halves and other field essentials) and then we were issued our jungle utilities and soft covers (hats). These were the typical, but relatively new, jungle uniforms that began as all dark green, and eventually ended up in a camouflage pattern. They were light, airy, and dried very quickly once they got wet.

When we finished, we went to the Officer's Club in our newly issued jungle gear, had dinner and a few drinks, and met the officers coming back from Vietnam. Besides their wide grins, their jungle utilities were sun bleached and well worn. We stood out like freshmen on our first day of school in our brand new, never been dirty jungle utilities and Vietnam combat boots, even though most of us had at least 14 to 18 years service in the Marine Corps. They told us many "sea stories," and it all sounded like some gung ho Hollywood movie because they never spoke of the Marines who were not returning and whose personal belongings were being shipped to their next of kin. Only the victories remained in their minds, as well they should be.

On September 19, we left Camp Hansen for Kadena Air Base where we would depart for the trip to Da Nang Air Base in Vietnam on a National Airlines 707 that was waiting for us. The plane had been chartered by the Defense Department to augment military troop movement aircraft, and we were all surprised to see that the plane was just like any other commercial airliner in the United States. There were five stewardesses on the plane, drinks were served, and it was just like flying anywhere back home except that we were flying off to war.

I sat down next to Lieutenant Colonel Ted Sargeant, whom I had known in Camp Lejeune in my 2nd Marine Division days. Ted was extremely gung ho and all he talked about was getting command of an infantry battalion. He got his wish and was assigned an infantry battalion in the 3rd Marine Division, and within a month he was dead. He was among the unlucky ones in my draft since the bulk of our group survived the tour and returned to the US as combat veterans.

I reflected on my life up to the current moment, and worried how I would act once on the ground in Vietnam. All officers aboard the plane loudly affirmed that they wanted to be assigned to front line combat units, but since we were all majors and lieutenant colonels, the chances of that happening were slight. There were only three field grade officers per infantry battalion; one lieutenant colonel and two majors, so the rest of us would be assigned to staff positions at the Division and Regimental levels. A few would be going to the Marine Expeditionary Force (MEF) headquarters in Da Nang City. We would find out when we landed in Da Nang. The press coverage of the Vietnam War was constant. Battles were shown in bloody details on the nightly news, and with all the fighting going on in Vietnam, you got the impression that just landing in Vietnam was a dangerous undertaking.

ARRIVAL IN-COUNTRY

I wondered why the stewardesses were not nervous, and why everything seemed like just another day in the air. In my mind, after watching the news and finishing pre-deployment training, I felt sure that our plane would land under mortar attack and that, once on the ground, some Punji staked whip would hit me in the face as I debarked from the aircraft. As we approached Da Nang Air Base, one of the stewardesses welcomed us to Da Nang, informed us what the temperature was on the ground, thanked us for flying National Airlines and hoped that our next trip would include a ticket on National Airlines. I almost laughed out loud, but as I looked around, the humor of the moment seemed to have been lost on everyone but me.

The plane landed uneventfully, no mortars, no surface to air missiles, in fact, not a gunshot was heard. The air base was immense, 2,350 acres to be exact, with two 10,000 foot asphalt runways, and support buildings plus a US Air Force base and a Republic of Vietnam Air Force Base. Aircraft with full loads of bombs and napalm tanks were taking off on the other runway as we were taxiing to our deplaning area. We deplaned and immediately boarded a bus which would transport those of us who had been assigned to the 1st Marine Division to the Division Headquarters located on Hill 327. Hills were given numbers as names which coincided with the height of the tallest landmass in meters; thus Hill 327 was 327 meters high above sea level. Those officers being assigned to the 3rd Marine Division waited for transportation further north to the Division Headquarters at Quang Tri near the DMZ.

The bus carrying the officers assigned to the 1st Marine Division, of which I was one, departed, and the first thing we saw was the mortuary, where metal coffins were piled up one on top of the other, waiting for the next KIA (killed in action) to arrive. The contract mortuary, filled with civilian undertakers and embalmers, worked inside a metal building, preparing bodies for their last trip home. I always felt that placing a mortuary right at the same location where incoming troops arrived was not exactly a smart thing to do for morale, but since all bodies were flown direct from Da Nang to the Dover, Delaware, Air Force Base for processing, it made sense to locate the mortuary as close to the planes as possible. Driving by the mortuary during my first few minutes in Vietnam, and seeing about a hundred metal coffins piled up like cordwood, was not exactly an uplifting experience.

The drive to the Division headquarters took about 20 minutes. We passed through several Vietnamese villages surrounded by rice paddies and drove by the 1st Medical Battalion and the 1st Recon Battalion camps on our way to Hill 327. As we approached the Division headquarters, we saw a sea of tents of all sizes located around a large, steel and concrete bunker that was the division headquarters complex. Before reaching the headquarters, we passed the biggest Post Exchange that I had ever seen since being in the Marine Corps. At the Division headquarters, we were directed to the Division Adjutant's office for incoming processing. We would be given our assignments and a large printed loose leaf binder, about as big as an average city Yellow Pages that contained the Rules of Engagement (ROE) for Vietnam. Since I was still worried about returning alive to my wife and family, I felt sure that when the Adjutant saw my extensive logistics and supply background, I'd be remaining in the Division headquarters area as a member of the staff. Secretly, I hoped this would happen.

The twenty-two field grade officers who had been assigned to the 1st Marine Division went into the Division Adjutant's office, one by one, to receive their assignments. I was in the middle of the pack and was, therefore, able to talk to each officer after he had received his assignment. The first ten officers were all going to staff positions within the Division. Prospects looked good for me I thought. I was the eleventh officer, and I reported to the adjutant and presented my orders. The adjutant told me I was being assigned to the 1st Battalion of the 7th Marine Regiment, a front line infantry unit. He went on to tell me I was going to the battalion as the Battalion Operations Officer (S-3), as a replacement for a Major Bill Uren, who had stepped on a land mine, lost his leg and was medically evacuated. I later met Bill Uren for the first time in 2004, in Las Vegas during a reunion of the 1st Battalion, 7th Marines. He was married to the daughter of Major General Paul Tyler, the former Quartermaster General of the Marine Corps, who had treated me so well at Headquarters Marine Corps in Washington, even though he had given me that Supply Officer's MOS.

The battalion had been without an operations officer for over a week, but the adjutant told me it was too late for the battalion to pick me up today, since we had to travel to the battalion headquarters by jeep, and we would be traveling through *Indian country* (meaning unfriendly or enemy infested areas where we might expect ground fire or land mines). I was given a copy of the rules of engagement (ROE), asked to read it and then sign a statement that I had read and fully understood the rules of engagement and that I would abide by them. I read the rules of engagement from cover to cover. I had never before read such nonsense.

It attempted to orchestrate almost every type of enemy engagement and then dictate when, and if, we could return fire. There were literally hundreds of examples that discussed friendly villages, liberated villages, fire free zones, harassing and interdiction fires, bombing runs, use of tanks and napalm, use of land mines, treatment of prisoners, and any other thing that some staff officer thought might happen in the field between two combatants. It was clearly a "cover your ass" document, which meant that once you signed the statement, the monkey was on your back to adhere to the rules. I read the ROE and immediately determined that unless the

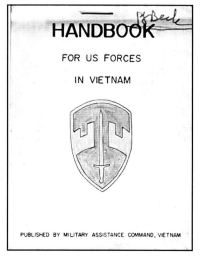

author was going to be standing next to me in the field, I'd use my own discretion and shoot first then ask questions later. I was not alone in this attitude. I also received a handbook from the Military Assistance Command, Vietnam, containing information about US Forces, North Vietnamese Army and Vietcong units, and how to conduct combat operations. This handbook proved more valuable to me.

I went to the Transient BOQ where I was assigned a canvas cot for the night, given a mosquito net and a poncho liner, and then went to the Officers Club for a drink. I needed one. The officers club was filled with division staff officers, each of them "wishing they could go to the field."

FIRST BATTALION, 7TH MARINES

The following morning a battered and road dirty jeep with two Marines in it came to the BOQ looking for me. I was ready and had on my helmet and flak jacket. Neither of the Marines were wearing flak jackets or helmets, choosing to wear soft jungle hats and dark green tee shirts instead. The Marine sitting in the passenger seat had a loaded M-16 rifle in his lap, and he gave me the driver's loaded M-16 to use in case we encountered any "Charlies" (slang for the enemy) along the way. Welcome to the bush!

We drove off Hill 327, observing all posted speed limits. Traffic at the Division HQ was very heavy, and by midday the roads were throwing up one dust storm after another, as trucks, tanks, amphibious tractors and jeeps, drove up and down the hill. The resulting dust covered everything, and even oiling the roads, which the engineers did almost every day, could not keep the dirt and dust from infiltrating everything on Hill 327. Thus, a speed limit of 15 miles per hour within the division compound attempted to at least slow down the inevitable daily dust storms.

Once we got out of the Division Command Post area, we headed down Route 587. While these routes had numbers on the map, they were dirt roads, wide enough to handle two small trucks going in opposite directions, and always cut through either low hanging brush, heavy tree lines or elevated dirt berms that ran parallel to rice paddies or dikes. In short, there were plenty of places for "Charlie" to hide if he were inclined to shoot at us, blow us up with a command detonated land mine, or simply hurl a grenade at us as we passed. The driver, Lance Corporal Mooney, from Pittsburgh, Pa., yelled at me to cover the left side of the road with my M-16 while the passenger, Lance Corporal Evans, from Hialeah, Fla., was covering the right side. We were locked and loaded and driving as fast as we could down the road that would be taking us to Hill 10, the command post (CP) of the 1st Battalion, 7th Marines. I tried not to look too nervous. I was clearly in the company of some battle hardened Marines and they were definitely evaluating me as we zoomed through the countryside.

Hill 10, the battalion CP, overlooked the village of Phu Hoa, and we entered a narrow road leading to the top of the hill. There were guard posts all around, and as we came closer to the camp on the top of the hill, I could see that an artillery battery had their 105 howitzers dug into positions covering 360 degrees around the top of the hill. In the center of the complex was a large wooden tower that also had a 360 degree view of the countryside. There were three Marines on duty in that tower, and there must have been at least 20 radio antennas around the top of it. I also noticed five tanks on the hill which were dug into the ground in what is called hull defilade. Clearly, the battalion was using the tank cannons as additional firepower. Vietnam was not a tank war country since the entire area in the south was covered with rice paddies. In the north, however, the 3rd Marine Division had fought the battle of Hue City using tanks to gain control of the Old Imperial Palace and the city. Tank platoon commanders were frustrated that they could not act like a little Rommel. The terrain would simply not support tank tactics.

As we drove through the camp, I noticed there were not enough troops on that hill to constitute a battalion of Marines. I asked LCpl Mooney about that, and he told me there were two other hills south of Hill 10, where units of 1/7 were based. We had two reinforced companies on Hill 22, located about one mile south of Hill 10 near the village of Phouc Ninh, and one reinforced company located on Hill 44, near the village of Dong Nghe, which was about another mile south of Hill 22. This meant that the 1st Battalion was providing security for that portion of the road leading from the 1st Marine Division CP and the Da Nang Air Base in the north, all the way to the village of Dong Nghe in the south. This road led further south to the industrial city of An Hoa, which was where the 5th Marine Regiment was located. We were also responsible for the Thoung Duc encampment of the Green Berets located several miles below our southernmost position, at Hill 44.

The jeep came to a stop in the center of the top of Hill 10, and I was directed towards an underground bunker that looked directly into a long, open valley ringed by a chain of mountains. I entered the bunker and found the Battalion Commander, Lieutenant Colonel Bill Bethel, sitting behind a field desk. Dug into the sides of the bunker were cots placed on metal supports that served as bunks for the people inside the bunker. The back wall was covered with a bank of radios, each radio having an operator in front of it, and obviously communicating with some unit in the field. As I entered the bunker, it suddenly became very still as I reported for duty. The Colonel welcomed me aboard, shook my hand, informed me I was going to be the Operations Officer of the battalion, and then he directed me to find Major Nick Carter, a mustang (ex-enlisted officer) Marine, who was the battalion executive officer.

After that, I would report into the battalion adjutant and turn over my Officers Qualification Record (OQR), a personnel file which contained all the important data pertaining to me such as pay, combat pay, next of kin notification information and previous military assignments and experience. Officers carried their own OQR's with them from duty station to duty station, however, just in case an enterprising officer decided to alter his OQR, an official copy of it was always maintained at Headquarters Marine Corps.

I found Nick Carter in the observation tower, and he climbed down and welcomed me to 1/7. Nick was wearing Vietnamese tiger stripe camouflage trousers and shirt with a matching soft cover (cap). After seeing the way Mooney and Evans were dressed when they came to pick me up at Division, I quickly got the message that in the front line combat units, the uniform dress codes were not exactly enforced. I liked that already!

Nick took me to a small tent erected on a wooden platform. It was his tent which he had shared with Bill Uren, and he would now share it with me. I stowed my gear then Nick took me to the battalion mess tent where we enjoyed a cup of field coffee in a tin cup. Nick told me that the mission of the 1st Battalion was unique, in that our sole function was to interdict and destroy any guerilla activity related to attacks on the huge Da Nang Air Base, located directly to our north, with the southern end of both airstrips being less than 3,000 meters from our positions at Hills 10, 22 and 44.

The battalion sent out patrols in a 360 degree area, day and night, with the emphasis being on night patrols. On any given night, 1/7 had at least forty 4 or 5 man patrols out in the bush looking for the enemy. The enemy, usually Viet Cong, but occasionally North

Vietnamese regulars, would spend all night positioning rockets and mortars that would be remotely detonated with the hopes they would impact the runways in the early morning. The purpose was to interdict American bombing and strafing runs going north from the Da Nang Air Base. Occasionally, living quarters, ammunition dumps and fuel farms were also hit by the enemy rockets, which would cause a temporary closure of all air operations until resupply and repairs were accomplished. The more effective 1/7 patrols were, the fewer attacks hit the air base. Thus, the battalion's effectiveness as a combat organization was directly related to the number of attacks on the air base, and the number of VC or NVA infiltrators we could kill.

There were over 50 villages around our general tactical area of responsibility (TAOR), each village having a village chief and sufficient villagers to farm rice and to either aid or support guerilla activities, while feigning allegiance to local American or Vietnamese forces. It was a difficult situation, and you truly never knew whom your enemies or friends were, consequently, you trusted no one because a bullet with your name on it could come from any direction. After our coffee break, Nick took me back to the bunker where LtCol Bethel began briefing me on my duties and responsibilities as the operations officer. The colonel took me up to the observation tower, and I could see almost the entire TAOR, from the mountain ranges to the west, the air base to the north, the An Hoa area to the south and Hill 55, the site of the Regimental Command Post, to the east.

There were only two main, improved, hard dirt roads that connected north to south in the entire area. One was Highway 1, the main supply route (MSR) between Da Nang and An Hoa, crossing the Song Vu Gia River at the Hieu Duc district headquarters over a two lane, pontoon bridge that was going to be replaced by a heavy timbered, wooden bridge being constructed alongside the pontoon bridge by the Seabees. The American troops had labeled this new bridge "Liberty Bridge." The other road, Route 540, ran directly along the base of our three, hilly outposts and, while nowhere near as good or straight as Highway 1, it also eventually got to An Hoa.

Located between these two main roads were over sixty small villages and three river tributaries of the Song Vu Gia and the Song Yon main rivers that supplied water to the rice paddies located in each village. In many villages, an intricate system of dikes, levees and foot operated pumps, powered by a bicycle frame mounted on a board and operated by one of the farmers, maintained the proper water levels necessary to grow rice. Many of the villages had been classified as free villages, meaning that they had sworn loyalty to the American and South Vietnamese forces, however, their loyalty often waned rapidly when nightfall came, and the VC began their nightly infiltration. The colonel told me I would be responsible for plotting all battalion patrols, coordinating intelligence reports, assimilating prisoner information and, whenever possible, launch operations aimed at interdicting supply lines and routes of entry and exit for guerilla forces operating within our TAOR. He then continued to give me a detailed summary of the type of action the battalion had seen in the past 30 days, and where we stood on the interdiction of guerilla weapons and personnel. Every time we captured some VC or NVA regulars, we usually wound up capturing a considerable amount of rockets and missiles that had found their way south from Hanoi by way of the Ho Chi Minh trail in North Vietnam and Laos.

Laos bordered Quang Nam province where the Da Nang Air Base and our hilltop command posts were located. The mountain ranges, clearly visible from any of our locations, were partially in Laos and partially in the Republic of Vietnam. We could not enter Laos legally, therefore, traffic of supplies, equipment and personnel on that trail went on almost uninterrupted. Only the bombing raids of B-52s out of Thailand, code named *Arc Light*, dropping thousands of pounds of bombs onto the jungle covered trail, could halt the influx of the enemy from the north. After the visual briefing, I was introduced to the operations staff. Captain Bob Stafford, a Stanford grad, and the current acting operations officer showed me the nightly patrol routes, and informed me that the operations section monitored all nightly patrols by radio and was prepared to provide support fires if any patrol became engaged or was attacked by the enemy.

I remained in the bunker through nightfall and then was indoctrinated into the two wars being waged in Vietnam. The first rocket hit the hill right after dark. It was a long whistle, followed by a very loud booming crash. The bunker rumbled and shook, yet no one in the bunker seemed particularly worried by the explosion. I knew that there was certainly one person in the bunker that was worried by the explosion, but discretion being the better part of valor, I kept my apprehension to myself, or at least I thought I did. The rockets kept coming in throughout the night and artillery from the hill began returning fire at the suspected enemy firing position. While the perpetrators may have been long gone from the site, a 105 howitzer shell does enough damage to render the site useless for several days. LtCol Bethel was watching me very closely, and I began to study patrol routes and monitor radio contacts with the foot patrols operating in our TAOR.

Several patrol leaders called in for mortar fire behind their patrol routes, believing that some VC had picked up their trail and were following them at a discrete distance. In three cases, the patrol leaders were correct, as the 81 mm mortars did their work and cut down some VC following our patrols in trace. Some patrols sustained casualties that required a medevac flight, and the helicopter squadron assigned to support the 7th Marine Regiment at Marble Mountain (the Marine Air Base below the Da Nang Air Base) was alerted. The Hueys, CH-34s and CH 53s were always ready to scramble and the *Purple Foxes* of HMM-364, were our direct support squadron. Hueys were in the air in less than three minutes, on the way to the site where our casualties were waiting for airlift to the hospital in Da Nang.

It was now past midnight, the patrols were moving around our TAOR looking for the enemy, rockets were hitting our position regularly, our artillery battery and our 81 mm mortar platoon were both returning fire, medevac choppers were in the air on the way from Marble Mountain, and I had just completed my first day in the field with 1st Bn, 7th Marines. Only thirteen more months before I could go home seemed like an eternity at that moment. I got through my first night, and then took a few hours rest on one of the cots in the bunker. I had to be ready to plan the next nights activities, based on the debriefings of the previous night's patrol leaders.

I woke up to see LtCol Bethel standing by my bunk. He asked me to go out with him to his tent, which was located directly outside the bunker. He asked me if I was married, and I told him I was, and that I had two children. He told me he could tell from last night's activities that I seemed too apprehensive to be useful to the battalion unless I immediately changed my attitudes. He told me that most married men came to Vietnam convinced that they had to do everything in their power to get back home alive. He said that this type of Marine didn't last long in combat, because their apprehension (he never used the word fear), made it impossible for them to think clearly in the heat of battle, a requirement that was mandatory in a front line combat unit.

He stressed that the first thought of any Marine has to be for his fellow Marines and NOT for his family back home. He told me to get ready to go on a patrol with him down one of the rivers surrounding our position. We would embark on a rubber raft that had a 50 horsepower motor on it and head down river for several miles. He told me there was a very good chance we would be engaging the enemy from the raft, and it was possible for the enemy to blow us out of the water. I put on my flak jacket and wore a soft cover and not a helmet, emulating what everyone else in the battalion seemed to be doing, and went down to the river bank with an M-16 rifle, and several, fully loaded extra magazines plus several bandoleers of ammunition.

There were three rubber rafts and one aluminum boat that certainly looked like a fishing boat to me. All it was missing was an L.L. Bean label. I got into one of the rafts with LtCol Bethel and off we went. It was very clear that this was a test for me. The colonel was taking me into Indian country, with a reinforced squad of Marines, to see how I'd act in a close combat situation. He was daring the enemy to engage us as we moved down river. I had taken the colonel's advice to heart. My only thoughts were of finding the enemy and killing him before he killed me. As we moved down the river, I noticed there was an M-60 machine gun, surrounded by sandbags, mounted in the aluminum boat, so at least we had some good fire power.

We did not have to wait very long. As we rounded a bend in the river, we received small arms fire from the left riverbank. The machine gun opened up, and we returned fire where we had seen the flash of rifle muzzles. The troops were yelling at each other, controlling their fire, and trying to concentrate their fire directly in the area from where we had been fired upon. We moved further down the river, and the same thing occurred three or four times.

I fired with the rest of the troops and kept trying to match my firepower with theirs. We concentrated our bursts of fire and hit a few VC in their black pajamas. We beached our boats and chased the enemy inland for about ten meters before LtCol Bethel ordered us back into the boats, and we took off back up river, continuing our waterborne search and destroy mission. After about two hours of this patrolling, we made it back to where we had started and beached our boats.

I had endured my baptism of fire. I wasn't scared, concentrating much more on hitting the enemy and supporting the rest of the troops in the unit. I said nothing but felt pretty good about myself and my reactions. I noticed that the troops seemed to accept me now, having proven to them that I could handle myself under fire. When we got to the top of the hill, LtCol Bethel looked at me and gave me a thumbs up, saying, "You'll do just fine out here." I have a picture hanging in my den that was taken just after we got back from that patrol, and I look like a cross between Rambo and Chesty Puller. I had proven to myself that I could handle combat, and I was very pleased with myself. You can see that in the picture, as I pose in front of the sandbagged battalion entrance to our operations bunker. I was now a "grunt" in a front line unit, and I had proven myself in front of the troops. I knew LtCol Bethel had devised this test, and I will be eternally grateful to him for doing that and making me become a combat veteran in a very short time. He was a Naval Academy graduate, the son of a Marine General and was a very good battalion commander, both brave and intelligent. Unfortunately, he was not promoted to colonel, which, in my opinion, he richly deserved.

The TAOR of the 1st Battalion was in full view of the Regimental Command Post, which was located on Hill 55, the highest hill in the entire area. Only the Division Command Post, which was located on Hill 327, was higher. Hill 55 was in "Indian country" and Hill 327 was well protected and fortified. Hill 55 was located southeast of Hill 10, and from Hill 55 all positions of both the 1st and 3rd Battalions could easily be seen. The 2nd Battalion was assigned defense of the Division CP, and remained in the hills surrounding Hill 327 to our north, with a mission to provide constant security for the Division headquarters. It was no wonder that when the Bob Hope Show came to our area, it always played on a makeshift stage built in the Hill 327 area. There was no way they would take a chance and let him go south to our positions, as there was too much of a chance of losing him or some member of his troupe.

Our battalion continued aggressive patrolling, and often we would kill the enemy before they killed us. As the Operations Officer of 1/7, I was responsible for planning and conducting the patrols to locate and destroy the enemy before he could attack the air base. This is a copy of the official written record showing one of my first actions in Vietnam taken from the 1/7 Command Chronology for October 1968. Obviously, the reproduction is not clear, particularly the patrol route map overlay.

As the month passed, Marines of 1/7 were getting killed and wounded on a regular basis, either from remote controlled booby traps, land mines planted in the roads

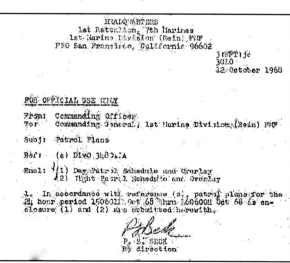

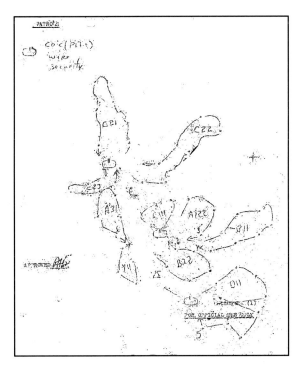

and trails, or small arms fire from enemy positions, hidden in the hundreds of tree lines and bushes that we walked through every day. Rockets and mortars continued to hit our positions on a regular basis, and our casualty rates increased with each new attack. The long and short of the situation was that the Marines owned the terrain in daylight, and the VC and the NVA owned the terrain after dark, because that's when they planted their rockets, buried their land mines and booby traps, fired on our patrols, and stole food from the villages.

Our rifle companies were able to interdict columns of VC carrying rockets and mortars down to the killing fields of our TAOR. With each interdiction, Division intelligence teams came down to check out the types of rockets finding their way south, and then there were pictures taken of the troops who had liberated the weapons just before blowing them up.

In October, we captured a group of NVA regular soldiers and the procedure was to have the prisoners taken back to Division for interrogation. One of the captured soldiers spoke a little broken English, and he was able to inform us he had been a barber in Hanoi. He seemed to be a personable fellow, and since we had no barber, we kept him in the battalion. His name was Ho, and he was the best barber I have ever met. He would take a double edged razor blade, break the razor blade in half, and then stick one half of the blade into a long wooden pencil. He gave me the very best razor cut I have ever had, using that pencil as though he were holding the finest straight razor that money could buy. He was fast, and his eye was perfect. The 1/7 Marines had the best sculpted, most perfectly cut heads of hair in the entire Division. His barbering skills saved his life, and his personality certainly endeared him to all of us.

Besides Ho, we had another Vietnamese resident of Hill 10. His name was Mr. Cu who was an entrepreneur, in that he ran a laundry and tailoring concession on our Hill. He did all the laundry for the troops, washing our clothes in rice paddies and then drying and starching our uniforms in the hot sun. He repaired torn canvas, torn uniforms and made jackets and hats for the troops. Since he was a South Vietnamese, he was paid for his services and was one of the richest men in our area. Mr. Cu was married, and he and

Mrs. Cu seemed to work 24 hours per day. They were always at work in their little tailor shop they had set up in a tent at the edge of our compound. Over time, the tailor shop also became a souvenir shop and our local PX.

I had noticed that Division was getting tired of coming down to our positions every time we captured rockets or mortars. The capture of these weapons made the Air Base area safer, however, the novelty of large weapons caches being liberated from the VC seemed to be wearing off, based on our continued success in finding them. LtCol Bethel lamented the fact that our battalion was not getting enough press for their deeds in the field. I noticed that every time we captured a new weapons cache, if we were lucky enough to also capture a North Vietnamese battle flag with the cache, the big shots from Division were on the next helicopter to our position, to "sight" the captured weapons. They were not fooling anyone. What they actually wanted was the captured battle flag, which was always taken back to Division for "intelligence purposes." The funny thing is that, while the troops could not keep the weapons they captured, they could certainly have kept a battle flag, but they were never around long enough to make sure one of the troops got one.

LtCol Bethel wanted more coverage for the troops, so I asked Mr. Cu to make twenty NVA battle flags. It was illegal to make these flags, so I asked him to make them at night when no one was around and bring the flags to me. I gave five flags to each rifle company commander, after we had taken the flags to the mess tent and soaked the flags in defrosting hamburger meat to make them look bloody. I instructed the company commanders that in the future, anytime they captured a sizable weapons cache and radioed the information into battalion, they were also to say they had captured an NVA battle flag.

Our battlefield communications were monitored by both the Regiment and the Division radio operators, and the fact that there had been some flags captured was quickly known in both command posts. Once we started reporting the captured flags, we never again had any trouble getting proper credit for the hard work our troops were doing. Only the 1/7 troops knew about the "home made flags," and we all got a great laugh out of the desire for battle flags in the rear, where obtaining them yourself was not very likely.

Some of the company commanders got a little more creative with the flags, because after we gave them the blood soaked flags, they wrapped the flags in a hand grenade and threw the grenade into the bush. The grenade exploded, ripping irregular fragmentation holes in all the flags. Now they really looked battle tested! We even sent one of the flags to the general manager of Caesars Palace in Las Vegas, asking him to send us some used playing cards in return for the flag. It worked, because several weeks later the battalion got a case of brand new Caesars Palace playing cards that we distributed throughout the battalion. The manager wrote that he had framed the flag, and placed it in his office. Oh well, what's one more fake thing in Las Vegas anyway?

Towards the end of September the monsoon season hit. It rained constantly, and it was almost impossible to remain dry. The monsoons made it more difficult for the VC to launch rockets and mortars at the air base, but our patrols had to keep pressure on the enemy, day and night. The troops in the bush were soaked to the skin, but I never heard them complain. We were always wet, but at least on Hill 10, we could find some shelter to get out of the heavy rains. The only dry place on Hill 10 was the operations bunker, but it smelled so bad that the benefits of being somewhat dry were overshadowed by the intense smell of wet clothing, wet boots and socks and wet bodies, not to mention the ever present mildew. It is amazing how quickly one can get accustomed to conditions less than favorable, when everyone else is experiencing the same thing.

The monsoon rains really hit us hard in October, making tactical operations difficult but extremely necessary, because the VC and the NVA were using the foul weather to their advantage. As an example of just how bad monsoon rains can be, on October 14 and 15, our area of operations received 10 inches of rain. This was followed by another 15 inches of rain on the 15th and 16th. Roads were impassable, temporary bunkers slid off their locations, bridges washed out and rice paddies overflowed, making foot traffic throughout our area nearly impossible. I used the term nearly, because our troops went out day and night and on the night of October 17, Alpha Company, on a night search and destroy mission, encountered a column of NVA regulars attempting to infiltrate an area near the air base, carrying brand new Russian made antitank missiles that could have done a lot of damage if they had been launched towards the air field. On that night, the troops made the biggest, single capture of enemy rockets in the history of the 1st Marine Division in Vietnam. In the radio report sent out, Captain John Rogers, the company commander, included the fact that he had captured one badly damaged NVA battle flag.

I took a picture of that cache the next morning when the photographers from Division headquarters came down with a colonel from the Division intelligence section, to inspect the rockets and, of course, take the flag back to division for the Commanding General. I still have that picture in my Vietnam photo album, and always smile when I look at it, thinking about those phony flags. We all got a laugh out of that report as we monitored our own unit transmissions.

Monsoon rains did not deter enemy activity. On October 22, after an eight day wait, a patrol sent out by the 1st Reconnaissance Battalion, called in artillery fire on a column of NVA regular troops, marching southward in a loose formation. The next day, the main body of that formation, not knowing that their advance column had been intercepted, continued marching into the same killing zone. Air strikes and additional artillery fire was called into the impact zone and destroyed the company.

The very next day, unbelievably, another company appeared in the very same impact area and suffered the same consequences as their previous comrades. By the time the carnage was over, the recon patrol had not lost a single Marine, had called in 15 air strikes and 12 artillery missions, and had killed 204 enemy soldiers. All members of that patrol received the Bronze Star Medal for valor, as well they should have, since they eliminated a certain threat to the Air Base and to our foot patrols south of the air base.

Conditions on Hill 10 were miserable. Water drenched every available inch of land, and bunkers, fighting holes, observation towers and living spaces were simply soaked all the time. We had to take care of our feet to avoid "jungle rot" which I'm sure must have been called "trench foot" in World War I. We did this by constantly switching socks and boots, putting on mildly wet socks and boots in exchange for socks and boots that were totally soaked.

As for uniforms, we simply remained wet all the time, wrapping ourselves in poncho liners (light weight, rayon blankets that easily dried in any kind of wind) to keep warm. I took out several two company sized, search and clear missions in the direction of the mountains that defined the Laotian border. It was from this position that the NVA troops were coming down into our area of operations. We met little resistance, getting into a few firefights, but never really being able to engage the enemy directly.

The tank platoon commander of the unit attached to our battalion was First Lieutenant Bill Higgins who had graduated from the Army Armor course at Fort Knox. He constantly bemoaned the fact that his tanks were being used only as artillery cannons, and questioned why his unit was even attached to an infantry battalion, since no one ever employed tanks the way they should be. I kept explaining to him that the terrain in our TAOR did not lend itself to tank-infantry tactics and that the only terrain that seemed suitable for the type of tactics that they taught at Fort Knox was probably up north with the 3rd Marine Division, where combat in built up areas had been fought around Hue City and the infamous Citadel. He was an extremely talented and intelligent officer, always volunteering to go out on patrols with the foot troops. On one such patrol, he was awarded a Bronze Star for valor, in the face of an overwhelming enemy force that had surrounded his patrol. Through his intrepid leadership, the patrol broke out of the ambush, taking their killed and wounded with them, and inflicting serious casualties on the surrounding enemy forces.

I liked Bill Higgins very much. He was a reserve officer from a Philadelphia Main Line family, with the promise of a great career in civilian life. Bill was a brave man and, on top of that, he was a genuine troop leader who had the respect and loyalty of every one of his troops. He just wanted to say he had been in a tank battle while he was in Vietnam. As the operations officer of the battalion, I could make that happen, but there simply had to be a reason for taking five tanks off Hill 10 and risking them on some foolhardy mission just to give a young Marine lieutenant some bragging rights back in Philadelphia.

I began to study the terrain very seriously, and looked for an opportunity to employ his tanks in the typical tank-infantry assault. If I was going to do this, I had to pick a time and a place that represented the lowest threat level, both for the tanks and the troops that I would have to employ on the operation. I discussed this with LtCol Bethel, and told him that if possible, I'd like to pull off the operation. Lt Higgins had joined us as an additional infantry troop leader and had shown his skill and bravery under fire, and I felt that the battalion owed him a shot at his most cherished desire. LtCol Bethel, true to his nature said, "Go for it, but if it gets screwed up, it'll be your ass!" I could live with that, so I began looking for an opportunity. I checked all the intelligence reports for the last month, and picked an area where there had been absolutely no enemy contact.

I contacted the operations officer of HMM-364, *The Purple Foxes*, and asked him if he could support a midday raid on a suspected VC choke point. I told him that I thought that we could be in and out of the area in about an hour and that I only needed one unit of infantry to be flown from Hill 10 to the village of Dong Phu, about three miles south of our position, to act as a blocking element on the banks of the Song Yon River. I told him that the main force would attack down Highway 540, mounted on five M-48 tanks. The Major on the other end of the line had me repeat what I had just said. "Did you say mounted on tanks,' he asked. "Yes, I replied. It's a long story, but can you do it"? The major was more than cooperative, with a, "Hell, yes, this should be a first in Vietnam, an infantry-tank-helicopter assault. Count us in."

During this planning phase, I told no one about what I was doing. Patrols kept going out, we kept engaging the enemy, and every morning, we sent mine sweeping patrols down Highway 540 to check for land mines that may have been buried in the road during the night. I checked the local meteorological data and found that we could expect a break in the rain around 23 October. If it stopped for a few days and dried out the road, we could realistically launch our attack on Friday morning at 0600, the 25th. I gave a warning order to Lt Higgins who thought he was dreaming. I told him I would command the assault, and we would mount one rifle company on his tanks (Alpha Company), and we would fly in elements of another company by helicopter (Bravo Company) to act as a blocking force and prevent any escape by way of the river. I did not tell him that I did not expect any enemy contact whatsoever.

On the morning of the 25th we briefed the two company commanders, the helicopter pilots and Lt Higgins on the mission. The tanks would move down Highway 540 at a very fast speed, with the infantry troops on them. The blocking unit would board their helicopters but would not take off until ordered to do so. After landing their troops, the choppers would return to Marble Mountain and await the call for extraction.

You may recall that my father received the Iron Cross while serving in the German Army in World War I. I took a replacement Iron Cross with me to Vietnam for good luck, put it on a dog tag chain, and carried it with me so I could wear it at an appropriate time.

THE "IRON CROSS" ATTACK ON DONG PHU VILLAGE

<u>Date/Place:</u> *25 Oct 1968; Đông Phú, Quang Nam Province*
<u>Units:</u> *Alpha and Bravo Companies, 1st Bn, 7th Marines*
Tank Platoon from 1st Tank Battalion attached to 1/7
HMM 364, The Purple Foxes, MAG 16
<u>Commander:</u> *Major Peter Beck, S-3, 1/7*

The assault force is in position and waiting for the order to launch an infantry/tank/helicopter attack on the village of Dong Phu. Major Beck hung his father's Iron Cross around his neck, got on the lead tank and gave the signal to attack. In a few seconds, the tanks roared off Hill 10 and barreled down Highway 540 at breakneck speed, raising huge spirals of dust and dirt high into the air which caused radios to begin buzzing, wanting to know just what the hell was going on in the 1/7 area of operations. The movement down Highway 540 was thrilling, and the troops mounted on the tanks were screaming like banshees. While the roar of the tanks drowned out their yelling, the adrenalin was pumping through everyone's veins. As they neared the village, Major Beck radioed the helicopters to land the blocking force, and shortly thereafter a vertical envelopment of the village began. Now comes the strangest twist of all. As the tank/infantry unit approached the village, it began receiving small arms fire from just about every hut in the village. The tanks returned fire, and the unit blocking the exits to the river began shooting VC as they tried to escape. By a stroke of luck, the attacking force had surprised a VC company unloading rockets and missiles and attempting to pick up rice and food supplies for units located deep in the mountains around the 7th Marines tactical area. Sporadic firefights broke out through out the village between the VC, NVA advisors and Marine attackers, and when it was over, numerous enemy had been killed, wounded or captured. Missiles, rockets and mortars were captured, which eliminated another potential threat to Da Nang Air Base. The first infantry-tank-helicopter assault in the 1st Marine Division TAOR was completely successful, achieving unexpected results.

During the planning, I did not notify the Regimental Command Center about the operation because I was sure they would not approve it. After it was over, I heard about not coordinating battle plans with the Regiment and Division in no uncertain terms from both Colonel Beckington, the regimental commander, and General Youngdale, the Division commander. It was only the unexpected success of the operation that kept me in my position of operations officer of the battalion, and which, along with everything else, branded me a "tactical genius." Thank God, no one outside of 1/7 knew the real story. LtCol Bethel, in the privacy of our operations bunker, thought the whole thing was hilarious and told me I should thank the VC for saving my rear end. Because the attack was never "approved," it does not appear in the Command Chronology or any other official record of that time.

I never saw Lt Higgins again after Vietnam, and I am sure he is telling his grandchildren about the tank attack in which he had participated. I do not believe he ever knew I conducted the attack just for him and his tankers, and that I never expected an enemy response. Not a stroke of genius ... just a stroke of luck!

After I returned to the United States, I was awarded a Legion of Merit with a combat "V" distinguishing device, partly because of this action. Here is a part of the citation: "... On one occasion, he planned, coordinated and led a helicopter assault deep into hostile territory and directed an operation which drove the Viet Cong from their long time sanctuaries."

On October 29, one of the most ridiculous things happened that really angered me and every fighting man in Vietnam. President Johnson made the decision to halt all bombing and fire attacks on North Vietnam and he got General Abrams, the commander of all troops in Vietnam, to agree with him on this. On October 31, President Johnson told the nation and the world, that he was halting all air, naval and artillery bombardment of North Vietnam, commencing at 8 a.m., Eastern Standard Time, November 1, 1968. He did, however, add the caveat that General Abrams would have the right to retaliate against enemy attacks across the Demilitarized Zone (DMZ), if he deemed it appropriate.

Talk about giving the enemy a license to steal. By bowing to civilian pressure in the US against the war, he was shortchanging the troops who were actually fighting the war in Vietnam. The enemy now began staging supplies in the north, directly across the Ben Hai River. Our troops could see the supplies but could do nothing about it. I am positive that several months later those same supplies resulted in the death and wounding of many Americans.

This is what happens when we fight "police actions" "undeclared wars" and other political wars, where our lily livered politicians are too afraid to declare war officially and activate a real national draft that includes all Americans. How could they have been so "selective" with our young men, as far as serving their country in Vietnam is concerned, in an effort that they deemed necessary? If a "war" is necessary, and we are going to ask Americans to risk their lives, then everyone should be treated equally. That never seems to happen, leaving the lower classes of America's youth (read disadvantaged) to fight and die in those wars, along with a cadre of career military personnel. The rich and privileged seem to escape all risks, all the time.

How very wrong this policy is for our population, and the results of this policy are truly sad for our country. We are now raising a nation of appeasers, self-centered and spoiled brats, and, most importantly, cowards. In my opinion, if this attitude persists, the United States will never win another war! I looked back at those last sentences and thought about taking them out of these memoirs, but, if I still have such an emotional reaction to the idiocy that was Vietnam forty plus years later, the thoughts are staying in this work.

On 10 November 1968, early in the morning, one helicopter landed at each one of our hill top command posts. They were delivering a freshly baked cake for the Marines at each outpost to celebrate the 193rd Birthday of the U.S. Marine Corps. This upheld a tradition within the Marine Corps that no matter where you are, the birthday of our beloved Corps will always be celebrated. In 1968, I celebrated the birthday by cutting the birthday cake under a tent in pouring monsoon rains and making sure that every Marine available got a piece of a somewhat soggy birthday cake. Looking back on that day, it was the best Marine Corps birthday I ever celebrated because it was a real celebration, not some formal event with speeches, dances and dinner. They certainly did not have a formal dinner dance at Tun Tavern in Philadelphia, where our Corps was founded on November 10, 1775, either.

In November we continued our patrols, and while several regimental operations were going on around us, our mission to protect the Air Base never changed. We continued to suffer casualties from land mines, booby traps and small arms fire, but we also interdicted enemy activity. During the month of October and into early November, the VC had only been able to launch two rocket attacks against the base at Da Nang, neither of which did very much damage, and none of which halted air operations for a single minute. Our support services, particularly during the monsoon rains, were provided primarily by helicopter. Mail, movies and replacements usually arrived by helicopter. We in turn, sent dead Marines in body bags to Graves Registration and wounded Marines back to the Naval Hospital in the same manner.

In any situation where you are removed from your particular civilization, mail is the single most important factor for maintaining morale. Each helicopter that landed on any one of our hilltop command posts always brought whatever mail was available. Mail is the single most important link to the outside world for every deployed Marine, and a lack of mail immediately becomes a severe problem that sometimes can result in suicide, depression and a lack of a desire to keep on living, which, on occasion, can lead to some people endangering the lives of others.

Because of the unpopularity of the war back home, many of our troops received *Dear Johns*, a letter from a loved one ending or severing a marriage or relationship. The receipt of these letters was so common that the 1st Marine Division had a policy concerning them. If a Marine received a "Dear John," he could show the letter to his commanding officer and get an immediate thirty-day emergency leave to the United States. This time would not count against his 13-month tour of duty in Vietnam, but it did allow him thirty days to attempt to either correct the situation that caused the "Dear John," or to take whatever measures were necessary to ease the problem or the pain. While this was a well-intentioned policy, 30 days could never be enough time to solve the type of problems that develop into "Dear John" letters, and, nine times out of ten, once the Marine is back in Vietnam, there is a very good chance that the problem will develop again.

On November 28, 1968, our battalion was celebrating Thanksgiving Day. I had gotten married on this day in 1960, and I had flowers sent to Sharron through the services of the big PX on Hill 327. I was sitting in a tent during another monsoon rain, eating kielbasa with the Battalion Chaplain and the Battalion Surgeon, whose sister had sent him the sausage from Milwaukee, when the word came that mail call was being held. There was a letter in the delivery for me from Sharron. It was dated November 20, and it was a "Dear John." Simply stated, the letter told me she had met a man whom she liked better than me, that she had moved him into her house and that she wanted a divorce. I was dumbstruck and went to my tent to try to figure out my next move. I went to see LtCol Bethel and told him about the letter. He cut right to the chase by saying that as far as he was concerned, I could leave tomorrow to return to Florida and try to correct the situation. He did tell me that if I did go, there was no way I would be coming back to 1/7, since if I left, he would need a replacement as I was the operations officer of the battalion, and the battalion could not function without an operations officer.

He then reached into his field desk, took out a bottle of Chivas Regal Scotch whiskey, gave me the bottle, and told me to go to my tent, have a few drinks, think about what I wanted to do, and let him know in the morning. That was the extent of sympathy and compassion I received from my commanding officer. I went to my tent and got fairly drunk. When it got dark, I went down to the front of the command bunker, took off my wedding ring and threw it into a rice paddy that was located directly below the hill. I then informed the colonel that I was staying, since I did not think that I could resolve the problem, or for that matter, given the contents of Sharron's letter, that I wanted to do so. Besides, I wanted to remain with 1/7, and I felt a stronger obligation to the troops that I had fought with than I did to what would soon be my ex-wife.

Based on certain laws existing in the military and the State of Florida, I was able to obtain the services of an outstanding lawyer who had been a Superior Court Judge in Florida. With the assistance of my father in New York, and the Judge in Miami, I obtained a final divorce decree from Sharron in a period of 28 days from filing to final. Thus, I would ring in the new year of 1969 as a bachelor. In exchange for this rapid dissolution, I gave everything I owned to Sharron, leaving me with the clothes on my back and the money I was earning in Vietnam. I felt I had gotten the better part of the deal, as Sharron and the children took off for their new life in the Florida Keys.

It also meant I had to cancel my plans for rest and relaxation (R&R), a program the military used to take combat troops out of Vietnam for a much-needed break. Married men met their wives in Honolulu for eight days while single men could go to Hong Kong, Tokyo, Bangkok, Manila, or Sydney, Australia, for their eight days. Since I was no longer going to meet Sharron in Honolulu, I notified the R&R coordinator that I would not be going on R&R and to take my name off any manifest.

I continued with "my" war. Vietnam was broken down into Corps areas with the Marine Corps assigned to I Corps, which encompassed all the districts from the DMZ to the area south of the Que Son Valley. The year 1968 in the I Corps Zone, was divided sharply into two halves. The first half of the year saw the enemy wage strong attacks in the north against troops holding the DMZ, Hue, Khe Sanh and finally, against the air base in Da Nang. At each point, the enemy was defeated and forced into retreat. By July 1968, there was a shift in the enemy's tactics. After his failures in the north and outside of Da Nang, he pulled his forces back to his bases in Laos, Cambodia, and North Vietnam where we were not allowed to attack. He gave up his strategy of gaining victory through a large-scale military victory, and concentrated on small-unit tactics and rocket and mortar attacks.

RESULTS OF STRATEGY SHIFT IN 1968

	First Half	Second Half
Enemy killed	40,144	22,093
Weapons captured	14,744	7,207
Marine fixed wing sorties	44,936	47,436
Marine helicopter sorties	333,000	639,194

The intensity of ground combat was reduced by 50 percent from July through December.

Marine troop strength in Vietnam in September was at an all-time high with 85,520 Marines in Vietnam, representing 24 battalions. Marine Corps end strength in Vietnam in December of 1968 was 81,000 Marines. With total strength of 195,000 Marines, that number represented 41.5 percent of the entire Marine Corps at the time. No wonder we met ourselves either coming from, or going to, Vietnam. Had I not been in Cuba in 1965 and 66, I would be on my second tour of duty in Vietnam in 1968.

Towards the end of November, the 7th Marine Regiment was ordered to redeploy further south from our positions around the Air Base. Our battalion moved down to Hill 37 in Dai Loc province, a distance of about 5 miles from our locations at Hills 10, 22 and 44. We occupied the site of an old French fort, located on the top of Hill 37, left over from the days when the French were fighting the Viet Minh and when Vietnam was known as French Indochina. Our two companies that were based on Hills 22 and 44 were now relocated to Hills 65 and 52, further south, along Route 4, and about a mile away from our base camp on Hill 37. On November 30, our Battalion Executive Officer, Major Nick Carter, rotated back to the United States, and 1/7 received a new Major who was junior to me, so he became the new Battalion Operations Officer, and I became the Executive Officer of the 1st Battalion, 7th Marines.

Major Bob Alexander had been a football player at the University of Maryland and looked as though he could still play. He was on his second tour of duty in Vietnam and had been awarded a Silver Star as a platoon leader during his first tour of duty. He had just been promoted to Major, and his first assignment as a field grade officer was that of the operations officer of our battalion. Bob was an imposing figure, and the troops took to him immediately. There was no question that he was experienced, and both LtCol Bethel and I were delighted to welcome him into the battalion. As the Executive Officer of the battalion, my duties now revolved more around maintaining the "good order and discipline" of the battalion, thereby leaving LtCol Bethel and Major Alexander all the time necessary to "fight the battalion."

I had observed Major Nick Carter accomplish this task with considerable competence, and I was determined to do the same. I had to run the entire staff of the battalion, oversee every aspect of administration and logistics, and carry out whatever requirements LtCol Bethel had. While I regretted leaving the position of operations officer, I enjoyed being the second in command of the battalion.

Our position on Hill 37 was unique. The top of the hill was commanded by an underground, concrete fort, which was built into the forward slope of the hill. From any portal in the fort, you could oversee the entire valley located below the hill, and the entire village of Dai Loc, which was the district headquarters of the region, and which housed the senior village chief of the region. The Song Thuy Bon River flowed below the hill and wound its way south through the village of Dai Loc. At the village of Dai Phuo, a large, two lane pontoon bridge, crossed the river from the south towards Dai Loc. The Marines had christened the bridge "Liberty Bridge" and it showed up on all of our maps with that name. South of the bridge, was the industrial city of An Hoa, and between the city of An Hoa and Dai Loc was the dangerous and always hostile area that Marines called the *Arizona Territory*, because it was truly the ultimate "Indian country" in our area of operations.

The 5th Marine Regiment secured the areas south of Liberty Bridge and the city of An Hoa, and the 7th Marine Regiment provided the same service north of Liberty Bridge, all the way up to Da Nang Air Base. The move to our new positions took about one week, and while we were moving south from Hill 10, elements of the 1st Marine Regiment, located south of the Marble Mountain Marine Air Base, moved into our old locations. The 5th Marines, who had been on Hills 37, 65 and 52 moved further south towards the industrial city of An Hoa. This placed an area of thick vegetation, isolated villages and heavily traveled jungle trails between the 7th Marine Regiment and the 5th Marine Regiment to our south. The area, the "Arizona Territory," lay directly in front of our positions, on the opposite side of the Song Thuy Bon, the river that separated the Arizona from the rest of our encampments. Going into the Arizona on patrol always meant having to make a river crossing to get into the area. If you did not come under fire immediately, you were guaranteed to be in a firefight with the enemy when you started your patrol inside the jungle areas of the Arizona.

Hill 37 was a large complex, compared to our small outposts up north. Since we were taking over an existing camp, we inherited a fully operational combat operating base, complete with a field messhall, an officer's club, a staff noncommissioned officers club and an enlisted club (all in tents or plywood huts). We had a motor pool, a tank park, a field hospital and aid station, company areas, administrative offices, a large helicopter landing field and 30 foot tall observation towers at each lookout point on the hill's perimeter. There was only one way to get to the top of our hill, and that was a dirt road that began from the center of Dai Loc, the district headquarters. The road was always guarded by Marines, stationed in bunkers on both sides of the road. The guard posts were always supported by machine gun positions above the guard posts, and these were further supported by a mortar platoon that fired H&I missions at random times throughout the hours of darkness.

The chief of the local population was based in Dai Loc, a large village directly below us, located on the banks of the Song Thuy Bon River. After we had moved the entire battalion into the Dai Loc area, LtCol Bethel received an invitation to a formal luncheon at the village chief's house. The chief had requested the Commanding Officer and the Executive Officer of the Battalion come to the luncheon, so I accompanied LtCol Bethel into the village of Dai Loc. I did not like going into Vietnamese villages. I did not trust the Vietnamese, and I had seen too many examples of supposedly friendly villages and village chiefs who were, in actuality, VC sympathizers and spies for the enemy. They were masters at making gullible American's believe they were on our side.

There was abundant proof of their treachery in the hundreds of troops who either lost their lives or were maimed for life, by the roadside mines and booby traps that were hidden along roads and paths almost every night. These mines and booby traps meant that every morning, we had to send road sweep teams, armed with mine detectors, out onto the roads and trails around our base camps so we could use them during the day. Often, members of these road sweep teams were either seriously wounded or killed, when they inadvertently set off some of those mines or booby traps. Nevertheless, LtCol Bethel and I drove off the hill down to the Dai Loc district headquarters building.

There were many Vietnamese people gathered around the building, and we were escorted into the office of the Chief. Through an interpreter, whom we had brought along, he welcomed us to the area and swore his everlasting allegiance to our pacification efforts. He then invited us into a back room where a dinner table had been set up with about twenty places. I looked around and saw there was only one way in and out of the room, and we were seated at the head of the table, with our backs against the rear wall. I liked that arrangement, as I could observe the whole room and keep the holster of my 45 caliber pistol open and ready to draw, if I needed it.

Obviously, I did not let on that I was suspicious of anyone, and LtCol Bethel was busy glad-handing everyone in sight. Finally, the chief motioned for everyone to sit down and LtCol Bethel and I were surrounded by the chief and several village elders on all sides of the table. Everyone appeared hospitable and I wondered how many of them were VC, since there was certainly no way to tell. The dinner was served by several Vietnamese women, all of whom were also gracious and hospitable, and I was beginning to enjoy myself as we progressed through each course of food.

One of the courses was a large plate of what appeared to be small, fried chicken legs. I told the colonel that this was mighty tasty, and he informed me that this was a great sign of respect by the village chief, because he was feeding us the greatest Vietnamese delicacy, puppy legs. I could not believe what I had just heard and asked him for a clarification. He replied that I had heard him correctly, we were indeed eating fried puppy legs. I stopped eating immediately and from then on just picked at my food. Eating a puppy was not my idea of a great feast, and I totally lost my appetite. We made it through the rest of the meal, thanked the chief for his hospitality, and headed back to the hill. My one experience with eating in a local village was over, and I was positive I would not repeat it. Besides eating a puppy, I had also eaten some other delicacy, consisting of some local beetles. At least I did not get shot, and we did make a favorable impression on the chief and the village elders.

Life on Hill 37 continued at a brisk pace. Because we had been assigned a larger TAOR, we increased foot patrols and search and clear missions into the Arizona Territory. We were taking so many casualties there that Division Headquarters decided that it was time to run several Air Force defoliation missions in the area. We were told to stay out of the area for one week and four old C-47 cargo airplanes began spraying the entire Arizona Territory. For several days, a large mist enveloped the area, and seemed to remain in the area with some clouds drifting over our positions. The area was being sprayed with Agent Orange, and after the spraying, our patrols began to suffer fewer casualties because most of the cover and concealment used by the VC had been killed and made useless to both us and the enemy. I have never seen a statistic concerning any Agent Orange damage suffered by our troops because of this effort, and so far, I have also not had any symptoms being experienced by some veterans of Vietnam who apparently have suffered considerably.

We celebrated Christmas and New Year's Day on Hill 37, and as a special Christmas treat, Martha Raye, the singer and comedienne, flew out to our Hill 65 and entertained the troops. In my entire time in Vietnam, she was the only celebrity that went out to the combat bases to entertain troops. While she was on Hill 65, the hill came under mortar and rocket fire, but she did not stop her show; however, her accompanist bolted for a bunker on several occasions, only to be told by Martha Raye to ignore the damn incoming and to keep playing. She won the heart of every Marine there and was forever remembered as a gallant lady and one hell of a woman. Many years later, I saw Martha Raye in the Los Angeles airport. I identified myself as one of the Marines she had entertained in Vietnam, and told her how much I had appreciated her efforts on behalf of the troops, especially during a mortar and rocket attack. She thanked me for my kind words, shook my hand and said, "Honey, I'm sorry I don't remember you, there were so damn many mortar and rocket attacks that I lost count." Incidentally, when I saw her in Los Angeles, she was wearing an Army uniform because she was also a nurse in the Army Reserve. They don't make them like that anymore.

A few words about USO shows: the troops were entertained from time to time by USO shows that were contracted to come to our camps by helicopter to entertain the troops and then fly to the next location. Almost all the USO shows that came to our combat bases were Filipino groups, except for two who were Australian. All of these groups did covers of the latest Rock and Roll and Country and Western songs that were popular in the States. They could not function without portable generators, since without power their electronic instruments would be useless. I never saw an American group that would come out into the field, choosing instead to stay in the relative safety of the Hill 327 complex.

THE REAL "JOE SHIT"

To pass the time when our troops were not on patrol or on some operation, I asked the Division Special Services Officer to send down three electric guitars and three electric bass guitars plus one drum set. We put these in the enlisted club on Hill 37, and I formed a rock and roll group called, *Joe Shit and the Ragmen.* This was a play on words, because in our radio transmissions, whenever we saw only one VC, he was invariably referred to as "one Joe Shit, if there were more VC with him, they were referred to as "Ragmen." Thus, "Joe Shit and the Ragmen" was a perfect name for our group. I put out the word that I was auditioning for the band and one lead singer, and that we would have auditions in the Enlisted Club as often as anyone could get there. If they were accepted for the band, they would be allowed time off to practice, and then entertain our own troops since USO shows did not come out very often.

Our battalion was composed of over 2100 Marines. Most of them were in the 18 to 21 year old age group, and almost all of them fancied themselves rock musicians. Looking back on it today, I guess it was an original version of "So you want to be in a Band." The word spread quickly throughout the battalion, and within a few days I was holding auditions at least 15 to 20 times per day. Some of the troops were awful, but they all got their turn, and within about three weeks, Joe Shit and the Ragmen became a reality.

Our two lead guitar players were both young men who had played in bands back home. One of them, Lance Corporal Bob Brentano, survived Vietnam and got a job as a studio musician in Hollywood. Our Bass player, Corporal Vernon Batteaux, from New Orleans, played in a funeral band back home and was an experienced blues musician. Unfortunately, that band had to play at his funeral, since he was killed while on patrol in the Arizona. Vernon was replaced in the band by a musician from New York City named Chester Rivington, who had cut his teeth on jazz in some small Harlem clubs, long before he reached a legal age to play in them.

Our lead singer, who quite naturally was dubbed "Joe Shit, was Lance Corporal Charlie Mooney, the Marine who had picked me up at Hill 327, and driven me to the battalion on my first day in Vietnam. Charlie had been a lead singer in a band in Pittsburgh, and he was very good. He sang all the rock and roll standards, and he got the troops into the mood. He could imitate almost all the current Rock and Roll stars, however, he was especially talented in imitating Wilson Pickett, The Temptations, Marvin Gaye, The Animals and Mick Jagger. This was enough ammunition to get the mood rolling, and our first show in the Enlisted Club was an enormous success. The band played *The Midnight Hour, My Girl, Satisfaction, Mustang Sally, We Got to Get Out of this Place*, and for the finale, *You Can't Always Get What You Want*. They were not experienced enough to take requests, however, in a few weeks, after practices that had to be scheduled between combat actions, they were good enough to keep our entire battalion better entertained than any other infantry battalion in Vietnam. I have always regretted that we never made any recordings of their songs, because if I had them today, they would be priceless for me.

As I had mentioned previously, our regimental headquarters was located on Hill 55, which was approximately three miles, as the crow flies, north of our position. At Hill 55, the 7th Marine Regiment had a forward logistics base and helicopter air base, complete with refueling capacity and a control tower to direct air traffic in and out of the area. All of our supply requests, whether for food, ammunition, weapons, beer, movies or whatever we needed, went through this forward base. It had to be able to meet all the requirements of all three battalions in their varied locations, and supplies had to be loaded onto cargo nets, which were then hooked up to the exterior cargo hooks of our helicopters, who then flew the supplies to the location dictated by the control tower.

This was no easy task, as each supply request was different, and each had to be loaded and dispatched quickly. Sending the wrong supplies to the wrong unit in the field could be critical. Unfortunately, supply shipments were often being misrouted or confused, and sometimes, a request for ammunition was answered with a week's supply of baked beans and dehydrated shrimp. More often than not, units in the field were held up waiting for the correct supplies, and helicopters were forced to bring the incorrect shipment back to Hill 55 so the routing could be corrected.

Running the logistics base fell to the Regimental Logistics Officer, a Major Jeff Kendall, who was a Naval Academy graduate, and the son of a Marine General. It was a demanding job and required a tremendous amount of skill and flexibility due to the constantly fluid situation of combat and the needs of the troops in the field. In all cases, medical evacuations (medevacs) took priority over all other helicopter mission, so if there were many casualties, the resupply chain was halted until all casualties had been air lifted to the hospital or, in the case of the dead, to the Graves Registration Platoon back at Hill 327. It was a difficult job to coordinate all these efforts, and it took its' toll on the major's assigned to the duty. Anytime we got a wrong airlift, we were on the radio to regiment asking why we can't get what we need when we need it? As usual, it was always the logistics officer who got the heat for any mistakes or hold ups.

In January of 1969, I had a major screw-up that could have cost me my life. Our Battalion Surgeon, a Navy Doctor named Bill Scranton, from Lima, Ohio, was scheduled to return soon to the States. He asked me for a favor, which was to take him on a combat patrol. I told him that taking the one doctor the battalion had out into the bush on a combat patrol would be crazy and that it would end my career if he got killed. He acknowledged my situation, but then told me that he couldn't tell anyone that he'd served in combat with Marines if he didn't go out on at least one combat patrol. I refused his request at least twenty times, but he kept bugging me and begging me and finally, in a moment of weakness, I told him I would check with Major Bob Alexander, our operations officer, and see if it was possible. I asked Bob if there were any areas that he felt were dormant without any enemy activity in the past 30 to 45 days. He told me that a village located southeast of Hill 37, called Phong Thu, located along the river's edge of the Song Thuy Bon River, had not had any enemy activity in over three months. I told him that I planned to take out a platoon sized patrol made up of cooks, bakers and truck drivers, all of whom wanted to play "Rambo" and go out into the bush on a patrol. I would take them out at midday and get back in two to three hours, maximum.

I did not tell him I would also take the doctor, figuring that if anyone was going to get into trouble for it, I would keep him out of it. We mounted out for our "meaningless" patrol the next day at 1130.

ON PATROL WITH THE DOCTOR
TO PHONG THU VILLAGE

At 1130 the troops mounted out for a "meaningless" patrol. Each members weapon and ammunition supply was checked and that everyone had flak jackets and helmets. Major Beck briefed them on the mission which was to check out the village of Phong Thu because there had been reports of VC activity in the area (which was a complete fabrication).

The patrol proceeded off the hill, stopped at the last guard bunker to be counted, and continued along Route 4 until they got to Phong Thu. It was very hot and all personnel were sweating profusely, wiping their faces with the ever-present green towels. The patrol approached the village and began to move through it to the riverbank.

The intention was to turn at the edge of the river, retrace the route and return to Hill 37, having completed a "combat patrol" for the benefit of the patrol participants, mainly the battalion doctor. As the patrol moved through the village, a few people were standing outside of their huts and a few were working in a nearby rice paddy. Everything seemed peaceful and fairly normal. As they got to the riverbank, the patrol sat down for a break and to drink water.

After about two minutes, small arms fire started coming from a nearby tree line. The patrol was caught in an ambush, and with their backs to the river, were stuck where they were and became sitting ducks. Small arms fire was returned. Major Back noticed that Dr. Scranton was crouched low behind the riverbank and was not returning fire. He yelled at him to start firing, because "our asses were on the line here, and we needed all the firepower we could muster." The doctor yelled that he was a noncombatant, and Major Beck yelled back that whoever was doing the firing didn't care much about his noncombatant status. The doctor seemed quite scared, but he attempted to return fire which was not particularly successful. The patrol was clearly in hot water, and it looked like they would have to fight their way out and probably suffer some casualties along the way.

Just at that moment, a HUEY helicopter flew overhead. The field radios had preset frequencies, and it was easy for Major Beck to ask the pilot if he had any ordnance he could fire at the enemy. The pilot replied that he had a full load of rockets in his pods and would be happy to assist. He was told that the patrol would throw green smoke grenades towards the general area from where they were getting fire, and if he could wait one minute before diving to fire his rockets, the patrol would get ready to run south along the river line and then get back on Route 4 towards Dai Loc. The pilot agreed to this scheme, and the troops were told that on the count of three, they were to hurl a green smoke grenade towards the tree line. When the HUEY started his rocket run, the patrol was to disengage, move quickly south along the river's edge, and then head back towards Route 4, about 500 meters south of its present position. Everyone was told to stay together and keep their weapons at the ready always.

The green smoke grenades were thrown and the HUEY started his descent, firing off his first rocket as he began his dive. When the rocket left the pod, the patrol moved out of its positions and headed south. The first rocket impacted right at the tree line and was quickly followed by three more rockets, all of them impacting with a tremendous roar and a huge fireball. By the time the second and third rockets hit, the patrol was out of the trap and heading south as fast as it could go. The rear guard kept checking for any followers, but there were none.

The patrol passed the final checkpoint where they were counted again, and returned to Hill 37. They had suffered no casualties. Doctor Scranton was very quiet, and his one combat patrol in Vietnam was a little more than he had bargained for. On the day he left the battalion he shook Major Beck's hand and told him that he would never forget that patrol. Major Beck wouldn't either.

The "Airedale" Marine had saved our collective butts, and as we headed back towards the village of Dai Loc, I got back on the Air Wing network and thanked our Good Samaritan profusely. Not only did he save our butts, he also saved my career, because if I had lost the doctor, my name would have been mud! As we returned to Hill 37 and crossed our final checkpoint where we were counted again, I thanked God that we did not lose anyone, because we came mighty close. Doctor Scranton was very quiet when we dispersed at the top of the hill. I think his one patrol in Vietnam was a little more than he had bargained for, and it certainly was more than I had expected, to say the least.

I went down to the operations bunker and briefed Bob Alexander on what had happened, and he told me that the entire operations bunker had been monitoring our transmissions. He never knew I had the doctor with me, and I don't think that Bill Scranton spoke much about it until he got home to Lima, Ohio. I'm sure that today, somewhere in Ohio, lives a doctor who has told his Vietnam war story so often that his colleagues are probably tired of hearing it. Somehow, though, I bet the doctor isn't tired of telling it. At least, I hope not.

Several days later, I drove to the Marble Mountain Marine Air Base and located the HUEY pilot. He was Major George "Whippet" Greystone, who happened to be the Executive Officer of VMO-1, the unit of which the HUEY that saved our collective butts was a member. I bought the Major a case of beer at his club, and told him he was welcome on Hill 37 anytime. He remarked that he was damn glad he had not expended his rockets earlier, because his rules stated that a helicopter could not land at Marble Mountain with a full load of rockets attached. If we hadn't needed him, he would have shot his rockets at any target of opportunity on the way back to his base. It turned out to be a "win-win" situation for both of us, with my side being a much bigger winner.

HEADQUARTERS, 7TH MARINES

Our resupply situation was continuing to be unsatisfactory. This was occurring at each battalion in the regiment, and Colonel Robert Nichols, who had replaced Colonel Herb Beckington as the Regimental Commander, was acutely aware of the problem. Unknown to me, he had requested a professional logistics officer from the Division to replace Major Kendall, who Colonel Nichols did not believe was up to the task. Unfortunately, Colonel Nichols spoke with the Division Supply Officer, a colonel by the name of Gene Schwartz, who told Colonel Nichols that he had such an officer in his regiment. I had known Colonel Schwartz in the Supply Department when he was the Commanding Officer of the Supply Depot in Philadelphia. Colonel Nichols asked Colonel Schwartz who that officer was, and the next morning I received a radio transmission at 1/7 headquarters instructing me to pack my things and get on a helicopter that would be taking me to Hill 55 the following morning.

Major Kendall would come down to Hill 37, where he would become the battalion Executive Officer, and I would become the Regimental Logistics Officer. My logistics background had caught up with me five months after I had arrived in Vietnam. I was heartbroken to have to leave 1/7, and I begged LtCol Bethel to intercede with Colonel Nichols on my behalf. I know he tried but to no avail. Colonel Nichols made it abundantly clear that I'd better be on that helicopter the following morning. My days in an infantry battalion had come to a premature ending. I would now be working out of Hill 55, and taking over the responsibilities of the Regimental Logistics Officer. The single most vital part of the job was going to be running the forward logistics air base and to get the right supplies to the correct units at the appropriate times.

I was on my way at 0800 the following morning, after saying goodbye to all my buddies in 1/7, and telling "Joe Shit and the Ragmen" that a new "manager" was arriving on the scene. Ho, the North Vietnamese barber and Mr. Cu, my North Vietnamese flag maker, were in tears, as was I. These were good people, and I would miss them. I am sure that they hoped that my replacement would take good care of them, and I implored LtCol Bethel to make sure that this would occur.

I had strong feelings about leaving the battalion. For the past five months, I had fought with the battalion, and I had seen many Marines killed and seriously wounded, wounds that they would carry with them for the rest of their lives, providing they survived whatever surgical procedures awaited them. I had lost close friends, I had seen almost every field grade officer wounded, except for myself. I did not suffer a single scratch from any combat engagement. I had gone down to Graves Registration and had the awful duty of having to identify the body of my air-ground control radio operator, who was killed on a road sweep patrol. When I got the word that he had been killed, I rushed down to Graves Registration, and when I got there, they had his body on a table, and one of the Marines was hosing his body off with a standard garden hose that had a pistol grip spray attachment on it. They stopped when I came into the room, but I could see that it was standard procedure to clean the body as much as possible before tagging the remains properly, and then putting it in a rubberized body bag, and placing it in a portable refrigerator. From there, the body would be transported to the morgue at Da Nang Air Base and processed for shipment home.

I identified the body and signed the necessary papers, then hitched a ride on a helicopter back to Hill 37. There is not a day that I do not think about my radio operator, usually when I'm taking a shower, as I remember my last glimpse of him. In 2008, I viewed his name on the Vietnam Wall monument in Washington, and I was as sorry over his death that day as I was when I heard the radio operator reporting his death back to battalion so many years ago. Like all the young deaths I witnessed, it was a terrible waste. I felt just as bad when I visited the Wall in Washington, and viewed the names of my friends that had made the ultimate sacrifice for their country.

Three days later, LtCol Bethel received orders to Okinawa for his last two months of duty overseas, and he was replaced as the battalion commander by LtCol Jack Dowd, a South Boston Irishman, and a close friend of mine from my tour of duty in Washington. This change was not a result of anything that LtCol Bethel did, but rather a bit of politics on the part of several senior officers who were very interested in getting a battalion command assignment for Jack Dowd. Jack was a "comer" in the Marine Corps, and an officer that everyone felt was a future general. I shared that belief, but I also felt that LtCol Bethel got a raw deal, even though he had already been the battalion commander for over six months. Jack was a jock from Holy Cross University, and when we were both assigned to Headquarters Marine Corps, he played basketball every day at noon. I met him at these pickup games and got to know and like him. He was a charismatic leader with a leprechaun sense of humor and an Irish gleam in his eyes. I envied Bob Alexander, the battalion operations officer, the opportunity to work with Jack in the field. I had missed working with him by three days.

One of Jack's trademarks was a green shamrock that he had sewn on to each set of his field uniforms. Jack was a true character, and had no trouble gaining the respect and loyalty of the 1/7 troops. He would have a great tour of duty with the battalion until he was killed. As the helicopter lifted me off of Hill 37 on my way to Hill 55, I looked down at the base camp of the unit that I would always identify with for the rest of my life.

I had been in two other infantry battalions before joining 1/7, but the outfit that you serve with in combat with always remains in your mind and your heart. There are too many memories imbedded in your brain to ever forget your combat unit, some good and many of them very bad. The bad was related only to the horrors of war, which are only discussed among those who suffered them together, while the joys are always recounted for anyone that will listen. Thus, the funny stories appear in these memoirs, recalled with fondness and love for the characters who participated in them, and the horrible stories are left untold, only to be shared with the survivors. It seems only right to me, and it is for that reason that this memoir does not contain many horrible war stories. Suffice it to say, war is horrible, and we should never subject our young people to the terrible experiences of having to fight one. History has proven that we never learn that lesson.

The helicopter dropped me off at the small helipad by the 7th Marines Regimental Command bunker. I went to the Regimental Adjutant to drop off my OQR. I would be dropped from the rolls of 1/7 and joined to Headquarters Company of the 7th Marine Regiment, effective Saturday, February 1, 1969. I reported to Colonel Robert Nichols, the Regimental Commander of the 7th Marines who was a tall, quiet man who looked a lot like Abraham Lincoln without the beard. He seemed genuinely happy to see me and told me I came highly recommended by all the supply and logistics people in Division. He was surprised I had been in an infantry battalion for five months when the Division needed qualified logistics personnel in the field. I reminded Colonel Nichols that my primary MOS was infantry, and I had been extremely happy to serve in 1/7. He laughed and told me he expected me to get the forward logistics operating base functioning properly soon.

He then took me to the command bunker, where he introduced me to the rest of the regimental staff. I met Bill Krulak again, having last seen him in AWS. Bill came from an exceptionally distinguished Marine family. His father, Lieutenant General Victor H. Krulak, the Commanding General of Fleet Marine Force, Pacific, was a Naval Academy graduate and a Navy Cross hero of World War II. Bill and his two brothers, Victor Jr., and Charles had attended the Naval Academy. Bill and Chuck had graduated from the Academy, but Nick, as Victor Junior, preferred to be called, had left the Naval Academy during his freshman year, transferred to William and Mary College and had become an Episcopal Minister. Nick was serving with the Marines as a Navy Chaplain, having already completed two tours of duty in Vietnam with front line Marine combat units. Later his brother, Chuck, would become the 31st Commandant of the Marine Corps, serving in that capacity from 1995 through 1999, earning one more star than his father. Bill would later leave the Marine Corps as a Major, go to Yale Divinity School, and become an Episcopal Minister serving a large congregation in Baltimore, Maryland.

I was also introduced to Major Bill Givens, the Regimental Air Officer. Bill was a fighter pilot who had been assigned duties as the Regimental Air Officer to coordinate all air traffic in and out of the regimental area of operations. This included all the helicopters that flew in and out of Hill 55's logistics base around the clock. I would be working very closely with Bill, and he took me to the tent that I would share with him and Bill Krulak. I stowed my gear and continued to the logistics tent where I would meet my staff in the Regimental S-4 (logistics) office.

My logistics chief was a very young Staff Sergeant by the name of Douglas Burke. He was from Milwaukee, Wisconsin, and had been in the Marine Corps only eight years, but was already on his second tour of duty in Vietnam. He was intelligent and extremely motivated to do his job to the best of his ability. He was a school-trained logistics NCO, a former Drill Instructor, and he was also an excellent troop leader. My Logistics Clerk was a Princeton University graduate, who had declined a commission in the Marine Corps and elected to serve his two years of active service as an enlisted man. His name was John Henry Brewer, and he was from Atlas, Georgia. He was an excellent clerk and served his country with honor and loyalty.

My driver and general utility man was a young black Marine from Philadelphia named Benjamin Moore. He was a willing and totally dedicated Marine who I immediately nicknamed "Bennie X," (think of Malcolm X), a name he liked as soon as I coined it. He stayed with me for the remainder of my tour of duty, and I have very fond memories of Bennie X. Those three Marines were my office staff, and after meeting and greeting them, I continued to the logistics air base where I would meet the rest of my crew.

Hill 55, as the Regimental Command Post, was almost three times as large as our battalion command post on Hill 37. It occupied the tallest landmass in the entire tactical area of operations south of the air base at Da Nang. It was situated at the confluence of the Song Yon and the Song Vu Ghia rivers, and it was directly above the village of Duc Ky, a smaller version of the regional district headquarters in Dai Loc. The village chief was supposedly friendly to the Marines, but like all village chiefs, it was hard to trust them, since their lives were usually endangered by nighttime VC incursions beyond their control.

Located on Hill 55 was a complete artillery battery of the 11th Marine Regiment, consisting of six 105 mm howitzers that were emplaced so they could provide artillery fire throughout the 7th Marines tactical operations area. A platoon of heavy trucks from the 1st Motor Transport Battalion was on the hill, as was a platoon from the 1st Bulk Fuel Platoon, which maintained our aviation fuel tank farm, located next to the logistics heliport. We had support troops from 1st Medical Battalion, a platoon of tanks from 1st Tank Battalion, ammunition support personnel to man our temporary ammunition dumps, as well as cooks and bakers that ran and maintained a large mess hall that operated 24 hours per day. They fed not only personnel located on the hill, but transient personnel like pilots, truck drivers, medical personnel and all others who were simply "passing through."

Our regimental mess hall had a very good reputation and our cooks were described as the best in the entire Division. Having eaten in that mess hall for eight months, I can attest to both the quality and the quantity of the food, prepared under the direction of Master Sergeant Edgar Robinson, who later became one of the first Master Gunnery Sergeants in the Food Services field.

Because the base was so big, it was constantly under mortar and rocket attack at night. This made it difficult to operate, however, the attacks never shut down the heliport for very long, and our supply chain continued unhindered by the random attacks. The heliport itself was located on the opposite side of the artillery battery and away from the two main roads that ran through our area. While the regimental headquarters overlooked the village of Duc Ky, the heliport stood by itself, with only the Song Yon River to its forefront. The Seabees had constructed the heliport out of pierced steel planking, and placed the steel plates on an area of ground that they had leveled, compacted, and then treated with used diesel oil, which served to reduce dust and harden the foundation of the landing site. The heliport was large enough to land and load four helicopters at one time, and the surrounding staging areas were large enough to stage eight external loads already put into cargo nets.

On one side of the heliport stood a three stories high control tower which was sandbagged up to the windows and which had withstood many rocket and mortar attacks. At the base of the control tower was a large wooden sign that proclaimed to all viewers that the name of the heliport was *Fort Courage*. Directly opposite the control tower across the heliport, was the fuel farm which was a series of large, rubberized bladders that were placed into holes dug out of the ground. There were several sizes of bladders, and one could hold 10,000 gallons of aviation fuel and another could hold 5,000 gallons. Besides the aviation fuel, we also stored the gasoline required to run the myriad types of gas driven vehicles, tractors and self-propelled guns. Each bladder was dug into holes which supported them in place. These holes were large enough to conceal the entire bladder, except the metal opening located at the top of the bladder. It was this opening that was hooked up to the refueling hoses that replenished the fuel supplies of the helicopters using the heliport. Large tanker trucks carrying aviation fuel departed from Da Nang regularly to keep the fuel bladders on Hill 55 full and ready for use by our support helicopters.

On January 1, 1969, Major General Ormond Simpson assumed command of the 1st Marine Division. As 1969 began in Vietnam, Quang Nam province, where the 1st Marine Division was located, was relatively calm. The Division continued to guard the approaches to Da Nang and the 2nd Brigade of the Korean Marine Corps, in conjunction with the 5th Marine Regiment, continued the mission of providing exterior security for the industrial city of An Hoa. While several tactical operations were underway, such as *Oklahoma Hills* and *Taylor Common*, the bulk of the 7th Marines efforts centered on continuous patrolling of all areas leading towards the Da Nang air base. The mission of all units within the TAOR was to stop any attempts by the VC or the NVA regulars to cut the roads between Da Nang and An Hoa, a distance of approximately ten miles south of Da Nang. Road travel was always risky due to the constant placement of mines and booby traps along all open roads. These mines and booby traps were always placed under cover of darkness and, while our constant patrols neutralized many of these guerilla attempts, there were always some that caused havoc when they were detonated.

This was the tactical climate of the combat area I was involved with and the units within that tactical area would be depending on me, and my troops, to get them the supplies they needed in an orderly and efficient manner. I inspected the heliport and then went up to the tower. The helicopters were working steadily with crews hooking up external loads and then waving the helicopters off the landing pad. The control tower operator would then dispatch the helicopter to its destination. This kept on throughout the time I was in the tower. I observed the control tower operator, a Marine Corporal, directing incoming and outgoing helicopters with complete calm and quiet authority. The radio transmissions were on a loudspeaker inside the tower, so that conversations between the pilots and the tower operator could be monitored.

The tower operator was Corporal Bob DePeau, who was serving his second tour of duty in Vietnam. He was the senior air traffic controller at the heliport, and an experienced combat air traffic controller, having served in the northern part of Vietnam with the 3rd Marine Division on his first tour of duty. He was relieved of his duties by Corporal Theodore Brown, a black Marine from East Los Angeles, and a former member of the wicked Crips Gang. Corporal Brown was every bit as good as Corporal DePeau in controlling the helicopters, but Corporal Brown added a lot of slang and quick talk to his interaction with the helicopter pilots. It was safe to say that while he kept things moving on the helipad, he also kept the pilots laughing. While he was about 40 years ahead of the Rap music craze, what he did in that control tower was every bit as good as what the current Rap musicians do in their songs, and his patter expedited helicopter air traffic and kept fatigued pilots entertained and attentive. Corporal DePeau told me that there were four tower operators and that the tower was manned 24 hours per day, 7 days per week. All the support personnel required to operate the heliport were on this schedule.

The external load Marines were members of the Shore Party Battalion, who, under normal circumstances, controlled beach landings and inward movement from the beach during an amphibious landing. Since there were no beach landings in Vietnam, the Shore Party Battalion was task organized to serve as helicopter loading and unloading support personnel at helipads throughout the Division's area of operations. The crew at Hill 55 was under the command of First Lieutenant Leon Russell, from Oklahoma City, Oklahoma.

Leon was a graduate engineer from the University of Oklahoma, and planned to return to his father's construction business when his tour of duty in Vietnam was completed. In the meantime, he ran an efficient and hardworking organization, always joining his troops on the helipad during load outs.

I returned to the logistics tent and spoke to Staff Sergeant Burke. I asked him why he felt that things were getting screwed up on the helipad. He told me that everyone was working their butts off, but there didn't seem to be an overall commander at the helipad and this caused a breakdown in communications. I then returned to the helipad and spoke with Corporal DePeau and asked him the same question. He said that the Shore Party personnel just did not pay attention and hooked up the wrong loads to the wrong helicopters. Lt Russell told me the staging areas were too narrow, and loads got mistaken in the staging area and then sent out to the wrong location.

I took all of these comments to heart and then spent the next four days in the control tower and at the helipad. I asked SSgt Burke to run the office and process the logistics requests and then send them directly to me in the tower. The requested supplies came from different supply dumps, and they had to be consolidated at a location before arriving at the helipad. The supply personnel on Hill 55 would assemble all requests, except ammunition requests, and then drive them to the helipad where Shore Party personnel began to stage the supplies for the field units. Ammunition came from our ammunition dump that was run by personnel of the Ammunition Supply Platoon. The main ammo dump was located in Da Nang and shipments for the regiment were trucked to our dump at Hill 55 almost daily. It was far too difficult to attempt to resupply ammunition directly from Da Nang. Keeping ammunition separated also decreased the possibility of a single attack paralyzing our ability to supply all of our varied weapons with the proper ammunition.

After a week of observing activities at the helipad and being very impressed with the dedication and hard work of everyone associated with the supply efforts, I reviewed the complaints from the field. We were still sending the wrong items to the wrong places. Pilots and the troops in the field were continuing to be frustrated. I decided to make a major change. I went to the regimental commander and asked him to let me take over the entire helicopter operation on Hill 55, using Major Jim Givens, the regimental air officer as an assistant. I told him that this was not an ego trip on my part, but rather an attempt to reduce the mistakes and to streamline the operations at the helipad. I went on to say that SSgt Burke would run the office and that we would be in constant communications.

He agreed to let me try, so I went to Jim Givens, the air officer, and told him of my plan. I asked for his help at the tower and the following morning at 0600, I had a meeting with all personnel who worked at the helipad, including all support units and their respective commanders. I told them that effective immediately, I was taking over all operations at the helipad, and that everything that happened there had to go through me. I told them that I would be very easy to find, since I would be either in the tower or on the helipad. I planned to sleep in a small bunker located directly behind the control tower.

The next thing we did was to change the staging areas. Since we were supporting three infantry battalions, I decided to color code each battalion. The 1st Battalion was red, the 2nd Battalion was blue, and the 3rd Battalion was yellow. Supplies coming to the helipad for each of those battalions had to be color coded before they were dropped off at the helipad. When the supplies arrived, they were taken to staging areas that were also color-coded. I asked Leon Russell to break his people down into three units and then made each of those units responsible only for one battalion, thereby making sure that each unit handled only those supplies designated for their battalions. I encouraged the units to place notes on the supplies, and they did this with great enthusiasm. Soon units were receiving supplies with notes in them that read, "Packed by Will the Thrill, your man on the Hill." The color coding seemed to eliminate much confusion, and it reminded me of the time in Camp Lejeune when I dyed all of our sheets green so the Navy would not steal them when we were aboard ship.

The helicopter operations improved dramatically, and we began getting kudos from the field. The fact that I had spent five months in the bush gave me a great deal of credibility with the support troops and the troops in the field. Pilots began coming into the tower while their helicopters were being refueled and complimenting the control tower operators on the new found efficiency of loading operations. We were molding the entire operation into a single unit, and it was working. Corporal Brown, our Crips gang leader, stole a large coffee urn, and we began furnishing pilots with hot coffee, another sure way to increase their appreciation for our operations on Hill 55.

We had no clubs on Hill 55, and all of our socializing was done at the large Regimental Mess Hall where an officers and staff noncommissioned officers dining area was set up. The mess hall was open all the time for hot coffee and "mid-rats" (midnight rations) for crews working around the clock. It was while we were seated here for meals that we got to know one another. One of the finest officers I ever met was on Hill 55, and he was our Regimental Executive Officer, Lieutenant Colonel Raymond P. Coffman. LtCol Coffman, like so many senior officers of his day, was the son of a former Marine general. LtCol Coffman did not attend the Naval Academy; however, he was a graduate of Virginia Military Institute, and he was the Marine Corps Open Handball Champion. On top of all that, he was also a true southern gentleman. We spent quite a few hours conversing over our meals, and he was a strong supporter of our efforts at the helipad. In short, he was probably our biggest fan and never missed an opportunity to compliment the troops working at Fort Courage. It was through the efforts of Colonel Coffman that I was able to get both Corporal De Peau and Corporal Goode meritoriously promoted to the rank of Sergeant.

Because LtCol Coffman's father was a friend of Major General Simpson, the Division Commander, I was able to pull off a little scheme on my two air traffic controllers. Once the paperwork was completed on the promotions, I arranged for both Corporals DePeau and Goode to be in the tower directing traffic. When they were working, they had to always look forward to observe the helicopter traffic in and out of the pad. While this was going on, I had asked a few of the helicopter pilots to keep them busy.

Major General Simpson climbed the tower, and unknown to the unsuspecting two corporals, was standing behind them observing operations. At one point, he asked a question, and Corporal Brown, without turning his head, gave him one of his usual wise guy answers. At that point, I asked both Corporals to turn around and there they were, staring right into the face of the Commanding General of the 1st Marine Division. The General laughed and told them they were both out of uniform. They couldn't figure out why, until the General handed each of them their new Sergeant's stripes, along with their official promotion document. Since I knew what was going to happen, I took a picture of both Brown and De Peau, with the General, and then thanked the General profusely for helping me to promote these two deserving Marines. From that day forward, General Simpson joined my list of favorite Generals.

One day in the Mess Hall, LtCol Coffman asked me if I had gone on R&R leave since I had been in Vietnam. I told him I had planned on going to Honolulu to meet my wife, but that since I had gotten a "Dear John" from her back in November and was now divorced, I had cancelled any plans for going on R&R and that I did not plan to go. He insisted that I should go anyway, however, I assured him that I had no interest in going.

Besides operating the helicopter-operating base, all troops on Hill 55 were also required to go out on night patrols to provide ongoing security. Sergeant Brown was one of the best patrol leaders on the hill. He was a natural born killer, and loved to go out on patrol and kill a few "gooks, something that he apparently did very well. I went out with him on one such patrol, (this was clearly against orders, as Majors did not go out on squad sized patrols) and was amazed at how effortlessly he moved at night, and the fact that he seemed to have a sixth sense about him when it came to any kind of suspicious activity or sounds. He was a natural, however, he was clearly in his element in Vietnam, and as he used to joke," I'm getting paid to pop people. Back in LA I'd probably be in jail!" When Sergeant Brown completed his second tour of duty in Vietnam, he volunteered for a third one. With his exemplary record, he was granted a third tour, but was forced into taking the obligatory thirty day leave in the United States before returning to Vietnam. He had indicated a desire to return to Fort Courage, and I whole-heartedly endorsed his request.

On the night before he was scheduled to return to the States for his 30-day leave, Sergeant Brown asked me if he could talk to me man to man and not Sergeant to Major. I told him that was always the case, and I hoped he knew that. He then proposed the following: "Look Major, I know you got a 'Dear John" from your wife, and I know she ran off with another man down to the Florida Keys." He knew this because he had heard me talking about it in the tower, or somewhere around the helipad. I told him that this was correct and then asked him why he was bringing it up. He told me he had a plan for me to consider. He said that once he got to LA, he would take a plane to Miami, rent a car and drive down to Marathon Key, which is where Sharron and her new boyfriend were living, stalk Sharron, and "pop" her, drive back to Miami, and return to LA immediately. He said there was no way either of us could ever get associated with the hit and she would be out of my hair for good. When I realized he was not kidding, I thanked him for his interest but told him that I didn't think I wanted to "rub out" my ex-wife. He said, "OK, but this is the only chance you'll ever have to do it."

He left for the states the next morning, without the contract on my ex-wife and returned to Fort Courage in less than two weeks, telling one and all that things back in the states were "really all screwed up" and that he was glad to be back in Vietnam where you knew where the hell you stood. I was glad to have him back and even happier that he had not decided to gratuitously "rub out" my ex-wife.

On April 27, 1969, there was some unfortunate logistics luck when a grass fire ignited Ammunition Supply Point One, located two miles west of the Da Nang airfield. The entire ammo dump went up in flames, exploding 38,000 tons of ammunition, valued at approximately 75 million dollars. Besides the ammunition, 20,000 fifty-five gallon drums of fuel also blew up in the fire. This represented 40 percent of all the Marine Corps ammunition in Vietnam, at that time. I remember that day very well, as it was a Sunday, and we were having a rare cookout on top of Hill 55 for all hands.

The ammo dump exploded around 1 o'clock in the afternoon, and it kept exploding for hours. Da Nang was only about eight miles north of us, but the ammo dump fire looked like the most fantastic fireworks display I had ever seen. Thinking about it today, it certainly was the most fantastic fireworks display any of the troops on the hill would ever see. We sat on our camp stools, ate our steaks, and watched the show from Hill 55. There wasn't anything else we could do, except be grateful that we had an ample supply of ammo in our dump at Hill 55 to tide us over until the big ammo dump in Da Nang could get resupplied. The investigation never determined who or what started the grass fire, and we'll never know. The dump was very well protected, and we always thought that some sentry's cigarette butt probably started the fire.

About one week after the ammo dump fire, my good friend, LtCol Jack Dowd was killed in the Arizona. He had led a three-company sweep for two weeks in that hellhole, and was coming out of the area when his command group came under small arms fire. He and Bob Alexander were caught in a rice paddy with their radio operators, and they had called in a helicopter strike on the area from which they were receiving fire. For some reason, Jack decided he wanted to see the air strike, and stuck his head over the berm to watch the incoming air strike. Bob Alexander was sitting down behind the berm talking to Jack, and then Jack sat down next to him, only he didn't sit down of his own will. He had taken a single shot between his eyes and he was dead.

I lost a good friend and the Marine Corps lost an outstanding officer. For his actions in Vietnam, and in particular, on that operation, Jack was posthumously awarded a Navy Cross, which was presented to his wife and surviving five children, in Washington, D.C. The good always seem to die young. The annual award of a physical fitness trophy to the second lieutenant who earns the highest score on the physical fitness test administered to all second lieutenants at the Basic School has been named the LtCol Jack Dowd Memorial Trophy in Jack's honor. He would have liked that, and it was right up his alley.

On Sunday, May 11, LtCol Coffman called me into his tent/office and asked me to drive to Da Nang Air Base and to see a Colonel Roberts at the Marine Corps arrival area. He told me that the colonel had something for him, and he wanted me to pick it up. I departed the Hill around 10 a.m. I had long ago decided that when I left Hill 55 in a jeep, I would drive myself and pick up a hitchhiker to ride shotgun. I figured that if I got blown up on the roads there was no need to take a driver with me just because I got unlucky. I had picked up a Marine going to the Da Nang Hospital to see a buddy, and he had his M-16 locked and loaded in the passenger seat. He had been in the bush long enough to know the score, so off we went hell bent for election. My theory, never proven, thank God, was that the faster we drove, the less surface there was for a command detonated land mine to blow up. Luckily, I never had to say I might have been wrong.

I dropped my passenger off at the Naval Hospital and continued to the USMC arrival area to see Colonel Roberts and pick up LtCol Coffman's package. I was met by a first lieutenant who informed me I was going to be the senior officer of an R&R flight departing for Sydney, Australia, at 3 p.m. LtCol Coffman had arranged the R&R flight for me. All I had to do was to check my weapons at the R&R Center, and SSgt Burke from the 7th Marines, would pick up my jeep. I was totally surprised, yet really glad to be going.

It was May 11, 1969, and I had been in country for nine months, and eight days of R&R, especially in Australia, didn't sound bad at all. I called LtCol Coffman and thanked him for his concern, but indicated I felt guilty leaving the helipad for eight days. He assured me that matters were being taken care of and to have an enjoyable time in Sydney. He had just returned from Honolulu, where he had seen his wife, and he said that R&R was a wonderful way to unwind. He hoped that this would happen to me.

The R&R process in Vietnam was an amazing operation. Troops were flown to their destinations aboard a commercial aircraft, usually a Boeing 707, belonging to World Airways, a contract carrier out of Oakland, California. There were eight destinations which the troops could select, such as Tokyo, Japan; Bangkok, Thailand; Hong Kong; Manila; Sydney, Australia and of course, Honolulu, Hawaii. A destination had to be reserved ahead of time and each individual Marine had to be placed on a manifest to allow him to go on the trip. I don't know how LtCol Coffman pulled it off to get me on a flight to Sydney, but I was not complaining. The first lieutenant told me my only duties as the senior officer of the flight were to get the troops on the plane at Da Nang, check the manifest to see that everyone was aboard, get the troops off at Darwin, Australia, where we would be held in a secured area until we could take off in order to land in Sydney after 6 a.m.

The airport in Sydney did not operate between midnight and 6 a.m. as a noise abatement measure. Getting the troops back on the plane in Darwin proved to be a little difficult, since we had a wait of approximately four hours during which time we all drank a lot of Australian beer, which came in 20 ounce cans and was a lot stronger than the 3.2 percent alcohol content beer we got in Vietnam. Once on the plane, everyone slept soundly. When we landed in Sydney, we were met by a US Navy officer, who was the resident R&R liaison officer for Sydney (Tough duty!).

I handed over the manifest, and the Liaison Officer informed me my responsibilities were through and in return for my duties, I would get the one room per flight which was available at the Wentworth Hotel (Australia's Waldorf-Astoria at the time) in downtown Sydney. As of 2012, the hotel is still a five star hotel, now called the Sofitel Wentworth Hotel. We boarded several busses and were driven to a large building. Here, we undressed, leaving our dirty combat gear in a well-marked cardboard box with our name and unit on it, and then we were issued complete toilet kits and instructed to shave and shower. After the shower, we were issued civilian clothing. I received three complete sets of underwear, three white shirts, two ties, two pair of gray slacks, a blue blazer, three pairs of socks and a pair of dress shoes. Everything was tried on to ensure it fit, and then we signed for the clothing, which would be returned in this building when our R&R was over, and where we would reclaim our washed and cleaned combat gear for the trip back to the war.

As the senior officer, I was the first person through the process and within thirty minutes, I was showered, shaved and dressed, in my new civilian clothes, and had converted my American money into Australian dollars. I hailed a cab to the Wentworth. In order for a city to be declared an R&R city by the US government, every hotel in the city had to participate in the program. This was designed so that cities did not just use their cheaper and less comfortable hotels to cash in on the R&R bonanza. The fancy hotels only allocated one room per flight, but, as far as the US government was concerned, this was "active" participation.

The majority of the R&R hotels were in the King's Cross section which was the wilder, more open, and far less sophisticated part of the city. This certainly didn't bother the troops, who, once settled down, immediately headed to that section of Sydney anyway. The cab driver told me that I was going to the best hotel in Sydney. At the standard R&R rates of around 40 dollars per night, I was getting a big bargain. We had landed at 6:01 a.m., the first aircraft to land for the day, and I was driving through downtown Sydney at 8:30 a.m. The taxi stopped at the hotel which was located in the heart of the thriving downtown section of Sydney, amidst business office buildings, banks, fancy restaurants, high couture retail stores, and very fancy clothing and shoe stores.

A uniformed doorman welcomed me to Sydney and the Wentworth. He carried my bag into the reception area and refused my offered tip saying only, "Thanks for your service, Yank." That was indeed a change from the virulent hatred that emanated from many Americans in the States towards the servicemen serving their country in Vietnam. I was secretly glad I was in Sydney, and quietly thanked Sharron for making it happen. The desk clerk was equally courteous and friendly. He informed me that check-in time was usually at 1 p.m., but since I had just arrived from Vietnam, and it was only 8:30 a.m. he was sure I must be tired, and they did have a dedicated room available for me and I was free to go up immediately. I welcomed the opportunity, took an elevator to the 14th floor, went to my room, undressed, took a hot shower again, and climbed into the first clean bed with clean sheets and fluffed pillowcases that I had slept on in over nine months.

I had noticed that the door of my room had a cabinet built into the center of it which opened from both sides and was used to place clothing into it that needed cleaning or pressing. I put my trousers and jacket in the small compartment along with my dress shoes and requested valet service. The valet would come up to my room, open the door from the outside, take my clothes and shoes out of the small cabinet, have them cleaned and pressed, and then return them to the cabinet. When I was ready, I would open the cabinet from the inside, and take out my freshly pressed clothes and shined shoes. I liked this fancy hotel life. It was very easy to adapt to luxury.

I did not realize how tired I was. I woke up at 4 p.m. after sleeping soundly for over seven hours. I went to the door cabinet and found my clothes beautifully pressed and my shoes shined to a mirror finish. I got dressed and took the elevator to the lobby floor. By now, the afternoon business crowd was beginning to come into the hotel. I followed a group of men, all dressed in suits, into a very upscale bar named, The Old Sydney Grill. The place was very elegant and impressive, however, since I was from New York City, it didn't look any different to me than the bars at the Algonquin or the Astor Hotels.

I immediately noticed that the room was crowded, but mostly with young men, almost all of them my age and all of them dressed in business suits. I did not see any women in the place. I went up to the bar and asked for a scotch and water. A young man about my age and dressed in a well-fitting suit that looked to be custom made was standing next to me asked if I was a Yank. I laughed and said, "What gave you the clue?" knowing that my accent was clearly American. He laughed with me and paid for my drink, and invited me to sit down with him and "his mates." It turned out my new found friend from the bar was the son of the owner of the largest investment bank in Australia, with offices all over Australia, but with the home office almost across the street from the Wentworth Hotel. He was an investment banker himself and "his mates" were all brokers, working at his father's firm. They had just gotten out of work, and had crossed the street for a drink before going home. They all looked to be about the same age, so in effect, I was sitting at a table of 33 year old bankers, all of whom could not have been more friendly, accommodating and genuinely interested in what life was like for me in Vietnam. We must have talked for over an hour with someone always buying another round of drinks and refusing to let me buy a round.

Finally, my friend from the bar, whom I only remember as Roger, said to the group, "Look lads, I'm sure Peter did not come to Australia to sit and talk with a bunch of guys. How about calling my secretary and ask her to join us." I looked surprised, and I was even more surprised when Roger told me that his secretary was a divorcee, was 28 years old, blond and blue-eyed and a very pretty woman. He thought that I might like to meet her, and he was about to arrange it.

After about half an hour, a very pretty, well-proportioned young woman, with blond hair and very blue eyes, dressed in a business suit and wearing high heels, came into the bar, looked around, saw us in the corner, waved at Roger and joined us at our table. Her name was Coral and not only was she a knockout, she had a great sense of humor, and I could see that she fit right in with the group. She was Roger's personal secretary and had been

272 • From Roaring Hate to Ramrod Straight

working for him for about five years. We all started joking around and then Roger asked everyone to be quiet for a moment, and he addressed Coral. "Coral," he said, "Peter here is on R&R from Vietnam and he just arrived today. He's going to be here for eight days, and then he will be going back to Vietnam. If you like him and he likes you, I'm willing to give you the next eight days off so you can show him around Sydney, and make sure that he will always remember his trip to Australia."

I was dumbfounded and I think Coral was also, but we looked at each other, and I certainly liked her, but I waited to hear what she had to say. Almost without any hesitation, she looked at Roger and said, "OK, where is he living?" Roger told her that I was staying at the Wentworth and Coral said that she would just have to go home to Coogee, get a few things, and she would move in with me for the next eight days. I did not believe what was happening, but that is exactly what happened.

Coral had a car, and I joined her on a short trip to Coogee, one of the beach suburbs of Sydney, where she packed a small bag and off we went to dinner and then it was back to my hotel room. For the next seven days we went everywhere together. She took me to Toranga Park, the Sydney Zoo, the new Opera House, a harbor cruise, a trip up the coast north of Sydney, and to a few of the nicer clubs and restaurants in Sydney proper. We visited a number of local RSL Clubs (RSL stands for Returned Serviceman's League, and is Australia's version of an American Legion Post) and in each club, we were warmly welcomed and hosted, by whoever was present. Having Coral with me certainly did not hurt the welcoming process.

We went to see an Australian Rules Rugby match, and we were invited to Roger's private club to watch him play Rugby against another private club team. After the match, we were invited to Roger's house for a victory party where he introduced me to his father and mother. Not a single person I met thought that the arrangement Roger had worked out with Coral about staying with me for seven days was either unusual or surprising. It was a whole new concept to me, which underscored one of the major differences between Australians and Americans. Australians simply did what they felt like, and didn't much care about what others thought. It was a great way to live, and one that I fully supported, especially at that particular time.

I mentioned to Coral that my uncle had immigrated to Australia in 1935, and lived in Bondi, another beach suburb of Sydney. She told me that Bondi was very near Coogee, and if I wanted to go and visit my Uncle, she would take me there. We looked him up in the phone book, found his address and, one night around 2 a.m., after we left a nightclub in Coogee, we drove by his house. I did not go in, and I did not visit him. I had decided that my time in Sydney would be better spent with Coral, than with Uncle Ken, whom I did not know. In that decision, I was 100 percent correct.

The 18th of May came around far too quickly. On Sunday, the 17th, I took Coral to dinner at a very fancy restaurant and gave her a gold wrist watch as a going away present and to thank her for really being a great escort and a wonderful companion both during the day and night. To my surprise, she presented me with a pair of engraved, gold cuff links and a tie tack. Each of the pieces was engraved with my initials. To this day, that present still is in my jewelry case. We had a tearful farewell and the following morning she drove me to the airport building where I would turn in my civilian clothes and get my cleaned combat gear back for the return trip to Vietnam.

I remember waving goodbye to her and being very grateful to LtCol Coffman and to Roger, the banker's son, for making my R&R trip to Australia both possible and memorable. Coral and I exchanged letters for several months and then she informed me she had met a man with whom she was getting serious and whom she felt she would marry. I wished her well, and I sincerely hope she has enjoyed a great life. She certainly made my stay in Australia one of the best eight days of my life. Obviously, I kept my promise to her that I would never forget her.

At the airport, I checked the manifest to ensure that all personnel had made it back and that we didn't have any deserters. There were certainly many good things about Australia to encourage desertion, however, all hands were accounted for, and we boarded our flight back to Vietnam. As we flew over the Pacific, I thought about how much I had really needed to go on R&R, and how much I appreciated LtCol Coffman's concern for my welfare. I left Vietnam a discouraged and somewhat deflated man, having been rejected by my wife in the form of the "Dear John." I returned from Australia secure in the knowledge that I was still apparently attractive to women and that once I returned to the States my life would continue and I'd find someone else down the line. This was an important milestone for me, and I will always have a soft spot in my heart for Australia because of my experiences there during my R&R leave.

We arrived in Da Nang and after retrieving my weapons (a .45 caliber pistol and an M-16 rifle, that I had stolen from Graves Registration because officers were not supposed to carry rifles). I hopped a helicopter to Hill 55 and went to LtCol Coffman's tent. He had a big smile on his face and so did I, so he could see that his idea about forcing me to go on R&R was the right thing to do. I will always remember LtCol Coffman for his interest in me and the fact that he went the extra mile for one of his officers. As it turned out, I served with him again after Vietnam.

I went to Fort Courage, where Major Jim Givens and First Lieutenant Leon Russell had been running the base during my absence. Everything had gone smoothly, and I was very happy to see everyone again. No one had been killed or wounded from my outfit, and that was always a big plus. The helipad had been mortared only twice, and the Seabees repaired the damage, almost as fast as it occurred. Supplies were making it out to the units much more efficiently, and our idea of staging all supplies strictly by battalions was working well and reducing incorrect deliveries.

The enemy began increasing attacks on Hill 55 and nightly barrages of mortars and rockets rained down on different sections of the hill on different nights. When these attacks occurred, the only thing we could do was to jump into some hole or nearby bunker and just lie still, waiting for the barrage to end. If it was your time to go, then if you suffered a direct hit where you were, it was over for you, but if you were lucky, you managed to live through another night of big noise, big shaking and flying metal fragments. That was the secret of trying to survive a rocket or a mortar attack. Once it started, you had to stay where you were. More people were killed running around in the open during one of those attacks than people who were secure in some hole or bunker, where they were relatively protected from flying metal fragments. I remembered LtCol Jack Dowd, if only he had kept his head down he might still be around.

On the night of May 27, Jim Givens and I were sitting in our tent sharing a drink from a bottle of Chivas Regal Scotch. All of a sudden, a huge blast erupted on the crest of the hill directly above our tent. We jumped into a hole in front of our tent, and hunkered down waiting for the attack to end. The rockets kept coming in, and there was no letting up to the bombing. Luckily, Jim had taken his bottle of scotch with him, and I was resting in the hole by leaning back on the frame of his radio, which was also in the hole with us. I had put my arms through the slings of the radio pack frame, to steady the pack and to get a comfortable position in the hole. The rockets kept coming in and we kept drinking the scotch. We couldn't go anywhere until the all clear sounded and from the looks of things, it didn't look like that would happen anytime soon.

We must have been in that hole for quite some time, because I remember feeling very high, when suddenly, almost directly behind us, came a huge explosion, followed by a large fireball. Somewhere behind us, something had taken a direct hit. For some inexplicable reason, both Jim and I got out of our hole and started running towards the fireball. What we saw was not pretty. Our artillery battery was in flames. Wounded and dead Marines were lying around the entire position, and the ammo dump, in the center of the battery, had also taken a hit and was burning. The ammunition in the dump would be cooking off very soon. I yelled to Jim to call for medevacs on his radio. He yelled back that he didn't have his radio. I felt behind me and realized that the radio that I was using for a backrest in the hole was still attached to my back. I started calling for medevacs, and then ran around with Jim, trying to stage the wounded for a quick load out.

As the first helo was landing the ammo dump went off. More explosions and fire, with fragments flying all around but the pilots kept coming in, and we managed to get all the wounded off the hill. The dead would be flown out in the morning. Just as the last helicopter was departing the hill with a load of wounded Marines, an explosion very close to me blew me up in the air and over the side of the hill. The radio pack frame broke my fall, but my back hit the bottom of the pack frame hard enough to make it impossible for me to walk very well. When the attack subsided, and the flames were being put out on the artillery position, I got to the sick bay tent and had the corpsman look at me. He said there was no broken skin, but I qualified for a Purple Heart. I looked around the tent and saw men with holes in them and blood all over the place. I laughed at the corpsman and told him that the guys that rated Purple Hearts were over there and certainly not me. I walked back to my tent and collapsed.

The next morning, Colonel Nichols called Jim Givens and me to his tent and informed us that we were to get on a helicopter and fly to Division Headquarters for a medal ceremony. Major General Simpson, the Division Commander, presented Jim and me with a Bronze Star Medal for Valor, for our actions the previous night on Hill 55. The real hero was Chivas Regal Scotch, because I remembered very little about what had happened the previous night. Apparently several witnesses submitted reports and these reports were sufficient grounds to award us the medal. Here is what the citation read:

"For heroic achievement in connection with combat operations against enemy forces in the Republic of Vietnam, while serving as Logistics Officer of the Seventh Marines, 1st Marine Division. On the night of 27 May 1969, a friendly artillery position on Hill 55 in Quang Nam Province was struck by several enemy explosive devices, which ignited an ammunition storage area and caused large secondary explosions. Although the area immediately came under a mortar attack, Major Beck rushed to the burning artillery site to assist in rescue operations. Ignoring the artillery explosions occurring all around him, he moved throughout the hazardous area, aiding the wounded and directing fire fighting operations. Fully aware of the imminent danger of additional mortar attacks, he disregarded his own safety and continued his lifesaving efforts until all casualties had been rescued and the fires brought under control. His heroic actions inspired all who observed him and prevented further serious injury or possible death to the already injured Marines. Major Beck's courage, bold initiative and unwavering devotion to duty, at great personal risk, were in keeping with the highest traditions of the Marine Corps and of the United States Naval Service."

I was glad to get the written citation because I honestly do not remember very much about what happened that night. I always felt that instead of a golden "V" for valor, which I wore on my Bronze Star Medal, I should have worn a golden "C" for Chivas Regal.

At any rate, that is the true story of my Bronze Star, and as Jim Givens said to me after the medal ceremony on the flight back from Division Headquarters to Hill 55, "What the hell, we did what the citation said, so what if we were drunk!" In the years since, I've come to agree with his assessment, and the Marines we saved could have cared less if we were drunk or sober. It just doesn't make a very good combat story.

On June 1, 1969, Colonel Nichols departed as the Commanding Officer of the 7th Marine Regiment and was replaced by one of the legendary characters of the Marine Corps, Colonel Gildo Codispoti. Colonel Codispoti had already been passed over twice for general, and there was no way he would ever be promoted to that rank. He was one of the wildest and craziest Marine officers on the roles of full colonels and had enjoyed a controversial career.

As a second lieutenant, he was one of the original members of Carlson's Raiders, having made several of his island assaults out of rubber boats launched from submarines. Once, while demonstrating how NOT to pull the pin on a hand grenade, he had the training grenade blow up into his chest, leaving him with a permanently scarred and disfigured chest. He thought the whole thing very funny, and he loved to show off his scars. As a junior Major, having just graduated from Junior School in Quantico, he publicly burned his diploma as a protest to what he felt was a lousy curriculum at the school. As a young lieutenant colonel in Washington, he felt there was too much socializing, and not enough serious work going on in his office, so he moved his own desk out into the hallway of the building to get away from all the "ass kissers." Short in stature, he stood about 5 feet 10 inches tall, and looked like the Italian Godfather that Marlon Brando tried to look like in the movies. He had a full head of thick gray hair with very bushy eyebrows and a face, punctuated by a large, several times broken, Roman nose that relayed the subliminal message that you did not want to get on his bad side.

He was tough on the outside and tough on the inside, but deep inside he possessed a heart of gold that only became evident when it suited him. Born in Brooklyn, New York, he grew up in one of the toughest sections of the borough, Williamsburg, under the Brooklyn Bridge by the East River, a known Mafioso hang out but still managed to graduate from St. John's College. He was a phenomenal troop leader and combat Marine, and a very close friend of Major General Simpson who felt that assigning him as CO of the 7th Marines, would be a fitting conclusion to Colonel Codispoti's brilliant but decidedly notorious career.

There was no question of his competence or his bravery, however, he was just a little erratic, with a terrible Sicilian temper, and a readiness to fight at the drop of a hat. In short, he was like every other guy I grew up with in New York City. In my particular case, just substitute Italian for Irish. The best way to describe Colonel Codispoti was to call him a no bullshit Marine. He gave an order, you performed, or else. He expected you to do your job, 24 hours a day, 7 days a week, and always, the troops came first, last and always. Everything else after the welfare of his troops was secondary. There were no second chances with Colonel Codispoti.

He was quite simply a mad man, who yelled, screamed, cursed and drove his people as hard as he drove himself. I absolutely loved him, but I'm afraid I was in the minority as almost everyone else was scared to death of him. There was a saying about Colonel Codispoti that inferred that he changed commanding officers working for him more often than he changed his socks. This was true, to some degree, however, I personally felt that every commander he relieved should have been relieved and he was one of the few senior officers with the guts to do it. I even witnessed him relieve a battalion commander for cowardice in battle, because he did not move his troops when Colonel Codispoti directed him to, and, subsequently, the enemy hit him in the position from which he did not move, resulting in the deaths of 15 Marines. That commander fought the relief through various official channels and courts of appeal but lost at each venue. In every instance, eye witnesses, myself included, corroborated the details of the events that led to his relief in combat. He was able to throw doubt on the cowardice portion of his official relief, however, the underlying cause of his relief was upheld, and, in the end, he retired in bitterness and disgrace. Colonel Codispoti had no regrets whatsoever, concerning that particular case, making the determination that the commander should never have been in the Marine Corps in the first place.

He was a terror as a commanding officer, but he knew what he was doing, especially in combat situations. He was fearless for himself, never wearing a flak jacket, helmet, or any other protective device. He practically dared the VC or the NVA to come and get him and fight him. He was that kind of strong personality. His daring and bravado aside, he was one fantastic troop leader, and all the enlisted men loved him because he was essentially one of them. Always rumpled and dirty with the dirt of the field, he carried a .45 caliber pistol in a shoulder holster, and always wore his old Marine Raider herringbone utility cap.

He yelled at every staff meeting, demanding answers and cutting off any officer he felt didn't know what he was talking about. Once he found out that I was from New York, he yelled at me the loudest, but no matter how loud he yelled, I would just keep going. Often times he would threaten me with bodily harm, but I would just ignore him. This was fine for him and me, and for some reason, he accepted that behavior from me, but he was absolute death to anyone else who would try it. Soon I became the Ombudsman between the Colonel and other officers on the Regimental staff, including LtCol Coffman, his Executive Officer. Colonel Coffman was a southern gentleman and Colonel Codispoti's roughshod ways and vulgar mannerisms were simply too much for him. Luckily, his tour of duty was over in one month, and he was eager to get away from the Mad Italian Godfather! He managed this without any blemish to his outstanding professional record and with no regrets. I was extremely happy for him.

I was the Colonel's favorite whipping boy, but I think that was because he knew that he did not intimidate me. It got to be a contest between us, how often he could he yell at me, and how often I kept coming back, as though nothing had happened. Whenever he flew out to see his battalion commanders, he always took me along because he felt I should see firsthand what logistical support was required. I also think he liked my company, but, of course, he would never admit that. LtCol Coffman rotated back to the States, and a new executive officer was assigned to the Regiment. Lieutenant Colonel Charles Evans Wright, another southerner, from William and Mary College, lasted about three weeks. He had never in his life encountered anyone like Colonel Codispoti, and dealing with him on a continuing basis was beyond his capabilities. Colonel Codispoti labeled LtCol Wright an out and out "pussy," and asked General Simpson to send someone out who had some balls!

On the evening of 25 July, I was working in the tower at Fort Courage, when Sergeant De Peau told me to standby for a personal telephone call from General Simpson. I thought he was kidding, but he was not, and in a few minutes, the Commanding General of the 1st Marine Division was on the phone with me. The subject of his telephone call was mind-boggling. He told me that since Gildo could not find an appropriate lieutenant colonel to be his executive officer, the general was going to designate me as the regimental executive officer and the logistics officer, and that was the way it was going to be. The general then asked me if I felt that I could do both jobs for Gildo, and I replied that I thought I could, and if not, I hoped he had a good job for me in Division. The General laughed and assured me he thought everything would be fine. Next, he called Gildo to inform him, and within three minutes after his phone call, I got a radio call to report to the regimental commander. I ran up to Gildo's tent, and he was sitting there, behind his field desk, with a bemused look on his face. "Well," he said, "it looks like it will be you and me. You better not let me down, or I'll cut off your legs!" I knew we were on the right track.

Under Colonel Codispoti, the 7th Marines continued aggressive patrolling of the areas assigned to us by Division headquarters. On July 20, the 5th Marine Regiment began Operation *Durham Peak*, pushing up into the Que Son Mountains south of An Hoa with three battalions. The 1st Battalion, 7th Marines, obligingly covered the entire Arizona territory during the absence of the 5th Marines. On August 12, 1/7 ran into two full battalions of the resurgent 90th NVA Regiment, and a battalion of the 368B Rocket Regiment. A two-day battle ensued in the Arizona in which 255 North Vietnamese were killed at a cost of 20 Marines killed and 100 Marines wounded and evacuated. *Durham Peak* ended on August 13, and the boundaries of the 1st Marine Division and the Army's American Division were about to be shifted southward to give the Marines responsibility for most of the Que Son Valley. This called for a major rearrangement of the respective areas of operations of the 5th and 7th Marine Regiments.

Some of this rearrangement was caused because soldiers of the 196th Light Infantry Brigade, a part of the American Division, had mutinied against their commanders. Ordered to take a hill three times, each time sustaining heavy casualties with no success, the beleaguered soldiers simply refused to advance a fourth time. This mutiny never made the press, and the Army moved quickly to suppress any repercussions. One fact was clear, the Army units had to be moved out of the area, and the 7th Marine Regiment was chosen to replace the 196th Light Infantry Brigade.

The geography of southern Quang Nam province requires some study if the problem that faced the 1st Marine Division is to be understood. The Que Son Mountains were a spur of a main mountain mass, running from southwest to northeast toward the city of An Hoa. Green, and incredibly beautiful, with hundreds of sparkling streams and tumbling waterfalls, and honeycombed with thousands of caves, the mountains offered the VC and the NVA regulars, a ready-made bastion from which to launch attacks against lowland targets. The Que Son Mountain range was also the natural boundary between Quang Nam province to the north and Quang Tin province to the south, however, the actual political boundary between the two provinces was established along the valley floor, below the mountain range, following the trace of the Song Ly Ly River. This was now established as the new boundary between the Army's American Division and the 1st Marine Division.

The 7th Marines were ordered to deploy the entire Regiment to the Que Son Valley, from their locations around Da Nang, which constituted seven separate, active combat bases. The movement of the entire Regiment, 54 kilometers south of where they were previously deployed on seven combat bases fell entirely on my shoulders. We received the warning order on Monday, July 28, and we were instructed that the first phase of the move would occur with one full battalion being moved south in a single day, that day having been designated as M-Day, (for moving out) and the date had been set for August 15, with the first elements deploying south at first light. This maneuver was a historic event, in that there had never been a relocation of this magnitude ever attempted into enemy terrain.

The best way to describe the following events is to quote a report of the movement from an official document entitled, "U.S. Marines in Vietnam in 1969," published by the

History and Museum Division of Headquarters, U.S. Marine Corps. Here, then, without any editorializing, is that account:

"The move of the 7th Marines, 54 kilometers to the southeast, was fraught with problems from the beginning. This was not to be a short tactical move, but a permanent one. In addition to men and equipment based at the regiment's seven cantonments scattered throughout, the soon to be vacated area of operations, all property assigned to the regiment would also be moved, necessitating use of the Division's entire inventory of rolling stock. First to go would be the 2nd Battalion. By the morning of the 15th, LtCol Lugger's Marines and their equipment were loaded on board 120 trucks at Dai La Pass, behind Hill 327, the 1st Division headquarters, and ready to head down Highway One. "This was," according to Major Peter S. Beck, the Regimental S-4, "the greatest single mistake we could have made, since it became readily apparent that it was absolutely impossible to control 120 vehicles in one convoy, on a narrow dirt road, many sections of which were only passable one way at a time." What occurred later in the day on the 15th could only be termed a fiasco. As Lugger's Marines moved south, without the aid of control vehicles or military police stationed at obvious choke points, unbeknownst to anyone on the division staff, a 35 truck convoy from the 9th Engineer Battalion, loaded with wide-angle bladed Eimco tractors, was moving north from Chu Lai. They met at the one place on Route One that could have precipitated the worst bottleneck possible: a one-way, one vehicle at a time, pontoon bridge. Riding at the front of the 120 truck convoy was Major Beck, and, as he later reported: "Needless to say, the tractor-trailers going North, completely blocked the road, so that the southbound convoy could not cross and could not pass, if they could cross. The northbound convoy, which was the tractor-trailers with the bulldozers, completely blocked their portion of the road. Consequently, we had a four and one half hour bottleneck at this bridge, which ate up most of the day, and additionally, at one point in the road, concentrated in excess of 150 pieces of large rolling stock, plus all of the equipment they were carrying, and the troops in the personnel vehicles. We finally managed to unsnarl the bottleneck, by allowing the northbound convoy, with the wide load angle blades, to pass first, because there was no way possible for the southbound convoy to pass. In doing this, we had to back up the 120 trucks off the right shoulder of the road, so that the convoy going north could pass. This was an unbelievable task, since Marines who can't move in either direction become very frustrated and all of a sudden we had 1,000 traffic control experts, everybody thinking they knew exactly what they were doing."

While this is the official report, you can imagine what Colonel Codispoti was doing while all of this was going on. Circling the convoy area in an observation helicopter, lent to him by the Army and flown by an 18 year old Warrant Officer pilot, he was especially concentrating on the blocked approaches to the bridge. As he kept circling over the bridge, he kept screaming at me through his radio to get the convoy moving. I guess he felt I had supernatural powers, because there simply was no way to get either of the convoys moving without letting the engineers move north as quickly as possible. I did not pay any attention to his screaming and worked on the ground to unsnarl the traffic as best as I could.

At one point, he landed his helicopter in a field near the bridge and came running up to where I was directing traffic. "That's it" he screamed, "you are relieved of duties. Why didn't you know that damn engineer convoy was coming north?" It was useless to explain to him that the 9th Engineers were part of the 3rd Marine Division, and apparently the 1st Division and the 3rd Division did not coordinate on this operation. I told Colonel Codispoti that he could relieve me later but that right now, I had to unsnarl this mess, and the best thing he could do was to get back in his helicopter, unless he wanted to direct traffic here on the bridge. He finally left the area, grumbling to himself, however, he never brought up the subject of the bridge fiasco until we both discussed the entire operation for an after-action report. Naturally, in the company of just each other, he thought it was quite funny, but, always aware of the image he had to project to the troops, he would never divulge that to anyone else.

We finally got the mess unsnarled, and our convoy continued south to Que Son. We were in the process of taking over two major combat bases from the Army. One was Landing Zone (LZ) Baldy, located at the intersection of Route 535 and Highway One, and Fire Support Base Ross (FSB), west of Que Son village, where Route 536 forks off to the Northwest.

On the 15th, the 2nd Battalion arrived at LZ Baldy so late in the day due to the fiasco at the bridge, that they could not continue to their final destination, FSB Ross, which was 16 kilometers inland from LZ Baldy. Again, we had a tactical nightmare staring us in the face, since now we had 120 trucks parked on LZ Baldy's landing strip, a lucrative target for enemy rockets and mortars. The enemy did attempt a mortar attack, but it was quickly silenced, and only one Marine was wounded. On the morning of the 16th, the battalion moved the 16 kilometers to FSB Ross without incident. Because of the huge screw-up at the bridge, the division staff decided they would move the remainder of the troops by CH-53 helicopters, while their equipment would be carried by 30 truck convoys, spaced over a period of several days, instead of attempting a single, 120 truck convoy. In addition, military police would be assigned to each bridge, choke point and "curve" while "road master" jeeps would patrol Highway One, regulating the flow of traffic. This was probably a great over reaction, caused by the fact that the 1st Marine Division and the 3rd Marine Division staffs had failed to coordinate a major truck movement between the two divisions, and now, they were all simply trying to cover their collective asses.

Nevertheless, between the 17th and 23rd of August, the rest of the regiment made the move south without incident, and on the morning of the 24th of August, the entire Que Son Valley and mountain range was under the control of the 7th Marine Regiment. We had a small change of command of the base camp at LZ Baldy on the morning of August 24. The Army Brigade Commander, a colonel, who appeared at the ceremony in pressed and starched field fatigue uniform (Army terminology), wearing a leather pistol belt with a gold buckle, infuriated Colonel Codispoti. He refused to go out to the ceremony, saying the Colonel was a phony, and he had just had a mutiny in his organization, and that we were going to relieve him because his unit couldn't do the job. I calmed Gildo down, telling him he had to go out there, and begged him to just go through the ceremony with no extra "histrionics" which were simply too easy for him to bring forth. He promised me that he "would behave," however, he changed into his muddiest and dirtiest field utilities, with no rank insignia, wearing boots that had never been shined or cleaned, and placed his old World War II Raider cap on his head, then went out to meet the Army colonel. I remember his name, but will not mention it in this memoir, however, he was a classic example of a West Pointer who clearly was not in touch with his troops. He was such an arrogant officer that I secretly hoped Gildo would blow his cool, but he did not. Later, this colonel was promoted to three star rank.

It was evident that the Army colonel did not like standing next to Gildo, however, after the ceremony the Army colonel invited the Marine officers into the Army officer's mess hall for a farewell drink. When we got inside the Army officer's dining room, Gildo began to laugh, and I knew that his period of behaving like a normal colonel was about to end. He asked the colonel if he really used this dining room while his troops were out in the field. Sensing that this was going to be a bad incident, I proposed a toast to the 196th Light Infantry Brigade, everyone had a drink and then I hurried Gildo out of there. "Can you believe that son of a bitch," Gildo screamed at me. "No wonder his troops mutinied, I would too if I ever saw that damn dining room." He then told me that the minute the last Army officer got out of LZ Baldy, he wanted the damn officer's dining room closed permanently and turned into an enlisted slop chute (Marine terminology for a beer hall). This was just another reason why I loved Gildo Codispoti.

Once our three infantry battalions were in place at Ross and Baldy, and they began their heavy patrolling activities, things began to change in the Que Son Valley. Several of the battalions were engaged in heavy combat, with casualties mounting, but never in the proportion in which the Marines were inflicting casualties on the enemy. In a two week period, following the 7th Marines occupation of Ross and Baldy, over 1,000 enemy troops were killed in the battle of the Hiep Duc Valley. Identification papers taken from the enemy casualties identified them as being from the 1st VC Regiment, and from the 3rd Regiment of the 2nd NVA Division. This indicated that regular North Vietnamese military units were fighting alongside Viet Cong guerillas. It also indicated to the Marines that the enemy had seen a need to reinforce units that were fighting Marine units by using regular NVA troops. After a pitched five-day battle, the enemy disengaged, and our units returned to their outposts at LZ Baldy and FSB Ross.

After we had been at LZ Baldy for about a week after the Hiep Duc battle, Colonel Codispoti told me that he wanted a "hooch" (temporary field living quarters) better than his friend, Major General Simpson. He wanted to have the thing in place for General Simpson's next visit to LZ Baldy. He then told me he didn't care how I got it, or where I got it, he just wanted it, and he wanted me to get it. I went back to the S-4 tent and told SSgt Burke my dilemma. "Where the hell can I get a fancy "hooch" for the Colonel?" I asked. SSgt Burke informed me that the Air Force had prefab houses that they used for temporary housing near air fields and that there were plenty of them available to the Air Force in Da Nang. The Air Force had an engineer battalion, called "Red Horse Squadron" that were the Air Force's Seabees. SSgt Burke suggested I go to Da Nang and ask the Red Horse squadron commander for assistance in this matter. The following morning, I took off in a jeep for the long drive up Highway One to Da Nang. I told Colonel Codispoti where I was going, and he was very enthused. I think he thought I'd be returning with his "hooch," I informed him this was an exploratory expedition, and I wasn't very sure where I was going to find what he wanted. I purposely did not tell him about the Air Force houses because, if I had, he would demand one immediately.

I picked up a hitchhiker for shotgun duties, and off we went, racing up Highway One. I got to Da Nang in a few hours, dropped off my hitchhiker and then continued to the Air Force base in Da Nang. I approached the main gate in a tactical jeep with Marine tactical markings which was covered with dirt and dings all over the jeeps' body. The main gate sentry saluted me, since I was wearing my rank insignia and I asked the sentry where I could find the Red Horse Squadron. All Air Force base personnel were in clean, starched utility uniforms, and I think I must have looked like something out of some old war movie. At any rate, I found the Red Horse Squadron and saw that the whole squadron was based in small, square wooden houses, each of which had an air conditioner hooked up to an exterior generator. The place looked like a trailer park in Florida.

I asked for directions to the Squadron Commander's house, and I was directed to the house closest to the air field. I knocked on the door and met LtCol Joseph Abbodonzo, USAF, the squadron commander of the Red Horse Squadron and an engineering graduate of West Point, who, because he was from an Air Force family, had upon graduation decided to go into the Air Force instead of the Army. He welcomed me, offered me a cold beer and asked how he could help me. I told him my entire story and asked him if the Air Force actually had prefabbed "hooches" that were used as temporary field living spaces. "You bet we do," replied Colonel Abbodonzo, "you are sitting in one." Any chance of getting one of them for my C.O., I asked. The Colonel, who by now had told me to call him Joe (the Air Force is very much different from all other branches of the service and I, personally, always liked them, and their attitude), told me he could get me a complete "hooch," but it would cost me two jeeps in trade. I told him that, as a combat unit, I couldn't give up a single vehicle that we had since we needed all the support we could find.

He then said that he didn't care where the jeeps came from, but if I brought him two jeeps, he'd get the house down to LZ Baldy, and even install it for me. I called SSgt Burke and asked him what he could do. He told me to tell the Colonel that he would have his two jeeps in two days. I thanked Joe and headed back to LZ Baldy, picking up another hitchhiker for the trip south.

When I got back to Baldy, I asked SSgt Burke what he planned to do. He told me that there were always many jeeps parked at China Beach, an R&R Center outside of Da Nang, right on the South China Sea. Jeeps did not have ignition keys, simply a switch to turn on the ignition. If the jeep was not locked with a homemade locking device all you had to do was turn the switch, start up the jeep, and drive off. Army jeeps were notorious for not having any locking devices on them. SSgt Burke was simply going to go to China Beach, lock up his jeep, and then he and Bennie X would look for two Army jeeps that were left unlocked. Once they found two jeeps, they would drive them directly to the Red Horse Squadron and then we would have met our part of the deal.

I approved this plan, and the next morning, SSgt Burke and Bennie X departed LZ Baldy for China Beach. They returned after about ten hours and informed me that the mission had been accomplished. Apparently, they had found two unlocked Army jeeps and drove them to the Red Horse Squadron where they were stripped and painted Air Force blue. Air Force markings were then painted on the jeeps, and the jeeps were reassembled. In three hours, the jeeps looked like brand new Air Force jeeps. LtCol Abbodonzo was so pleased that he had his cooks prepare a steak dinner for SSgt Burke and Bennie X. An airman drove Burke and Bennie X back to China Beach to pick up their jeep and then invited them back to the base for a few drinks. This is why they were gone for ten hours, however, Joe had told Burke to tell me that the Colonel's "hooch" would be delivered in two days, and would be installed by the Air Force. I still said nothing to Colonel Codispoti strongly supporting that adage, "don't believe it until you see it."

Two days later, in the middle of the afternoon, I get an urgent radio message informing me that a single Air Force lowboy, (a truck with a low trailer attached) was driving down Highway One, unaccompanied and with no security. The military policeman that had stopped them at a checkpoint asked them where they were going, and they said to a Major Beck at LZ Baldy. The military policeman asked them if they had any idea where they were, and they said no, they were just told to deliver the load they had to a Major Beck, and that they would get there by driving south on Highway One.

When the MP told them they were in the heart of enemy held territory, and that they were subject to attack, they suddenly became worried. I sent a team of troops up to the checkpoint to greet them and ride shotgun with them all the way down to Baldy. In about two hours, the large Air Force truck with the Colonel's "hooch," arrived at LZ Baldy. The Air Force Sergeants who had driven the load down told me that they were given instructions to assemble the "hooch," and then go back to Da Nang. I got them flak jackets and helmets, plus two cots I put up in the S-4 tent, and we went to see Colonel Codispoti. He was absolutely thrilled and wanted the men to start erecting the "hooch" right away. The men told him they need level ground and then asked him where he wanted the "hooch" built. In typical Gildo fashion, he replied, "Right here on the very top of this hill, where every son of a bitch gook can see it, and I dare any of those bastards to try to shoot up my hooch."

That is where it was built. It took three complete days to build the hooch from the prefabricated parts. There was a back bedroom, a toilet and a shower, even a urinal, fed by a gravity tank, on the roof of the building, a kitchen, complete with electric stove and refrigerator, powered by a portable generator, and a front living room, that Colonel Codispoti would use as an office. The entire building was painted Air Force blue, and to the best of my knowledge, it remained Air Force blue as a testimonial to the Air Force. There was a foam roof, which kept the place insulated, and a portable air conditioner set into the wall of the bedroom. A large 55-gallon tank was also on the roof, which supplied the water to run the utilities in the hooch. The only thing that had to be done was to paint the inside of the water tank with a primer and a waterproof paint, to inhibit rust in the extremely damp and humid climate. The Air force men painted the primer in the barrel and told us to paint the inside with the waterproof paint after the primer dried. The job was completed quickly, and before leaving for Da Nang, Colonel Codispoti made both Air Force Sergeants honorary Marines. Each of them received a 7th Marines Plaque and, of course, one of my "North Vietnamese flags" (I had brought ten of them with me when I left the 1st Battalion).

The colonel became very impatient with me because the primer in the barrel was taking a long time to dry. He told me not to paint the interior with waterproof paint, instead, when the primer was dried, he wanted me to fill the barrel with water so he could take a shower in his new bathroom. Every morning I checked the primer, and every morning it was still sticky. I kept telling the Colonel that he would have to wait, but Gildo finally ordered me to fill the barrel with water because, "By God, I'm going to take a shower today, I've waited long enough!" I told the Colonel again that the primer was not dry, but he overrode my objections and told me to fill the damn barrel. I had the water tanker driver fill the barrel, and then informed the Colonel that it was full. The Colonel took his shower. In about ten minutes, I heard a scream from his hooch, and I went running up the hill to his hooch and went inside. Colonel Codispoti was standing there, naked, in his new shower, covered from head to foot in deep rust colored primer. He was yelling, and I couldn't stop laughing. I had to get some kerosene, and gave it to him to clean off the primer, and then he went to our communal shower, which was an empty napalm tank that had a single shower head welded into the center of the tank. The shower head had a chain on it which you pulled when you wanted water. By leaving the water in the tank until about two in the afternoon, we always had a sun-heated, hot shower. The primer took a week to dry and then the Colonel finally had his private shower, but the scene of him standing naked in that shower covered with red primer paint, is my most cherished memory of Vietnam.

August turned into September and on 10 September, I received my orders to Quantico, Virginia, for duty. If I were still married, this would have been a good assignment, but under the circumstances, I wanted to get as far away from the East Coast as possible.

I asked Colonel Codispoti for some help in this matter. He got me on a direct telephone call to HQMC in Washington where I spoke to a Major Joe Hoar, who was the officer in charge of Major assignments. I told him my problem, and in one minute he reassigned me to the Marine Corps Recruit Depot in San Diego. I was getting as far away from the East Coast as possible. Major Joe Hoar completed his career in the Marine Corps as a 4 star general commanding the US Central Command at MacDill Air Force Base in Florida. He was the first Marine to hold that job, and the first Marine, except for the Commandant, to wear 4 stars in a joint command, which is composed of all services.

In Vietnam, when you approached your overseas control date (OCD, the date that you were scheduled to return to the US) the common practice was to let Marines go home two weeks early, thereby, turning a 13 month tour of duty into a 12 ½ month tour of duty. My OCD was October 16, 1969, which meant that on that date, I would have competed exactly 13 months in Vietnam. As that date approached, I kept waiting for Colonel Codispoti to indicate on what date he would let me go home. One afternoon, he asked me what my OCD was, and I told him that it was October 16. "Good," he replied, "Be prepared to go up to Da Nang on October 15 to ship out for the States." I really did not care what my end of tour date was going to be, and, in a way, it showed me that the Colonel did not want me to leave the Regiment. I was perfectly happy with his decision and, as far as I was concerned, that was the end of the matter.

On October 1, Major General Simpson came down to LZ Baldy to see Gildo. The 7th Marines were having tremendous success in the Que Son area, and enemy activity had decreased considerably. After his meeting with the Colonel, I drove the General down to the Landing Zone from Gildo's hillside mansion. Gildo loved to entertain high-ranking officers in his Air Force hooch, and everyone came away shaking their heads. Comments like, "Only Gildo!" were common, and the one individual who got the biggest kick out of Gildo's mansion was General Simpson. He made it a point to tell Gildo, every time he was in the 7th Marines area, that no one had a better "hooch" than the CO of the 7th Marines, including himself! To Gildo, this made all the effort worthwhile.

On the way back to the LZ, the General asked me when I was going home. I told him that I was scheduled to leave on October 16, just two weeks into the future. He then asked me when I had arrived in Vietnam, and I told him on September 16, 1968. The General said that he was sorry to see me go, but he was certain I would enjoy the Recruit Depot in San Diego. This surprised me because I had no idea that General Simpson knew anything about where I was going from Vietnam. We drove the rest of the way in silence, and when we got to the LZ, the General's helicopter was waiting. I walked him to his helicopter, saluted him and returned to the Regimental Command Post.

That afternoon, I got a call from Colonel Codispoti, and he sounded furious. "What the hell did you tell General Simpson, you son of a bitch," he screamed at me as I entered his hooch. "Nothing," I replied, "what happened?" Apparently, the General had called Gildo and asked him to send me up to Division on Saturday 11 October, as he wanted to treat me to dinner in the General's dining room that evening and that he was going to send me home on 12 October. Gildo was convinced I had whined to the General, but I finally got him to believe me, that I had nothing to do with my invitation to eat in the General's Mess. He calmed down and then smiled at me saying, "Well, I damn near had you staying till the very last day!" On the evening of October 10, I ate dinner with Gildo in his hooch. He was now a combat veteran of World War II, Korea and Vietnam, and soon he would be retiring from the Marine Corps after 30 years service. He was planning to retire on February 1, 1970, and he planned to settle in San Diego, pointing out that he expected me to visit him once he retired. I promised him that I would. I then asked him if there was anything I could send him from the States. "Yes," he replied, "a box of Dunhill cigars." Gildo knew I was from New York City, and he knew that I knew what Dunhill cigars were, and how much they cost, but I assured him that the first thing I would do when I got home was to buy him his cigars. We said our good-byes and I thanked him for everything. He was a tremendous leader and a great and brave combat Marine. I knew this first hand, having observed him in battle on many occasions. That night I packed my seabag, got my qualification record from the Regimental Adjutant, and boarded the General's helicopter the following morning for my last ride out of LZ Baldy.

War is a horrible experience and one that I would not wish on anyone. The events I have written about in this chapter have purposely omitted all the deaths, injuries, killings, and heartbreaks that occur in a war. I have seen many terrible things, and I never speak of them, preferring to leave them deep in the recesses of my mind, hopefully, never to surface. On rare occasions, when I am with others who have shared my experiences in Vietnam, I will bring those memories to the surface. Vietnam, like all wars, was a stupid war. It did not serve any purpose, and in the end, it cost the lives of 58,000 young men and women. Vietnam today is a communist country, and that is what we were trying to prevent. We were unsuccessful, because Vietnam was a political war run by politicians who had neither the courage nor the experience to see it through to a favorable conclusion.

In spite of all the mistakes, I was proud to serve with my fellow Marines. As for serving my country, I looked upon my assignment to Vietnam as a natural result of being a professional soldier, without a lot of patriotic overtures. Our country was never threatened by Vietnam and we had no reason for being there. We wasted millions of dollars and thousands of lives for nothing. Unfortunately, we never learn, because throughout the history of the world, man has found a reason to go to war. It is extremely stupid to fight wars, and I hope that someday the world will find some other way to solve the problems that seem to crop up regularly. One thing is certain, unless you have fought in a war, it is impossible to describe the horrors you experience. After Vietnam, I understood why my father never spoke about his World War I service.

I had a wonderful evening in Da Nang with General Simpson, and on the morning of October 12, 1969, I departed Vietnam, alive and in one piece. I had made it and was heading back to the United States. I had weighed 195 pounds when I arrived in Vietnam, and I was leaving Vietnam weighing 155 pounds. While skinny, I was perfectly healthy, and had no mental problems, no drug problems and, as far as I knew, no financial problems, as I was flying out with over 10,000 dollars in cash, which represented all of my pay plus my combat pay while I was in the field. I had bought a Rolex Oyster watch, which I still have today, for the grand sum of 99 dollars, a one-time benefit for all returning US military personnel, provided they wanted to buy one. I was looking forward to spending thirty days of leave in New York City before driving across the country, to my new duty station in San Diego.

I was one lucky Marine. As another side benefit, I had arrived in Vietnam with one ribbon to wear on my uniform, and I was returning with 14 ribbons. I would never again be mistaken for a "rookie," since I had served my time in hell. In closing this chapter, I am reminded of a poem written by Rudyard Kipling. It is a short poem, and it tells the story of all soldiers, in all wars, since the beginning of time. Here, it is:

God and soldier, we adore,
in time of danger, not before.

The danger past and all things righted,
God is forgotten and the soldier slighted.

Sadly, this poem tells the story that all of us experienced upon our return to the States, except the American public vilified our returning heroes. Since I was a career Marine, I could live with it, but the damage that the American public brought down on the poor survivor/veterans of Vietnam, was unconscionable and did irreparable damage to thousands of young men and women, many of whom are still suffering today (2012).

There is no justification for a war, the only way to stop war is to make the politicians and their families fight the wars they declare, or vote for, while I think that every combat veteran would dearly love to see this happen, I am afraid that we will never see it, either in my lifetime, or the lifetime of the reader. At least, in the history of mankind, to date, no means to end war has ever surfaced. It seems to be a curse of mankind, and I only hope and pray that no one else in my family will ever have to experience the horrors of a war. I think my father, and I have paid our dues for the Beck family when it comes to war.

After we departed from Hill 55, my crew at Fort Courage remained at the forward air base on Hill 55, and continued providing logistics support for the entire TAOR. Sergeant Goode finished his third tour of duty in Vietnam and returned to East Los Angeles, I never heard from him again. He was an outstanding Marine, and I hope that all went well for him in the States. Sergeant De Peau finished his third tour of duty in Vietnam and returned to the States to be discharged at Marine Barracks, Treasure Island in San Francisco. While walking through San Francisco International Airport in his uniform, two teen-aged girls spit on him and called him a baby-killer. He was so infuriated by this action, that immediately after discharge, he left the United States and immigrated to Australia, where he became an Australian citizen and a State Policeman. Based on his experiences in Vietnam, he established the Australian Helicopter Branch of their Highway

Patrol and remained on active duty, in the helicopter division of the police department, until he suffered a severe case of Post Traumatic Stress Syndrome, fourteen years after leaving Vietnam. He was treated in Australia for four years and is now retired in Queensland, Australia. I saw him as recently as 2005, and he is in good shape today. He still harbors a great deal of bitterness about the way he was treated by the American public, but we have remained in contact with each other, and in 2008, he came to the United States, with a group of Australian Vietnam War Veterans, to embark on a cross-country motorcycle ride with American Vietnam veterans, from Los Angeles to the Vietnam Memorial in Washington. His wife, Cheryl, a beautiful Australian woman, accompanied him on this epic ride, as did members of the 1st Marine Division Association, based in Oceanside, California.

I have attended several reunions of the 1st Battalion, 7th Marines, and am extremely proud to be included in their brotherhood of warriors. We share experiences that only those who have gone through them, could ever understand. It is my privilege to join them as often as possible, and share the brotherhood that was forged on the battlefields of Vietnam. We shall never forget, and we honor both the living and the dead, at each of our reunions, remembering that famous line:

> **All gave some, Some gave All.**
> **May God Bless us all.**

CHAPTER 15

MARINE CORPS RECRUIT DEPOT, SAN DIEGO

The day I left Vietnam, October 12, 1969, happened to be a Sunday. I can remember everyone in the National Airlines plane being very quiet, and I experienced a tension inside the aircraft that was so intense that you could cut it with a knife. No one spoke, and everyone seemed to be lost in their personal reflections. As the aircraft taxied for takeoff, all eyes were intently looking out the windows on both sides. I can't speak for others, but I was thinking that I hope we can make our takeoff and clear the surface to air missile (SAM) range as quickly as possible. I also recalled I did not notice the same level of tension on our R&R flight to Australia. Maybe that's because when we went on R&R, we were going back to Vietnam, and this time we were not going to see Vietnam again.

The aircraft sped down the runway, lifted off over Marble Mountain, then turned east over the South China Sea. As we cleared the landmass of Vietnam, a wild and loud cheer erupted inside the aircraft. People shook hands, bumped fists, slapped backs and screamed, "We got out of that god damn place." I felt exactly the same way and joined in the screaming and cheering. As the noise died down, National Airlines served everyone one free cocktail or one free beer. I never forgot that simple act of kindness.

On the day I left Vietnam, President Richard Nixon announced he would make a major policy address to the nation on Vietnam in early November and that he would not be swayed or influenced by the ever-growing antiwar movement in the United States. On October 14, Radio Hanoi broadcast a long, open letter to American war protestors, congratulating them on their efforts. In my opinion, a large percentage of the casualties of the Vietnam War can be laid at the feet of the war protestors, and Hanoi's "open letter of congratulations" said it all.

Our plane landed safely in Okinawa and busses took us to Camp Hansen where we would reclaim our personal gear and wait for transportation to the United States. Planes left every day, however, there always seemed to be more people than aircraft, so it was not unusual to wait for a few days on Okinawa. There wasn't much else to do while waiting, so a lot of alcohol was consumed in the various clubs and off base at the many clubs and bars surrounding Camp Hansen. Sitting in the Officer's Club, I saw the new officers getting ready to go to Vietnam, and secretly felt very sorry for them. They were going to a place where some politicians were playing Russian roulette with their lives. Some would win, and some would lose; hopefully, there would be more winners than losers.

On Tuesday morning, I boarded an Air Force plane at Kadena Air Base for Travis Air Force Base in California. I landed at Travis AFB, took a bus to San Francisco where I called American Airlines and booked a flight to New York City for early next morning. I stayed at the Marine's Memorial Club and took off the next morning at 8 a.m. I had called Dad and Dora, and they were going to meet me at JFK Airport (renamed from Idlewild Airport, in honor of assassinated President Kennedy). I landed in New York City, and Dad and Dora were delighted I was home again. When we got to their apartment, I took off my uniform and changed into civilian clothes. I then asked if they would mind if I went down to the corner of 31st Street and Lexington Avenue where a hot dog push cart was always stationed.

While in Vietnam, people fanaticize over two things, sex and food. I had been telling myself that the first thing I would do when I got back to "the world," as we called the United States, was to go to the push cart on 31st and Lexington Avenue and eat a hot dog, with onions and spicy mustard. Luckily, the cart was still there, and I ordered a hot dog with onions and mustard. It tasted exactly the way I had imagined it would taste. I ate 12 more hot dogs before I was finished. The push cart vendor was in awe of my eating abilities, but I chose not to tell him what I was doing. I was eating one hot dog for every month I spent in Vietnam, and I was savoring every hot dog as though I was eating the finest meal at the Waldorf-Astoria. In my mind, I was, and the memories of all the places in Vietnam where I had thought about doing this flooded my brain like an emotional tsunami.

I went back to Dad and Dora's apartment and explained my actions to them. They seemed to understand, and Dora told me she had planned to feed me my favorite meal of Weinerschnitzel, (veal cutlets) red cabbage and hot potato salad. I told her I was sure I could eat again if she felt like cooking. She did, and we sat down to a wonderful German style dinner. I was glad to be home, and we drank Champagne in honor of my safe return. After dinner, Dora took out a copy of my Bronze Star citation, which I had sent to her from Vietnam, and showed it to my Dad. He had never seen it until that moment because Dora said he worried himself sick over my welfare every night, and she did not want to add to his worries by showing him what I was doing in combat. My Dad read the citation and began crying. I comforted him immediately and assured him that anything I did could not even begin to equal what he had done in World War I. To ease the tension of the moment, I told him about leading a tank charge wearing his Iron Cross around my neck. He laughed and shook his head and things quickly returned to normal.

The following morning, I went to the Alfred Dunhill store in Manhattan, one of the finest cigar stores in the world. Dunhill was a British company, and from its' original location in London, it had supplied cigars to many world famous cigar smokers, including Winston Churchill, for whom they had named a cigar. I bought a box of Dunhill Churchill's. I simply couldn't see Gildo Codospoti smoking anything else. I had taken several hundred dollars with me, and it cost all of that, and considering that it was 1969, that was a lot of money. I mailed the box to the colonel. I had enclosed a short note that told him, again, how much I respected him and how much I had enjoyed serving with him in combat.

By the time I got home, there had been a telephone call for me from Sharron. She was tearful and asked me to come to Florida to see the boys. She told me she was now living at home with her parents, and that the "new boyfriend" was apparently out of the picture. I told her I had no desire to see her, but since I wanted to see the boys, I would come to Deerfield Beach within the next few days.

I took a train to Florida, the *Orange Blossom Special,* since I was in no hurry to see Sharron and I had to calm down my innermost anger to arrive at some emotional place that would allow me to see my children without causing some kind of scene. I arrived in Miami, rented a car, and drove to Deerfield Beach. It was not my intention to stay overnight in Deerfield, but I was prepared for whatever might occur. I drove to Sharron's house, and by coincidence, she was in the front yard playing with Eric and Paul. Sharron came up to me, and the boys also ran up to me. "I'm your Dad," I said, afraid they would not recognize me. "No, you're not, you're Peter" said Eric. Welcome to Florida.

Apparently, her "boyfriend" had swindled her out of the money I had given her in the divorce, even being brazen enough to buy a house in the Florida Keys, using her money and putting the house in his name. Sharron did not find out about this until he threw her and the boys out of the house and told them to go back to Deerfield Beach. The few remaining hours I spent with her and the boys were strained and uncomfortable so I drove to Miami and flew back to New York City.

Back in New York City, I called a few of my college buddies and arranged to meet them at Jimmy Ryan's Club on 52nd Street for a night of Dixieland jazz and a few beers. It was fun visiting with them and, as always, the music was great. The big Broadway musical at the time was "Hair" and I got a single ticket for the following night. I was not impressed.

My orders directed me to report for duty at the Marine Corps Recruit Depot in San Diego, on Monday, 10 November, so I had plenty of time to spend in New York. While in Vietnam, I had read about a new car the German auto company, Opel, was building for the American market. It was a two-seater that looked very much like a small Corvette. It was called the Opel GT. I asked my Dad to look into it for me, and he had all the information I needed, plus a dealer who was holding one for me. The dealer showed us the car, which was a royal blue model with black leather interior, and it was selling for $3,495. I bought it.

I was planning to drive to the West coast beginning on Friday, the 31st of October. After visiting some friends in Washington, I would then head for San Diego. The distance I planned to cover between New York and San Diego would be around 2800 miles. I looked forward to the drive.

On October 30, the Defense Department announced that for the previous week, deaths in Vietnam had reached 100 per week for the first time in the past five weeks. I felt guilty for not being over there, and angry as hell at all the people I saw in New York just walking around, living their daily lives without even a thought for those poor bastards over there fighting a war they didn't want.

On the morning of the 31st, I took off for San Diego, with a first stop in Washington, where I went to Headquarters, Marine Corps, to review my official records. My fitness reports from Vietnam were all outstanding, and they would certainly help me for promotion. I then headed to San Diego, and I was thrilled to be going to California. Being an East Coast Marine, it was rare to get an assignment clear across the country. If you were from the East Coast, you usually stayed on the East Coast. This is why I was scheduled to be assigned to Quantico, Virginia, upon my return from Vietnam, and why I had already had a tour of duty at a Recruit Depot, only it had been Parris Island in South Carolina. As far as a tour of duty in the Fleet Marine Force was concerned, East Coast Marines went to Camp Lejeune and the 2nd Marine Division, where I had already spent three years, while West Coast Marines went to Camp Pendleton and 1st Marine Division.

My newly made friend, Major Joe Hoar, the Major's assignment officer in Washington, had pulled some strings for me, and that is why I found myself in a wonderful city, with great climate, fantastic beaches, many single women, and a recruit depot that was located in the heart of downtown San Diego, right across from the city's international airport. I was really looking forward to reporting for duty on Monday, November 10, 1969. It seemed to be a lucky day to begin a new portion of my life.

Monday morning, before reporting to MCRD, I checked in with the BOQ manager at the Naval Training Center and requested a permanent assignment of quarters. I was given a two-room suite on the second floor of the BOQ. I unloaded my car, hung up my clothes, got into a green uniform, took my orders, and reported in to the Recruit Depot for duty. I handed my orders to the Depot Adjutant and waited to hear where I was going to be assigned. While the main mission of the Recruit Depot was to train recruits, there were plenty of support facilities on the Depot that required officers and getting assigned to the Recruit Training Regiment was not easy.

Obviously, everyone wanted to be in the Recruit Training Regiment, but there were only so many vacancies, and, as you got higher in rank, there were even fewer vacancies. As a regiment, there was only one colonel, the regimental commander, and four lieutenant colonels, one commanding officer for each of the three recruit training battalions, and one regimental executive officer. There were a few major billets in the regimental headquarters, since each of the staff divisions in the Headquarters, was headed by a major. Each of the three training battalions had a major for an executive officer. With such a limited amount of openings for a major, getting into the recruit training regiment was going to be difficult.

I did not know anyone at the Depot Headquarters, including the Commanding General, Major General John N. McLaughlin, a hero of the Korean War. General McLaughlin was another one of the Marine Corps' "Southern Gentlemen." Born in Savannah, Georgia, and a graduate of Georgia Tech, he had been awarded the Silver Star during the Korean War for his "gallant actions while confined as a prisoner of war in North Korea" for over two years. I was escorted into General McLaughlin's office, and he informed me that he had received two letters of recommendation from General Simpson and Colonel Codispoti concerning my assignment to the Recruit Training Regiment. When I told General McLaughlin I had completed a tour of duty as a Series Officer at Parris Island, my new assignment to recruit training at San Diego was settled. I'll never forget the fact that two senior officers took their time to help advance my career, and I have done the same for personnel working for me.

Since it was the Marine Corps Birthday, the Depot was in a festive mood. In those days, the Birthday was always celebrated on 10 November, no matter on what day of the week the birthday happened to fall. The Depot was poised to celebrate the 194th birthday of the Corps and my arrival went unnoticed.

The Marine Corps Recruit Depot had been in San Diego since 1924 when it was opened as a recruit training facility under the command of Major General Joseph H. Pendleton. The base itself, while having grown considerably in physical plants, was always just 388 acres, set in the heart of downtown San Diego bordering the San Diego International Airport. With the immense rectangular parade ground and drill field commanding the center of the base, the Depot Headquarters is located at one end of the rectangle and the Recruit Training Regiment is located at the other end.

All the buildings located on the north side of the parade ground look like Spanish mission buildings and comprise the original buildings of the depot when it was constructed from 1919 to 1923. It was these buildings that opened for business on March 1, 1924, and they have since remained in place. The remaining buildings around the parade ground are new construction, but fit into the general atmosphere of the depot, underlying its' primary mission of training basic Marines for the Fleet Marine Forces. After reporting in to the Depot, I went to the Provost Marshall's office to obtain my base decal which was required to drive aboard the base.

I drove to Recruit Training Regiment (RTR) Headquarters and reported for duty to Colonel William R. Joslyn, the Commanding Officer. Colonel Joslyn informed me I was being assigned to the 1st Recruit Training Battalion as the Executive Officer. He then told me the Commanding Officer of the 1st Battalion was a Lieutenant Colonel Barney Chen. I tried not to go completely haywire and simply stated I looked forward to meeting LtCol Chen. I then reported to my best friend and best man at my wedding in New York, Barney Chen. (After he retired, he changed his name to Schenn because he was tired of being identified as Chinese and receiving Chinese mail!)

We kept up our pretense until we got into his office, and then I couldn't hold it in any longer. I simply asked Barney, "How in the hell did you pull this one off? "It was easy," replied Barney, 'Depot Headquarters sent out a list of incoming officers and asked if there was anyone on the list we knew or wanted. I simply said I needed an Executive Officer and this Major Beck looks like a good man, so I'll take him. I just didn't tell them I knew you.

The next thing I knew, you were assigned to the battalion." I said this calls for a celebration. It was a great reunion with promises of at least three years of good times. The next thing I did was to seek a good civilian law firm because I wanted to allocate an appropriate amount of my monthly income to provide child support for Eric and Paul. This was rapidly and efficiently accomplished.

The fact that both Barney and I were bachelors made our time spent with the troops far greater than the other battalion commanders and executive officers. We didn't have anything else to divert our attention and so we were able to devote more time to the business of training recruits in the 1st Recruit Training Battalion.

In those days, most off-duty social life was centered at the Officer's Club. Every evening, beginning promptly at 1600 (4 p.m.), Happy Hour would start and this lasted until exactly 1800 (6 p.m.). During those two hours, officers would stop by for a drink on their way home. The club always served several kinds of finger foods to go along with the very cheap drinks (martini's and scotch for 25 cents a drink) and, besides the socializing, quite a bit of business was also conducted at happy hour. The club was a very large facility, given the rather small and singular mission of the recruit depot, and some units on the base had their "de facto" seating areas. Our 1st Battalion area was off the main bar, where promptly at 1630, the battalion officers would assemble for some serious socializing and a "farewell cocktail." The married men went home at 1800, but Barney and I would usually close out happy hour, and then stay longer. We rarely got drunk, as it was not a good thing to be drunk on base, or to allow senior officers to notice you could not handle your liquor.

Barney and I were really having a great time together in the 1st Battalion. When we weren't working, we would go out for dinners and go to San Diego Charger football games. Barney had found a girlfriend named Mary Felix, and we would often go to her apartment for breakfast before the games. We always had a few drinks with breakfast, and by the time we got to the football game, we were well on our way to total relaxation.

Just a few weeks before Christmas in 1969, Sharron called from Florida and implored me to move her and the boys to San Diego so the boys could be "closer to their father." On December 20, 1969, Sharron and the boys arrived in San Diego. Sharron was 30 years old, Eric was 7 years old, and Paul was 4 years old. Little did I know that, 40 plus years later, they would still be living in San Diego.

In spite of Sharron being back in my life, albeit only on the periphery, I was enjoying a rather full social life. San Diego was full of eligible women, and the officer's clubs around San Diego had weekly dances to live music which assured any available bachelor that meeting women was never a problem. There were hundreds of couples in the military who met at these events and then got married. These events were nicknamed "the Meat Market," and the name was not only descriptive, but also accurate.

Meanwhile, life in the battalion was outstanding. We were turning out recruits to fill the pipeline for Vietnam, and on December 1969, the Department of Defense announced that it was withdrawing 60,000 troops from Vietnam by December 15. This was good news to at least 60,000 families across America. The following day, December 16, Secretary of Defense, Melvin Laird, announced that based on the troop reductions, the draft would reduce the number of men being called up to active service by 25,000. Thus, the year ended on Wednesday, December 31, 1969, and we began to look at the New Year with greater hopes for some kind of end to the war in Vietnam.

The new year of 1970 was rung in with appropriate celebration, and while it was the holiday season, recruit training never ceased. The only concession to the holidays for the recruits was a festive holiday dinner in the mess hall, where, in honor of the holidays, the recruits ate a delicious holiday meal of turkey and ham and all the trimmings. This was and is a standard procedure on Thanksgiving Day, Christmas and New Year's Day.

I received word that I was going to receive a medal at the regularly scheduled Friday recruit graduation parade. Graduation was always on a Friday with a final parade, which allowed the recruits' parents the opportunity to watch their son graduate. There were always medals to be presented to both officers and enlisted men for service in Vietnam. Usually, the paperwork did not catch up with them until several months after they had returned from the war.

My turn came on Friday, January 9, 1970, when I received the Legion of Merit with a combat "V" for my services in Vietnam. I was totally bowled over, since Majors rarely got that medal; it was usually awarded to generals and colonels or lieutenant colonels who had held positions of great responsibility. Again, Gildo Codispoti and General Simpson had gone to bat for me with the Awards and Decorations Branch and had gotten my recommendation for that medal through the Awards Board. It was a great day for me, and I remember celebrating the day later that evening with my newest girlfriend, Marybeth Rowland.

On January 5, 1970, the Commanding Officer of the Recruit Training Regiment, Colonel Bill Joslyn, received orders to Headquarters Marine Corps, and he was replaced by Colonel Ed Derning, a tough infantry officer, who came to the regiment from the 1st Marine Division in Vietnam. Colonel Derning was an impressive officer. Born in Chicago, Illinois, he grew up on the streets of the city and enlisted in the Marine Corps at the age of 17. He began his Marine Corps career as a Private and worked his way up to Colonel. He was a great leader and earned the respect of his troops through personal example.

Where Colonel Joslyn was somewhat reserved and totally professional as a commander, Colonel Derning believed in being out with the troops and mixing with the drill instructors. In a very short time, it was common knowledge throughout the regiment that the colonel would show up at any time of the day or night, seven days a week, to check on the training and the morale of the troops, both the recruits and the drill instructors. He also monitored all classroom instruction and was always at the physical fitness fields to observe training. He was particularly concerned at the high number of drill instructors who were washed out at DI School and the increasing number of drill instructor offenses towards recruits during training.

Each month, the three battalion executive officers sat on a screening board that evaluated marginal students at Drill Instructor School, to determine if they should continue their training or, whether they should return to the Fleet Marine Force. When I attended the January Screening Board, I was unfavorably impressed by the manner in which the Director of the school, a mustang captain, was addressing the students. It felt as though the students were again in boot camp, and I did not feel this approach was suitable for training instructors. I began to feel that an atmosphere of constant harassment, such as they were experiencing at DI School, would only encourage students to increase the levels of harassment on the recruits, once they graduated and went to a recruit training battalion for duty as drill instructors.

I made these concerns known to Colonel Derning, and he asked me in great detail what I thought was wrong with the school and what I thought could be done to improve it. After about an hour, he said, "Major Beck, effective February 1, you will be the new Director of Drill Instructor School. I want you to take it over, rework the curriculum, evaluate the instructors at the school, and make the school into a training ground for drill instructors, and not a duplication of Boot Camp!" I asked Colonel Derning if my going to Drill Instructor School wasn't a little extreme, since the Director's job called for a captain and not a major. Colonel Derning informed me that he was making the job a major's job, until I got the place redirected along the lines that we had discussed.

I returned to the battalion and informed Barney about what had just happened in Colonel Derning's office. He looked at me and said, "Well, that's what you get for not keeping your big mouth shut. Good luck, it's a very good job, and you'll do well. They need you there." On February 1, 1970, I left the 1st Recruit Training Battalion and became the Director of the Drill Instructor School. It was time to put my theories into action.

I began by calling the staff together and informed them that they were to treat all students in the school with the respect that their rank entitles them. I emphasized that they were not "boots" or "recruits, but rather, they were Marines who were being trained to become drill instructors. I told them that I intended to respect them as instructors, and I expected them to respect the students as Marine Noncommissioned Officers, which each one of them was, because they had earned their rank. I also informed them that if they did not like my approach, they were free to request immediate reassignment.

I brought in a young Captain who would be the Assistant Director of the School, and, who, if he met my expectations, would take over the school once we realigned the curriculum and the manner of instruction. The next thing we did was to change the manner of instructing the students. There would be no more yelling or harassment. Students would continue to meet the same standards and requirements, however, they would simply be expected to perform, and they would be evaluated on their performance. The staff at the school was there to help them graduate and become drill instructors, and not to see how many they could wash out of the program.

All instructors would make up a course outline with a check sheet and examinations that specifically addressed every item that would be graded to complete that particular subject successfully. We would simply shift the responsibility to the students. They would be given a complete course outline at the beginning of the 9-week course of instruction, and they would also be given a complete copy of all testing criteria.

There would be no surprises, and there would be a professional atmosphere at the school at all times. The easiest thing to fix was the physical fitness classes. Instead of yelling at the students during periods of extended running or working on the obstacle course, instructors were to encourage, train and assist students in achieving the required physical fitness standards. This worked particularly well because the primary instructor, Staff Sergeant Bill Dower, immediately went from Drill Instructor to Coach, thereby getting the most from all of his students. After retirement, Bill Dower made some exercise CD's called, "Train like a Marine," that became very popular, and earned him quite a bit of money. In my mind, he deserved all the success he attained.

The drill portion of instruction was a bigger challenge. We finally arrived at a point where we split the drill instruction into two phases, with the first part being voice projection, and the second part being the ability to instruct on the drill field. We felt that if a student could not project his voice so that 75 recruits, standing on the drill field, could hear him, and clearly understand what he was saying, there was no point in going any further. This worked well for us, since students who simply could not master the skill of imparting knowledge orally and having their students understand what they were teaching, could clearly not advance any further, and would have to be terminated. Not because they failed, but because they did not possess the necessary skill to become a drill instructor. Within three months, the entire mindset of the school and its' instructors was changed. I am also extremely proud of the fact that during the transition period, I did not lose a single instructor. They all bought into the new system.

Another innovation was to have recruits who had washed out of boot camp explain to the students why they washed out. Accompanying these washed out recruits was the Depot Psychiatrist, a US Navy medical doctor. After the recruits finished telling their stories, he discussed each case with the students. This allowed the students to be eye witnesses to some of the mistakes that were being made on the drill field and gave them a chance to discuss how they would have done things if they had been the drill instructor of the failed recruit. This turned out to be one of the more popular classes in the school, and the Depot Psychiatrist made the classes particularly interesting and meaningful.

He became a big supporter of DI School, where previously he had been one of the more vocal critics of the school. As this new crop of drill instructors were assigned to recruit training duties, offenses against recruits began to decrease. My tour of duty at Drill Instructor's School was proving to be highly successful, and I was proving my theories clearly to Colonel Derning. Of course, as you might expect, the "old school" drill instructors who were products of the previous administrations, openly derided the "new wave" of drill instructors. The success rate of the new drill instructors, however, soon silenced even the harshest critics.

On the social scene, I went through a series of women. My longest association during this time seemed to be with Marybeth, who used to say that she appeared to be a "bad penny," because I always wound up coming back to her. In the interim time, there was a school teacher, an investment banker (who would leave telephone messages for me with my clerks saying that a Barb Wire or a Kitty Litter had called) who urged me to marry her, assuring me that she would make me rich, and several other women, all except one, eager to marry and settle down.

I maintained my long friendship with Barney, and we continued our usual antics, except he was beginning to become serious with Mary Felix and it looked like, after years of being a bachelor, Barney might just be deciding to get married. I continued to see Sharron and the boys in Chula Vista, and found myself spending a great deal of time in Chula Vista.

In December, Colonel Derning surprised me with a new assignment. Beginning January 1, 1971, I would be leaving Drill Instructor School and assuming the job as the Operations Officer for the Recruit Training Regiment. This new job made me responsible for the implementation of all recruit training at the Recruit Depot. In two short years, I had been fortunate enough to have the three best assignments possible at the Recruit Depot for an officer with the rank of major. I had been a recruit training battalion executive officer, the Director of Drill Instructor's School, and now, the operations officer of the Recruit Training Regiment. It just didn't get any better than that, and I felt that my chances for promotion to lieutenant colonel were getting stronger by the minute, provided that I didn't screw up along the way. My friend, Barney Chen, had been promoted to colonel and reassigned as the RTR Executive Officer and my new office would be near his.

Socially, again, the amount of available women in the San Diego area was a continuous surprise. I was able to go out just as often as I wanted, and with my friend, Barney, now permanently occupied with Mary Felix, I was pretty much left to my own devices, however, between my job as the Operations Officer of RTR, and my semipermanent connection with Marybeth Rowland, there wasn't very much time left to explore new horizons.

The Recruit Training Regiment had a tremendous amount of pressure placed on it by the ever-increasing demands for well trained, battle ready Marines for the war in Vietnam. The training syllabus required constant attention to be completely in harmony with the demands of the field. While we continued to train the recruits physically, we also had to train them to be able to withstand the rigors of jungle combat and thus more emphasis was placed on being self-reliant and flexible, while still remembering that Marines were always part of a team, designed to be the finest fighting machine in the world.

We became even more selective, and began to wash out recruits we felt could not measure up to jungle warfare and the demands of a highly unpopular war. Training intensity centered about preparing infantry troops, with just enough support troops, to make the life of an infantry Marine as comfortable as possible. Infantry Training School became a one-month school at Camp Pendleton, after boot camp was completed. Marksmanship training, always important in the Marine Corps, became even more important, as every recruit had to qualify as a basic marksman. It was certain that over 90 percent of all recruits graduating from boot camp, were on their way to Vietnam as their first tour of duty. In three months time we rewrote the training syllabus at least four times. Each revision was in response to new requirements issued by Headquarters Marine Corp. There wasn't much free time for other things during this critical period while the war in Vietnam was raging.

Luckily, my work requirements kept me very busy, and, in a short time, I met an investment banker named Elizabeth, who decided she liked me and wanted to see more of me. Elizabeth was a highly intelligent woman with a very successful business practice, however, she was also very intense and the type of woman, who once she made up her mind about something, usually got what she wanted. At the same time as I was dating Elizabeth, I met a very attractive divorcee' who lived in a beautiful home on Point Loma, who I was more interested in than she was in me. Marybeth's departure from my life was not a very traumatic event, although, again, I had been involved with an unsuccessful relationship. The Officer's Club continued to be our social center. Along with the regular Thursday and Friday night mixers, Happy Hour every afternoon remained a good jumping off point for whatever activities were of interest.

One of the fixtures at the club was a young cocktail waitress, who also occasionally served as bartender, especially on Thursday and Friday nights, when the club was packed. Her name was Cathie Frasher, and she was a single mother with two small children. She was a very attractive woman and the 1st Recruit Training Battalion had christened her "Miss 1st Battalion" and even had a banner made for her, which she wore during Happy Hours, especially when she was serving the officers of the 1st Battalion. She was a real sweetheart and was working hard to support her two young children, and attending Mesa College whenever she could fit the classes into her schedule to improve herself, and her life with her children.

She was an active part of the 1st Battalion officers group and several of the single officers dated her during their free time. She was everyone's sweetheart and was very well liked by all the officers on the Depot, from the Commanding General on down. I got to know her because I spent time at the Officer's Club bar. She, in turn, had an opportunity to meet every one of my girlfriends, and, on rare occasions, my ex-wife Sharron, who would make appearances at the club with either me, or some other date of the moment. In conversations across the bar, I learned that she was 10 years younger than I was, but I never tried to date her.

In January of 1971, Barney informed me he intended to ask Mary Felix to marry him. At age 44, he had never been married, so I wished him well and told him I looked forward to the wedding. He asked me to be his best man, and, in what had to be the freakiest twist of fate, Mary asked Sharron to be her Maid of Honor. The wedding was held at the Depot Chapel on Wednesday, May 15, with a large reception at the Officer's Club.

In May 1971, the Commanding General, MajGen John MacLaughlin, asked me to rewrite the annual Marine Corps Birthday Ball pageant. He said it was far too predictable, and he wanted a new and different type of pageant that would be introduced at the 1971 Marine Corps Birthday Ball in November, which was going to be held at the Mission Bay Hilton Hotel in San Diego. He informed me that Colonel Derning had recommended me to him because Colonel Derning had been impressed with my writing skills and my creativity. The General told me to think about a concept and then come and brief him on it to get his approval.

My idea was to replace the uniform portion of the pageant with movie clips of old time Marines in the same order as the uniformed Marines came on stage. I felt that if we could access a Hollywood film library, there were certainly enough movies about Marines made over the years to provide us with film clips from each period. This was a tall order, since accessing a Hollywood film library was certainly no small task, however, as I said to the General, it would certainly be a unique pageant if it were possible. Not only did the General love the idea, he had a contact for me in Hollywood that he was sure would be able to help me. He gave me the name and telephone number of Colonel Bill Hendricks, U.S. Marine Corps Reserve, who just happened to be the senior film editor at the MGM Studios in Hollywood.

I scheduled an appointment with Bill Hendricks, and I arrived at the MGM gate at 10 a.m. Friday and was directed to his office. His office was in one of the old stucco offices that were so frequently filmed in movies when they wanted to show you the "back lot." The movie *Singing in the Rain* comes immediately to mind, because of all the activity that took place in the back lot in that movie. Bill proved to be a warm and genuine man who had a deep love for the Marine Corps and was very proud of his service on active duty, and his many years of service as a reserve officer. He loved my idea, and immediately began to write down the names of movies we could use.

I told him that my plan was to put the film clips together and then, after the film clips were completed, I would write a timed narration to coincide with the running film playing on a screen. I had not planned to start and stop the film, instead, I would write the narration to coincide with the entire movie, as it ran, uninterrupted, from start to finish. As luck would have it, MGM owned "John Paul Jones," and we would use that movie to introduce the visual pageant. General MacLaughlin had given me four days to complete the film loop.

Typical Marine mentality; if you're going to do a job, do it, complete it, and get back to duty. I had orders to Hollywood for "temporary additional duty on matters pertaining to official Marine Corps matters." Bill Hendricks cancelled his other appointments, and we got down to serious business. I told him the period in history, and he came up with an appropriate movie. Once we had all the time periods covered, we had to go to the MGM film library and get the film, place the film on a viewer, called a "movieola," and look for appropriate scenes. Some of the movies we wanted belonged to other studios, however, a telephone call from Bill to the chief film editor of the studio owning the print, got us use of the print to make our scenes at absolutely no cost. Talk about knowing the right people, Bill Hendricks knew everyone important person in Hollywood and he could get the job done.

He is no longer alive today, but I count those four days with him in Hollywood among my most prized memories. Once we had the scenes, Bill would mark the scenes on the original, and then place the can of film on a special pile. The movieola was nothing more than a very high-speed viewer. Once we identified the films and the chronological sequence, Bill Hendricks would take the clips from the movies we had selected and put them all together into one continuous 14-minute movie that had no music, and no sound. I said farewell to Bill and headed back to San Diego. Bill promised to send me the film, in 16 mm format, within one week. I could then begin to match the music and the narration to the running film.

I briefed General MacLaughlin on Monday and, at that meeting, the General decided that besides the film and narration, he also wanted to incorporate the period uniforms into the pageant. The Depot had spent a great deal of money buying the period uniforms to always have a set of accurate, historical uniforms available for the birthday ball pageant. This new twist made it necessary to revise my game plan. Once I understood that the period uniforms had to be in the pageant, the end product was much better because the uniforms were included.

Three copies of the film were delivered to me. I took them to the audiovisual section of the Depot and viewed the result. It was wonderful. Bill had understood exactly what I was trying to accomplish and the movie he put together supported every aspect of the script. Now all I had to do was to tape some appropriate background music and write a narration which included the period uniforms. Part of the fun surrounding this project is that no one knew what we were doing. The pageant would be a complete surprise to everyone attending the ball, and that was exactly what we wanted.

On the day of the Ball, the pageant went off like clockwork. The music was timed perfectly, the film ran smoothly, the period uniform Marines came in on cue, and I, as the narrator, did not screw up my lines. When the pageant concluded, we received a standing ovation from the entire ballroom, and I breathed a big sigh of relief. The General called me over to his table and congratulated me on a job well done, while I secretly promised I would never get involved in another Birthday Ball pageant.

Looking back on that pageant, it turned out to be the most personally creative thing I did during my 22 years in the Marine Corps, however, the Marine Corps is not exactly an "artsy-craftsy" organization. In the interim time, my classes at USIU, where I was studying for an MBA degree, were also going well, and I had completed almost two semesters of work. The training syllabus was also being developed with great work by my two assistants, Captain Buzz Buse and Captain Pete Metzger. Strangely enough, both Buzz and Pete were the sons of active duty Marine three star Generals, but, in their own right, they were both outstanding officers, who deserved to be deep selected for promotion, based on their dedication, intelligence and innate leadership abilities. They were great fun to work with, and I considered myself extremely lucky to have two such fine officers working as my assistant operations officers.

As the Christmas holidays approached, I made my annual contribution to the welfare of my fellow officers by volunteering for duty as the Depot Officer of the Day on Christmas Day. Sharron had decided to take Eric and Paul to Mexico for the holidays. She was going to go with her friend, Sally, (a friend from our Marine Barracks, Washington days) and her two children who were about the same age as Eric and Paul. The children were out of school for the holidays, and since they attended the same school, I was sure they would have a good time together.

It was not until a week after school started for the boys that they returned. I became extremely angry with Sharron and "lost my cool." I calmed down, left the house, and went to the Officer's Club bar. Since it was a Tuesday evening, there weren't many people at the bar, and I began drinking one scotch after another. It happened that the bartender that evening was Cathie Frasher and I'm afraid she got an earful that evening. I do remember that I kept drinking and that I got progressively drunker as the evening wore on.

At some point, I must have lost any control that I had, because the next thing that I remember is waking up in a strange bedroom, all by myself, with a tremendous headache. As I shifted in bed, got up and started to walk around to see where I was, Cathie came into the room. She told me that I had gotten so drunk last night, that she decided to take me home with her, and she took my car keys away at some point in the evening because she felt I was in no condition to drive. Cathie drove me back to the club where I got my car and returned to the BOQ. I was extremely hung over, but the breakfast Cathie had made for me helped alleviate some of the agony and a few cold Cokes helped me get to my office without anyone thinking I was some alcoholic showing up late for work.

I was still very upset with Sharron, but after the incident in her house, I decided that it would be better to stay away from her and the boys and not try to run their lives. I got through the day without incident and decided I would return to the Officer's Club to thank Cathie for her help the previous evening. As luck would have it, she was working at the club, and I asked her if she would be interested in dinner after her shift. I told her that it was the least I could do to repay her for her kindness. After assuring me that it was unnecessary to buy her dinner just for helping me, I told her that I wanted to buy her dinner because I liked her and that seemed to be an entirely different issue. She agreed to go to dinner, and we had our first "date." After dinner, I asked her out again and before long, we became an item. I realized that Cathie was ten years younger than me, but it didn't bother her and I was certainly very happy to be dating such a young and beautiful woman.

By July 1971, almost all Marine units had deployed out of Vietnam. These redeployments eased the requirements on the Recruit Depots to continue to feed the Vietnam pipeline with recruits, and in a very short time, we extended recruit training back to 12 weeks, allowing us to spend more time training and conditioning basic Marines. The finished products of the new, revised 12 week program didn't look any different from the finished products of the nine week program, however, the stress levels on drill instructors were noticeably decreased. The new 12-week syllabus allowed us to spend longer time with physical fitness, marksmanship training and leadership skills and, most importantly, it allowed us to provide drill instructors with more time off between recruit training cycles. Troop harassment cases decreased incrementally, and domestic violence problems, always high among drill instructor families, also decreased. Useless deaths in combat ended immediately.

In February 1972, I moved in to Cathie's house and began to live with her and her two boys, Tim and Don. There was very little difference in age between Eric and Paul and Tim and Don. While I saw my boys occasionally, I saw Tim and Don daily and in a very short time, we became a sort of "family." I helped Cathie as much as I could, by shopping for her in the commissary, and I bought a very serviceable and reliable Datsun station wagon for her.

We went everywhere together, and Cathie decided to quit her job at the club and go to work for a local San Diego company that published automotive repair manuals. In this job, she had a steady income, and was able to attend Mesa College on a fairly predictable schedule. I continued working as the Operations Officer of the Recruit Training Regiment, and attending classes in the evenings at USIU in pursuit of an MBA degree.

In September of 1972, the promotion list for lieutenant colonel was published, and I had made the list. Considering my position on the list, it would probably be at least six months before I would be promoted, however, any future assignment would be made as a lieutenant colonel. This meant that there was about a 95 percent chance that no matter where I would be assigned, it would be in a staff officer's position, since there is a limited amount of command billets for lieutenant colonels, and the Marine Corps tends to assign commands based on experience, competency and, most importantly, seniority. It was clear to me that I would be getting orders fairly soon.

Since I only had nine more credits remaining on my MBA degree requirements, I petitioned the Marine Corps to extend my tour of duty in San Diego by six months which would allow me to complete my degree. My argument was that with my supply and logistics background, an MBA degree would be an additional asset for the Marine Corps. If the Marine Corps refused my request, all of my credits at USIU would be meaningless, because graduate schools do not accept credits from other graduate schools.

The answer came back from Headquarters Marine Corps that my request for an extension had been denied, and I could expect orders transferring me in November 1972. This was the second time I had attempted to earn an MBA degree while on active duty and the second time that the Marine Corps had decided that they apparently did not want me to get an advanced degree. In early September, I received a call from the Officer Detail Section of Headquarters, Marine Corps, informing me I had been selected for a very special duty assignment with the US Second Fleet in Bahrain, in the Persian Gulf. I would be the senior Marine on the staff of the Commander, 2nd Fleet. This would serve to complete the requirement that all lieutenant colonels have for assignment to a joint or combined services staff before being eligible for promotion to the rank of colonel.

The 2nd Fleet, known as *The Great White Fleet*, because all the ships were painted white, to reflect the searing heat of the sun in the Middle East. While Headquarters Marine Corps may have thought this was a great assignment, I was devastated and did not want to go. I called the assignment officer and asked him if there was any way possible to get another assignment in lieu of the one to Bahrain. He said absolutely not, just pack your bags and standby for official orders. I slept in the BOQ that night, perhaps fueled by a few too many cocktails, based on my impending trip to the Middle East. Sometime around 3 a.m. I woke up and flashing across my mind was the one thing that would keep me out of the Middle East. I was surprised that I hadn't thought of it before.

I called the Officer Assignment Section and spoke to the same officer who had told me that there was no way he would change my assignment. I asked him to look at my service record and to very carefully read what was shown as my religion. I heard him say something along the line of "Oh, Shit!" and then he told me that there was no way the Marine Corps could send me to Bahrain. Along with the job being a joint staff assignment, there would also be a great deal of interaction with the various emirates of Bahrain, Qatar and Kuwait, none of whom were particularly fond of Jews! I was told I would not be going to the Middle East and that I would be receiving a new set of orders. For once, being Jewish had paid off and I could now look forward to a different assignment. Considering the hoops I had just put the assignment officer through in Washington, I did not hold out any hope for a choice assignment, but at least I would not be joining the "Great White Fleet."

One week later, I was shocked to receive orders to serve on the staff of the Commander-in-Chief, Pacific, in Pearl Harbor, Hawaii. I had just hit the lottery. I was being transferred from one of the best duty assignments in the Marine Corps, to one of the best duty assignments in the US Navy. The Marine Corps had just sent me a three-year ticket to live in Hawaii. It didn't get much better than that and, in lieu of their failure to allow me to finish my MBA degree work, I felt it was the least they could do. I could not believe my good fortune. Hawaii was the kind of duty station you never asked for, because you might be considered to be a "candy ass." In other words, the duty was just too good to be true, and assignments to Hawaii were hard to get. My orders directed me to report to CINPAC (the DOD acronym for Commander-in-Chief, Pacific) Headquarters at Camp Smith, Hawaii, for duty with the Operations Directorate, by November 27, 1972. I was to contact the Base Transportation Officer in San Diego, to arrange my reassignment transportation to Hawaii.

I told Cathie about my orders and told her I planned to spend a year in Hawaii as a bachelor just to see in what direction our relationship would develop. I told her I was not ready to consider marriage at this time, but that I would certainly keep her informed about my feelings towards a permanent relationship with her and her boys. She was perfectly supportive of my intentions, and made absolutely no demands on me, as I prepared for my Hawaii adventure.

I had experienced three wonderful years in San Diego. I was privileged to have had the three best jobs possible for a Major at the Recruit Depot, I was leaving as a soon to be promoted lieutenant colonel, and I had almost completed a wonderful year living with Cathie. I had made many friends in San Diego, and, as I look back at that time, it is very easy to say that the three years I spent in San Diego, were easily the best three years of my entire career in the Marine Corps. I say this knowing that I had experienced a tremendous amount of great duty stations during my 22 years of service, however, taken as a whole, the San Diego experience was the best. Great duty, good friends, who remain good friends today, and, unbeknownst to me at the time, I had also met my life partner to be.

I reported to the Base Transportation Officer and began my travel arrangements. I was informed that everyone flew to Hawaii and that the government would transport my car by ship, and I would be without a car for approximately three weeks after I arrived in Hawaii. I looked over the travel regulations to Hawaii, and noticed a sentence in one of the regulations that stated that personnel being transferred to Hawaii "could elect surface transportation." I asked the Transportation Officer what this meant, and he told me that this was a holdover from the old days when the military shipped most personnel to Hawaii by ship. This really got my attention, and I asked if these regulations were still in effect. The Transportation Officer said they were, but no one used them anymore. Guess what? I decided I would exercise my right to elect surface transportation and requested transportation to Hawaii by ship. This request created quite a stir in the office. I told them I was sure they would figure it out and to please let me know what I had to do to go to Hawaii by ship.

In a few days, I was informed I had a ticket on the American President Lines ship, *President Cleveland*, an American flag registered cruise ship which would be departing from San Pedro, California, on Friday, November 17, 1972. Based on my ticket, I was also authorized to ship my car on the ship, so I would be able to drive to San Pedro, and watch my car being loaded aboard the same ship that was taking me to Hawaii. This meant that along with everything else, when I arrived in Hawaii, I'd have my car ready and waiting for me at the dock.

I had the usual round of farewell parties and happy hours and, finally, on Wednesday, November 15, 1972, I departed the Recruit Depot for San Pedro and an ocean voyage to Hawaii. Cathie had decided to see me off, and I was very touched by her love and loyalty. I was really sorry to be leaving her, but as I told myself, if I ever got married again, I wanted to be sure I was doing the right thing. There was another aspect to my reluctance to get married. I had lost everything in my divorce from Sharron and with her child support payments and the other monies that I seemed to constantly provide her, I found myself with no money in savings and living from payday to payday. Except for my clothes, my uniforms, and my car, I owned nothing else. Getting married seemed out of the realm of possibility.

CHAPTER 16

HAWAII

CINCPAC

T he American President Lines must have contracted with a local band to play music as the ship departed from the pier at San Pedro. Passengers were given rolls of colored confetti to toss over the side of the ship to the people on the pier. It was a snapshot of a different era when ocean voyages and shipboard life were desirable and sought after by tourists who could afford the luxuries of an ocean liner. The confetti unfurled its way down to the people on the pier and the ship slowly left its' mooring. The people on the pier held on to the paper confetti coils as they caught them, and as the ship slowly departed from the pier, each coil was slowly broken. It was a symbolic parting gesture as contact between the passengers aboard the ship and the people on the pier, was slowly severed.

I waved to Cathie and detected tears in my eyes as I was leaving behind the only woman who had been 100 percent loyal and loving to me, but sure in my heart we would meet again. I stayed on the deck until I could no longer see her. As the ship entered the Pacific Ocean, I looked forward to five days of total relaxation. The Marine Corps had been able to book a single cabin from Los Angeles to Honolulu. Luck was with me simply by doing something different, and insisting on a surface mode of transportation to Hawaii instead of the routine airplane flight.

I had been assigned a sponsor, meaning an officer who was already stationed in Hawaii, who would meet me at the ship, and answer any questions I might have, or provide any assistance I might need. Major Gerry Reczek and his wife, Lisa, were my sponsors, and they were waiting for me at the dock when the ship arrived. Jerry Reczek was a person-able and energetic officer, who informed me that I had been granted 15 days leave to get settled in Hawaii. He informed me that I could move into the Navy BOQ at Makalapa in Pearl Harbor immediately, or I could look around for an appropriate apartment. Jerry recommended I at least look for an apartment, because I could always move into the BOQ whenever I wanted.

He also informed me that I had been assigned to the J-3 section of CINCPAC (Com-mander-in-Chief, Pacific then, but now known as Commander, Unites States Pacific Command (CDRUSPACOM) for duty as the Executive Assistant to the J-3 and the Assistant J-3. He told me that the Marine Headquarters Company that would be monitoring our records was co-located with CINCPAC at Camp H. M. Smith, located in the mountains above Aiea, a small city on Oahu, with a commanding view of the entire Naval Facility at Pearl Harbor.

As we were speaking on the dock, my Opel GT was being unloaded in front of my eyes. I tried to drive it off the dock, but I was informed that I could pick it up on Sand Island in about an hour. Jerry told me that they would drive me over to Sand Island, after I checked into wherever I was staying. I checked into the Reef Hotel (today it is known as the Outrigger Reef Hotel) right on the beach at Waikiki.

I was given a room with an ocean view, and the price of the room was lower than the government per day rate for housing. I told the hotel that I had a vehicle, and they gave me a free parking space on the hotel grounds. I don't think that would happen today. After I moved in, Jerry and Lisa drove me to Sand Island where I picked up my car. We said our good-byes and said that we would see much more of each other once I reported in for duty at CINCPAC.

I drove back to the Reef Hotel and went for a swim in the ocean. I felt as though I was on top of the world. Tomorrow I would begin my apartment hunting in earnest. I had one more thing to do, and that was to call Lieutenant Colonel Johann S. Gestson, USMC. Joh, who was an Icelandic-American, was a classmate of my good friend, Barney Chen, and had already been in Hawaii for over a year, assigned to the J-8 section of CINCPAC.

Joh was a legendary character in the Marine Corps. Joh (apparently the Icelandic way to spell Joe) was quite a drinker and carouser. He hung his hat, at the time, in a local bar in Laguna Beach called the Sandpiper. As a young captain, stationed at Camp Pendleton, he pulled off a caper that brought him nationwide notoriety, and forever secured a place for him in the almanac of zaniness. It was all about a drunken phone call he made one night to a wrong number in Peoria, Illinois, that wound up being a "Hollywood production," when Joh managed to get the man he called by mistake out to the West Coast for a free trip to meet him. Along the way, stars like Jayne Mansfield, Sammy Davis, Jr. the L.A. Dodgers and the mayor of Laguna Beach got involved. It was a wild caper and probably helped shorten Joh's career in the Marine Corps.

I reported to CINCPAC Headquarters on Monday morning, November 27, 1972. After processing my paperwork in the Marine administrative section of CINCPAC, I reported to the J-3 Division for duty. The J-3 Division was the Operations Branch of the combined staff and was directly responsible to the Commander-in-Chief, Pacific, for all operations taking place in the entire Pacific region.

In 1972, Vietnam was still going on, although a cease-fire would be signed in Paris between Henry Kissinger and Le Duc Tho on January 28, 1973. We continued bombing Cambodia, attempting to interdict and neutralize the Ho Chi Minh trail and cut off what later became the occupation of South Vietnam by the North Vietnamese. When the United States, later in the year, decided unilaterally to end the bombing on August 15,

1973, the road to a North Vietnamese victory became stronger and inevitable. Even with the cease-fire having been signed, the prisoners of war were not freed from the "Hanoi Hilton" until February 12, 1973, when the first contingent of prisoners were released, and lasted until March 29, 1973, when the final group arrived at Clark Air Force Base in the Philippines.

My job, as the Executive Assistant to the Director of Operations, allowed me information on these events not available to many people, either then or now. Many varied and separate regions of the Pacific theater, such as Laos, Cambodia and South Vietnam, were still teetering on the edge of chaos. American troops remained in Southeast Asia, and the political climates throughout the Pacific Rim were highly unpredictable and susceptible to almost any provocation.

The J-3 Division, to which I reported for duty that Monday morning, was charged with the responsibility to respond to all threats in the Pacific theater of operations. In discharging this duty, two, round-the-clock command centers were maintained, staffed by officers trained to take immediate, emergency actions. One of the command centers was located in a bomb proof bunker at Camp Smith, located at the site of a former US Naval Hospital in Aiea, Hawaii, while the other command center was airborne and located inside a specially configured Boeing 707 that remained airborne throughout its two week tour of duty, using aerial refueling procedures to keep that command center airborne and fully operational. Both command centers were staffed by officers from all four branches of service, and the command center crews were broken down into four teams, with three teams working 8 hours per day, every day for two weeks, and then one of the crews would take one week off before they would again begin another two week shift.

Each shift was dictated by the time of the day so that one crew worked from 8 a.m. to 4 p.m., the next shift worked from 4 p.m. to midnight, and the third shift worked from midnight to 8 a.m. The fourth shift was off for two weeks, and this rotation kept everyone working equitably, although changing working hours every two weeks was somewhat of a strain on all watch-standers. The airborne group did the same thing, although, they remained airborne for two weeks, and then returned to Honolulu to replenish crews, and then took off again.

When I reported for duty, I was informed that my security clearances had not yet arrived from Washington, and I was encouraged to take another week off in Waikiki, since, without the security clearances, I could not even set foot inside the complex where I was supposed to be working. I was also informed that I would be a watch-stander until a separate set of security clearances arrived, at which point I would be assigned duty as the Executive Assistant to the Director of Operations and the Deputy Director of Operations. These two officers were both General Officers, the Director being a Marine Major General and the Deputy was an Air Force Brigadier General.

The security clearances that I was waiting for, were so classified, that it is against the law, then and now, to even name the type of clearances. Suffice it to say that very little of what went on in the United States government would be unknown to me, once my clearances came through, and I began my assignment. I was told that my clearances would come through in sections, and after the arrival of the first section, I would be qualified to become a command center watch-stander. When the final section arrived, I would transfer to my assigned position with the two generals. In the interim, I had another week off, and more time to hang out in Waikiki, and enjoy all the benefits of a Hawaiian vacation, with pay.

I met Joh again in the evening at the *Top of the I* at the Ilikai Hotel for several drinks, and to check over the available stock of single women. After about an hour, we went to the Chart House, where Bobby the piano player, began playing old Hawaiian songs, and the mood of the place became far more mellow than the frenetic pace of the Top of the I. The bar began to fill up rather quickly, and Joh and I retained our seats at the far end of the bar. During the evening, I began to realize that I did not want to live my life the way Joh did.

While the idea of going out every night in Waikiki and becoming a regular at almost all the well-known night spots was appealing, the reality quickly sank in and convinced me that, even though I had just moved into a Waikiki Beach penthouse, my life would go in another direction. Perhaps these thoughts, coupled with several days of making inane conversation with a succession of single women, influenced my thinking. Towards the end of the evening, I asked the bartender for the Ericaphone, which was kept behind the bar for the use of bar patrons, and Keoki, the bartender, brought it to our location at the end of the bar. I dialed Cathie's number in San Diego, realizing that besides it being very late, it was even two hours later in San Diego, and asked her to marry me. I was very happy she accepted my proposal, and I told her I would call her in the morning to discuss exactly how we were going to pull it off. I hung up the phone, and bought a round of drinks for everyone at the bar, then informed Joh that I had proposed to Cathie and that she had accepted my proposal.

Joh was quite supportive and happy for me, and the evening ended on an upbeat and euphoric note that left me very pleased with the new direction my life was about to take. I called Cathie the following morning and filled her in on a few more details, the most important of which was the fact that I had signed a six-month lease for my apartment, and couldn't move out of it until May 1973. The lease stipulated no children, so if she came over to join me in Hawaii, we didn't have a place for Tim and Don to stay. She told me that we would work this out, and I told her that I would come to San Diego for Christmas, where we could develop more detailed plans. I began to spend my days playing racquetball at the Central YMCA in downtown Honolulu. Since I couldn't go to work without my clearance, a fact I thought was ridiculous since the Marine Corps could have begun the clearance process long before I reported for duty, I spent many hours at the Y.

I noticed that I was one of the few haole's (Hawaiian for a white man), playing during the day. There were many local men, including several well-known entertainers, who regularly played racquetball at the Y. I had decided that the best way to get along, was to say nothing, other than hello, thank you, and good bye, and began playing games on courts where the loser left the court, and the next man waiting went in. I began to win quite a few games, and remained on the court longer than usual, thereby meeting many of the day time players. They said nothing to me, except a perfunctory hello, thanks and goodbye, however, I did notice that after several days, while not necessarily friendly, they began to accept my presence, and did not scowl in my direction.

This, by the way, is the real "aloha" spirit, which says, if I want to accept you at all, I'll let you know when. It was not the tourist type aloha commercialism spouted by the Hawaii Convention and Visitors Bureau, which seems to convey the message that all Hawaiians sing songs, dance the hula and love tourists. Each morning I called CINCPAC to check on my clearance and each day I was informed that it had not yet arrived. My racquetball skills were improving dramatically, and after one week, a few of the locals at the Y began to at least acknowledge that I was alive.

On 4 December, the first part of my clearance finally arrived, and I was assigned duty as a command center watch-stander on the midnight to 8 a.m. shift. I was also very happy to find out that this shift was going to get the Christmas holidays off, so I made immediate plans to fly to San Diego to spend Christmas with Cathie and the boys.

The duty in the command center consisted of maintaining contact with all military units in the Pacific theater. The center was full of closed circuit TV monitors, dedicated channel radio frequencies and all other types of ultra-secure communications, which enabled constant contact with all military organizations, actively in the field, in the entire Pacific theater of operations. Besides maintaining contact with all the Pacific theater forces, we were in constant contact with the *Blue Eagle* (the code name given to the airborne command center) and the NMCC (National Military Command Center) located in the bowels of the Pentagon (Like our Blue Eagle Airborne Command Center, the Pentagon had the same setup in the air over the European and Middle Eastern sectors of the world.)

All of our communications were integrated, and at any time, each senior watch commander could communicate with his opposite number at the other command center locations, including any of the airborne command centers. Each watch crew was commanded by a full colonel or Navy captain and they, in turn, had seven other officers ranging in rank from major or lieutenant colonel, serving on their watch teams. As a Marine member, my responsibilities included monitoring all Marine units in the field.

Every morning at 8 a.m., the Commander-in-Chief of the Pacific Command, a Navy 4 star Admiral named Noel Gayler, was briefed on the previous day's activities. This meant that every morning at 5 a.m., the briefing officers arrived to prepare the daily briefing. This was a high stress job, as Admiral Gayler was a tyrant, and took out all of his frustrations/anger on briefing officers who did not get their facts straight. If he could not satisfy himself by bullying the briefing officers, he would then begin to harangue the General and Flag officers on his staff, who were required to attend the 8 a.m. briefings.

With this type of pressure, the midnight to 8 a.m. shift worked diligently to make the daily briefings flawless. I was glad that I wasn't assigned duty as a briefing officer, not because I couldn't do the job, but because it would be very difficult for me to maintain my composure, once Admiral Gayler took off on one of his raving critiques of everything from the briefer's uniform, to the accuracy of his reports. Later, when all of my clearances finally came in, and I was assigned as the Executive Assistant of the two General officers who were the directors of operations, I witnessed Admiral Gayler's petulant, personal vendettas on a daily basis.

My first two weeks of watch standing went off without incident, and on Friday morning, December 22, 1972, I flew to San Diego to spend Christmas with Cathie and the boys. I left my penthouse in the hands of a house sitter who I had met on the nightlife scene of Waikiki who was a friend and drinking buddy of Joh Gestson.

My first Christmas with Cathie and the boys, who would become my permanent family, turned out to be a wonderful experience. Stockings, gifts and all the Christmas traditions were observed with great gusto and enthusiastic support. Wonderful moments around a tree, a great dinner, and the warmth and comfort of a family, and a loving partner helped to make the Christmas of 1972, one of the most memorable in my life. During my visit, Cathie and I talked about the logistics of both our wedding, which would be set when Cathie could get to Hawaii, and, what we would do with the boys, since they could not live with us in the penthouse in Waikiki. It was determined that Cathie's parents, who lived in Long Beach, California, would take care of the boys until I had secured permanent living quarters in Hawaii. It looked like everything was ready to go, and, as I boarded the flight back to Honolulu, I was counting the days until Cathie could join me in Paradise.

I returned to Honolulu on Friday 5 January 1973, just in time to begin a new watch schedule beginning on Sunday, January 7. I was lucky in that my watch schedule was going to be from 8 a.m. to 4 p.m. for the next two weeks, which would give me some time to begin planning for my upcoming wedding.

On Monday morning, January 15, I was informed that my security clearances were still in the works and that I would remain as a command center watch-stander until they arrived. When that occurred, I would be transferred to the office of the Director of Operations for duty as his Executive Assistant. I was scheduled to relieve Lieutenant Colonel Wally Fogo, USMC, who had spent the past few years in the assignment, and his tour of duty would be extended until all of my security clearances were completed. I remember Wally Fogo, not only as a classmate from my Basic School days, but an outstanding Marine. Wally and his wife, Dot, were a credit to the Marine Corps and the Hawaii officers community.

Based on my impending assignment to duty as an Executive Assistant, I was informed that the job came with a set of fully furnished quarters in the primarily US Naval officers housing area of McGrew Base Housing, located right on the water, on a spit of land overlooking the infamous Ford Island, where the Japanese attack on Pearl Harbor occurred on December 7, 1941, the singular event that propelled the United States into World War II.

The housing area, while near to the main Pearl Harbor Naval Base, was an overall part of the base itself. This stroke of good luck would make my transition from bachelor to a married man with two children, almost painless. Since both Cathie and I had hardly any money between us, the fact that we were going to be assigned completely furnished quarters, at no expense to us, was going to be of great assistance as we began our lives together. Since Cathie was Catholic by birth, I thought that a Catholic ceremony might be possible. The Navy Chief of Chaplains in Hawaii was a Jesuit Priest by the name of Jake La Boone, Captain, USN.

Father La Boone was one of the most interesting priests/chaplains in the US Navy. He graduated from the US Naval Academy as an Ensign in 1942, and was assigned submarine duty, serving as a submarine officer throughout the remainder of the war. During one patrol in the Pacific he had been awarded a Silver Star for valor, and at war's end, was a lieutenant (equivalent to a Marine Corps rank of captain). It was at this point that he decided that he wanted to become a priest, and he resigned his commission and went into the seminary.

Many years later, as a full-fledged Jesuit priest, Jake volunteered for duty as a Navy Chaplain and served with both Navy and Marine units. I had met Jake in Vietnam, where a priest who was a graduate of the US Naval Academy, who wore a Silver Star ribbon, and the gold submarine insignia with four patrol stars on the wings, had very little trouble relating to the troops at any level. When you included his native intelligence and his quick-witted good humor, he was the complete package and a model chaplain, of any denomination, for military personnel.

Besides everything else, Jake and I shared a love of poker, and we played together wherever we could find a game. When Jake was assigned duty as the Chief Chaplain of the Pacific Command, it did not take long before I was invited to join in on his weekly poker games, which were always played at his quarters in the Makalapa housing area of Pearl Harbor, an area reserved for Captains, Colonels, Generals and Admirals. It was at one of these poker games, that I asked if I could speak with him after the game, and requested his assistance in getting married in a Catholic ceremony.

While Jake was my friend, he was also a hard line priest, and a devout Jesuit. After hearing that both Cathie and I were divorced and that the marriage would be our second marriage, he absolutely refused to participate in my wedding. Furthermore, he refused permission for any Catholic Navy Chaplain to marry us in a catholic ceremony. While it wasn't exactly the answer that I was looking for, I respected his candor and understood his position. I vowed to take all his money at our next poker game.

Sitting in on this particular poker game was another Jesuit priest, who had been a battalion chaplain in Vietnam, and, whom I knew from the fact that he had served with the 7th Marine Regiment and at MCRD, San Diego when I was there. His name was Vincent Germano, and as we walked out of Jake's quarters, he whispered to me that he would marry us, provided that I never said anything about the ceremony to Jake La Boone. He went on to say that he could not marry us in a Catholic ceremony but that he would improvise a ceremony, and sign our wedding certificate as a Catholic priest. I was elated with this turn of events, and told him that I would get in touch with him a soon as I found a place to get married.

Vinnie told me that he could get the small and very charming chapel located on the Submarine Base at Pearl Harbor, and that the chapel would be a great location for a small wedding. Being at the Submarine Base, it was also pretty removed from any CINCPAC activities, and I realized immediately that Vinnie meant that it was far removed from the watchful eyes of Jake La Boone. I agreed immediately, and we shook hands on the deal, waiting only for an appropriate day and time.

In the meantime, Cathie arrived in Hawaii on Friday, January 26, 1973. She had closed out the house in San Diego, moved her children to her parent's house in Long Beach, and was joining me in Hawaii to get married and to begin preparations for moving into our quarters at the McGrew Housing Area. In the meantime, we would enjoy Hawaii together and have an extended honeymoon. The ban on children in The Tradewinds, had, unwittingly, provided us with a wonderful time together without any distractions, except for Joh Gestson, of course.

Immediately after Cathie's arrival, Joh and I took her to the weekly luau at Fort DeRussy. Fort DeRussy, now no longer in existence, was located on the beach between the Hilton Hawaiian Village Hotel and the Reef Hotel. It had been an old coastal artillery base before the First World War, and the wooden, tropical buildings were still in use as an island recreational center. The Fort stood on what was probably the longest and smoothest section of Waikiki Beach, and it boasted an elegant Officer's Club, a wonderful Staff Non-commissioned Officer's Club and an Enlisted Club, all on the grounds of the Fort, and all facing a pristine, white sand beach.

 Only military personnel could enter the Fort, and its' location and private use by the military, had long been a sore point with the local inhabitants of the island. Fort DeRussy was apparently located directly over the grounds of one of King Kamehameha's royal fishing ponds. Nevertheless, in 1973, it was a private enclave of the military, right in the heart of Waikiki Beach. Every Friday evening, Fort DeRussy sponsored the largest Luau in the islands, using a professional caterer from the islands, and the most prominent Hawaiian dance troupe in Honolulu. The sounds of the music drifted from Fort DeRussy throughout Waikiki Beach, but only military personnel and their dependents, were in attendance.

The following day, we met with Vinnie Germano, who told us that he was able to obtain the Submarine Chapel for Wednesday, the 7th of February, at 5 p.m.. It was to be a quick and very private wedding, which would include only him, Cathie and me, and two witnesses. He was worried about Jake La Boone discovering him, and the faster he could officiate at the wedding and clear the chapel, the more comfortable he was going to feel.

I asked Major Tom Campbell, a Marine I knew from Vietnam, who was also a fellow watch-stander, to be my best man, and his wife, Nancy, became Cathie's Maid of Honor. On Wednesday afternoon, we were married in a lovely ceremony that Vinnie Germano had constructed especially for us, and upon the conclusion of the ceremony, Vinnie presented us with a certificate of marriage, attesting to the fact that we had been married in the Submarine Chapel of the Submarine Base of the Pearl Harbor Naval Station in Honolulu, Hawaii. The certificate was dated February 7, 1973, and it was full of anchors and nautical logos, in keeping with its' naval origins.

When the chapel was finished, the crew of the USS Argonaut (SS 166) donated their ship's bell just before they departed on their next wartime patrol. It was a patrol from which they never returned. The submarine was sunk by the Japanese, somewhere in the western Pacific Ocean. The bell remains in the belfry to this day, sounding the unusually haunting sound of a submarine bell as the tolling of the bell summons Sailors and Marines to services. I was very proud that we had gotten married in this building, and Cathie and I return to this chapel every time we visit Hawaii.

On January 28, just a few short days before our wedding, the United States and North Vietnam signed a cease-fire, and American troops began an orderly withdrawal from Vietnam. Life in the command center was hectic, as operations and troop movements were monitored all the way up to the White House. While still living in Waikiki, I continued working the various shifts at the command center, and preparing for our eventual move into government quarters. My clearances were somewhere between Washington and Honolulu, however, I was not yet cleared to assume the job for which I had received orders in November of 1972.

On February 12, 1973, the first POW's were released from Hanoi, and they continued coming home until the final group touched down on the tarmac of Hickam Air Force Base in Hawaii, during the first week of April 1973. Unknown to the American public, the POW's were not immediately released to their families. When the first contingent was released, a group was set up, staffed by the CIA, Naval Intelligence, the Defense Intelligence Agency and the FBI. These intelligence groups were augmented by psychiatrists, psychologists and social workers, and then, all personnel were flown directly to Clark Air Force Base in the Philippines. No press or photographers were allowed anywhere near the POW's and the operation was highly classified. The purpose of this operation was to debrief each POW immediately upon their release from prison. As the POW's arrived, they were immediately segregated into individual hospital rooms, where they were joined by their debriefing team. This team remained with the POW until the entire regimen of debriefings were completed. This allowed each POW to report independently, what exactly happened to him, and to recall as many names and incidents as possible.

The debriefing reports were all classified Top Secret. Later, in my capacity as the Executive Assistant to the Directors of Operations in the Pacific theater, I was able to read almost all the debriefings. They were poignant, complimentary and damning, naming names of American traitors and heroes, war criminals, and compassionate jailers, plus a great deal of never divulged information concerning Jane Fonda, and the results of some of her actions in North Vietnam. Since these documents are still classified today, it is sufficient to say that words alone could never describe the treachery of Jane Fonda, and I only hope that someday, these facts become known to the American public.

When the POW's began coming home to their families at Hickam Air Force Base in Hawaii, all of them had already undergone debriefings at Clark Air Force Base in the

Philippines for close to three weeks, plus fittings for new uniforms, complete with new rank insignia, and appropriate ribbons. Nevertheless, Admiral Gayler, the egocentric and narcissistic Commander-in-Chief of the Pacific, met every POW as he came down the steps from the aircraft at Hickam, assuring himself a place in military history, since he was photographed with each POW as they arrived on American soil. After the Admiral shook hands with each POW, their families were then allowed to run to them as they walked away from the plane, making for many memorable photographs. Unfortunately, not all POW's came home to happy households, as was later well documented, upon their return to "normal life" in the United States.

About a month after Cathie's 28th birthday, we were notified that a 3-bedroom house had become available at 22 McGrew Loop in the McGrew Housing area on the base at Pearl Harbor. The housing area was located in the small town of Aiea, Hawaii, which became both our mailing address and our school district. We had enjoyed our short residence in Waikiki.

Another interesting event that occurred while we were living in Waikiki was our acceptance into a very tightly knit local community. I continued going to the YMCA, where I was playing racquetball when I wasn't working. One day, out of the blue, one of the local Hawaiian players approached me and asked me if I wanted to go to a party that they were having at the Primo Brewery Picnic Area (then, Primo Beer was the most popular beer on the islands, and it was a local company that had been brewing beer in Hawaii since 1898).

The Company had only one brewery in downtown Honolulu, but after it was sold to the Joseph Schlitz Brewing Company of St. Louis. Missouri, a brand new brewery was built in Pearl City, located practically right on the water, near Pearl Harbor, and, as a gesture of community involvement, the company maintained a beautiful picnic area on the grounds of the brewery, which they allowed local groups to use for no fee. The only requirement was to reserve the area, through the brewery public relations department, a process that required almost six months of prior planning, due to the large number of groups who wanted to use the picnic area.

There had been a tremendous outcry from all the locals, begging the owners not to sell, but the price offered was just too good to pass up, and the sale was completed. Since Joseph Schlitz took over the company and retained all the local workers, and continued to run the local brewery, making Primo only in Hawaii, business continued to prosper. In 1981, the company was again sold, this time to the Stroh Brewery, who shut down the local brewery, and moved the entire brewing operation to the mainland. Local jobs were lost, and the local flavor of Primo disappeared.

Life in downtown Waikiki continued for us until the middle of April 1973, when we had to decide whether to move into the 3-bedroom house that had become available in the McGrew housing area in Pearl Harbor. We had exactly two weeks, from April 15 to make a decision on this house, or we would lose it to the next person on the list. For us, it was a godsend, and I felt that the possibility of losing one month's rent on the penthouse was well worth moving into our first house together.

It would also enable us to bring Tim and Don to Hawaii almost immediately, and reunite them with their mother, not to mention relieving Cathie's parents of the responsibility of taking care of the boys. We moved into our new home at 22 McGrew Loop in the McGrew Housing area of Pearl Harbor on Friday, April 20, 1973. It was the easiest move we would ever have in our life together. We only had the clothes on our backs and what we had hanging in our closet at The Tradewinds. Since we had no furniture or personal possessions, we moved into a fully furnished Hawaiian-style house and by the end of the weekend, we were firmly established in our new home.

The Tradewinds management gave me further good news, in that they already had a prospective tenant for the penthouse, and therefore, I would not lose any money on my early departure from our Waikiki retreat. A memorable story that occurred after we moved in to our new quarters happened between the maintenance department and me at Pearl Harbor. The custom in Navy housing areas was to have a blue and gold sign placed in the front yard of each house, which contained the complete name and rank of the inhabitant of the quarters. Since these were US Navy quarters, all the signs were in Navy "blue and gold." Since I was a Marine, I asked the maintenance department if they would mind making my sign in Marine Corps "red and gold." They had never received such a request before, and indicated that there were 7 other Marines living at McGrew, and no one had ever asked for such a differentiation.

Luckily, one of the maintenance workers was a retired Marine, and he agreed with me. Not only was he willing to make a red and gold sign for me, he was going to replace all the Navy "blue and gold" signs that were placed at Marine's houses at McGrew with the new Marine "red and gold" signs. In a few weeks, for the first time in the history of the McGrew Housing area, every Marine living in the housing area had a red and gold sign in front of their houses. To this day, the sign remains a treasured possession and currently is on the wall of my garage. On a recent visit to Hawaii, Cathie and I drove through the McGrew housing area, which is now under strict security regulations, and we were happy to see that the "red and gold" signs still exist at McGrew.

I continued working in the Command Center as a watch-stander throughout April, May and June, but with a family trying to live a normal life, working three different shifts and trying to sleep in between,"normal" life for me became a challenge.

In the middle of July, I received word from the Headquarters Company office at Fleet Marine Forces, Pacific, which was co-located with CINCPAC at Camp Smith, that my promotion to lieutenant colonel had arrived. I called the company office and asked them when they wanted me to come in for the promotion. The company clerk told me that I could come in anytime, so I informed him that I would be there the next day at 10 a.m.

The day of my promotion, I put on a clean uniform, Cathie got dressed up in a perfect "Officer's Wives Club" outfit, looking every bit the part of an officer's wife, and we both drove up to Camp Smith for my promotion. Together we walked into the company office, and I informed the clerk who I was and why we were there. The previous day, I had bought a set of lieutenant colonel's silver oak leaves, which Cathie was going to pin on my collars.

The clerk seemed surprised to see both of us, and simply reached into a file cabinet and handed me my promotion. It had been properly signed and endorsed and indicated that I was now a lieutenant colonel. There was no ceremony, and no ceremony had even been planned. The commanding officer was not in his office, and as far as the clerk was concerned, I was promoted, and the issue was closed.

Cathie and I left the office and looked for a place to change my major's gold oak leaves for my new lieutenant colonel's silver oak leaves. We found a broom closet in the hallway of the Camp Smith wing, where the Headquarters Company office was located, and Cathie took off my major's leaves and put on my lieutenant colonel's leaves in the closet. We had a good laugh about the "promotion ceremony," but it really hurt me, and I never forgot it. It was another leadership lesson taught by an unfeeling and uncaring commanding officer, who apparently didn't think that promoting a Marine to a higher rank was very important.

I never forgot how I felt that day and, in my heart, I am sure that it was one of the contributing reasons to my early retirement from the Corps I loved so much. We walked to the Officer's Club and toasted my new promotion. Little did I know at the time, that this would be my last promotion. We went out to dinner before I reported for duty on the graveyard shift at the Command Center. I walked into the Command Center, wearing my new rank insignia, and no one noticed until I informed everyone that I had been promoted and that they had all missed the "wetting down" party.

In the Marine Corps, it is customary to give a party at the Officer's Club bar when you get promoted. You buy everyone present a round or two of drinks, and this "wets down" your new rank and promotion. At the mention of a wetting down party, my peers took notice, and I received a chorus of forced congratulations. Nothing else changed in my duties since I had been assigned to the Command Center as a prospective lieutenant colonel.

On August 1, 1973, I was called into the office of Major General Ralph J. (*Smoke*) Spanjer, USMC, who was a World War II fighter pilot and who was the Director of Operations of the Pacific Command. He informed me that my clearances had finally come through and that I would assume the duty as the Executive Assistant to the Director of Operations on Monday, August 6, 1973.

I would spend the next five days understanding all the security clearances that I had been assigned, and learning the job from the outgoing Executive Assistant, Lt Col Wally Fogo, USMC, a classmate of mine from Basic School, where he had been the only First Lieutenant in the class. Besides serving as the Executive Assistant, I would also serve as the Aide-de-camp for Major General Spanjer and for Brigadier General James A. Young, USAF, one of the legendary heroes of the US Air Force, who was the Deputy Director of Operations for the Pacific Command.

General Young had been horribly burned in an aircraft crash while serving in Korea as a fighter pilot. He spent the next four years in burn hospitals, where he went through extremely painful restorative surgeries. It left his face disfigured, in that his eyebrows and lips had to be surgically replaced. Along the way, he became addicted to pain killer medicines and alcohol. Through his own self-control, he was able to break his addictions and return to flight status. Reader's Digest published a long story about his determined recuperation entitled, *The Man Who Would Not Die.*

During the Vietnam War, General Young was the Group Commander of an F-105 Fighter Group. He flew 105 missions over North Vietnam, even though he knew that if he had to eject from his aircraft in an emergency, the gravitational forces exerted on his body would destroy all the skin grafts and restorative surgery. It never stopped him for a minute. Besides all of this, General Young began his military career as an Army enlisted paratrooper, who applied to flight school, was accepted, and then went into the Air Force.

Working for General Young was one of the highlights of my career, and I learned a great deal about leadership and interpersonal relationships from this truly great American Warrior. One of my prized possessions is an autographed photograph of him, which he gave me and inscribed it with the statement, " To Pete Beck, A true Marine and Friend, Keep Charging. Jim Young, BGen, USAF."

I said my goodbyes to the watch standers in the Command Center and moved into the General's office immediately. There, I met Chief Master Sergeant Rod Rodriquez, USAF. Rod was a rare breed in 1973, in that he was an official Air Force stenographer, who took shorthand and typed faster than any human being I had ever seen. Rod spent his entire career in the Air Force, going from one sensitive assignment to another, and I felt privileged to work with him. Rod and I ran the office for the two Generals. We set up all meetings, briefings and interviews, and while Rod managed the office, I accompanied the Generals whenever one or the other left the office.

My duties were extremely time consuming, and as I took hold in my new job, I discovered that 14 to 16 hour days were normal, and certainly not the exception. Besides dealing with all personnel in the J-3 Directorate, which is the official military title of the Operations Department of CINCPAC, I had to come to work every morning by 6 a.m., to debrief the Command Center personnel for any late breaking news concerning any military events in Southeast Asia. Then, I would continue to the Message Center, where I would get all incoming message traffic for the Operations Division, and begin to read and classify the information, so that by 7 a.m., when the General's arrived, they could begin to prepare for their daily morning briefing with Admiral Gayler.

While these briefings should have been simply routine updates, with Admiral Gayler, they were anything but that. The briefings became daily hunting trips for Admiral Gayler, as he worked diligently to make at least one General Officer look like a complete idiot at each briefing. With the tremendous volume of activity in Southeast Asia, occurring all over the region, it was impossible to know every detail of each event, every day. While each Directorate Chief gave the Admiral his daily update in their respective areas of interest, Admiral Gayler would routinely pick out some arcane and almost irrelevant item, which he culled from their briefing, and ask some specific question, which the Admiral knew that the General conducting the briefing did not know. When the briefer was forced into admitting that he did not know the answer, the Admiral would begin to lecture the General, in front of all attendees, that he should have known the answer to his question.

He generally followed up this lecture by directing the General being questioned to provide him with the answer to his question within the next ten minutes after the briefing concluded. It became a game with all the Generals and Admirals, where they all tried to figure out what a ridiculous question the Admiral was going to ask. The only Generals who did not play this game were General Spanjer and General Young, my two bosses, who preferred simply to classify Admiral Gayler as a complete asshole, and answer questions they thought were relevant.

This show of strength seemed to put off the Admiral because, like all bully's, he tended to direct his questions towards those senior officers who became flustered at his questions. I sat in the back row of the briefing room, with all the other Executive Assistants, and marveled at the idiocy that was going on in front of me. I remember thinking that if that was what it took to become a General, I didn't want it. I always enjoyed the post-briefing meetings in General Spanjer's office, when he and General Young would just laugh at how up tight and arrogant Admiral Gayler behaved.

I was aware of the high level of stress that these briefings placed on the other General officers and their Executive Assistants, and thanked my lucky stars to be working for such true warriors as Generals Spanjer and Young. The geopolitical situation in Southeast Asia in 1973, was, at best convoluted. Almost every day, news from that part of the world surfaced which affected the lives of all people in the region, and those of the American forces stationed in Southeast Asia.

Admiral Gayler, as the Commander-in-Chief of the Pacific was directly answerable to the Chairman of the Joint Chiefs of Staff and the President of the United States, for anything that occurred in the Pacific theater. This fact alone, provided undue stress on every member of the Pacific Command, and accounted for round the clock surveillance of the entire region by radio, airborne command posts, and field reports, that arrived at Camp Smith in Hawaii, twenty-four hours a day. Admiral Gayler insisted on being briefed at any time of the day or night, depending on the severity of the event in the region. Since almost 95 percent of any events were of an operational nature, the Operations Directorate never slept, and, like a local fire station, was always open.

In January of 1973, then President Richard Nixon, together with the governments of North Vietnam, South Vietnam and the Viet Cong political party, reached what became known as the Paris Peace Accords. The document was signed in Paris, France, on the 27th of January, and stipulated that all US forces would withdraw from Vietnam within 60 days after the signing of the accords. On the same day as the peace accords were signed, the United States ended the draft, making service to the country voluntary.

In my opinion, this was the single worst result of the Vietnam War, because it ended, for all time, any requirement for an American citizen to have to serve his country. Henceforth, only the poor, the disadvantaged, people who were unemployed or could not get a job, or the truly dedicated patriot, would serve their country. This left a huge majority of young people who had no allegiance to their country, and no desire to serve anyone but themselves. We are still seeing the results of these attitudes in 2012, where the new generations seem to have a feeling of entitlement, without ever having to work for it and where reliable national surveys have proven that only 1 percent of the eligible population of the United States has ever served their country in the military services. This fact extends from the current President of the United States, (2012) to over 95 percent of our elected representatives and our population as a whole.

The strength of the antiwar riots and demonstrations that were almost a daily occurrence throughout the country, fueled a move in Congress to draft and pass the Case-Church amendment, which forbade further US military involvement in Southeast Asia effective August 15, 1973. The amendment was veto-proof and passed by overwhelming margins in both the House (278 to 124) and the Senate (64 to 26). This amendment, while greeted enthusiastically by the American people, also signaled the North Vietnamese that henceforth, the United States would not oppose any actions that they took in their efforts to conquer South Vietnam. To the South Vietnamese government, it was an admission of defeat and loss of resolve that has become the bellwether of American foreign policy, and, based on our internationally perceived lack of will to "stay the course," allows revolutionary movements throughout the world to thrive.

In June of 1973, Graham Martin was appointed the US Ambassador to South Vietnam, and on August 14, 1973, two weeks after I became the Executive Assistant to the Operations Directorate of the Pacific Command, US bombings in Cambodia, a major supplier of the North Vietnamese Army, were halted. This constant level of activity throughout the Pacific Command kept everyone occupied for long hours, day and night. Social lives were put on hold, and my life revolved around the command bunker, daily briefings, emergency meetings, last-minute changes, and strategic updates that seemed to change almost as fast as the time of day.

Cathie became the bedrock of our family, in that she had to take care of the boys, and the quarters, attend Marine Officer's Wives Club functions, do all the commissary shopping, take care of medical emergencies, attend school functions, and participate in after-school activities, such as Little League, Pop Warner Football and the Pearl Harbor Swim Club. She performed all of these myriad tasks and responsibilities while attending Leeward Community College, a branch of the University of Hawaii. She was pursuing an Associate of Arts degree in Liberal Arts. Before departing Hawaii, she accomplished this goal, graduating with honors, and receiving an AA Degree from the University of Hawaii. I was then, and still am, very proud of her and her accomplishments.

As I settled into the job, I became very comfortable with both General Spanjer and General Young. They were both real human beings, who never acted superior in any way, and who were both very people-oriented. On top of that, though they were in different branches of the service, they were both fighter pilots, and had a genuine liking for each other that made working in the stressful environment of the Operations Directorate a far more pleasant experience. They absorbed all the invective that emanated from the Admiral, and never passed it down the line. They were both living leadership examples, and every member of the Operations Directorate was aware of their skills. There wasn't an officer or an enlisted man who did not like and respect both Generals.

Another one of my jobs was to be the unofficial "Marine Corps Spy" at the Pacific Command and to report on a daily basis, to Lieutenant General Louis Wilson, the Commanding General of the Fleet Marine Forces, Pacific (FMFPAC), whose Headquarters were also located at Camp Smith. The age-old rivalry between the Navy and the Marine Corps was very much alive and well at Camp Smith in 1973. Admiral Gayler ran his command very much like a personal fiefdom. Everything went through him, and he dispensed information to subordinate commands only if he felt that it was necessary. Unfortunately, he rarely felt it was necessary, and, therefore, his subordinate commanders, all at least three star Generals or Admirals, were often left in the dark, and caught short when a crisis erupted, and they were not fully informed. General Wilson, a Medal of Honor recipient during World War II in the Marine Corps campaign on Guam, did not appreciate this attitude. He asked General Spanjer to keep him informed daily, and General Spanjer selected me to brief the General daily, immediately after the morning briefing given to Admiral Gayler.

Since FMFPAC headquarters was on the fourth floor of the building at Camp Smith, and CINCPAC occupied the lower three floors, it was easy for me to simply walk up one flight of stairs each morning, and brief General Wilson and his staff. I did this for three years and never did anyone at CINCPAC find out about it. It must have surprised Admiral Gayler how well informed General Wilson always appeared to be, however, he never openly demonstrated any curiosity. It was just another way for the Marine Corps to "one up" the Navy, in particular, Admiral Gayler, and his self-important demeanor.

When the Headquarters of the Commander-in-Chief, Pacific co-located to Camp Smith in October of 1957, the Marine command retained the top floor of the former hospital (the only floor with a great view of the Pearl Harbor base and the entire surrounding areas) and gave the remainder of the building to the Joint Command. In 1973, this arrangement was still in place, and LtGen Wilson was in an office that had been the hospital room where he had been treated in 1943 after the battle of Guam. It was to this office that I reported each day, immediately following the daily CINCPAC briefings.

I was required to take copious notes during Admiral Gayler's briefings, and I remember that all the other Executive Assistant's wondered why I was such a diligent note taker. Obviously, I was preparing my briefing for General Wilson during Admiral Gayler's briefing, a fact that gave me a great deal of personal pleasure.

Cathie and I enjoyed all the wonderful aspects of life in Hawaii during the times in my schedule that allowed me to participate. All Hawaiian restaurants and show venues would give a "kamaaina" (local, in Hawaiian) discount. All that was required was showing a local Hawaii driver's license. This would automatically get you a better table, a lower price, and quicker service, than any of the tourists who were visiting Honolulu.

My days at the Downtown YMCA playing racquetball, also made me a friend of several of the local entertainers, and it was easy for me to get tickets to see Don Ho, Dick Jensen and Danny Kalikini, all racquetball players from the Downtown Y. We went to Michel's at least once a month, and our headwaiter friend, Horst, always gave us a wonderful table, right on the beach. I am sure that guests wondered who we were, especially the night that Mark Spitz came into Michel's, and couldn't get a beachfront table, because Horst had just given us the last one available.

General Spanjer enjoyed going out in Waikiki, and there were several nights where we would go out together, wearing white turtle neck sweaters, blue blazers and sleek trousers, looking for all the world like a couple of real big spenders. I remember thinking at the time, how lucky I was to be working for such a great guy, who was a real joy to be with, and who never seemed to care that I was very much his junior, a fact that I never forgot.

Meanwhile, work at CINCPAC did not slow down. In October of 1973, Vice President Spiro T. Agnew was forced to resign, due to some inappropriate transactions that occurred during his tenure as the Governor of Maryland. The press was relentless in its coverage of his misdemeanors, and finally, on October 10, he resigned, and was replaced by Gerald Ford, the Senator from Michigan.

On November 7, 1973, Congress passed the War Powers Resolution Act, which required congressional approval, 90 days in advance, before sending any troops overseas to engage in hostile action. This resolution was like telling our prospective enemies exactly when we would begin to send troops overseas to counter any enemy action. It gave our prospective enemies a huge advantage, and served to further place our own troops at a tremendous disadvantage. This is what happens when untrained politicians think they can develop a strategy against a foreign aggressor.

In December of 1973, the North Vietnamese Army and the Viet Cong, destroyed 18 million gallons of fuel stored in tanks near Saigon. There was no response from either the South Vietnamese government or the United States. We had now officially left the South Vietnamese government alone to deal with Ho Chi Minh and the oncoming invaders from the North.

With all of these developments in Southeast Asia, the Pacific Command continued to be at the forefront of the action. Constant communications between CINCPAC and Washington were commonplace, and the pressures to somehow end the involvement in Vietnam, in an honorable and successful manner, continued to mount. Unfortunately, the thing that the politicians wanted so desperately, would never happen, thanks to their own reluctance and cowardly legislations that forever prohibited a military victory on the ground.

Many years later, we would find out, from our former North Vietnamese enemies, that had we simply pursued the enemy to the North when we were able to do so, the war in Vietnam would have been over, and we would have secured a victory. Obviously, that never happened, and the political restrictions placed on troops engaging the enemy by politicians half a world away, who had never heard a shot fired in anger, handed Vietnam to the Communists.

In January of 1974, I was able to take two weeks leave, and Cathie and I visited every island in Hawaii, except for the "Forbidden Island" of Niihau, a private island belonging to the Robinson family that controlled all entry and exit from the island. Our favorite island was the Big Island of Hawaii. The tourist overflow from Oahu and the Waikiki strip had not yet begun. In short, it truly was an island paradise, and we traveled between the islands in the small commuter planes of Royal Hawaiian Airlines, another casualty of over population and too many tourists. The chief pilot of the airlines, a close friend of ours, let our son Donald sit behind the controls on a flight from Oahu to the Big Island. Those days are gone forever, and we are all poorer for not being able to relish the small town, local atmosphere that had been Hawaii.

I'm only glad that we were able to get in on the end of the era. We have memories from those times that will last a lifetime. One day, while visiting General Young, at his quarters at Hickam Air Force Base, I met his young son, a college senior, who wanted to go into the service, but because his name was Jim Young, Jr., he did not want to go into the Air Force, where he would always have to live in the shadow of his father's fame. I told him about the Marine Corps aviation programs, and told him that I felt he would make an outstanding Marine pilot. He took my advice and did become a Marine Corps pilot. He decided that he really liked helicopters and became an excellent helicopter pilot. Unfortunately, while on maneuvers in Italy, he crashed into some overhanging electrical wires and lost his life. I always felt that, in some way, I was responsible, however, his father, the consummate pilot, told me that this was one of the risks of being a pilot, and every pilot understood this. It didn't make me feel much better, but it did alleviate the guilt I felt over convincing young Jim to become a Marine.

Besides manning a 24-hour a day, 7 day a week command center, the CINCPAC Operations Directorate also maintained another 24/7 command center. This command center was capable of performing all the functions of the command center at Camp Smith, however, it was airborne at all times. This was in case the command center at Camp Smith was ever taken out of operation. The airborne command center, code named *Blue Eagle,* would take off from Hickam Air Force Base in Honolulu and fly over the entire Pacific Ocean area.

The aircraft was a military version of the Boeing 707 that contained all the communications necessary to assume control of the CINCPAC area of operations in an emergency. At one point of the deployment, the aircraft would land on the island of Taiwan, at CCK Air Base, (whose real name was Ching Chuan Kang Air Base), where a visual inspection of the aircraft would be conducted. If some small repairs were required, the command center staff would remain aboard the aircraft and continue all command and control functions. During my deployment on the Blue Eagle, which I did one time, we encountered communications problems, and we were forced to remain at CCK for two days.

Upon my return from the Blue Eagle deployment in September of 1974, I was greeted by the very sad news that Major General Spanjer and Brigadier General Young were going to be transferred in November. General Spanjer would be relieved by Major General Frank Lang, another Marine aviator, and General Young would be relieved by Brigadier General Fritz Treyz, another Air Force fighter pilot. I had truly enjoyed working for both Generals, and while I never felt that either of them were my close buddies, I did feel that we were more than simply two senior officers with a Lieutenant Colonel Aide-de-camp. We had socialized privately, and Cathie had gotten to know both Mrs. Spanjer and Mrs. Young, both of whom always treated us as family, rather than as "subordinates."

On December 1, 1974, LtGen Louis Wilson, the Commanding General of the Fleet Marine Forces, Pacific, was selected to become a four star General, and would subsequently serve as the 26th Commandant of the Marine Corps, effective January 1, 1975. At that time, his deputy, Major General Tom Miller, became the Commanding General of FMFPAC. Thus, in a few short months, all of my "friendly Generals" would be departing, and I would be left with a largely unknown group of Generals for the remainder of my tour of duty in Hawaii. As an Executive Assistant, this can always prove to be disastrous.

Most General's like to select their own aides/executive assistants, but in a joint staff, such as CINCPAC, that decision is taken out of their hands, and they must accept the officer who is already in the job. If the aide and the general do not get along, then the general can always replace the aide, however, such an action always proves detrimental to the career of the aide who is being relieved. In short, chances for further promotion for the aide rapidly deteriorate to zero. General Lang and General Spanjer had two weeks of overlapping duty in order for General Spanjer to brief General Lang on his new duties as Director of Operations.

The Marine Corps is small enough so that all Generals know one another, and it became very clear to me that General Spanjer and General Lang would never be drinking buddies under any circumstances. Where General Spanjer was relaxed, considerate and possessing of a great sense of humor, General Lang was all business, with a taciturn manner, which rarely allowed a smile or a chuckle. General Lang was the serious drama mask, to General Spanjer's smiling one. Perhaps the old saying, "As different as night and day" was most appropriate to describe the two Generals, who now, at least temporarily, occupied the Director of Operations offices. During the transition, both General Spanjer and General Young went out of their way to recommend me to their replacements. General Treyz, who had German roots and had grown up in New York City, and I hit it off almost immediately.

I could tell that we would share a very good working relationship, based on mutual respect. On the other hand, it was very difficult determining General Lang's emotions. He seemed to say all the right things, but I felt a definite reticence, perhaps caused by his less than adoring respect for General Spanjer, and the fact that General Spanjer seemed to constantly tell General Lang how great I was as the Executive Assistant of the Operations Directorate. It got so bad that I secretly asked General Spanjer to stop touting me to

General Lang, and, after my request, the effusive comments concerning my work at the Operations Directorate disappeared.

Towards Christmas of 1974, the turnover was complete, and I attended my first briefing of Admiral Gayler with General Lang. The Admiral must have smelled fresh meat, because he immediately began quizzing General Lang. It took about five minutes before it was fairly obvious to everyone in the briefing room, that General Lang was going to be easily rattled by the Admiral. General Lang knew what the Admiral was doing, but just couldn't bring off the old "What me Worry?" attitude of General Spanjer. This became even more obvious after the briefing, when Master Sergeant Rodriquez and I began to get the brunt of General Lang's frustration with the Admiral.

We were immediately tasked to revise the daily briefing books, and to put far more detail into each subject listed to try to preclude any nit-picking questions that the Admiral might ask. The General began to come in to work by 6 a.m., so that he could adequately prepare for the morning briefing. This meant that my working hours had just been increased, but, as I rationalized, that was the price one paid for having my "prestigious" assignment. General Lang also stopped my daily briefings of LtGen Wilson. Since General Wilson was going to be the next Commandant of the Marine Corps, General Lang decided he would brief him each morning. While this might have been politically astute for the Marine Corps, Admiral Gayler, should he ever discover these daily trips, would not look upon General Lang's sojourns to the top floor with great enthusiasm.

In day-to-day work, General Lang went out of his way to appear cool, calm and collected. The officers and enlisted men of the Operations Directorate took an immediate liking to him, and only his "inner circle" (meaning me and Master Sergeant Rodriquez), suffered through his daily and continuous mood swings. General Spanjer had placed a parabolic mirror on the corner of his office door, so that I could always see if he was in his office while I was sitting at my desk. He thought it was quite jazzy, and it allowed me to answer immediately, the question that I was most often asked by the staff, when they walked into the office, to wit, "Is the General in?". I thought it was very clever also, and both Sergeant Rodriquez and I used that mirror constantly.

One morning, after General Spanjer's departure, I came into my office and noted that the parabolic mirror had been ripped out of the wall, and the broken mirror was sitting on the center of my desk. I knew immediately that General Lang had done this, but I played dumb and went in and asked him about the mirror. He began to shout at me to get that god damned mirror out of the office, and never, ever think of replacing it. He did not like it and did not want to use it. I "Yes Sired" him and walked out of the office, thinking how much simpler it would have been to simply ask me to take down the mirror. In addition, I think that General Lang felt I had put up the mirror, and I never told him otherwise. I had approximately two years remaining on my tour of duty, and it did not look like the remainder of my tour was going to be very enjoyable.

Several days later, allowing the General to cool down and having thought the matter through rationally, I went into General Lang's office and asked to speak with him on a personal basis. He seemed very agreeable, and I then told him that I had given the matter a lot of thought, and I wanted him to know that I would understand if he was interested in interviewing for a new Executive Assistant. I told him that I realized that I was essentially "handed down" to him by a previous incumbent, and that, perhaps my personality, my ways of doing business, and the fact that I was an infantry officer and not an aviator, might not exactly be what he was looking for as an executive assistant.

I was dumbfounded by his reaction. He stated that I was just fine and that he would tell me when he wanted a change. The matter was closed and was never surfaced again. My extremely cold relationship with General Lang was destined to continue for the remainder of my tour of duty, or, at least until he relieved me, whichever came first. I could only wonder what this would do for my career in the future. I returned to work, and continued to do everything asked of me to the best of my abilities, and with great concern for General Lang's sensibilities. This seemed to work, because over time, General Lang began to treat me, and Sergeant Rodriquez, in the same manner that he treated the rest of his staff. As we worked together more often, we began to understand how to deal with General Lang, and, while he was not at all like General Spanjer, he was not a bad guy, just a very controlled individual, who seemed to lack any kind of a sense of humor.

On December 13, 1974, the armies of North Vietnam broke the Paris Peace accords and waged a full-scale attack of Phouc Long Province in South Vietnam. This province was located north of Saigon but certainly close enough to represent a threat to the security of Saigon. While the South Vietnamese government asked for American intervention, which was called for under the terms of the accords, President Ford responded with only diplomatic sanctions, and no military action of any type. The enemy had tested the water again, and found that America was not going to respond. This was a bad indication for the South Vietnamese government, but another feather in the cap of General Giap and Ho Chi Minh.

By January 8, 1975, North Vietnam began plans for the final invasion of Saigon, and the toppling of the government of South Vietnam. These plans were given a great deal of support on January 21 when President Ford, addressing a joint session of congress, stated that the United States was unwilling to reenter the war.

On March 10, 25,000 North Vietnamese soldiers attacked the Central Highlands of South Vietnam, and on the next day, Ban Me Thout, the regional capital, fell and 4,000 South Vietnamese soldiers surrendered. This victory began a series of military victories for the North Vietnamese Army. On March 19, 1975, Quang Tri City fell, on March 24, 25, and 26, Tam Ky, Hue City and Chu Lai fell. On March 30, the major port city of Da Nang was captured, and over 100,000 South Vietnamese soldiers surrendered after being abandoned by their officers.

This high level of activity in Vietnam had the watch-standers and staffs of CINCPAC working around the clock, trying to anticipate any kind of contingency or emergency actions by the United States. Plans for every type of military action were put into active status, and a wide variety of options were evaluated and anticipated. As it turned out, nothing developed, and we simply were placed in the unenviable position of watching a former ally go down in defeat.

During all of these actions, the Admiral was briefed often and regularly, and direct communications between the Admiral, the Joint Chiefs of Staff, the Secretary of State and even POTUS (the Secret Service nickname for the President of the United States) were coming over the Hawaii airwaves. Those items that dealt with operations, which included about 99 percent of all radio traffic always included General Lang, and, therefore, also included me.

I was in the communications bunker when we listened to the actions that resulted in the eventual fall of Saigon on April 30, 1975. The Ambassador, Graham Martin, who wound up becoming the scapegoat, was, in fact, a hero, and a man who followed the power of his convictions, up to and including the point at which President Ford and Secretary of State Henry Kissinger directed that U.S. Marine guards at the US embassy in Saigon, to forcibly escort the Ambassador to a waiting helicopter. He was finally evacuated from Saigon at the last possible minute. The interactions and conversations between national and international leaders concerning the fall of South Vietnam during the period of April 1 through April 30 of 1975 is a period of my life that I can never forget.

I remember wondering, as a lowly lieutenant colonel, just who was in charge, as I listened to orders being given that were immediately countermanded by a higher authority, sitting in some conference room in Washington. While political actions in Washington certainly underwrote the eventual fall of Saigon and the capture of South Vietnam, the last days of Saigon were a study in individual valor and complete frustration with our government in Washington by the people on the ground in South Vietnam. For example, the fall of Saigon on April 30, 1975, was preceded by the evacuation of almost all the American civilian and military personnel in Saigon, along with tens of thousands of South Vietnamese civilians, most of whom worked for, or were closely associated with, the US Government in South Vietnam.

When the North Vietnamese Army was on the outskirts of Saigon, and defeat was inevitable, massive evacuation flights were conducted out of Ton San Nhut Airport. Huge American transport aircraft began a ferry service out of Vietnam that saved the lives of thousands of South Vietnamese. This ended on the night of April 28, when the North Vietnamese decided to strafe the airfield with rockets and heavy artillery. In the initial shelling, an American C-130 taxiing to pick up evacuees and flown by an aircrew out of Clark Air Force Base in the Philippines was struck. The crew evacuated the burning aircraft, and ran into another C-130 that had landed previously, and was leaving to return to the Philippines.

The continuing rocket fire made Ton Son Nhut Airport unusable for any further aerial evacuations, and General Homer D. Smith, the US defense attaché at the US embassy in Saigon, advised Ambassador Martin that the runways were unfit for use and that any further evacuations from Saigon would have to be accomplished by helicopter. The plan was even further complicated when a South Vietnamese pilot decided to defect to the North Vietnamese, and jettisoned his ordnance on the only remaining serviceable runway at Ton Son Nhut, thereby closing the airfield for use by anyone.

Until that time, the major evacuations from South Vietnam were planned out of Ton Son Nhut, now, this plan would have to be scrapped, and all subsequent evacuations had to be implemented by helicopters. Under pressure from Secretary of State Kissinger, Ambassador Martin ordered U.S. Marine embassy guards to take him to the airbase, in the middle of the shelling of the airfield, so that he could make an on the spot, personal assessment of the gravity of the situation. After seeing that fixed wing evacuations were no longer an option, Ambassador Martin gave the green light for the helicopter evacuations to begin. This new operation was quickly code named, *Frequent Wind.*

Reports came into the embassy that the North Vietnamese were on the move towards the center of Saigon. Ambassador Martin had to ask Secretary Kissinger, back in Washington, for permission to begin the massive helicopter evacuations. Approval was granted in three minutes, however, I remember thinking how ridiculous it was that the man in the field, who was in the middle of the entire operation, could not implement the plan without getting approval from Washington. No wonder we lost the war!

When Kissinger gave the approval to evacuate Saigon, Armed Forces Radio in Vietnam began playing Irving Berlin's song, "White Christmas" every few minutes. This was the prearranged signal for all US forces remaining in Saigon to move immediately to evacuation points. Operation Frequent Wind planned to use all the CH-53 (troop and vehicle transport) and CH-46 (troop transport) helicopters available, to begin ferrying American and friendly South Vietnamese personnel to ships of the US Seventh Fleet that were anchored off of Saigon, in the South China Sea. The evacuation point had been designated as the Defense Attache's Office (DAO) compound at Ton Son Nhut.

The first helicopters landed in the early afternoon and by 11 p.m. of the 29th of April, 395 Americans and 4,000 South Vietnamese had been evacuated. At 11 p.m., the Marine security guards blew up the DAO compound and evacuated all American equipment, files and cash. All of these actions were being monitored at CINCPAC in Hawaii. Where assets in Thailand and the Philippines could be diverted to assist in the evacuation, orders were issued, and the aircraft were dispatched. The US Air Force redeployed refueling and support aircraft as close as possible, to support the operation. The airborne command center circled Saigon at 40,000 feet, and monitored all ground communications, from both sides, to provide whatever communications intelligence became available.

The original evacuation plan had not called for a large-scale evacuation from the embassy grounds. Helicopters and busses were supposed to shuttle people from the embassy to the DAO compound, however, several thousand people were stranded at the embassy. Additional South Vietnamese civilians gathered outside the embassy walls and begged for asylum. Soon, these people began scaling the walls, hoping to claim refugee status. The evacuation continued, through violent thunderstorms, throughout the day and night. The underlining mood at CINCPAC was one of quiet desperation.

We listened and monitored communications, fully realizing that there was nothing that the world's largest military power could do to avert what would soon become, America's most crushing defeat. At 3:45 a.m. on April 30, 1975, the refugee evacuation was halted.

Ambassador Martin, true to his obligations to the Vietnamese who had supported the United States, had ordered that South Vietnamese and Americans be given the same evacuation priorities. Both President Ford and Secretary Kissinger were livid with this directive, and ordered Ambassador Martin that henceforth, only American's would be evacuated. Ambassador Martin reluctantly complied with the wishes of the Washington brain trust. This action was taken by the politicians in Washington because they were worried that the North Vietnamese would soon occupy Saigon, and the Ford Administration desperately wanted to announce that all Americans had been evacuated from Saigon. Ambassador Martin had to be ordered personally by President Ford, to board an evacuation helicopter.

The Marine Embassy guards had been sent a top secret message, from President Ford through CINCPAC, that if Ambassador Martin refused to board an evacuation helicopter, the Marines were to forcibly place him on the helicopter, insuring his evacuation from Saigon. The embassy evacuation had flown out 978 Americans and about 1,100 South Vietnamese, the Marine Guards, who were the last to leave, departed at 7:53 on the morning of April 30, and thus ended any American presence in Vietnam. Later that day, a day that the North Vietnamese now call Reunification Day, Saigon officially became Ho Chi Minh City, a name that it still has to this day (2012).

The most famous photograph to come out of these events, is the photograph of the human ladder on the rooftop of the American Embassy, taken by Photographer Hubert van Es, that shows South Vietnamese civilians trying to board the last helicopter, an Air America (the CIA's not so secret airline in Vietnam) HU-1E, hovering on the roof of the embassy. Sadly, they did not all make it, and the fates of the over 200,000 South Vietnamese government officials, military officers and soldiers sent to "reeducation centers," after the fall of Saigon, has never been either documented or discovered. To this day, no information on their fates has ever been released by the current government of Vietnam.

Unfortunately, I was only an ineffective listening post during these traumatic times, however, I can state that the chain of events, as described in this memoir, are exactly the way I remember them happening. As Saigon fell, and the North Vietnamese occupied all of Vietnam, the finger pointing and blame began in earnest in Washington. At CINCPAC, we could finally attempt to regain some semblance of routine. Our contingency plans for additional military actions in any part of the Pacific Theater became our most important function. With the occupation of Vietnam by the Communist government of North Vietnam, we did not know in what direction this newly found power might propel the North Vietnamese.

In actuality, the efforts to capture the country had so depleted the abilities of the North Vietnamese armies to wage any further incursions anywhere else that the reunification and consolidation of their victory took up their entire time and no further threats to the region would emanate from Vietnam. The loss of Vietnam, at a cost of 58,000 American lives and hundreds of thousands of wounded men and women, would never prove worth the fight. Vietnam veterans were vilified at home and returned in disgrace, a situation that developed thousands of additional mental and emotional problems in our veterans, many of which are still evident to this date (2012). Just check any Veteran's Administration Hospital.

You would think that the disasters of Vietnam would have taught the politicians in Washington a hard lesson, but, unfortunately, there was one more major fiasco waiting in the wings, one in which I was able to observe and listen to every decision made, and then deal with the aftermath of a situation that should never have happened. After the April 30 fall of Vietnam, countries around the Pacific began to explore their options. Laos, Cambodia and Vietnam clearly were embracing Communism and, besides these political inclinations, all were harboring a deep dislike and distrust of the United States.

In addition, the United States was being viewed as a "paper tiger," a position that our political machinations in Washington seemed to reinforce on a daily basis. Perhaps it was this general attitude towards the United States that caused the final episode of the Vietnam War, and an incident that has been placed down in the history books as the "last official battle of the Vietnam War." Again, I was able to monitor the entire battle from the CINCPAC Command Center Communications Room, in the company of Admiral Gayler and General Lang.

At 11:21 a.m. on Monday, May 12, 1975, the US merchant ship *Mayaguez*, was seized by the Khmer Rouge, the Cambodian communist army, in the Gulf of Siam, about 60 miles from the Cambodian coastline, and eight miles from Poulo Wai Island. The ship, owned by the Sea-Land Corporation, was enroute to Sattahip, Thailand from Hong Kong, carrying a non-arms cargo destined for military bases in Thailand. Captain Charles T. Miller, a veteran of more than 40 years at sea, was on the bridge in command of the ship. He had steered the ship within the boundaries of international waters, but the Cambodians had recently claimed territorial waters 90 miles from the coast of Cambodia. The thirty-nine seamen aboard the ship were taken prisoner.

In response to this action by the Cambodians, President Ford ordered the aircraft carrier, USS *Coral Sea*, the guided missile destroyer USS *Henry B. Wilson* and the destroyer USS *Holt*, to the area of the seizure. By nighttime, an airborne reconnaissance aircraft located the *Mayaguez*, at anchor off Poulo Wai Island. Plans were immediately made to rescue the crew. A U.S. Marine Corps Battalion Landing Team comprising 1,100 Marines was ordered flown from bases in Okinawa and the Philippines to assemble at Utapao, Thailand, in preparation for an assault.

The first casualties of this operation to free the *Mayaguez* occurred on May 13, when a helicopter carrying Air Force security team personnel crashed enroute to Utapao, killing all 23 aboard. I remember a shudder running through the Command Center as the helicopter crash and the casualty count was relayed to CINCPAC headquarters. This was certainly not a good way to begin the operation. Early in the morning of May 13, the Cambodians ordered the *Mayaguez* to head for Koh Tang Island. Its' crew was loaded aboard a Thai fishing boat, and taken first to Koh Tang Island, then to the Cambodian mainland city of Kompong Song, where they were moved again to Rong Sang Lem Island.

US Intelligence had observed a cove with considerable activity on the island of Koh Tang, a small five mile long island about 35 miles off the coast of Cambodia, southwest of the city of Sihanoukville, the communists name for Kompong Song, and they believed that some of the crew might be held there. They had also seen the Thai fishing boat loaded with what appeared to be Caucasians, but they could not determine how many Caucasians were on the fishing boat.

The USS *Holt* was ordered to seize and secure the *Mayaguez*, which was still anchored off Koh Tang Island. Marines were to land on the island and rescue any of the remaining crew. Navy jets from the USS *Coral Sea* were to make four strikes on military installations on the Cambodian mainland. The very nature of this plan was suspect from the beginning. We were launching an intricate, three service operation (Air Force, Navy and Marine Corps), with units that had never previously worked or trained together, into a very restricted geographic area (a small, five mile long island for which we had no previous intelligence and even fewer maps). Planners, watch-standers and action officers at CINCPAC looked at each other with that "I wonder what we're going to screw up next" look. It was very obvious from the beginning that the entire operation was being run by the State Department and the President, sitting in a command center in Washington.

On Saturday morning, May 15, the first wave of 179 Marines headed for the island, aboard eight Air Force "Jolly Green Giant" helicopters. These helicopters were primarily used by the Air Force for search and rescue operations, and the pilots flying these helicopters had no experience in flying troops into potentially "hot" combat zones. They flew to the USS *Holt*, the destroyer that had been tasked to occupy the *Mayaguez*, and unloaded the Marines on the helicopter landing pad, located on the fantail (rear) of the ship.

These Marines, from the 1st Battalion of the 4th Marine Regiment, would serve as the landing force that would occupy the *Mayaguez*. After the Marines had boarded the USS *Holt*, an Air Force plane flew over the *Mayaguez* and dropped tear gas on it. The USS *Holt* then pulled alongside the ship and the Marines stormed onto the *Mayaguez* only to discover that it was totally deserted. At the same time that the boarding of the *Mayaguez* was taking place, Marines from the 2nd Battalion, 9th Marines, based on Okinawa, landed at two separate sites on Koh Tang Island. One group landed on the eastern side of the island, which was where the cove was located and where intelligence personnel had observed enemy activity from the air. It was also the area where the Cambodian compound had been detected. The second group of Marines landed on the western side of the island, behind the compound, where the Marines hoped to surround the compound and capture the enemy on the island.

It is important to remember, that no one in the entire chain of command, all the way up to the White House, had any knowledge of the size of the enemy force on the island, if, in fact, there even was an enemy force on the island. The entire operation was planned and executed in two days, using three branches of the service and almost no hard core intelligence. As the first Marines began to land on both designated landing areas on the island, the Cambodians opened fire. At the western landing zone, one helicopter took a direct hit, but managed to fly off the island. Since the helicopter had landed its' troops before being hit, the pilot was able to fly the helicopter out to sea, where it crashed into the ocean. The pilot of the helicopter was saved, but the copilot perished in the crash.

In the meantime, the eastern landing zone had become a disaster. The first two helicopters that landed were met with heavy enemy fire. The ground commander, Lieutenant Colonel Randy Austin, a friend of mine with whom I had served in the 2nd Marine Division, had been told to expect no more than 20 to 40 enemy soldiers on the island. What he encountered on that first wave, was between 150 and 200 enemy soldiers. One of the helicopters, loaded with Marines, was hit in midair, tore apart and crashed into the surf, right before the landing zone. All aboard survived the crash and ran through the surf into the tree line at the landing beach.

One of the CH-53 Jolly Green Giant helicopters, with a crew of three and carrying 23 Marines and 2 Navy Hospital Corpsmen, all from 2nd Battalion, 9th Marines was caught in a cross fire and was hit by surface to air rockets. The severely damaged helicopter crashed into the sea, and the survivors had to swim out into the ocean to avoid small arms fire from the shore. A total of 12 personnel aboard the helicopter survived, including the pilot, however, the remaining 16 were all killed in the crash. This was what we were listening to at CINCPAC, as only the first wave of Marines attempted to land on the island.

Other helicopters were more successful in landing on the island, except one more CH-53 that was shot down. In that case, all but one passenger survived the crash. A Marine Staff Sergeant was lost at sea in that crash. Radio traffic from the island was chaotic. The ground commander, with his troops spread all over the island, some swimming in the ocean, and others dispersed throughout beachfront tree lines, was finding it almost impossible to get a head count of his unit. Enemy resistance compounded the problem, but those Marines on the ground were able to return fire and begin to neutralize the enemy threat.

By midmorning, when the Cambodians on the mainland began receiving reports of the island assault, they ordered the crew of the *Mayaguez* to get on a Thai fishing boat, and they left the island. The *Mayaguez* crew was recovered, unharmed, by the destroyer, USS *Wilson*, before the second wave of Marines were deployed, but the second wave was ordered to attack anyway.

Here was another case of poor control, this time from the White House, since they were calling the shots on the ground at Koh Tang Island. Sensing that things had deteriorated quickly, they probably felt that more Marines on the island would expedite a successful conclusion on Koh Tang. Late in the afternoon, the assault force had consolidated its position on the western landing zone, and the eastern landing zone was evacuated by 6 p.m. After a 14-hour long operation, most of the Marines were extracted from the island safely. On the ground, one Marine was killed, but his body was not recovered, and 50 Marines were wounded. A total of 40 Americans were lost on this operation, counting the helicopter crashes. When Lt Col Austin, the Marine ground commander, began accounting for his troops before the helicopter extraction, he determined that there were four of his men missing. He refused to board the helicopters until these Marines were found. He radioed that he was mounting a search team to find these Marines, and was calling off the extraction until these Marines were found.

This single action on Randy Austin's part saved his career in the Marine Corps. Marines are taught from the very beginning of their training that they never leave any troops, dead or wounded, behind after an operation. Randy was taking the correct course of action, and at CINCPAC, the Marines in the command center looked at each other and acknowledged the fact that common sense had returned to the battlefield at Koh Tang. Imagine our shock when an order came directly from President Ford and Secretary Kissinger, to evacuate immediately and overrode Randy Austin's orders. Randy was instructed to load his Marines aboard the helicopters, and return his troops to Utapao in Thailand. This meant leaving his four missing Marines on the ground. He reluctantly complied with his orders, but never forgot what he considered a cowardly act by the leaders of his country.

The after-action report listed 18 servicemen missing in action from the Koh Tang Island raid, and to this date, their remains, or any information concerning these men, has ever been uncovered. Koh Tang was the last battle of Vietnam, and like so many things about Vietnam, it was a total disgrace. Randy Austin was awarded a Silver Star for his heroic actions on Koh Tang. He was subsequently promoted to Colonel and retired from the Marine Corps. He is still very bitter about the Koh Tang raid, and refuses to discuss it with anyone other than those who were directly involved. I wrote this narrative because I do not want that raid to ever be forgotten. It is a prime example of why politicians will always lose wars, unless they allow their ground commanders to fight the battles on the ground, making decisions, as required, in real time, during the battle. I personally do not believe that the United States will ever win another war, because everything we do today is politically driven and controlled.

As a lieutenant colonel, my next step was getting selected for a top level school which would enhance my chances of getting promoted to colonel. Top level school selection is a difficult process, and each year, a few lieutenant colonels are selected to attend these schools with lieutenant colonels and commanders from the other branches of the service. These schools are very prestigious, and among them are The National War College, The Industrial War College in Washington, D.C., The Army War College, located at the Carlisle Barracks in Pennsylvania, The Navy War College, located in Newport, Rhode Island, the Air Force War College located at Maxwell-Gunther Air Force Base in Alabama and several international War Colleges located in Australia, New Zealand, England, Scotland and Canada. Selection for any one of these schools practically guarantees selection for promotion to Colonel.

While in Hawaii, I received a letter informing me that I had been selected as a "first alternate," meaning that if any of the primary selectees were unable to attend, I would be ordered to the school in their place. The letter informing me of this selection would be made a part of my permanent record. I was happy about the selection, but disappointed that I was not a primary selectee.

In late April of 1975, I finally came up with an idea that would get me away from General Lang, in a manner that he would not be offended by, and which, I hoped, he would endorse. Since he was a Naval Aviator and I was an infantry officer, I appealed to him to let me leave my position early, to get to the 3rd Marine Division in Okinawa, early enough in June or July, to be assigned the command of an infantry battalion.

The bulk of Marine permanent change of station orders are issued in June, July and August, to accommodate those personnel with children, and to allow the children to enroll in new schools at the duty stations to which they have been ordered. My game plan was to arrive at the 3rd Marine Division in late June, to get the first battalion that became available. I had already been informed that I was again heading for a year of an unaccompanied tour (meaning no family) in Okinawa, with an infantry unit. I felt that with an early arrival, perhaps my chances for a command would be greatly improved.

All infantry lieutenant colonels dream about commanding a battalion. This is the only ground combat sized unit that a ground specialty lieutenant colonel can command in the Marine Corps (Marine lieutenant colonels aviators want to be squadron commanders and there are fewer squadrons than there are battalions) and, unfortunately, there are more lieutenant colonels in the Marine Corps (1,500 in 1975) than there are battalions or squadrons to command (approximately 100 when you include supply, logistics and aviation units). Competition for these commands is fierce, and all kinds of political favors are often called upon to insure someone gets his command. General Lang agreed to support my efforts, and even volunteered to write a letter of recommendation for me to the Commanding General of the 3rd Marine Division. I thanked him and told him how much I appreciated his support.

I departed CINCPAC with orders to report to the 3rd Marine Division on Okinawa on June 23, 1975. Based on new legislation, officers receiving orders for an unaccompanied tour of duty, who lived in public quarters, were authorized to have their families remain in those quarters until their unaccompanied tour of duty was over, so Cathie and the boys could remain in Hawaii, while I was in Okinawa. This was a source of comfort for me, since we had made many friends in the housing area, and with husbands constantly on deployments (especially submariners), there was a very active support group in the housing area, which made separations much easier for the families left behind.

On Monday morning, June 23, 1975, I boarded a Military Airlift Command troop aircraft at Hickam Air Force Base on Oahu and departed Hawaii for Okinawa. I had great hopes of finding a battalion somewhere in the 3rd Division in need of a commander.

My tour in Hawaii had been very rewarding. My marriage to Cathie was greatly aided by the wonderful luck of getting a nice home, fully furnished, in a secure and supportive housing area for officers at Pearl Harbor. Our boys, Tim and Don, had met many new friends, and participated in a myriad of interesting and educational activities that would not normally have been available to them. Donald, who was born with a bilateral cleft palate, which required constant surgical repair as he grew, (22 separate surgeries by the time he was finished with the reconstruction of his palate, mouth and nose) was fortunate to find one of the Army's leading plastic surgeons assigned to the Army Medical Center at Tripler Army Hospital on Oahu. The doctor performed several very important surgeries on Donald's face and nose, all of which had amazing results, and restored Donald's appearance to normal.

Cathie and I enjoyed Hawaii immensely. We visited all the islands, with the exception on Niihau, the private, restricted island. We became very "island like," adapting to both the local customs and language (pidgin). Our life together began in an idyllic setting, and I am only sorry that I did not have more time to enjoy our surroundings. Cathie had earned her AA Degree, and Hawaii will always have a special place in my heart, and even General Lang, who was certainly not the easiest man to work for, prepared me for future assignments with demanding bosses.

In retrospect, considering all the difficult bosses that I have since encountered in both the Marine Corps and in civilian life, General Lang was a pussy cat, and a decent and highly principled man who lived his life the way he wished others to behave and never wavered from his high personal standards. Overall, he was an outstanding role model for conventional behavior and compassionate living, something all of my other difficult bosses were most certainly not.

During my tour of duty with CINCPAC, the Marine Corps ceased participation in the Vietnam War on April 30, 1973, when the last ten Marines departed the US Embassy in Saigon in a helicopter, officially ending the United States presence in Vietnam. Just before I left Hawaii, the United States declared the end of the Vietnam War on May 7, 1975, which, I suppose, is when all diplomatic efforts towards Vietnam ceased. For the Marine Corps, the War started on August 7, 1964, which was the date that Congress passed the Gulf of Tonkin resolution, however, there is a great deal of doubt that the confrontation ever took place. There was, and continues to be, a great deal of misinformation and incorrect perceptions of the Vietnam War among Americans. This needs to be corrected.

Here are some facts about the war:

- 9,087,000 military personnel served on active duty during the war
- 2,709,918 served in uniform in Vietnam (which is only 9.7% of their generation)
- Two-thirds of the men who served in Vietnam were *volunteers* and not draftees
- 97 percent of all Vietnam veterans were honorably discharged
- 91 percent of those say they are glad they served their country. 74 percent of those 91 percent say that they would serve again, even knowing the outcome.
- 247 Medals of Honor were awarded; 57 to Marines
- 489 Navy Crosses were awarded; 360 to Marines. Two men earned TWO Navy Crosses. At least 175 awards of the Navy Cross were posthumous awards of which 139 were Marines.
- The 2000 Census reveals that the surviving US Vietnam Veteran population estimate was 1,002,511. During this same Census count, the number of Americans falsely claiming to have served in Vietnam is 13,853,027. **Thus, four out of five who claim to be Vietnam veterans *are not*!**

VIETNAM WAR CASUALTIES (US)

One out of every 10 Americans who served in Vietnam was a casualty.

KILLED (KIA)

- 58, 260 were killed:

- The average age was 23.1 years

- 61 percent were younger than 21

- 17, 539 were married

- Five men killed were only 16 years of age

- The oldest military person killed was 62

- 86. 3% of those killed were enlisted men (50,274)

- 70 percent of those killed in Vietnam were volunteers

- 86 percent of the men killed were Caucasian

- 12. 5 percent killed were African-American

- 1.2 percent killed were from other races

WOUNDED (WIA)

- 304,000 were wounded out of the 2.7 million who served in Vietnam

- 75,000 were severely disabled, with 23,214 of those being 100 percent disabled

MISSING (MIA)

There are still 1,875 Americans unaccounted for from the Vietnam War

CHAPTER 17

OKINAWA —
FOR THE LAST TIME

3RD MARINE DIVISION

Traveling to Okinawa in 1975 was different from the trip I had taken there in 1968, when I was on my way to Vietnam. The stop over at either Midway or Wake Island was no longer required, since our more advanced aircraft had longer ranges, and refueling for a relatively long-range flight had become a thing of the past. The trip from Hickam Air Force Base in Hawaii to Kadena Air Force Base in Okinawa went smoothly, and the reception center for all incoming personnel quickly directed each of us to our designated areas for further transportation to our respective units.

All incoming Marines were taken by busses to the Marine Expeditionary Force (MEF) Headquarters at Camp Courtney, which was located in Uruma City, just south of Ishikawa Beach, and near the village of Teragawa, which was situated right outside the main gate of the camp. It was the Headquarters of both the III Marine Expeditionary Force and the 3rd Marine Division.

The camp itself was opened as a Marine Base in January 1956, when select units of the 3rd Marine Division were transferred there from Camp McGill, Japan. Originally, the base kept its' Japanese name, and the Marines of 1956 called it Camp Tengan. A new base, called Camp Courtney, was constructed nearby to house the major headquarters.

In 1975, Camp Courtney was a complex of concrete, typhoon proof buildings which included two major Marine headquarters. The buildings themselves and, for that matter, the entire camp, looked like a small enclave of the United States which had been placed right in the middle of a typical Japanese city.

As for Okinawa, that was indeed a different story. In 1969, which was the last time I was on Okinawa on my way home from Vietnam, it was still a separate island, in a chain of islands called the Ryukyu Islands, which the American forces had liberated from the Japanese during World War II. While belonging to Japan, it was governed by the High

Commissioner of the Ryukuan Island Command, an American appointed State Department official

All roads and customs were according to American standards, especially vehicular traffic, which always drove on the right side of the road, just as it did in the United States. Police and fire support agencies in local cities were modeled after American organizations, as was the public transportation infrastructure. This system lasted for 27 years after our 1945 landings on the island and had been in force on my two previous visits to the island.

In 1972, the US government returned the islands to Japanese administration. This became a huge undertaking for the Japanese, because they immediately set out to "de-Americanize" Okinawa and return it to its' prewar status as a prefecture of Japan. This was no small task. First, all traffic on the island had to be switched from right side driving to left side driving, mirroring the way things were done in Japan. Vehicles, especially busses, had to be changed to left hand drive, and all bus stops and road interchanges had to be switched. Police and fire services were changed to reflect the Japanese way of conducting these services. All road signs were changed, and Japanese, not English, became the primary administrative language used on the island.

A Treaty of Mutual Cooperation and Security was signed between Japan and the United States, formally returning the islands to Japan, and agreeing to operate under Japanese law, except for retaining the Status of Forces Agreement, which allowed the United States to discipline American forces in Japan, which now included Okinawa. As of 2008, there were over 15,000 Marines stationed on Okinawa, with 18 percent of Okinawa occupied by US military bases. Another interesting statistic is the fact that 75 percent of all American forces in Japan are stationed on the island of Okinawa. The distribution of bases and military population is such that the entire island of Okinawa, from south to north, houses some kind of military base, either Army, Navy, Marine Corps or Air Force. The Marines, who have the largest force on the island, are spread across the island in ten permanent bases, which does not include terrain dedicated simply to training.

When I arrived in Okinawa in 1975, the bases that existed were: Marine Corps Air Station, Futenma; Camp Foster and Camp Sukiran, all in the southern portion of the island; Camp McTureous and Camp Courtney, which were in the central part of the island; and the large bases of Camp Hansen and Camp Schwab, located in the northern part of the island. Besides these camps, there were six training areas, dedicated to Marine and Navy amphibious training exercises, scattered throughout the island. In 1968 and 69, when I had passed through Okinawa on my way to Vietnam, all personnel moved through the Marine Corps' largest island camp which was Camp Hansen, located directly opposite Kin Village. This relatively small Okinawan village, had 242 bars in an area of four blocks by six blocks, catering to the 52,000 Marines that were traveling through Camp Hansen, either going to, or returning from, Vietnam.

Things were far less hectic in 1975, and the islands' Marine population, while still large, had been reduced in size from the Vietnam War days. All incoming personnel for the 3rd Marine Division were processed through Camp Courtney. As we boarded the bus at

Kadena Air Force Base for the 45-minute trip to Camp Courtney, I wondered what the 3rd Marine Division had in mind for my next assignment. The Marine Corps, like any large sized organization, is influenced by internal politics. Obviously, a senior officer will assign an officer he knows to a job before he will assign an officer with whom he is totally unfamiliar. Essentially, if you know a senior officer, usually a General, your chances of receiving a good assignment, usually a command, are far better than if you have never worked for, or served with the General.

Up to the time I reported for duty in the 3rd Marine Division, I had benefited greatly from knowing or working for senior officers responsible for making specific assignments. Reporting for duty with the Division at Camp Courtney, I discovered that the Division was commanded by a General who I did not know existed before arriving at Camp Courtney. Major General H. L. Wilkerson, the Division Commander, insisted on interviewing all incoming lieutenant colonels and colonels, before assignment. My interview went very quickly, the General had never heard of me, was impressed by my previous assignments, was made aware, by me, that I would like to have a command, and wound up assigning me to the G-1 Division of the Division Headquarters Staff (G-1, in military terminology, means the Admin/Manpower Division). I would be staying at Camp Courtney in a staff job, in the Personnel Section, where all assignments were coordinated and implemented. I would not be getting a command.

I was totally devastated and went to the Officer's Club, where I checked in, and received my room assignment in one of the permanent officer's barracks. I was now officially buried in a ponderous group of staff officers assigned throughout the Division and the MEF. I moved into my room, hired my personal maid and reported for duty to the Division G-1 Officer, Colonel Dave Wagner. I had known Colonel Wagner when he was a captain at Parris Island, and he knew I was arriving. He was a very straight-laced officer who remembered my wild escapades in Parris Island. He assigned me duties as the Division Alcohol and Substance Abuse Control Officer. In my mind, this was a dead-end assignment that would do very little to embellish my portfolio for consideration to promotion to the rank of colonel.

The irony of the entire situation was not lost on me either, here I was, assigned to the Division personnel section, which made all the assignments in the Division, and I couldn't assign myself to a battalion. What a terrible position to be in, and, on top of everything else, I was powerless to change anything. I settled into my job and continued to campaign actively for a transfer to a battalion. I'm afraid that I overdid my campaigning, as I was called into the General's office, and ordered to stop asking for a battalion. Furthermore, the General warned me, that enough was enough, he understood my frustration, however, he did not want to hear from me again concerning command of a battalion. July went into August, and my life at Camp Courtney became an exercise in mediocrity. I really did not have much of a job, and I found I could perform my duties in about 20 minutes a day, leaving the rest of the day with plenty of time to feel sorry for myself.

I volunteered to teach freshman English for Los Angeles City College, which had a branch on Okinawa, dedicated specifically for military personnel. I taught one semester, and derived a great deal of personal satisfaction out of this, not to mention some additional pay from the college. I had a class of 22 Marines, and at the end of the semester, one of my students, a grizzled Gunnery Sergeant, showed me a letter from his wife, in which she commented on how much more interesting his letters had become, and what a great writer he had become. I'm afraid the Gunny gave me too much credit for his writing improvement, however, it was a definite highlight of my tour of duty in Okinawa.

For the first time in my Marine Corps career, I had an office job that was totally meaningless (in my mind). Since there had been such a large alcohol and drug problem in the military services, each service was tasked to conduct vigorous anti-drug and alcohol indoctrinations, and continuing classes. These classes were conducted by Marines who had been trained in drug and alcohol counseling, and had an MOS that designated them as "professional" drug and alcohol counselors.

My job was to insure that the appropriate classes were being conducted and that all units within the division were maintaining their records properly, to show that all required instruction had been completed. In short, it was a CYA (cover your ass) operation, because, no matter how hard you tried, or how many classes were taught, the troops that wanted to use and abuse drugs and alcohol, always managed to accomplish the task.

While at Camp Courtney, I spent a lot of time exercising, usually during the noon hour, where a one and a half hour lunch break could easily be stretched into two hours, if you were running around the base. Evenings after dinner, the officer's club always showed a movie, which would stretch the time into bedtime around 10 p.m.. There were other choices available for officers at Courtney. You could turn yourself into an alcoholic, or, if you were so inclined, you could tour the overly friendly bars of all the surrounding towns that circled the base. Neither of these two options appealed to me, so I stuck with the workouts and the daily movies, plus teaching college freshman English, three evenings a week.

The year 1975 was a highly memorable year in Marine Corps history because it was the year that the U.S. Marine Corps would celebrate its' 200th Birthday on November 10, All of us thought that we would have a fantastic traditional birthday ball at our base in Camp Courtney. Birthday celebrations on the 10th of November, each year, are a tradition throughout the Marine Corps, and it is a tradition that has never changed, since its' inception in 1923, by the then Commandant of the Marine Corps, General John A. LeJeune. Our infantry battalion even had a birthday cake flown into our jungle base camp, in 1968, while we were in Vietnam, so that we could properly celebrate the birthday of the Corps.

We were all very disappointed to learn that our 200th Birthday Ball would be an island wide celebration, to be held in the large field house in Camp Sukiran, down in the southern part of the island. This negated all unit celebrations in the individual camps throughout the island. I felt that this was not a proper way to celebrate our 200th Birthday, and my rebellious mind immediately went into action. I determined that with so many people at that consolidated ball, no one would notice if you chose not to attend (It was not a command performance).

I contracted with a local restaurant owner in the city of Teragawa (the largest city on the outskirts of Camp Courtney), to close his restaurant for a special party on Monday, November 10, 1975. The restaurant could easily accommodate 200 people, and it also had a bandstand for entertainment. Since we were all single, (a tour of duty for Marines on Okinawa was an "unaccompanied" tour of duty, which meant that families were left back home, to be prepared to deploy anywhere in the Pacific theater within 24 hours) I contracted for a "kabuki-like" show, and Geisha type musical entertainment.

At the time, Korea was making almost anything you could want in the way of US products, knockoff gifts, collectables, or gadgets to take home as souvenirs. One of our officers regularly traveled to Seoul to coordinate with the Korean Marine Corps and so the task to develop a truly meaningful souvenir of our "renegade birthday ball" fell on his shoulders. He came up with a great idea, which was to have a Korean foundry manufacture 200 solid brass belt buckles, with the 3rd Marine Division Crest in the center of the buckle and the words "USMC 200th Birthday, November 10, 1975," underneath the crest. Each attendee at our birthday party would receive one, however, no one except me and Lieutenant Colonel Ort Steele, (the project officer for the belt buckles, who would later become a Major General) would know about the surprise gift. I found out that quite a few officers were disappointed about the "consolidated birthday ball," and in a matter of a few days, my party was sold out.

We charged $25 each for the dinner and party, where there would be unlimited drinks, and the restaurant owner thought that he had struck the Mother Lode. A $5,000 night never had happened before in Teragawa City, and soon his restaurant was the talk of the town. The dinner and party was a great success. We celebrated our 200th Birthday with great warmth and personal feelings for our beloved Marine Corps, complete with a reading of the obligatory messages and letters, required at all birthday celebrations, large or small, across the face of the earth, on the 10th of November. It turned out to be a memorable birthday celebration, and one which all the participants, recall with great nostalgia, even to this day. The belt buckles, which later became highly prized collector's items, are still the proud possessions of the attendees of that magnificent event.

Unfortunately, I lost my belt buckle in 1979, when British Airlines lost my bags at Heathrow Airport, and never found them again. While I was compensated for my loss, I was truly sorry that my precious belt buckle had disappeared. Again, my rebellious nature had pulled off another memorable event, which also gained me additional notoriety, because the joint officer's ball at Camp Sukiran had been a huge disappointment for all attendees. The celebration at Camp Sukiran proved to be too big, too impersonal and had no unit cohesiveness.

My job at Camp Courtney continued in its' uneventful manner. Except for the fact that I was stationed in Okinawa, the job could easily have been a 9 to 5 office job with absolutely no additional duties. It was a shame that Cathie and the boys were not in

Okinawa, since my job assignment could easily have accommodated a family life. Thanksgiving came and went, and we celebrated Thanksgiving in the Officer's Club, with a traditional turkey dinner with all the fixings. At Christmas time, Cathie mailed me a small artificial Christmas tree with decorations attached, that I assembled and placed in my room at the BOQ. It was not a particularly happy time for any of us who were separated from our families, no matter how many times in our lives we had endured the separation.

Back in Hawaii, Cathie's parents had come over to spend Christmas with her and the boys, and immediately following Christmas, Cathie was going to come to Okinawa to spend a few weeks with me. Since the Marine Corps prohibited families from being on Okinawa, Cathie obtained a passport and visitor's visa and traveled to Okinawa as a US tourist, which was perfectly legal, and which was also impossible for the Marine Corps to prohibit.

I was not the first Camp Courtney officer who had his wife visit them in Okinawa, and the complete boredom of the staff jobs at Courtney, together with the huge amount of available free time after work, encouraged those officers stuck in these jobs, to bring their wives over for a visit. Cathie's parents watched the boys in Hawaii, and Cathie arrived the second week in January, to spend two weeks with me. The decision to bring Cathie to Okinawa for a visit was not one which I made lightly. As an unaccompanied tour of duty, the Marine Corps did not encourage visits from family members to Okinawa.

Technically, there was nothing that they could do about it legally, however, there might be subtle means of "getting even" with officers who chose to circumvent the existing regulations, and enjoy the companionship of their wives, while the bulk of the Marine officer's on Okinawa were living in their "forced celibacy" mode (subtle comments on the semiannual fitness report were the most obvious form of "retribution" open to reporting officers who did not bring their wives to Okinawa). I was so disgusted with my assignment, and the lack of any professional challenge, that Cathie's visit quickly became the highlight of my tour.

I had bought a rebuilt Nissan four-door sedan (in the United States this brand was called a Datsun, because the Japanese company who manufactured this automobile felt that the company name of Nissan was too close to Nippon and, therefore, might have some derogatory implications from World War II in the United States) from Teragawa Sam, who had the most unique used car dealership in the world. Sam, which was his "American" name, had a huge junk yard on the outskirts of Teragawa City. Personnel arriving for a 13 month tour of duty on Okinawa who wanted transportation, would go to Teragawa Sam's, from all over the island, to buy a "custom-made" used car.

The process was always the same. You would walk through his junkyard until you spotted a car with the body style you wanted, either a coupe or a four-door model. Together, you and Sam would inspect the body, to insure that the car was "salvageable."

Once that determination had been made, Sam would move the body into a large workshop, which was his "assembly line." Before any work being performed, Sam would give you a price, which was usually elevated enough to allow for limited haggling, until a solid price was agreed upon, by both parties. The next step was to agree on a color for your "new" car. After that, Sam would tell you when you could pick up your car, which would be guaranteed to operate for the length of your tour of duty on Okinawa. This was a 13 month guarantee, at the most. I selected a family sedan, requested that it be painted a dark burgundy color, and then was informed that the car would be ready in a week.

During that week, Sam would rebuild the entire car, repair or replace the engine, check the electrical system, repair or replace the brakes, and insure that all liquids remained in the car for a reasonable time. This would insure that the automobile passed the military inspection, required before obtaining a base sticker, which would allow you to enter any American military base on Okinawa. My car, which Cathie and I named The Red Baron, required a daily check of the brake fluid and the transmission fluid, along with a check of the radiator, however, it was a good running car, and it served us well, exactly as Teragawa Sam had promised, as long as all fluids were topped off daily.

Cathie and I had a wonderful visit at Camp Courtney. I took her all over the island, including Kin Village, up in the Northern part of the island, near Camp Schwab, where she and I hit the local bars on payday night, to observe and participate in the trooper's fun, on one of the few days in the month when they all had money. Cathie met the Momma-sans of the bars, and whorehouses and was a big hit with all the local women because of her long blond hair. They could hardly keep their hands off her hair because it was so fine and so blond.

Cathie's attitude helped as well, since she treated all the people she met with respect and deference. I took her to Camp Schwab, where the Commanding Officer of the 9th Marine Regiment took her on a tank ride, an LVT ride, where the hatch hit her in the head (luckily she was wearing a helmet) and gave her a tour of the base on a mechanical mule, which was a four wheeled platform used to transport ammunition and supplies in a forward operating area under combat conditions.

We ate our meals at the Officer's Club, except for occasional meals at our favorite Japanese teppan-yaki restaurant in Teragawa City, (the place where we had our Marine Corps Birthday party and where I was now treated as a VIP, thanks to the tremendous payday that the owner had realized from that party), and enjoyed each other's company.

In the process, because she had been a bartender at the Recruit Depot in San Diego and was familiar with Marine Corps customs and traditions, and the fact that both her parents had been Marines, she charmed everyone on the base, and she became a mini-celebrity just because she was good looking, friendly and took time to talk to everyone. When she left to go home, everyone was sorry to see her go, especially me. Shortly after Cathie left Okinawa, the top level schools list came out, and again, I had been designated as a "first alternate." I also found out that several officers, whose tours of duty on Okinawa were relegated to remaining at Camp Courtney for their entire tour of duty, were bringing their families to Okinawa.

This was truly a "semi-defiant" gesture, since, if the Division was ever totally deployed from Okinawa, the families would be left on the island to fend for themselves. The reality of the situation was that the chances of the entire division being deployed from Okinawa were remote! One of my good friends, Lieutenant Colonel Russ Porter (later the Aide to the Secretary of the Navy and a Brigadier General), the assistant Division Supply Officer, had already brought his family over, and they were living in a Japanese house in Ishikawa Beach, as the only non-Japanese family in the entire village.

Speaking to both Russ and Nancy, I found out that they loved living in Ishikawa and that living in a totally Japanese environment was educational, safe and exciting. Their children were attending the American school located on Kadena Air Force Base (the Air Force allowed dependents on Okinawa, and had a full range of services for dependents), Nancy was shopping at the Kadena base PX and Commissary, and, when necessary, was taking her children to the Air Force medical facility, for treatment. Apparently, all she needed to use any or all the services available at Kadena Air Force Base, was her dependents ID card. The Air Force did not care that her ID card said U.S. Marine Corps instead of U.S. Air Force.

As news of Nancy Porter's success spread, a small, US family enclave began to develop in the various rental houses at Ishikawa Beach. The Air Force base began running school busses to Ishikawa Beach to pick up the children who were now attending the Air Force Base school. I immediately decided that since I had been told I would spend my entire tour of duty at Camp Courtney, Cathie and the boys, along with our dog, Kiumakahiki, would soon be joining me on Okinawa.

This decision was not one I made lightly. I was defying Marine Corps orders in the sense that I was doing something that the Marine Corps specifically did not allow Marines to do if they were assigned to combat unit in Okinawa. Legally, there was absolutely no restriction on an American family visiting and living in Okinawa for a specific time. It was like visiting Japan, which, in fact, was exactly the case. I also realized that by taking this course of action, I might jeopardize any future chances for promotion. With my apparent difficulty for being selected to a top level school, and my guarantee by General Wilkerson, that I would remain in a staff job for my entire tour of duty on Okinawa, I did not think that I had much to lose by bringing Cathie and the family to Okinawa. I knew that I would be a lot happier, and if that stopped me from becoming a colonel, so be it. I toured Ishikawa Beach, and found a Japanese man who was willing to rent me a three bedroom house on a month-to-month basis. The house was a first class Okinawa style house, which means that it was built out of solid concrete, including the roof, and it was definitely typhoon proof, a very important factor on Okinawa, especially in a beachfront village. I furnished the house with military cots, and the standard brick and board shelves throughout, while Cathie was busy cleaning up our government quarters in Hawaii, in order to be released from housing, so she could move out of quarters.

Moving out of government furnished quarters is one of the most harassing and difficult procedures ever established by the US military. On the one hand, the procedure was greatly appreciated by every military family moving into a government furnished set of quarters, and, it was despised by every family moving out of that set of quarters. The thing that made the moving out process so oppressive was the "final inspection." All quarters required a final inspection before a military family was released from their quarters. These inspections were conducted by full time housing inspectors, who came to the quarters and inspected every inch of the quarters, including inside stoves, underneath heating elements, inside toilet tanks, floorboards, lighting fixtures, electrical outlets, ceilings, in short every inch of the house. If any dirt, rust, mildew or discrepancy was found, the house "failed," and required re-inspection. The inspectors literally used white gloves to inspect each house. All inspectors had a ready-made excuse for their actions, which, not surprisingly was, "Wouldn't you want to move into a perfectly clean house?" This question obviously had only one answer, and explained why thousands of military families spent hundreds of hours "clearing quarters." Some families simply hired professional janitorial companies to come in and clean the house from top to bottom, but these services were expensive, and, therefore, most junior officers, like myself, simply bit the bullet and did it themselves.

While I was preparing our new "home" in Okinawa, Cathie worked like a slave, all by herself, and cleared quarters on her first try, an effort that did not go unappreciated by me, even if I was several thousand miles removed from Hawaii. I knew how hard the work had been. Finally, all arrangements were made, and Cathie, Tim, Don and our dog, Kiumaka-hiki departed Hawaii on a Northwest Orient Airlines flight direct to Naha International Airport in Okinawa. By the time they arrived, the house in Ishikawa was ready, and the family moved into our new "Ishikawa home."

Cathie enrolled the boys in the Kadena Air Force Base School, and a bus from the base picked them up at Ishikawa, because there were some Americans living there, and they had decided to support this small "expatriate" community. Since officers who had decided to bring their families to Okinawa were no longer a rarity, I took the family to the Officer's Club for meals, which were very inexpensive, and allowed the boys to use the ice cream machine every night that we ate there. The machine was a soft ice cream machine, which the club staff kept supplied with a different flavor every night, and much to the delight of the boys, they could go back as often as they liked. To this day, they remember the Camp Courtney Officer's Club Ice Cream machine, with fondness and a bit of longing, as well. Our Japanese adventure was enhanced when Cathie's sister, Joan, came out for a visit. Joan was a very good racquetball player, and soon she was playing officers at the Camp Courtney racquetball courts, and, what is more important, winning quite regularly.

While life on Okinawa was most enjoyable for the entire family, we were also faced with the ongoing threat of the ever-present South China Sea Typhoons. Typhoon season, roughly every year from about November through April, can cause tremendous damage. Generally, the typhoons dissipate at sea, and the islands of the South China Sea are left with only high winds, however, when a typhoon makes land, destruction and, sometimes death, often follow. The military, having been on Okinawa since 1945, was fully prepared to deal with typhoons, and all units, including aircraft and ships, participate in preparations for typhoon conditions. There are often typhoon drills, where personnel go to shelters, aircraft and ships leave Okinawa, and head to calmer and less vulnerable locations and all buildings are fortified for the tremendous winds which can wreak havoc on anything they encounter, should the typhoon make land.

Generally, the typhoon dissipates, and everyone just enjoys a period of hunkering down in bunkers, or staying inside in protected areas, playing cards, watching movies, or taking a sip from a pre-staged "typhoon fifth." On April 1, a warning was issued by the Typhoon Weather Service, which stated that a typhoon was forming in the South China Sea and that it might become strong enough to hit the island of Okinawa. Preparations were made to fortify the island, and as the typhoon progressed at sea, it was given a name. By the afternoon of the 2nd, Typhoon Marie was on course to strike a direct hit on the entire Ryukyu Island chain, and it appeared that Okinawa would be at the center of the storm. Everyone was evacuated to their storm shelters, and since my location was supposed to be at my BOQ room, I hurried out to Ishikawa, where the entire family, minus Kiu, prepared to sit out the storm in our typhoon-proof house. Kiu, our dog, had taken off with a pack of wild dogs, and he was running with the pack, which occasionally ran by our house. He refused to acknowledge us, or even show that he recognized his name, when he ran by our house, so we figured that we had lost him to the wild dogs of Okinawa.

Typhoon Marie hit Okinawa on the morning of April 3, 1976, and was immediately classified as a Category 4 Typhoon, meaning that according to the SSHS (Saffir-Simpson Hurricane Scale), the typhoon had minimum winds of 131 miles per hour, and was causing a surge in the waters surrounding Okinawa, of at least 13 to 18 feet more water than normal. The entire island of Okinawa secured during the typhoon. All Navy ships put to sea before the typhoon struck land, and all Air Force and Marine aircraft flew off the island to sanctuaries on Guam, Taiwan, Mainland Japan and the Philippines.

The house we had in Ishikawa was definitely typhoon proof. Heavy winds and rains struck the island, and while we lost power and were constantly inundated with heavy rains, our small group was safe inside our house, subsisting on C-Rations, pre-positioned water, with flashlights and candles for lighting. Only our dog, Kiu, who had been running with the pack of wild dogs, was unaccounted for, and we feared that we had lost him in the storm.

On April 13, the typhoon finally subsided, and things returned to normal. As the all clear sirens sounded all over the island, we went outside to survey the damage that had been caused by the typhoon. As we walked out of our house, we immediately noticed a dirty ball of white fur and blood, huddled at the base of an uprooted palm tree. It was our dog Kiu, who somehow had found his way home, and rode out the storm, huddled under a tree in our front yard. We were all happy to see him again, and while he was weak and dazed, we took him inside, and began an immediate term of rehabilitation. Kiu recovered nicely, with the aid of a veterinarian from the Air Force base in Kadena, and he remained a loyal family member for the remainder of his life, which lasted until 1989, in San Mateo, California.

During the month just before the typhoon, Major General Wilkerson was transferred and he was replaced by Major General George Smith, my old Basic School platoon commander and fellow 8th and I Marine. Timing is everything, whether you are in the military or anywhere in life, and, had General Smith been the Commanding General when I reported in for duty with the 3rd Division in June of 1975, there would have been no doubt that I would have gotten an infantry battalion to command.

As it was, General Smith called me into his office immediately after taking command of the division, and informed me that since I had less than five months remaining on my overseas tour, he could not give me a battalion. I was scheduled for orders in July of 1976, and as things were, I would be happy to return to the states. After Colonel Wagner, the Division G-1 was transferred to the States, General Smith made me the Assistant Chief of Staff, G-1, giving me a full colonel's job to make my over-all performance record possibly more impressive for the selection board to colonel.

My final tour in Okinawa saw many changes to the island, as it took its' place as a newly minted prefecture of Japan. In 1976, 85 percent of Okinawans opposed the presence of the US military on their island. Much of the resentment had been fueled by the behavior of a few American military personnel, who had raped and murdered Okinawans, and, who were protected from local prosecution by the Status of Forces Agreement, which allowed the United States Government to punish American offenders. While American punishment was harsh, it was nowhere near as harsh as it might have been had the miscreants been turned over to the Japanese government for both trial and punishment. In 1995, the rape of a 12-year old Okinawan girl, by an American Marine, triggered huge protests against the United States and their military presence on Okinawa.

Several bases on Okinawa were relocated away from urban areas, and other bases were consolidated. The current climate in Okinawa is extremely anti-American, and, this is a shame, as my times on Okinawa were happy, and our relationships with our local hosts were always one of mutual respect, and genuine friendship. The adage that a few rotten apples can spoil everything is never better illustrated than by the current US Military-Okinawan relationships on the island. In 2012, Okinawa is a tropical paradise for Southeast Asia, boasting the best beaches, and the most favorable climate in the entire Pacific Rim.

We enjoyed our stay on Okinawa, and I was particularly glad that I had taken the "professional risk" of bringing my family to Okinawa. As it turned out, their presence in Okinawa did not affect my job performance, and since I was working in a "9 to 5" office staff job anyway, it turned out to be a blessing for me, and a great adventure for the rest of the family. The remaining months of my tour of duty on Okinawa progressed fairly rapidly, and uneventfully. In June, as I celebrated my 41st birthday, and my completion of twenty years of service in the Marine Corps, I received orders to report for duty at Headquarters, U.S. Marine Corps in Washington, D.C.

This assignment would be my third trip to Washington, however, this time I was going to be assigned to the Plans and Policies Division, the most prestigious division in Headquarters, and the division which seemed to spawn the most future general officers. From the point of view of an assignment for a lieutenant colonel, who was competing to be promoted to the rank of colonel, I could not have received a better set of orders. While

I was somewhat disappointed with my third assignment to the Washington area, and a guaranteed desk job, my assignment to the Plans and Policies Division, certainly indicated that I was still in the running for promotion to the rank of colonel when my turn for consideration arrived.

As the family made plans to depart Okinawa, we had one final duty to perform. The lieutenant colonel who was going to relieve me at the G-1 office at Camp Courtney, a former enlisted Marine named Glen Hickey, had determined that he would probably spend his entire 13 month tour of duty at Camp Courtney, and as such was the case, he needed a reliable car. I suggested that he buy the Red Baron from me, and he agreed. We drove the Red Baron down to Teragawa Sam's place of business, so that Sam could conduct a safety and reliability check on the car.

Sam looked the whole vehicle over, and determined that it had another 13 months of reliable performance still in it, so Glen and I agreed that he would pay me exactly what I had paid Sam for the car. Sam agreed to stand by a "limited warranty," meaning that he would replace any part that failed from his vast storehouse of used parts, and the deal was done. We all hated to part with the Red Baron. It had been a good car, and to this day, it is the car that we all remember. We always wondered how many parts from different cars were in the Red Baron, however, we all agreed that it was the "best" car we ever had, in sentimental terms and in unforgettable experiences. At some time, every member of our family had "fluid refill" duties, and we still laugh when we think about our adventures in Okinawa, with our jury-rigged vehicle that we so lovingly dubbed, "The Red Baron."

Cathie, the Boys and Kiumakahiki, departed Okinawa together on the same aircraft that was taking me back to Washington. It was a direct flight to Dulles International Airport, with a stop in Anchorage, Alaska, to clear US Customs. I will never forget that stop, because since we were all required to clear Customs, the entire plane had to be unloaded and checked by Customs agents. It was still cold in Alaska and I remember watching our dog, Kiu, being unloaded from the plane. All the animals on the flight were in Japanese manufactured metal pet cages, and I recall watching Kiu dancing around the inside of his roomy cage. It took us a few minutes to realize that the floor of the cage suddenly became cold, and he was trying to keep his paws warm. We had an opportunity to visit him in the holding hangar, and he was very happy to see us.

After several hours, the plane was cleared, and we boarded the aircraft and were finally on our way to Washington and Dulles International Airport. Our Southeast Asian adventure was over, and our East Coast experience was about to begin.

CHAPTER 18

WASHINGTON, D.C. — THE THIRD TIME

THE LAST HURRAH

We arrived in Washington in late July 1976. Washington had certainly gone through some very traumatic situations in the years since my last tour of duty in 1968. The Vietnam War had finally ended on April 30, 1975. The loss of over 58,000 American men and women is forever memorialized on the granite tablets of the Vietnam Memorial Wall in Washington. The war had taken its' toll on the soldiers, Marines, airmen and sailors who fought it, on the citizens of the country who protested and lived through the war years at home, and, most definitely, on the politicians that eventually received the blame for America's involvement in Vietnam.

The war had begun under President Eisenhower, when he offered aid to French Indochina in 1959. It had escalated under President Kennedy, when he employed Special Forces to assist and advise units of the South Vietnamese Army in 1960 through 1963. At the time of his assassination, Kennedy had committed over 16,300 troops to Vietnam, and had decided to "draw a line in the sand" in Vietnam, primarily based on two huge political failures of his, the ill-fated Bay of Pigs invasion of Cuba, and the building of the Berlin Wall. He simply could not tolerate a defeat in Vietnam, and thus, supported efforts to shore up and reinforce a poorly led and corrupt South Vietnamese military. In 1964, Lyndon Johnson, unwillingly, committed more troops to Vietnam, so that by 1968, 1.2 million troops were fighting 520,000 North Vietnamese Communist forces.

As one can well imagine, this amount of activity in Vietnam, coupled with the American populations resistance to the War in Vietnam, turned Washington into a center of protest and political activity on a scale seldom seen since the American Civil War. The war made it impossible for Lyndon Johnson to run for a second term as President, and thus, Richard Nixon became President in 1970. He began a slow but methodical evacuation of American troops from Vietnam, and engineered the release of American prisoners of war held in North Vietnam. He opened up Communist China to the rest of the world, through his diplomatic efforts, but he was not popular with the American public. They did, however, view him as a person who got things done, and he was subsequently reelected for a second term as President in 1974.

All of this turned out very badly, when he was directly linked to the infamous Watergate break-in of the Democratic National Headquarters in June of 1972. By early 1974, evidence was piling up that showed that while not directly involved in the break-in, President Nixon had knowledge of the events, and did nothing to bring any of the perpetrators to justice. It was determined that he had actively participated in a long and extremely devious cover up operation. The FBI discovered secret tapes of conversations that President Nixon had with his staff concerning the Watergate break-in. On August 9, 1974, to halt impeachment proceedings that were underway in the Congress, he became the first President of the United States to resign from office. This made the Vice President, Gerald Ford, the new President, with a term that would end on January 20, 1977. This was the climate that our family met in the Washington of July 1976, in the midst of a heated political campaign for President between Gerald Ford and Jimmy Carter.

In short order, we rented a four-bedroom, southern style, two-story home, in the Mount Vernon section of Alexandria, Virginia. The house was near Headquarters Marine Corps, close to the Army base at Fort Belvoir, with complete support facilities, including dispensaries, commissary and post exchanges, and it was in an excellent school district for the boys. This tour of duty was starting out very positively, and I had not yet reported in for duty. On August 2, 1976, I drove to the Navy Annex in Arlington, Virginia, to be processed for duty at Headquarters Marine Corps. The Navy Annex housed the headquarters of the Bureau of Naval Personnel and the Headquarters of the U.S. Marine Corps. Although many people still think the Marine Corps is a part of the US Navy, by law (National Security Act of 1947) it is a separate Military Service within the *Department* of the Navy. The Commandant of the Marine Corps reports directly to the Secretary of the Navy as the head of a separate service. Fortunately, most Americans think of the Marine Corps as a separate service anyway, and in the end that is what really matters.

After turning in my records, I was further directed to report for duty to the Plans and Policies Division. The Division was located on the second floor of the building, and its' offices were next to the offices of the Commandant of the Marine Corps. It was clear that the importance of the Plans and Policies Division was underscored by its' proximity to the seat of power. The Director of the Plans and Policies Division was Lieutenant General Andrew O'Donnell, a Marine aviator, and a senior officer whom I knew personally. Andy O'Donnell was a close friend of MajGen Spanjer's, and the two of them had raised a little hell together in Honolulu during General Spanjer's tour of duty at CINCPAC. On several occasions, I had accompanied them on their tours of some of the finer "watering holes" of Honolulu, serving as their designated driver. General O'Donnell recognized me immediately and welcomed me to the Division. He informed me that I was being assigned to the

Service Plans section, which was responsible for writing all possible contingency plans in which the Marine Corps might be involved around the world.

It was the responsibility of the Service Plans section to evaluate all geopolitical situations, worldwide, evaluate military threats, and then write possible contingency plans for the consideration of the Plans and Policies Director and for the final approval of the Commandant of the Marine Corps. There were many other sections within the division, and each section dealt with highly classified material and was entrusted with positions and constraints not known by anyone outside of the division. For example, the division made accurate assessments of the abilities of the Marine Corps to perform its' duties, including prioritizing contingency and emergency assignments, which always were dependent on the current strength and deployment of all active and reserve Marine forces.

Officers assigned to the Plans and Policies Division, were considered frontrunners for promotion, and all of their records were carefully screened before assignment. It was generally understood that all officers in Plans and Policies were promotable, and historically, had not been passed over for promotion in recent history. Looking back on the officers who were assigned to the Plans and Policies Division with me in 1976, one of them later became Commandant of the Marine Corps, two of them became three star general's, two became two star general's and three became one star general's. Not a bad track record.

I was introduced to the head of the Service Plans section, a Colonel Robert Albany, who, like all the other colonels in the Division, had his eyes on a future star. It took me all of a day working in the office with him, to recognize that the colonel's dream of attaining a general's star would never happen. He simply wasn't cut out for the rank, lacking style, humor, intellect and charisma. The atmosphere in the Service Plans section was mirrored in all the other sections of the Plans and Policies Division. I was escorted to the Service Plans section, where I was assigned a desk in a room where nine lieutenant colonels sat at desks facing the walls of the large office. The head of the section, Colonel Albany, was the only colonel in the section, and, as the head of the section, his desk was in the center of the room, with the desks of the "action officers, as we were all called, ringed around the center desk.

Each desk had two or three heavy, fire proof top security file cabinets that contained all the information we needed to function in the area of interest to which we were assigned. I was assigned to the four countries of Scandinavia, and I was required to write and develop any service plans that would include an American presence in any of these four countries. With their proximity to the former Soviet Union, their locations and possible support functions for American or NATO operations were critical.

These were high visibility jobs, meaning that if you did well, you were recognized as an officer with promotion potential, but if you did not do well, you were finished with your career. While this may sound draconian, it was generally the way that things were done in the Plans and Policies Division and, for that matter, throughout the Marine Corps Headquarters, where officers were constantly screened for their potential as future senior officers in the Corps. This accounted for the fact that so many future generals were developed within the Headquarters, which made assignment to HQMC so necessary, especially if one wanted to advance to high rank. The competitive nature of the place reminded me of the pressures of Stuyvesant High School, which was the last place where every student was pitted against one another to see who could get the scholarships to the Ivy League schools.

Each action officer would spend a minimum of eight hours per day, writing plans or going to various research locations to obtain necessary background information. It wasn't long before I discovered a group of lieutenant colonel action officers who regularly met in the rear of the Navy cafeteria, located in the basement of the Navy part of the building, where we would spend many fun filled hours doing "research." Looking back on that group, we had a lot of fun, and all of them who stayed in the Corps attained the rank of colonel, but not a single one of them made general officer. Their attitude, coupled with a "love of life," rather than a willingness to sacrifice everything for the sake of a possible promotion to flag rank, is clearly what drew me to them. They were smart, witty, and recognized the need to prepare for a life outside of the Marine Corps, whenever that might occur.

It didn't take long to settle into the job. I had been at HQMC before, albeit in the Supply Department, however, my success during my previous tour of duty gave me a decided advantage over my peers, since I was intimately aware of how things got done at the HQMC level. The role of the action officers in each Division is to insure that a General or other briefing officer is fully prepared and with sufficient back-up information so he is able to deliver an impressive and accurate briefing. This means making him "look good" during Commandant of the Marine Corps briefings, Joint Chiefs of Staff briefings at the Pentagon or even during testimony in front of either the Senate or the House Armed Services Committees.

In each instance, if your area of expertise was the subject, you accompanied the General to the briefings after many hours of pre-briefing preparations. All action officers had large, square, leather briefcases in which they carried the "back-up." If a question was asked that required more detailed information, your function was to reach into your bag and provide the General with the appropriate information. It took a tremendous amount of thought to prepare for these briefings because you had to anticipate the questions that would be asked and always have the back-up data available in your briefcase. One slip, which might make the General look bad during a briefing or be detrimental to the Marine Corps, and you were no longer an action officer. While this was obviously very stressful, I always looked upon it as a game, in which I was pitted against whoever the General might be briefing, and I was determined to always win the game.

As it turned out, I always did, however, my area of expertise, the Scandinavian countries, was an area about which few people were particularly conversant and this made my job fairly easy. My role within the Division was to develop military plans for the Marine Corps, which included either support or participation of one or all Scandinavian countries in any future conflict in that area with a hypothetical enemy, loosely disguised so as not to mention the Soviet Union by name. While the job was intellectually stimulating, sitting at your desk in a room full of lieutenant colonel's, all of who were also busy writing plans, made for a rather dull and stifling work environment. Every officer in the Division knew they were constantly "under the gun," and that the price of success was to always be prepared for any situation.

The primary emphasis for the Scandinavian countries was to use their countries for the pre-positioning of needed supplies if there is a war. This would preclude a huge movement of supplies and equipment after hostilities broke out and it would enable the United States to simply move the troops and the airplanes to a location within the battle area where the supplies were already available. This scenario made a great deal of sense, required detailed logistics experience, and had to be maintained at a Top Secret classification, since it allowed the US forces a tremendous amount of flexibility against any possible aggressor in the geographic area.

The plans, once written, were constantly being modified, adjusted and tailored to specific war scenarios. Thus, a battle in Finland would be different from an incursion into the Soviet Union, and the political climates in the Scandinavian countries had to be considered, especially when outright support of the United States might not always be a top priority for the sitting government.

Marines of any rank join the Marine Corps for adventure and excitement. Infantry troops and officers are particularly attracted to this life, and the rugged demands of life in the field and, for officers, the challenge of leading troops in both peacetime and combat. I was fortunate enough to have had these experiences up to the rank of major, however, my tours of duty as a lieutenant colonel turned out to be staff jobs, very far removed from any troop leadership.

My biggest disappointment during my tour of duty with the 3rd Marine Division was the fact that I had been unable to obtain a command and spent my entire 13 month tour in an office staff job. This environment existed in every job at HQMC and, while assignment to HQMC was a definite steppingstone to higher rank, the amount of leadership positions in the Marine Corps decreased exponentially as your rank increased. In short, lieutenants and captains were in much higher demand as troop leaders than lieutenant colonels and colonels. This fact began to hit home with me as I contemplated my future in the Marine Corps.

Another aspect of duty at HQMC in 1976 was the fact that it was extremely expensive to live in the Metropolitan D.C. area. Most of the officers working at HQMC lived in Virginia in homes they owned from previous tours of duty. Others lived in Maryland, right on the D.C. line, making their commute horrible, because they had to cross a bridge to work twice each day. When I had been stationed at the Marine Barracks in Washington after my first marriage, I commuted over the 14th Street Bridge twice each day. The commute was awful, and a distance that should have taken less than 30 minutes often took over an hour each way. On that tour of duty, after being stuck in traffic for over two hours, on days when there was snow on the ground I promised myself that I would never, for the rest of my life, place a bridge between myself and my place of work.

Since parking at HQMC was at a premium, I soon found a colonel with a designated parking space who lived near me in Mount Vernon. We decided to carpool to HQMC, and this resulted in savings for both of us, and company on the often torturous commute of only 12 miles that often could take an hour and that was without crossing any bridges. The colonel was an engineer, and we spent many pleasant hours stuck in traffic, discussing anything from how they obtain octane ratings on gasoline, to the possibility of the Redskins winning their football games. Colonel Dick Evans was a good man, and on occasion, we would stop for a drink on the way home. He was good company, and a very intelligent man from whom I learned many new things. He retired from the Marine Corps in 1980 and accepted an engineering teaching position at Lehigh University.

There was a limited social life for members of the Service Plans section. Colonel Albany had his usual Christmas party at his home in Alexandria, but besides that, officers of the section were so busy working, that socialization took a back seat to working on getting yourself promoted. At HQMC, my job continued uneventfully until Col Albany received orders and he was replaced by an aviator colonel named Paul Pirhalla. Colonel Pirhalla was a rare breed at HQMC, in that he had no desire to become a general officer and was admittedly on his final tour of duty before retirement. Colonel Pirhalla was from New York City and this established an immediate bond between us. The fact that he liked to tell jokes and maintain a fairly lighthearted atmosphere in the office endeared him to many, but also turned off the officers who were there to make general. Col Pirhalla got the assignment because he had been one of General O'Donnell's squadron commanders and General O'Donnell, an aviator out of the Smoke Spanjer and Pappy Boyington mold, liked Colonel Pirhalla, and wanted him in his division.

Soon, Colonel Pirhalla and I placed "whoopee cushions" on everybody's office chair, and every Friday was "Groucho Day, in which every officer in the section wore those famous Groucho glasses that came with a plastic nose and a fake mustache for the first hour of the day. It really broke the tension, and soon, even the uptight officers in the section participated in our "fun and games" with enthusiasm. I loved the fact that Colonel Pirhalla was our section chief, probably more than anyone else in the entire division.

In late 1976, I heard about an after-hours class that was being taught at Catholic University by a Professor Stanley Kaplan called, "The Strategy of Career Transition." The Marine Corps provided Catholic University with a briefing room within the Headquarters building, complete with slide projectors, audiovisual equipment and a top quality sound system. The capacity of the briefing room was 150 seats, and within a very short time, the class was totally booked. I had heard about the class from the Headquarters Marine Corps Education Officer who was responsible for booking the class into HQMC, so I was assured a space. The cost of the class was $100, not exactly a bargain in those days, but the subject matter appealed to me, and, somewhere in the recesses of my mind, lingered a thought that I might need the information that was being taught in this class.

During my previous tour of duty at HQMC, the thought of possible retirement never entered my mind. On this second tour of duty, I had already attended many retirement ceremonies for lieutenant colonels and colonels. The one thing that all of these ceremonies had in common was the fact that the retirees seemed to me to look like deer that had been caught in the headlights of an oncoming car. Almost universally, it was clear that the retirees in question thought they would stay in the Marine Corps forever, never even considering the fact that, down the road, their time would be up, and due to the famous "up and out" law, they would have no choice.

I had attended too many of these ceremonies that turned into wakes and left the retiree with the awesome task of having to plan for a future outside of the Marine Corps, a future that had not been considered or properly planned. Early on, I vowed that I would not allow that to happen to me. Perhaps, subconsciously, the specter of forced retirement is what led me to enroll in Professor Kaplan's class.

A few words about the "up and out" law, and its' effect on the promotion of officers in the Marine Corps: Until almost 1900, officers in the Marine Corps were promoted whenever a vacancy in the next higher rank occurred. Thus, it was not unusual for a captain to remain a captain for his entire career and never attain the rank of major. This effect was similar for every officer rank throughout the Corps. Naturally, this caused a great deal of disillusion and dissatisfaction, since qualified officers would see not so qualified senior officers, remain on active duty permanently, thus denying them a chance for promotion. Using a recent business term, there was no "upward mobility" for the junior officers and consequently, many left the Corps. The Marine Corps began losing almost all of its' young, junior officers, and what was left were 55 or 60 year old captains who could no longer lead troops into battle.

In 1899, a law was proposed that would require officers to be promoted after being considered for promotion twice over a two-year period. If the officer failed to be selected for the next senior rank twice, he would be required to either leave the service immediately, if his rank was that of captain or below, or, if his rank was major or above, he would be required to retire immediately upon completing 20 years of service. The law was approved and passed and remains in effect today as Title 10 of the United States Code. What this does, is ensure upward mobility for everyone, and an officer who decides to make a career of the Marine Corps, understands from the very beginning that he either successfully gets promoted to the next higher rank as he progresses in his career or he will be passed over and required to leave the Corps.

Besides the destruction of an existing lifestyle, being passed over for promotion, with the fact being published for all to see, resulted in severe psychological changes, and many officers, who had been passed over, became bitter, angry men. Many of them never recovered from the ultimate "shame" of not being found acceptable by the very institution to which they had dedicated their lives. Some were never able to put back the pieces of their lives and lived them out in isolation, depression and abject anger. It was certainly not a pretty sight to behold, and I swore that it would not happen to me.

In 1975, a group of civilian psychiatrist's at Georgetown University published a study about military service and the effect of being "passed over" for promotion. The study found that many passed over personnel developed severe psychological problems, based on the rejection syndrome, from which recovery was not always guaranteed, primarily based on the single issue that they had been forced out of the service. It also came up with a startling actuarial table that showed that the average military retiree did not survive more than five years after retirement. These were sobering facts, and they were not taken lightly by those who took the time to familiarize themselves with the contents of the study. With such high percentages for possible failure built into the system, it was no wonder that Professor Kaplan's class on the Strategy of Career Transition was fully subscribed and even boasted a waiting list.

The class began on January 10, 1977, in one of the 2nd floor briefing rooms. It would meet for two hours on Mondays and Wednesdays, for the next six months, after which, those officers or senior staff noncommissioned officers who felt that a career change was in order, would have the necessary tools with which to implement the change. The initial class was fascinating. Most of the students in the class had already completed 20 years of service in the Marine Corps, or, were within two years of doing so, and we were listening to a Clinical Psychologist instruct us on how to market ourselves to the civilian world. While most people in the room had certainly thought about the possibility, this class was a first, solid step in the direction of separation from the Marine Corps.

The most important requirement for success after the Marine Corps, according to Dr. Kaplan, was to de-program your attitudes from Marine Corps ways and to begin to assimilate into the civilian world. He spoke of the preconceived ideas that civilians have about the military, and compared them to the preconceived ideas that the military has about civilians. It was clear that the next six months would prove to be an eye-opening experience for each student in the class.

Along with the requirements for the class, my regular duties were filled with developing contingency plans and action plans for U.S. Forces deploying to the Scandinavian countries. It was no secret that the importance of Denmark, Sweden, Norway and Finland to the United States was directly proportional to their proximity to the Soviet Union. In 1977, the Iron Curtain, which had been pulled down shortly after the end of World War II over the Soviet Union and its' satellite countries in Eastern Europe and East Germany, produced the largest, single "enemy threat" to freedom, to the United States and its' NATO (North Atlantic Treaty Organization) allies. It was this threat that required military planners from all NATO nations to be prepared for any kind of action at any time and under almost any circumstances. The Marine Corps would most probably be required to conduct amphibious landings in the North Sea, the Baltic Sea, the Gulf of Bothnia or the Norwegian Sea.

To make these possible landings as rapidly as possible and to move inland over long distances to a combat area, it was necessary to preposition supplies in warehouses and open field locations within the four Scandinavian countries. These pre-positioned supplies became my responsibility and, while the climate in Scandinavia allowed longer term storage without rotation, a detailed list of pre-positioned supplies was maintained by the Supply Department at Headquarters, and it was my responsibility to continuously review the equipment lists and ensure that any landing force would have adequate, usable, and fully functional supplies available, in country, to support their missions. This included rations, fuel, ammunition and clothing, and any other items that a landing force might require for sustained operations ashore.

I had also been assigned as the Marine Corps representative to the Program Operations Memorandum (POM) Task Force. This group of senior Navy and Marine officers prepared an analysis of all programs requiring funding for the next budget cycle, and attempted to prioritize the programs in order of importance. Both services were adamant that all of their programs were critical to the survival of their service and the United States and, therefore, should be fully funded at the expense of other, less important programs. The analyses were prepared for General and Flag officers of both services, who would argue the relative merits of each program in front of the House and Senate Armed Services Committees, which would be the entities that would approve final budget allocations.

The action officers on the Board were responsible for presenting the case for each program assigned to them and then briefing the general officer who would testify in front of the congressional committees. In all cases, the briefing officer always accompanied the general officer to the committee hearings. It was in this environment that I learned the Marine Corps had, for years, been placing programs into the memorandum that had high price tags and that they wanted the congressional committees to cut out of the budget. By using this approach, the Marine Corps always looked like the most cooperative service and always got the programs they really wanted approved without any problems from Congress. To say that games were played at every level would certainly be redundant.

Both of my assignments were definitely intellectually stimulating, however, they were office, desk jobs, and there was no opportunity for command. Furthermore, I was beginning to realize that my chances for any command in the future were rapidly diminishing as I attained success as an action officer at the Headquarters level, This marked me as an outstanding staff officer who was valuable on the staff of important divisions within the Headquarters, and in addition, I was becoming an excellent candidate for future assignments to joint staffs at the Joint Chiefs of Staff level within the Pentagon.

My class in Career Transition was progressing very nicely, and one of our assignments was to construct a resume for ourselves that detailed our military experiences using purely civilian terminology. I understood the concept immediately, and perhaps my two attempts at obtaining an MBA degree while on active duty, assisted me in the completion of the assignment. When we handed in our completed resumes, Dr. Kaplan asked me if he could use my resume as an example of how to do it properly. I agreed, and very soon I became an "onsite consultant" to many officers who asked for, and received, help from me, in constructing their own resumes.

Further classes discussed the sending of unsolicited letters to prospective employers and discussed the importance of dressing appropriately for the interview. In this regard, we were all introduced to a classic book entitled, *Dress For Success* by John T. Molloy, which discussed, in both words and pictures, how to dress appropriately, in the business world of 1976. Another assignment in the class required each of us to buy an appropriate business outfit that included shoes, shirt, tie and suit. With my father's background in the fashion industry, this was not a problem, as I already owned all the required clothing outlined in the book.

Since my job at Headquarters required many edits and revisions, the Plans and Policies Division was provisioned with state of the art computer support, The use of these computers was closely regulated, and only action officers and administrative personnel, were authorized to use them. This did not preclude extra use of these computers on nights and weekends, and on one weekend, I prepared 300 letters of introduction and resumes that I sent to various companies all over the United States to test the waters of future civilian employment.

On my 42nd birthday, Friday, June 3, 1977, I decided to take some definitive action. I made an appointment with Colonel James McMonagle, later Major General, who was assigned duties at Headquarters as the Colonel Monitor. This assignment meant that Col McMonagle was responsible for the assignment of all colonels in the Marine Corps, a very powerful and influential position, however, it was a position that Col McMonagle performed with the greatest integrity and the highest degree of morality.

There were no deals made and everyone received exactly the same level handed treatment. Since I was going to be considered for promotion to the rank of colonel in 1977, I asked Col McMonagle what my future assignments might be if I were selected for promotion. Col McMonagle told me that he would review my record and then asked me to come back the following Friday.

Upon my return, Col McMonagle informed me that based on my service record, my fitness reports, and my assignments in the Marine Corps since 1956 he would think that I would be selected for promotion to colonel. I then asked him a far more important question which dealt with possible future assignments. Since I had recently returned from an unaccompanied overseas assignment, I would not be eligible to return overseas, as a colonel, for the next 7 years. This meant that I would complete my three year tour of duty at Headquarters, and then, as a colonel, I would be assigned to a joint services assignment in the Pentagon. This policy was in place because the Marine Corps was trying to save money on relocation costs, and by assigning me from Headquarters to the Pentagon, this eliminated the need for any relocation costs and still transferred me to a totally different assignment within the metropolitan Washington area.

In short, Col McMonagle was assuring me at least 5 more years of office work as an action/staff officer even if I was now wearing eagles. I asked Col McMonagle if I had any chance to get a command. Since commands for colonels were as scarce as hen's teeth, he told me that my chances for a command, based on the detailed level of experience that I had as a staff officer, were zero. I thanked the colonel for his time and candor, and I decided to make an effort to get a civilian job before the Colonel's Promotion Board convened in December 1977. I called my father in New York and told him that based on my discussions with Col McMonagle, I did not want to spend the next five years of my life in an office job while still in the military.

If an office job was the only prospect that I had in the Marine Corps, I might as well look for an office job in the civilian world where, I felt I could make more money, and at the age of 42, begin a new career. I asked him to keep his ears open for any possibilities among his business contacts, another trick that Dr. Kaplan had taught us. (Use your personal contacts often, you'll never know where the next job comes from!) My letters were beginning to have results, although they were all rejections. Dr. Kaplan had warned us about this, and told us to remain diligent because, with effort on our part, something would develop.

In November 1977, our family drove to New York City for Thanksgiving dinner at Dad and Dora's house. While visiting, my father told me that a business acquaintance of his had recommended me to the president of a stuffed animal manufacturing company in San Francisco, as a prospective employee. He told me I would soon hear from a Mr. Harry Nizamian, the President of the company, who would schedule an initial interview with me. We returned to Washington, and in early December 1977, I received a call from Mr. Nizamian asking me to meet him at Dulles International Airport for an initial interview. He asked me to bring my wife with me to this interview. Mr. Nizamian was returning from a trip to Europe, and he took the opportunity to see if there might be a fit for me with his company. Cathie and I met Mr. Nizamian in the lounge of United Airlines, and he conducted a lengthy interview. He told me that he was looking for a Director of Operations for his company and that perhaps I might be a very viable candidate for the position. He seemed impressed with my qualifications and was equally enthusiastic when he discovered that Cathie was a San Francisco native, since the company, R. Dakin and Company, was an old San Francisco firm.

He told me I would hear from him after Christmas. I remember driving home from Dulles with mixed feelings. I was glad that the process was obviously underway, but I was also very nervous inwardly that the time to leave the Marine Corps might be approaching faster than I had thought, or planned. The first week in January 1978, I received a call from Mr. Nizamian asking me to fly to San Francisco for a day of interviews at the Company's headquarters. The interview date had been set for Monday, January 9 at 9 a.m. and on Sunday, January 8, I flew to San Francisco. On the flight, all the lessons from my classes on career transition ran through my mind. Don't seem to anxious, don't try too hard, appear calm and knowledgeable, know something about the company, be prepared to discuss compensation, but only in an indirect manner, dress appropriately, and always pay attention to whoever is speaking, and be prepared to answer a question when the questioner has completed his question.

The primary question on my mind was compensation. As a lieutenant colonel in 1978, my pay with all allowances was about $45,000 a year. This was my goal in civilian life. If I could earn $45,000 a year, when I retired, I could begin my second life exactly even with my earning power in the Marine Corps as a lieutenant colonel. The folks from Dakin would pick me up at the hotel at 8:30 a.m. Monday. Facts about R. Dakin and Company ran through my mind, and I wanted to appear knowledgeable about the company. R. Dakin and Company was, in 1978, the largest domestic manufacturer of stuffed animals in the United States. It was an extremely successful company and the company was privately owned by the Dakin family. From various financial journals, I had memorized the annual revenues, the growth of the company and the future of the company as seen through the eyes of financial experts. I had done my homework, and I was prepared, as much as possible, for my first civilian world interview. I noticed immediately that I seemed overdressed in my sincere business suit and tie. I was escorted into Mr. Nizamian's office where I was given an overview of the company, followed by a complete tour of the facilities. I was introduced to each department head, and senior executive, noticing again, that I was the only person in the entire building in a business suit.

At noon, the senior executives joined Mr. Nizamian and me for lunch. Most of the questions directed at me were about the Marine Corps, Vietnam, a military career, and why I wanted to begin a second career in civilian life. During the entire time I spent at R. Dakin and Company, no one ever asked me a single question concerning my knowledge of their company, or why I was interested in joining the company. So much for some of the training that I received in Dr. Kaplan's class.

I discovered upon my return to work that the Colonel's Selection Board would convene on Monday, January 16th and was expected to report out by February 24, 1978. This board, composed of seven Generals, was tasked to review the records of all lieutenant colonel's in the zone of consideration and to select 125 of them for promotion. Those not selected would be considered passed over for promotion. Those who had only been passed over once, had one more chance at promotion the following year, and those passed over twice, would have to retire immediately upon reaching 26 years of active duty. Since I was in the promotion zone, my name was being considered for promotion by this board.

On Wednesday, January 25th, Mr. Nizamian called to inform me that R. Dakin was interested in hiring me for the position of Director of Operations at a salary of $25,000 per year. Also included in the package was a company car and gas credit card, plus full participation in the company's annual bonus program, and a 90 day free rent allowance while I found a place to live in the Bay Area. He asked that I consider his offer and call him back by Friday, January 27th, with my answer. I was truly excited about the offer. I felt that the financial deal was definitely favorable, especially since the total package exceeded my projection of having to earn $45,000 a year, to make the break from the Marine Corps.

Now came the hard part, deciding to leave the Marine Corps. I discussed the matter with Cathie who did a very wise thing. She informed me that the decision was entirely mine. She was fine with staying in the Marine Corps, and she was fine with leaving. Saying this put the decision squarely on my shoulders, where it truly belonged anyway. She further stated that the decision to leave the Marine Corps was such an important one for me that it had to come exclusively from me, so that in the future, when looking back on the moment of the decision, there would be no one to blame or praise, but myself.

Since I had only two days to make my decision, I decided to call Col McMonagle one more time. I asked him if his forecast for my future assignments was going to hold true, and if there was some chance for a command. He told me that anything was possible, but that if he were a betting man, the odds in my favor of getting a command as a colonel were about 1000 to 1. He then gave me the logic for his analysis and sadly, the logic was quite accurate, and reflected the needs of the Marine Corps, the economic impact of change of station orders, and my recent return from an overseas tour of duty, all of which dictated at least a five year stay in a current geographic area. Col McMonagle did say that instead of the Pentagon, I might be assigned to Quantico, however, there were far more billets for colonels in the Pentagon than Quantico. Thanks to Col McMonagle, my choices were simple either remain in the Washington area for the next five years, as a staff officer, or begin a new career as a civilian, in a new world and in a new place.

Two days were not a very long time to make a life changing decision. I was rushed by Mr. Nizamian's deadline, however, my dreams of command at a senior level had essentially been crushed by my experiences in the 3rd Division, where serving as the Division's Personnel Officer, I was deemed "too important to the needs of the Division" and, therefore, I was unable to get a command, and, by Col McMonagle's forecast for my future as a colonel.

I spent two sleepless nights and then accepted the job. I had decided, in a few days, to make the big jump and to leave the *Green Cocoon* and to see what the next stage of my life had to offer. To accommodate my retirement from the Marine Corps, Mr. Nizamian told me that he expected me to begin work on May 1. I now knew I was going to retire from the Marine Corps, and I went in to work on Monday the 30th of January as though nothing had happened. I had decided that I would wait to announce my retirement until after the Promotion Board had announced their findings. That way, I would know if I had been selected for colonel, or if I had been passed over. I remained in this state for about a week. Each evening I would go home and decide to tell someone about my decision, however, I really wanted to know if I was going to be selected for colonel.

The Marine Corps has a strange system as far as promotion boards are concerned. Once a list is published, if anyone on that list decides to retire and not accept their promotion, no alternates are ever selected, and it simply means that someone who was passed over might have been selected had that promotion space been available. However, once the list is published, if someone on the list decides to retire, the slot is simply not filled, and there are just fewer Colonel's promoted that particular year. That thought kept gnawing at me, and I began to feel that by being selfish, and waiting to announce my retirement until the list came out, I would be taking away a promotion opportunity from someone else. I wrote a letter to the Promotion Board and requested my name be taken out of consideration for promotion, because I planned to retire on March 31, 1978. I walked the letter to the Promotion Board conference room and gave the letter to the colonel recorder and returned to my office and formally announced my decision to retire on March 31.

I felt very conflicted, neither elated or very sad, just apprehensive, as to what my future would bring, and wondering how I would accomplish everything in time to retire and depart Washington with my family, my dog, and my cat, sell our second car, and drive across the country in our VW bus, on our way to a new life in San Francisco. The reaction to my decision was very surprising. Most of my peers, who were also in the zone for promotion to colonel, told me that I was making a big mistake, especially since I was so close to promotion. Once I explained my rationale to them, they still could not understand why I was leaving the Marine Corps at this particular time. I explained, in detail, my future as a staff officer and further explained that if I did not take this opportunity to retire, at age 42, I might not be able to retire for at least another four or five years, which would make me at least 47 and future retirement would be far more difficult in the civilian world at that age.

I thought that 42 was pushing it to begin a new life, and I wanted to give myself the best shot at success. As a career officer, to retire, I had to formally request permission from the Secretary of the Navy. This was a letter detailing my request to retire and the date that I desired to retire. This process was a holdover from World War II, when the needs of the service were the single most important thing, and an individual's desires were secondary. The process remained because it was still a vehicle whereby the services could retain personnel that they deemed critical, and circumvent their own desires to leave the service. It was rarely done, and in my case, my request for retirement was returned approved in less than one week.

February of 1978 went by in a flash. There were several retirement parties held in my honor and the officers in my section presented me with an engraved sterling silver cigarette case (a sign of the times) that I still have to this day. I don't think that there has ever been a cigarette inside the box, but it is still a treasured memento. On Wednesday, March 1, the colonel's list came out and was published throughout the Marine Corps. Obviously, my name was not on it. Within a few hours, I began to receive calls from friends all over the Marine Corps, calling to commiserate with me over having been passed over for promotion. When I told them that I had voluntarily taken my name out of consideration and that I was retiring on March 31, they seemed incredulous. Nevertheless, the word seemed to circulate that I was retiring, and the calls coming in were more calls of curiosity than concern. In March, my orders to retirement were published indicating that March 31, 1978, would me my last day of active duty and that this day would be the day that I would be transferred to the Retired List.

The events leading up to this date were hectic, to say the least. Besides completing the required "paper work" a retirement physical examination must be conducted to determine that the retiree had no service connected disabilities which might be claimed later. I was ushered into an examination room, and in a few minutes, a female in a white coat came into the room. I asked her if she was the nurse, and, of course, she was the doctor. I informed her that I was uncomfortable with a woman doctor, and could she please let a male doctor give me my physical exam. She looked at me and in the softest of voices said," Colonel, the way I see it, you have two choices. Either I examine you, or you don't get to retire. Which one will it be?" Needless to say, she examined me, and I retired. It was the first experience I had ever had with a woman doctor in the military.

At 11 a.m. on March 31, Cathie, my peers, and other interested parties assembled in General O'Donnell's office for my official retirement ceremony. I was surprised by the turnout. Several general's with whom I had served in Vietnam attended, as did my entire division. General O'Donnell read the retirement orders, gave me my Certificate of Retirement, and then presented me with the Meritorious Service Medal. Col Pirhalla, my section chief, had decided that since I already had a Legion of Merit, won in combat, he was recommending me for a Meritorious Service Medal so I would then have one more medal to wear at the Birthday Balls.

General O'Donnell then asked me to say a few words. First I thanked everyone for attending and then I told them about my decision to retire. I informed everyone present that I was leaving the Marine Corps on my terms, never having been passed over for promotion, which meant that I would never have any bitterness towards the Marine Corps. I went on to say that everyone who stays in the Marine Corps to the end will eventually get passed over and since only one person in the Marine Corps, who remains on active duty, never gets passed over for promotion, which is the Commandant of the Marine Corps, everyone in the room who doesn't make Commandant will experience being passed over at some point in their career.

I was happy I had taken myself out of that huge disappointment. Little did I know that Lieutenant Colonel Carl Mundy, a contemporary of mine, who was at my retirement ceremony, would one day be the Commandant of the Marine Corps. After my speech, I called Cathie to the front of the room and pinned a miniature Legion of Merit medal on her for all of her support during my career. Everyone thought that it was a wonderful gesture, and several of them, including General O'Donnell, told me that they were going to borrow my idea for their retirement ceremonies.

Almost all of them agreed with my statement about everyone getting passed over at some point in their career, and all of them said that they had never even looked at it that way. It was a very nice ceremony, and, following the retirement, Cathie and I had only one more stop, and that was to pick up my Retired Identification Card and to sign some final forms before retirement. At around 1 p.m., we were done, and I was retired. We drove home to Alexandria to finish packing and prepare for our trip to San Francisco. It was beginning to settle in that I was finally retired, and, if it was the correct decision, it was made and completed, and there was no turning back.

On Monday morning, April 3, as Cathie and I were putting the final things into the VW bus, the telephone rang. I went inside the house to answer our last telephone call in Alexandria, Virginia. I was absolutely shocked to hear Major General Lang at the other end of the phone. He told me that he had just heard that I had retired, and he was truly sorry that I had made that decision. He asked me why I had decided to retire, and I told him that I had always been disappointed in not being able to get a command as a lieutenant colonel and the prospect of five more years of staff work simply did not appeal to me. He listened quietly and then wished me well in my future endeavors and added, just before he hung up, that I had been selected for Colonel by the promotion board on the first round and that when my letter was delivered to the board, I had already been selected for promotion. He said he wanted me to know that because I had taken the high road and notified the board about my retirement, to allow someone else to be selected. I thanked him for his call, and told him that I would always appreciate the call he made to inform me about my selection, and wished him well in the future. With this last minute conversation with General Lang, I ended my career in the Marine Corps, locked the door of our house and put the key in the mail box, got into our VW bus, and drove out of Virginia, heading to San Francisco and a new life as a civilian.

Twenty-two years of my life had just ended, and the memories, good and bad, would remain with me for the rest of my life. The adage that there are no ex-Marines only former Marines holds true for every Marine. To this day, I am, and will always be, a Marine, and the thirty plus years of civilian life that followed, is just icing on the cake. I consider myself extremely lucky to have been a member of the finest fighting organization in the world, and I treasure my "comrades-in-arms" who have remained my most loyal and reliable friends throughout my life.

I still tear up whenever I hear the *Marine's Hymn* played, and if I am not standing when the hymn is played, I jump to my feet and honor the memory of all Marines, past, present and future. I am proud of my service to my country, but I am proudest of the fact that I served my country as a United States Marine. The lessons I learned as a Marine helped me become a successful civilian professional and assured me and my family a stable and rewarding future life outside of our Green Cocoon.

It will always be *Semper Fidelis* for me.

THE LAST WORD

This book ends in 1978 when I retired from the U.S. Marine Corps. The cast of characters in my life through that period of time were as varied as the people in the lives of every reader of this book. My experiences with those characters influenced, changed, altered and impacted my life in either a positive, negative or neutral manner. I learned something from each of the people in my life, and I used that knowledge to help me live my life in the best possible manner.

Having said that, there were people in my life whose impact is still felt and who have influenced me to this very day.

- At the forefront is my father, whose spirit, heroism and unconditional love sustained me and my mother through terribly difficult times. His unwavering loyalty to me throughout my life is directly responsible for the conscientious and reliable person I believe I became.
- Mr. Milbut at The Mohonk School was especially supportive and compassionate, and I can never forget his kindness to me in the year after my mother's untimely death.
- Mrs. Margaret Stovall of Waynesville, NC became the mother I lost and longed for, and for three years, she filled a needed and necessary role in my life by serving me in that capacity.
- I am indebted to Stuyvesant High School in New York City for providing me with the very best public school education obtainable in the United States. I am only sorry I did not take greater advantage of the options available to me at the time.

- The Boy Scout movement of the 1950s in America instilled in me a pride of country and a sense of responsibility that have remained an important part of my everyday life.

- The faculties at Champlain College and Syracuse University provided me with a strong intellectual foundation which I have tried to enhance and improve throughout my life.

- The Officers, Staff Non Commissioned Officers and Enlisted men of the U.S. Marine Corps formed the basis of my life for twenty-two years, and I accumulated memories of shared experiences that remain imbedded in my brain and sustain me in the autumn of my life.

Like an Awards Show on television, the list of people in my life who have been positive influences is far too long to list here, but there are a few who need to be mentioned. They are, in no particular order: Catherine Marie Johnson Beck, Byron Thomas Schenn, Charles Edmund Davis, William Rivers Von Harten, John Henry Bateman, Jonas Mansfield Platt, Arthur James Rauchle, Gildo Codispoti, Ormond Simpson, Ralph Spanjer, James A. Young, George W. Smith and James McMonagle. The others, who are too numerous to mention here, know who they are and know how deeply I appreciated their involvement in my life.

Researching this book took many forms. There was some information available to me about almost all phases of my life, however, as is often the case, the details surrounding specific incidents needed fleshing out. My father refused to talk to me about his experiences in Germany. Although I wondered all my life what made my father remain in Berlin after Hitler came to power in 1933, I never found out the answer to this burning question. To get the details of what Berlin was like before I was born and why Hitler came to power, I used a book entitled "Jews in Berlin" published by Henschel Verlag, Berlin in 2001 and edited by Andreas Nachama, Julius H. Schoeps and Hermann Simon. The facts and statistics in this book derive from some of the contents of the book, however, I have written these facts and statistics in my own style. The numbers are the same, much as the fact that 6 million Jews died in the Holocaust. No matter how you say it, the number never changes.

As I write these lines, I am happy to report that my stepbrother, Tom Selldorff has received from the Austrian government, the first increment of art works stolen from his grandfather's collection by the Nazis. While his mother, who became my stepmother, graciously made me a direct heir of her assets, I waived all rights to any art work belonging to her father, Richard Neumann, and believe that their rightful place is with his grandson, Tom Selldorff, and his family.

The looting of art works by the Nazis in Europe has been well documented. I have been unable to uncover much information about my stepmother and her family and their life and exit from Austria after Germany annexed the country. I do know that my stepmother's father was Richard Neumann, a manufacturer of textiles in Austria before World War II. He owned a well-known art collection which was completely expropriated by the Nazis after the annexation of Austria (German Anschluss) in 1938. Neumann managed to flee to France, then Spain and finally, on to Cuba. For many years, Dora's family worked tirelessly to retrieve the stolen art work and in 2002, the first of these treasures was finally returned to his grandson, his only living direct heir. Recently, the French government has begun proceedings to return some of the stolen art work currently in their possession to the family. The success of these proceedings is far from accomplished as of this date.

Other sources that proved invaluable were the Vietnam archives at the Texas A&M University, the Encyclopedia Britannica Books of the Year for 1968, 1969 and 1970 and of course, all the information available on the Internet, with a special tip of the cap to both Google, Wikipedia and Ancestry.com. Often, information from these internet sources took only seconds to obtain, and this included obscure photographs and passenger manifests long thought to be either destroyed or unavailable. Several of those documents are reproduced in this book. I cannot imagine how much time would have been required to obtain these same results without the use of electronic media.

I had retained a lot of information of a personal nature from my days in the Marine Corps consisting of old orders, pamphlets, field manuals, combat maps and other memoranda which also served to fill in a lot of blank spaces in my recollections.

The documents made available to me by my stepbrother Tom Selldorff of Weston, Massachusetts provided a tremendous amount of personal information concerning my father and my mother, all of which was new information about which I had no previous knowledge and which was used throughout this book.

Since this book is being written in 2012, it goes without saying that I was fortunate to live a second life as a civilian in the San Francisco Bay Area. Thanks to Pepperdine University, where I paid much more attention than at any previous institution, I earned an MBA degree in 1980 and embarked on a highly successful "tour of duty" as a civilian.

There is an equally long list of people who supported me throughout my civilian endeavors. These are people who also became close friends in some cases. I found them to be interesting, loyal (to a degree) and generally reliable. They could not replace a single Marine "comrade-in-arms," but in many instances, they came into my life willingly and have remained in it to this day.

I am convinced that my success in the Marine Corps and in civilian life was heavily influenced by the solid core of very good friends that I was fortunate to meet and keep throughout the years of my life. I treasure all of them and thank each and everyone from the bottom of my heart.

I could not have succeeded without my friends, both in and out of the Corps, and while the bonds of our friendships are strong and enduring, the bonds of friendship forged in the heat of battle can never be replaced, forgotten or broken.

* * *

THE CURTAIN

I see a curtain in the distance, how far away I do not know.
And soon this distant curtain will run down upon my show.
Oh, there were many scenes in my long play, they happened every day.
Some were good and some were bad, how many is hard to say.

I look at all of them much more, as time becomes my enemy,
And wonder if I'd change a few, if I had the opportunity.
Hindsight is always twenty-twenty, or so the Sages say
But when you live a life so full, patience rarely comes into play.

There are things from childhood, school and my old neighborhood,
and memories I had forgotten that I thought I never would.
There are friends and old acquaintances and events I just forgot,
And yet each one appears to tweak my mind, within their designated spot.

There seem to be so many, that in my brain are resident,
That just remembering each event is not always so pleasant.
My breath is short, my heart beats strong I also feel a pain,
And hidden thoughts within my mind become much harder to explain.

The reasons swirl around in time, and answers still elude me,
You had your chances, more than most and choices came abundantly.
Why did you take that crooked course, when others were much better?
You had to go against the grain and live your life unfettered.

Upon reflection that's the way it went and now it's far too late to change,
The only thing that could be done is my memories to re-arrange.
But even so, they're all still there and sometimes each comes calling,
If nothing else just to remind you of some things that were appalling.

You had a good run over all with far more laughs than tears,
And in the twilight you reflect on all those vibrant years.
When bones were strong and goals achieved and illness wasn't there
And life continued for you recklessly, you lived without a care.

What would you change at this late date in all the things you've done?
The answer isn't very hard to guess, for it's not a single one.
So ring the curtain down at the end of my last act
There's no need for any revision, I'd leave my life intact.

Peter Steven Beck